BRAHMS

BRAHMS

Malcolm MacDonald

Schirmer Books
A Division of Macmillan Inc.
New York

Schirmer Books
A Division of Macmillan, Inc.
866 Third Avenue, New York, N.Y. 10022

First published in Great Britain by
J.M. Dent & Sons Ltd.
91 Clapham High Street
London SW4 7TA

Musical examples set by Tabitha Collingbourne

Library of Congress Catalog Card Number: 90-8545
Schirmer Books paperback edition 1993
Printed in the United States of America
printing number
1   2   3   4   5   6   7   8   9   10

Library of Congress Cataloging-in-Publication Data

MacDonald, Malcolm, 1948–
    Brahms / Malcolm MacDonald. — 1st American ed.
        p.   cm.
    Includes bibliographical references (p.   ) and index.
    ISBN 0-02-871393-1 (hc), 0-02-872851-3 (pb)
    1. Brahms, Johannes, 1833–1897.
    2. Composers—Germany—Biography.
I. Title.
ML410.B8M113   1990   90-8545
780'.92—dc20   CIP
[B]   MN

Seiner lieben Freundin
Regina Busch
in Wien zugeeignet

1 Brahms at the piano: a tempera painting by Willy von Beckerath (1911) after a sketch made in the 1890s.

Preface

Brahms had a lively sense of his music's worth, but was less sure how it would be understood by posterity. In his gloomier moments he forecast that he would become a 'neglected master', his works the preserve of specialists only, like those of Cherubini whom he so admired. He might have been surprised, even a little embarrassed, to learn that since his death, nothing has in fact seriously damaged his popular status as one of the supreme masters of European music. Some works may recede or advance in favour, but in general his compositions sit comfortably in the mainstream of the genres he most adorned – orchestral, chamber and piano music, and songs. (With some obvious exceptions, his choral output is probably under-performed.)

Yet those works have represented very different things to different generations, a fact that has been reflected in the 'Master Musicians' series itself. The present study is the third since the series was founded in 1899. The first, by Lawrence Erb, appeared in 1905 and was one of the first books on Brahms to appear in English; accordingly its content was more biographical than musical, and Erb wrote polemically about a composer whose music was still 'modern' and a matter for debate. A revised edition was issued by Eric Blom in 1934, just after Brahms's birth-centenary; Blom consciously toned down some of Erb's pronouncements, explaining that since 'Brahms is now a Classic' he no longer 'required explaining and defending'. This shift in opinion was taken a stage further when Peter Latham's book on Brahms replaced Erb/Blom in 1948. For Latham, in a memorable phrase, Brahms was 'no founder of a new dynasty, not even an intermediate name in a long continuous line, but the very last of the classical Caesars'; in other words, a dead-end – a view he found no reason to modify for the revised edition of 1966.

Two decades later the picture of 'Brahms the last Classic' may still be the one with which music-lovers are most familiar; but the advance of scholarship, and increased understanding of the music of our own century, has done much to retouch it. Brahms is indeed a vital component in a line that stretches down to the present day; in particular, the music of Schoenberg and his pupils, the so-called 'Second Viennese School', which once seemed to represent a break with all past music, can now be seen to have been deeply influenced by Brahms's musical practice and compositional cast of mind. It was Schoenberg himself who began this process of rethinking Brahms, in his deliberately controversial article 'Brahms the Progressive' (published, as it happens, the year before Peter Latham's book). Although the article is to some extent a justification of his own procedures, and highly selective in its arguments, Schoenberg's understanding of many aspects of Brahms's technique was profound, and his polemic still has force and point today.

Meanwhile Brahms's commitment to the music of the past, to the Baroque and pre-Baroque composers from whom he learned so much, and the mastery of whose techniques was a vital ingredient in the 'progressive' aspects of his own music, has begun to be much better understood than it was in his own lifetime – partly because of the vastly increased interest in early music that has arisen since the middle of the current century. Here, too, Brahms begins to seem a pioneer rather than a conservative. And with the simultaneous expansion of the theoretical discipline of musical analysis, a new generation of scholars has found Brahms's *oeuvre* an especially rich field of study, concerned as he was with the practical exploration of compositional questions that now concern them; and they have begun to discover compositional subtleties previously unsuspected.

This, the third 'Master Musicians' study of Brahms, is not a theoretical treatise (nor even, I hope, over-complex in its treatment of analytical issues). But it could not in any conscience ignore the advances in understanding that have been made in the recent Brahms literature, and therefore the picture of the composer which emerges from it is rather more complex than in its predecessors. This is all to the good; he was a complex man. But while mindful of the twentieth century's debt to him, and his debt in turn to the centuries before, I have tried to locate him very much in the intellectual and artistic currents of his time: not a 'classical Caesar' but one of the great synthesizers of the conflicting elements within that powerful yet elusive movement we call Romanticism.

The book interweaves biography and music, but the balance must nowadays be weighted towards the latter. Though new Brahms material still occasionally comes to light, the essential shape of his biography was established very early, and all writers attempting to give some account of his life and character are forced to use the same broad group of primary sources. No doubt Brahms was fortunate in that the two decades after his death saw the publication of Max Kalbeck's massive and – for its time – exhaustively researched biography, a huge collection of the composer's correspondence, and a host of first-hand memoirs and reminiscences. The result, however, was that this primary source material was presented to the public (at least in German) very much in the way that his friends wished him to be remembered. The material is immensely valuable, and their view of him was no doubt largely accurate – though perhaps constrained by the social and literary conventions and reticences of the pre-1914 era. It makes any fresh biographical approach almost impossible, though the attempt might be well worth making.

In the discussion of the music I have, as in the 'Master Musicians' *Schoenberg*, endeavoured to give some account of virtually everything the composer wrote. I have deliberately dealt with the music chronologically rather than by category, the better to trace the growth of Brahms's thought from work to work and to show how his activity in one genre could impinge upon others within a given period. The Appendices (Latham's book took over the Chronology unaltered, and the Personalia nearly so, from Blom's revision of Erb) have been completely rethought *ab ovo*, as has the List of Works, which is intended to be as complete as possible and reflect the most up-to-date research.

Two recent major works of Brahms scholarship have been of especial assistance in the preparation of this book. Michael Musgrave's *The Music of Brahms* (London, 1985) is an exhaustive and usually penetrating survey of the whole of Brahms's *oeuvre* by one of the main authorities among the present generation of Brahms scholars, sometimes to an analytical depth that recommends it more to the graduate student than the general reader. It is, however, indispensable further reading. The second work is Virginia Hancock's *Brahms's Choral Compositions and his Library of Early Music* (Ann Arbor, 1983) – an in-depth study of a seemingly limited area of Brahms studies which has enormous ramifications for the understanding of his music as a whole. Both books have been constant companions, and I here acknowledge my general debt to them beyond those pages where they are directly cited.

The large number of quotations from the correspondence of Clara Schumann and Brahms is generally drawn from the two-volume English edition, anonymously translated as *Letters of Clara Schumann and Johannes Brahms 1853–1896*, ed. Berthold Litzmann (London, 1927), and are not separately credited in the text. I have not had uninterrupted access to the much fuller original German edition, but where I have been able to compare the translation with the German versions I have sometimes preferred a different reading.

I am much obliged to the Research Fund Committee of The British Academy, whose award of a personal research grant enabled me to visit

Brahms

Vienna during the course of writing this book; and I am grateful for the kindness and co-operation I then received from the staffs of the Vienna Stadt- und Landesbibliothek, the Musiksammlung of the Öster- reichisches Nationalbibliothek, and especially the Archiv of the Gesellschaft der Musikfreunde in Wien. To the last two institutions I am indebted for the use of photographs, as also to the Robert-Schumann- Haus in Zwickau, the Mary Evans Picture Library, and George Newman. The few copyright music examples are reproduced by kind permission of their publishers: Breitkopf & Härtel, Wiesbaden (Exx. 14 and 15), Ludwig Döblinger (Bernhard Herzmansky) K. G., Vienna (Ex. 43c), and Boosey & Hawkes Music Publishers Ltd (Ex. 67b). Among the many friends and acquaintances who supplied me with materials, information, ideas, advice and encouragement during the book's ges- tation were Regina Busch, Paul Chipchase, Raymond Head, Peter Hill, J. Barrie Jones, Oliver Neighbour, George Newman, Mike Smith, Ronald Stevenson, and Harold Truscott. David Brown read the typescript and made several helpful suggestions. Special thanks are owed to Ingrid Grimes for her meticulous and supportive sub-editing, which has materi- ally contributed to the evolution of the text and must have removed nearly all the avoidable blemishes from it. For those that remain, and all the unavoidable ones stemming from the limitations of its author, I take full responsibility. And last (though it should be first), thanks to Lib.

Brahms has been my favourite composer ever since I was old enough to be able to think about music; but to live with him as intensively as I have done while writing this book is to be constantly reminded that music is a language of truth, operating by its own principles but not therefore 'abstract'. I have tried to write out of my personal experience of it, but in the end Brahms's music still speaks for itself, and for him, magnificently independent of any exegesis.

London, 8 July 1989   M. M.

x

Contents

Preface vii

List of illustrations xiii

Prelude, in canon 1

1   Young Kreisler (1833–54) 3
2   The Romantic foreground 23
3   Storm and stress (1854–60) 39
4   Fully armed like Minerva: the music to 1860 60
5   Not quite a Viennese (1860–72) 123
6   The sense of the past 143
7   The music of the middle years, 1860–75 157
8   'Frei aber froh' 229
9   The music of the middle years, 1876–82 245
10 The final phase 292
11 The later music, 1883–96 302
12 Music and *Menschenbild* 383
13 A Music of the Future 402

Appendices

A   Calendar 419
B   List of works 436
C   Personalia 459
D   Select bibliography 469
E   Who wrote the A major Trio? 475

Index 477

Illustrations

Between pages 242 and 243

1 Brahms's birthplace, No. 60 Speckstrasse, Hamburg, photographed in 1891. (*Österreichisches Nationalbibliothek*)
2 Brahms in 1853. (*Robert-Schumann-Haus, Zwickau*)
3 Clara Schumann; a portrait by Franz von Lembach. (*Robert-Schumann-Haus, Zwickau*)
4 Joseph Joachim and Clara Schumann performing in Berlin, by Adolph von Menzel. (*Robert-Schumann-Haus, Zwickau*)
5 Brahms in 1857. (*Mary Evans Picture Library*)
6 Brahms in the 1880s. (*Gesellschaft der Musikfreunde, Vienna*)
7 Brahms with Hans von Bülow. (*Gesellschaft der Musikfreunde, Vienna*)
8 Elisabet von Herzogenberg. (*Gesellschaft der Musikfreunde, Vienna*)
9 With Viktor von Miller zu Aichholz's wife and daughter in Gmunden in the 1890s. (*courtesy of George Newman*)
10 Squiring Alice Barbi in the Ringstrasse, Vienna, 1892. (*Österreichisches Nationalbibliothek*)
11 Easter Monday, 1894: a photograph by Maria Fellinger. (*Gesellschaft der Musikfreunde, Vienna*)
12 A page from Brahms's manuscript of the String Quintet no. 2, op. 111. (*Gesellschaft der Musikfreunde, Vienna*)

Illustrations in text

1 Brahms at the piano: a tempera painting by Willy von Beckerath. vi
2 A page from Brahms's manuscript of the 'Schumann' Variations, op. 9. (*Gesellschaft der Musikfreunde, Vienna*) 38
3 Bohemian dance-tunes written out by Brahms. (*Gesellschaft der Musikfreunde, Vienna*) 382

Prelude, in canon

Einförmig ist der Liebe Gram,
Ein Lied eintöniger Weise,
Und immer noch, wo ich's vernahm,
Mitsummen musst' ich's leise.

(Monotonous is love's sorrow,
A song with but one note;
Yet always when I heard it,
I had to hum along with it.)

Friedrich Rückert

Some seven years before his death, Brahms published a set of thirteen Canons for female voices. Its opus number, 113, is misleadingly high. These miniatures of the contrapuntist's art, setting aphoristic texts by arch-Romantic poets such as Eichendorff and Rückert, or treating some of his favourite folk-melodies, mostly date from his youth and early manhood, from the 1850s and 60s. The exception is no. 13, the last (and most elaborate) of them, which sets the little poem by Rückert given above.

Brahms divides the female chorus into six parts for a particularly intricate design, with the main tune in four-part canon in the sopranos, accompanied by a separate, two-part canon in the altos. This is a very ancient polyphonic form: indeed it resembles the canonic structure of the famous thirteenth-century 'Reading Rota', *Sumer is icumen in.* But here the mood is utterly different. Brahms's beautiful canon, tinged with melancholy, is rendered particularly haunting by the pathetic, repetitive (indeed, *'einförmig'*) tune in the sopranos. Yet the tune is not his own – it is the melody of the last song of Schubert's cycle *Die Winterreise, Der Leiermann*, the famous, chilling song about the ragged organ-grinder on the ice, who is perhaps the figure of Death.

This canon seems to me to encapsulate many of the significant things about Brahms as a composer. It shows him as someone standing in an intensely personal relationship to the musical past. On the one hand he has become absolute master of the forms of strict contrapuntal writing, an art that for a time had been well-nigh lost; on the other he forges deliberate links with his predecessors, and invests their vision with a new and personal interpretation. It may be unusual to find him

1

basing an entire piece on someone else's tune, but he is in effect treating Schubert's melody as he might – and often did – treat a folksong, as part of the common heritage of the people. And in making a canon of it he makes a small demonstration of his powers of variation, such as he often brought to bear on other composers' themes, and on his own.

Above all, this little work is *symbolic*. Nothing is there simply for itself. The ancient form, the Schubert tune, the Romantic melancholy (enhanced by the memory, which Brahms means to conjure up, of the words to which the tune was sung in *Winterreise*) combine to provide a powerful symbol of musical continuity, of the persistence of musical ideas and meaning despite surface change. Brahms had a very highly developed sense of musical history, and his works are full of symbols of this kind, though usually subordinate to the demands of a larger design, and very seldom effected, as here, by direct quotation.

The Rückert text is important too. By setting it Brahms was making an ironic comment on his own personal life, as one who had 'hummed along' with the chorus of love but always stood apart from it. The poem implies the reliving of memory, always for Brahms an emotional process; and the Schubert tune, symbolizing old things, may be taken as a symbol of memory as well. Love is a song, says Rückert. Music and love were, for Brahms, very closely allied – the women he loved were musicians; musical creation competed with his emotional life; love was sometimes sublimated into composition. In this he was completely a Romantic; yet, remaining unattached, and creating in his work a revived polyphony – a song not on one note but on many – he was effectively writing Romanticism's epitaph.

Young Kreisler (1833–53)

Keinen hat es noch gereut,...
Um in frischer Jugendzeit
Durch die Welt zu fliegen....
Lorbeer und Rosen
Führen ihn höher und höher hinan....
Dann wählt er bescheiden
Das Fräulein, das ihm nur vor allen gefällt.

(No man has yet regretted it....
In the first flush of youth
To speed through the world....
Laurels and roses lead him onward and upward....
Then modestly he chooses
The damsel who pleases him most of all.)

Ludwig Tieck, first *Magelone* Romance
(set by Brahms in his op. 33)

Twenty years after Brahms's death, when many critics still maintained that, whatever his greatness as an 'absolute' musician, he had possessed no sense of instrumental colour, it fell to the Marxist philosopher Ernst Bloch to place within his first culture-spanning *magnum opus, Geist der Utopie*, an elegant characterization of Brahms as a master of the orchestra:

> He does have colour: his orchestral sound has been compared, not unfavourably, to the North German heathland, which appears from a distance like a broad, monotonous expanse, but whose greyness, as we enter, suddenly dissolves into a myriad little blooms and specks of colour.[1]

Behind that poetic comparison lurks an unstated pun on the composer's origins, and even on his name. The sweet-flowering broom, *planta genista*, is known throughout North Germany by the dialect name *Bram*: from Hanover to Schleswig people bear variations of that name, usually in a possessive form ending in 's' – Brams, Brahms, Bramst, and so on. In a French-speaking culture, therefore, the composer might have borne

[1] Quoted here from Ernst Bloch, *Essays on the Philosophy of Music*, translated by Peter Palmer (Cambridge, 1985), p. 30.

the resoundingly aristocratic name 'de Plantagenet'; but in German 'Brahms' has no connotations of noble birth – rather the opposite, for it means 'a child of the heathland'.

The family – whose members seem, up to and including the composer's father, to have spelt themselves indifferently Brahms or Brahmst – was in fact of peasant stock. Records do not extend further back than the composer's great-grandfather, Peter Brahms, who left lower Saxony in the mid-eighteenth century, searching for work, and after extensive wanderings settled in the small seaport of Brunsbüttel in Holstein, where he plied the trade of carpenter and wheelwright. His son Johann (1769–1839) married a Holstein girl and became an innkeeper in the village of Heide further to the north – in the so-called 'Dittmarschen' country, near the Danish border, a region noted for its independence of character. They had two sons, Peter Hoeft Hinrich (born 1793) and Johann Jakob (born 1806); grandfather Peter joined the family in Heide on his retirement. The poet Klaus Groth, born in the same village in 1819, thus came to know four generations of Brahmses, and many of his lyrics were set as songs by Johann Jakob's son.

Peter Hinrich may have been the first of the family to manifest something resembling an artistic temperament: he remained in Heide as a pawnbroker by trade, but in spirit a somewhat eccentric collector of antiques. However Johann Jakob, his junior by thirteen years, was the first Brahms to aspire to be a professional musician. He achieved his ambition against stern parental opposition, three times running away from home to look for tuition before old Johann allowed him to become apprenticed to the town musician of Heide at the age of fourteen. Indentured for five years (the last two under a member of the town band of Wesselbüren), Johann Jakob trained as an orchestral player, learning to play flute, bugle, and all the stringed instruments. His instruction over, the nineteen-year-old guild musician left home to seek his fortune in the nearest big city: Hamburg.

In this pre-revolutionary Germany of little kingdoms and principalities Hamburg, situated between Schleswig-Holstein and the kingdom of Hanover, was a wealthy city whose independence dated back to the thirteenth century, when it had been one of the principal seaports of the great mercantile confederacy of the Hanseatic League. In recent decades it had received a new influx of wealth as the major trading link between Europe and the newly independent USA. The city supported a prosperous merchant class, but near the harbours the poorer citizens crowded in close-packed slum areas, among the bars and brothels that catered to the appetites of sailors from all over the world.

It was in this more squalid part of the city that Johann Jakob lodged, and found his first employment playing in taverns and dance-halls. By dogged persistence he eventually rose to become a horn-player in the town guard and an occasional member of a popular sextet that played light music at the Alster Pavilion on the fashionable promenade of the Jungfernstieg. It was mainly as a double bass-player that he made his living; but in these early Hamburg years, however much he relished the career he had chosen for himself, he remained a poor man. In 1830, having acquired the right of citizenship in the city, he took lodgings in the Ulricusstrasse with a family called Detmering: and within a week had proposed to Frau Detmering's younger sister Johanna Henrike Christiane Nissen, a skilled seamstress who helped in the family shop. After she had got over her surprise (for at forty-one she was seventeen years her suitor's senior, slightly lame, in delicate health, and – despite a rather more exalted ancestry traceable back to the fourteenth century – quite as poor as he), Christiane accepted the young musician. It proved a surprisingly successful match, for she was an intelligent, kind-hearted, and eminently practical person, well able to organize a household and family for her easygoing husband.

They were married in early June, and their first child, a daughter Elizabeth (Elise), appeared promptly in February 1831. They were then living at the Bäckerbreitergang; shortly afterwards they moved to a first-floor dwelling in no. 24, Specksgang, Schluterhof, a vast, shabby, gabled tenement[2] in the Gängeviertel (Lane Quarter), a thoroughly disreputable area known locally as 'Adulterer's Walk'. Here, on 7 May 1833, Christiane gave birth to her first son, who was named Johannes – 'son of Johann' – after his father, mother, and his grandfather, the innkeeper Johann Brahms, who stood sponsor at his baptism.

The future composer spent his infant years in the most cramped surroundings. The unsalubrious nature of 24 Specksgang is evident from surviving photographs of the building, which was set back in a gloomy court in a slum area near the city walls, where dirt and disease were commonplace. The fastidious Florence May, who visited the birthplace in 1902, wrote that

> the house and its surroundings testify only to the commonplace reality of a bare and repulsive poverty.... On entering [the first-floor dwelling], it is difficult to repress a shiver of bewilderment and dismay. The staircase door opens on to a diminutive space, half kitchen, half lobby, where some cooking may be done and a child's bed laid up ... this communicates with the sleeping-closet, which has its own window, but is so tiny it can

---

[2] The building (more often known by its later renumbering as no. 60 Speckstrasse) was destroyed by bombing in 1943.

scarcely be called a room. There is nothing else, neither corner nor cupboard..[3]

Brahms's parents and their two young children lived in these two rooms until 1835, when the third and last child, Friedrich (Fritz) was born.[4] After this they moved into slightly larger quarters in Ulricusstrasse, where Christiane started a modest haberdashery business to augment the family's means. This was one of her husband's many money-making ideas, but it was difficult to make a success of it as she was already so harassed by domestic responsibilities; throughout Johannes's childhood they were always chronically short of money.

The boy 'Hannes', fair-haired and blue-eyed, inherited his mother's short stature and delicate features, but his father's sturdy constitution: he grew up remarkably unaffected by the diseases endemic to the rat-infested area where he lived. His home luckily escaped the great fire of 1842 which consumed so many of the wooden houses in the old quarter; and though the next year Johannes was run over by a cab on his way to school, he recovered without serious consequences.

He was sent to a private school at the age of six, transferring soon after to another run by J. F. Hoffmann, an imaginative teacher who included foreign languages on his curriculum. It was here that Brahms picked up a sound reading knowledge of French and English, though he was never able to speak them. He was brought up in the strict Protestant faith of North Germany, receiving instruction from Pastor Johannes Geffcken at the Michaeliskirche, where he had been baptized. Geffcken became a good friend, and awakened the boy's interest in Lutheran chorales and church music: these were his first encounters with the music of earlier times.

Surrounded by music from his infancy, Johannes had soon shown appreciation and talent. Although his father started teaching him violin and cello when he was about four, he was fascinated by the piano from the first time he heard one. After three years of Hannes's stubborn determination Jakob (perhaps remembering his own youthful persistence) bowed to the inevitable, even though the instrument seemed to offer scant commercial potential, and arranged for his son to have lessons with a local piano-teacher. Luckily he chose a man of real gifts and character. In Otto Friedrich Willibald Cossel, the boy for the first time encountered an artist for whom music was not merely entertainment and livelihood, but a calling. Working with Johannes through

---

[3] Florence May, *The Life of Johannes Brahms*, 2nd ed. (London, 1948), p. 55.
[4] Fritz, too, pursued a musical career and became a piano-teacher in Caracas and Hamburg, where he was known in later years as 'the wrong Brahms'.

the studies of Czerny and Cramer, and Clementi sonatas, Cossel discovered him to be dedicated, intelligent, and blessed with such natural
aptitude that within three years he felt that there was little left that he
could teach him. He had noted, also, Johannes's first stirrings in the
direction of original composition; and when it proved impossible to
quench his pupil's thirst for such distraction from the pianistic career
pure and simple, Cossel tried to get his own teacher, the locally renowned
pedagogue and composer Eduard Marxsen, to accept the boy for further
tuition, but at first without success. Later, when Jakob himself
approached him, Marxsen consented to give one lesson a week, but only
on the understanding that Johannes continued to study with Cossel
(who by now was also teaching his brother Fritz).

Meanwhile Jakob, eager to turn his son's talent to advantage,
arranged a private benefit concert to raise funds for the ten-year-old's
future education. Johannes appeared as pianist in Beethoven's op. 16
Quintet and a Mozart piano quartet, and played a bravura Etude by
Henri Herz. An impresario who attended the concert now suddenly
presented Jakob with a glowing vision of financial gain – he offered to
take the boy on a tour of America, promising this would bring rich
rewards. The dazzled Jakob was disposed to accept the scheme (according to one account, he actually sold Christiane's shop at a loss in
preparation for the journey to the other side of the Atlantic), but
Cossel was horrified at the idea of his young pupil's being commercially
exploited as a *Wunderkind*; he immediately persuaded Marxsen to
intervene and insisted that he take overall responsibility for Johannes's
musical education. Perhaps to salve Jakob's angry disappointment,
Marxsen refused to accept any payment for his teaching.

Thus Johannes became a pupil of one of the most cultured
musicians in the area. Marxsen was a prolific and versatile composer
whose works ranged from the florid virtuoso piano variations so popular
at the time, to symphonies, and even an orchestral version of Beethoven's
'Kreutzer' Sonata. He had studied composition in Vienna with Ignaz
Seyfried, a pupil of Mozart and Albrechtsberger, who knew both Haydn
and Beethoven; and piano with Carl Maria von Bocklet, a close friend
and early champion of Schubert. His initial unwillingness to take on the
young Brahms evaporated as he began to recognize the boy's potential
as a composer. He instructed him in harmony, counterpoint, and theory;
encouraged him to develop the skill of transposing at sight; introduced
him to much of the then-unfashionable repertoire of the Classical and
earlier periods; and lent the already avid young reader many books he
would not otherwise have seen. Brahms had his lessons in the neigh-
bouring town of Altona, practising in the meanwhile at Cossel's or in

7

piano showrooms (there was of course neither room nor money for a piano of his own), while continuing to attend school. It was a punishing schedule, and it is hardly surprising that throughout his youth he suffered from migraine. His relations with Cossel remained warm and valuable, for though Marxsen's Classical tuition was to stand him in good stead in later life, the young Brahms shared his first teacher's enthusiasm for the works of contemporary Romantic composers. However, Marxsen's sets of variations on peasant dances and Finnish folksongs set him a different and important example in the art of incorporating folk material into original compositions.

While receiving this excellent musical education, Johannes could not avoid putting his gifts to practical use to alleviate his family's acute poverty. In particular, from the age of thirteen he had – like his father before him – to take engagements playing the piano in the many drinking and wenching dives of the notorious St Pauli area near the harbour. English accounts of his early life usually render these establishments as bars, taverns, or dance-halls; our language in fact provides no exact equivalent for the now-archaic German terms *Animierlokale* or *Animierkneipe* – literally 'stimulation saloons', where the stimulus on offer was musical, alcoholic, and sexual in convenient combination. Providing non-stop dance music late into the night in rooms thronged by prostitutes and sailors straight off their ships, the sensitive Johannes saw a daunting amount of low life in the raw just as he himself was entering puberty. Upon this background some biographers have erected elaborate speculations concerning his later difficulties in relations with women; whatever the truth may be, the experience undoubtedly left its scars. At a very early age, he could retain few romantic illusions about the opposite sex, let alone about his own.

Nevertheless when he grew up he deeply resented any suggestion that he had been exploited by his parents, to whom he always remained strongly attached. Usually he hated to talk of his innermost feelings, protecting them with a reserve that grew ever more forbidding. Yet over forty years later, walking through the Central Cemetery in Vienna with his friend and eventual biographer Max Kalbeck, he felt the need to make them clear. As Kalbeck wrote:

> Brahms recalled his own youth in disconnected but deeply felt words, words that came from the depths of his heart, as if he wanted to defend himself against the charge of a 'neglected upbringing' that had been made against him. He talked about how much his parents had loved him, and he them, about how dispiriting they and he found the constant struggle to make ends meet, about the humiliation and injuries to which he and they had been exposed in his home town, and about how he had calmly

accepted everything. Undeterred by praise or blame he had gone his own way, and always the recognition of a few friends had rendered him immune to the hatefulness of a hostile world.

One may wonder, however, whether Johannes's fierce dedication to the creative side of music, and his quickening intelligence, arose merely of themselves or rather in self-defence – not simply against the clientele of the *Animierkneipe* but against a home environment that, however affectionate, was absolutely lacking in privacy. The mind is the ultimate private place, and Johannes furnished his through a vast, instinctive appetite for learning and literature. He started collecting old volumes from the bookstalls dotted along the Hamburg canals, and even as he played in the *Lokale* he read poetry, propped upon the music-stand. He became a devotee of the fantastic fiction of E. T. A. Hoffmann – who as both composer and writer had been one of the early geniuses of the Romantic period, and for whom music was a constant touchstone of spiritual value. In particular Brahms responded to the grotesque irony of his novel *Kater Mürr* (1821), in which the sardonic tomcat Mürr indites his autobiography on the backs of the passionate meditations on Art written by his master, the neurotic, idealistic musician Johannes Kreisler. Brahms began strongly to identify with Hoffmann's hero, building up for himself an alter ego as 'Johannes Kreisler Junior'. Hoffmann's Kreisler, unable to cope with philistine society, always found solace in his Art; this 'Young Kreisler' would do likewise.

By the winter of 1846–7 the strain of his double life, of serious musician by day, bar-pianist by night, was taking its toll – Johannes was near collapse with anaemia and nervous exhaustion. He once told Klaus Groth that eventually he had to hold on to the trees while walking down the street, to prevent himself from falling. Luckily, at the Alster Pavilion his father had meanwhile befriended a wealthy paper-mill owner and farmer, Adolf Giesemann; and hearing that Johannes was in poor health Giesemann invited the boy – who had never been further than Altona in his life – to spend some weeks at his country home at Winsen an der Lühe, where he could supply the family's musical needs. The summer months at Winsen, taking long walks in the woods and swimming in the river, returning to Hamburg occasionally by steamboat for his piano and school lessons, soon restored the boy's health; but they also broadened his cultural horizons and fed his creative imagination. Here he formed the lifelong love of nature for which his Romantic reading had prepared him. He gave piano lessons to Giesemann's daughter Lieschen, a year younger than himself, who shared his love of reading; they became close friends, and she afterwards came to stay with his family in Hamburg. Together in Winsen they befriended a Jewish boy, Aaron Lowenherz, who for a small consideration brought them volumes temporarily purloined from the lending-library owned by his mother. One of these was the romance *The Beautiful Magelone and Count Peter of the Silver Keys*, which years later was to supply Brahms with the basis of his most substantial song cycle. He played piano-duet arrangements of Beethoven with a local bailiff, Herr Blume. Most important of all, he gained his first experience of conducting with the Winsen Choral Society, about a dozen strong, for whom he wrote some small partsongs.

Back in Hamburg in the autumn, Johannes returned to his studies but not, apparently, to the *Lokale*. Instead he played in restaurants and took part in a few concerts, without attracting much attention. The following spring he left school at the age of fifteen, and again spent some weeks at Winsen, where he arranged two folksongs for the choral society. This year, 1848, was one of revolutionary ferment across Europe, which resulted, in Germany, in the first steps towards a Prussian-dominated unitary state. At first Hamburg was little affected, and Brahms's attention was presumably fixed upon musical matters (such as his first hearing of Beethoven's Violin Concerto, played by the phenomenal seventeen-year-old Joseph Joachim; and his first visit to the opera, to see Mozart's *Le Nozze di Figaro*, at Giesemann's expense). He was beginning to take piano pupils of his own, and preparing for his first public recital. He gave this in Hamburg on 21 September, with two singers and a cellist, and – in a largely 'contemporary' programme of virtuoso trifles by Rosenhain, Döhler, Herz and Marxsen – he was bold enough to play a fugue by J. S. Bach: very severe and unfamiliar concert-fare for the time. The following April, again with a number of supporting musicians, he returned to the concert platform with a much more ambitious (and much better attended) recital that included Beethoven's 'Waldstein' Sonata, an operatic fantasia by Thalberg, and – most significant of all – a work of his own, a 'Fantasia on a Favourite Waltz'.

The piece has not survived, but the fact that Brahms was daring to come before the public not just as a pianist but a *composer*–pianist shows how important to him his creative work had now become. Marxsen, who had initially forbidden composition until his pupil acquired sufficient technique, was by now encouraging Brahms to contribute fantasias of this type and hack arrangements to the catalogue of the Hamburg publisher Cranz.[5] But there is no doubt that, even at this

[5] For more details see p. 60.

early stage, Brahms was more interested in serious forms of composition. For some years now he had been friendly with a young pianist and song-composer, Louise Japha (who recalled in later years that as early as 1844 the eleven-year-old Johannes had played her a piano sonata of his own!); and he now began to show her his current pieces. Louise was a passionate enthusiast for the music of Robert Schumann; and when this leading contemporary composer visited Hamburg in 1850 with his wife Clara, one of the greatest piano virtuosos of the age, Louise persuaded Brahms to send a parcel of his works to their hotel – but to his bitter disappointment it was returned unopened.

The revolutionary stirrings of 1848 impelled a wave of political refugees towards Hamburg from the Austro-Hungarian Empire. Many of them simply passed through on their way to America; one who stayed was the Hungarian violinist Eduard Reményi, born in 1830, who had studied in Vienna alongside Joseph Joachim. On his arrival in Hamburg he gave some recitals, and for one of these engaged Johannes as his accompanist. Few biographers can bring themselves to give Reményi a good character, and he does seem to have been a boastful, temperamental, opportunistic person. But he was the catalyst for dramatic changes which were to thrust the obscure young Hamburg pianist onto the international musical stage. Reményi was impressed with Johannes's playing, while for his part Brahms was fascinated by the Hungarian's spirited performances of his 'national' music, gypsy-style folksongs and dances. For a time, the personal chemistry between them was right, and the two played together a great deal in the period 1850–52 – with a brief interruption when Reményi was temporarily expelled by the police as a politically undesirable alien.

At first, however, Reményi was simply one among a number of potentially useful professional contacts which Brahms was making while he applied himself to composition with markedly greater enthusiasm than to public performance. In the Hungarian's absence he partnered the celebrated Hamburg pianist Otto Goldschmidt (composer of the famous carol *Stille Nacht*) in a piano duo; he played his new Scherzo in E flat minor (eventually to be published as his op. 4) to the visiting composer Henri Litolff; and in July 1851 he took part in a private chamber concert with the cellist d'Arien (who had participated in some of his earliest recitals) and the Danish composer–violinist Niels Gade. Among the items they played were a Piano Trio and a Duo for cello and piano ascribed to one 'Karl Würth'. Brahms's own annotated copy of the programme shows that this was a pseudonym for himself; but these, his first known chamber works, were never heard of again.

Nevertheless it was with Reményi, who returned to Hamburg in late 1852 after some time in the USA and Paris, that he was forming the closest association. Already (at least as early as 1848) Brahms had become a passionate collector both of old vocal and instrumental music and of folksongs; the Hungarian's large repertoire of Magyar and Zigeuner melodies fired his enthusiasm, and was eventually to leave an indelible imprint on his musical language. Early in 1853 the two of them gave a recital in Winsen including Beethoven's C minor Violin Sonata, a concerto by Vieuxtemps, and Reményi's renditions of Hungarian melodies; such was the enthusiasm of Brahms's Winsen friends that there and then they conceived the idea of making this same programme the basis of a concert tour of other north German towns, specifically Celle, Lüneburg, and Hanover (where Reményi hoped to gain the interest of Joachim, who had recently taken up a court appointment as Konzertmeister there). The two young musicians set off on 19 April. For Brahms, a month short of his twentieth birthday, it was a great adventure, the longest journey he had yet made; but he could hardly have dreamed that he would be away from Hamburg for eight months that were to change his life utterly.

After successful concerts in Celle (where Johannes, finding the piano tuned flat, nonchalantly transposed the piano part of the Beethoven up a semitone, from memory), Lüneburg, and Hildesheim, they made for Hanover, where Reményi speedily renewed his acquaintance with Joseph Joachim, already at twenty-one renowned as violinist, conductor, and composer. Joachim, however, soon found himself more attracted by the flamboyant Reményi's reserved and self-effacing accompanist; and when Johannes was persuaded to play some of his piano pieces and the song *Liebestreu*, he realized that he had encountered a musical mind of a quite extraordinary order. Moreover, the two young men discovered a strong temperamental affinity, and Brahms, probably for the first time in his life, found he had gained a close friend with whom he could discuss every subject, personal and artistic, that lay close to his heart.

Foreseeing that Brahms and Reményi were an ill-matched pair of individuals, Joachim advised Johannes to seek him out at Göttingen in the summer if he ran into difficulties. He also procured an engagement for the duo to play to the court of his patron, King George of Hanover; but within days the Hanoverian police interrogated Reményi on suspicion of being a political troublemaker, and ordered the two of them out of Hanover at the double. They decided to head for Weimar, where Reményi hoped to contact Franz Liszt, the greatest Hungarian musician of the age; and Joachim, who had been *persona grata* with the

Liszt circle for some years, obligingly supplied them with the necessary introductions.

At Weimar Johannes for the first time found himself seriously out of his depth. Liszt was living in grand style at the palace of his mistress, Princess Carolyne von Sayn-Wittgenstein, amongst a throng of pupils and acolytes of the 'New German' school, whose would-be revolutionary musical principles were far removed from the tenets of Marxsen. Amongst them were prolific and fashionable composers like Raff, Cornelius and Karl Klindworth. As always with young aspiring musicians, Liszt himself was the soul of kindness; but the boy from the Hamburg docklands was overawed by the sumptuous lifestyle, and recoiled almost through blind instinct from the atmosphere of insistent adulation that surrounded the great man. Though Liszt and Reményi coaxed him, he was too unnerved to play his compositions to the assembled company; and seeing this Liszt himself volunteered for the task. He performed Brahms's E flat minor Scherzo and part of his C major Sonata, at sight, with sovereign ease, keeping up a running fire of comment and compositional advice as he did so. A little later some of those present begged the master to perform his own Sonata in B minor, which was then still in manuscript. This Liszt did, magnificently – but glancing across to Johannes during a particularly affecting passage, he discovered the young Hamburger had fallen fast asleep.

That at least was the story as transmitted by Liszt's American pupil William Mason; but though present on this occasion he had been unable to see Brahms's reactions, which were later described to him by Reményi (a very unreliable source). Yet given the exertions of the journey to Weimar, Johannes's general disinterest in Liszt's music, and the emotional strain of having his music exposed in such a gathering, he may well have nodded off in psychological self-defence. Liszt was not offended, and was to maintain cordial if distant relations with Brahms for the rest of his life.

Nevertheless, Brahms now wished to leave Weimar as soon as possible. Reményi, however, found Liszt's circle and surroundings eminently congenial; he was outraged by Johannes's apparent lack of gratitude, and saw it as directly threatening his own career prospects. For some time, too, he had resented the disproportionate amount of attention which musical notables had lavished upon his socially awkward accompanist. The duo had come to the parting of the ways; Reményi went off without him (they never met again) and Brahms was left to his own devices. Remembering Joachim's parting words, he wrote to him on 29 June, the very epitome of Romantic dejection:

If I were not named 'Kreisler', I should now have well-founded reasons to curse my art and my enthusiasm . . . I really did not need such another bitter experience; in this respect I had already quite enough for a poet and composer. I cannot return to Hamburg without anything to show . . . I must at least see two or three compositions in print, so that I can cheerfully look my parents in the face . . . may I visit you [at Göttingen]? Perhaps I am presumptuous, but my position and my dejection force me to it.

At Göttingen Joachim was improving his education by attending courses in philosophy and history at the University. He welcomed Brahms warmly, and there was an instant renewal of their friendship, which deepened and flourished throughout the two months in which Brahms joined Joachim's circle and enjoyed all the advantages of student life without actually needing to do any academic work. Instead he devoted himself to reading and composition – not all of it serious, to judge by the *Hymne zur Verherrlichung des grossen Joachim* ('Hymn to the Veneration of the Great Joachim'), a burlesque serenade for string trio which Brahms and two mutual friends, Otto Brinkman and Arnold Weber, played to Joachim on the latter's twenty-second birthday. Joachim too was making a name for himself as a composer, and he and Brahms seemed to have whetted the edge of each other's creativity. In August, Joachim and Brahms gave a concert which raised enough funds to enable Johannes to carry out a long-cherished ambition: a walking tour along the Rhine.

Parting from Joachim, he wandered northward on his own with the flow of the great river through rocky and Romantic landscapes. In September, staff in hand and knapsack on back, he arrived in Bonn. Here he met the violinist J. W. von Wasielewski, a pupil of Mendelssohn, who introduced him in turn to the Deichmann family, prominent patrons of the arts, at Mehlem across the Rhine. He stayed with them for a while, walking in the countryside and working on a new and very ambitious Piano Sonata in F minor. The Deichmanns were ardent proselytizers for the music of Schumann, who lived further down-river at Düsseldorf; and it was in their house that Johannes finally began to study Schumann's works closely and to recognize that this was a master whose musical ideals accorded with his own far more than he had hitherto suspected. He even recognized his own enthusiasms for E. T. A. Hoffmann in Schumann's *Kreisleriana*, musical impressions of the novelist's Kapellmeister Kreisler. Until now – despite Joachim's urging – Brahms had fought shy of approaching Schumann, perhaps anticipating a rebuff as in 1850, or having to penetrate another 'court circle' such as surrounded Liszt. But he finally resolved to call at Düsseldorf and make the acquaintance of the man whose support could mean a great deal to him in artistic terms. He continued his walking-tour with the Deichmann brothers as far as Cologne, where he met the composers Carl Reinecke and Ferdinand Hiller; and then boarded a train for Düsseldorf.

Brahms presented himself at the Schumanns' house around noon on 30 September 1853. They were not at home, but their eldest daughter, Marie, who opened the door (to a person she long afterwards remembered as 'a very young man, handsome as a picture, with long blonde hair'), told him to come the next day at 11 a.m. This he did, and was cordially received by Robert Schumann himself, who immediately asked Brahms to play for him. Much more at ease in the comfortable domesticity of the Schumann household than he had been at Liszt's establishment, Brahms suffered no loss of confidence and attacked the opening bars of his C major Piano Sonata. But he had only been playing for a few seconds before Schumann stopped him and ran out of the room saying 'Please wait a moment, I must call my wife'. He brought Clara back with him, sat her down, and signed for Brahms to continue, telling her 'Now you will hear music such as you have never heard before.' Brahms played for them throughout the forenoon, and promised to stay nearby so as to be able to visit his new friends every day. Afterwards at lunch the Schumann children found their parents bubbling over with excitement about the fair-haired young man. That evening Schumann wrote in his diary: 'Visit from Brahms, a genius.' Clara's diary entry shows she was equally impressed:

> Here again is one of those who comes as if sent straight from God. He played us sonatas, scherzos etc. of his own, all of them showing exuberant imagination, depth of feeling, and mastery of form. Robert says there was nothing he could tell him to take away or add. It is really moving to see him sitting at the piano, with his interesting young face which becomes transfigured when he plays, his beautiful hands, which overcome the greatest difficulties with perfect ease (his things are very difficult), and in addition these remarkable compositions.

Schumann himself, at forty-three, had attained the height of a fame founded chiefly upon his early piano compositions (in which he had set new standards for the purposeful application of Romantic fantasy), and which was now augmented by a prolific output of vocal, choral, symphonic and concertante works. In the faction-riven artistic world of his time his music still fell short of universal esteem, and was a 'cause' to be fervently promulgated by friends and associates; nevertheless, he was recognized as one of the leading musical personalities in Germany. His courtship of the young Clara Wieck, the foremost woman pianist in Europe, culminating in their marriage against the wishes of her tyrannical father, had added a lustre of romance to both the Schumanns, and thirteen years of married life had brought modest material prosperity and a large family. Clara, despite her domestic commitments, was a rare example for that time of a dedicated woman professional, who continued to pursue a demanding concert schedule while acting as her husband's artistic deputy; Robert was employed as music director of the Düsseldorf Municipal Orchestra and Chorus, with responsibility for ten concerts and four church services with music each year.

Brahms must at first have been unaware how precarious Schumann's position actually was, both professionally and mentally. Since adolescence, and much more frequently in the past decade, the composer had been ill with a series of recurrent nervous complaints which had made him increasingly dependent on Clara and had undermined his constitution and his ability to function in public. His symptoms at various times included general weakness, headaches, vertigo, insomnia, ringing in the ears (always alarming to a musician), extreme nervousness and emotional agitation, irritability, and manic-depressive swings of mood. Habitually awkward and diffident in company, in recent months he seemed to be experiencing difficulty in speaking or formulating his thoughts, and was troubled by auditory hallucinations. Friends were alarmed by his new enthusiasm for contacting the spirit-world in table-rapping séances; and not surprisingly his conducting duties appeared to be quite beyond him. Schumann had never been a good conductor, unable to keep discipline or convey his intentions clearly to performers; now his apathy and abstractedness, combined with an obsessive sense that the music was always being played too fast, was convincing the authorities that he was unfit for his post.

Within the Schumann circle it had long been believed that he suffered from an ill-defined 'nervous condition' aggravated by continual overwork. Although Clara had adopted a routine of shielding her husband as much as possible from social and professional stresses, she seems not to have faced the possibility of a looming mental collapse, but it is clear that Schumann was suffering from a major personality disorder. Conjecturally, he made have contracted syphilis in his teens which was now causing an additional degeneration of the nervous system – but medical opinion was then (and is now) still divided on the precise nature of Schumann's malady.[6]

---

[6] The symptoms are surely consistent with schizophrenia; but the most recent detailed study of the case, Peter F. Ostwald's *Schumann: Music and Madness* (London, 1985) finds too little hard evidence for a sweeping diagnosis, plumping for a 'major affective disorder' aggravated by a number of other but separate conditions.

Brahms's arrival coincided with (and may have helped to sustain) one of Schumann's increasingly rare spells of energy, interest, and apparent good health. The very day he arrived Clara had discovered she was pregnant with her seventh child. During Brahms's stay in Düsseldorf Schumann conducted several unsatisfactory concerts, had a number of confrontations with the increasingly worried members of the orchestra (who wished to replace him with his deputy Julius Tausch), and entertained several visitors including Bettina von Arnim, Joachim, and the French artist J.-B. Laurens; but he gave most generously of his time to Brahms, and threw himself whole-heartedly into assisting the career of this 'young eagle' from Hamburg in every way he could think of. Most importantly, he wrote to his publishers Breitkopf & Härtel in Leipzig, urging that they consider whatever Brahms could offer them.

So began a wonderful month for Brahms. He saw the Schumanns practically every day, playing music with them and to their distinguished visitors, talking, reading, or accompanying them on walks. He renewed his acquaintance with Louise Japha and made a new, lifelong friend in Schumann's composition pupil Albert Dietrich, only a few years older than himself. The two breakfasted together daily, and Dietrich introduced Brahms to a number of painters, kindling a strong, enduring interest in the visual arts. This congenial and admiring atmosphere clearly suited Brahms: several observers commented on his natural boisterousness and sense of fun. Clearly he took the Schumanns out of themselves, giving them a new mutual enthusiasm and helping to confirm Robert in his own compositional path. As if in recognition of this, the older composer dedicated to Brahms his latest large-scale work, the Introduction and Allegro for piano and orchestra, op. 134.

Joachim was to play in Düsseldorf at the end of October and Schumann had the idea of writing a work for him in collaboration with Brahms and Dietrich. Thus was born the so-called 'F-A-E' Sonata for violin and piano, based upon the initials of Joachim's personal motto *Frei aber einsam* (Free but lonely). The result was served up to Joachim on his arrival, and on 26 October he played it through with Clara Schumann accompanying: the joke was that he was supposed to guess who had written which movement, but he can have had little difficulty. Schumann had given of his best in the Intermezzo and Finale,[7] as had the talented Dietrich in the expansive first movement, but by far the most striking portion of the work was the splendidly taut Scherzo that was Brahms's contribution. Much more successful than many collaborative works of this kind, the Sonata stands as a living symbol

---

[7] Which he forthwith incorporated into his own Violin Sonata no. 3.

of the hopeful, optimistic atmosphere that prevailed in Düsseldorf during October 1853.

Brahms finally departed the town on 2 November, returning to Joachim's quarters at Hanover. There he found a new issue of *Neue Zeitschrift für Musik*, the journal Schumann had founded in 1834. He had abandoned the editorship ten years previously and had not written for it since then: but there, in the issue dated 28 October 1853, was an article by Schumann – about Brahms. Joachim had been consulted about it, but Schumann and he had carefully concealed it from the essay's subject, so Brahms was astonished by Schumann's ringing pronouncement. The article 'Neue Bahnen' ('New Paths') was nothing less than the announcement to the musical world of a new genius in its midst.

'Many new and important talents have appeared, for a new force in music seems to have notified its existence', wrote Schumann, going on to instance such composers as Joachim, Dietrich, Niels Gade, Woldemar Bargiel, Theodor Kirchner, Stephen Heller, and Robert Franz:

> I thought, while following the tendencies of this chosen band with the deepest sympathy, that sooner or later after this preparation someone would and must appear, fated to give us the ideal expression of the times, one who would not gain his mastery by gradual stages, but rather would spring fully armed like Minerva from the head of Kronion.[8] And he has come, a young blood at whose cradle graces and heroes mounted guard. His name is Johannes Brahms, from Hamburg, where he has been creating in obscure silence... recommended to me recently by an esteemed and well-known master. He carries all the marks of one who has received a call. Seated at the piano, he began to disclose wonderful regions... There were sonatas, or rather veiled symphonies; songs whose poetry would be clear even if one were ignorant of the words, though a profound singing melody runs through them all; individual piano pieces of almost demonic nature and charming form; then sonatas for violin and piano, quartets for strings – and all so different from one another that each seemed to flow from a fresh spring...
>
> When he waves his magic wand where the power of great orchestral and choral masses will aid him, then we shall be shown still more wonderful glimpses into the secrets of the spirit-world. May the highest Genius strengthen him for this... His contemporaries salute him on his first journey through the world where wounds may await him, but also palms and laurels; we welcome him as a powerful fighter...

Brahms was clearly taken aback – not so much by the extravagance

---

[8] English translations usually render this name as 'Jove', to harmonize with the Latin form Minerva; but Schumann, curiously mixing mythologies, uses the Greek epithet of Zeus meaning 'the son of Kronos'.

of Schumann's language, which was characteristic both of him and his times – but because he was wise enough to know that this heartfelt praise had thrust him irrevocably into the limelight before he felt ready for it. He had become an immediate object of attention and, he must have realized, of scepticism, for Schumann had pronounced in similar terms (though never with such fervour) on other composers who had failed to fulfil their promise. He immediately began to revise the works he intended to submit for publication, and it was a fortnight before he felt able to write to Schumann in thanks:

> The public praise you have deigned to bestow on me will have so greatly increased the musical world's expectations of my work that I do not know how I shall manage to do even approximate justice to it. Above all it forces me to exercise the greatest caution in the choice of pieces for publication. I think I shall not publish either of my trios, but shall select the sonatas in C major and F sharp minor to be my opus 1 and 2, songs for opus 3 and as opus 4 the Scherzo...

In addition to the shadowy 'trios', a String Quartet in B flat which had previously been discussed as publishable now vanished into obscurity. Whatever else Schumann's article did for Brahms, it certainly strengthened his already formidable powers of self-criticism. As soon as he had made his revisions, and a fair copy of the new Piano Sonata in F minor (completed in draft just before he left Düsseldorf), he resolved to go to Leipzig and present his works to Breitkopf & Härtel in person.

On 17 November he arrived in that great musical centre, where the memory of Mendelssohn was still fresh, and was greeted almost immediately by a friend of Dietrich's, Heinrich von Sahr, who became his host for the first part of his stay and set about introducing him to important local musicians. The advent of 'Schumann's young Messiah' excited considerable interest (mingled with disbelief) in Leipzig circles. Brahms met the violinist Ferdinand David (with whom he gave the last known performance of his Violin Sonata in A minor), the composer–pianist Ignaz Moscheles who had studied with Beethoven, the publishers Härtel and Senff, Clara Schumann's formidable father Friedrich Wieck and her sister Marie, and the young choral conductor Julius Otto Grimm, who soon became an influential friend. He introduced Brahms to the Countess Ida von Hohenthal, who invited him to spend a few days on her estate; while there he persuaded her to offer his brother Fritz the post of music-teacher to her children, which Grimm had just resigned, and repaid this kindness with the dedication of the new Piano Sonata. His hopes of publication were richly rewarded: Senff took the

new Sonata[9] and a group of songs; Härtel paid a reasonable advance
and immediately set about putting the first two Sonatas, the Scherzo,
and some other songs into print.

Instead of staying continuously in Leipzig he snatched another
few days in Hanover at Joachim's lodgings so that he could continue
composing in peace. 'How enviable is a nature like Brahms's, on whom
work has the most soothing effect', wrote Joachim on 27 November to
his close friend Gisela von Arnim:

> He is sleeping peacefully now, after his day's work, on my sofa in the
> next room, where he has already camped out for two nights – I am glad
> to think he is getting so much at home with me that he hardly ever leaves
> my rooms ... Brahms has been here since Friday, when, on coming back
> from a late walk, I found the young green and gold tiger lying in wait for
> me, greener than ever by reason of his laurels and newly gilt by publishers
> who are printing all his things ... You have really seen deep into his
> nature – he is egotistic and always on the lookout for something to his
> advantage – but at any rate he is sincere in the expression of his feelings,
> with none of the false sentimentality with which others of his kind like
> to deceive themselves ...

Brahms soon returned to Leipzig, where he played his works in
several semi-private venues and at a public concert with David's quartet;
but he was by no means the only new musical attraction in the town.
In early December Hector Berlioz came from Paris to conduct a concert
of his works, and Liszt arrived from Weimar to see the French composer.
Brahms met them both. Liszt was cordial as always, and when Brahms
performed at a salon held by Franz Brendel, the editor of *Neue Zeitschrift für Musik*, Berlioz was deeply moved, and embraced the young
Hamburger, whom he likened to Schiller (the comparison must have
delighted Brahms). 'I am grateful to you', Berlioz wrote to Joachim on
9 December, 'for having let me make the acquaintance of this diffident,
audacious young man who has taken it into his head to make a new
music. He will suffer greatly ...'.[10]

[9] Apparently as a substitute for the Violin Sonata. Senff had intended to publish this,
but it seems that Liszt (who liked the work) borrowed it from him to perform with
Reményi, who – typically – decamped with it on an English tour. A recently discovered
letter from Brahms to Clara Schumann (see the essay by George Bozarth in *Brahms
2*, ed. Michael Musgrave, Cambridge, 1987, pp. 84–5) suggests, however, that it did
not remain lost: Liszt made it his business to get the manuscript back and probably
returned it to Brahms in 1855. It was therefore not fate but its composer who made
sure it subsequently vanished; he probably destroyed it, although in 1872 Dietrich saw
a solo part, unreported since, among the papers of Brahms's Bonn friend Wasielewski.
[10] This and the previous quotation from *Letters from and to Joseph Joachim*, selected
and translated by Nora Bickley (London, 1914), pp. 40 and 49 respectively.

The production of Brahms's first printed music proceeded at that lightning nineteenth-century pace which so often astonishes publishers of our own day; when Brahms departed from Leipzig with Grimm on 20 December, he had engraved copies to take with him. Some he sent to Schumann, referring to them as 'your foster children' – the older composer, not much younger than Brahms's own father, was coming to occupy a parental role in his imagination.

Grimm had business in Hanover; but Brahms went on to Hamburg, arriving there in time to spend Christmas with his parents. Johann Jakob had recently secured a post with the Hamburg Theatre Orchestra, enabling the family to move to a slightly larger flat; but this recent success paled before the achievement of his brilliant son. Johannes had been absent from home for fully eight months, and the interval had transformed him from an obscure provincial pianist into an extravagantly acclaimed new talent, supported by some of the leading figures of the age, and on whom the eyes of the musical world now rested to see how he should fulfil Schumann's promise. Despite the warmth of his welcome from his family, Brahms was acutely aware of these expectations, and after a few days spent at home over Christmas as the conquering hero, he set off once more for Hanover to stay near Joachim, in surroundings where he could more easily work.

At Hanover he threw himself into the composition of a new, very large-scale Piano Trio in B major. Joachim and Grimm were on hand most of the time, and Brahms was also soon introduced to the pianist Hans von Bülow. Although Bülow was a leading advocate of Liszt's 'New German' school he was deeply impressed with Brahms's works and soon became the first pianist, other than Brahms himself, to perform some of them in public. Meanwhile preparations went ahead for a small Schumann-Festival in Hanover, centred around a performance of the master's cantata *Das Paradies und die Peri*. In anticipation of this, Schumann wrote to Joachim for news of Brahms, again urging that he should attempt orchestral composition as soon as possible:

> Is he flying high – or only amongst flowers? Is he putting drums and trumpets to work yet? He must remember the beginnings of the Beethoven symphonies; he must try to do something of the same kind. The point is to make a beginning...

At the end of January Robert and Clara Schumann arrived. Schumann had meanwhile been forced to give up his conducting position in Düsseldorf but they had just concluded a successful concert tour in Holland, and he was in good spirits. The concerts went well – they included performances not only of the cantata, but also of Schumann's

Fourth Symphony and Beethoven's 'Emperor' Piano Concerto (with Clara as soloist). Joachim conducted, and took the solo part in the première of Schumann's new *Fantasia* for violin and orchestra under the composer's baton. Nevertheless Clara noted that Brahms and Joachim seemed more subdued in her husband's presence than when they had previously met; possible they were disturbed by something in Schumann's behaviour, for his illness was approaching its climax.

The Schumanns departed for Düsseldorf on 29 January; for a while Brahms and his friends heard little of them except for a curious letter from Schumann to Joachim on 6 February which hinted at increasing mental disturbance. Indeed, his final breakdown began about four days later. Headaches, auditory hallucinations and feelings of mental anguish began to afflict the composer with greater force and frequency than ever before, despite the attentions of two doctors; he imagined the spirits of Mendelssohn and Schubert were dictating music to him in the night, and felt at the same time that he was no longer in control of his mind. By 21 February even Clara (by then five months' pregnant) realized that her husband's sanity was failing, and she, her daughters, or friends took turns sitting with the sick man at all times. The catastrophe came on 27 February: Schumann gave his family the slip, left the house, and threw himself off a bridge into the middle of the Rhine. The crew of a passing steamboat were able to fish him out and bring him home; but his spirit was so broken that it now seemed imperative to remove him to a sanatorium. At his own request Schumann was taken to one at Endenich, a suburb of Bonn. He was never to leave it.

2

The Romantic foreground

Alles verwandelt sich; nichts stirbt. In schöner Verwandlung wird das Verlorene Gewinn.
(Everything changes itself; nothing dies. In beautiful transformation, the lost is gained anew.)

Johann Gottfried Herder

Klarer Verstand mit warmer Phantasie verschwistert, ist die echte, Gesundheit bringende Seelenkost.
(Clear understanding mixed with warm fantasy is the true, health-giving food of the Soul.)

Novalis (Friedrich von Hardenberg)

(Quotations entered by Brahms in Des jungen Kreislers Schatzkästlein)

Popular music-history names the century into which Brahms was born 'the Romantic era'. The label identifies a period that asserted instinctive drives of feeling and imagination, of individual and collective identity, long pent up by the cosmopolitan rationalism of the eighteenth-century Enlightenment. We trace it from late Beethoven and Schubert to late Mahler, and situate it between the age of Viennese Classicism, and the 'modern' period initiated by Schoenberg, Stravinsky, Bartók and others. Romanticism's musical manifestations include the 'magical' operas of Weber and Marschner, the virtuoso instrumental writing of Paganini, Liszt and Alkan, the hybrid dramatic forms of Berlioz, Liszt's symphonic poems, the music dramas of Wagner, Chopin's and Schumann's cultivation of the intense lyric piece, Meyerbeerian grand opera, Italian opera (Verdi above all), Mendelssohn's essays into the picturesque, the tonally enlarged epic symphonism of Bruckner, and the nationalist aspirations of Russians, Czechs, Scandinavians and even Britons.

This then was a period of many opposing tendencies and contradictions. Moreover, few of these composers would have called themselves 'Romantics'. They regarded the 'Romantic' age as the recent past, the age of the French Revolution, and of writers such as Schelling, the Schlegels, Novalis, Arnim, Brentano and Tieck; its composers were, above all, Haydn, Mozart, and Beethoven – those whom we call the 'Classical' masters, but who had been defined as Romantic by their contemporary E. T. A. Hoffmann, himself a literary (and musical)

23

Romantic of the first order. The composers *we* call 'Romantic' thought of themselves as contemporary, 'of the future' – part of 'the progressive avant garde', as Schumann said of Robert Franz, Niels Gade and others. Brahms made no claim to write music of the future, but certainly considered himself his contemporaries' contemporary. Though by convention we regard him as a central figure of the Romantic era, he is often represented as a composer swimming against its currents, a 'conservative', even a 'neo-Classicist', staging a return to Classical ideals of structural balance and 'absolute' music, in contrast to the headily emotional and over-literary music of his day.

That clichéd view has a kernel of truth, but is of limited use if it is not seen in historical perspective. There is no space to explore adequately the imaginative phenomenon known as German Romanticism, which as a historical movement had already run its course before Brahms was born. But its ideas and ideals profoundly influenced nineteenth-century European creativity, and continued to develop – especially in music, always considered the Romantic art *par excellence* and always (until our own century) the last to absorb the effects of any radical new departure in aesthetic thought. Its influence on Brahms, the supposed 'Classicist', has seldom been given the prominence it deserves; but it hardly exaggerates the case to say that Romanticism was the determining intellectual influence of his impressionable years. At twenty he was already deeply, indeed voraciously read in the literature of Romanticism. His favourite authors were Schiller and Hoffmann, especially the musical novels of the latter; and a personal anthology of favourite quotations, kept from the age of fifteen in a notebook with the Hoffmannesque title of 'Young Kreisler's Treasure-Chest', contains nearly 650 epigrams and apothegms, largely drawn from the poets and aestheticians of the Romantic movement.

Accordingly, this chapter outlines some aspects of Romantic thought, especially as it pertained to music, that find a resonant echo in Brahms's life-work. It is vital to grasp that, however Olympian his eventual orientation to musical tradition, he was essentially a child of his times.

Whatever guises it assumed, Romanticism in art implied the primacy of subjective, imaginative and individualized modes of expression. Its initial motive force was political, stemming from Rousseau's call (especially in the *Discours sur l'origine de l'inégalité*, 1755) for a 'return to nature' to redress the imbalances in human society: not to re-enter Eden, which was forever lost, but to construct a radically new and more equitable social order. This was an important strand in the thinking that led to the French Revolution, but the echo it found in eighteenth-century Germany, fragmented among myriad quasi-medieval principalities, was of greater significance for the arts; an emerging sense of German nationhood was effectively denied political expression, but instead became a focus of cultural progress. Herder, theoretician of the proto-Romantic *Sturm und Drang* ('storm and stress') movement, preached the separate and undilutable cultural identity of different peoples; an identity conceived as a *linguistic* rather than racial heritage whose value transcended mere political nationalism.[1] Shakespeare's plays and, perhaps even more significantly the Scottish poet James Macpherson's 'translations' of ancient Gaelic fragments in his manu-factured 'Ossianic' epics, struck Herder with the force of a revelation. His *Briefwechsel über Ossian und die Lieder alter Völker* (1773) made a decisive break with the literary tenets of the Enlightenment. Holding that all forms of human self-expression are in some sense artistic, and that such self-expression is part of the essential nature of Man, Herder contended that the truest poetry is folk poetry — since, in his view, it springs spontaneously from the creative genius of an entire people: not as the result of intellectual ratiocination, but as direct inspiration born of strong and primal emotions. This belief spurred him to collect and preserve 'Germanic' (by which term he included British) folk poetry in the enormously influential anthology *Stimmen der Völker* (1778–9, revised 1807). It was a shining example to the Romantics Arnim, Bren-tano, the Grimm brothers, Ludwig Uhland, and their successors, who followed it in creating a literature of preserved folksong and folk music — a literature of which Brahms was the first composer to make systematic use. (As an early example, his 1854 piano Ballades were directly inspired by Scottish Border ballads he encountered in *Stimmen der Völker*. He set passages from *Ossian* too. Macpherson's epics retained a perennial attraction and enhanced authority for composers, after Schubert set nearly a dozen passages from them. Schubert's *Ossian* songs, seldom heard today, were greatly esteemed in the nineteenth century and were the first of his Lieder to be posthumously published in 1830; Brahms certainly knew them.)

At Weimar, Herder exercised a strong influence on Goethe and Schiller, whose position in regard to literary Romanticism is comparable to that of Beethoven and Schubert to musical Romanticism — gigantic figures whose actual modes of discourse remained Classically 'balanced'

---

[1] The fact that later and lesser thinkers distorted Herder's thought into a strident German nationalism does not diminish its original humanity. In his view, 'the German mission is not to conquer; it is to be a nation of thinkers and educators': cf. Isaiah Berlin, *Vico and Herder* (London, 1976), p. 161.

but instinct with a dynamism and commitment to strong, spontaneous emotion that prepared the way for the increased subjectivity of the Romantics. Goethe's aesthetic theories, especially those derived from his direct study of nature, proclaimed the need for 'organic' unity in artistic work – that, indeed, works of art are 'brought forth as Humanity's works of nature, according to true and natural laws'. These ideas had profound resonances for the following generation, the Romantics proper. But Goethe believed Man should recognize and abide by the limitations of his nature; the Romantics hoped to overcome them, and thus to open up new resources and cross-connections.

The German Romantics, above all in the aesthetic writings of Friedrich Schlegel, the fragmentary novels of Novalis, and the pantheistic nature poetry of Hölderlin, therefore elevated art to the status of religion. The artist, moved by inspiration, communicates an experience of nature which is both sensual and spiritual. Novalis's mysticism unites the earthly and the supernatural: he saw human love as the equivalent of God's love of the cosmos (an idea which is perhaps at the root of Brahms's *Deutsches Requiem*). Developing ideas from the Renaissance hermetic philosopher Jakob Böhme, he regarded the natural world as a vast reservoir of spiritual meaning. It provided the Romantic artist with an inexhaustible repertoire of objects – stones, stars, water, flame – which could be used as symbols or mirrors of the highest spiritual truth. This whole conception of nature, it was believed, had been better understood in ancient and medieval times, before the 'soul-destroying' Classicism of the Enlightenment; and so the Romantics were fascinated by 'primitive' (i. e. pure, untouched) cultures like that of India, folk art, the ancient world, and medieval chivalry. In some, the result was merely conversion to Catholicism. But Novalis's novella *The Apprentices at Sais* (1798) describes a search for inner wisdom at an Egyptian temple; his unfinished *Heinrich von Ofterdingen* (posthumously published in 1802) attempts the same on a larger scale in a medieval setting; Ludwig Tieck and others explore the glamour of medievalism and pre-Renaissance Italy in their novels and poetry. Among contemporary painters, Caspar David Friedrich in Dresden brilliantly adapts the vocabulary of light and landscape into a symbolic language irradiated by an intense spirituality; while the group known as the Nazarenes travelled to Italy and worked in a pre-Raphaelitic style, living in a Roman monastery like monkish craftsmen, drawing many other German artists to the city.

The Romantics regarded music as the ultimate art form. By its very nature, it could embody conflict of forces, depict interior states, suggest the infinite and invisible, encompass emotional change, mental flux, the

26

process of becoming, with a completeness and immediacy unavailable to painting or poetry. It avoided both literalness and pictorial imagery, communicated 'meaning' without committing itself to specific content. Music alone, they maintained, was capable of direct translation from the language of nature: it directly embodied the same principles of correspondence, harmony and organic unity that sustain the fabric of nature itself.

This mystical value placed upon music, celebrated as an untrammelled expression of the language of the spirit, was an ideal far beyond the range of response open to most of the contemporary Classical composers (although the last quartets of Beethoven might well be viewed as its perfect fulfilment). The Romantic authors – with the important exception of Hoffmann – were acquainted less with Beethoven than with more minor figures. In particular, the now-forgotten Johann Friedrich Reichardt (1752–1814) played an important role: his house at Giebichstein Castle was a meeting-place for major literary luminaries of the Romantic movement, and his considerable output (which Mendelssohn greatly admired, and Brahms also esteemed) marks an important stage in the evolution of German Singspiel and Lieder (he set voluminous amounts of Goethe, whom he knew personally, as well as Schiller and Shakespeare). E. T. A. Hoffmann studied composition with him.

Music on the desired Romantic pattern, breaking with the balanced tonal principles of the Classical era, got under way partly through the new cult of the virtuoso performer, the Romantic hero incarnate, whose rhapsodizing and improvisation seemed to fulfil the ideal of complete emotional spontaneity. The Mephisto-figures of Paganini (whose wild playing is celebrated in Heine's *Florentine Nights* as a kind of 'automatic writing') and Liszt were catalysts for a changed conception of music's function. Paganini's compositions are skeletal frameworks upon which to hang his personal brand of virtuosity; Liszt, however, under the influence of the Romantic theory of correspondences, was drawn in the direction of combining musical with other artistic impulses, in his 'symphonic poems' inspired by literature and painting, and his symphonies, conceived as character-portraits from Goethe's *Faust* and Dante's *Divina Commedia*. In France, Berlioz explored similar paths with his literary overtures, his works based on Shakespeare, his *Symphonie Fantastique* whose structure is 'programmed' by a symbolically autobiographical drugged dream. The climax of musical Romanticism, however, is generally considered the achievement of Wagner, with his concept of the *Gesamtkunstwerk* – the epic drama embracing myth, music, poetry, and scenic effect in a single, unified conception, for performance in a specially designed theatre, in the spirit of an over-

27

whelming public ritual, a man-made substitute for religion. Wagner's operas vastly surpassed the earlier 'magical' operas of Hoffmann, Weber, and Marschner, and the 'exotic' ones of Spohr. By centering his music dramas on the Germanic creation-myths (in *Der Ring*), on the supernatural (*Der fliegende Holländer*) and on aspects of idealized medievalism (in, for example, *Lohengrin*, *Tristan*, and *Meistersinger*), Wagner gave some of the chief Romantic preoccupations their most potent expression, and did so in an arch-Romantic way, evolving a musical symbolism which could denote emotion, ideas, relationships, character, and even inanimate objects in a vast network of 'leading-motifs' (*Leitmotiven*). Their transformation is elevated into a structural principle that can be deployed on an immense scale, most elaborately in the *Ring* tetralogy. Wagner, Liszt, and the numerous followers who gathered around them, felt justified in declaring their methods to be the 'Music of the Future'.

This was the situation when Brahms arrived on the scene. But there had always been a sense in which Romanticism was deeply concerned about the music of the past, and it was this tendency – not a 'conservative' one, but just as fundamentally 'Romantic' as the path taken by Liszt and Wagner – that was to shape his future achievements. The Romantic concern with the ancient and medieval worlds, with folk poetry and folksong, with pre-Raphaelitic painting, with Shakespeare and with 'Ossian' – in short with *old things*, because their greater proximity to the original wells of inspiration gave them unique authority – naturally extended to old music, even if few of the writers could have any clear idea of what this was. The revival of the works of the almost forgotten Leipzig Cantor Johann Sebastian Bach[2] – initiated by Mendelssohn[3] and his teacher Zelter in the 1820s and 30s – was not an act of 'neo-Classicism' (like Stravinsky's Bachian interests a century later) but a symptom of this Romantic fascination with the 'purer' music of earlier times; and it had a direct impact on the formation of contemporary musical style. As Charles Rosen has observed:

> Schumann set down only the literal truth when he wrote that his music (and that of Chopin, Mendelssohn, and Hiller) was closer to the music of Bach than to the music of Mozart. The impulsive energy of the Romantic work is no longer a polarized dissonance and an articulated

---

[2] Bach's keyboard works were always admired, but the rest of his output had fallen into obscurity.

[3] Mendelssohn, the most Classically-minded of the Romantic composers, knew Goethe, and his aunt Dorothea had married Friedrich Schlegel after an affair celebrated in the latter's influential, autobiographical Romantic novel *Lucinde*.

rhythm, but the familiar Baroque sequence... The music of Schumann in particular (Chopin retains some of the Classical clarity) comes in a series of waves, and the climax is generally reserved for the moment before exhaustion... With the change in style came a change in the tonal language itself. The chromaticism of Chopin, Liszt, and Spohr is only a surface manifestation of this change... The sources of the new style... are, above all, Bach and Rossini... Clementi, a figure from an earlier generation, remained a force in his development of loose, basically melodic structures; and by his importance for keyboard pedagogy, he transmitted a part of the heritage of Scarlatti...[4]

Brahms's reverence for Clementi (and Scarlatti) is well attested, and his explorations of Baroque and even earlier music were to be far more systematic and far-reaching than those of Mendelssohn or Schumann, crucial though their example was. It might be said, indeed, that though he always avoided the most obvious forms of musical Romanticism – the music drama, the symphonic poem – his special destiny was to reconcile, within the development of his own language, Romanticism's conflicting musical demands for intense expression of feeling *and* for closeness to the spirit of the oldest, 'purest' music; and to synthesize these with a revived mastery of the large-scale dynamics of Classical structure. He would once again build movements on 'a polarized dissonance and an articulated rhythm', but with vastly enlarged harmonic and rhythmic resources.

From this point of view Brahms's early and avid devotion to the writing of that arch-Romantic E. T. A. Hoffmann is especially significant, for Hoffmann, in his own person, embodies the conflicting Romantic conceptions of music.[5] Principally known to posterity as a brilliant writer of grotesque fantasy, several of whose novellas examine the problem and agonies of the creative artist (often with withering irony), he was also perhaps the most penetrating music critic of his age – and a prolific, exploratory composer whose own music is liberally, though unevenly, illuminated by genius.

Every writer notes Brahms's enthusiasm for Hoffmann. As previously related, Brahms identified so strongly with the composer–hero of several of Hoffmann's novels and stories, Kapellmeister Johannes Kreisler (musically embodied in Schumann's *Kreisleriana*), that he used the alias of 'Kreisler Junior' intermittently until at least 1860. He was familiarly addressed thus by his friends Joachim and Grimm, signed his

---

[4] Charles Rosen, *The Classical Style* (London, 1971), pp. 453–4.
[5] The ensuing discussion of Hoffmann is partly indebted to Gerhard Allroggen's study in the *New Grove*. David Charlton's English edition of E. T. A. Hoffmann's *Musical Writings* (Cambridge, 1989) appeared too late to assist the writing of this chapter.

manuscripts as Kreisler, and in 1855 sent Joachim two volumes of 'Kreisler's' piano works (now mostly lost, but they included the Variations on a Theme of Schumann, alternate variations of which are signed 'Brahms' or 'Kreisler' in the surviving manuscript). All this is well known (and intriguing enough). But it is usually represented as an adolescent retreat into a fantasy-world, as if fantasy were not in any case the necessary stuff of art. What has not been recognized – partly because, until recently, Hoffmann has been so undervalued as a composer in his own right – is that this profoundly stimulating musical mind must powerfully have affected Brahms from the first years he began to compose. We must therefore give Hoffmann closer attention.

Hoffmann's Kapellmeister Kreisler, who in boyhood found that a folksong his father sang became inextricably associated in his mind with a moss-covered stone concealing the grave of a murdered girl (consider the depth of emotion behind Brahms's earliest folksong settings, their dramatic treatments in his piano sonatas), is introverted, unstable, self-torturing, yearning for perfection in love, unable to accommodate himself to the manners of polite society; he experiences life as a series of professional failures and rebuffs. He is sustained by the rapture of creation and the intensity of his inner life; and Brahms must have found *him* very sustaining, propped up on the music-stand in the *Animierkneipe*. Kreisler's ecstatic conception of music descends directly from the vision of Novalis, with its mystic 'correspondences' between the arts and Nature. 'It is no mere image or allegory', says Kreisler,

> when the musician says that colours, scents, and light-rays appear to him as musical sounds, that their blending is to him a magnificent concert. An ingenious scientist has claimed that hearing is a form of internal sight; and in the same way sight is to the musician a form of internal hearing, a means to the deepest consciousness of the music that streams from every object that presents itself to his eyes, and vibrates to the same rhythms as those of his spirit... the sudden promptings of the musician's mind, the birth of melodies, are the unconscious – or rather the verbally inexpressible – recognition and grasping of the secret music of Nature as the principle of all life and activity.[6]

Kreisler's creative forte is improvisation, a halting, frustrating, yet desperately sincere, attempt to realize his inner visions in music. Yet the 'musical–poetical club' which Hoffmann describes in the *Kreisleriana* mocks his pathetic attempts and devotes its attention to much older music – such as the seventeenth-century Italian violin music also exalted

[6] Translated by Martin Cooper in two BBC radio talks, broadcast June and December 1951.

in Hoffmann's tale 'Councillor Krespel' (1816), or the works of Gluck, so uncannily conjured from blank music pages by the eccentric protagonist of Hoffmann's first story, 'Le Chevalier Gluck' (1809). Old music in Hoffmann's writings has a disturbing, almost magical power.

His own music manifests something of the same dichotomy, but from a different perspective. It was long believed (while his works lay unperformed) that as a composer Hoffmann was simply an inept imitator of Classical models, unable to invest his notes with the transcendental power he assigned to music in his fiction. But after all, the 'Classical' masters were his musical contemporaries, and revivals of some of his major works in recent years have begun to replace that negative view (which in any case minimized Hoffmann's wide practical experience as conductor, composer, and operatic producer) with something far more interesting. Certainly his sturdy Symphony in E flat (1806) could be considered a skilful amalgam of late Mozart, Gluck and early Beethoven, not without some personal touches. However in opera, the genre he cultivated most tenaciously, he achieved much that was original and had lasting effect. His eighth and last, *Undine* (1816), with its water-sprite heroine and magical meeting of human and spirit worlds, is a pioneering example of German Romantic opera, an inspiration to Weber (who praised it) and Wagner. A work long relegated to a footnote in opera's development, its recent revival has shown that it shaped history, not because of a fortuitous good idea but by the sheer force and integrity of Hoffmann's inspiration. Despite occasional dull patches *Undine* is a masterpiece of sorts, remarkable for a fiery rhythmic dynamism that owes much to Beethoven, a telling sense of instrumental colour, a fluent mastery of counterpoint, and a genuine capacity for large-scale thinking, integrating solos, choruses and even scene-changes into a single dramatic sweep – a stage on the way to the *durchkomponiert* approach of Wagner. But there is another area of Hoffmann's music which has more immediate relevance to Brahms: his conscious study of the music of the past. His numerous piano sonatas of 1807–8, with their elaborate application of fugue and strict counterpoint, were consciously essays 'in the old style', and undoubtedly helped Hoffmann gain the contrapuntal mastery just mentioned. Even more significant is his attempt to establish a new polyphonic church music idiom in his D minor Mass (1803) and the striking B flat minor *Miserere* of 1809. In these works the Protestant Hoffmann drew upon the Catholic church music of the Renaissance, above all Palestrina, whose style he claimed as a direct inspiration, and advocated as the ideal for a renewed and purified choral style in his 1814 essay 'Alte und neue Kirchenmusik' (which Brahms undoubtedly read):

In Palestrina's music each chord strikes the listener with its full force; elaborate modulations will never have that same power over the spirit as have bold strong chords such as his, bursting upon us like dazzling rays of light.

Sentiments such as these lay behind Brahms's voracious collecting of pre-Baroque music, and spurred him to a close study of it that began to bear fruit in his own choral works of the later 1850s. But he was also familiar with Hoffmann's writings on Beethoven, important not merely for their profound understanding of that composer (which Beethoven himself had acknowledged) but for their stimulating development of the cardinal Romantic concepts of correspondence and organic unity in relation to actual musical forms.

As already mentioned, Hoffmann saw the Viennese masters as 'Romantic' geniuses, 'opening up the wondrous realm of the Infinite' in different ways: their 'Romanticism' was in fact the individual stamp they imposed upon their musical subject-matter – Haydn in terms of the most human qualities, Mozart (especially in *Don Giovanni*, a work that deeply influenced Hoffmann himself) extending his grasp to the miraculous and superhuman, while Beethoven, using music as a moral force, evoked the infinite awe and cosmic yearning that were such fundamental parts of the Romantic response to life. In his celebrated review of Beethoven's Fifth Symphony (1810), Hoffmann drew attention to the fact that

> The inner arrangement of the movements, their development, instrumentation, the manner in which they are ordered, all this works towards a single point: but most of all it is the intimate relationship among the themes which creates this unity, which alone is able to keep the listener held in *one* sentiment...

And elsewhere, in a famous admonition to those listeners who professed to find Beethoven's music too difficult and obscure, he writes:

> what if it were only *your* weak sight which misses the profound unity of inner relation in each composition? If it were only *your* fault that the language of the master, understood by the consecrated, is incomprehensible, if the door of the holy of holies remains closed to you? In truth, the master... carves his essential being from the inner kingdom of tones, and reigns over it as absolute ruler.

To create an 'intimate relationship among themes', a 'profound unity of inner relation'; to be 'absolute ruler' of an 'inner kingdom of tones' that expressed 'his essential being' (*sein Ich*) – these were goals that the impressionable Brahms would work towards in his own music throughout his life. His preoccupation with structural unity, subtle architecture, and the Classic instrumental forms is usually represented as a commitment to 'absolute' music – but it is an 'absoluteness' of a distinctively Romantic kind.

Brahms's first discovery of Schumann's *Kreisleriana* and *Fantasiestücke* at Mehlem in September 1853 must therefore have been an epiphany of extraordinary force. An established master – of whose music he had not until now made any close study – was suddenly revealed as having entered the Hoffmannesque imaginative world before him. But Schumann's example was to remain largely that: an example, validating for Brahms the imaginative and creative development he had already undergone on his own. Schumann was to encourage him to study folksong and early church music; Brahms had already embarked on it. Schumann's library was to be an immense source of knowledge; but at twenty Brahms was extraordinarily well read. Already he had filled *Des jungen Kreislers Schatzkästlein* with passages from such writers as Pope, Young, Jean-Paul Richter, Lessing, and the Greek poets – but the entries are firmly centred on the Romantics and their immediate forebears, especially Goethe, Herder, Schiller and Novalis. Another notebook-anthology, the so-called *Zweites Schatzkästlein*, is much concerned with Goethe's philosophy of art. From such reading he would have discovered the principle of the work of art as a self-consistent organism, if Hoffmann's critique of Beethoven had not already shown him this principle in operation in music.

What he was to gain from the encounter with Schumann was something different, though equally fundamental to Romantic thought: a symbol-system. Symbols of the natural world were expected to form the vocabulary of the Romantic work of art, and Wagner had taken this furthest in the leitmotivic methods of his music dramas. But the mysteries of musical notation, already a symbolic representation of sound, lend themselves to the evolution of secret speech, code, cryptography. Composers had amused themselves with this approach for centuries, for instance in the common practice of writing a piece on the letters of someone's name: the most famous name in music is BACH, which according to the German nomenclature of notes spells a musical motif, B flat, A, C, B natural. Bach himself used it, and it is central to his contrapuntal 'testament', *Die Kunst der Fuge*.

The Romantic enthusiasm for symbolism stimulated afresh the possibilities of musical ciphers, and no composer was more passionately devoted to them than Schumann, whose love of codes and cryptograms found its way into the very structure of his music. His opus 1, the

'Abegg' Variations (1830), is based on the notes ABEGG, the name of a girl he had known in Heidelberg, Meta Abegg. When he was briefly engaged to a girl from the town of Asch, he based his piano masterpiece *Carnaval* on the notes ASCH (A, E flat, C, B), which are also the only four 'musical' letters in the name 'Schumann': their relationship is made clear in the movement called 'A.S.C.H.–S.C.H.A. (Lettres dansantes)'. But once he became engaged to Clara Wieck, he evolved many musical ciphers of the name Clara, which yielded a characteristic melodic shape, expressed in its most basic form by the notes C-B-A-G sharp-A, a 'Clara-theme' that, whether at this pitch or transposed, resounds in the op. 17 Fantasy for piano, the Piano Concerto, the Fourth Symphony and many other works.

This symbolism, now widely recognized in Schumann's music,[7] was a private affair known only to the Schumann circle. But Brahms, entering that circle, was initiated into it, and was thus able to recognize it and use it (most significantly the prime 'Clara' symbol, and for much the same reasons as Schumann) in his own works. The result was to be a lifelong use of such musical symbols, less obsessive but more diversified than Schumann's, to express secretly the 'specifics' that music allowed him to avoid saying outright. 'I speak in my music', he once wrote to Clara Schumann; he was stating the literal, and the Romantic truth.

Schumann's influence, personal and posthumous, was not confined to this, of course. A recent and stimulatingly wide-ranging study has suggested Schumann's creative path led him away from Romantic subjectivity towards an (equally Romantic) 'objectification' of music; and that by the time Brahms met him Schumann had subsumed the musical representation of extra-musical or poetic ideas into a 'poeticization' of musical form itself, the ideal form being the spacious, resonant epic of the Symphony, sounding in concert-halls of the mind to evoke the wide spaces of Nature, so close in the Romantic imagination to that other mystically resounding interior space, the Gothic cathedral.[8] A culminating work in this regard is the 'Rhenish' Symphony (his Third but

---

[7] The basic literature is quite recent, and principally the achievement of Eric Sams: see his essays 'The Schumann Ciphers', 'A Schumann Primer?' and 'Brahms and his Clara Themes' (*The Musical Times*, May 1966, November 1970, and May 1971 respectively). Though not all his arguments have found equal acceptance, the general principle of Schumann's and Brahms's employment of such musical ciphers is not now seriously disputed.

[8] Reinhard Kapp, *Studien zum Spätwerk Robert Schumanns* (Tutzing, 1984), especially pp. 142ff. See also his introduction and analysis in the Goldmann/Schott edition of the 'Rhenish' Symphony (Mainz, 1981).

last, published in 1851 yet conceived as long before as 1837), and a work
to which Brahms paid several homages, not least in his own Third
Symphony. Schumann's earlier exploration, in so many piano works,
of variation technique, approaching themes from such different angles –
in the *Etudes symphoniques*, Impromptus on a Theme of Clara Wieck,
C major Fantasy, for example – with differing structural consequences
for the work as a whole, can be understood as 'controlled experiments'
in mastering aspects of symphonic form. If this is so, it surely helped fuel
Brahms's interest in methods of motivic transformation. Schumann's
use of combinatorial letter-symbolism, as in the 'Lettres dansantes'
movement previously cited, seems sometimes to test to destruction what
it is that constitutes a musical idea or motif. The example must have
helped Brahms in his quest for methods of achieving large-scale thematic
unity, even if his eventual practice was very different. Schumann's free
working with motifs Brahms termed 'fantasia variation': he studied it
closely, and emulated it in his own 'Schumann' Variations, op. 9. His
later approaches were to range from a neo-Baroque strictness to an
astonishing freedom.

From our vantage point, the Romantic musical landscape seems
dominated by a few towering figures, most of them already named in
this chapter. That is the conveniently tailored view of a music history
which subscribes to theories of evolution, a history concerned to identify
the stylistic trends which became dominant, and their chief practitioners.
At the time, when 'contemporary composers' were as thick on the
ground as in any age, the situation felt very different. Brahms, writing
about variation form to friends in 1876, named not only Schumann but
also Gustav Nottebohm as a modern master of 'fantasia variation'.
Nottebohm is remembered now only as a Beethoven scholar, but was
also the composer of some finely crafted chamber and piano music
including a striking set of piano-duet Variations on a Bach Sarabande
which Brahms sometimes performed with him. Such 'minor figures' (in
history's view) did not look so minor then – even less so in 1853, when
the name of Schumann's discovery, Brahms, stood on a par with Liszt's
latest protégé, the agreeably talented Bronsart von Schellendorf. Brahms
took note of his contemporaries: many he knew personally; some he
deplored; several he admired, and the extent to which their music
contributed to his is a subject that remains for musicologists to
explore.

Though hostile (and friendly) critics saw Brahms as the last member
of a 'Schumann school', his musical personality was already establishing
itself before he ever met Schumann, and his tastes and interests always
extended far beyond the Schumann circle. When in the early 1880s

Wagner rediscovered and performed his own youthful Symphony in C (1832), Brahms was able to compare it with the contemporary works of the long-forgotten Dresden Kapellmeister Karl Gottlieb Reissiger (1798–1859) – to Reissiger's distinct advantage.

Certainly Brahms befriended several composers who had actually studied with Schumann, notably Theodor Kirchner and Albert Dietrich. Both men's outputs are worth exploration for their own qualities, and for the light they cast on their more famous contemporary. Kirchner extended the tradition of the Schumannesque piano miniature in a voluminous keyboard output; Dietrich worked rather in chamber and orchestral music. Brahms seems to have been less than overwhelmed by Dietrich's Symphony in 1868 while he was working on one of his own; but his friend's highly attractive D minor Violin Concerto (1874) – broadly in the Schumann mould, but with a distinct character of its own – could well have been a spur for Brahms to compose his in 1878.

The slightly older composer Robert Volkmann deserves consideration in this context. Brahms knew him, corresponded with him, and sometimes performed his music; his letters of the 1850s contain admiring comments on Volkmann's chamber works. The British writer Harold Truscott maintains that Volkmann's early piano trios, especially that in B flat minor, op. 5, contributed to the formation of Brahms's personal idiom. The claim should bear investigation, especially since Volkmann also wrote Variations on a Theme of Handel for piano some years before Brahms, and his Symphony no. 1 (D minor, op. 44) shows an assured symphonic use of a 'Hungarian' style (Volkmann spent much of his professional career in Hungary) astonishingly reminiscent of some of Brahms's own achievements in that direction in chamber and orchestral music.

But for Hungarian influence Brahms had, of course, a much closer and dearer example. Joseph Joachim – to Brahms's dismay – relegated his own composing to a sideline after about 1860 (partly because of performing commitments, partly because he felt Brahms far outreached him); nor have his works had much reputation since. Yet he was very gifted, and his music gave Brahms an important example at a very formative period. Joachim's friendship with Bettina von Arnim and her daughter Gisela gave him a direct connection to some of the leading Romantic writers. Although he made a painful break with the Weimarites not long after he first met Brahms, he had begun as a friend of Liszt and, as a composer, was as committed as any Liszt follower to the principles of psychological programme music. His dramatic overtures after Shakespeare (*Hamlet, Henry IV*), Herman Grimm (*Demetrius*, a subject also treated by Schiller), and in memory of Kleist, were all admired by Brahms, and are conceived as Romantic character-studies, however Classical their architecture. His historically important near-masterpiece, the Concerto in the Hungarian Manner, applied extended Classical principles to a Lisztian 'exotic' idiom in a way that had significant repercussions for many Brahmsian slow movements and finales.

Last but not least there was Clara Schumann herself, one of the few women composers of the age. She had been writing mainly piano pieces since her girlhood, and though composition had taken a reluctant back seat to her piano playing, domestic duties, and the need to give Schumann prior use of the piano as a composing facility, she had continued to produce in halting fashion pieces of charm and some individual character, among them a set of Preludes and Fugues in neo-Bachian style, and a fluent if somewhat Mendelssohnian Piano Trio that compares quite favourably with her husband's own essays in the medium. In the summer of 1853, just before Brahms arrived in her life, she had produced what are perhaps her finest works – the Variations, op. 20, and the three *Romanzen*, op. 21, both for piano solo; a further set of *Romanzen* for violin and piano, op. 22; and the six *Jucunde* Lieder, op. 23. With Schumann's death she virtually gave up composing, although Brahms – whose op. 9 Variations essentially takes her op. 20 as its starting-point – valued her music and made several unsuccessful attempts in later years to persuade or cajole her into renewed creative work.

An exploration of now even more obscure figures might include Woldemar Bargiel (Clara Schumann's half-brother, whom Brahms knew well and whose works he praised in early letters); the rather older Jacob Rosenhain (whose music he performed in one of his first public appearances, and whom he later came to know); the chamber and choral music composer Friedrich Kiel (noted in his time as a master contrapuntist); Brahms's Hamburg friend Karl Grädener; the symphonist and concerto composer Friedrich Gernsheim; or the slightly younger Adolf Jensen, who wrote some fine piano music and many songs encompassing a comparable range of folk poetry to that which Brahms treated, from Herder's Scottish ballads from *Stimmen der Völker* to the Giebel/Heyse *Spanisches Liederbuch*. Such an exploration might well yield equally fruitful parallels and similarities; no one of them decisive, perhaps, but together adding up to a spectrum of contemporary endeavour in which Brahms might be seen much less as a lone 'Classicist', single-mindedly reacting against his times, than as someone who responded intelligently to a whole range of currently available musical and imaginative stimuli, and created from them a powerful personal synthesis.[9]

2 A page from Brahms's manuscript of the 'Schumann' Variations, op.9: the end of Variation VIII and the whole of Variation IX, showing the signatures 'B' and 'Kr' for 'Brahms' and 'Kreisler'.

[9] To give one further example: Brahms was certainly aware of the music of the short-lived Düsseldorf composer Norbert Burgmüller (1810–36), an early Romantic whose death Schumann considered a tragedy second only to Schubert's. Brahms wrote admiringly to Clara about Burgmüller's Rhapsody for piano as early as August 1854. In the mid 1860s Burgmüller's Symphony no. 1 in C minor and (unfinished) Symphony no. 2 in D major were posthumously published: Hans Vogt, writing in the March–April 1989 issue of *Musica*, pointed out illuminating parallels between these works and Brahms's first two symphonies, not confined to the fact that they are in the same keys.

3

Storm and stress (1853–60)

> ...*Und doch ist's Wahnsinn, zu hoffen sie!*
> *Und um sie schweben,*
> *Gibt Mut und Leben,*
> *Zu weichen nie.*
>
> (...and though it is madness to hope for her!
> To hover near her
> gives me courage and life
> never to retreat.)
>
> 13th century French sonnet, attrib. Thibault IV of Provence,
> translated by Herder, set by Brahms in op. 14, no. 4

Brahms and Joachim learned of Schumann's suicide attempt from a newspaper report. Appalled, they wrote to Dietrich for news: but without waiting for an answer, Brahms hurried to Düsseldorf on 3 March and announced to Clara Schumann that he was there to help her and her six children in any way he could. 'She wept a great deal,' he reported to Joachim, 'but was very glad to see me'. His action was both practical and characteristic: whereas Joachim, Grimm, or Dietrich had their professional commitments, he was practically a free agent. He was also Romantic, quixotic, and aware of an especially deep personal obligation. For the next three years he was seldom far from Clara Schumann's side.

To begin with Clara was in shock. The doctors thought it inadvisable that she should see her husband; moreover, to her distress and confusion, Schumann expressed no desire to see her – though he asked constantly for Brahms, and Brahms's music. With the help of Dietrich and others of the Schumann circle in Düsseldorf, Brahms did all he could to ease Clara's burdens. He had virtually no money, but found some piano pupils and otherwise lived for the next few years on what he could borrow from his friends. Joachim, when his Hanover duties allowed, came on short visits; Grimm returned to Düsseldorf. Brahms took over some of Clara's teaching, helped the servants to look after the children, took charge of the running of the family's financial affairs (rent, servants' wages, school fees, investments), and regularly visited the incarcerated composer in Endenich. Schumann was kept in reasonably pleasant surroundings with access to a piano and opportunities for walks: he became much calmer and more rational, and there began to be hopes for a recovery.

Though it might seem an arduous life, Brahms clearly felt himself fulfilled and invigorated by his double duties as creative artist and guardian angel to the stricken Schumann family. His youthful energy and buoyant high spirits speedily revived. 'He is as mad as can be', Grimm reported to Joachim in April,

> – as the artistic genius of Düsseldorf he has adorned his room with beautiful frescoes in the style of Callot, *i.e.* with heads of Madonnas and brats – so as to have something worthy of his contemplation whilst he is at work...[1]

In an effort to justify Schumann's expectations of him, Düsseldorf's new 'genius' threw himself into composition. Within days of his arrival he began turning a projected two-piano sonata into a grandly tragic symphony, while for the piano, he wrote his Variations on a Theme of Robert Schumann as a special act of solace for Clara, and began a set of Ballades, partly inspired by the Scottish Border ballads he discovered in Herder's *Stimmen der Völker*. He was introduced to the volume by Julius Allgeyer, a new friend who was studying copperplate engraving in Düsseldorf.

Brahms's delight with himself and his good fortune was clearly something of a self-defence against having to live in a situation underpinned by tragedy and fraught with uncertainty; but even his friends found it a trial on occasion. Joachim (himself inclined to be thin-skinned and depressive, despite his much securer public position and reputation), writing to Gisela von Arnim after Brahms paid him a flying visit on his way to Hamburg in October 1854, was moved to pen an analysis of what he saw as his young friend's character faults and virtues:

> As for Brahms, who put up here on the black sofa for a few days, I did not really feel at ease with him, although I once more realised his good, his unusual qualities... whereas I used to live, purposely, in a kind of twilight, so far as my friendships were concerned, so as not to be disillusioned in that which I cared for – now my reason insists on seeing what my affection feared to discover. Brahms is egoism incarnate, *without himself being aware of it*. He bubbles over in his cheery way with

---

[1] *Letters from and to Joseph Joachim*, p. 60. The French artist and engraver Jacques Callot (1592–1635), renowned both for his fluent realism and his vein of ultra-detailed symbolic fantasy, was much admired by E. T. A. Hoffmann, whose first book of stories, including the 'Kreisleriana', is entitled *Fantasiestücke in Callots Manier*, and in turn influenced the *Fantasiestücke* of Schumann.

exuberant thoughtlessness – but sometimes with a lack of consideration (not a lack of reserve, for that would please me!) which offends because it betrays a want of culture. He has never once troubled to consider what others, according to their natures and the course of their development, will hold in esteem; the things that do not arouse *his* enthusiasm, or that do not fit in with *his* experience, or even with *his* mood, are callously thrust aside, or, if he is in the humour, attacked with a malicious sarcasm . . . He knows the weaknesses of the people about him, and he makes use of them, and then does not hesitate to show (to their faces, I admit) that he is crowing over them. His immediate surroundings are quite apart from his musical life, and from his attachment to a higher and more fantastic world. And the way in which he wards off all the morbid emotions and imaginary troubles of others is really delightful. He is absolutely sound in that, just as his complete indifference to the means of existence is beautiful, indeed magnificent. He will not make the smallest sacrifice of his inclinations – he will not play in public because of his contempt for the public, and because it irks him – although he plays divinely. I have never heard piano playing (except perhaps Liszt's) which gave me so much satisfaction – so light and clear, so cold and indifferent to passion. His compositions, too, are an easy treatment of the most difficult forms – so pregnant, rejecting all earthly sorrows with such indifference. I have never come across a talent like his before. He is miles ahead of me.[2]

Brahms's 'exuberant thoughtlessness', if that was what it was, was already undergoing a severe test in the complex of emotions that were gathering around the woman to whom he had pledged his service.

Clara Schumann was a very resilient and determined person. As soon as her new child was born – a boy, Felix, to whom Brahms became godfather – she began making plans for a return to the concert platform in order to earn sufficient to support herself and her family and pay her husband's hospital fees. During 1854–6 she threw herself into a punishing schedule of touring and concert giving that took her to Berlin, Vienna, Prague, Budapest, Belgium, the Netherlands, and England as well as many places nearer to home. Several of these tours were made with Joachim, and some with Brahms as well, but for much of the time Brahms remained in Düsseldorf, running her affairs so that she could be freed for this major effort. As Clara's travelling and acceptance of every public engagement became almost obsessive, Brahms and other friends became concerned she was wearing herself out; but in fact it was probably her instinctive method of pulling herself through the disaster that had overwhelmed her marriage.

[2] Ibid., pp. 91–2.

In addition to the plausible economic necessity to gain an income, Clara had been dedicated to the life of a musician since her childhood: studying and performing were absolutely necessary to her, the only activities which could wholly take her out of her grief. And these were pursuits which, as Robert Schumann's wife and mother of his children, she had been forced to curtail. Since she was a girl she had been reckoned among the finest pianists in Europe; during her marriage she had felt her reputation was slipping in comparison with her rivals such as Liszt and Thalberg. Always rather solemn, she was an earnest, thoughtful artist, perennially described as a 'priestess'. She had little of the egotism of the crowd-pulling virtuoso, and was well known for her 'serious' programming – yet she thrived on the excitement of live performance, the tributes of audience applause. These at least she could have once again in full measure, and now there was an added urgency to her specialization as the principal exponent of Robert's works.

Most of all, however, she was sustained by Brahms's unstinting loyalty. She could hardly have failed to find him an attractive and congenial companion – young, handsome, passionate, and like herself a dedicated artist, with the undoubted creative genius that she had found in Schumann. To Brahms, Clara in her turn soon came to represent his ideal among women. She never thought of herself as beautiful, but drawings and photographs show a striking, somewhat melancholy face of great expressiveness; many pupils and acquaintances testified to the magnetic power of her dark-blue eyes and the warmth of her personality. Compared to Brahms she was mature and experienced in life; she was also highly intelligent, a great pianist and musician with the widest possible interest in her art – and the fact that she was herself a composer of definite gifts gave her additional insight into his own creative predicaments. Their friendship had begun in enthusiasm and mutual admiration; within months it was immeasurably deepened by Brahms's devotion and companionship in crisis; before long it had ripened into love.

As early as June 1854, while writing his 'Schumann' Variations, op. 9, Brahms had confessed in a letter to Joachim that

> I believe that I do not have more concern and admiration for her than I love her and find love in her. I often have to restrain myself forcibly from just quietly putting my arms around her and even – : I don't know, it seems to me so natural that she could not misunderstand.
>
> I think I can no longer love an unmarried girl – at least, I have quite forgotten about them; they only promise heaven, while Clara shows it revealed to us.[3]

[3] See Artur Holde, 'Suppressed Passages in the Brahms–Joachim Correspondence Published for the First Time', *Musical Quarterly*, Vol. XLV, no. 3 (1959), p. 314.

The letters he wrote to Clara when she had embarked upon her concert tours or on his rare absences from Düsseldorf give some indication of the developing emotional situation. In November Clara decided they should use *Du*, the intimate form of the personal pronoun, in correspondence. On 15 December Brahms wrote from Hamburg 'I am dying of love for you', though he camouflaged this in a quotation from the *Arabian Nights*. But on 25 January 1855, by which time he was back in Düsseldorf but Clara was touring Holland, he wrote quite openly '...I can do nothing but think of you... What have you done to me? Can't you remove the spell you have cast over me?' Even so his letters still began formally 'Most Honoured Lady' or 'Dearest Friend'. It was not until March that she became 'My Dearly Beloved Clara'; in June he was writing 'I can no longer exist without you... Please go on loving me as I shall go on loving you always and forever'. As many years later Clara destroyed nearly all of her earliest letters to Brahms we lack her detailed responses to his ardent outbursts, but she was clearly anything but indifferent. 'There is the most complete accord between us', she confided to her diary:

> It is not his youth that attracts me: not, perhaps, my own flattered vanity. No, it is the fresh mind, the gloriously gifted nature, the noble heart, that I love in him.

However far this love might take her, part of the time she must also have been amused. Often Brahms's letters to her remind us forcibly how young he was; and in falling headlong for this remarkable woman, he did not immediately throw off a somewhat coltish streak. Clara was expected to share his enthusiasm for toy soldiers, his delight in running and jumping and his cracking walking pace, and his accounts of horseplay with her children. Brahms's early biographers tended to quote these details at somewhat tedious length, doubtless eager to draw a healthy contrast with what they saw as the neurasthenic decadence or morbidity of the young composers of their own day. But they are partly evidence of how hard he worked to cheer Clara up; and of how brim-full of nervous energy he was, released from the physical and mental constrictions of Hamburg into the wider and more stimulating world.

For both of them, the situation was exquisitely complex. In many ways circumstances had forced Brahms to step into Robert Schumann's shoes, as protector of his family and household and closest confidant to his wife; moreover, it was now *his* newly emerging music that formed the focus for Clara's hunger to share the act of artistic creation, as she had done with Schumann for most of the previous two decades. Yet Robert, to whom Clara remained utterly devoted and Brahms felt an overwhelming sense of obligation, was still alive: indeed, for at least a year his return to health and home was periodically expected. Schumann's doctors at Endenich, fearing the excitement would destroy such mental stability as remained to him, forbade any visit from Clara during the whole of his illness; and so it was primarily Brahms who visited him and carried greetings and messages to and fro; and Brahms also who interviewed other doctors and inspected other asylums in the hope of discovering a superior standard of care. The experience left him ever afterwards with a horror of mental illness. Schumann was generally lucid but often very agitated, obsessed with the need to consult atlases; and gradually it became clear there would be no speedy recovery. Even as the prospect receded, Clara's sense of dedication to his reputation and the furtherance of his work increased. So the growing warmth of personal feeling between herself and Brahms was occurring in circumstances where any romantic attachment was likely to involve a certain amount of subconscious guilt and would be prone to inevitable misunderstanding by the outside world. They came very quickly to love each other deeply, but in a situation where the emotional constraints on their relationship (let alone those of conventional morality) were intensely strong.

Whether their love was ever physically consummated is a question that has provoked endless speculation. Since there is no incontrovertible evidence in either direction (the two of them took care there should be none) it ought perhaps to be left on one side. The wide disparity in their ages, which inevitably introduced a surrogate mother/son element into their relations, and their highly developed senses of honour, would perhaps have been additional restraints. On the other hand they had opportunity (though probably less than we imagine in the large Düsseldorf household); and recent evidence that some years later Clara conducted a discreet affair with Theodor Kirchner (a Schumann pupil significantly nearer her own age)[4] shows she did not consider her sexual life at an end with the removal of her husband.

Whatever the answer, in terms of what they *meant* to each other Brahms and Clara were certainly lovers. For nearly twenty years Robert Schumann had been the most important man in her life; for the next forty it was Johannes Brahms. On Brahms's side, chivalric fantasy and genuine attraction merged in an utter devotion to the person of Clara

[4]The evidence is in letters between them now in the possession of Kurt Hofmann; see Nancy B. Reich, *Clara Schumann, the Artist and the Woman* (London, 1985), p. 209.

Schumann that he never really managed or wanted to shake off. He knew himself to be attractive to women; his head and heart were certainly available to be turned. Throughout his life, even more than in his many close male friendships, he would delight in the company of gifted, intelligent, musical women – Agathe von Siebold, Bertha Porubsky, Elisabet von Herzogenberg, Hermine Spies and others; of these, Clara was the first and the supreme archetype. Her age, gifts and the special circumstances of the relationship gave her an authority that surpassed any other, if she was minded (as she often was) to be possessive; it also gave Brahms an excuse if he wanted to pull back from total involvement (as he usually did). Whether he would have pulled back had he never met her seems doubtful; but in 1854–5 he was constantly at the side of his chosen lady, his 'fair and haughty dame', as one of his letters addressed her – with no inkling that he would remain unmarried, and have to settle for one of musical history's longest and closest platonic friendships.

In the autumn of 1854, Clara launched her concert career with a tour of North Germany, accompanied by Joachim, including several of Brahms's piano works in her repertoire: among them the new F minor Piano Sonata, whose first complete performance she gave in Magdeburg. Her travels brought her in November to Hamburg, so Brahms joined her there in order to introduce her to his family; she and Joachim then continued to Berlin, Frankfurt, and Leipzig while Brahms travelled back to Düsseldorf to spend Christmas with her and her children. In January 1855 Clara resumed touring in Holland, and Brahms used up most of his money to follow her to Rotterdam; otherwise he spent most of the year in Düsseldorf, free to explore Schumann's library, which he was rearranging. In August, when Clara finally moved house to 135 Poststrasse, Brahms assisted her and moved in to a first-floor room.

Not surprisingly, he had published little in 1854, and in 1855–6 it appeared to many that Schumann's 'someone... fated to give us the ideal expression of the times' had fallen silent, for almost nothing of consequence appeared in print. In fact he was wrestling with major works fated never to appear in their intended form (such as three movements of the D minor Symphony and a C sharp minor Piano Quartet), and keenly feeling the need for further grounding in technique. He suggested to Joachim that every fortnight they should exchange exercises in counterpoint, submitting them to each other's mutual criticism. Whoever failed to provide an exercise was to pay a fine, which the other could spend on books or music. The two friends kept up the practice for some years, but it rapidly became quite one-sided: the busy Joachim much preferred to pay numerous fines (incidentally con-

Brahms

tributing to Brahms's burgeoning library), while Brahms dedicatedly
pursued studies of strict canon which gradually bore fruit in the marvellous polyphonic textures of his mature music.

His reputation, however, was continuing to grow during 1855. His
op. 8 Piano Trio received its first performance as far afield as New York,
the performers including the pianist William Mason, a Liszt pupil who
had been present when Brahms visited the master in 1853. In order to
increase his slender finances, Brahms decided that he must after all
appear as a concert pianist, and accordingly attached himself to another
tour that Clara was undertaking with Joachim. From contemporary
accounts the events of the previous eighteen months seem to have drained
his exuberance and left him shy and nervous. He played in Danzig and
Bremen – in the latter town as soloist in Beethoven's G major Concerto
(the first occasion on which he had played with an orchestra), and
repeated the work in Leipzig a few months later. In Danzig the pianist
Anton Door was somewhat nonplussed by the appearance and lack of
social graces of this 'slight young man with long fair hair marching up
and down ... incessantly smoking cigars' who hardly deigned to notice
his presence. Late in the year Brahms visited Hamburg, where he played
Beethoven's 'Emperor' Concerto (in a manner the local press criticized
as 'reticent in the extreme') before returning to Düsseldorf to be with
Clara for Christmas. By this time she had organized her life so that
Brahms's constant attention was no longer required; thus, early in 1856,
he returned to Hamburg and stayed with his parents for some months,
appearing as soloist in Mozart's D minor Piano Concerto at the Mozart
birth-centenary celebrations there, and making trips to play in Leipzig,
Kiel, and Altona. On his way to Hamburg he stopped over to see
Joachim, and here encountered the Russian composer–pianist Anton
Rubenstein – who reported to his master, Liszt:

> I have made the acquaintance of Brahms and Grimm at Hanover, and
> also of Joachim ... as for Brahms, I do not exactly know what impression
> he has made on me; he is not polished enough for the drawing-room; he
> is not fiery enough for the concert-room; for the country he is not primitive
> enough; and not cosmopolitan enough for the town. I have no faith in
> that sort of nature.

At the beginning of April he moved to Bonn, to be near to
Schumann, as Clara had embarked on a long concert tour in Britain
(where she introduced Brahms's music to this country by playing two
of his recent neo-Baroque studies, a Sarabande and Gavotte, in London).
Here he formed two important friendships when he met the poet Klaus
Groth (from his ancestral Dittmarschen) and the great baritone Julius

Stockhausen at the annual music festival. There was an instant rapport with Stockhausen, who was to become the first real champion of Brahms's songs, and the two young men were soon performing together in Bonn and Cologne. The period, however, was dominated by concern about Schumann. As early as September 1855 the doctors at Endenich had warned Clara that her husband's sanity would never fully return; and he had been growing gradually weaker (in fact, it appears that he was starving himself, refusing all food except wine and calves'-foot jelly). When Brahms visited him on Schumann's birthday, 8 June, he was shocked by the deterioration in his condition. He immediately telegraphed Clara that, in his view, the end was near. Clara was just coming to the end of her English concert tour, and hurried home. Robert lingered for almost a month, however; Brahms visited him several times, but it was only on 27 July that Clara saw her husband, for the first time since he had been taken from Düsseldorf. Schumann seemed by now to have lost the power of speech, and looked terribly ill, but he knew her, and she remained with him that day and the next. On 29 July she and Brahms went to the railway station to meet Joachim, but when the three of them returned to the sanatorium Schumann was dead.

Considering his pathetic condition, death probably came as a blessed release to him, and a relief to his family and friends. At the funeral in Bonn on 31 July Brahms, Joachim, and Dietrich were chief mourners; it was left to Brahms to place Clara's wreath on the coffin. Joachim and he supported Clara through the funeral and brought her back to Düsseldorf, staying to see her through the period of most intense grief and also helping to put Schumann's papers in order.

'All happiness has gone with his passing,' wrote Clara in her diary. 'A new life begins for me.' She was greatly in need of rest and recuperation, and in the late summer Brahms escorted her on a holiday to Switzerland, at Gersau on Lake Lucerne. They did not, however, travel alone, but with two of the Schumann boys and with Brahms's own sister Elise, who was in delicate health (she remained a simple Hamburg body to the end of her days, and never ventured so far afield again; the trip was the adventure of her life).

This holiday was in some way decisive for the future of Brahms's relationship with Clara, but we have no firm idea of what was said or done. It was the time when marriage could reasonably be discussed. Some writers have opined that only now, with Schumann dead, did Clara return Brahms's feelings with undisguised passion, and that he in turn drew back. It may be that he was afraid she would be undermined by too great a dependence on him, or that the confusions of the son/lover role made it too complicated for him to play it to a satisfactory

47

conclusion. But all we know is that by the end of the holiday they had agreed to part, so that Brahms returned to his home town in October.

This was painful for both of them, and though in the next few years it was usually Brahms who urged Clara to abide by their decision, he still felt a proprietorial interest in her, and a lover's concern for her well-being. This often emerged in tensions about money, which he was always trying to help her with, when he had anything more than sufficed for his Spartan immediate needs. In one such disagreement in 1861, when she turned down the offer of a few days' rest in Hamburg with her daughter Julie at Brahms's expense, he complained, only half-humorously:

> In all things that concern me you have always treated me, and always will, as though I belonged to you, and yet in all things that concern you I am allowed to do nothing. If I had not a farthing I should live with you. If I had a house you would certainly live with me. But now I have a purse full ... [which] I am not allowed to spend ... I can assure you I shall really be furious if you refuse to be my guest ... I shall throw all my money out of the window within a month. For what is the good of the trash otherwise?

The fact of the matter seems to be that they were both proud and independent people who had been thrown into mutual dependence by the prolonged tension of Schumann's illness. With that controlling factor removed, they had personal destinies that they knew were better worked out apart from one another. But their love did not diminish, and made the separation difficult to bear – sometimes harder for Clara, sometimes harder for Brahms.

The Swiss holiday with Clara over, Brahms resumed his contra-puntal correspondence with Joachim, and appeared at the Hamburg Philharmonic Concerts as soloist in Beethoven and Schumann concertos. Otherwise he occupied himself with quiet musical study and in cultivating the society of his friends among Hamburg musicians, notably the music-teacher Theodor Avé-Lallemant and the composer Karl Grädener, while he considered how he could develop his career.

In the interval between Schumann's funeral and the Swiss holiday, Brahms had relieved Clara of some piano pupils, and had taken over a course of lessons she was to give to Laura von Meysenbug, sister of a high official at the court of Lippe-Detmold. She and her family were so impressed with him that they invited him to visit them in the tiny but cultured principality, where Clara had already played and where Prince Leopold II was an avid music-lover, maintaining a choral society and a small court orchestra. In May of 1857 Brahms took up the invitation and spent a few days in Detmold, where despite his social awkwardness he was generally liked and his playing in Beethoven's G major Concerto and Schubert's 'Trout' Quintet was much admired. The result was that he was engaged to spend the months of October to December at Detmold, his duties including giving piano lessons to the Princess Frederike, conducting the choral society, and playing at court. As the appointment was renewable, it held out some prospect of financial security while leaving him free for the bulk of each year; equally important, it would broaden his experience of handling chorus and orchestra.

Shortly before Brahms took up the Detmold appointment, in September 1857, Clara Schumann sold her house in Düsseldorf and moved to Berlin, where she believed her children would be better looked after close to other members of her family (her mother, her half-sister Marie, and her half-brother Bargiel all lived there). But leaving the Rhineland was a painful wrench, and it may well be that it appeared to write an even more painful *finis* to the earliest and most passionate part of her lifelong relationship with Johannes Brahms, even though the move to Berlin followed the logic of their decision of the previous year. Brahms and Joachim helped at the Düsseldorf end, but Clara seems to have been in a highly emotional state. Just after her arrival in Berlin she wrote to Joachim on 6 October: 'When Johannes left me in the morning my heart bled...' What she wrote to Brahms has not survived, but his response has. The gently remonstrating tone of his first letter from Detmold, on 11 October, almost suggests that the age-difference has been reversed, that she is the inexperienced girl and he the fatherly figure:

> My dear Clara, you really must try hard to keep your melancholy within bounds and see that it does not last too long. Life is precious and such moods as the one you are in consume us body and soul. Do not imagine that life has little more in store for you... You must seriously try to alter, my dearest Clara... Passions are not natural to mankind, they are always exceptions or excrescences. The man in whom they overstep the limits should regard himself as an invalid and seek a medicine for his life and for his health. The ideal and the genuine man is calm both in his joy and in his sorrow.

'*Passions are not natural to mankind*' – this from the composer of some of the most passionate music of the 1850s, to the widow of Robert Schumann! Small wonder that she found his words hard, even cold. He was not cold; he was striving to do the right thing, even if that led to self-absorption; and he was making a better outward show of it than Clara. He loved her and always would; none the less, he had devoted four crucial, formative years, body and soul, to the Schumann circle, and by now desperately needed some independence from her too.

The pattern of his life was set for the next three years: three months in comfortable lodgings in Detmold, the rest divided between Hamburg, Hanover, Göttingen and Düsseldorf, composing and performing. At the Detmold court, where over three seasons he played an immense number of concerted and instrumental works, he was generally popular and seems to have valued the opportunities for quiet introspection and walks in the vast Teutoburger forest, where centuries before Arminius had annihilated the legions of Varus and turned back the Roman invasion of Germany. But though he enjoyed conducting a choral society 'richly adorned with Serene Highnesses', he was lonely, and chafed at the social restrictions and etiquette of the protocol-bound society at the Residenz, and having to perform such duties as accompanying the Prince in songs he had composed. Most of all he seems to have felt the lack of a congenial and understanding circle of musicians, although the Prince's orchestra was led by a protégé of Joachim's, Karl Louis Bargheer, who became a good friend. A few years later he ironically recalled to Clara

> ...how attractive a post at one of these little Courts is. One gets plenty of time to play to oneself, but unfortunately one cannot always feel happy at heart, for, after all, one would become nauseated by the faces one sees there, they are enough to make anyone a misanthropist. One can enjoy the beauties of nature alone, but when playing music in the drawing-room before people, one does not wish to be alone.

Nevertheless, he spent three seasons at Detmold, and (now no longer in Robert Schumann's shadow) at last found himself back on the road to self-discovery as a composer. At Detmold he worked on his two orchestral Serenades, several choral pieces, a preliminary version of the G minor Piano Quartet, and the beginnings of a string sextet, as well as wrestling with the very large-scale Piano Concerto which was gradually emerging from the ashes of the unfinished D minor Symphony. This work in particular was causing endless trouble, partly resolved in continuous correspondence with Joachim, who was advising him on the details of the orchestration. On 30 March 1858 Joachim was able to conduct a private rehearsal of it with his Hanover orchestra. Brahms, of course, was the soloist; but he remained dissatisfied with the Concerto as it stood and nearly a further year passed before he could commit the work to a public performance.

These creative efforts also proceeded in Hamburg and elsewhere. Brahms was again living with his parents: he now had some space to work, as they occupied considerably roomier apartments than those of his childhood, though still in the old district. He hung around the town not only from filial duty but because of a strong sense that his roots lay there (perhaps this helped him maintain his identity, along with his 'rough, Northern' manners in the ultra-cultured Schumann–Joachim circle), and partly also because he had begun to entertain the hope he might secure a permanent position that would bring home to his fellow citizens the reputation he had already won in the larger musical world – perhaps even as conductor of the Hamburg Philharmonie, the focus of the city's musical life.

He was also much in Göttingen. Grimm already held a conductor's post there, and had recently married; Brahms stayed with him and his wife Philippine in the summer of 1858. Clara joined them (with five of her children). So did Woldemar Bargiel, and Konzertmeister Bargheer from Detmold. It was in this circle that Brahms's D major Serenade was performed for the first time, in its original form as a Nonet for wind and strings. He was amusing himself with – and drawing new compositional strength from – the study of folk music; already that summer he had sent Clara a collection of thirty-two folksongs arranged for voice and piano. During their time together in Göttingen he delighted his friends further with a set of children's songs, the *Deutsche Volks-Kinderlieder*, for Clara's children, and with a number of wild, gypsy-style piano pieces – the first examples of his Hungarian Dances.

Göttingen held a further attraction: Agathe von Siebold, daughter of one of the University professors and Philippine Grimm's closest friend. From the first Brahms felt a natural affinity for this dark-eyed, lively, intelligent girl with long, black hair and a hauntingly beautiful singing voice ('like an Amati violin', said Joachim), whom he accompanied in many of his songs; and he soon found himself falling in love. This had its dangers in the company he kept in summer 1858: when Clara discovered 'her' Johannes with his arm round Agathe's waist, she was so upset she left Göttingen the same day. Although she often urged Brahms to find 'a nice young wife' for himself, she was too possessive of him to cope with the concrete possibility.

During the 1858 season in Detmold he corresponded assiduously with Agathe through the Grimms, sending her new songs and duets (some of which became his opp. 14, 19 and 20) and a choral setting of Ludwig Uhland's *Brautgesang* (Bridal Song) that he was later to destroy. At the beginning of 1859 he returned to Göttingen for a fortnight, primarily to see Agathe, and took the seemingly unmistakable step of secretly exchanging engagement rings with her. In the little town his attentions could not pass unnoticed. The Grimms (who would have been delighted if the liaison could be formalized) attempted to extricate Agathe from the centre of current gossip by writing to Brahms and telling him to make a public declaration of his intentions. Thus forced to the point of irrevocable decision, he instinctively shied away. The expectant Agathe received only an awkward letter avowing (as she quoted it from memory decades later) that 'I love you! I must see you again! But I cannot wear fetters. Write to me, whether I am to come back ...' Deeply hurt, she consented to release him from the engagement, but refused to allow him to return. They never saw each other again, and both felt the effects of the emotional upheaval for a long time. After ten years Agathe married someone else, but only in old age put the affair in perspective in a slim autobiographical novel which testifies that knowing Brahms had been the crucial romantic experience of her life. Meanwhile memories of Agathe (even her name, spelt out in the G major Sextet) became one of the principal impulses behind Brahms's works of the early 1860s, not least those many songs and choral works in which the principal figure is that of a girl abandoned by her lover.

It was an unfortunate affair all round, and hardly shows Brahms in a favourable light. The contemporary reader has difficulty even in accepting Agathe's final novelistic gloss on the situation, which was that the heroine could never have adequately filled the life of her young man, who 'like every genius, belonged to humanity'. Brahms's genius surely had little to do with the matter, except insofar as that his sense of it was an aggravating factor. The mundane truth is more likely that he had a more complicated emotional life than most people; but in common with many, he tended to make a mess of it. Only in his art could he put it right, or at least put his impulses into a justifiable shape. Seemingly, Agathe would have made an ideal companion for a composer who, on his own admission, often yearned for a wife: in addition to her intelligence and talent she was, unlike Clara, near his own age and unburdened with children. But Brahms was a warm, proud, impulsive man (in his friendships and his rudenesses) who often came to regret his impulses on mature reflection. He was, perhaps, perennially more attracted by the *idea* of domesticity than its reality; and however strongly he felt about Agathe, he had lost his heart first and most decisively to Clara Schumann – of whose continuing feelings he was only too aware. To marry Agathe would be to risk a permanent rift with Clara, though he rationalized it as more a betrayal of himself – a loss of independence, a diversion from his duty as a creative artist. The artist eventually took over, translating these conflicts of loyalty into mythic patterns re-enacted in his *Magelone-Lieder* (with its references to the giving of rings, and love-triangle story) and *Rinaldo* (with its enraptured knight rudely disentangled from the snares of love). It was not the last time his heart would flutter over a beautiful girl, but he never again wounded one by raising her hopes and then withdrawing. In an age when a solitary bachelor was something of a social scandal, a bachelor he stubbornly remained.

Providentially or otherwise, the break with Agathe coincided with one of the biggest challenges of his professional career. He was finally appearing before the public as soloist in the most ambitious work he had yet composed – the massive Piano Concerto in D minor, begun as the Symphony that would justify all Schumann's predictions of greatness, and which had since cost him four years of compositional struggle. On 22 January 1859 the première took place in Hanover under the baton of Joachim, who had already given the work in two provisional forms in semi-public rehearsals the previous year. The audience was sympathetic rather than enthusiastic, for the Concerto's immense length and seriousness made it difficult to grasp, but Brahms was pleased enough with the result. He departed at once for a second and far more prestigious performance in Leipzig, at that time still the virtual musical capital of Germany, where he intended to stay if the work was a success. On 27 January he presented the Concerto at a Gewandhaus concert, under the baton of the composer–conductor Julius Rietz. Rietz seems to have disliked the music, though Brahms felt the performance went well; but in any case it fell utterly flat, and he experienced the most hostile reception of his career. At the end he was hissed by a public who, expecting a virtuoso showpiece, found themselves having to endure a grim, uncompromising work far more intellectually demanding than the average symphony. No concerto of such ambitions had been heard since Beethoven, and the musical press found no joy in that fact. Edward Bernsdorf, the influential critic of the *Signale*, dismissed the concerto as

> a composition dragged to its grave. This work cannot give pleasure ... it has nothing to offer but hopeless desolation and aridity ... for more than three quarters of an hour one must endure this rooting and rummaging, this straining and tugging, this tearing and patching of phrases and flourishes! Not only must one take in this fermenting mass; one must also swallow a dessert of the shrillest dissonances and most unpleasant sounds. Herr Brahms has deliberately made the pianoforte part as uninteresting as possible ... finally, Herr Brahms's piano technique does not satisfy the demands we have a right to make of a concert soloist today.

Bernsdorf was an old-style conservative, who held that real music had died out with Mendelssohn; but he probably spoke for the bulk of the audience. The few supporters of the Weimar-based 'New German' school were more discerning, but they too failed to appreciate the work's truly prodigious nature: the Liszt partisan Ferdinand Gleich, in a largely sympathetic review, nevertheless declared that

The work suggests a condition of indefiniteness and fermentation, a wrestling for a method of expression commensurate with the ideals of the composer, which has indeed broken through the form of tradition, but not yet constructed another sufficiently definite and rounded to satisfy the aesthetic demands of art... The first movement, especially, gives us the impression of monstrosity...

'Fermentation' was clearly the critical metaphor of the hour. 'I am still quite dazed by the sublime delights which have assailed my eyes and ears by the sight and sound of the wise men of our musical city', Brahms wrote ruefully to Joachim on the morning after the concert:

My Concerto has had here a brilliant and decisive – failure... At the conclusion three pairs of hands were brought together very slowly, whereupon a perfectly distinct hissing from all sides forbade any such demonstration. There is nothing more to say about this episode, for not a soul has said a word to me about the work!

He added, with a fine show of taking things philosophically:

In spite of everything, the Concerto will meet with approval when I have improved its form, and the next one will be quite different. I believe this is the best thing that can happen to one; it forces one to concentrate one's thoughts and increases one's courage. After all, I am only experimenting and feeling my way as yet. But the hissing was too much of a good thing, wasn't it?[5]

There was nothing for it but to return to Hamburg; however, Joachim and Brahms's Hamburg friends were eager to neutralize this reverse, and by dint of various manoeuvres were able to programme the Concerto at the Hamburg Philharmonic Society on 24 March with Joachim conducting, Brahms as pianist, and Julius Stockhausen as soloist in some supporting items. The combination of two such renowned artists with the controversial local composer (playing one of his own works in Hamburg for the first time since his childhood benefit concerts) sufficed to draw a large audience, and the work was politely if not rapturously received. Moreover, they gave a further concert on the 28th at which Joachim conducted Brahms's recent D major Serenade in its brand-new (and still intermediate) guise for small orchestra. The welcome for this work was equally restrained – the *Hamburger Nachrichten* advised Brahms to 'learn to say what is plainly in his heart, and cease going to the trouble of performing peculiar antics' so that 'the man in the street may be able to understand what professional musicians admire so much about [his] works'. Brahms was dissatisfied with the

[5] *Letters from and to Joseph Joachim*, p. 180.

performance, which probably led to his re-scoring the work yet again; yet, as he reported to Clara:

> Yesterday the Serenade was played to nearly twelve hundred people and you were not among them ... It really seemed to reach the audience. The applause continued until I showed myself on the platform. You would scarcely have known the Hamburgers.

Brahms himself was soon to know some female Hamburgers rather well. Among his piano pupils was a girl called Friedchen Wagner who was also an enthusiastic choral singer; she had collected a group of friends, including a visiting Viennese girl, Bertha Porubsky, to sing some of Brahms's small choral works and folksong arrangements in her home, under his direction. Bertha had a large repertoire of Austrian folksongs, and a close but platonic friendship grew up between herself and Brahms; her brother Emil came to lodge with Brahms's parents after Brahms himself moved out to more commodious apartments in the suburb of Hamm. It was the Porubskys who first awakened in him the desire to visit the great city of Vienna.

In May 1859 Brahms played the organ accompaniment for a motet for women's voices by his friend Grädener in a wedding at the Michaeliskirche, and was so impressed with the acoustic effect that he began to desire a performance in the same great building of the *Ave Maria* he had composed the previous autumn. Friedchen Wagner collected a sufficiently large band of girl singers (mostly pupils from Grädener's singing school), and rehearsals at her home led to a performance at the Michaeliskirche – after which this *ad hoc* group was put on a permanent footing as the 'Hamburger Frauenchor', with regular weekly meetings and a repertoire chosen and composed by their conductor: Johannes Brahms. No salary went with the post, but this ladies' choir (which soon numbered about forty voices and was active until the spring of 1861) provided him with continued conducting practice and a valuable stimulus to the composition of small-scale choral works, allowing him to try out in a congenial genre the polyphonic techniques he was learning from his attentive study of the pre-Bachian composers, such as Gabrieli, Schütz, and Eccard. He was able to explore old music in actual performance, as his curiosity took him: the Frauenchor performed works by Bach, Byrd, Caldara, Eccard, Gallus (Handl), Hassler, Isaac, Lotti, Palestrina and others, some of them specially arranged for female voices by Brahms or transcribed by him from old part-books.

It also gave him a focus of activity in Hamburg as in Detmold, and (no small consideration) a circle of enthusiastic female admirers. It is no unusual phenomenon for choristers to have a 'crush' on their choirmaster, and likely enough several members of the Frauenchor – among them Marie and Betty Völckers, Laura Garbe, and Marie Reuter, who formed a female-voice quartet under Brahms's special direction – lost their hearts to the handsome Johannes. He was careful not to lose his; but as he always relished female company – all the better if it was young, bright, and musical – he must have felt himself reasonably well compensated for the loss of Agathe. His letters to Clara are full of teasing references to 'my dear girls', who '. . . will walk quite calmly into a garden and wake the people up at midnight with their singing' (the choir would, indeed, accompany him on walks, and at least once he conducted them sitting in a tree). But before long Clara was elected to honorary membership, and her signature – she was passing through Hamburg at the time – appears on the grandiloquent 'Avertimento' of the rules of the choir, drawn up by Brahms (still signing himself here 'Johannes Kreisler Jun.') in April 1860: a document largely devoted to stipulating, in deliberately quaint and archaic language (parodying the macaronic style of treatises by such eighteenth-century German music-theorists as Mattheson), that everyone should turn up for rehearsals on time.

It was for the Frauenchor that, in 1859–60, he wrote his setting of Psalm 13, the *Marienlieder*, the *Geistliche Chöre*, the spellbinding partsongs, op. 17, for female voices with horns and harp, folksong settings, and many canons (including several published towards the end of his life in op. 113). Parallel to these efforts he was writing works for mixed chorus, some of which he could try out in Detmold: these included more folksong settings, the *Begräbnisgesang*, two motets ultimately to appear as op. 29, and a number of partsongs including those published nearly a decade later as op. 42. His conductorship of the Detmold and Hamburg choirs gave rise to parallel versions of several of the smaller works, for female chorus and for mixed voices; though Brahms tended to publish only one version of each.

His sojourn at Detmold in the last three months of 1859 was, however, the last, for he resigned his post at the end of the year, too dissatisfied with the standard and possibilities of musical activity there. Henceforth he was largely based in Hamburg, working with the Frauen-chor. One reason why he stayed so closely tied to his home town, with no salaried position, was a growing hope that he might soon be chosen to succeed Wilhelm Grund, the ageing conductor of the Hamburg Philharmonic Orchestra. In February, indeed, he conducted the orchestra in the première of his new A major Serenade, op. 16 (having tried it over privately first in Hanover), and the work had a fairly friendly reception. Two months later, however, playing the solo part in a repeat presentation of his Piano Concerto, Brahms felt the hostility of the audience so keenly that at the end of the first movement he nearly left the stage and had to be persuaded by the conductor to finish the performance.

Indeed, 'modern music' was capable of arousing the uglier face of Philistinism then as now. Joachim always kept among his papers a letter from an unknown correspondent, signed 'M. H.', which he received after performing the A major Serenade in Hanover in March of this year, and which shows the kind of hostility he and Brahms had to face:

> Brahms's Serenade is a monstrosity, a caricature, a freak, which should never have been published, much less performed *here* ... whilst the piano concerto served up to us last winter still sticks in our throats! It is inexcusable that such filth should have been offered to a public thirsting for good music. That was an hour – a fiendish torture that can never be forgotten. Poor Mozart, poor Beethoven! ... May we be spared grimaces of this kind in the future! We all unite in bidding farewell to Herr Brahms and Herr Konzert Meister [i.e. Joachim]: do not tax the patience of your audience too severely, and do not impose on them a taste for that which can only be the greatest torture to people with *sound* ears.[6]

It was at this time that Brahms made his sole (and as it proved, futile) entry into the field of musical polemic. The proselytizing of the 'New German' school of composers – especially the Weimar circle headed by Liszt and including such figures as Raff and Bülow – had been irritating him ever since he had become part of the Schumann circle. Liszt and Schumann had been good friends despite wide differences in aesthetic outlook; but the 'New Germans' seemed to assume that all contemporary composers were in sympathy with the aims of programme music and poetically determined form, and the journal *Neue Zeitschrift für Musik*, which Schumann had founded, was now largely a 'New German' propaganda sheet. Brahms, Joachim and Clara Schumann thought Liszt an amazing pianist and a likeable personality (Brahms's liking may have been tempered by embarrassing memories of their first encounter), but none of them could find much to admire in his music, least of all the orchestral 'symphonic poems' which were being so strongly publicized at the time. Brahms, deeply engaged in the study of older masters and attempting to learn from them what he could, saw these works as a light-minded renunciation of the essentials of the art; he wanted no truck with a 'Music of the Future' that possessed no past. Joachim, originally a favoured member of Liszt's circle, had already made a painful break with it, on like principles. The lesser Weimarites

[6] Ibid., p. 191.

57

looked upon this as a betrayal (though Liszt, characteristically, later declared that since Joachim disliked his music it was incumbent on him to like Joachim's music all the more); and though they felt some interest in Brahms, they were sufficiently aware that he already represented a contrary tendency – as shown by a contemptuous reference, in a letter from Bülow to Liszt, to 'Joachim and the statue of which he is making himself the pedestal'.

These disputes now seem very petty and far away. It is important, however, not to represent them as a contest between composers of contrary 'Romantic' and 'Classical' outlooks. They were all Romantics: Schumann's piano works, Brahms's early compositions including the Piano Concerto, and Joachim's dramatic overtures are as 'Romantic' as such things come. But to Brahms it seemed that the 'New Germans' were in fact demoting music to the position of a handmaid of the other arts, allowing literature or paintings to dictate essential form, with more or less catastrophic results, rather than developing their art by its own inner logic, from the basis of the riches provided by past tradition which lay at hand to be rediscovered and studied anew.

Perhaps feeling the more isolated since Schumann's death, and by the fact that Joachim spent so much of his time playing and conducting and so little composing, Brahms now persuaded Joachim to co-write for publication a manifesto criticizing the claims of the 'New Germans', and the editorial policies of the *Neue Zeitschrift*. He had just been enraged by an editorial declaring that 'all the most prominent musicians of the day' supported the cause of the 'Music of the Future', and that at last 'even the North Germans' had finally been won over. It was difficult to find a form of words on which everyone could be expected to agree, and Brahms himself caused problems by wanting to draw a distinction between Liszt's works and those of Berlioz and Wagner, for which he had a wary respect. In the end no composers were directly named: the manifesto declared, in part, that

> The undersigned have long followed with regret the activities of a certain party whose organ is Brendel's *Zeitschrift für Musik*. The said journal continually spreads the view that earnestly striving musicians agree with the tendencies it represents, that they recognize in the compositions of the party's leaders works of artistic value, and that the argument for and against the so-called Music of the Future, especially in North Germany, has been fought out and decided in its favour. The undersigned ... declare that, in their view ... the products of the leaders and followers of the 'New German' school, which partly put their principles into practice and partly enforce ever new and unheard-of theories contrary to the inner spirit of music, are to be deplored and condemned.

In March Joachim sent out copies to a large number of distinguished musical acquaintances, soliciting their signatures as a sign of their support, and explaining his attitude to one of them as '*Amicus Liszt, magis amica Musica*'. Max Bruch, Theodor Kirchner, Dietrich, Bargiel, and Grädener agreed to sign; Hiller and Gade also agreed on condition that Julius Rietz, who was uncertain about the wisdom of the plan, signed too; Volkmann did not reply; a few others refused outright.

But a draft of the document was somehow leaked to the Berlin journal *Echo*, which printed it forthwith with the four signatures which were all that had yet been affixed to it – those of Brahms, Joachim, Grimm and a Hanover conductor, Bernhard Scholz. Brahms's polemical labours had brought forth a mouse. With such inadequate backing, the 'Manifesto' encountered general derision. Within a few days the *Neue Zeitschrift* responded with a spirited parody attributed to the signatories 'J. Geiger' ('Fiddler', i.e. Joachim), 'Hans Neubahn' (a reference to 'Neue Bahnen', the article in which Schumann had sponsored Brahms), and the German equivalent of 'Tom, Dick, and Harry'. Brahms learned his lesson once and for all. Though he continued to hold strong opinions about the music of his contemporaries, and to judge it by exacting standards, he never again ventured into public criticism, and endured many critical attacks in silence.

4

Fully armed like Minerva: the music to 1860

I have never come across a talent like his before. He is miles ahead of me.

Joachim, to Gisela von Arnim, 1854

I feel so imbecile . . . I cannot understand how you can take any interest in my things, in little Variations and Sonatas like mine!

Brahms, to Joachim, 1854

Brahms's famous capacity for self-criticism appears to have been a native trait, active from his earliest years. There are plenty of indications that he was a prolific composer throughout his early and middle teens – we hear of a piano sonata written at the age of eleven; pieces for the choral society in Winsen; songs, even song cycles; early attempts at chamber music; and, among the better-documented items, a Piano Fantasia 'on a Favourite Waltz' which he performed at his second public recital in Hamburg in 1849. All of these seem to have been destroyed, and the earliest work which he allowed to be published under his own name is the E flat minor Scherzo of late 1851.

The qualification 'under his own name' is important. It is now generally accepted that by the late 1840s Brahms was one of a number of composers contributing – under the shared pseudonym 'G. W. Marks' – to a long-running series of light-music arrangements and potpourris being issued by the Hamburg publisher Cranz. Presumably Marxsen, himself a contributor to the 'Marks' *oeuvre*, introduced him to Cranz and suggested the ploy to Johannes as a useful source of income (and possibly as good practice in technique). Brahms's low opinion of his efforts in later years can probably be gauged from the fact that he was content to let them remain buried under a pseudonym. But they reveal a taste for the popular music of the day, and an interest in the art of transcription, that remained with him throughout his life. (Its next flowering was in two technical studies: a Chopin Etude arranged for right hand only, and a Weber Rondo similarly arranged for the left; the latter is dated to March 1852 and was written, though not published, under the pseudonym of 'Johs. Kreisler, jun.'.)

The lost *Phantasie über einen beliebten Walzer* may well have been intended for the Cranz catalogue, or as an essay in that general style. But only one of Brahms's incarnations as 'G. W. Marks' seems to have been identified with certainty: and his earliest known surviving work, of about 1850, turns out to be the composite composer's 'op. 151', a Suite for piano duet entitled *Souvenir de la Russie*. This is a sequence of six 'transcriptions en forme de Fantaisies' on Russian songs (the National Hymn and three numbers attributed to Titov, Varlamov, and Alabiev) and two unattributed Bohemian airs − by far the earliest instance of the 'gypsy' music that exercised such a perennial fascination for Brahms.

For a 'pot-boiler', the *Souvenir* is surprisingly substantial, and its lack of empty virtuosity is one of the main pointers to its true authorship. Except for the opening rendition of 'Hail to the Emperor' (a tune we are well familiar with from Tchaikovsky's '1812' Overture, combined in this version with something that sounds suspiciously like the 'Rákóczy' March already made famous by Berlioz),[1] Brahms tends to eschew showy passage-work for a concentration on musical essentials and a firm grasp of the duet medium which make for thoroughly enjoyable listening. The second movement, 'Chansonette de Titoff', is in fact his earliest surviving set of variations, though a modest and decorative one. In the version of Alabiev's 'The Nightingale' which forms the fourth number, the essential manner of the future Hungarian Dances is already established. The rhythmic intricacy of the 'Chant bohemien' fifth movement, and the efficient canonic writing of the Finale, provide further strong hints of the composer who would develop from such unassuming beginnings.

From the little we can gather of Brahms's first compositional efforts, the picture that emerges − however incompletely − is of someone who, despite instincts and training unusually 'Classical' for his time, remained in intimate contact with popular song and dance. Given his father's profession, and his own partial adaptation to it, this is no surprise; and his own taste for folksongs (he arranged two for the Winsen choir in 1848) is further confirmation.

It was natural, therefore, that he first began to impress his individual stamp on the music of his time in an area where dance, song, and the Classical style meet: in movements of a scherzo type. The Classical scherzo and trio is, after all, a dance that has been sublimated into a miniaturized sonata movement, with a song-like melodic contrast in the middle. Brahms established his mastery of the form at the outset; and even the earliest examples furnish evidence of his potential for

---

[1] In the early 1850s Brahms made a solo piano transcription of this famous Hungarian march, which he played to Wasielewski. It has remained unpublished, although the manuscript (no longer quite complete) is extant at the Robert-Schumann-Haus in Zwickau.

symphonic thinking, both in his handling of structure and in the sheer dynamism which found its outlet in a powerful rhythmic drive, allied to motivic concentration.

First piano works

Brahms's earliest surviving wholly original work is, in fact, the Scherzo in E flat minor for solo piano, composed in 1851 and published three years later as his op. 4. Although its form is comparatively simple, it is laid out on an impressively large scale with two Trios, extending the customary A–B–A design into A–B–A–C–A with a developing coda. The organic development of the themes is already remarkable for its subtlety and continuity, both from the Scherzo to the first Trio and from one Trio to the other; and the scherzo sections are propelled by an unremitting rhythmic urge that might fairly be called demonic. They mark the eighteen-year-old composer instantly as a child of the Romantic era with their whiff of Hoffmannesque devilry, and their secondary theme which is a reminiscence of Heinrich Marschner's 'troll opera' *Hans Heiling*. It is little wonder that Liszt found the piece so congenial at Weimar. Whether Brahms had a specific model in mind is less certain (he claimed ignorance of Chopin's scherzi at that time, and the resemblances to them are in any case rather generalized). The obsessiveness of the rhythmic working suggests Beethoven rather than any more contemporary source of inspiration – among Brahms's contemporaries, only Alkan was developing this aspect of Beethoven's Classicism.[2]

The first major form to which he applied himself with sustained attention and success was that of the piano sonata. He wrote at least five of them, of which those we possess are (probably) the last three. The earliest, in F sharp minor, was actually published as no. 2, but it

[2] The one work of Alkan which Brahms certainly possessed, and apparently from an early period, is the fearsomely difficult toccata forming the third of the French composer's *Trois Grandes Etudes pour les mains séparées et réunies* (published in Prague, 1838). His copy, now in the collection of the Gesellschaft der Musikfreunde, Vienna, shows signs of frequent use and is covered with pencilled fingerings. He seems never to have performed it in public, and possibly regarded it primarily as a practice study; but he can hardly have remained unaware of its musical quality – the work is one of Alkan's first major and characteristic achievements – and he may, of course, have had opportunities to examine others. (His great friend of later years, Elisabet von Herzogenberg, was the daughter of Bodo Albrecht von Stockhausen, who had studied with both Alkan and Chopin in Paris, and Brahms consulted her father's copies of Chopin, with fingerings she believed to be Alkan's, when he was assisting Breitkopf & Härtel to revise their Chopin Edition in 1877.)

dates from 1852, whereas all but the Andante of the C major, issued as no. 1, was written the following year. Both works, however, were among those that Brahms played to Schumann at their first meeting.

The F sharp minor Sonata reveals its young composer as a thorough Romantic. It is a species of 'Fantasy-Sonata', influenced by the manner rather than the matter of middle-period Beethoven, and much afflicted by attacks of *Sturm und Drang*. The best movements are the middle ones. The Andante, which was the first part to be composed, is among Brahms's earliest surviving set of variations – upon *Mir ist leide*, an old German song ascribed to the Minnesinger Kraft von Toggenburg ('It makes me sad, that winter has bared the wood and heath'). Brahms stays close to the tune throughout, increasingly elaborating its surrounding texture; and though the first variations are beautiful, the last one, *con molt'agitazione*, is overloaded with 'dramatic' juxtapositions of loud and soft, changes of register, and chordal complexities. But the terse, epigrammatic Scherzo, which follows without a break, is a gem, showing that the E flat minor Scherzo of the previous year was no fluke. Moreover, the scherzo theme is itself fashioned out of the opening notes of *Mir ist leide*, indicating that even at the age of nineteen Brahms was much concerned with subtle and large-scale structural unity (perhaps inspired by the 'cyclic' forms of Liszt). This is a highly effective, through-composed little movement: the scherzo section itself takes up less space than a lilting, melodious Trio in D major; and the buzzing, dissonant note-repetitions that lead back to the scherzo material must have seemed extraordinary to early audiences. The Trio neatly manages a brief return in the coda, enveloped in trills.

The outer movements are less satisfactory, because less personal. Both are burdened with a great deal of hammered, teeth-gritting octave writing and virtuoso display, exhilarating for the pianist but not especially rewarding to listen to. The first movement's jagged and turbulent first subject, an arresting idea in itself, accords uneasily with a second group reminiscent of Schumann at his most sententious. The Finale, the most complex structure in the Sonata, is more interesting – and it is revealing, too, that Brahms should already be throwing the architectural weight towards the end of a sonata-style work, as he was to do in such later compositions as the First Symphony. There is an 'Introduzione' that contrasts a gaunt theme in octaves with florid, improvisatory passages of runs and trills. Once the main movement is under way the gaunt theme turns into a tune with an ambling grace worthy of Schubert, its *bonhomie* subtly and delicately undercut by acid minor-second clashes with the accompaniment. But Brahms cannot rest content with this: there is a lengthy second group in an inflatedly 'dramatic' style, some of whose ideas are decidedly inconsequential. Thereafter the proceedings are dominated by its febrile *agitato* character, which infects the Schubertian tune, until in a final *sostenuto* page Brahms re-invokes the spirit of the 'Introduzione' and the Sonata, its tensions unresolved, concludes in vertiginous, cadenza-like keyboard flourishes. Taken as a whole, it is one of the least appealing of Brahms's piano works, but it cannot merely be dismissed: its energy and originality already proclaim a composer of unusual quality.

Nevertheless the C major Sonata of next year is a substantial advance – as powerful and assured an opus 1 as any composer has published. It is not merely an improvement on the F sharp minor, though they have many features in common, but a work that is travelling a different path. The rhapsodic, improvisational aspects of the earlier Sonata have all but disappeared, and in their place is a bold concentration on the essence of musical ideas. The passionate nature of those ideas is given greater direction and scope for action through an increased understanding of Classical models. Not since Beethoven had there been such a first movement.

Ex. 1
(a)

The trenchant first subject (Ex. 1a) reveals the influence of both the 'Hammerklavier' and Schubert's 'Wanderer' Fantasy; but the handling of the spacious sonata form it initiates is already original, traversing a richer and more complex key-sequence than the Beethovenian model, with disciplined and effectively organic development of themes.

The slow movement, like that of the F sharp minor (which it actually slightly pre-dates), is a short set of variations on 'an old German Minnelied' – though the folk-like melody, *Verstohlen geht der Mond auf* ('The furtive moon is rising': Ex. 2) is now known to be the work of Zuccalmaglio, in whose collection Brahms found it. The tune is treated throughout with tenderness and restraint; responding to its nocturnal evocation, the movement is almost wholly lyrical, looking forward already to the mood of the Ballades despite a faint whiff of Mendelssohn in some of the more decorative writing. Unlike the Scherzo of the earlier sonata, the 6/8 Allegro molto e con fuoco has a formal repeat; but it is laid out on a much larger scale, approaching the dimensions and character of the E flat minor Scherzo. Once again we are treated to a decisive display of rhythmic vitality in Brahms's favourite galloping scherzo-metre, with a warm, more Romantically chromatic trio melody that rises and falls in smooth, sweeping arches without any loss of forward movement.

The exhilarating Rondo-finale, too, is marked *Allegro con fuoco*, and retains something of the scherzo character in its 9/8 metre: while – in another attempt at 'cyclic unity – its staccato main theme (see Ex. 1b)

Brahms

Ex. 2

is a cunning derivation from that of the first movement. The *sforzando* arpeggios on weak beats, usually the ninth, give the music an irresistible rhythmic *élan*. A graver, more poised chordal idea, in G major, forms the first episode, but despite its quiet dignity (in its latter stages it begins to sound like Fauré) it is never to return. The second episode, in A minor, is also chordal in texture, with a fine, vaunting tune that seems to blend Chopin and Schumann in their most heroic moods. As the rondo theme returns once again, in F, this tune dovetails with it until a brilliant, rather breathless *Presto* coda brings the Sonata to a crisp end. These concluding pages seem rather lightweight in comparison to what has gone before, but their bubbling, optimistic vitality is highly infectious.

The Third Sonata, in F minor, seems to have been composed at intervals throughout 1853, and was not complete when Brahms had his first meeting with the Schumanns. In five movements rather than four, it is his largest single piano work, and as decisive an advance on the C major as that had been on the F sharp minor. But again the nature of the advance is not merely technical. This Sonata is a grand synthesis of and capitalization upon everything he had learned in the earlier ones and in the op. 4 Scherzo. It re-engages the Romantic passion and fantasia-like construction of the F sharp minor, tempered by the formal grasp and power of thematic evolution achieved in the other works. The result stands with Liszt's B minor Sonata and the *Grande Sonate* of Alkan as one of the three greatest piano sonatas of the mid-nineteenth century.

Ex. 3

The very opening (Ex. 3) has a Promethean strength of aspiration; but it proves to be protean in its potentialities. The first movement is large, eventful, and displays all the character and contrasts of a particularly rich sonata design. Yet the structure is concise: the richness and breadth comes from the nature of the ideas themselves – and they are all derived, by thematic metamorphosis, from this initial statement, especially figure (x), which expands and contracts to form new tunes and motifs through augmentation and diminution. Deeply serious, passionately assertive, the movement seems truly Beethovenian in its apparent desire to burst the boundaries of the medium with its fiercely virtuosic and taxing pianism.

In the first two sonatas Brahms had turned to 'old songs' as the basis of his slow movements, providing extreme lyric contrast to strenuous first movements by simple, closed forms. Here he makes a song (without words) of his own, for the opening melody (Ex. 4a) of

the A flat major Andante seems to fit the quotation from the poet
Sternau which he placed at the head of the page: 'The twilight falls, the
moonlight gleams, two hearts in love unite, embraced in rapture'.The
nocturnal mood, exquisitely conjured by the music, recalls the slow
movement of the C major Sonata; however, this is no sequence of
decorative variations but a broad, finely proportioned form of almost
symphonic implications. Ex. 4a alternates with an equally delicate *ben
cantando* idea, before an expansive central episode that gives rise to a
new, Romantically ardent tune (Ex. 4b) presented over a sensuously
undulating left-hand figure. The first two themes return, fulfilling a
ternary design; but the mood becomes shadowed, bringing in a long
ecstatic epilogue in D flat, built upon Ex. 4c, which is a wonderful hymn-

Ex. 4

(a)

(b)

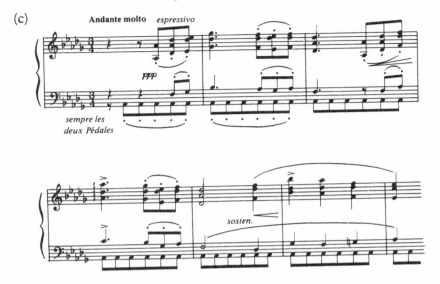

(c)

like variant of Ex. 4b. It rises songfully over a sinister throbbing A flat in the bass, and mounts to the most splendid, full-hearted climax Brahms had yet composed, only to sink to rest with memories of Ex. 4a's descending chain of thirds.

The Scherzo, *Allegro energico* in F minor, is as fiery as anything we have so far encountered, with thunderous octave writing and a mephistophelean swagger which gives it something of the character of a daemonic waltz. The Trio, in D flat, is taken at the same pace, but its full, sustained chordal texture greatly broadens the momentum with an almost tidal rise and fall of melody. Ideas from both Scherzo and Trio are succinctly developed in a masterful transition back to the repeat of the scherzo-section.

So far this Sonata has followed the general pattern of the other two. But now Brahms inserts a mysterious little movement which he calls an Intermezzo, with the subtitle 'Rückblick' (a backward glance). What it looks back to is the Andante, whose opening theme (Ex. 4a) undergoes a spectral transformation in B flat minor (relative minor of the warm D flat in which the Andante ended), enveloped in a sad panoply of trumpet and drum effects. At several points in these early works Brahms has seemed in need of rather more than a single piano to project his ideas with the requisite force. Here he has discovered how to make an orchestra speak through the medium of the keyboard, and the result is the closest he ever comes in texture and sonority to Alkan

69

(whose specific genius that was): see Ex. 5. In its depiction of sorrow and suggestion of inexorable fate, the conception is as Romantic as anything by Berlioz or Schumann.

Ex. 5

The Finale is a modified rondo form. Its opening, like that of the C major, is scherzo-like in character. There the similarity ends. The 'Rückblick' movement demands something less simply ebullient in conclusion; and the restless rondo theme, with its sardonic, loping rhythm, admirably answers the mood. As in the Finale of op. 1 the first episode (in F major) is a self-contained lyric interlude, never to return; instead the rondo theme is developed so that its tramping staccato semiquavers, over a nagging D flat pedal, begin to sound obsessive. But darkness is banished by a grand, swinging, chorale-like tune, again in D flat, which is soon developed canonically, evoking the quiet tollings of great bells. Henceforth this *echt*-Brahmsian subject is in competition with the rondo theme, while the pace and excitement increase throughout a lengthy F major coda – and it is the chorale that triumphs, to the rondo theme's final joyful agreement.

Although Brahms occasionally thought of revising this Sonata in his later years, it is difficult to see what could need doing to it save for the tidying and possibly simplifying of some details, and a tightening up of the helter-skelter coda. With it, the twenty-year-old composer had put his mark indelibly on the piano music of his time. Yet he wrote no more in this form. From now on in his large-scale works he seems to have felt the need for larger forces. But he may not at first have been conscious of relinquishing the genre. Doubtless he saw himself as writing a natural successor when, in early 1854, he started a new Sonata for *two* pianos; but that work was rapidly to turn into the draft of a Symphony, which would eventually see the light – five years later, and then only in part – as his First Piano Concerto.

Earliest songs

Brahms's impulse to write songs was as native to him as his ambitions in piano music. His earliest efforts (which are believed to have included cycles on poems by the Romantic nature-mystic, Eichendorff) are lost; but the eighteen songs which he published in 1853–4 in three sets of six *Gesänge* – opp. 3, 6, and 7 – all predate his meeting with the Schumanns. They are contemporary with the first two piano sonatas, and the earliest of all, *Heimkehr* (1851), setting a text by Uhland, is placed circumspectly at the end of the op. 7 group. By contrast, in the first item of op. 3, he announced himself to the world as a song-writer with one of his most recent examples – the one which had so impressed Joachim on their first meeting. This is *Liebestreu* (see Ex. 6). The memorable melodic line, shadowed and dragged down by a deep canonic imitation in the left hand, against an inner agitated chordal pulse that rises to the top of the texture like the unsuppressible sorrow of the speaker, proclaims a powerful song-writing gift, of a naturalness and immediacy that had scarcely been heard since Schubert.

However, it is instructive to compare this song with the earlier *Heimkehr* – for, as has frequently been remarked, *Liebestreu* is in effect a recomposition of it, and Brahms had come immensely far in a scant two years. *Heimkehr*, too, has the pulsing triplet chords, the imitations between voice and the piano's bass. Yet its expression is much more melodramatic, with something of the rodomontade of grand opera; and the effect is much weaker and ill-proportioned – the gestures (starting with the introductory piano solo) too grandiose for the song's twenty-

Brahms

Ex. 6

('Drown, O drown your sorrow, my child, in the sea, in the deep sea!')

odd bars: it is just about tolerable in its role as the brief, barnstorming coda which Brahms effectively made it, by allowing it to round off his op. 7 collection.

This 'quasi-operatic' mode (by no means unaffected by early Wagner) is felt in some of the other early songs, notably in the *Lied aus 'Ivan'* (op. 3 no. 4). But elsewhere, in strong contrast, there is a piercing simplicity of utterance – especially in the settings of folksongs, a source of inspiration that was to refresh Brahms's lyric gifts throughout his career. The palmary specimens are op. 7 nos. 4 and 5, *Volkslied* and *Die Traurende*. The latter especially – in the slow, drooping melancholy of the melody, the austere purity of the harmony in its suggestion of archaic modality – perfectly matches the mood of the forlorn girl, and does so with astonishing economy.

Between these extremes Brahms discovers plenty of scope for his already prodigal song-writing powers, while paying graceful debts to

72

his predecessors: Schubert in the sad *Parole* (op. 7 no. 2), Mendelssohn in the youthful élan of *Juchhe* (op. 6 no. 4), Schumann in the two op. 3 songs called *Liebe und Frühling*. The first of those, with its covert quotation of Zerlina's aria 'Batti, batti' from *Don Giovanni*, recalls (so he confessed in later life) a youthful passion for a girl who had sung that part in Mozart's opera. The texts of these songs – to poets of very variable quality, from Eichendorff to the decidedly inferior Robert Reinick (who, nevertheless, provides the words of *Liebestreu*) – already concentrate upon certain themes that would always excite an immediate emotional response from Brahms: constancy in love, often a hopeless constancy, and a concomitant feeling of isolation (sometimes expressed through the metaphor of homelessness) in the absence of an actual or even any potential beloved.

Thus the crowing high spirits of *Juchhe* and the lazy satisfaction of the sensuous fandango-rhythm in *Spanisches Lied* (op. 6 no. 1) are exceptions: far more typically Brahmsian in their melancholy are *Treue Liebe* (op. 7 no. 1), where the girl seeks her drowned lover in the sea; or *Anklänge* (op. 7 no. 3) where she sits spinning for the wedding dress that presumably she will never wear; or the extremely beautiful *Nachtigallen schwingen* (op. 6 no. 6, to a text by Hoffmann von Fallersleben), whose piano part is loud with suggested birdsong as the long, elegiacally arched melody leaves the poet with the sense that he is the one flower in the world that refuses to bloom. The mood in these songs is no less genuine, and intensely memorable, for being ever so slightly indulgent.

Chamber Music

As we know from Schumann's 'Neue Bahnen', Brahms was already well versed in chamber music composition before he came to Düsseldorf. Yet only one pre-Düsseldorf piece has survived: the curious little *Hymne zur Verherrlichung des grossen Joachim*, which is a kind of musical joke. A waltz-serenade for two violins and double bass, with a mock-classi-cal main theme and a ludicrously florid gypsy-style violin cadenza, it was written for Joachim's twenty-second birthday in July 1853 and – to judge by the flowery dedication – actually played to him 'by his travelling admirers: Gioseppo, Ottone and Arnoldino' (for whom read Brahms, Otto Brinkmann, and Arnold Weber), 'artists from Arcadia'. But as for the Duo for cello and piano and the Piano Trio performed in Hamburg in 1851 (the latter may be the same as the *Phantasie* Trio in D minor mentioned in letters to and from Schumann and Joachim), the B flat String Quartet composed in the summer of 1853 and shown to Breitkopf & Härtel, or the Violin Sonata in A minor, nothing now remains.

The *Hymne* aside, therefore, Brahms's earliest extant chamber music achievement is, as in piano music, a scherzo: the splendidly decisive Scherzo in C minor which he wrote in 1853 for the so-called 'F-A-E' Sonata, whose origins are described on p. 17. Joachim would have had little difficulty guessing the author of this movement: no one but Brahms was writing scherzi with that kind of rhythmic drive, and nobody who knew the early piano sonatas would mistake it. It shows all his early mastery of the genre in its clipped concision, cumulative rhythmic power, and sudden generous efflorescence of *cantabile* melody in the second subject and Trio; even while he keeps the rapping rhythm ♪♪♪ ♩. – the germ from which the entire structure has sprung – nagging away in the bass. The violin writing is confident, spanning the instrument's full range; and the grandiloquent trills of the coda are a witty homage to Joachim's virtuosity.

The 'F-A-E' Sonata stands now as a poignant memorial of the brief and happy period in which Brahms was accepted into the Schumann circle and he and the older composer were able to collaborate on something like equal terms. Schumann's suicide attempt some four months later, and his subsequent confinement to the sanatorium, were emotional disasters of the first magnitude, disrupting the pattern of Brahms's life, the course of his blossoming artistic career, and leaving its mark indelibly on the music he was to compose for the next few years. Many pieces, begun in an attempt to justify Schumann's faith in him, did not find their proper shape for years; others emerged with their emotional travail written upon them more explicitly than Brahms would ever have allowed in later years.

When Brahms received news of the Schumann catastrophe he was hard at work on a major chamber work which is nowadays virtually unknown – the Piano Trio in B major. Begun at the start of 1854 and essentially complete in June (the month of the 'Schumann' Variations), it was published as op. 8 about the end of that year. Thirty-five years later (as related in Chapter 11), Brahms – very unusually – chose to produce a completely revised version of this Trio. Although it was his declared intention that the two versions should circulate on equal terms, posterity's unfortunate passion for over-simplification has led to the effective suppression of the 1854 score. Almost invariably it is the 1889 version we encounter in performance, conventionally described as 'Brahms's First Piano Trio'; whereas it should more accurately be considered his last. The recasting, masterly as it was, resulted in a radically different piece – and the original Trio of 1854 demands to be described at this point as a work in its own right.

It was not his first essay in the medium, and may partly have originated from his work on the Trios (in the plural) mentioned in a letter to Schumann of 1853, which are otherwise lost.[3] It is a very ambitious conception indeed, laid out on a scale that suggests familiarity with Beethoven's 'Archduke' Trio (and perhaps those of Schubert); crammed with a plethora of memorable and highly disparate ideas, it is one of the few early Brahms scores where his expressive aim clearly surpasses his structural reach. Yet its very imperfections are part of its fascination, and none of his early works more poignantly intertwines his burgeoning compositional skills with elements of passionate auto-biography. Nothing else – not even the F minor Piano Sonata – so clearly proclaims the twenty-one-year-old composer's astonishing potential, the master in the making.

The work begins magnificently, with a murmuring groundswell of piano figuration to emphasize the tidal ebb and flow of perhaps the sublimest tune he had yet composed (Ex. 7a). This long, leisurely theme accumulates power as its exposition progresses, punctuated by wide-spaced piano chords in contrary motion that outline and hammer home the descending figure (x). But the listener is soon rudely jolted by a drastic change of gear: a transition passage based on an almost comically

Ex. 7

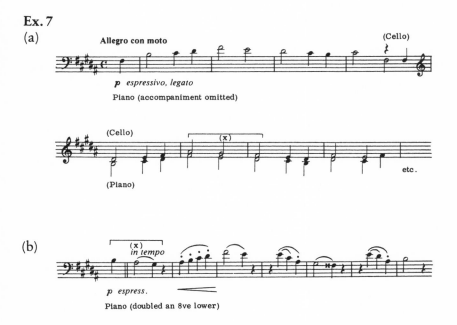

(a)

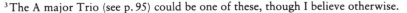

(b)

[3] The A major Trio (see p. 95) could be one of these, though I believe otherwise.

diminished version of the same figure. The second subject proper then grows from another treatment of (x) into a wayward, recitative-like melody, first heard in bald octaves on the piano and then in canon on the strings.[4] Whereas the first half of this theme (partly shown in Ex. 7b) is diatonic, its second half is meanderingly chromatic, evoking in a general way the late contrapuntal works of J. S. Bach. The exposition concludes with a new, *poco scherzando* version of Ex. 7a in the manner of a country dance, complete with rustic drone fifths in the bass; after a complete repeat, quiet augmentations of figure (x) lead on to the development section.

Manifest in the exposition's abrupt and unprepared contrasts is Brahms's eagerness to pour into the movement all his musical experience to date: but it leaves a patchwork impression, and a problem of structural reconciliation which the ensuing development hardly solves. This draws together most of the material so far heard, often in varied form or contrapuntal combinations (but omitting the 'Bachian' ingredient). Ex. 7b, and then the 'country dance' adaptation of Ex. 7a, appear along with a new dotted version of the first theme, plus a pattern of *sforzato* triplet repetitions in the cello which gives rise to some striking and rhythmically complex textures. These elements, intermingled with (x), are worked upon in the spirit of an uneasy pastoral, and prepare the way for a punctual and orthodox recapitulation of the grand tune Ex. 7a in its original guise. This time Brahms side-steps the embarrassingly flimsy transition passage, only to produce something even more unsettling: a fully-fledged fugue upon the 'Bachian' chromatic subject, perhaps over-indebted to study of *Die Kunst der Fuge*. This neo-Baroque phenomenon sits rather oddly and scholastically within an otherwise ultra-Romantic movement; but it initiates what is, in effect, a second development. Fragments of both main subjects, alternating with figure (x) in triplet rhythm, are followed by a lingering farewell to the first phrase of Ex. 7b (itself a form of (x)) that momentarily looks forward thirty years to the Fourth Symphony! (Ex. 7c). Finally a choleric coda (marked *Schneller*) storms to a decisive close with yet further development of its main elements in a rich, chordal texture. The result is a powerful, highly inventive yet undeniably awkward movement whose very flaws are so deeply a part of its essential expression that, as Brahms recognized thirty-five years later, any mere revision would amount to

---

[4]Eric Sams sees this theme – which certainly sounds vocal in its inspiration – as a 'message' to Clara Schumann couched in the form of a résumé of salient phrases from Schumann's opera *Genoveva*, whose love-triangle plot could have had autobiographical resonances.

falsification. (In the event, his recomposition would jettison everything save the opening tune.)

Ex. 7
(c)

There are no such problems with the second movement, an *Allegro molto* Scherzo in B minor. The opening, almost Mendelssohnian in its delicacy (with specific reference, perhaps, to the Scherzo in *A Mid-summer Night's Dream*) soon explodes into a continuation in Brahms's heroic 'hunting' style, seeming to demand the orchestral sonority of massed horns. Towards the close a note of pathos enters with a longer-spanned tune which proves to be the subject of the *espressivo* Trio, in the major, where the Scherzo's nagging rhythm still haunts the bass. This section reaches a full-textured climax, crowned by a rather rhetorical high tremolo from the violin, before the *da capo* of the Scherzo; Brahms unexpectedly freezes its hectic motion into a coda of long-held piano chords and soft pizzicato exchanges between the strings.

Serene, chorale-like chords on the piano and *espressivo* responding phrases on the strings begin the Adagio non troppo in B major; then it moves to E for a warmly lyrical second theme which bears an unmistakable resemblance to the song *Am Meer* from Schubert's *Schwanengesang*. Here the tune – to which Schubert sets a poem of hopeless love by Brahms's fellow Hamburger, Heinrich Heine – is lapped in plangent pizzicato figuration, emphasizing its pathos and serenade-like qualities. The first subject resumes, and is elaborated; but a second episode, partly derived from the *Am Meer* theme, abruptly shatters the reflective mood with an agitated, Schumannesque *Allegro*. Its climax is perhaps the least effective music in the work, but the serene opening theme returns for the last word.

That agitated episode, however, is an unmistakable presage of the *Allegro molto agitato* Finale. Unusually and revealingly, Brahms chooses to end his ostensibly major-key work with a tragic and disturbing movement in the minor. The urgent yet febrile opening theme, given first to the cello, features a nagging figure of repeated notes in the dotted rhythm ♩ ♪ ♪♪♪♩ , which is rarely absent throughout the movement, and an angry answering phrase in his most passionate 'Hungarian' vein. A battering climax on the dotted-rhythm figure then gives onto the calm of the dominant major, and the glorious assuagement of a radiant *espressivo* theme (Ex. 8c).

Ex. 8

(a) Beethoven

Nimm sie— hin   denn,   die - se Lie - der

(b) Schumann

This theme has a specific and significant heredity. Essentially it is a version of the phrase 'Nimm sie hin, denn, diese Lieder' – 'Take, then, these songs' (and the poem continues '...which I wrote for you, Beloved') from the last song of Beethoven's cycle *An die ferne Geliebte*; but it is more than just that. Schumann, too, had adapted the same melody in his op. 17 Fantasy as a lament for his separation from Clara in the period before their marriage. Ex. 8 gives the genealogical tree; Brahms's soaring F sharp major tune, burgeoning soon into a love-duet for violin and cello, is incontrovertible evidence that the Trio contains intimate messages readable (at that time) only within the immediate Schumann circle. Yet even here sinister iterations of the ♩ 𝄾 𝅘𝅥𝅯𝅘𝅥𝅯 ♩ figure infiltrate themselves into the accompaniment, and the music soon plunges back to B minor for an emotionally turbulent development of that inescapable figure, now hectoring, now spectral in bare string octaves interspersed with tolling piano chords. A new, vaunting theme of unmistakably Schumannesque cut then arises in the strings, but its heroic assertiveness has arrived much too late in the proceedings to affect the outcome, and is undercut and immobilized by a tapping ostinato on the fateful dotted rhythm. The tonality darkens to D minor and the first theme returns – a 'false' recapitulation that is turned aside by a brief glimpse of the 'distant Beloved' tune. But the tapping rhythm is now as insistent as the strokes of Mephistopheles's whip, and the music gallops on into B minor and a true, intensified recapitulation of the first subject in stretto. A final, but now *sempre agitato* reminder of the distant Beloved on the piano merely heralds a furious coda in which the dotted-rhythm figure carries all before it, and the Trio's enormous energies expend themselves at last in a grim B minor.

Brahms brutally suppressed most of this Finale in his 1889 revision – but it is a remarkable movement nonetheless. Unlike the first movement (or indeed the Finale of op. 5), there is nothing amiss with its larger structure; if the opening theme tires the ear with its ubiquitous presence, this very obsessiveness is precisely what the music seeks to convey. As it stands, the 1854 Trio is more than half a masterpiece; but the whole masterpiece Brahms was to make of it thirty-five years later is not even the same artistic entity.

Piano Variations and other pieces

Brahms wrote no more piano sonatas after the three completed in 1852–3; but overlapping them is another group of three piano works in variation form which – in different contexts and instrumental media – he was to pursue for the rest of his life. The order of publication, however, obscures that of their composition. The Variations on a Hungarian Song, issued eventually in 1861 as op. 21 no. 2, is a work of 1853; the Variations on a Theme of Schumann, op. 9, is firmly and poignantly located in the summer of 1854; while the Variations on an Original Theme, op. 21 no. 1, can safely be described only as 'after 1854' – but not very long after.

Op. 21 no. 2, as befits its early date, is the shortest and simplest of all Brahms's independent variation sets. In April 1853 he had sent Joachim piano settings of three Hungarian tunes obtained from Reményi, with a friendly dedication from Reményi and himself. This manuscript still exists in Leipzig – and the second tune proves to be the theme of these Variations: a rugged eight-bar melody, rhythmically enlivened by its alternating bars of 3/4 and 4/4. Probably the obstacle to variation posed by that very feature was what attracted Brahms in the first place. His first eight variations all retain this metrical irregularity, and the theme remains throughout as a kind of cantus firmus, though often subtly transformed – as in the 'gypsy' colouring of variation 5 (Ex. 9), whose repeated notes and rhythmic hesitations evoke the sonority of the cimbalom and (perhaps only from similarity of inspiration) passages in the Hungarian Rhapsodies of Liszt. From the ninth variation onward Brahms standardizes the metre to two beats in the bar although keeping the eight-bar structure: but the thirteenth and last variation finally overspills these confines, developing into an extended and increasingly brilliant finale at doubled speed that entails several further variations and culminates in a triumphant restatement of the theme.

The expressive contrast offered by the Variations on a Theme of Schumann is extreme: its great sensitivity and almost overwhelming pathos faithfully mirror the circumstances of its composition within the ambience of the stricken Schumann household. Brahms composed it in late May and early June of 1854, bringing each variation to Clara ('to comfort me', she noted in her diary) as she convalesced after the birth

Ex. 9

of her seventh and last child. Clearly, Clara herself was as much in his mind as her hapless husband. The theme he had chosen, from the fourth of Schumann's *Bunte Blätter*, op. 99, was the same one that Clara had taken the previous year as the basis for a searching and beautiful variation set of her own, composed for Schumann's birthday in 1853. That work was still in manuscript when she played it to Brahms on 24 May 1854; his is therefore unmistakably a response to Clara's. Moreover, Brahms arranged for both sets to be published by Breitkopf & Härtel, almost simultaneously, in November. Clara's, her op. 20, appeared under the title 'Variations on a Theme of Robert Schumann. Dedicated to Him'. The manuscript of Brahms's op. 9 bore at first the imitative title 'Little Variations on a Theme by Him. Dedicated to Her'.

Originally there were fourteen variations, but in August Brahms wrote two more which were inserted as variations 10 and 11, to make sixteen in all.[5] Perhaps at this point he ceased to think of the set as 'little' (it was in any case more elaborate than Clara's), and it was printed under the title we know today. But at about that time Clara presented him with a copy of her own set, inscribed 'For the creator of the most glorious variations, these little ones'; and later still he begged her manuscript from her.

But Schumann himself presides over Brahms's Variations in far more than the choice of theme. There are reminiscences in style and

[5] Fourteen years later, he composed one further, separate variation on the same theme, as a gift for Clara's sister Marie Wieck.

texture of several of his other works,[6] and the variation techniques as such, predicated especially on the free melodic transformation of the theme or its bass in 'fantasy' style, show Brahms absorbing some of Schumann's most personal innovations. Moreover, many of the individual variations are signed – the more lyrical ones 'B' (for Brahms) the faster, more ardent ones 'Kr' (for 'Kreisler'). This was a clear emulation of Schumann's ascription of different variations of his *Davidsbündlertänze* to Eusebius and Florestan – and for Clara's eyes only, as these signatures were not carried over into the published edition.

The first four variations adhere to the plaintive theme's twenty-four-bar outline, and the first eight to its key (F sharp minor); but as the work proceeds Brahms alters tonality and proportion much more freely than in the 'Hungarian Song' set. And throughout, he is much more resourceful in presenting a varied sequence of musical character and mood – though all the moods are tinged with varying gradations of melancholy. This atmosphere is never allowed to sap the structural control, which is reinforced by a contrapuntal mastery that in some respects already surpasses Schumann – not least in the strict canons that articulate several variations.

Variations 1–7 seem to make up a structural unit. Against the sadness inherent in the theme itself these make progressively more vigorous attempts towards positive activity, climaxed by the passionate Allegro of variation 6 (marked 'Kr') – only to be brought up short by the numbed stillness of no. 7 (marked 'B'): the essence of the theme presented in a drastically compressed form. Thereafter no. 8 (also 'B') reintroduces the theme in a sad, serenade-like evocation of its original shape, with a murmurous canon in the figuration of the accompaniment. The key now shifts at last, to B minor, for 'Kreisler's' windswept no. 9, an allusion to Schumann's *Bunte Blätter* no. 5, companion-piece to the one from which the theme derives.

Originally the music now returned to F sharp minor, but the two later-inserted variations artfully and satisfyingly extend the exploration to other keys. Now variation 10 brings a further shift to D major. This is an exquisite song-like inspiration that feels almost like a self-contained Romance. Brahms, ultra-Romantically, headed the manuscript sheet '(Fragrance of Rose and Heliotrope)', and both variations are ascribed to 'B': if there is a symbolic significance to the flower names we do not know it, but there is certainly a musical symbolism here. The warmest, most glowing music in the set, no. 10 opens with a striking example of

---

[6] See Oliver Neighbour, 'Brahms and Schumann: Two Opus Nines and Beyond', in *19th Century Music*, Vol. VII no. 3 (April 1984).

melodic inversion between treble and bass, while the lapping figuration in the middle of the keyboard soon develops into an expressive tenor part that, at the final cadence, quotes the 'Theme by Clara Wieck' on which Schumann had based his op. 5 Impromptus.[7] The delicate variation 11 is transitional in character, avoiding its nominal tonic of G, beginning on the dominant and modulating to C sharp major – a result perhaps of his more recent study of Schumann's *Carnaval*, and a much more original approach to the F sharp minor of the next three variations. No. 12 is quiet but staccato and *scherzando*, rapid quaver movement punctuated by sudden stillnesses, something like a virtuoso piano study in thirds. This 'study' aspect is maintained into the toccata-like no. 13, with its streams of legato quaver figuration. No. 14 is a kind of nocturne, marked *Andante*, the left-hand quavers rising and falling in limpid accompaniment to a barcarolle-like variant of the theme, treated in close and plangent canon at the second.

The nocturnal mood darkens and intensifies in the penultimate variation: an Adagio in the tonic major (but written as G flat). A long-spanned augmentation of the theme tolls out, once again in canon, between treble and bass, while sonorous arpeggios span the intervening gap like an Aeolian harp. Then the key-signature changes to sharps, and the final variation (by 'B') comes as a very slow, stark, almost skeletal coda. The bass of the theme is augmented to form what feels like a hushed chaconne-type ground, above which the melody is fragmented into poignant, isolated chordal sighs. Despite the use of the major mode, this ending conveys a sense of infinite regret. The work is a masterpiece, perhaps the finest thing Brahms had yet written: but its elegiac quality, the intensity of private feeling it expresses through musical symbols, make it an achievement of a very idiosyncratic kind, not easily repeated.

The fact that Brahms originally imagined op. 9 as at least partly the work of his Hoffmannesque *alter ego* is an indication of how thoroughly his youthful Romanticism suffused the whole conception. 'Kreisler' was rather active at this period. Already Joachim had received from Brahms a volume of short, possibly playful piano pieces, entitled

---

[7] See Brahms's letter to Joachim of 12 September 1854: 'My Variations have had two new additions, in one of which *Clara speaks!*' (*Letters from and to Joseph Joachim*, p. 77). Furthermore, the bass of her theme – not quoted by Brahms but much used in Schumann's op. 5 – closely resembles the *Albumblatt* theme on which Brahms's Variations are based, which is itself a version of one of the most common 'Clara-motifs' that Schumann employed in many works. Brahms seems to be enlarging in very Schumannesque fashion on Schumann's private, Clara-directed musical symbolism – to suggest that Schumann's op. 5 and op. 99, Clara's op. 20, and now his own op. 9, form a sequence whose connecting thread is Clara herself.

Leaves from a Musician's Diary and ascribed to 'Johannes Kreisler'. They included a Minuet, a Scherzino, and a 'Reminiscence of M.[en-delssohn] B.[artholdy]': but they have not been preserved. In mid-1854 'Kreisler' sent Joachim a second volume: it is also lost, but we know it contained a copy of the 'Schumann' Variations, and probably the first of his essays in neo-Baroque dance forms, discussed later. However, almost simultaneously Brahms was working on a different kind of piano composition, of greater significance for his ultimate development. The four Ballades, op. 10, written in the summer of 1854 but not published until 1856, mark a new departure: the first example (unless the little 'Kreisler' works were a true forerunner) of the groups of short, essentially lyrical pieces which were to become the hallmark of his piano output in later life.

In a recent study of Chopin, Jim Samson has remarked that 'the genre title *Ballade* carries no formal *expectations* whatever ... the innocent ear will have no *a priori* reference point'; he goes on to mention the 'narrative' quality of the four Chopin Ballades, and that they 'draw heavily upon the sonata principle, and particularly upon the thematic dualism of the sonata'.[8] To some extent, Brahms must have had Chopin's works in mind, but except in his first Ballade (where Samson's latter comments could certainly be applied) there are striking differences of approach. On the whole his formal organization is simpler than Chopin's, each Ballade assuming an approximately ternary form with clear divisions; but he achieves extraordinary variety within that basic shape. Moreover, while each Chopin Ballade was published separately, as an independent work, Brahms's form a coherent group, and are best experienced as such. He seems to have understood the term 'Ballade' as suggesting a form and mood evocative of ballad poetry: and the first of the set, in D minor, is self-proclaimedly 'after the Scottish ballad *Edward*' as Brahms had read it in Herder's German translation. Indeed, the two intimately related halves of its first theme – the one plaintive, the other sombre – alternate in a manner that enacts the ballad's question-and-answer form. Even more: they fit its words, be they in Herder's German or the original Scots (Ex. 10).

In musical language, too, there is an advance. The austere yet resonant spacing of the chords, with plaintive thirds at the top and 'archaic' fifths at the bottom of the texture, creates a haunting sound that is characteristic of Brahms alone and is to persist throughout his output. The piece's middle section provides strong contrast of character, with heroic fanfare-figures pounded out in triplet rhythm, but there is

[8] Jim Samson, *The Music of Chopin* (London, 1985), p. 175.

Ex. 10

Andante

Dein Schwert, wie _ ist's von Blut so rot? Ed - ward, Ed - ward! Dein
Why dois your brand sae drap wi bluid? Ed - ward, Ed - ward! Why

Schwert, wie ist's von Blut so _ rot, und gehst so
dois your brand sae drap wi _ bluid, and why sae

dimin.

Poco più mosso

trau - rig da? 'O ich hab' ge - schla - gen mei - nen Gei - er
gang ye o? 'O I hae _ killed my hawk _____ sae

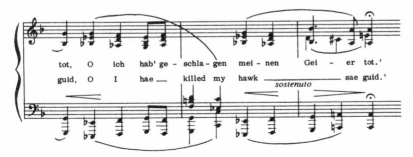

tot, O ich hab' ge - schla - gen mei - nen Gei - er tot.'
guid, O I hae _ killed my hawk _____ sae guid.'

sostenuto

no new theme as such: the passage constitutes rather a miniature sonata-style development, enveloping and overwhelming fragments of Ex. 10, whose second strain returns at the climax. The bleak opening music resumes, and grows bleaker as its bare accompaniment fragments, and ebbs away into gloom. As a re-creation of the ballad in purely musical terms it is brilliantly effective. Perhaps we would transgress the bounds of propriety to speculate why Brahms should have chosen, in the aftermath of Schumann's tragedy, to evoke this tale of the son who has slain his father at the mother's behest: but one suspects that the symbolism must have held a strong significance for him.

The second Ballade, in D major, is perhaps even more archetypally Brahmsian. Its first part presents a warm, serene *Andante* tune, almost like a lullaby, over a gentle syncopated accompaniment. A sudden switch to B minor brings in the extensive middle section, at double the speed and characterized at first by stern groups of hammered quavers, conveying a sense of controlled anger. Triplets invade the rhythmic pattern, and Brahms now seizes on the main triplet figure to create a new 6/4 section – a kind of restless gallop in B major, the hands moving in contrary motion in a relentless crotchet pulse, the notes plucked *molto staccato e leggiero*, while an internal pedal sounds out insistently. This music subsides back into B minor, where the hammered-quaver idea resumes and rises to a climax, then reduces itself to a rumble in the bass; and the initial *Andante* theme now returns – but in B major, whose colours are even richer and warmer than the original D. (The entirely different character created by the use of B major here and in the 6/4 section is not the least of Brahms's subtle achievements in this movement.) D major is eventually regained, however, and the piece ends with a melting, long-drawn-out coda.

Brahms gave the title 'Intermezzo' to the third Ballade, which is in the plainest ternary form of all; but this 6/8 Allegro in B minor is in fact another tautly rhythmic scherzo of the kind for which he had manifested such a strong native gift. Schumann, writing to Brahms about the Ballades from the asylum in a period of lucidity, suggested the epithet for it should be 'demoniacal', but this could really only refer to the opening, where the turbulent mood is established by abrupt, stamping left-hand fifths on the upbeat and a choleric, scrambling main subject. The texture is soon refined and the dynamic level drops to *piano*, leaving the music to work itself out in a mood of suppressed excitement.

The Trio, in F sharp major, is a simple tune rendered bright and ethereal by wide spacings and chiming harmonization in bell-like triads at the top of the keyboard. The transition back to the scherzo music is achieved in a remarkable few bars which freeze harmonic movement at different levels while the fateful knocking of the original left-hand ictus intrudes once more (Ex. 11). When the scherzo section returns it is compressed *sempre pp* and *molto leggiero*, a vanishing wraith of itself.

Ex. 11

The fourth and final Ballade, in B major, has been less widely admired than the other three; yet it is not the least original, and its expansiveness of approach makes it in some ways the most surprising. The long, sighing tune which forms its first section, over a gently cascading quaver accompaniment, sounds more like Schumann than Brahms; but it gives way to a mysterious middle section in F sharp, *con intimissimo sentimento*, which conceals a graver and more characteristic tenor tune in the middle of a sombre, murmuring texture of right-hand triplets against left-hand quavers. Brahms explores this crepuscular mood at length before returning to the opening theme and key – only to abandon it soon for a new idea entirely, predominantly chordal in texture, with something of the resonance of a chorale. At one time critics were wont to term this interlude 'a trifle dull'; but these days its gravity and inward poise seem to mark it out as the most Brahmsian page in the work. The Ballade concludes, not with the Schumannesque tune, but with the murmurous woodland music, now in B minor, brightening to major only in the dreamlike final bars.

The form of the last Ballade is thus not a strictly ternary A–B–A, but a chain-like A–B–A–C–B; and something of the same sort is observable in the succession of tonalities through all four Ballades, which are arranged around the major and minor modes of the three keys D, B, and F sharp. That certainly lends them a feeling of internal unity; and it may be that in this set of apparently disparate pieces Brahms was attempting a new form, a kind of looser, lyrical approximation of a four-movement sonata. Ballade no. 1 is itself a miniature sonata first movement, while no. 2 – at least in its outer sections – is the slow movement of the four, no. 3 the Scherzo; and no. 4's melodic breadth and chorale might be felt appropriate to a finale. Whether or not this was Brahms's purpose, op. 10 remains a fascinating collection, greater than the sum of its parts.

During this same period Brahms was experimenting with a group of short dance movements in the then unfamiliar Baroque forms. A Sarabande in A major and Gavotte in A minor were composed by June 1854, followed early in 1855 by another Sarabande (in B minor), another Gavotte (A major)[9] and two Gigues, in A minor and B minor. It seems likely that Brahms intended to produce a number of piano suites after the model of Bach's 'English' Suites, and practically certain that in September 1855 the four movements in A were combined with a Prelude and Aria (both now lost) to make a complete Suite in A minor. However, the practice arose of performing the dances in pairs (in June 1856, in London, Clara Schumann played a Sarabande and Gavotte, announced as 'in the Style of Bach' – the first music of Brahms ever heard in this country), and the manuscript sources arrange them as to type.

Brahms did not bother to publish them (the Gavottes were only printed as recently as 1979). Doubtless he regarded them principally as composition exercises, and they are undeniably slight; but effective pieces nonetheless (as he must have realized, since he later raided their ideas for the G major Sextet and F major Quintet). They may have struck his contemporaries as an antiquarian conceit, but they are something better than pastiche – Brahms's compositional personality is

[9] The end of this piece is in fact missing, but has been reconstructed by Robert Pascall on the basis of Brahms's reuse of the material in the String Quintet in F, op. 88.

merely refracted through Bach's phraseology and contrapuntal skills. The palm must go to the exquisite A major Sarabande – a mere sixteen bars of music (with repeats) whose rich chain of thirds and florid right-hand figuration bring to Baroque formulae a decidedly Romantic intensity (Ex. 12 shows its second half).

Ex. 12

Vocal and instrumental studies

History conceals composers' difficulties from us. We remember the great masters by their achievements, not their aborted projects; and Brahms is pre-eminently a composer who steadily made good his claim to a mastery that had been early prophesied. But he did not necessarily feel that. By the summer of 1855 he must have been plagued with doubts about his creative direction and capacities. With the partial exceptions of the piano sonatas, especially the last, his most characteristic successes to date had been the 'Schumann' Variations and the Ballades – small, concise forms disciplining the ardent passions of his youthful Romanticism.

In larger structures he had serious problems. The op. 8 Piano Trio is so ambitious it threatens to come apart at the seams. Since then he had devoted much of his time and energy to a massive Symphony in D minor that was refusing to come right, and was already running into similar difficulties with an explosively emotional Piano Quartet in C sharp minor. Into these works he was pouring his heart and soul – the Symphony as a response to Schumann's fate, and also an attempt to justify Schumann's faith in him; the Quartet as an embodiment of his emotional predicament with Clara. In a few years' time the Symphony would re-emerge as the First Piano Concerto, but the Piano Quartet would need *two decades* before it found its proper shape in a flatter key. From his present vantage-point, Brahms could not foresee a successful outcome for either of them.

So the 'young blood' who 'would not gain his mastery by gradual stages' but 'spring fully armed like Minerva from the head of Kronion' seems to have embarked on a rigorous programme of musical self-education. It was at this time that Brahms began exchanging counterpoint exercises, strict canons, and mutual criticism with Joachim – and, feeling a greater need, was far more assiduous in the enterprise than he. And indeed the majority of the works Brahms wrote in the next few years, in the shadow of the major creative effort required to convert his Symphony into a piano concerto, are to a greater or lesser extent studies in the art of composition, in contrapuntal technique and in mastery of form. This is as true of the complex and highly developed Variations on an Original Theme, and perhaps even the orchestral Serenades, as it is of the little dance movements in Baroque style, or the choral canons. Even these latter works he was content to publish or incorporate into other compositions many years later; and in truth none of the 'study pieces' which have survived are without some solid artistic quality.

It is in this context that we should approach Brahms's earliest essays for a medium in which he was ultimately to be very prolific – that of choral music. Canons with words had perhaps more intrinsic interest, and a reason to be more expressive, than purely instrumental ones, and so his first works for combined voices grew directly out of his canonic studies. Among these is the *Geistliches Lied* for mixed chorus and organ, a beautifully lyrical setting of a text by Paul Flemming. Composed in Hamburg in April 1856 (but not published till eight years later, as op. 30), this is specifically indicated in a subtitle on the manuscript as a 'Double Canon at the Ninth'. Tenor and bass imitate soprano and alto, with tranquil organ interludes and a glowing canonic Amen to conclude.

At least two of the three *Geistliche Chöre*, short unaccompanied settings of sacred Latin texts for female voices, op. 37 (all of which are canonic), are probably contemporary with the *Geistliches Lied*. They are traditionally dated 1859, when Brahms's 'dear girls' first sang them in Hamburg, but they look like studies (mellifluous but not entirely assured ones) in the style of Palestrina, whose *Missa Papae Marcelli* he was studying in 1856. In the first, 'O bone Jesu', Brahms's conscious archaism extends to the Latin specification of his chosen technique: *Canone per arsin et thesin, et per motum contrarium* – a double canon in contrary motion with the strong beats of the leading voice imitated on weak beats by the answer. The second chorus, 'Adoramus te', is a canon at the fourth, fifth and octave with a few final, non-canonic bars which sound distinctly like an afterthought. (The last of the *Geistliche Chöre*, 'Regina coeli laetare', is however a more elaborate affair, with two soloists in canon by inversion and freely composed choral support; it probably comes from the end of the 1850s, though it was not performed until Brahms was established in Vienna.)

The bulk of the eleven short Canons for female voices which he published many years later as op. 113 – simple, direct settings of folksong texts and proverbial verses by poets such as Goethe and Rückert – also probably date from this period. Considerably more substantial, but strongly related in technique, was an unaccompanied Mass for five-part chorus in canon form, the so-called *Missa Canonica*,[10] partly composed during 1856. The work may never have been completed to Brahms's satisfaction: we do not know if he ever gave it a Kyrie and Gloria, while the Credo gave him such trouble it was not finished until 1861 (and is now lost). In 1857 he sent the other three movements – a Sanctus and 'Hosanna', a Benedictus, and an Agnus Dei with 'Dona nobis pacem' – to Julius Otto Grimm in hope of a performance; and it is these portions of the Mass which have survived in a copy which Grimm made, along with a fugal Kyrie for voices and organ unrelated to the larger work.

Brahms would much later (1877) recompose the music of the Benedictus, Agnus Dei, and 'Dona nobis' for portions of his German-language motet *Warum ist das Licht gegeben?*; and it may be that in attempting a Mass he was more attracted by the archaic associations of the form, and the opportunity for choral canonic working on a large

---

[10] This was Grimm's name for it. Brahms's own references are merely to a Mass (*Messe*) in C major; the fact that so many of its sections deviated from that key caused him some disquiet – and indeed, of the surviving music, only the 'Dona nobis pacem' is in C.

canvas, than by the text of the traditional Catholic liturgy. However, since the slow movement of the First Piano Concerto also has links with the words of the Benedictus, celebrating the man whom Brahms referred to as 'Domine', it seems possible that there could be a Schumann connection here too. The music has an ardent purity that lifts it well above the level of a mere exercise, and this applies even more strongly to the fine sombre Kyrie in G minor – longer and more elaborately worked than the Mass movements, and in a more neo-Baroque idiom.

The four compositions for organ which Brahms wrote in 1856–7 – his only solo works for that instrument apart from the Choral Preludes assembled at the end of his life – could also have been conceived as studies, though he thought well enough of two to allow them to be published, albeit long after the event. These were a Fugue in A flat minor and a Chorale Prelude and Fugue in A on the chorale O *Traurigkeit, o Herzeleid*; the other pieces, a pair of Preludes and Fugues, appeared posthumously. All four compositions, therefore, contain (or are) fugues, while the three preludes explore different aspects of Baroque form; and all are of greater substance than the Baroque-style dance movements for piano.

The two Preludes and Fugues have a solid, virile brilliance, and owe much to many Bachian models, such as the Chromatic Fantasia and Fugue which was in Brahms's piano repertoire – indeed, the writing is more often pianistic than organ-based. The A minor, dedicated to Clara (who had worked in this form herself), has a short Prelude that itself begins fugally, continues mainly in two-part texture, and culminates in dramatic chordal writing. The fugue subject develops triplet patterns in its second half, and as the Fugue proceeds these give rise to much characteristically Brahmsian two-against-three rhythmic complications (anticipated, as four-against-six, in the Prelude). A forceful passage of chordal writing over a chromatically descending bass appears twice, like a refrain, and the Fugue concludes in a bravura cadenza that combines the subject with the Prelude's opening figure in a blaze of Neapolitan harmony.

The G minor Prelude and Fugue is laid out on a bigger scale. Its fiery Prelude is a free fantasia weaving rapid manual passage-work and descending chromatic figures around emphatic, strongly rhythmic chord-sequences. The Fugue is earnest in tone and masterful in its polyphony. Again, descending chromatic sequences direct much of the harmony, enhancing the Bachian feeling. Brahms himself is easily recognizable in the triplet rhythms of the central episode, and the impressive and closely worked counterpoint of the extensive coda seems to blend the two composers into a single musical personality.

The most intimate of these early organ pieces is the Chorale prelude and Fugue on *O Traurigkeit*. Brahms's choice of this obscure, anonymous Passion chorale ('O sorrow deep, who would not weep with heartfelt pain and sighing, God the Father's only Son within the grave is lying'), published in a Mainz *Gesangbuch* in 1628, reflects his early-music explorations; but it may, too, be intended as an allusion to the fast-failing Schumann, who went to his grave a month later. The Prelude sets the tune as a cantus firmus in the right hand, with gentle triplet figuration in thirds and sixths in the left; but the mood darkens as the first phrase of the chorale returns only to dissolve in drooping melismata. There follows the most beautiful of Brahms's organ fugues. Its subject, only tenuously connected with the chorale, nevertheless echoes its sorrowful descent, but then rises again (perhaps the sacred pun is intentional) in leaping phrases, brightening into the major key. Its intricate and peaceful counterpoint, in three voices, is confined to the manuals, while the chorale sounds in the pedals, line by line.

None of these works is negligible; but the Fugue in A flat minor is a pearl of particularly rare colouring. Slow in tempo and subdued in dynamics, its mood is searching, deeply introverted, spiritually withdrawn – seeking the unseen light, with anguished persistence, through the manipulation of the elements of music in their most abstract essentials. Contrapuntally it is the strictest of the four works; the fugue subject is answered (as in the *O Traurigkeit* Fugue) by its own inversion, a device later extended (along with that of augmentation, diminution, and stretto) to most of the episode material and other figures that entwine within its sombre discourse. The unusual tonality and high degree of chromaticism involve numerous accidentals and double-flats, giving the music an arcane, almost occult appearance. Here Brahms draws nearest (and more appropriately than in the op. 8 Trio) to the late contrapuntal works of Bach, especially *Die Kunst der Fuge* – a 'pure' music whose very concentration on technical problems is suffused by a mystical intensity of vision. A switch to B minor around the middle of the Fugue seems to be a notational convenience rather than a relaxation in the fervent meditation. Towards the end the note values broaden, and the work attains at last a quiet, painful serenity as mysterious and otherworldly as anything Brahms ever composed.

On a larger scale than any of the organ pieces is a sizeable piano work of the same period, the Variations on an Original Theme. This is no compositional study but a searching and personal creation of considerable poetry and substance; yet it does investigate and seek mastery over new aspects of variation technique. It also has something of the aloofness of the A flat minor Fugue. Instead of the bluff vigour of the Hungarian Song Variations, or the elegiac intensity and regret of the 'Schumann' set, these variations on a theme of Brahms's own devising are pensive and self-communing in mood; perhaps even self-questioning – 'Where have I got to, and where next?' – even while they mark a technical advance.

The theme is a noble melody in D major, presented in a rich setting (with graceful cadential turns and active middle parts) that leaves it almost over-supplied with possibilities of variation. But Brahms pays little further attention to those features. In all his previous variation sets (including those in the first two piano sonatas) he had been much concerned to keep the theme itself constantly before our ears. Here, he concentrates to a new degree on the theme's basic harmonic structure to provide a framework for fresh invention. Paradoxically, however, the harmonic structure is itself dominated and somewhat restricted at each end by a pedal bass, whose implications Brahms sometimes accepts and sometimes ignores.

All except the last of the eleven variations adhere strictly to the theme's unusual dimensions: two nine-bar halves, each half repeated. The first seven variations are all in D major, and quiet and introspective (another contrast to the strongly characterized individual numbers of the 'Schumann' Variations). No. 5 is a Romantic canon in contrary motion, the left hand mirroring the right at two bars' distance during

Ex. 13

the first half and then, through an elision of the mid-point cadence, at one bar's distance in the second half. The bareness and angularity of variation 7, where wide-leaping four-note groups in either hand pursue each other ceaselessly at a quaver's distance, has an almost Webernian appearance on the page, and introduces a piano texture that is wholly original to Brahms (Ex. 13).

Only with variation 8, a vigorous study in martial dotted rhythm, does the pace increase, the volume rise to *forte*, and the tonality shift to the minor. Variation 9 forms the dynamic climax of the work, turning the pedal bass into rumbling drum effects to bolster powerful and emphatic chordal writing. From there the music subsides uneasily through a further *espressivo agitato* variation to variation 11, which returns to D major and to the tempo of the theme, recalling it in varied form. This final variation, unlike the rest, is open-ended, freely evolving into a large-scale coda. Brahms transforms the bass pedal into a sonorous, continuous trill that bears up a sudden efflorescence of melodic invention, and he alludes to aspects of some of the earlier variations. The music eventually achieves a subdued but very beautiful resolution with final reminiscences of the theme in berceuse-like rhythm.

Something of the same mood is perceptible in what I take to be his next major composition, a Piano Trio in A major which may also date from this 1856–7 period.[11] This work (which Brahms did not see fit to publish, and which appears to have survived only by chance) has seldom received the attention it deserves. Its many strong similarities (and equally strong contrasts) with the previous trio suggest that Brahms may have conceived it very much in the light of op. 8, as a more Classically-disciplined attempt at a large-scale, sonata-style chamber work. Perhaps he then discarded it because he felt he had succeeded too well. Certainly this Trio lacks op. 8's fierce Romantic ardour, but it remains an impressive composition by any standards, subtler in its moods; while in formal organization it marks a positive advance.

Altogether less dramatic in conception than its predecessor, the *Moderato* first movement of the A major Trio is constructed with great economy, yet unfolds at a seemingly leisurely pace. There is a sense of latent power held in reserve; the movement impresses through its fluent

[11] A degree of mystery surrounds this Trio, which survives only in a copyist's manuscript and was not discovered until 1924. Most English writers have preferred to regard it as spurious, or at best a very early work. As will be evident from the discussion above, I believe it to be genuine, later in date than the B major Trio, and of sufficient importance to deserve attention on its own merits; but rather than engage in controversy here I have confined my reasons for this view to Appendix E, 'Who wrote the A major Trio?' (p. 475).

and unassertive mastery of sonata style. The meditative tone of the lyrical first theme (entrusted to piano against low cello, thus reversing the state of affairs at the opening of op. 8) is amplified rather than contradicted by the more expansive melodies of the second group. This may have something to do with key-character: certainly the prevailing atmosphere seems to presage two maturer works in A major – the Serenade, op. 16, and the Piano Quartet, op. 26. The main element of contrast within the exposition is confined to a brief transitional idea, a C minorish fanfare-like figure in abrupt dotted rhythm, introduced quietly and redolent of suppressed excitement.

The development is straightforward, reviewing each of the themes in ordered sequence, rising to a central climax on C sharp and then subsiding again, with none of op. 8's parentheses, changes of direction, and possibly extra-musical associations. Brahms concentrates here on motivic and emotional continuity – and nowhere more strikingly than at the point where the recapitulation begins. In all his previous sonata-style movements this had been very obviously defined; in some cases a moment of high drama. Here (Ex. 14) it is covert, unannounced – the cadence beautifully judged but unemphatic, the first subject gliding in upon the piano, dovetailed with the strings' final working-out of the last development idea, enhancing the movement's overall effect of a seamless, organic flow.

The recapitulation is quite regular, but then gives way to a coda that furnishes further evidence of Brahms's increasing structural subtlety. Based largely on a wide-ranging treatment of the first theme, it is suddenly curtailed by the clipped, dotted rhythms of the fanfare-figure. Originally a mere transition, it is this idea, its rhythms broadening to produce the effect of a *ritardando*, which brings the movement to an unexpectedly severe close, all the more effective for its concision and quality of understatement.

As in op. 8 the Scherzo (in F sharp minor) comes second, and is a wholly characteristic example of Brahms's approach to the genre, with tumultuous galloping figures held under steely rhythmic control and high, faintly sinister violin writing. The Trio, in B, is itself ternary in form, a gentle, ambling *dolce* tune on the piano enclosing a more soulful *cantabile* development of it, first heard on solo cello. The return of the Scherzo bursts in brusquely upon these lyrical proceedings. As further proof of his growing command of the medium, Brahms avoids the comparatively ineffective stratagem with which he had slowed and ended op. 8's Scherzo. This time there is no coda; instead a transfigured development of the trio section's closing portion is deftly inserted into the middle of the Scherzo's *da capo*, beautifully and effectively delaying

Ex. 14

what might otherwise have been the movement's over-prompt completion.

The Lento is in D major (the Trio's key-scheme, while orthodox, shows much greater variety than the obsessively B-centred op. 8). Its basic form is very simple, alternating two principal ideas. The first is a quiet hymn-like melody, stated first like a chorale in the piano with answering elaborations on the strings; the second, thematically more diverse, derives its motive power from a nagging dotted rhythm with the character of a slow, quasi-funereal, march. Three times these themes are heard, becoming more varied in texture and venturing tonally further afield, the movement's central climax coinciding with the second appearance of the march. The varied hymn and march characters betoken no such emotional swing between hope and despair as we might read into op. 8's slow movement: both ideas proceed at exactly the same calmly inexorable pace, creating a movement whose surface beauty seems to repress a deeper sense of underlying melancholy. This latter streak becomes overt in the coda, where the two principal ideas merge and are liquidated with a typically Brahmsian 'dying fall' into D minor, the major key only being regained with the piano's final chord.

The Finale is in some ways the most original movement. An energetic Presto in sonata form, it shows much of the contrapuntal mastery towards which Brahms was striving throughout this troubled period, but manifests it in unorthodox ways. The vigorous opening theme (Ex. 15), with its descending chromatic sequences, harks back (as did an element in the first movement of op. 8) to Bach, and would seem an inevitable subject for a fugue. But though Brahms makes much use of it in augmentation, in stretto and in imitation, he is careful (perhaps with op. 8 in mind) to avoid formal fugal procedures. Instead the movement displays a remarkable amount of writing in contrary motion and against insistent pedal-points (whose stress on the basic tonalities offsets the chromatic inflections); while Ex. 15's characteristic rhythm can be heard in many of the accompaniments to the other themes. There are several of these – including, in the second subject group, a soulful tune in Hungarian style – but Ex. 15 eventually sweeps all before it, and has the coda to itself. This inventive movement is a fitting culmination to a work which, even if its authenticity were to be universally recognized, would never occupy the first rank of Brahms's chamber music, but which chronicles an important stage of his development and is no mean achievement in its own right.

Ex. 15

Earliest orchestral works

Throughout the period 1854–8, as background to all his other endeavours, Brahms was engaged on one particularly Herculean compositional labour – a large-scale, tragic conception of symphonic dimensions. It had started life in March 1854 as a Sonata for two pianos, conceived very soon after Schumann's suicide attempt; before long it began to turn into a four-movement symphony, doubtless intended to fulfil Schumann's hopes that Brahms would take over from him the mantle of leading German symphonist. This Symphony in D minor (a very large one, to judge by the little we know of it) was sketched in two-piano score during the succeeding year, but its Finale was never finished. Virtuoso piano writing kept intruding into the fabric of the music; and though Brahms did prepare an orchestral version of the first movement with help from Grimm and Joachim, he felt too inexperienced, and was dissatisfied with the result.

Even at this stage, the inchoate symphony was probably the most powerful, original, and personal orchestral achievement in German music since Beethoven's Ninth. That was clearly part of Brahms's problem: the very explosiveness of his material demanded treatment not only on the largest scale but in the most dramatic personal manner, and with an instrumental technique to match. Only in 1856, shortly before Schumann's death, did Brahms hit upon the solution of combining the resources of piano and orchestra to create a piano concerto of symphonic stature, the like of which had not been seen since Beethoven's time, of quite unprecedented emotional intensity. It forms the creative climax of the immensely rich artistic harvest of the 1850s.

From the unfinished symphony Brahms kept only the first movement, discarding the incomplete Finale, the slow movement, and the slow Scherzo in sarabande tempo (whose main theme, years later, found its destined role as the basis of the funeral march in the *Deutsches Requiem*). The first movement was reworked and re-scored (with much advice from Joachim), and united to a new slow movement and Finale. The Concerto was essentially complete by March 1858, when Brahms first played it in a private rehearsal under Joachim; but he continued tinkering with it right up to the first public performance in January 1859, and was hardly satisfied even then. Yet despite its teething troubles the work had emerged with a grandeur and scope that no piano concerto had attained since Beethoven's 'Emperor'; and though the initial public response was at best puzzled and cautious, within Brahms's lifetime the Concerto had become recognized at its true worth.

The huge first movement is by far the most extended single musical

Brahms

structure Brahms had attempted by 1854, and one of the largest he was
ever to write. It is nearly the longest, and probably the most dramatic,
symphonic movement since Beethoven.[12] It is also the direct and climactic successor to the *Sturm und Drang* moods of the early piano
sonatas, as is immediately apparent from its extraordinary opening
(Ex. 16). According to Joachim, this theme reflected Brahms's state of
mind on hearing that Schumann had thrown himself into the Rhine:
and it certainly begins the Concerto with a palpable sense of catastrophe.

Ex. 16

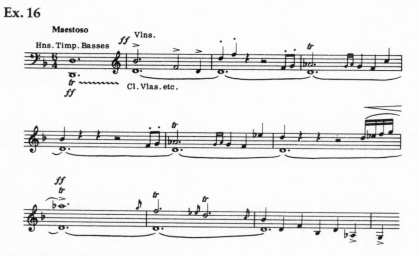

The air is chill with tonal instability. The key-signature says D minor,
but the theme starts by outlining B flat major; D is asserted by the
leaden, rumbling bass pedal, while the theme immediately develops
a rebellious chromaticism, a prominent, shivering A flat trill which
repeatedly grinds against the D to form a tritone dissonance. The theme
itself has something of the Bachian chromatic character Brahms had
favoured in the op. 8 Trio, and though used here for the highest Romantic expression it immediately displays its contrapuntal possibilities,
going into close canon while the pedal shifts to C sharp. These long
pedals, keeping the bass movement slow, already suggest the immense
scale of the movement that has begun.

The orchestral exposition is unusual enough in structure, with two
separate statements of Ex. 16, enclosing smooth, sad *cantabile* music

[12] The colossal first movement of Alkan's Concerto for Piano (without orchestra) from
his op. 39 Etudes is even longer – and, though published in 1857, may well have been
conceived around the same time that Brahms began work on his.

that looks forward to the second subject yet remains essentially preludial in character. It ends with an impassioned theme characterized by repeated quavers, combined with a would-be heroic figure of leaping fifths and fourths that gives way, with infinite pathos, to the first entry of the soloist, who is discovered quietly and meditatively developing the repeated-quaver idea in a manner that Tovey thought 'worthy of Bach's ariosos in the *Matthew Passion*'.

In a movement whose prodigal richness of themes is another indication of its enormous scale, it is noticeable that, in contrast to the fevered intensity of the orchestra, the piano at first propounds only the more emotionally soothing ones: as at its first entry, and then – after a comprehensive review of the other material in company with the orchestra – in its unaccompanied presentation of the second subject proper (Ex. 17a). The warmth and serenity of this majestic, flowing tune make it the principal counterbalance to the tragic and pathetic character of the other themes. Only with the onset of the development does the soloist have a chance for display, plunging us back to D minor with a fusillade of double octaves. Even so, the piano is never treated in this movement as a vehicle for exhibitions of bravura – and though it has significant solo passages, there is no formal cadenza at all.

Ex. 17

(a)

The development is stormy and comparatively brief, though it reveals important new aspects of the themes. With a fine sense of irony, Brahms steers it into D major for an unexpectedly sunny episode in a quick waltz-time – only to snatch away this glimpse of illusory happiness in an unremittingly tragic build-up to the recapitulation, which is prepared by a long, sinister dominant pedal and a choleric chordal outburst, ending with orchestra and piano crashing together onto a unison D. Drums and basses now hold the D pedal, as in Ex. 16, but in a dramatic stroke the piano blazons forth the theme from a chord of E major (the dominant of A) above it. As this gestures presages, the recapitulation of the whole group of first subject themes is practically a further development, for new harmonic relationships are constantly being explored, until the soloist, unaccompanied once more, presents an almost literal and extremely orthodox restatement of the second subject (Ex. 17a) in the tonic major.

This very orthodoxy excited the exasperation of the late Glenn Gould, for whom it represented the ultimate surrender of Brahms's 'incredible imagination' to an 'academic situation . . . the exigencies of formal symphonic behavior'. It is certainly possible (though given what happens at the analogous point in the op. 8 Trio, by no means certain) that this literal restatement was an unmalleable aspect of the movement as the young Brahms conceived it in 1854. But he could have had good reasons for retaining it – as the main source of stability (emotional as well as motivic) in an otherwise extremely turbulent movement. And his reasons perhaps extended further than that – to the new Finale that he came to compose in 1856–8, where Ex. 17a seems to have some significant repercussions. At any rate it is here able to impose its calm on the remainder of the recapitulation, until the piano intrudes a memory of the development to begin the coda, which concerns itself stormily with Ex. 16 and its subsidiaries and concludes the movement in as grim a mood as it began.

The following Adagio in D major is certainly a peaceful contrast, but there is something almost numbed about its lyricism, as if the experience of the first movement had left it in shock. When sketching the serene first theme, Brahms wrote above it the text 'Benedictus qui venit in nomine Domini', which fits the tune exactly. Indeed the music has much in common with the sacred choral works he was writing in the mid-1850s, such as the *Missa Canonica*. There is little doubt that the reference here is to Schumann – whom Brahms often addressed as 'Mynheer Domini' – perhaps with the idea of an instrumental requiem for his troubled spirit; though Brahms also spoke of it as a portrait of Clara. Whatever the truth, it stands as one of his profoundest evocations of a withdrawn, almost mystical spirit. Despite two more assertive ideas in its central section, nothing really disturbs the movement's quietude, its expression of intimacy on a grand scale. It develops into a grave dialogue between piano and orchestra, with touches of filigree fantasy in the piano writing of the central section, which issues at last in a brief and tenderly undemonstrative cadenza.

The muscular, grimly energetic main theme of the Rondo (Ex. 17b) returns us to D minor and the realities of the physical world. A light-hearted Finale would be emotionally false: there is no attempt to escape the profundities of the preceding movements – rather, there is a sense that they can only be given meaning by a continuing commitment to vigorous and creative activity. This strongly rhythmic and lithely contrapuntal music is serious in its import but engenders its own exhilaration, and the broader, more lyrical tunes of its episodes are more optimistic in character.

Ex. 17

It has been little remarked that all the main subjects of this remarkable Rondo share a basic shape: indeed, that the themes of its principal episodes – the passionate Ex. 17c, in F major, and the more suavely lyrical Ex. 17d, in B flat – are in the nature of free variations on the rondo theme Ex. 17b. This shortly becomes clearer as Brahms turns the music's energy to precise, constructive use in a sinewy but light-fingered fugue on Ex. 17e, which points up the similarities between Ex. 17b and d. Now this same basic shape is also the kernel of the first movement's second subject, Ex. 17a, where it seemed to stand for stability and affirmation. Perhaps the reason for that theme's 'academically' verbatim recapitulation was to fix its shape more strongly in the listener's mind, so that the Finale might at length be sensed as the true fulfilment of a promise made in Ex. 17a.

At any rate the movement soon expands into a vast and calmly eventful coda, like a sunset after a storm. It contains not one but two short cadenzas – both giving an impression of release into improvisatory freedom – and a moment of pure country landscape, with bagpiping oboes and drone fifths in the cellos, before Brahms brings this astonishing Concerto to an end in a final blaze of fierce triumph.

From Symphony to Concerto, the work's instrumentation had been so thoroughly worked over, so often revised in consultation with more experienced friends, that it had amounted to a self-education in the art of orchestral scoring. As such it is a triumphant, and revealing, success. Many great masters before Brahms had used heavier orchestras for works of far less weight; but instinctively (with Joachim showing the way) he went for economy of means. He had a strongly personal sense of orchestral timbre, favouring dark, rich, low-lying sonorities – but it was never to be 'applied from outside'. He sought rather to bring the essential colour out of the musical ideas themselves. The final form of the Concerto is an astonishing demonstration of the intimate relation of colour to structure. This fiery, passionate, huge-limbed music is scored for a severely 'Classical' orchestra of double woodwind, four horns, two trumpets, timpani and strings, yet there is nothing small (or 'Classical') about the sound Brahms obtains from it. How many listeners, hearing the tremendous first movement for the first time, even notice that there are no trombones or tuba? In later life Brahms would use those instruments (and extras such as the contrabassoon) whenever he felt the need of them: but only then, and always with maximum economy. A proper study of his orchestral technique still waits to be written, and it ought to examine the many places (the close of the first movement of the Fourth Symphony is another celebrated instance) where Brahms does *not* use heavy brass yet achieves the effect of an overwhelming orchestral tutti.

Very different examples of the union of colour and form are afforded by his other orchestral works of this period, the two Serenades – the first of which had almost as difficult a gestation as the Piano Concerto. Though they have been overshadowed by Brahms's later orchestral masterpieces, they are important and deeply characteristic scores, exploring that paradise of natural harmony briefly glimpsed at the end of the Concerto with a wealth of unconstrainedly delightful music. They also display a quite different side of Brahms's involvement with the Classical tradition: the ancestors of these works include

Mozart's Divertimenti, Beethoven's Septet, the Schubert Octet, as well as the symphonies of Haydn and the early Beethoven symphonies.

The First, in D major, was in fact conceived as a Nonet for wind and strings in 1857–8 (and seemingly as a three-movement Octet before that), only to be recast for a small orchestra (apparently single wind and about fifteen strings) and then re-scored again in 1859 for a full orchestra (with trumpets and drums, but no trombones). Meanwhile (from 1858) Brahms was composing the Second Serenade, which emerged as a work for a small orchestra of double woodwind, two horns, and a string section without violins.

Charles Rosen has characterized Haydn's symphonies as 'heroic pastoral', a designation we could aptly appropriate for the Brahms Serenades. Otherwise the two had very distinct identities. The First (in D major, op. 11) is almost recklessly expansive, in six movements lasting nearly an hour, and contrasts rustic simplicity with practically symphonic scope, especially in its first three movements: indeed it was commonly referred to by Joachim and Grimm as the 'symphony-serenade'. The Second (in A major, op. 16) is smaller in dimensions, has only five movements, and is marked by a greater intimacy of expression – partly achieved by some of his subtlest and most poetic orchestration. As Tovey pointed out, the absence of violins makes it essentially a work for wind instruments with string accompaniment, and this is reflected in the whole character of the writing. But indeed the wind have the lion's share of the glory in both Serenades: the First begins, over bagpipe-drone fifths in the bass, with a bucolic horn theme worthy of Haydn (Ex. 18).

Ex. 18

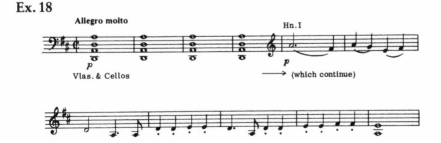

The D major Serenade has come in for some criticism, right up to the present day, for the extent and complexity of its working-out, in apparent conflict with the downright plainness of such material as Ex. 18; it is sometimes deemed an unsuccessful experiment. Certainly it had no clear successors, in his own output or that of others; but on its own terms the work succeeds admirably. Brahms knew he was attempting something new, not merely an imitation of Classical style, and rather than viewing thematic and contrapuntal elaboration as an academic conceit he delighted in it for its own sake. What his contemporaries found tedious and laboured, modern audiences are finally discovering to be rich and leisurely, delivered at a length as 'heavenly' as that for which Schubert is customarily praised.

The extensive scale of Brahms's thought is well illustrated by the flowing and sinuous nature of the second subject, rising from a tiny two-note figure in a long arching line that weaves his typical triplet rhythms into its contours; by the elated 'hunting' cadence theme (which develops the triplet rhythm); and by the direction that the entire exposition should be repeated. The development is cheerfully eventful, modulating more widely than a Classical composer would attempt in a work of this nature: and the coda, in which Ex. 18 finally stutters to a halt in dialogue between solo flute and pizzicato strings, is perhaps the prime example of the whimsical wit so dangerously evident throughout this beautiful score.

There follows an unusually subdued Scherzo in D minor: its rather spectral first theme, often treated in canon, brings an unwontedly shadowy mood to the proceedings (and in its outline curiously anticipates by twenty years the grim Scherzo of Piano Concerto no. 2). Its recurrences frame a sturdy Trio in B flat, whose swinging tune and homogeneous scoring are the work's only hints of Schumann (specifically, perhaps, a reminiscence of the 'Rhenish' Symphony). The crepuscular aspects of the Scherzo, and the key of the Trio, prepare in some measure for the ensuing slow movement: a long, leisurely – and in some performances somnolent – Adagio non troppo in B flat. Cast in a full sonata form with an elaborately varied recapitulation, its resemblances to the 'Scene by the Brook' movement of Beethoven's 'Pastoral' Symphony (especially in the second of Brahms's three chief themes) have often been noted; the horn solo of the third theme is evocative of forest depths. The mood is peaceful, entranced; perhaps nowhere else in his music has Brahms presented himself so frankly as a passive devotee of landscape.

After this slow, dreamy movement, two faster and extremely concise ones provide welcome relief. The fourth movement alternates a pair of delicate little Minuets (in G and G minor), whose scoring for wind instruments and a few strings probably corresponds closely to the chamber instrumentation of the Serenade's original form. Next comes a short second Scherzo (in D), cheerfully extrovert and dynamic this time, glorifying the horn, and clearly modelled on the Scherzo of Beethoven's Second Symphony; its Trio is even faster, with racing quaver motion on the strings. The movement makes a splendid introduction to the Finale: a bucolic Rondo with a vigorously striding main theme in march style that diverts its course into several lyrical byways for the sake of contrasting episodes and piquant detail. As the Finale proceeds Brahms introduces subtle reminders of the first movement – nowhere more strikingly as when, with a bird-like semiquaver roulade on the solo flute, the solo horn gives out one of the episode themes against a drone bass in the low strings. (The effect is the more delightful for the fact that the theme in question, first introduced by violins earlier in the movement, has always sounded like a natural 'horn tune' and has now found its proper medium.) The pastoral landscape has never been forgotten, and the lyrical sunset on the dominant that precedes the ebullient coda is a trademark of Brahms alone. This First Serenade, whose structures of Haydnesque wit and formal clarity are propelled by a Beethovenian sense of motion, yet imbued with Brahms's own very personal breadth and flexibility of melodic thinking, is in its way as remarkable an orchestral début as was the First Piano Concerto.

The calm, upwardly-unfolding phrases which begin Serenade no. 2 indicate at once a less symphonic, more intimate approach. This rich wind-instrument sound, already explored in Serenade no. 1, is even more subtly deployed here. Brahms scored this work for just double woodwind (plus a piccolo which plays only in the Finale), two horns, violas, cellos, and basses: an ensemble whose constitution has a profound effect on the presentation of the music. With no violins to give out or double primary thematic statements, almost all the principal melodies are assigned to the wind, and the violas are used with unusual freedom.[13] Above all, the score is an education in itself for the subtle and expressive blending and mixing of tone colour. Brahms must greatly have enjoyed solving the problems of texture and sonority imposed by his chosen ensemble; and his solutions are the perfect refutation of the old canard that he was not a good orchestrator. On the contrary, he applied himself as tenaciously to mastering orchestration as he did to

---

[13] Brahms revised the work in 1860 very shortly after its first performance (in which form it was his first composition to be published by Simrock), but we do not know how far the revision extended: certainly a later revision of 1875 was chiefly concerned with dynamics. Several writers have speculated that Brahms dispensed with violins following the example of Méhul in his Ossianic opera *Uthal* (1806). Brahms certainly admired this work; it is not certain that he knew it in the late 1850s, but in view of the op. 18 choruses (see below), it seems quite likely.

all other aspects of his art, and the Serenades, even more than the Piano Concerto, were his proving ground in the discipline.

The interest of the A major Serenade is by no means simply colouristic, however. Its first movement, eschewing the broad, simple outlines of that of the D major, is a much closer-knit structure, growing organically from the initial statement of the first subject (whose gentle triplet-rhythm extension seems metaphorically to put out roots and branches), with little of the earlier work's sharp contrasts. In this movement there is no repeat of the exposition: instead Brahms feigns one by opening the development with a restatement of the first subject in the tonic – and when he arrives at the recapitulation, the reappearance of that subject is insinuated into the texture as deftly and unassertively as in the A major Piano Trio. After this compressed and refined opening movement comes a brief, uninhibited Scherzo in the manner of a fast country dance (the wind scoring here enhancing the effect of a village band). The other dance movement in the work is the fourth, marked 'Quasi Menuetto' – a delicate, rather pensive invention in a halting rhythm which sounds rather like a foreshadowing of some of Elgar's little genre pieces in dance rhythm. These two movements enclose the Serenade's chief glory: its central Adagio non troppo is among the most poetic things Brahms was ever to write. Here most of all we find infinite resource in tonal blending, as the strings in octaves rise and fall with a ground bass in brooding 12/8 rhythm, and the woodwind muse upon a plaintive, haunting theme (Ex. 19).

Ex. 19

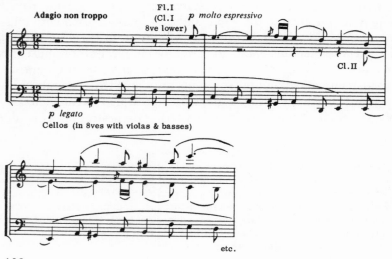

The movement is in an elaborately worked-out ternary form, full of contrapuntal ingenuity, with a sombrely dramatic central episode and the main section led back to by means of a fugal invention upon the bass of Ex. 19; but what lingers in the memory is its shadowed, introspective lyricism, suffused with a hint of tragedy. There is no other movement quite like it. This mood perhaps sufficiently explains the subdued atmosphere of the following Quasi Menuetto; and it is only with the Finale that Brahms completely abandons his brown study. This is another good-humoured Rondo with a march-like main theme, terser in its rhythmic quips than that of Serenade no. 1, but no less outgoing; and the bright, clear timbre of the piccolo liberally embellishes the proceedings to the end.

Songs and duets

As the first three sets of *Gesänge* had demonstrated, song was a genre in which Brahms had more than found his feet at an early age; but the songs he composed in the later 1850s almost consistently surpass that first achievement. They do so with an increased range of expression, a broadened gamut of song forms, and an enhanced psychological depth; although paradoxically he achieves this greater richness and variety through a much firmer self-discipline, aligning his inspiration more closely with the folksong models which had contributed an element of such striking simplicity to the op. 7 group. The 'folk' expression of the next body of songs is sometimes much more complex, and pervades the music in many different ways – in text, melody, expressive stance or a combination of all three. To a large extent, it is clear, folksong *was* for Brahms the classic model to follow in song-writing. His songs of this period centre upon – but are not confined to – two sets encompassing 'Songs, Ballads, and Poems': the eight *Lieder und Romanzen*, op. 14, and the five *Gedichte*, op. 19, both of which were composed in 1858–9 (and which are traditionally associated with his love for Agathe von Siebold, whose fated impermanence we may, if we wish, read into the choice of texts). It is important to remember that these 'art songs' were surrounded by the preparation of two much larger collections of folksong arrangements for voice and piano: the fourteen *Volks-Kinderlieder* written for the Schumann children, and the twenty-eight *Deutsche Volkslieder*, both completed in 1858.

Though the melodies of op. 14 are all Brahms's own, their texts are all 'folk': six German folk poems, a Scottish Border ballad, and a thirteenth-century 'sonnet' by the troubadour Thibault IV, Count of Champagne, whose very antiquity would elevate it to folk status in

Brahms's eyes. However, the range of treatment is now very wide. It can be heard at its simplest in no. 6, the exquisite strophic lovesong *Gang zur Liebsten* and in the sorrowful epilogue of the group, *Sehnsucht*, which recalls *Die Traurende* from op. 7 with fuller, bittersweet harmony. A progressively more sophisticated approach informs no. 2, *Vom verwundeten Knaben*, a ballad whose sense of comprehensive desolation is enhanced by the pathos of its oft-repeated, quasi-modal cadence; no. 7, *Ständchen* – a strophic serenade with a long, finely poised melody and wandering harmonies whose range is disguised by the guitar-like casualness of the piano's repeated chords; and the quasi-dramatic dialogue form of no. 1, *Vor dem Fenster*, with its tender consummation as the lovers bid each other farewell.

The theme of parting, which lies lightly but inescapably over op. 14, receives a different emphasis in no. 5, *Trennung* ('Separation'). Rousing a pair of sleeping lovers with its cock-crow fourths, galloping rhythm and roguish tune, this seems at first blush thoroughly if splendidly conventional: we may need several hearings to note how the music does not quite disregard the darker tones of the last two verses. Can Brahms really mean us to take seriously his throw-away insertion of a little lachrymose chromatic scale in verse 4 where 'parting is hard as death', or the (quite unillustrated) reference to the girl's 'great sorrow'? In all probability the music says: *she* feels these things, the boy doesn't.

A different kind of folk impulse comes to the fore in op. 14 no. 3, *Murrays Ermordung*, a setting of Herder's version of the Border ballad known to every Scot as *The Bonny Earl o' Moray*, and thus a kind of counterpart to the piano Ballades, op. 10: but it is a peculiarly uningratiating song, and in its episodic construction one feels Brahms is still exorcising the rhetorical, 'operatic' manners of some of the first *Gesänge*. The contrast with his slightly earlier setting of the German ballad *Das Lied vom Herrn von Falkenstein* (1857 – but not published until 1868, as op. 43 no. 4) is all in favour of the latter, whose robust tune carries a nominally strophic form but is dramatically and effectively varied by the requirements of dialogue and the emotional situation. Another song which had to wait ten years for publication is a treatment of an Old German poem. *Ich schell' mein Horn* (eventually op. 43 no. 3), so determinedly archaic that on the page it resembles something from three centuries earlier. The chorale construction, long note-values, and homophonic accompaniment clinging to a single stave as if in lute tablature, give it the appearance of an antiquarian conceit – dispelled immediately in performance by its unforced expression of a noble melancholy.

A different kind of archaism touches the beautiful *Ein Sonett* (the troubadour setting in op. 14), with the hint of a stately, courtly dance underlying and objectifying the passionate sadness of its overt Romanticism. The text is not, strictly speaking, a sonnet; but about this time Brahms turned to a true sonnet by Goethe, set already by both Schubert and Mendelssohn. His *Die Liebende schreibt* (which also only appeared in 1868, as op. 47 no. 5) more than equals the effect of theirs in its sensitive demarcation of form, and gently supplicative declamation.

The op. 19 *Gedichte* extend his fondness for folk models in other directions: towards graphic onomatopoeia in the setting of Uhland's *Der Schmeid*, with its swinging melody, battering fifths in the bass, and the ringing hammer-strokes of the piano postlude; and into a greater structural range with the set's two other Uhland settings, *Scheiden und Meiden* and *In der Ferne*, which are actually complementary halves of the same poem. Brahms treats them so: the first song seems initially a closed, perfectly self-sufficient little structure of two strophes – and then *In der Ferne* actually begins as a third strophe, *L'istesso tempo*, with selfsame key and melody, only to flower literally 'far away' into a through-composed song with its own internal balance, transforming though not forgetting the lyric simplicity of *Scheiden und Meiden* ('Parting and Separation').

There is only one song of this period which entirely escapes the influence of folksong, popular ballad, or archaic stylization – yet that is perhaps the supreme masterpiece among all his Lieder of the 1850s. *An eine Äolsharfe*, the final song in op. 19, sets a famous poem by Eduard Mörike (occasioned by the death of the poet's brother, yet a celebration of the mystical twinning of nature and music). Brahms uses a wonderfully flexible and evocative combination of recitative and impassioned, self-questioning arioso, lapped around with the liquid arpeggios, faint strummed chords, and mysterious harmonies which are Romantic music's chief metaphor for the wind-stirred strings of the Aeolian harp – never used with greater fitness or poetic logic than here. It is also his most ambitious song to date, freely ranging with the movement of the poet's thought in spontaneous association of motif, key and texture – and thus it anticipates his more exploratory songs of the 1860s.

In the totality of Brahms's output the area that is currently most unfamiliar is that of the duets and quartets for solo voices and piano. In his own time this was an established, 'mainstream' musical form, and he contributed to it as naturally and willingly as had Schubert, Mendelssohn and Schumann, or the multitudinous glee composers of Great Britain. But with the decline of domestic music-making in the first half of the twentieth century (allied to the rise of interest in the unaccompanied madrigal among professional groups) the entire genre went decisively out of fashion, and has yet to experience an effective revival. As a result, with the partial exception of the series of *Liebeslieder* Waltzes, some of Brahms's most characteristic inspirations languish unperformed.

The idea of duets and quartets as a separate, 'dated' kind of music is in any case an absurdity of categorization. Brahms treated such pieces as extensions and complements of his Lied style, merely making use of the special possibilities for dialogue and/or choric effects which they afforded. The interdependence of Lied and multi-voice song in his output was to be demonstrated towards the end of his life by the op. 103 *Zigeunerlieder*: a set of vocal quartets (discussed on p. 353) most of which he recast in an alternative form as solo songs. His models, at least in the earliest duets, veer towards Mendelssohn rather than folksong – but folk texts remained a primary stimulus, and in his settings Brahms tended to treat them as strophically as if they were fitted to folk-melodies.

This is certainly the case with the three Duets for soprano and contralto, op. 20, two of which were written at Göttingen in 1858 with the third following in 1860. All three set texts collected by Herder in *Stimmen der Völker*, and the first two (*Weg der Liebe* I and II) use different parts (separately culled from two eighteenth-century collections) of a Northern English folk poem, *Love will find out the Way*. They are highly contrasted, the first a fast, lightly bouncing song, and the second a much more serene and harmonically resonant slow treatment. An Italian poem provides the text of the concluding number, *Die Meere*, which Brahms sets as a charmingly sinuous barcarolle. Throughout this op. 20 set the voices move in consort, typically paired in thirds or sixths. An even earlier duet uses much the same technique but with more resource. This is *Klosterfräulein*, a song of restlessly immured nuns to a poem by Justinus Kerner, which we know Brahms wrote in Hamburg as early as 1852 though he waited over twenty years to publish it as part of his op. 61. Here the voices are allowed their own grave cadence-figure, moving up to a resonant tenth apart.

By contrast Brahms's next duets, the four for contralto and baritone (1860–62), published in 1864 as op. 28 and dedicated to Amalie Joachim, are cast almost throughout in dramatic dialogue form. They are also considerably more personal in idiom. Brahms reverts to poets he had already set in solo song – Eichendorff, Hoffmann von Fallersleben, Goethe, as well as anonymous Old German texts – and the neo-medieval imagery and situations strongly relate to the concerns of the *Magelone–Lieder*, which were begun in this period.

Three of the pieces inevitably present pairs of lovers, star-crossed or otherwise: most conventionally in the hunting/dancing strains of *Der Jäger und sein Liebchen,* not at all conventionally in the grave, nocturnal G minor strophes of *Die Nonne und der Ritter,* amplified by expressive piano interludes and the piercing entwining of the voices as the parted lovers for a moment draw near without knowing of each other's presence. It is as haunting a meditation on the theme of fate-enforced separation as Brahms achieved in any of his solo songs. *Vor den Tür,* the facetious number in which the lover's importunings are comprehensively rebuffed by the object of his desire, is a deliciously irreverent adaptation of his own scherzo style (compare the Scherzo of the op. 8 Trio). The odd number out is Goethe's *Es rauschet das Wasser,* treated in more Schubertian manner as a directly appealing lyric.

Other choral works

Brahms's close involvement during the last years of the 1850s with two choirs, in Hamburg and Detmold, ensured that a steady stream of small choral compositions issued from his pen, in a relatively wide variety of idioms, and soon showing distinct advances upon the canonic pieces of the mid-decade. For example, the gentle *Ave Maria* in F major, op. 12, for female voices and organ, written in Göttingen in September 1858 (there is also an orchestral version, which Brahms first conducted in Hamburg the following year) has little in common with his Mass movements save the Latin language and a characteristic motivic concentration. This is Brahms's choral writing at its simplest, sopranos and contraltos sweetly entwined in thirds around a mellifluous tune in lulling berceuse-rhythm. The organ accompaniment is entirely confined to a supporting role (and in his orchestration Brahms went no further than to add some discreet woodwind detail); the harmony, seemingly unremarkable, conceals some almost Wagnerian chromaticisms beneath its placid surface; but the overall effect is charming, and emotionally uncomplicated.

The same could hardly be said of the *Begräbnisgesang* (literally 'Burial Song'), op. 13, for mixed chorus, twelve wind instruments and timpani, which followed a month later in October 1858. Little larger in dimension than the *Ave Maria,* this is a compressed, tragic masterpiece with few parallels in the choral repertoire. On one level, the work is another essay in archaism: it sets an Old German text to a melody which – though Brahms's own – has the character of an early chorale tune, even to the obdurate 'mis-accentuation' of the words; and just as the middle section seems indebted to Bach's then recently published

Cantata no. 4, *Christ lag in Todesbanden,* so the resonant and spacious deployment of the wind band[14] almost certainly reflects his study of Giovanni Gabrieli.

Yet the result is a monumental, thoroughly Brahmsian creation which, cast in the manner of a slow march in C minor, powerfully anticipates the second movement of the *Deutsches Requiem.* (Or rather, it parallels it – that movement already existed to some extent in the abortive D minor Symphony.)

The quasi-biblical text clearly moved Brahms profoundly. The vision of the judgement of the dead man, who 'will rise up from the earth when God's trumpet sounds' has a terrible splendour (Ex. 20 – from the work's very first bar, the music has been moving towards this climactic cadence, whose intensity is worthy of the First Piano Concerto). The assuaging glow of the major-key central section, with its calmly expanding modulations at 'God will transfigure him and give him joy'; and the fatalistic simplicity of the quiet coda (where the mourners go their separate ways, knowing that 'Death comes to us likewise') defines a deeply elegiac conception of perfect proportions and almost symphonic scope. Perhaps, like several contemporary scores, the *Begräbnisgesang* enacts a symbolic ritual of expiation, and the body it

Ex. 20

[14]Brahms had originally intended to use low strings as well, but discarded them so that the piece might be performed in the open air.

(... And from Earth will rise again, when God's trumpets sound.
His soul lives for ever in God...)

inters (of one who has 'suffered anguish here') is that of Robert Schumann. But its artistic significance is universal; the work deserves to be much better known.

One might have expected Brahms's contemporary setting of Psalm 13 ('How long wilt thou forget me, O Lord?') to have drawn similarly profound and searching conclusions from his chosen text: in our own century Alexander Zemlinsky did just that in a sombre, granitic setting of the same psalm for mixed chorus and orchestra, one of the final masterpieces of the post-Brahmsian tradition. But Brahms's own treatment, for female voices with organ or harp (in Vienna he also provided an optional version with string orchestra support, very seldom performed) is altogether a slighter affair. Written presumably to sound bright and effective without causing his singers too many difficulties (though the first soprano part has a taxing tessitura), it alternates between comparatively homophonic textures and passages of imitation, concentrates on the more optimistic elements in the psalm and has a busy, festive organ part. The effect is not far removed from some of Mendelssohn's psalm settings.

More distinctive, indeed idiosyncratic, are the *Marienlieder*, op. 22, a cycle of seven songs (virtually madrigals) dating from 1859–60, which Brahms described to Simrock as 'somewhat in the manner of old German church chorales and folksong' but which integrate their archaic traits into a personal evocation of the objects of simple religious faith. Settings of some of the many folksong texts devoted to the cult of the Virgin, Brahms first conceived them for four-part women's chorus. So low were the contralto parts that the Frauenchor was forced to introduce some tenors to sing them at their first performance; so they were eventually published as arrangements for mixed voices, though at least one of the female-voice originals survives. Brahms also made independent arrangements of some of the folk-melodies associated with his chosen texts, and though he did not quote these in the *Marienlieder*, their influence can sometimes be traced on the new melodies he provided. The op. 22 settings are largely syllabic, not without a certain hymn-like quality that is largely transcended by the sheer radiance of mood. Generally strophic in construction, they still find space for appropriately naïve word-painting (the church bells of no. 2, *Marias Kirchgang*, the hunting horns of no. 4, *Der Jäger*), and sometimes save up a surprise for the final verse – the hushed canon as the angels sink to their knees at the close of *Der Englische Gruss* (no. 1), or the sternly aphoristic ending to *Marias Wallfahrt* (no. 3), for instance. The curious mis-accentuation of *Magdalena* (no. 6) recalls that feature of the *Begräbnisgesang* and several of the choruses, especially *Marias Kirchgang* with its Dorian tune, display modal features; by contrast no. 5, *Ruf zur Maria*, is the least archaizing in its approach, its sensuous chromatic harmony thoroughly of the mid-nineteenth century.

A similar mixing of styles affects, to varying degrees, many of the other vocal works which Brahms poured forth in such abundance in

1859–60. The twelve *Lieder und Romanzen* for female chorus and piano (published only in 1866, as op. 44) are a case in point. These are small-scale pieces, almost choric miniatures, usually in strophic form and to be distinguished from the contemporary solo Lieder by the complete subservience of the piano part, which has no more than a discreet accompanimental role. They bear some resemblance to Mendelssohn's works in this genre, but the choice of texts is characteristically Brahmsian: by a variety of authors, these tend to imitate the themes and vocabulary of folksong, and most of Brahms's settings accordingly imitate the manners of his folksong arrangements, though the themes are all his own. Several of these charming songs, nonetheless, make use of unobtrusive devices of strict imitation after the manner of early vocal composers – sometimes in the service of word-painting, as in the series of large vocal leaps which convey the motion of the windmill sails in no. 5, a song about a miller's daughter. Elsewhere illustration is achieved by lush Romantic harmony (the moonlit woods in no. 2, *Der Bräutigam*); and the group ends with the very curious no. 12, a poem by Uhland about the contrary moods of a March night – set with archaic strictness as a double canon at the sixth, but whose lines breathe an *echt*-Romantic character of sighing, windswept chromatic sequences.

Of greater moment and textural elaboration are the three partsongs for six-part choir Brahms was to publish in 1869 as op. 42: the first, *Abendständchen*, was actually completed in October 1859 at Detmold, and the others, *Vineta* and *Darthulas Grabgesang*, date from the following year. *Vineta*, which sets a poem by Wilhelm Müller using the legend of a city sunk beneath the sea as a symbol of extinguished love lying deep within the heart, is a gorgeous example of a Romantic *Chorlied*, its warm harmony and strophic verse-form opening out the musical space to provide telling metaphors for the undersea bells and sinking to the ocean's floor. All three partsongs explore such poetic images of Romantic literature. But the flanking pieces bear a clearer imprint of Brahms's early-music interests, and have attracted the attentions and sympathies of twentieth-century commentators more.

Indeed the very employment of six-part chorus – which Brahms often splits into a virtual double chorus of three male and three female voices – had probably sent him back to the study of Renaissance models. The harmonic austerity and antiphonal choral exchanges of *Abendständchen* recall some of the Gabrieli pieces he studied, though their evocation of ancient, far-off manners of word-setting accords perfectly with the Romantic nature-mysticism of the text, proving once again that a sense of the past was an essential component to the moods of the Romantic present. *Darthulas Grabgesang* sets a passage translated by Herder from James Macpherson's *Ossian* (1762), that vital source-text of Romanticism which had retained respect (and therefore the power to inspire other artists) far longer on the Continent than in Britain. In this dirge for a dead Celtic prince, Brahms again creates a female/male vocal antiphony, his use of bare unison phrases at the opening underlining the archaic effect. The piece is in fact remarkably varied in texture: its austere opening and closing music in dialogue frames a more conventional, rather Mendelssohnian central section, with 'modern' chromatic harmony, where the choral groupings finally merge into a unified texture.

Closely contemporary with *Darthulas Grabgesang* Brahms made an even finer setting from Macpherson's 'ancient epic' to conclude another set of partsongs whose idiom is far more consistent and very much 'of its time'. The *Vier Gesänge*, op. 17, for women's chorus, two horns, and harp definitively rebut the view of Brahms as a 'Classicist' in reaction against the prevailing aesthetic climate. Composed in early 1860 for the Hamburger Frauenchor, everything about these entrancing, seldom performed choric songs bespeaks their Romantic orientation. Brahms chooses two instruments beloved of all Romantic composers – the horn with its associations of forest mystery, and the harp, nearest in tone to the rippling music of the wind (already evoked in his great Mörike song *An eine Äolsharfe*) and water. He writes for both with perfect understanding of their most evocative effects – his paramount consideration seems for once to be sheer instrumental colour. And the texts are symbols of the Romantic sensibility in literature: another Ossianic lament, from *Fingal* (translated by an unknown German author);[15] Shakespeare (a song from *Twelfth Night*, translated by Schlegel); a lyric by Eichendorff, quintessential German poet of the Romantic age's mystical response to Nature; and, to begin, some lines by a minor contemporary, Ruperti, which nevertheless apostrophize the power of sound in unmistakably Romantic terms, equating the harp notes with falling tears.

The prelude to this, *Es tönt ein voller Harfenklang* (a *Naturthema* on solo horn enwrapped in liquid harp arpeggios), is as evocative of Romantic mystery as anything in Schumann,[16] and the sad, poised syllabic setting of the words above the still-resounding harp preserves

---

[15] It is not the translation by Edmund von Harold, which Schubert set in 1815 as the song *Das Mädchen von Inistore* (D281).

[16] In *The Music of Brahms* (London, 1985), p. 74, Michael Musgrave notes similarities with the horn call and piano figurations at the opening of Schumann's Introduction and Allegro (he means the op. 92 *Concertstück*, not op. 134); but Brahms, unlike Schumann, actually derives his harp figurations (by diminution) from his horn theme.

the rapt mood unbroken. There follows a simple, rather austere setting of Shakespeare's *Come away, Death*, the harp punctuating the texture with staccato chords, and then a scherzo-like treatment of Eichendorff's *Der Gärtner* with a continuously bubbling harp accompaniment that brings it close in character to Mendelssohn (who set the same text as a duet). These three songs are strophic, with appropriately atmospheric instrumental preludes and postludes. The concluding *Gesang aus Fingal*, however, is a twilit funeral march which evolves its own large ternary form over 160 bars. Rhythm, harmony, melody and colour here combine to produce a powerful mood of sustained pathos. The doleful opening theme and its accompaniment share a fateful, insistent dactylic rhythm which Brahms seems to have associated with the working-out of indifferent Destiny: similar examples colour the later Horn Trio (see Ex. 28, p. 176) and the much later *Gesang der Parzen*. Its ultimate model could well be the Allegretto of Beethoven's Seventh Symphony. The 'archaism' of the choral part is confined to its chant-like character; indeed the vocal writing in op. 17 is almost entirely homophonic, with very little of Brahms's typical contrapuntal elaboration. But as the lament grows impassioned he introduces expressive cross-rhythms between the voices and their accompaniment. A contrasting middle section, beginning *a cappella* (and, for the only time in op. 17, in four parts rather than three), uses sinister semitone oscillations in the lower registers of the horns for a graphically atmospheric depiction of the growling hounds and the restless ghost of the chieftain slain by the hand of the Gaelic hero Cuthullin; and the foreshortened recapitulation resounds with plangent windswept horn and harp sonorities in response to the poem's mountain and sea imagery. Had Brahms written nothing but these four choruses he would deserve to be remembered as one of the lyric masters of the Romantic period.

If the op. 17 partsongs represent the fullest choral expression of Brahms's innate Romanticism, his painstakingly acquired skill in the 'archaic' techniques of Renaissance polyphony was crowned by the achievement of three remarkable Motets to Lutheran religious texts for *a cappella* mixed chorus. Two of them (*Es ist das Heil* and *Schaffe in mir, Gott*) were completed in 1860, and published together four years afterwards as op. 29; while the third, *O Heiland, reiss die Himmel auf*, though probably composed not long after, was held back for many years and only appeared in 1878 as op. 74 no. 2.[17] In these impressive and

---

[17] Virginia Hancock (*Brahms's Choral Compositions and His Library of Early Music*, Ann Arbor, 1983, p. 16) gives force to the generally accepted date of 1863 (probably with subsequent polishing) by pointing out that Brahms's MS notation of the text gives a reference for the chorale tune to Meister's *Das katholische deutsche Kirchenlied*, a

moving works Brahms shows he has absorbed the polyphonic language into his compositional bloodstream to an extent unmatched by any other nineteenth-century composer (with the partial exception of Bruckner, whose teaching at St Florian gave him a direct link to polyphonic tradition).

All three motets set verses which, if they do not approach the carefully constructed text of the much later *Warum ist das Licht gegeben?* for theological subtlety and confessional doubt (see p. 256), at least concentrate on tenets of Christian belief which struck a responsive chord in Brahms: salvation through faith (*Es ist das Heil*), spiritual cleansing (*Schaffe in mir, Gott*), renewal of the natural world and removal of barriers between heaven and earth (*O Heiland*). The music of all three is based on Old German chorale tunes, in the tradition of J. S. Bach, some of whose cantatas and chorales Brahms studied very closely and performed in Detmold;[18] but their approaches to this material are very different – though united by consistently elaborate (not to say virtuosic) contrapuntal thinking. *Es ist das Heil*, for five-part chorus (SATBB) to words by the sixteenth-century religious poet Paul Speratus, opens with a full harmonization of its chorale, but this is merely the prelude to the motet proper, an extended, vigorous fugue in five voices which takes the various component phrases of the chorale tune from which to derive successive subjects, while restating the tune itself, long phrase by phrase, in bass I: a development of methods employed in the organ fugue on *O Traurigkeit*. The whole work is in E major, but throughout Brahms persistently flattens the leading-note to obtain a modal feeling.

Schaffe in mir, Gott, also officially for five voices (though the total number fluctuates), displays a much more varied treatment; Brahms divides it into three short contrasting movements, corresponding to the three verses from Psalm 51 which form its text. The first of these dates back as far as 1857 and, despite its sonorous harmonies, is polyphonically based as a canon by augmentation: the tune is at the bottom of the texture, in long note-values in bass II – and twice as fast in the soprano line; while the middle of the texture is filled out with freely derived parts. Although the harmony here is a warmly diatonic G major, the second movement is an anxious G minor fugue in four voices on a

collection only published in 1862. The rival dating to 1860, based on a letter in which Clara Schumann acknowledges receipt of a motet, must therefore be abandoned, and that motet becomes an unknown, 'lost' work. Nevertheless, *O Heiland* so usefully complements the op. 29 pair that it remains convenient to discuss it in this context.

[18] As regards *Schaffe in mir*, Virginia Hancock suggests Brahms may also have studied a setting of the same text by the seventeenth-century composer Andreas Hammerschmidt (ibid., p. 118).

flowing but uneasily chromatic subject. The third movement begins lyrically, dividing the choir into two three-part male and female choruses for a flowing dialogue between them on music which is smoothly (and unobtrusively) canonic within each chorus; Brahms then concludes with an exuberant five-voice fugal exposition on a subject derived from the motet's opening theme.

O Heiland, reiss die Himmel auf is for four-part chorus (SATB) throughout, to an anonymous rhymed German translation of a Latin hymn ('O Saviour, tear the heavens asunder, /Flow down to us from heaven, /Tear from heaven gates and doors, /Tear open every lock and bolt'). There are five stanzas in all, and Brahms sets them as a series of chorale variations: in verses 1–4 the chorale tune is always present in one voice as a cantus firmus while the others surround it with derived canons or freer imitation, while verse 5 varies the tune in all four voices, with a mirror-canon between soprano and bass, and concludes with a canonic Amen. Tonally this motet is more exploratory and eventful than the two op. 29 pieces, opening in a Dorian F minor, moving through A flat and C minor to an F minor conclusion from which the hint of modality has finally been purged. None of these motets could really be taken for the work of 'some old ecclesiastic of Palestrina's time' (see p. 143), but their employment of Renaissance techniques and harmony is remarkably pure and natural. In no sense can they be considered 'studies': they are beautifully achieved, and within their ordained limits eloquent, works of art. Brahms's personal voice may be heard in them at many points, and especially in *O Heiland*, whose individual verses are vividly and sensitively characterized. The fourth, *Hie lieden wir die grösste Not* ('We suffer here in direst need'), features impressively dark chromatic writing in groping canon by inversion, while the third's invocation to nature (*O Erd', schlag aus, schlag aus, o Erd', /Dass Berg und Tal grün alles werd', /O Erd', herfür die Blümlein bring,* – 'Break forth, O earth, /That hill and dale all blossom green. /O earth, bring forth this flower') causes Brahms's own highly characteristic triplet writing to break out, putting forth motivic shoots in what nowadays seems an admirably ecological passion.

Brahms

Ex. 21

122   etc.

5

Not quite a Viennese (1860–72)

As a man I suppose I am a little bit old-fashioned; in any case I am certainly so in this respect, that I am not a cosmopolitan, but am as attached to my native town as I might be to my mother.

Brahms to Clara Schumann, 1862

Shortly after the 'Manifesto' episode Brahms attended the Rhine Music Festival in Düsseldorf, taking three of the girls from the Frauenchor to sing vocal quartets with Clara Schumann. Proceeding afterwards to Bonn with Joachim for the baptism of Dietrich's first child, he encountered the young Fritz Simrock, junior partner in the Bonn–Berlin music publishing firm of N. Simrock. As a direct result of this meeting Simrock published Brahms's A major Serenade, the op. 17 partsongs, and the recently completed B flat major Sextet. By this time Brahms was in the fortunate position of being able to distribute his works between several publishers, with Breitkopf & Härtel and the Swiss firm of Rieter-Biedermann as his usual outlets; but Simrock was gradually to supplant them as his principal publisher. More, over the years Simrock became one of Brahms's closest friends, an adviser in business affairs, and trustee of the considerable wealth the composer was to accumulate.

For the remainder of 1860 and right through into 1862 Brahms continued to base himself in Hamburg – principally devoting himself to composition but also conducting the Frauenchor until its dissolution in the spring of 1861. He fulfilled a large number of concert engagements in the city and elsewhere in Germany, usually in company with Joachim or Stockhausen, and spent occasional periods with Joachim in Hanover. In November 1860 the two friends appeared together in a concert at the Leipzig Gewandhaus (the scene of his failure with the Piano Concerto), both as composers and executants – Brahms conducted his A major Serenade and Joachim, under his baton, was the soloist in his own recent Concerto in the Hungarian Manner, which Brahms greatly admired. Both compositions were tepidly received, but the critics were friendlier to Joachim than to Brahms. Clara Schumann, who was in the audience, arranged for Brahms and herself to play the Serenade in a piano-duet arrangement at the Leipzig Conservatoire, and wrote afterwards to Joachim:

My heart is so full on account of our dear Johannes ... I felt with you as deeply in your joy as I did with Johannes in his sorrow – maybe more than you yourselves did. My grief at Johannes's bad reception was somewhat lessened by the evening at the Conservatoire, when nearly all the musicians had to admit, after hearing the Serenade, that it was beautiful.

During that winter, and the next, Brahms spent some time with Theodor Kirchner at Winterthur in Switzerland, where his music met with warm appreciation. In Hamburg itself, because of tensions in his parents' household, he moved out in the summer of 1861 to the suburb of Hamm, where Frau Dr Rosing, the aunt of the Völckers girls from the Frauenchor, had offered him rooms in her house (next door to the Völckers) together with a balcony and the use of her garden. The creative activity of the last few years had already been impressive in its scope and dedication; in these new and highly congenial surroundings he applied himself even more vigorously to composition. Here he began work on the large cycle of *Magelone-Lieder* which was to occupy him over several years, and produced a series of ambitious instrumental works – the G minor and A major Piano Quartets, the piano-duet Variations on a Theme of Schumann, and the Variations and Fugue on a Theme of Handel for solo piano. His friend Dietrich, on a visit, was immediately presented with the manuscript of the latter. When Clara came to Hamburg for three concerts in November she saw all this music and started learning and discussing it forthwith. 'Interesting talk with Johannes on form', she noted in her diary for 11 November:

> How it is the older masters who are perfect in their use of form, while modern compositions are confined within the most rigid small forms. He, himself, emulates the older masters and especially admires Clementi's large, free employment of form.

During her stay she took part in several Brahms performances, including the premiere of the G minor Quartet. She also gave the second performance of the 'Handel' Variations in December (Brahms gave the first the preceding month), and appeared as soloist in Brahms's Concerto with the Hamburg Philharmonic, with Brahms conducting. Not even her reputation and musicianship, however, could add much zest to the Hamburgers' reception of it.

In the following spring Brahms performed at Oldenburg, where Dietrich was now the kapellmeister to the Grand Duke; the A major Serenade was played as far away as New York; Clara proselytized for him in Paris; and the String Sextet had several well-received performances in various parts of Germany. Despite the débâcle of the

Manifesto, Brahms's reputation was steadily growing; indeed the much criticized *Neue Zeitschrift für Musik* now began to publish a laudatory series of articles about him. In June he again attended the Rhine Festival at Düsseldorf, after which Dietrich and he spent a holiday at the mountain village of Münster-am-Stein, near Kreuznach, with Clara and some of the Schumann children. Brahms continued composing the *Magelone-Lieder*; he also showed Dietrich a draft movement of a symphony – destined to appear as his First only after many revisions and hesitations fourteen years later.

A few months later Dietrich received a hasty letter from his friend:

> I am leaving on Monday for *Vienna!* I'm looking forward to it like a child. Of course I don't know how long I shall stay; we will leave it open, and I hope we may meet some time during the winter. The C minor Symphony is not ready; on the other hand a string quintet (2 cellos) in F minor is finished. I should like to send it you and hear what you have to say about it, and yet I prefer to take it with me... Pray do not leave me entirely without letters.

Brahms was fulfilling a long-held wish to see for himself the city of Haydn, Mozart, Beethoven, and Schubert. He had nearly gone there in 1861; in the summer of 1862, as the question of a Hamburg appointment still remained unresolved, he had decided at the promptings of Bertha Porubsky and the Viennese singer Luise Dustmann (whom he had met at that year's Rhine Festival) to make an extended visit to their city. He left Hamburg on 8 September, little knowing that he was opening the second great chapter of his life.

Brahms had intended staying in Vienna merely for a few weeks, but no sooner had he arrived than he was captivated by the beautiful city with its parks, coffee-houses, and gypsy music, and found the easygoing warmth of the Viennese more congenial than the habitual reserve of the North Germans. A warm welcome awaited him from such old friends as Bertha Porubsky, Luise Dustmann, and Grädener (who had recently left Hamburg to teach at the Conservatoire), and he rapidly made important new ones: the influential music critic Eduard Hanslick (whom he had first met in Düsseldorf in the 1850s); the composer–pianist Carl Tausig – a young Liszt pupil, whose piano technique and character both fascinated Brahms; and the musicologist Gustav Nottebohm, already at work on the study of Beethoven's sketchbooks that was to bring him his principal fame. Nottebohm was also, however, an avid collector of pre-Bach music and a not untalented composer; and of the several musicologists Brahms was to consort with, was to be the closest, and perhaps most influential, friend. Julius Epstein, professor of piano at the Vienna Conservatoire, and the violinist Josef Hellmes-berger, director of the Conservatoire and leader of his own string quartet, soon arranged for Brahms to appear in public as composer–pianist, and by November he had taken part in performances of both his (as yet unpublished) piano quartets and played the 'Handel' Variations in a recital, while his A major Serenade had been heard at the Gesellschaft der Musikfreunde under the leading conductor Johann Herbeck.

With such a reception (even though Hanslick's reviews of his works were at first distinctly unenthusiastic), it was hardly surprising that Brahms extended his sojourn in Vienna throughout the winter until the following spring. His favourable first impressions of Vienna were to influence the later direction of his life, in which he became ever more closely attached to the Austrian capital; and during his visit he was given a further push in that direction – by Hamburg. In mid-November he received an embarrassed letter from his friend Theodor Avé-Lalle-ment, who was on the committee of the Hamburg Philharmonic Orches-tra, telling him that in Brahms's absence the long-awaited post of conductor was about to fall vacant, but that the committee had already chosen another man as deputy, and warning him that they planned to bestow the conductor's job on – Julius Stockhausen!

It might, of course, have been anticipated that a celebrated visiting artist would seem a more attractive proposition than a 'difficult' local composer, focus of a minor 'cult', whose taste both for modern and outlandishly archaic music was presumably well known. Brahms did not allow the affair to affect his friendship with Stockhausen, even though he had been partly responsible for bringing him to perform in Hamburg in the first place. But as his own hopes, perhaps irrationally, had been fixed on the conductor's post for several years, he was bitterly disappointed, as he let Clara know in a letter of 18 November:

> ...I don't suppose it has occurred to you what a heavy blow it has been to me... If I could not fasten my hopes on my native town, what claims have I elsewhere? Where should I care to go even if I had the chance? Apart from what you experienced with your husband you know that, as a general rule, what our fellow-citizens like best is to be rid of us and leave us to drift about in limbo. And yet what one wants is to be bound, to acquire the things that make life worth living, and one dreads being alone...

Clara was actually in Hamburg at the time, and after talking with Avé-Lallement was inclined to make light of Brahms's chagrin:

What artist has ever been so lucky as to be able to settle down in his native town? That is precisely what is always so sad. And yet, dear Johannes, you are so young. You will find a permanent niche yet, and 'if a man has a loving wife with him he finds heaven in every town'. My husband said that . . . I can well understand that you still feel strange in Vienna. But you will certainly lose this feeling after a longer stay, and in time there will be many things to rivet you to the spot.

At all events, Brahms found plenty of reasons to linger in Vienna, and appeared there on several further occasions as pianist or accompanist, and once as the illustrator of a lecture by Hanslick on Beethoven. Richard Wagner, the arch-apostle of the 'New German' school, was also in Vienna that winter, to conduct three 'monster concerts' of excerpts from his operas. Tausig, who was one of the young musicians who surrounded the controversial master, suggested Brahms as someone who could assist in copying orchestral parts. As a result he was given part of *Die Meistersinger* to copy, and attended all three concerts; Wagner for his part attended one of Brahms's recitals on 8 January 1863, though the two composers were not to meet face to face for another year. Writing to Joachim about the work he was doing for Wagner, Brahms commented:

> I shall probably be called a Wagnerian, but it will, of course, be chiefly owing to the spirit of contradiction that cannot fail to be aroused in any sensible man by the frivolous way in which the musicians here talk about him.

Whatever else he felt about Wagner's music (and for some of it he had a lively respect), Brahms always recognized the quality of dedication which the senior composer brought to his art, and that was bound to win his support – the more so as Wagner, striving to complete *Tristan und Isolde*, was very much down on his luck at this period.

Another important element of this first Viennese visit was the opportunity to get to know a large amount of the music of Schubert, many of whose greatest works were only beginning to find their way into print, thirty-five years after the composer's death. The publisher Carl Anton Spina, who had assembled a large collection of Schubert manuscripts, invited Brahms to study them and make copies of pieces that interested him. To the music critic Adolf Schübring, Brahms wrote that he had the impression of Schubert's

> being still alive. Again and again one meets people who talk of him as a good friend; again and again one comes across new works, the existence

of which was unknown and which are so untouched that one can scrape the very writing-sand[1] off them...

Among the treasures he discovered was Schubert's Easter Cantata *Lazarus*, which so excited his admiration that he copied substantial parts of it. That work bears a perceptible relationship to his own cantata *Rinaldo*, composed the same year, while the wholesale absorption of Schubert in general had important consequences in the major chamber compositions Brahms was to work on in the mid-1860s. When he finally departed from Vienna on 1 May 1863 one of the most treasured acquisitions he carried with him was Spina's gift of all the Schubert volumes so far published by his firm.

Having nowhere else to go, Brahms returned to Hamburg, by way of Hanover to visit Joachim. His great friend had recently become engaged to Amalie Weiss, a young opera singer who was now, at Joachim's urging, retiring from the stage in favour of concert work. Brahms (not without a tinge of envy for Joachim's good fortune) hit it off with her from the first; and Amalie, with her dark lustrous contralto voice, was to become a leading interpreter of his vocal works. He arrived in Hamburg in time for his thirtieth birthday, but found his home no longer the tranquil environment of his childhood. Friction between his parents had been growing for some years past and had finally come to a head. His mother, never very strong, was now seventy-four and an invalid, while his father, still in the prime of life, had reached the peak of his profession (through Brahms's influence with the recently appointed Stockhausen he had become a bassist with the Hamburg Philharmonic), and was inclined to resent the necessity of looking after her. Most of that responsibility had devolved on Brahms's sister Elise, who was herself often in poor health; Fritz Brahms had become a rootless, dandified wastrel, ever ready to sponge off his successful elder brother. Johannes did his best to induce his parents to live together in harmony in the same house, but was only temporarily successful.

As Hamburg, in any case, no longer held out career prospects for him, it was inevitable that Brahms's sojourn there would not last very long. He considered reviving the Frauenchor, though this would have been at best marking time; but before May was out an invitation arrived from Vienna for him to return as conductor of the Singakademie, a long-established but now struggling choral society whose founder, Ferdinand Stegmayer, had just died. This was a major appointment, but Brahms hesitated, writing to Dietrich that he 'could not make up his mind to

[1] The old substitute for blotting-paper. Brahms actually had a little box in which he preserved the sand from Schubert's MSS.

shorten the little time he had with his parents'. It was only after a peremptory letter from Hanslick virtually demanding immediate accept- ance that he acquiesced, and returned to Vienna as early as August to take rehearsals and prepare for the coming season. On the way he stayed for a few days with Clara Schumann in her new house at Lichtenthal near Baden-Baden, a beautiful part of the Black Forest where he was to spend many subsequent summers.

Brahms's season with the Singakademie was controversial to say the least. He was an excellent trainer of small choirs, but in attempting to bring new and exploratory programming to a large choral society with a moribund repertoire, he encountered stiff resistance both in the Viennese public and in the Singakademie itself. Brahms's choice of music followed his own interests and introduced his singers to many important but unfamiliar pieces, creating an unusual amount of hard work for them; and in the event, he had to abandon his plans for presenting Handel's then practically unknown *Acis and Galatea*. His first concert, on 15 November 1863, featured the first-ever Vienna performance of Bach's Cantata no. 21 (with an organ continuo part specially composed by Brahms), a work by Isaac, folksong arrangements, a Beethoven item and Schumann's *Requiem für Mignon* (also a Viennese première). This programme was enthusiastically received: one critic hailed it as 'the most noteworthy achievement in the record of the Singakademie', and remarked on the clearness and precision of Brahms's conducting tech- nique, so unexpected in an artist 'who has shown himself, in his creations and performances, so essentially a Romantic and a dreamer'.

Despite this promising beginning, the 'antiquarianism' of the next concert, on 6 January, mainly devoted to austere unaccompanied pieces by Eccard, Schütz, Gabrieli and Rovetta, was altogether too strange and serious for the popular taste. The ill-preparedness of the singers and the poor standard of the participating instrumentalists pointed up a contrast with the much more flourishing Gesellschaft der Musikfreunde, made all the clearer when Brahms performed three parts of Bach's 'Christmas Oratorio' in his third concert. Even though this was the first time the work had ever been heard in Vienna, it was quite overshadowed by Herbeck's performance of the *St John Passion* two days later. However, Brahms recouped the position with his fourth concert, a request pro- gramme devoted entirely to his own works, including the *Ave Maria*, some of the *Marienlieder*, one of his op. 29 Motets; and premières of the vocal quartet *Wechsellied zum Tanze* and of a new Sonata for two pianos (culled from the stillborn String Quintet), played by Brahms and Tausig. This was a considerable success, and after a fifth and final concert (which included some Elizabethan madrigals, as well as Haydn and Schumann), he was re-elected conductor for the next three years. However, Brahms had found the administrative duties very irksome, and was dismayed by the public reception of music that he venerated; so on reflection that summer he resigned the conductorship to allow himself to be once again a free agent.

Throughout the 1862–3 season Brahms also taught piano in Vienna. One of his star pupils was a beautiful, aristocratic blonde girl called Elisabet von Stockhausen (no relation to his friend the famous singer). Warm, humorous, talented and perceptive, she was an obvious snare for the lonely and susceptible composer (who had just, with some effort, fought off an attachment to another Viennese girl, the singer Ottilie Hauer). Finding himself in danger of falling head over heels for Elisabet, he once again withdrew and cancelled the piano lessons. Not long afterwards, she married the composer Heinrich von Herzogenberg, and Brahms felt able to renew the friendship. Elisabet von Herzogenberg was to become one of his closest confidantes, and a discerning critic of his music. The lively three-cornered correspondence between her, Brahms, and her husband which occupied the next decades is delightfully eloquent testimony to the sheer affection and admiration he could arouse in his friends.

It was during this winter (and not, as is often stated, the previous one) that Brahms and Wagner finally met face to face, on 6 February 1864. Wagner had remained in Vienna and conducted further operatic concerts there; the introduction was effected by Tausig and another of Brahms's new friends, the composer Peter Cornelius. Now over fifty and about to be harried from Austria to Bavaria by his numerous creditors, Wagner received the young Hamburger at his villa in Penzing with a display of his considerable grace and charm, and they spent a cordial evening together. Brahms played his 'Handel' Variations, and the pioneer of epic music drama was quick to grasp the significance of this outwardly 'old-fashioned' work, admitting that 'It shows what can still be done with the old forms by somebody who knows how to handle them.' The two composers never encountered one another again, and Wagner was later often scathing about Brahms in print and conversation; but Brahms, despite grave reservations about many of his works, continued to admire Wagner's single-minded vision and immense creative energy.

At this juncture Brahms still had no settled intention of making his home in Vienna, and he left the city all the more hurriedly in June because of continued bad news from Hamburg. Relations between his parents had continued to deteriorate, and had finally arrived at the point where Brahms was forced to admit that it was better for them to separate. His brother Fritz was becoming a successful piano-teacher, and lived on his own in considerably grander style than his parents, but volunteered no assistance. Although his means were still quite modest, Johannes provided all necessary finance for Johann Jakob to move into lodgings away from his invalid wife and daughter, who were left in possession of their old home but soon moved to more pleasant quarters with a garden. Brahms undertook to support them, but he still thought his father should be responsible for helping his mother with this move and with her financial upkeep, and so sent additional money via him, as well as other funds for his father's personal use. Had Brahms himself not been used to the strictest personal economy, the strain on his resources at this time would probably have bankrupted him.

After attending to these family problems he paid a surprise visit to Clara at Lichtenthal, and found a particularly glittering collection of celebrities in the spa town that summer. Here Brahms renewed his acquaintance with Anton Rubinstein, whom he admired as a man if not as a composer, and who generously made his villa available to Brahms. The engraver Julius Allgeyer, Brahms's friend from Düsseldorf days, now lived nearby, after having spent some years in Rome with the painter Anselm Feuerbach, whose biography Allgeyer was to write and who was now also staying in Baden. Here, too, Brahms now met the 'Waltz King' Johann Strauss; the conductor of the nearby Karlsruhe Opera, Hermann Levi, destined to be a close friend and an important champion of his works; the Landgräfin of Hesse, who presented him with a notable addition to his collection of composers' autographs – Mozart's manuscript of his great G minor Symphony; the pianist–composer Jakob Rosenhain; and the Russian novelist Ivan Turgenev, who was there to be near to the great love of his life, the brilliant and flamboyant Franco-Spanish singer, composer and pianist Pauline Viardot-Garcia. She had studied with Liszt, owned Mozart's autograph of *Don Giovanni*, was building a grand villa on the same street as Clara Schumann's and had opened a miniature 'Palace of Art' in Baden where she and her circle performed music and drama. Though of radically different temperaments, Clara and Pauline had already been firm friends for over a quarter of a century: sometimes appalled, occasionally envious, Clara thought her 'the most gifted woman I have ever met'; and Pauline now became Brahms's friend too. He also took greatly to Turgenev, virtually exiled from his native Russia by the radical press even though he had been imprisoned for anti-tsarist political tendencies. The novelist was already supplying libretti for Pauline's operettas (which she composed, orchestrated and produced herself), and he and Brahms seriously discussed the possibility of collaborating on an opera –

although the project came to nothing. In Baden, though, Brahms did finally complete his F minor Piano Quintet and wrote the bulk of a new String Sextet in G major. And in honour of the birth of Joachim's son in September – the baby almost inevitably being christened Johannes – he wrote one of his finest songs: the *Geistliches Wiegenlied* (not published until many years later as the second of the two *Gesänge* for alto, viola, and piano, op. 91) which quotes the famous carol *Resonet in laudibus*, known in Germany by the folksong text *Joseph, lieber Joseph mein*.

He returned to Vienna in October and spent the first part of the winter there. But at the end of January 1865 his mother suffered a stroke; a telegram from Fritz brought him dashing back to Hamburg to be at her bedside, but the frail old lady died at the age of seventy-six, shortly before he arrived. Brahms brought his father to the death-bed and, having overseen the funeral and made sure the other members of his family were provided for, he returned to Vienna. But his mother's death had been a severe psychological blow. The cellist Josef Gansbacher, calling on him unawares, found him practising Bach keyboard music; Brahms told him of his loss with tears streaming down his cheeks, but never stopped his playing. Clearly creative work was the only possible solace, but he was restless, undecided what to do next. Certainly at the moment Vienna seemed no fit place for him, as he wrote to Clara on 20 February:

> .... the kind of life I lead here makes Vienna as a whole seem every day more pleasant to me, but the people and especially the artists ever more repulsive. The way the latter behave towards the public and the critics, and play before them and depend on them, takes away all one's desire to join in the swindle with them ...

Almost immediately, it seems, he began a new work under the impact of the loss he had suffered. By April he had sent Clara two slow, benedictory movements for chorus and orchestra to texts from the Lutheran Bible: 'How lovely are thy dwellings, O Lord of Hosts', and 'Blessed are they that mourn: for they shall be comforted...'. The latter was, he told her,

> probably the weakest part of a *German Requiem*...the [other] chorus...is number four. The second is in C minor[2] and is in march time. I hope that a German text of this sort will please you as much as the usual Latin one. I am hoping to produce a sort of whole out of

[2] It is not. For an ingenious explanation of this slip see Musgrave, op. cit., p. 84.

the thing and trust I shall retain enough courage and zest to carry it
through...

Over the next few years this *Requiem* – the largest work he was ever to
write – was added to and carefully refined, and the composition of it
sustained Brahms through his depression, bringing himself and his art
to philosophical maturity.

Brahms once again spent part of the summer in Lichtenthal, where
he composed his Horn Trio, with its deeply elegiac slow movement.
Otherwise much of the year was taken up in restless travelling; like
Clara after Schumann's incarceration he accepted an unusual number
of engagements as a pianist, redoubling the energy he devoted to music
and society, and to earning money to help support his father and
sister. These concerts included a triumphant performance of the Piano
Concerto under Hermann Levi at Mannheim, where that difficult work
was finally received with public enthusiasm, and a Brahms-Festival
mounted in Oldenburg by Albert Dietrich. It was only in early 1866 that
he eventually found the stability and peace of mind to put his *Requiem*
in order, by dint of sustained work at Allgeyer's house in Karlsruhe and
then in Switzerland, where he spent the summer near Theodor Kirchner
in a house overlooking the glaciers of the Züricherberg. Here he made
new and long-lasting acquaintances: the violinist and conductor Friedrich Hegar, the poets Joseph Viktor Widmann and Gottfried Keller.
More significantly, he played duets and chamber music with a distinguished German surgeon and keen amateur musician, Theodor
Billroth, who was destined to become one of his most valued friends.
At this time too, a friendship developed between Brahms and Mathilde
Wesendonck, whose love-affair with Wagner had inspired the composition of *Tristan und Isolde*. Wagner had long discarded her for Liszt's
daughter, Cosima von Bülow; but in Brahms, the poetess found a
sympathetic comrade in art (whom she felt was 'one of the best and
most unprejudiced men of our time'), and they kept up a lively correspondence for many years.

In the winter of 1866 Johann Jakob Brahms decided to remarry.
His choice had fallen upon the owner of the little restaurant where he
had been taking his solitary meals. Announcing this to his son, who had
returned to Vienna after an absence of eighteen months and was spending Christmas with Bertha Faber (the erstwhile Bertha Porubsky) and
her husband, he asked if he would approve his choice. With some
trepidation Johannes learned that Caroline Schnack was nearly twenty
years younger than his father and had already been twice widowed; but
when he finally met the lady in Hamburg he greatly warmed to her (and

to her sixteen-year-old son Fritz Schnack) and gave his blessing to the marriage, which took place in March 1867. It was a considerable relief that there was now someone capable and sensible to look after his father, but he became genuinely attached to his new stepmother.

In the early months of 1867 Brahms accompanied Joachim on a series of concerts in Switzerland and Alsace, followed by a tour of Austria and Hungary which produced a gratifyingly large profit. This enabled him to bring his father to Vienna for a holiday and take him on a tour of the Austrian Alps: an exhausting but unforgettable experience for the old man, who had never seen mountains in his life, and who now became an enthusiastic traveller under the rejuvenating influence of his new marriage.

The next few months were dominated by the production of the *Deutsches Requiem*, which at this stage had stabilized as a work in six movements. Three sections were given in Vienna by Herbeck's Gesellschaft der Musikfreunde, but with near-disastrous effect: the performance was under-rehearsed and after a chaotic rendition of the third movement Brahms was hissed – Hanslick called it 'A Requiem for the decorum and good manners of Viennese concert rooms'. Billroth, who had moved to Vienna from Switzerland to take up a professorship at the University, was also present at the concert and confided in a letter to a friend: 'I like Brahms better every time I meet him ... His Requiem is so nobly spiritual and so Protestant-Bachish that it was difficult to make it go down here.'

Meanwhile, Albert Dietrich had sent a copy of the score to the organist and musical director of the cathedral in Bremen, Karl Martin Reinthaler. He was so impressed that plans were soon being laid for a complete performance in Bremen Cathedral to take place on Good Friday (10 April) 1868, to be prepared by Reinthaler and conducted by Brahms. The composer therefore based himself in Hamburg at the comfortable new flat his father and stepmother now occupied, to be near enough to consult Reinthaler, with whom he was keeping up a steady correspondence about the work. The kapellmeister was exercised about the *Requiem*'s lack of any strict doctrinal statement. Proposing that Brahms should write a further movement of incontrovertibly Christian content, he wrote:

> The central point about which everything turns in the consciousness of the Christian is absent. 'If Christ is not risen then is our faith vain', says St Paul. All the same you say [in the final movement] 'Blessed are the dead which die in the Lord *from henceforth*', which can only mean since the accomplishment of Christ's work of redemption...

Brahms's response is deeply interesting from the point of view of his own spiritual beliefs:

> As regards the title I will confess I should gladly have left out 'German' and substituted 'Human'. Also that I knowingly and intentionally dispensed with passages such as St John's Gospel Ch. 3 verse 16.[3] On the other hand, I have no doubt included much because I am a musician, because I required it, because I can neither argue away nor strike out a 'henceforth' from my venerable extracts.

In the interim he embarked on a series of concerts with Julius Stockhausen in Berlin, Dresden, Kiel and Copenhagen. Stockhausen was now no longer the conductor of the Hamburg Philharmonic: he had resigned at the beginning of the year, and once again the committee failed to award the post to Brahms. This second rebuff, though less wounding than the first, finally determined him that, if he should settle anywhere, it had better be Vienna. The concerts with Stockhausen were a success, especially at Copenhagen where their old acquaintance Niels Gade had helped prepare the way; but the tour was cut short when a casual remark of Brahms's was misconstrued by his hosts, still very touchy about the 1864 war with Prussia over Schleswig-Holstein, as an anti-Danish insult.

The Bremen première of the *Requiem* aroused enormous interest, and many distinguished musicians came from all over Germany and abroad to hear it. Brahms was especially eager that Clara should attend, though he did not seem to expect any great results when he wrote to her on 2 February:

> If only you could be a listener on Good Friday I should be more happy than I can say. It would be as good as half the performance for me. If it goes at all as I wish it to, you would certainly have good reason to marvel and rejoice. But unfortunately I am not the man who succeeds in getting more than people deign to give me of their own accord, and that is always very little. So I am resigning myself to the thought that this time, as in Vienna, it will go too fast and too sketchily. But do come! ...

In the event, the performance was a triumphant and memorable occasion. Clara had finished her concert tour in England and arrived with her daughter Marie just in time for the performance; Brahms met her at the cathedral door and led her up the nave on his arm. To his pride and delight his father was in the audience, as were the Joachims (who performed in some preliminary items), the Grimms, the Dietrichs,

[3] Authorized Version: 'For God so loved the world, that he gave his only-begotten Son, that whosoever believeth in him should not perish, but have everlasting life'.

Minna Völckers, Rieter-Biedermann, Max Bruch and other old friends; only Marxsen was prevented by illness from making the journey to Bremen. Stockhausen sang the baritone solo;[4] the chorus even included some former members of the Hamburger Frauenchor. The performance itself was excellent. 'The effect... was simply overwhelming,' wrote Dietrich, 'and it at once became clear to the audience that the *Deutsches Requiem* ranked among the loftiest music ever given to the world'. The English composer John Farmer approached Johann Jakob as they made their way out of the cathedral afterwards to ask his opinion: 'It was pretty well done,' said the elder Brahms, and took a pinch of snuff. Afterwards his son was fêted at a banquet in his honour and was prevailed upon despite all his protests to make a speech – which he limited to calling for three hearty cheers for Kapellmeister Reinthaler. Critical acclamation was almost universal, and it was generally acknowledged that the *Requiem*, his first really large work for chorus and orchestra, had finally fulfilled Schumann's prophecies of Brahms's greatness. Less than three weeks later, by popular demand, the work was repeated under Reinthaler's baton.

Brahms meanwhile had returned to Hamburg to prepare it for publication, and in so doing enlarged it yet further by adding, at Marxsen's suggestion, a seventh movement (placed fifth in the overall scheme) for solo soprano. This final form of the *Requiem* was heard in Leipzig under Reinecke in February 1869, and by the end of that year had been given in over twenty German and Swiss cities; premières followed in 1871 in London (a private performance without orchestra)[5] and Vienna, Utrecht and St Petersburg in 1872, London (with orchestra) in 1873, and Paris in 1875. No work did more to win Brahms international recognition in a short time; and from now on, he was regarded by all but the most partisan supporters of the 'New German' school as one of the leading composers of the age.

From Hamburg in June he travelled to Cologne for the Rhine Festival. Here this year he became friends with the composer Friedrich Gernsheim; with Hermann Dieters, critic of the *Allgemeine Musikalische Zeitung*, who was later to write the first book-length study of Brahms; and with the composer Max Bruch, five years his junior, whom he had already known through correspondence. Bruch, as we have seen, had

---

[4] The soprano solo movement did not yet exist, but Amalie Joachim sang 'I know that my Redeemer liveth' from Handel's *Messiah* as part of the performance.

[5] Which marked the last public appearance of the distinguished composer Cipriani Potter (1791–1871), a friend of Beethoven, who took one part of the piano-duet accompaniment with lively enthusiasm at the age of eighty.

attended the première of the *Deutsches Requiem* and had been greatly impressed – though not as wholeheartedly as some: his own gifts lying in a more purely lyrical and melodic direction, he resented (as did many other contemporaries) the intellectual effort required by Brahms's polyphonic textures. 'The work is very greatly conceived and deeply felt', he had written[6] to Ferdinand Hiller:

> It makes a meaningful impression not only on artists, but also on the people. It appears that Brahms has achieved something here which had failed him hitherto. Nevertheless I believe that one will feel more respect and awe for this work of his, rather than love. I am frank enough to say that a powerful ravishing melody is preferable to the most beautiful imitations and contrapuntal tight-rope walk. There is now a Philistine Party in Germany which places work above all else, and gives at best a disdainful shrug of its shoulders to every fresh, impartial, uneducated expression of Life in Art...

Despite these misgivings, the two composers became firm friends when they met in Cologne, and before the end of the year Bruch had dedicated his First Symphony to Brahms.

The latter now made his base in Bonn for a working summer, adding a large final chorus to the cantata *Rinaldo* composed five years previously, and assembling several collections of songs. After that he took his father to Switzerland for a second mountain holiday, and then stayed for a while with the Dietrichs in Oldenburg, dividing his time between them and Reinthaler's family. At this juncture another important work was conceived, in the unlikely circumstances of a visit with the Dietrichs to the great naval dockyard at Wilhelmshaven, which Brahms (whose Hamburg childhood had left him with a lifelong interest in ships, though he seldom ventured aboard one) had particularly asked to see. 'On the way there', Dietrich recalled in his published memoir of Brahms,

> our friend, who was usually so lively, was quiet and serious. He told us that early that morning (he always rose at dawn) he had found Hölderlin's poems in the bookcase, and had been most deeply moved by 'Hyperions Schicksalslied'. When, later in the day, after having wandered about and seen everything of interest, we sat down by the sea to rest, we discovered Brahms at a great distance, sitting alone on the beach and writing. These were the first sketches for the *Schicksalslied* (Song of Destiny)...

Later that year, on another visit to Oldenburg, Brahms partnered Clara Schumann in what seems to have been the first complete performance

---

[6]In a letter quoted at greater length in Christopher Fifield's *Max Bruch: his Life and Works* (London, 1988), pp. 86–7.

of his Hungarian Dances (ten so far) for piano duet, although some had already existed (and been played) in solo piano form for over a decade.

Despite their continuing professional amity, 1868 had in fact been one of the most difficult years in Brahms's relationship with Clara. Now nearly fifty, she was burdened with increasing family difficulties: her daughter Julie and her youngest son Felix were both in very fragile health, while Ludwig Schumann had already manifested signs of the mental instability that would soon consign him, like his father, to an asylum. She urgently felt the need to earn money to support them by extensive concert giving; together with this went a professional concern not to be outshone and supplanted by other, younger pianists. Her attitudes alarmed and exasperated Brahms, who became anxious both that she was wearing herself out (in fact she was extremely resilient), and that by her peripatetic life she often failed to give her children what they needed most: her company and undivided attention. He tried to put this tactfully to Clara in a letter of early 1868, but tact was never his strong point, and she was deeply offended. There were complicating resentments on his side; for the past few years he had felt he no longer occupied the prime place in her life that she did in his, and that he was no longer, as previously, welcome at all hours in her house or within the bosom of her family.

Clara, for her part, seems to have become tired of Brahms's moodiness, the often curt manners and acid wit which he was cultivating as a self-defence and which she felt were especially unsuitable when in the company of her children. It is clear that on occasions, even in his ebullient vein, she found him trying company; herself inclined to seriousness and melancholy, she had little patience with his delight in practical jokes or wild, playful humour, and his ill-disguised impatience with social conventions and the niceties of refined behaviour. A gulf had opened between them, a space occupied perhaps by their mutual awareness of the might-have-beens of the 1850s. Perhaps Clara had subconsciously divined the attention Brahms was currently paying to her daughter Julie, and was jealous of it. (Possibly, too, Brahms had divined some hints of Clara's affair with Kirchner, although this seems to have been one of the best-kept secrets of nineteenth-century music.) At any rate the atmosphere between them was highly charged, and though Brahms was overjoyed when Clara turned up for the première of the *Deutsches Requiem* the occasion rapidly went sour when his behaviour the following day gave further offence (we do not know how). As will have been noted, he did not visit Lichtenthal in 1868, and it took a painful, loving, yet recriminatory exchange of letters that autumn to restore the friendship to something like its previous level.

Brahms spent part of November giving recitals with Stockhausen in North Germany, and before Christmas he made his way to Vienna, having first taken a goodly portion of his library from Hamburg. He had spent a large part of each year in the Austrian capital since 1862, but had not really maintained a house of his own, living rather at hotels or with friends. In February and March 1869 Stockhausen and he gave a series of concerts in Vienna and Budapest, and these proved to be Brahms's last appearances as a concert pianist, except in his own works. From now on he was to devote himself to composition, and occasionally to conducting (he directed the première of *Rinaldo* in Vienna that same February). On 30 April he informed his father that it would no longer be necessary to reserve rooms for him in Hamburg. He had finally decided to make his home in Vienna.

Hardly had he made this decision, and moved into a house near the Prater, than two professional positions in Germany seemed to be his for the taking. Ferdinand Hiller asked him to accept the post of Professor of piano in Cologne; Joachim, recently appointed director of the newly founded Hochschule für Musik in Berlin, urged Brahms to join his staff. After some hesitation he turned down both proposals. Not that he had wholly given up the idea of a post; but one more to his taste would be the directorship of the Gesellschaft der Musikfreunde in Vienna: Herbeck was close to retirement, and Brahms had reason to believe that his chances of being considered as the successor were better than they had been for the Hamburg Philharmonic.

In the summer of 1869 he was once more at Lichtenthal, within easy reach of the Schumann family. Here he worked on string quartets (almost certainly preliminary versions of his op. 51), and completed the *Liebeslieder* Waltzes for vocal quartet and piano duet, settings in *echt*-Viennese waltz style of simple love-songs by Georg Daumer. These spontaneously lyrical waltz-songs, a refined apotheosis of domestic music-making, could well have been the outward expression of his current daydreams about the beautiful Julie Schumann, whom he was seeing every day at her mother's house. But in early July Julie announced her engagement to a young Italian nobleman, Count Victor Radicati di Marmorito, whom she had met during a sojourn in Italy for her health. 'Of course I told Johannes first of all', Clara noted in her diary on the 11th. 'He seemed not to have expected anything of the sort, and to be quite upset'. She certainly seems to have harboured no conscious inkling of his feelings about Julie; but soon afterwards Hermann Levi told her Brahms had been 'devotedly attached' to her daughter. By 16 July, she observed

Johannes is quite altered, he seldom comes to the house and speaks only in monosyllables when he does come. And he treats even Julie in the same manner, though he always used to be so specially nice to her. Did he really love her? But he has never thought of marrying [her], and Julie has never had any inclination towards him.

In fact Brahms felt the betrothal as a personal blow. He was undoubtedly very fond of Julie, and though his 'love' for her may have been no more than a private fantasy, there was real pain involved in acknowledging its groundlessness. Clara had long been unattainable, yet he still yearned to become in some way a real part of the Schumann family, rather than the ambiguously placed surrogate son/brother he often felt himself to be. At the height of their disaffection the previous year he had written to Clara: 'I speak through my music. The only thing is that a poor musician like myself would like to believe that he was better than his music.' His response now was musical. Julie and Marmorito were married at Lichtenthal on 22 September; later that day Brahms called on Clara, who confided to her diary:

Johannes brought me a wonderful piece...the words from Goethe's *Harzreise*, for alto, male chorus, and orchestra. He called it *his* bridal song. It is long since I remember being so moved by a depth of pain in words and music. This piece seems to me neither more nor less than the expression of his own heart's anguish. If only he would for once speak as tenderly!

The piece in question was the so-called Alto Rhapsody, destined to become one of Brahms's most famous works – a portrayal of isolation concluded by a prayer that this state should not degenerate into misanthropy. In October Hermann Levi rehearsed it in Karlsruhe, and the *Liebeslieder* Waltzes were premièred there with Clara and Levi sharing the piano part: these carefree evocations of the Viennese waltz may by now have sounded ironic to the composer's ears, but they were an immediate success, and soon became one of his most popular compositions in lighter vein.

The Rhapsody received its first public performance in Jena, sung by Pauline Viardot-Garcia, early in 1870. (It was however Amalie Joachim who later became almost inseparably associated with it as an incomparable interpreter.) During this year Brahms was being actively considered as Herbeck's successor as conductor of the Gesellschaft concerts in Vienna; however, he insisted on being responsible for the chorus as well as the orchestra, and as the Society was unwilling to concentrate so much responsibility in one individual the post was eventually awarded to Anton Rubinstein on a temporary basis. In late summer the Franco-Prussian War broke out. Despite his resolve to live in Vienna, Brahms was in his bones a German patriot, and had tremendous admiration for Bismarck, the Prussian Chancellor. He had taken scant interest in the Austro-Prussian campaign of 1866, but paradoxically the events of the war with France seemed to touch him more closely. Ferdinand Schumann, Clara's only healthy and successful son, was called up for army service – only to contract such debilitating rheumatism that its treatment left him a morphine addict for the rest of his life.[7] Brahms was anxious at the thought that Clara was in a possible war-zone, and he had seriously considered volunteering after the initial German reverses; however wisdom prevailed and instead he channelled his energies into the composition of a species of victory Te Deum – but, like the *Requiem*, to German words of his own choosing. This was the *Triumphlied*, whose first part he conducted in Bremen Cathedral at a concert in memory of the war dead in April 1871; the rest of the work was not completed for another year.

He spent the early part of 1871 in restless travelling and concert giving, relaxing in the summer at Lichtenthal. This was the summer during which Clara Schumann turned over to him her new English pupil Florence May, to learn how to improve her piano technique. Although technique interested him profoundly, once he no longer had the need Brahms almost never took piano pupils, and then only at Clara's special entreaty. Many years later, Florence May was to be Brahms's first English biographer, and has left a charming and perceptive memoir of Brahms's teaching methods, scrupulous musicianship, love of nature and capacity for friendship. In her opinion (which is amplified and confirmed by other, shorter accounts of his teaching, for instance in Eugenie Schumann's autobiography):

> Brahms united in himself each and every quality that might be supposed to exist in an absolutely ideal teacher of the pianoforte, without having a single modifying drawback. I do not wish to rhapsodise; he would have been the first to object to this . . .
>
> He was strict and absolute; he was gentle and patient and encouraging; he was not only clear, he was light itself; he knew exhaustively, and could teach, and did teach, by the shortest possible methods, every detail of technical study; he was unwearied in his efforts to make his

---

[7] Only a few months earlier his elder brother, the gentle, eccentric and erratic Ludwig Schumann, had finally been pronounced incurably insane (an effect of a spinal disease) and was confined to a mental asylum in Colditz castle at the age of twenty-two. There he outlived both Clara and Brahms.

pupil grasp the full musical meaning of whatever work might be in hand; he was even punctual.[8]

Brahms returned to Vienna in the autumn. He had occupied several lodgings in the city in the past few years, interspersed with stays in hotels or with friends, but in December he rented a pair of rooms from a family called Vogl at no. 4 Karlgasse, a nondescript apartment-block very near to the great Baroque Karlskirche, and just a short walk from the new building housing the library and concert-halls of the Gesellschaft der Musikfreunde. As much as he ever had a home, this was to be it for the rest of his life. By now he was a 'Viennese' in spirit if not by birth – and one who was finally, if not happily, resigned to remaining a bachelor.

Within the month, however, grave family news brought him hurrying to Hamburg: his young stepbrother Fritz Schnack, who had been working as a clockmaker in Russia, had been brought home from St Petersburg with a spinal injury, and the doctor attending him had diagnosed Brahms's father, who had complained of vague indisposition, as fatally ill: in fact, Johann Jakob was dying of cancer of the liver. While Caroline Brahms looked after her son, Johannes was able to be with her husband for the last few days, never leaving his side until the old man breathed his last on 11 February 1872. He then stayed on in Hamburg to make sure that his sister, his stepmother and stepbrother were properly provided for. His steadily increasing income allowed him to give them regular financial aid, and in the coming years he often bore the expense of holidays for their health. Elise, rather to his concern, had lately married an elderly widower with six children; but it proved a successful match, and Johannes provided her with an annuity as well as paying for the education of the youngest child. Caroline went back to her catering trade: Brahms and she continued to correspond in the warmest terms, and he established Fritz Schnack in a clockmaker's business in Pinneberg, the Holstein town where he convalesced from his injury. With his own brother Fritz, returned from a few years teaching in Venezuela, there was a formal reconciliation, but no closeness on either side. The death of his father had sundered the last real tie with Hamburg, and from now on Brahms's life was concentrated further south.

---

[8] May, op. cit., pp. 9–10.

6

The sense of the past

As Grimm was distributing the parts of the *Ave Maria* and the *Begräbnisgesang* at one of the practices, my neighbour, a glib University student with the experience of several terms behind him, said in a surprised tone: 'Brahms! Who is that?' 'Oh, some old ecclesiastic of Palestrina's time,' I replied – a piece of information which he accepted and passed on.

Brahms's friend Carl von Meysenbug[1]

Brahms's lifelong fascination with what we now call early music, going back as far as the Renaissance period in Germany and Italy, and to composers such as Isaac and Palestrina, is well known. But to most of his contemporaries it seemed an eccentric enthusiasm, and his first biographers were ill-equipped to understand its significance. During his lifetime, although the works of Bach and Handel were gradually gaining appreciation, the value of music earlier than the Classical period was hardly generally accepted; the majority of critics and music-lovers would have considered it outmoded, 'primitive', uncouth, and above all boring, and would have questioned whether it was worth performing at all. Only in recent years – with the enormous explosion of interest in the whole early music field that has taken place since the mid-twentieth century in performances, editions, musicological discussion and recordings – have Brahms's attitudes begun to seem important, even prophetic and pioneering. He was, of course, by no means the first composer to admire and learn from pre-Classical music: Mozart studied Bach and made his own version of *Messiah*, Beethoven's late music gained much from his study of Bach and Handel, Mendelssohn was a prime mover in the Bach revival, Schumann was an enthusiast for Palestrina and co-founder of the Bach-Gesellschaft. But Brahms's involvement with early music (whether 'art music' or folksong) was very different from theirs. He was in the forefront of its exploration, just as the field was beginning to be opened up by contemporary scholars. His study of it was both wide-ranging and systematic; it was of long duration, pre-dating his contact with Schumann and extending as far as the conception of his last work, the eleven Chorale Preludes for organ. It was a scholarly

[1] Quoted by Florence May, op. cit., p. 264.

interest, insofar as he studied the music for its own sake; it was also a performer's interest, for he brought much of it before the public; and above all it was a composer's interest – an absorption in early music techniques which had a whole range of continuing repercussions on his own musical language.

In his explorations, Brahms (who in any case had the natural instincts of a bibliophile) amassed over the years a personal library of music and music books which probably surpassed that of any other composer of his time. (Most of it, totalling over 2,000 volumes, remains in the collection of the Gesellschaft der Musikfreunde in Vienna.) From his early teens he was an avid collector, spending what money he had at second-hand book-dealers' stalls; he also made it his business to acquire important works which remained unpublished (as most of Bach or Schütz still were when he began investigating them). The only practicable method of doing this was to make his own autograph copies (*Abschriften*) from manuscript sources or rare editions beyond his means. Friends such as Clara and Joachim, who knew his tastes, would buy him music or books as presents, and make or commission *Abschriften* of particularly choice items; in some cases they were able to present him with rare original manuscripts, which he also bought and collected. At one time or another Brahms owned such treasures as Mozart's autograph of the G minor Symphony, K550, Haydn's op. 20 String Quartets, songs and piano pieces by Schubert, a Beethoven sketchbook including the sketches of the 'Hammerklavier' Sonata, Schumann's *Davidsbündlertänze* and the original version of his D minor Symphony, and even for a while Wagner's holograph full score of *Tannhäuser* (which he was exceedingly loth to return to its composer when it became clear that the person from whom he received it had been acting without Wagner's consent!).

As suggested in Chapter 2, one of the Romantic movement's achievements was a revaluation of older works of art and their techniques; previously dismissed and neglected as outmoded, they became shining examples worthy of study, even of veneration. Allied to this was an antiquarian streak that Brahms certainly shared: the Hoffmannesque delight in old music partly because it *was* old, the repository of a purer, more magically powerful form of expression. But Brahms soon came to appreciate the music for its own sake, realizing that, far from 'primitive spontaneity', much of it represented a highly developed art from which music had since retreated. This became all the clearer to him as soon as he had the chance to rehearse and perform the choral music with actual choirs. As he wrote to Clara during his first season in Detmold in 1857: 'We intend to do [Schumann's partsong] *Zigeunerleben* and I am sure it will go splendidly. How childishly easy such things are compared with old church music...' As he studied and learned from the editions he collected, his fascination developed into meticulous scholarship. In an age when performers still regularly took liberties with music as written, Brahms was unusually concerned to establish the composer's original intentions and to compile an accurate text of everything he acquired. The manuscripts and editions in his library are liberally marked and annotated as a result of his researches – for which he visited most of the major libraries in Austria and Germany – among competing editions or manuscript sources. Over a very wide range of music, from the Renaissance to the work of his contemporaries, he would correct misprints or scribal errors, supply missing accents or accidentals, resolve typographical ambiguities, add citations and references to other editions or books which cast light on interpretative problems, mark passages which seemed to him especially effective (or the reverse) and so on. This was no longer antiquarianism but scholarship of a rather impressive order; Brahms clearly had the makings of a first-rate musicologist. Musicology was still a young science – but it is highly significant that Brahms numbered some of its foremost figures among his close friends.

Musical scholarship had itself experienced a similar progress from the initial impulses imparted to it by Romanticism. In the early decades of the nineteenth century had appeared the first major folksong collections and studies of Renaissance music. Among the most important of these latter was Carl von Winterfeld's three-volume *Johannes Gabrieli und sein Zeitalter* (published 1834, the last volume entirely devoted to musical examples), which Brahms acquired and absorbed early, and continued to study throughout his life. In presenting this panorama of 'the Age of Gabrieli', Winterfeld provided what was in effect a handy anthology of late Renaissance music, much of it unavailable elsewhere. Though he printed pieces by Lassus, Monteverdi and Marenzio, by far the bulk of his examples was given over to Giovanni Gabrieli and, even more significant, to Heinrich Schütz; Winterfeld is sometimes said to have accomplished, practically single-handed, the nineteenth-century rediscovery of the seventeenth-century German master. Winterfeld's cast of mind is, however, thoroughly Romantic in his prolix, ecstatic enthusiasm for his subject, and his Lutheran fascination with its religious aspects.

Authors like Winterfeld (and Friedrich Rochlitz, whose collection of Renaissance pieces Brahms also possessed) nevertheless laid the groundwork for the next generation of scholars, among whom Brahms had many friends: Friedrich Chrysander, Otto Jahn (the biographer of Mozart, and co-founder with Schumann of the Bach-Gesellschaft),

Brahms

Gustav Nottebohm, C. F. Pohl (biographer of Haydn), and younger men such as Eusebius Mandyczewski (Nottebohm's pupil, who edited the works of Haydn and Schubert, and eventually Brahms himself) and Philipp Spitta. He was deeply interested in their work, and his correspondence and conversations with them enlarged his knowledge and understanding of the music of former times. They in turn greatly respected his learning, opinions, and critical instinct; and were clearly encouraged that their activities should be so warmly supported by one of the leading composers of the times. These scholars were concerned to make available accurate texts and documentation (such as work-catalogues and composer-biographies), and to understand better the dynamics of musical creation. Among their monuments are epoch-making complete critical editions of major pre-Classical composers; and although by modern standards their editorial methods leave much to be desired, succeeding generations of musicologists remain vastly in their debt. During the whole of Brahms's adult life, the Bach-Gesellschaft was publishing the first-ever Complete Edition of Bach's music, at the rate of one volume per year. The first volume appeared in 1851, and he was a subscriber to the Edition from 1856 onwards, though he had access to older editions or manuscript copies of works that the Gesellschaft Edition had not yet arrived at. Sometimes – as in the case of Bach's Cantata no. 150, which gave Brahms the idea for the Finale of his Fourth Symphony – this material was supplied to him by Spitta, who was at work on his monumental biography of Bach. Spitta also edited the first Complete Edition of Schütz, published by Breitkopf between 1885 and 1894, and the organ works of Buxtehude; Brahms and he kept up a lively correspondence over the years, though it was interrupted by disagreements arising from Spitta's religious scruples about musical setting of scripture.

Chrysander's name is inextricably associated with that of Handel, whose biography he wrote in the decade 1858–67, and whose works he edited in his monumental 96-volume Complete Edition (1858–94): Brahms subscribed to this too, and realized the continuo parts for the vocal Duets and Trios published in Volume 32. Chrysander was also general editor of an important series of *Denkmäler der Tonkunst* (1871) including motets by Palestrina, Corelli's trio sonatas (edited by Joachim), works by Carissimi, and Couperin's *Pièces de Clavecin*. Brahms owned all the volumes, and himself edited the Couperin at Chrysander's request: moreover, with Chrysander and Spitta he co-founded a *Denkmäler deutscher Tonkunst* which began with an edition of Samuel Scheidt's *Tablatura Nova*: and in 1892, with Bülow, he organized a fund to enable Chrysander to publish a facsimile edition of Handel's *Messiah*.

The somewhat older Gustav Nottebohm was perhaps an even more

146

significant figure for Brahms, partly because their friendship seems to have been closer, and because of the sheer range of his work. He is nowadays almost solely remembered for his pioneering work on Beethoven's sketchbooks, for he was the first scholar to see that these documents afforded illuminating insights into the growth and transformation of Beethoven's musical conceptions. This was a subject Brahms and he must have discussed closely, not least because Brahms himself owned various Beethoven sketches; indeed it is sometimes thought that he was so scrupulous about destroying his own sketch-material because he wanted to avoid any future Nottebohm laying bare his compositional processes after his death! But Nottebohm also carried out studies of Mozart and Schubert, edited Bach, Handel, Beethoven and Mendelssohn; and he was, like Brahms, a passionate collector of early music. Soon after they first met, during Brahms's first visits to Vienna, Nottebohm allowed Brahms to transcribe items from his own manuscript copies of polyphonic folksong settings by composers such as Zirler, Walther, Förster and Senfl; and after Nottebohm's death in 1882 (Brahms was at his bedside, and gave the oration at his funeral) he inherited not only this collection but Nottebohm's six remarkable, mainly manuscript volumes of 'Alte Instrumentalcompositionen' – a gigantic compendium featuring many transcriptions from early-sixteenth-century lute tablature and literally hundreds of pieces by such composers (and this is merely a random selection) as Arbeau, Buxtehude, Banchieri, Bononcini, Byrd, Caldara, Carissimi, Campra, Cavalli, Cesti, Corelli, Dandrieu, Dowland, Erbach, Frescobaldi, Froberger, Hasse, Johnson, Keiser, Kerll, Lully, Marchand, Pachelbel, Pasquini, Playford, Quagliati, Rameau, Scheidt, Titelouze, Vivaldi, Willaert, and Zarlino – not only beautifully copied but meticulously edited, annotated and provided with textual variants by Nottebohm himself. (There seems never to have been a thorough study of the collection, which remains part of Brahms's library; so this aspect of Nottebohm's scholarship, as an early music pioneer, remains so far unexplored and unappreciated.)

Brahms took his place with these musicologists as an editor, bringing little-known works to publication and performance. His Couperin Edition and Handel continuo realizations, both carried out at Chrysander's request, have already been mentioned. But he also produced editions of concerti by C. P. E. Bach, oboe sonatas by the same composer (with continuo realizations), a Sonata for two claviers by W. F Bach (interestingly enough he was working on this about the time of his own two-piano Sonata, op. 34); and carried out the vitally important task of revising Mozart's Requiem for the critical Collected Edition, attempting to establish what Mozart actually wrote and separating this from

Süssmayr's subsequent additions and changes. While these were all published in his lifetime, Brahms also edited various small choral works by Bach, Eccard, Mozart and Ahle for his own performances, and for the same reason provided new continuo parts for Bach's Cantatas nos. 4 and 21 (the latter was unfortunately lost in a fire that largely destroyed the archives of the Vienna Singakademie in 1979). He was equally active in editing more recent music, especially for the Complete Editions being published by Breitkopf & Härtel – such as Schubert (whose Symphonies he edited for the Complete Edition, as well as much piano music for other publishers), Chopin (four volumes for Breitkopf, including the Sonatas and Mazurkas); and of course Schumann. Between 1879 and 1893 Breitkopf issued Schumann's Collected Works, officially under the sole editorship of the composer's widow. In fact Clara sought and received advice from many Schumann disciples, and there is no doubt that Brahms was her chief adviser and helper in this strenuous undertaking – although it was the cause of many tensions between them, especially their bitter quarrel over publication of the first version of the Fourth Symphony, which almost threatened to wreck their long association. He himself edited the supplementary volume, including the *Etudes Symphoniques* with the five variations Schumann had discarded.

One is, as often, amazed at the energy of the man. It is a mystery how he found the time to carry out all his studies and editorial work; yet one is tempted to say that had he never composed anything of his own, he would still have been reckoned as one of the leading musical scholars of his age. Not that he would have agreed. '...I am sorry to say I know by experience that I am not a good editor', he wrote to Clara in 1891:

> I have often tried my hand at it, and brought love and enthusiasm to bear, but it is impossible for me to give myself a testimonial for such work and I have to confess that others are far better fitted for the task...

Beyond his editorial endeavours it is perhaps significant that he made no contributions to the scholarly literature: no book, no articles in learned journals (not even the *Vierteljahrsschrift für Musikwissenschaft* jointly edited by Chrysander, Spitta and Guido Adler, which Brahms subscribed to from time to time but did not always bother to read). He did, perhaps, once plan a treatise on a subject that particularly interested him: at any rate he left a manuscript (finally published by Heinrich Schenker to mark the centenary of Brahms's birth) which looks like a collection of music examples to an unwritten main text, begun sometime in the 1860s and added to at intervals; Brahms entitled it *Octaven u. Quinten u. A.* ('Octaves and Fifths, et cetera'), and it is a document of very great interest, although its precise purpose remains enigmatic.

Essentially, it gives examples of voice-leading in polyphony that result in situations which are traditionally 'forbidden' or considered 'inadmissable' by strict contrapuntal theory – in particular, consecutive octaves and fifths. The chosen specimens – over a hundred of them – testify to the astonishing breadth of Brahms's studies; ranging as they do from Caldara, Clemens non Papa, Gabrieli, Hassler, Lassus, Marenzio, Palestrina, Praetorius and Schütz through Cherubini, Gluck, Haydn, Méhul and Mozart, to Hiller, Schumann and even Bizet's *Carmen*. He records comparatively few instances of crude parallel motion; but many where the parallelism is disguised in various ways, or results from decoration of the principal polyphonic lines – and nearly all of them are carefully identified, cross-referenced, and annotated with brief (and occasionally obscure) comments. The important thing that emerges from the material is that Brahms did not necessarily consider consecutive octaves or fifths evidence of faulty composition; on the contrary, he distinguished between good and bad, skilful and unskilful employments of these polyphonic formulae, and clearly relished what he considered especially effective cases. What he seems to have been trying to establish in *Octaven u. Quinten* were the circumstances in which such violations of contrapuntal doctrine were justified by the expressiveness of their effect.

This helps to clarify the nature of Brahms's commitment – to all music, but especially to early music as the repository of the contrapuntal mastery he wished to repossess. His instincts and capabilities were scholarly, but they were not academic: he wanted accuracy and availability so that the repertoire could be enlarged and the music performed, not just discussed. His approach was rigorous but not doctrinaire: his ultimate criterion was expressive rightness, fidelity to the nature of the work as a whole. It goes without saying that the composers most capable of that fidelity would be those with the greatest technical skill. But the skill should not be a barren one. He detested arid displays of mere technique, as he detested lifelessness in performance. From the performing materials that survive from the concerts he conducted, we can see that – once he had arrived at a 'correct' musical text – he added many detailed expression marks, dynamics, crescendi and decrescendi to enhance the work's effect, and was quite prepared to change details of orchestration (adding violas to the cellos and basses at the opening of a Handel organ concerto, for instance) if he felt this would give a more satisfying sound. Although he paid much greater attention than many of his contemporaries to what the composer had actually written, he would not have shared the modern passion for 'authenticity' in performance. He was no purist; he was committed to the clearest and most vivid presentation of musical ideas.

By the same token he had no qualms about arranging other composers' works for new media: he provided orchestral accompaniments for some Schubert songs and produced a number of piano transcriptions (which he called 'Studies') partly for his own interest and partly to enlarge the keyboard repertoire. Though much less active in this field than, say, Liszt or Busoni, he would clearly have agreed with Busoni's dictum that the act of composition is itself an act of transcription, and his few examples take their place among the classics of the arranger's art – none more so than the magisterial version of Bach's D minor Chaconne for unaccompanied violin, transcribed as a piano work for the left hand alone. Most of his piano arrangements do indeed have a technical purpose, usually to do with strengthening the left hand or ensuring absolute equality between hands (as in his two versions of the Presto from Bach's G major Violin Sonata: the second assigns the first version's right-hand material to the left, and vice versa). But the impulse was also sheer pleasure, as he made clear to Clara when he sent her the manuscript of the Chaconne transcription in 1877:

> The *Chaconne* is in my opinion one of the most wonderful and most incomprehensible pieces of music. Using the technique adapted to a small instrument the man writes a whole world of the deepest thoughts and most powerful feelings. If I could picture myself writing, or even conceiving, such a piece, I am certain that the extreme excitement and emotional tension would have driven me mad. If one has no supremely great violinist at hand, the most exquisite of joys is probably simply to let the *Chaconne* ring in one's mind. But the piece certainly inspires one to occupy oneself with it somehow ... and in any case Joachim is not always there, so one tries it otherwise ... There is only one way in which I can secure undiluted joy from the piece, though on a small and only approximate scale, and that is when I play it with the left hand alone ... The same difficulty, the nature of the technique, the rendering of the arpeggios, everything conspires to make me – feel like a violinist!

Brahms's dealings with the music of the past are most clearly illustrated in his attitudes to German folksong, with which he occupied himself for practically fifty years, producing multitudinous settings of pre-existing tunes and absorbing their contours and cadences until they became an essential ingredient of his own melodic idiom. In 1880, his earliest biographer, Hermann Dieters, was already pointing out Brahms's unusually strong debt to secular and spiritual folksong, averring that he had thus remained in closer touch with the essential elements of music than had Schumann. Brahms certainly valued folksong no less than he did polyphonic church music: both genres were to be considered 'old music', with the peculiar virtues that attached to age – above all, closeness to the sources of primal creation. As study of the latter genre schooled him in the skills of counterpoint, the former enabled him to respect the demands of direct, expressive melody and preserve a fundamental lyric impulse.

The revaluation of folksong, like that of older art music, was one of Romanticism's cardinal achievements. Herder's *Stimmen der Völker* had stimulated Achim and Brentano's famous folk poetry collection *Des Knaben Wunderhorn* (1805–8), and this in turn had inspired the work of pioneering collectors of folk melodies – most notably August Kretzschmer and Anton Wilhelm von Zuccalmaglio, joint editors of *Deutsche Volkslieder mit ihren Original-Weisen* (1838–40), and Friedrich Wilhelm Arnold. In the 1850s Brahms met and corresponded with Arnold, who lived near Düsseldorf and had known Schumann, and Brahms was allowed to copy out materials from his collection. He first studied the Kretzschmer–Zuccalmaglio anthology in Schumann's library; his own copy was a present from his friend Karl Grädener in 1856. Despite its shortcomings (the editors plundered the work of previous collectors without acknowledgement, 'Romanticized' some of the tunes, altered others to regularize their rhythms, and included recently written melodies and texts, sometimes even of their own composition, which they occasionally identified as '*Altdeutsch*'!) it remained his favourite source for the tunes he dealt with throughout his life. He did not himself 'prospect' for folksongs in the field;[2] but he made a more thoroughgoing use of such printed and manuscript sources than any composer before him, to bring the melodies and poems into the field of concert and domestic performance.

Between the late 1840s and the mid 1890s Brahms made well over two hundred folksong arrangements, generally for unaccompanied voices or for voice(s) and piano. Some tunes were set several times for various media. The most numerous arrangements date from the late 1850s and early 1860s, and can be associated with his need to provide a repertoire for the Frauenchor, the Detmold choir, and the Singakademie. There are also many simple settings for voice and piano from the

[2]Nor did any of this generation of folklorists, of course. Few of their 'folksongs' actually derived from the peasantry; a larger proportion of what they culled from old manuscripts and part-books were urban or domestic songs, often composed by professionals (such as the relatively 'learned' Minnesingers). On this basis it has sometimes been claimed that Germany has no true folk music – an exaggeration, needless to say, and in any case irrelevant to the fact that Brahms believed the melodies represented a genuine musical culture of the people.

same period. Most of these Brahms did not himself think worthy of publication (one of his exceptions was the *Volks-Kinderlieder*). In general the choral settings were simple harmonizations of his chosen melodies with little or no polyphonic movement, rigorously adhering to a plain strophic design with the same music for each verse. The settings with piano allowed rather greater variety in the accompaniments, but were equally uncomplicated in form. (The *Volks-Kinderlieder* have a couple of modest piano solo interludes and codas.) A few found their way into his official 'art song' output. An example is *Sehnsucht*, composed in 1858 as the last of the op. 14 Lieder: a typical specimen of Brahms's setting of folk text (and folk-melody) at its most unassuming, the melody at the top of a simple chordal texture, mainly triadic and usually in four parts. A couple of years later he made an even simpler version for the Hamburger Frauenchor, a setting for three-part female chorus that merely omits one note from each chord (often but not always from the lowest voice, so the movement of the harmony is sometimes different).

His principal monument in folksong setting, however, is the superb set of forty-nine *Deutsche Volkslieder* for voice and piano (the last seven also with chorus refrains) which he published in 1894. Brahms took enormous pride in this undertaking – as much as, and probably a good deal more than, in many of his 'original' compositions. Here he brought to bear a lifetime's experience in dealing with folksong material, to create highly personal works of art. His purpose was partly polemical. A new generation of folksong collectors had arisen (for example, Ludwig Erk and Franz Böhme), and though Brahms studied their works he found them deficient in aesthetic sense. In particular he felt that in the cause of 'scientific' completeness the later collectors included far too many songs that were of negligible musical interest; and he frankly resented the fact that they cast doubt on the authenticity of many tunes he had relished since his youth. His 1894 *Volkslieder*, drawn almost entirely from the collections of Arnold and his beloved Kretzschmer–Zuccalmaglio, and including many melodies that he had worked with before, was therefore intended as a summation of what he considered the choicest folksongs: not necessarily the most authentic ones, but the most beautiful, the most affecting, the most stimulating to creative endeavour.

The result is a series of miniature masterpieces worthy to stand with any of his art songs of the same period. Indeed in all essentials these *are* art songs. Perfectly complementing texts grave, gay, homely, pious, teasing, macabre, or discreetly erotic, they are full of unobtrusive harmonic subtleties, poetic detail, and formal ingenuity; the tunes are absorbed into an overall conception so thoroughly and self-consistently Brahmsian that he might well have written them, too. His ultimate structural ideal remains the simplicity of the strophic song; but this is enlarged, enlivened, and varied in many cunning ways – for instance with slightly different music for later verses of the text, repetitions of one half-strophe but not the other, or (especially in narrative songs) progressive and expressive variation of the accompaniment as the tale proceeds.

The immense advance in Brahms's setting manners (and his song-writer's art as a whole) is most graphically illustrated in those *Volks-lieder* which look anew at tunes he had set many years before. Consider for instance no. 28, *Es reit ein Herr und auch sein Knecht*, a ballad about a squire's jealousy of his knightly master, the knight's murder, and his lady's grief. Brahms had made a setting of text and tune in 1858: Ex. 22a shows the result. Look now at Ex. 22b, the start of his 1894 setting. The entire conception has been rethought. In 1858 a single harmonization served for all eight verses; the 1894 setting has five varied, atmos-pherically developing sections, involving only three exact repetitions. There is a tiny but effective chordal prelude (destined for development at the song's mid-point). The key has descended from C minor to the deeper and darker E flat minor, necessitating very slight reshaping of the tune itself. The bass line's scalic descent is augmented both rhythmically and intervallically into a tenebrous chain of falling thirds, a Brahmsian trademark shared with the Fourth Symphony and the *Vier ernste Gesänge* (the way the right hand echoes the left is especially reminiscent of the Symphony's opening). The accompaniment, in short, no longer apes the tune and provides it with harmonic filling, but develops from it motivically – and the gain in substance and expression is incalculable.

In lighter mood, we might look at the case of the hump-backed fiddler of Frankfurt. Brahms found this song (in which four witches engage the fiddler to play for their dance on Walpurgis night, and reward him by magically removing his hump) in the Kretzschmer–Zuccalmaglio collection, identified as a 'Rhenish folksong'. He was clearly very fond of it, for he set the tune three times, and used the text for a fourth, independent composition. In the early 1860s he made two strictly strophic, modestly homophonic choral versions of the tune, both under the title *Der Fiedler* – one for the Frauenchor and the other an SATB setting for the Vienna Singakademie. About twenty years later he set the words of the song to a tune of his own as *Der bucklichte Fiedler*, the first of the op. 93a partsongs. This progressively varies Brahms's tune and has much more sophisticated chordal textures, including a

Brahms

Ex. 22

(a)

Lebhaft und Schauerlich

Bass Voice

1. Es reit ein Herr und auch sein Knecht wohl üb'r ein' Hei - de

Piano

p

legato

die war schlecht, ja schlecht, und al - les was sie re-d'ten da, war

all's von ei - ner schö-nen Frau - en, ja Frau - en.

rit.

(A lord and his squire rode over the gloomy moor,
and all their talk was of a beautiful lady.)

154

(b)

quite daring vocal imitation of open-string fiddle sonorities. After
another decade had passed, he returned to the original folksong and
produced a final version as one of the 1894 *Volkslieder*, now titled
according to the text's first line, 'Es wohnet ein Fiedler'. This voice and

155

piano setting begins strophically but has a much elaborated second half – separated from the first two verses by a piano imitation of the violin's open strings, completely different from but clearly suggested by the one in op. 93a. Here again, the boundaries between what constitutes 'folk' and 'high' art are not so much blurred as deliberately ignored. In any case, the issue is further clouded by the fact that this 'Rhenish folksong' is almost certainly Zuccalmaglio's own composition – which clearly in no way diminished Brahms's affection for it. He had thought it a good tune thirty years previously, and a good tune it remained.

The fact that he was prepared to defend such gravely suspect 'folksongs', and indeed glorify them by his attentions, bespeaks a strong emotional attachment that took precedence over scholarly scruples. Perhaps we should expect that, from a researcher who religiously scraped Schubert's writing-sand from his manuscripts and kept it in a little box. Brahms may have possessed a much clearer and better informed sense of the past than most of his contemporaries, but it was still irradiated by a Romantic imagination. The 1894 *Volkslieder* present a world of gallant knights, deserted maidens, enchanted fiddlers, repentant nuns, lovers both sad and happy, and Death the Reaper – an idealized medieval world, fit for the dreams of Young Kreisler. Yet Kreisler could not have envisioned it with such serene sincerity. We may, if we wish, stigmatize Brahms's passion for folksong as a sentimental escape from nineteenth-century urban society. It was left to the young Gustav Mahler to invest such folk sources with the overwhelming sense of dissociation and loss that irony and parody can bring, and it is astonishing to think that his *Des Knaben Wunderhorn* songs were being composed during the very years that Brahms was compiling his *Volkslieder*. For Brahms, no less sceptical in his everyday thinking than Mahler, but less self-tortured in his Romanticism, the folk vision deserved to be presented straight, with all the power that 'high' art could bring to its support. The past might be another country, but it needed loving conservation if people were to visit it in their minds.

7

The music of the middle years, 1860–75

The whole winter I have been studying counterpoint most assiduously. What for? To be able the better to run down my beautiful things? – I do not need counterpoint for that. To become a Professor at the Academy? – no not that either. To be able to write MS music better? – I do not even aspire to that! But there certainly is an element of tragedy about becoming in the end too clever for one's needs.

Brahms to Clara Schumann, Easter 1872

Brahms's music does not easily group itself into 'periods'. The lineaments of his style were foreshadowed in the first years of his compositional activity, and were not subject to abrupt change. Even his earliest music has such strength of character and technical command that it is difficult to speak of immaturity giving way to maturity. There is, certainly, a gradual development by which ever more thorough mastery of the essentials of his craft led to an ever closer match of means and manner with expression; to a deepening profundity; and to the ability to say more and more with fewer and fewer notes. But this was by no means as easy for Brahms as it now looks to us, and it was achieved only by unremitting hard work. The 1860s found him capitalizing on the gains he had made with his contrapuntal studies in the previous decade, and experimenting in large but intricate forms, especially in the field of chamber music. It was only with the *Deutsches Requiem*, largely composed between 1865 and 1867, that he created a grand synthesis of all he had learnt, and deployed a comprehensive mastery upon the largest scale. The *Requiem* was a watershed: only after its remarkable success was Brahms able to finish many projects that had lain incomplete for years, and to advance with total confidence into the great abstract forms – especially symphony and string quartet – that had tantalized him for so long.

157

Chamber works of the 1860s

The String Sextet in B flat, Brahms's first published chamber work without piano, forms a convenient bridge into this quite large group of pieces, for it was begun in 1859 and could be regarded as the final fruit of his Detmold period. It is also a direct successor to the orchestral Serenades, displaying a good measure of their genial expansiveness of atmosphere and form. At this stage Brahms seems to have felt more at ease with the comparatively large string ensemble – two violins, two violas, two cellos – than the string quartet. It must have suggested something less strenuously polyphonic, more relaxed melodically and motivically: there were no daunting Classical precedents that he must equal. Not that the work lacks subtleties in all these areas; but it wears its learning (including, in the slow movement, the close study of strict Baroque variation forms) very lightly, cloaked beneath an almost rustic squareness of themes and the rich sonorities which the ensemble affords. The presence of two cellos frequently allows Brahms to entrust cello II with the bass line while freeing cello I for the principal melodic statements: indeed it is this instrument, rather than the violins, which seems to lead the ensemble much of the time, enhancing the mellow colouring of the work as a whole. The start of the first movement is a case in point. Joachim found the original fuller opening, at what is now bar 11, too abrupt, and on his advice Brahms prefaced this with an announcement of the initial theme on cello I. The movement's Schubertian breadth has often been commented upon: it has two subsidiary themes – one gravely angular, growing out of the first theme's cadence-figure, with pizzicato responses from viola and cello, the other a lyrical cello theme with an undulating accompaniment – and behind all three lurks the spirit of the Ländler, the slow waltz of the Austrian countryside, of which Schubert left so many examples. The development is based on the first two themes, while the third comes into its own in the coda, taking over the pizzicato characteristics of the second to produce a particularly atmospheric and delicate close.

The ensuing slow movement is a set of variations in D minor on a stern but noble theme of archaic cut, whose rigid adherence to the theme's proportions suggests a debt to Bach's great D minor Chaconne. An important example of Brahms's developing variation technique, fully comparable with the various piano variations,[1] it clearly provided him

---

[1] Brahms indeed made a solo piano version of these Variations at Clara Schumann's request. Most modern writers seem to find his arrangement ineffective, but it became a great favourite of his own, and his performance of it to Florence May became one of her most treasured artistic memories.

with valuable experience for the Variations and Fugue on a Theme of Handel, soon to be composed. These Sextet variations so transform the theme, and are so rich in their contrasted sonorities, that they completely surmount the strictness of the form. The third variation, with its turbulent ebb and flow of rapid scales on the two cellos; the magniloquent fourth, giving the theme its most impassioned expression in the major; and the sixth – a spectral coda, with the theme returning as a shadow of itself on solo cello – are perhaps the most memorable features in a movement that, while not among Brahms's subtlest, is nevertheless worthy to stand with his greatest.

The Scherzo is very short but high-spirited, with a fiery Trio that returns in the coda; the country-dance character of both portions is another link with the Serenades. The Finale, by contrast, is the longest movement of all – an unhurried, loose-limbed Rondo whose ambling motion and melodic generosity are again reminiscent of Schubert. With its initial solo cello statement of the rondo theme and striking use of pizzicato towards the end, it creates several deliberate parallels with the first movement. It also takes over a subsidiary rhythmic figure from that movement and turns it into an important three-note motif which is cannily developed: in the form of two crotchets plus a minim this becomes the accompaniment to the first-episode theme and then the focus of the second episode, which assumes the character of a spirited development. (Ex. 23 shows the main features of the process, a good example of Brahms's capacity to create a large-scale organic unity out of the simplest motivic materials.) The rondo theme itself is wittily treated at later appearances despite its peaceful character. Brahms first splits it into two halves, violins and viola I answered by viola II and cello; later, just before the coda, these instrumental groups reduce it to its bare bones, lobbing it back and forth as a series of simple two-note groups.

Ex. 23

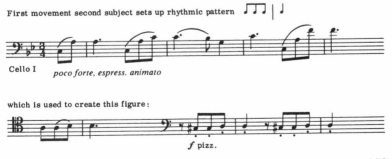

First movement second subject sets up rhythmic pattern

Cello I   *poco forte, espress. animato*

which is used to create this figure:

f pizz.

Brahms

In Finale this becomes:

(Cellos)

then:

then in the Coda:

Animato, poco a poco più

If this Sextet seems near kin to the Serenades, the Piano Quartets and Quintet which followed it are altogether more 'symphonic' in their formal ambitions and range of contrast. The Piano Quartet in G minor, op. 25, is Brahms's official 'no. 1' in this form, but he had already expended considerable efforts on one in C sharp minor, which would appear many years later as his op. 60, in a different key and a greatly

160

rethought form. Although the shape of that early quartet is now impossible to reconstruct, it appears to have had several boldly unorthodox features (perhaps combining the functions of scherzo and finale, for instance). Its G minor successor (possibly conceived about 1857, drafted in Detmold in 1859 and polished up in Hamburg until 1861) has a more outwardly conventional four-movement design, yet each movement produces its share of structural and stylistic surprises. Clara and Joachim both seem to have thought the work a little undisciplined, and the first two movements bear some of the marks of *Sturm und Drang* – but its vigour and capriciousness are among the qualities which have most endeared it to audiences ever since.

In fact the work seems continually to strive beyond its chosen medium, towards an orchestral sense of colour, scope of expression and developmental range. (To a repertoire which had almost forgotten Beethoven's last quartets and hardly knew Schubert's C major Quintet, such impulses seemed stranger than they do today.) The sombre, spacious first movement presents an unusually large number of distinct ideas, linked by a complex network of shared motivic and rhythmic elements, in strangely fluid tonal perspectives (Clara complained it was 'more D major than G minor'). It was the most searching sonata movement Brahms had yet written, counterposing a ruthless concentration (in the comparatively brief development section) on the one-bar motif that makes up the very first theme, with a reckless expansiveness in the outer sections and an unparalleled reshuffling of the exposition's elements in the recapitulation, even introducing a completely new idea. There is energy and lyricism in plenty, but the movement is never untroubled, continually questioning its own premises; and no comforting answer is found, for the coda, beginning hopefully with sweet *tranquillo* writing for strings alone, blazes up in a passion only to gutter out quietly in implied frustration. But there is no trace of the problems that afflicted the corresponding movement of the op. 8 Trio; this one imposes its own expressive logic with masterly force.

Brahms originally called the C minor second movement a Scherzo, but it has little in common with the dynamic scherzi of his earliest works, and the later title of Intermezzo suits it better. It is one of the first examples of a species of movement Brahms was to make peculiarly his own (most conspicuously in the first three symphonies): a delicate, moderate-paced, rather subdued interlude full of expressive half-lights, whose poignant understatement throws the larger movements into relief. This is certainly the effect of the main theme, a haunting version of the 'Clara-motif' unfolded by viola and muted violin against a throbbing pedal in the cello. The Trio, in A flat, is brighter and more animated, with rippling piano figuration, but retains the characteristic rhythm of the scherzo theme.

The Andante con moto, in E flat, presents itself first as a full-hearted song, the long arching lines of melody calmly flowing on the string instruments, with the piano in a mainly accompanimental role. As it develops, however, a sprightlier dotted rhythm makes itself felt, and this leads to a C major central section in the form of a strutting, almost military march, whose rumbustious good spirits strongly suggest orchestral textures, and which works up to a climax that cries out for trumpets and drums. This colourful parade somehow resolves the expressive tensions that had shadowed the work until this point, making possible the sheer animal vitality of the Finale, a 'Rondo alla Zingarese' which belongs to an occasional tradition of 'gypsy' finales that goes back to Haydn.

Yet it startingly extends that tradition, and is the most flamboyant and unbuttoned episode in Brahms's long love-affair with the popular and exotic Hungarian idioms he had imbibed from Reményi and Joachim. If the main theme, with its headlong rhythmic impetus and curious three-bar phrasing, could be an unusually choleric Hungarian Dance, the structure which Brahms proceeds to build on it is much more elaborate: yet the music's devil-may-care abandon takes us very far from the intellectual concentration of the first movement. The movement's extremes of pulse, virtuosity and emotional affliction suggest that his tongue was at least half in his cheek, while the extravagant piano cadenza that forestalls the whirlwind coda seems to parody Liszt himself.

(While connoisseurs of chamber music have revelled in this work for generations, it has more recently become familiar to a much wider audience in the brilliant transcription for full orchestra made in 1937 by Arnold Schoenberg, who had often played it as a violist and cellist. At the time, this *tour de force* of the arranger's art was thought merely eccentric, but in the past twenty years it has achieved the wide currency Schoenberg hoped for through many performances and recordings. Schoenberg's notorious embellishments to the Finale, including trombone glissandi and a large percussion battery including xylophone and glockenspiel, only serve to emphasize the uproarious nature of Brahms's invention.)

The Piano Quartet no. 2 in A major, which followed in short order and was presented to the public at the same time (as op. 26), makes a fascinating contrast. Clara Schumann preferred it, and in Brahms's lifetime it was the more frequently performed of the two; but subsequently it seems to have gained a reputation for excessive length and worthiness, perhaps because three of its four movements are cast in expansive sonata form, and is less often heard in the concert-hall than the other quartets. This is unfair: the work is a masterpiece – more obviously 'Classical' in conception, perhaps the 'Apollonian' response to its 'Dionysian' G minor cousin, but with plenty of the same gypsy energy directed now to less picturesque but equally satisfying ends. It manifests a comparable though less emphatic tendency to a 'symphonic' scale of argument, and a 'heavenly' length that testifies to Brahms's (by now) close study of Schubert. The first movement, one of the broadest and most exquisitely poised sonata designs he ever wrote, is as closely worked as that of op. 25 and yet essentially lyric in effect. The opening idea (Ex. 24), whose two rhythmically distinct halves are apt for separate courses of development yet achieve a statuesque balance of force, easily dominates the movement despite a rich supporting cast of subsidiary themes, and has the last word as it had the first. The Poco Adagio, at least, has always been admired, its large but subtle ternary form articulating what Joachim called its 'ambiguous passion'. The muting of the strings until the reprise throws the piano, with its mysterious desolate Aeolian-harp flourishes and ardent second theme, into unusual relief, looking twenty years forward towards the style of Brahms's Second Piano Concerto. The 'shadowing' of the piano's tranquil, song-like opening theme by the strings, and its gypsy-style cadential turn, are developed at length in ever more floridly decorated thematic statements that put this among Brahms's most beautiful slow movements. The muted sonorities return in the coda, hushing and chastening the full-hearted lyricism.

Ex. 24

That sonata-form Scherzo is yet another new venture in this genre that Brahms used so resourcefully. The easily flowing quaver motion of the first subject seems at first too mild for a scherzo, too plain for a character-intermezzo like the comparable movement of op. 25 – yet it proves apt for an inexorable build-up of immense melodic spans, emphasizing the symphonic scale of the music. A more animated rhythmic interest is relegated to the quaver figuration of the transition passage that leads to the second subject. Yet the Trio proceeds to base itself on a variation of this transition theme, now turned fiery and Hungarian but treated with ruthless discipline as a canon at the unison between piano and strings. Previous generations of critics accordingly labelled the movement 'dry' and 'academic', a mistake which is unlikely to be made again since the contrapuntal masters of the early twentieth century, Schoenberg and Busoni, have taught us to recognize the life-giving energy and precision of thought that proceeds from strict canonic principles, imaginatively applied.

The last movement is not a rondo but another fully worked sonata design, yet its first subject has plenty of the capricious Hungarian colouring of op. 25's 'Zingaresca' Finale. Its exotic flavour and idiosyncratic rhythms are, however, subordinated to an ample and unhurried overall form whose length proceeds Schubert-like from the sheer size of the melodic paragraphs themselves, creating an Olympian mood of relaxed strength that satisfyingly balances the stability of the equally large first movement. This is a Finale that takes its time, and enjoys the taking of it, and it aptly rounds off a work whose perfectly achieved mastery is all the more remarkable for being so consistently understated.

Brahms's next work for piano and strings, the Piano Quintet in F minor, op. 34, is one of the most eloquent testimonies to the mood of *Sturm und Drang* that still possessed him in the early 1860s, and one of the several crucial works which underwent a complicated genesis – in this case, one that parallels the First Piano Concerto. What Brahms first wrote, in 1862, was a String Quintet, for the Schubertian (as opposed to Mozartian) ensemble of a string quartet with a second cello: its relations to Schubert's C major Quintet were probably even clearer in this form than they are now. He remained unsure about the piece, however, and Joachim convinced him it would be too difficult and not sufficiently effective for strings alone. Brahms accordingly suppressed that version, and recast its material as a Sonata for two pianos – which he premièred in public with Carl Tausig in 1864. But at the urging of Clara, who saw this Sonata as 'only an arrangement', he returned to the music for a third time and reworked it as the Quintet for piano and strings, generally acclaimed as its most successful realization – although the two-piano Sonata has its champions (Brahms remained sufficiently pleased with it to have it published), and has maintained a foothold on the repertoire.

Whatever the claims of its different media (there are certainly passages where the sheer percussive capabilities of two pianos seem to have the edge, especially in the Scherzo), op. 34 is self-evidently one of Brahms's most significant compositional statements so far, perhaps the archetypal masterpiece of the early 1860s. In many respects it synthesizes and capitalizes on the different advances he had already made in the chamber music genres, particularly the piano trios and quartets, and brings his attempted unification of the 'dynamic' Beethovenian impulse and the 'lyrical' Schubertian one to its most intense expression yet. The formal solutions by which he achieves his goal are masterly, but the result is a work full of tension and shadowed by minor-key conflict, magnificent in utterance but often sombre or thunderous in its moods.

One of the principal forces behind that tension – and a fine example of Brahms's increasing ability to compose a large-scale unity outward from the smallest motivic elements of his design – is the extent to which the Quintet's very varied materials are dominated by the interval of the minor second: the semitonal fall or rise which has always been among music's most graphic metaphors for emotional disturbance. This in turn reflects an aspect of Brahms's large-scale tonal planning, which lays unusual stress on keys that have a semitonal (or Neapolitan) relationship to the tonic and dominant of his principal tonality (e.g. F sharp minor and C sharp minor/D flat major in relation to his main key of F minor). Ex. 25 illustrates how comprehensively the principal ideas throughout the work are linked by the feature of a significant semitone (bracketed(x)); it also reveals some larger, surprising thematic correspondences of shape and rhythm (bracketed (y)) established across the movements, especially between first movement and Scherzo.

The sinuous idea announced at the outset (Ex. 25a) not only contains this semitonal seed but establishes a melodic shape that is varied throughout the entire work; indeed the variation process begins at once with the arrival of the theme's second half (Ex. 25b), a dramatic interruption which gives both (a) and (b) a merely introductory character until a grand unison statement of (a) gets the movement on its way (this has important consequences for the Finale, with its full-blown formal introduction). The transition to the second subject produces further dramatic semitonal stresses (Ex. 25c) and the various elements of the second subject (Ex. 25d, e, f) are almost exclusively concerned with different aspects of it, most atmospherically in the sinister bass tremolo of Ex. 25e. As Ex. 25e shows, this second group largely centres around

Brahms

C sharp minor, a semitone above the orthodox dominant. During the recapitulation, when it might have been expected to appear in the tonic F minor, Brahms presents the material a semitone higher, in F *sharp* minor, reinforcing a parallel Neapolitan relationship, and deliberately withholding the clinching and confirmatory effect of conventional sonata structure. Note too how the melancholy Ex. 25d varies the shape of (a). Despite its prevailing mood of grim determination against the claims of sorrow, the coda of this movement contains some wonderfully tranquil writing for strings alone that gives some idea of the sound of Brahms's original String Quintet.

Ex. 25

(a)

(b)

(c)

(d)

166

(e)

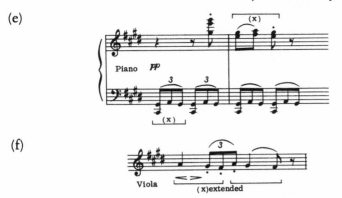

(f)

Some of that tranquillity adheres to the A flat major slow movement, a calm ternary structure whose main theme, built out of an infinitely extendable one-bar refrain with a charmingly hesitant accompaniment, brings to mind the character of a Schubert song. The second theme, in E major, with the piano's strummed accompanying chords, is more dramatic and instrumental in conception, but the mood remains comparatively untroubled. This polarity of A flat/E mimics, in the relative major, the F minor/C sharp minor contrast of the first movement, providing emotional respite while reinforcing its tonal argument. The movement seems at first to stand outside the motivic preoccupations of the rest of the work; but in the transition back to the first theme motivic fragmentation emphasizes the semitone once again (Ex. 25g), casting that theme's continued pensive alternations of major and minor in a new light, and this is further stressed (Ex. 25h) in the lead-in to the coda. Thus the peaceful beauty of its last bars contains a tiny cloud in the viola's E flat – F flat oscillation.

Ex. 25
(g)

(h)

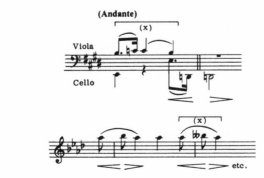

The Scherzo, approaching the key of C minor via A flat with a theme (Ex. 25i) that unwinds in serpentine syncopation over a pizzicato cello pedal, soon blazons itself forth as the supreme example thus far of those taut, virile, dynamic scherzi that Brahms had been cultivating since his earliest piano works. The insistent, convulsive dotted rhythm of its second theme (Ex. 25j) reveals a kinship with the equally obsessive Scherzo of Beethoven's C minor Symphony (and, surprisingly, to Ex. 25d from Brahms's first movement); the third theme (Ex. 25k) makes more specific reference to Beethoven's famous triplet figure while remaining thoroughly Brahmsian in its grand striding motion (and transforming Ex. 25d in a different way). This is perhaps the most 'demonic' of all Brahms's scherzi, driven by an apparently unquenchable rhythmic impulse; Ex. 25j's obsessiveness is underlined by fugal treatment and a fusillade of hammered syncopation between strings and piano. Again there is a concentration on the D flat area, leading to snarling semitonal appoggiature at the close (Ex. 25l). The Trio is taken at the same inexorable tempo, its broad singing tune and forthright C major apparently a strong and positive contrast: yet the tune develops straight out of the Scherzo's third theme, and the nagging triplet rhythm never really departs from the accompaniment.

Most surprising of all is the Finale, which virtually creates its own form. Insofar as labels convey anything it is a concise, moderate-paced

Ex. 25

(l)

sonata form whose recapitulation doubles as development, enclosed by a slow introduction and a huge, very fast coda. Brahms was to return to this kind of design in the finale of his First Symphony – not least the dramatic effect of the *Poco sostenuto* introduction: numb, ghostly string figures (Ex. 25m), groping their way in glacial imitation into perhaps the most emotionally afflicted music the work has yet encompassed, the rising semitone emphasizing the Neapolitan relationship once again. The arrival of the Finale proper, with a sturdy cello tune of almost Haydnesque aplomb and Classical cut (Ex. 25n) comes as a witty relaxation that Haydn himself might have appreciated. But the second subject brings back the fevered Romanticism of the introduction, starting with a string theme of pronounced lyric pathos (Ex. 25o) and proceeding to a vigorous subsidiary idea (Ex. 25p) whose fast triplet rhythms are more agitated than exuberant. The transition back to the first subject, almost in salon style, comes as further humorous relaxation, but the darker moods prevail, and are massively confirmed in the Presto, non troppo coda. Beginning in C sharp minor, this turns the first subject Ex. 25n into a staccato blizzard of triplet quavers (Ex. 25q) – a move that simultaneously reinstates the spirit of that memorably obsessive Scherzo, while emphasizing the augmented-dominant relationship encountered

Ex. 25

(m)

(n)

169

(o)

p espress.

N.B. *(n)* is form of *(k)* from 6/8 bar.

(p)

poco *f* marcato

(q)

in the other movements. The second subject's lyric tune returns with drastically intensified emotional rhetoric, and the work ends with an angry outburst of characteristic syncopation, the triplet rhythms and the shape (y) turned finally into a gruff cadential epigram.

'And what is this C minor Sextet?' asked Clara by letter on 21 February 1861. Had she heard rumour of the F minor Quintet, or the other ambitious chamber work of this period, the String Sextet no. 2 in G major? The several versions of op. 34 complicate its already obscure chronological relations *vis-à-vis* the Sextet, which was not published (as op. 36) until 1866. But the theme of the Adagio existed as far back as February 1855; the Scherzo cunningly reworks an idea from one of his neo-Baroque piano dances, composed in 1854; and the first movement, if not written in 1858–9, certainly arose from memories of that time – and one memory in particular which plainly speaks its name as lyrical climax to the second subject: A–G–A–D (= T) H–E (Ex. 26). These features would argue for a piece substantially contemporary with the B flat Sextet, but in fact almost every feature in the composition, from the smallest to the largest elements of structure and texture, suggest a later, maturer and more integrated manner of expression. The bulk of the work on it seems to have occupied him in 1864–5.

Ex. 26

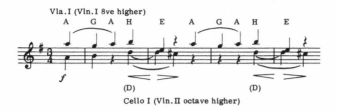

An exact contemporary of the Quintet's final version, then, but conventionally contrasted with it as much more sunny and serene, the Sextet boasts a richness of sonority seldom paralleled elsewhere in Brahms's chamber output. Yet there is a dark hue to the Sextet's 'charming suavity', and he makes us aware of this in many insidious ways. At the very outset of the nominally G major Allegro non troppo, persistent semitonal inflections twist the key towards the harmonically more unstable minor mode and establish something like an 'axial tonality'[2] with E flat, vastly increasing the potential for tonal exploration and giving the opening theme (Ex. 27a below) an almost febrile grace. The semitonal inflections – and the music's vastly increased sensitivity to string colour – are adumbrated in microcosm by the first viola's hollow, monotonous semitone oscillation across two strings, which is the first sound we hear. This figure persists through the first half of the first subject, develops into a transition theme, is usually present (literally or by implication) throughout the rest of the exposition, is a principal pivot for unexpected modulation – and, like the unstoppable flywheel of some perpetual-motion machine, becomes the obsessional motive force of the development (which ventures into the remote key of C sharp minor). The music is never less than beautiful, and the second subject contains one of Brahms's most gracious and glorious tunes; but it has a manic edge. The spiritual progenitor, as Michael Musgrave has rightly pointed out, is surely Schubert's C major Quintet. And here again a 'Classical' poise is actually disciplining Brahms's 'Romantic' sense of anguish – which is allowed its frankest expression at the crucial moment of lead-back to the recapitulation: a long, despairingly chromatic swoon from the first violin over a flurry of catastrophe-laden tremolo effects on the other instruments.

The rather slow and appropriately subdued Scherzo which follows is unequivocally in G minor, and a considerably more elaborate affair

---

[2] Lionel Pike's useful term for coexistence between a key and its relative major or minor: see his 'The Tonal Structure of Brian's *Gothic* Symphony', *Tempo*, no. 138 (September 1981), pp. 33ff.

Ex. 27

(a)

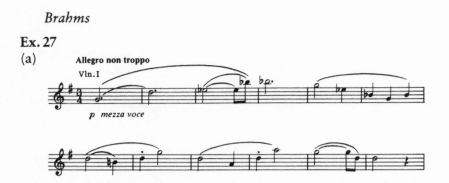

than the comparable movement of the B flat Sextet, although like that movement it exploits a stylized dance-character. The dance from which it stems, as noted above, is Brahms's A minor Gavotte of June 1854, whose first bars are reworked in a subtly growing, open-ended design that still retains a certain air of courtly formality, along with a new gracefulness, rhythmic irregularity and wistful, shadowed charm. In sharp contrast to this music's poignant interplay of light and shade, the Trio bursts out with a hectic, rumbustious Presto giocoso – again redolent of the dance, but now of surprisingly Bohemian accent, less a waltz than a furiant, so close is the anticipation of one of the Dvořák Slavonic Dances. The return of the Scherzo (via an imaginative transition that annuls the Trio's contrasting character) restores a bittersweet tranquillity, but a brief *Animato* coda brings the movement to an abrupt, even angry close.

As in the op. 18 Sextet the slow movement is a set of variations in the relative minor; in op. 36 this means E minor, and it comes third rather than second. The theme (Ex. 27b) quoted with its accompaniment but without any attribution in a letter Brahms sent to Clara from Düsseldorf on 7 February 1855, has its own faint Baroque tinge (given the context, one is tempted to speculate that it came from a missing movement of his neo-Bachian keyboard suites). But its initial pair of rising fourths harks back to the rising fifth of the opening movement's first subject (Ex. 27a), contriving a large-scale structural link of a characteristically understated kind; and the first variation is wholly Romantic in coloration, its misty, long-drawn chromatic sighs likewise recalling a ghost-image of the end of the first movement's development. The pensive and closely worked second variation leads to a vigorous fugal third, again with hints of the Baroque (it is the first to have a formal repeat) and now with relation to the Finale of the Cello Sonata that Brahms was writing during the same period as this Sextet. The fourth variation then develops the motives of the third in an even more sophisticated stretto, and a smooth transition leads, via a reminder of the ascending-fourth figure, into E major. Here, virtually for the first time, the work attains an unruffled tranquillity in the *Adagio* fifth variation, whose closely interwoven tracery of rippling semiquavers evokes the contentment of a late summer evening. Whereas in op. 18 the major-mode variations lead back to the minor, here Brahms remains in E major for a coda that maintains and confirms this transfigured mood, ending with a long, luxurious melodic descent in thirds, over Ex. 27b's rising fourths in the bass.

Ex. 27

(b)

The *Poco Allegro* Finale is a species of sonata design with a single (but bi-partite) subject. The excited rapid repeated-note idea, almost a tremolando, which constitutes the subject's first element has been seen as a reference to the climactic tremolo writing of the first movement, but it reflects even more strongly the persistent semitonal oscillation-figure which haunted that movement. It has parallel consequences in this one: 'straightened out' into insistent note-repetitions, broken by the accents of a melodic line, it imparts an ever-present momentum, and provides stability where the oscillation ensured its opposite. The under-lying motion, however, is slower and even more assured than its semiquavers suggest: the subject's second element is a warm, majestically lyrical tune that symbolizes the confidence and peace of mind the music has progressively won through the previous movements. The spirit of the dance is never far away, but for all its vibrancy and gladness this is a stately dance, appropriate alike to self-aware players of life's tragi-comedy, and to the stars in their courses.

Alongside these two superbly formed chamber works evolved a third, the Cello Sonata in E minor, op. 38, which has a curious formal balance that seems almost arbitrarily arrived at. Brahms wrote three movements for cello and piano in 1862, only completing the work, with a fugal Finale, in June 1865 for the amateur cellist Josef Gansbacher, who had been instrumental in securing his appointment to the Sing-akademie. But before publication he suppressed one of the 1862 move-ments, an Adagio (though a manuscript of this apparently survived at least into the 1930s), and issued the Sonata in the oddly proportioned three-movement form we know today: a very large, moderately paced first movement, followed by a dance-scherzo in the manner of a minuet and a vigorous but severely worked fugue, without any slow movement *per se*. Since the main subject of the fugal Finale is closely (and surely consciously) modelled on that of Contrapunctus XIII from Bach's *Die Kunst der Fuge*, and the opening idea of the first movement bears a strong resemblance to Contrapunctus III of the same work, the Sonata must be said to have a strong archaizing tendency, reaching back beyond the conveniently available models in Beethoven (despite the fugue in the second of Beethoven's op. 102) to more purely Baroque examples, possibly even Bach's own sonatas for bass viol and harpsichord, which the Bach-Gesellschaft Edition had printed in 1860. It has also been suggested that Brahms's Cello Sonata reflects close study of one (also in E minor, and also op. 38) by the respected Hamburg composer Bernhard Romberg (1767–1841).

Yet the result is distinctively Brahmsian, most of all in the first movement, whose brooding, ruminative character is reinforced by Brahms's concentration on the cello's lower register and the warm, dark tone of the bottom strings. The piano, however, is never confined to a merely accompanying role. Brahms in fact followed Classical practice in designating the work a 'Sonata for piano with violoncello', empha-sizing the two instruments' parity; and in their co-projection of thematic material the textures are minutely interwoven, sometimes to the point of thickness. It may be that Brahms stressed the register in which the cello is strongest in order to weight it against the very full piano part, but there remain some unsolved problems of balance and part-writing. All of this may be heard in the first movement, a broad sonata structure distinguished most of all by the plainness of its themes and its mel-ancholic homogeneity of mood. The first subject, with narrative earn-estness and sauntering gait, is so self-sufficient that the more impassioned subsidiary elements of the movement can make little headway against its all-enfolding brown study.

The atmosphere is lightened somewhat by the ensuing Allegretto quasi minuetto, whose courtly formality, partly secured by a Phrygian modal colouring which itself develops tendencies from the harmony of the previous movement, escapes any hint of pastiche through a prevailing spirit of wry irony – indeed, though it appears to look backward, the movement strikingly anticipates the ambiguous flavour of some of Mahler's scherzi in similar dance steps. The main theme is introduced by a mock-sententious cadence-figure; and this, in hesitant repetition, becomes the germinal cell of the central Trio, whose franker Roman-ticism wreathes it in arpeggios and a delicate tracery of quaver figuration. The Finale, less well-liked than the other movements on the work's first appearance, is really the most original portion of the Sonata. The most elaborate instrumental fugue Brahms had yet written, it in fact represents a resourceful combination of fugue with elements of sonata form, most notably a non-fugal 'second subject group' (actually derived from the fugue's countersubject) which enters at the appropriate junctures between the main groups of fugal entries, both to create the impression of binary exposition and recapitulation, and to provide a much-needed textural contrast. Nevertheless the main fugal idea is worked out with exhaustive command of contrapuntal technique, in stretti, inversion, imitative episodes, and so on. If Brahms intended a homage to the spirit of Bach, this is a marvellously effective one.

The remaining chamber work of this important group from the early 1860s, the Trio for piano, violin and horn in E flat, op. 40, shares a few of the Cello Sonata's archaizing traits. As Brahms's first major instrumental work to dispense with a sonata-form first movement, and to create an overall design that alternates two slowish movements with two fast, dance-like ones, it establishes some resemblances with the slow–fast–slow–fast design of the Baroque sonata as typified by the Trio Sonata in Bach's *Musikalisches Opfer*. But in other respects this is one of Brahms's most openly Romantic scores: not least in sonority, where the natural dignity and mystery of the horn establish an 'atmospheric' dimension unavailable to the more straightforward combination of strings and piano.[3] Possibly this reflects its conception in the highly poetic surroundings of the Black Forest around Baden in 1864; an equally strong and even more personal source of inspiration was the death of Brahms's mother, which deeply coloured the elegiac slow movement. Brahms himself played the horn in his youth (it was one of his father's principal instruments), and the need to evolve themes suitable for its participation on equal terms with the other instruments probably influenced him in the direction of simpler forms. His choice of a natural horn (*Waldhorn*), rather than the valved horn then coming into general use, caused him to limit his notes to those of the harmonic series obtainable on that instrument, whose strong natural sonority he clearly preferred.

The opening Andante therefore deliberately eschews many of the challenging intellectual aspects of Brahms's characteristic first-movement designs. He casts it in an extended song form, A–B–A–B–A, the 'A' idea a long and hauntingly vocal 2/4 melody introduced with the

---

[3] The work was published as for horn or cello; Brahms regarded the substitution of the cello as a very poor alternative, but later became considerably more enthusiastic about using a viola in the absence of a horn, and a new viola part was published in 1884. Performances with either substitution are prodigiously rare, however, whereas the Trio has become one of the mainstays of the non-orchestral horn repertoire.

simplest of accompaniments (though its second half is treated with some simple but exquisitely dovetailed imitation). Michael Musgrave has rightly drawn attention to – but I think insufficiently stressed – the parallels between this opening idea and the brooding Ossian setting from the op. 17 partsongs with horns and harp (Ex. 28). The 'B' material is faster (*Poco più animato*), providing a necessary contrast of key (C minor), tempo and metre (a lilting 9/8) while the mood tautens and intensifies in the return of both ideas. This gives way to an ebullient, dancing movement similarly straightforward in expression, but in that concise sonata-scherzo form of which Brahms had already long been a master. Here he frankly exploits the horn's 'hunting' associations to the full, while subjecting the movement's basic, galloping 3/4 momentum to his full battery of rhythmically enlivening devices: off-beat accents, grandiloquent cross-rhythms, as well as more subtly deployed syncopations. The Trio, in A flat minor, is very much slower, unfolding an extensive, song-like melody that harks back to the spirit of the first movement.

Ex. 28

(Weep on the rocks where the storm-winds are breaking,
Weep, o Maiden of Inistore!)

The heart of the work is however the E flat minor slow movement, openly labelled 'sorrowful' (Adagio mesto): here the melancholic tones of the horn come into their own in creating an unmistakable mood of funereal lament. The quiet, oppressed first theme, in a lulling berceuse rhythm, leads to a contrapuntal presentation of the second, led off by solo horn, that develops over an ethereal slow tremolo accompaniment in the piano and returns, marked *ppp quasi niente*, on solo violin: the movement's deepest point of emotional desolation. The appearance of a flowing (but closely related) new theme in F major strikes a note of ambiguous hope and releases the movement's repressed emotions in a climactic coda, but the berceuse, with an uneasy grinding semitone at the bottom of the keyboard, has the last word.[4]

Darkness is finally banished by the Finale, a vivacious 'hunting' gigue whose main theme turns out to have been adumbrated by the new theme that entered the latter stages of the slow movement. This is one way that Brahms binds these last two movements together, despite their very different characters; another is that the obstinate bass semitone also plays an important role in the Finale. The sombre, elegiac moods may be exorcised here, but there is no attempt to deny or forget them.

Piano Variations

It was in November 1861, in Hamburg, that for the second time in his career Brahms produced a set of Variations on a Theme of Schumann – op. 23, for piano duet: his first published work in that medium since the very early *Souvenir de la Russie*, although some of the Hungarian Dances probably existed in duet form by this time. The op. 23 Variations should perhaps be associated with Dietrich's contemporary visit to Hamburg, as the two composers enjoyed playing as duet partners, and sometimes performed the work in public in later years. It has little of the exploratory pianism and almost painful intimacy of expression that characterized the solo piano Variations op. 9, but is nonetheless rife with personal associations. After the *Sturm und Drang* of the works conceived in the aftermath of the catastrophe of 1854, op. 23 seems as if it might be Brahms's formal farewell to Schumann, before he turns at last to his own concerns, no longer looking to the past but to the future. Its dedication, not to Clara but to her daughter Julie (eighteen when the work was published in 1863) is perhaps symbolic of this.

More symbolic still is the theme Brahms chose for op. 23, a simple E flat tune of rather wan pathos which constituted the dead composer's 'last musical idea'. In the final days before his suicide attempt Schumann noted down a theme which he believed had been dictated to him by the spirits of Mendelssohn and Schubert, and began a series of variations of his own on it – failing to recognize a version of a tune from his own

---

[4] This 'sad and distant' music, one of Brahms's most heartfelt slow movements, seems to have been the starting point for György Ligeti's Horn Trio, subtitled '*Hommage à Brahms*', though it uses no direct quotation.

Violin Concerto, written the previous year. Since both the Concerto and the Variations were to remain unpublished until the late 1930s,[5] the provenance and significance of the theme was hidden from all but the Schumann family, Joachim, and a few others.

Despite these melancholy associations Brahms makes no attempt to exploit the theme for pathetic effect. Although his Variations keep strictly to its proportions (and repeated second half), they modulate more freely than is his normal practice in this kind of work, and each is decisively characterized; there are vivid elements of keyboard colour that occasionally evoke orchestral sonorities. The prevailing mood is serious but generally extroverted, as if Brahms is determined to celebrate Schumann in his more positive moods; and perhaps only variation 4 (with its fateful drum-beat in the second half) can really be described as elegiac. More often the variations are strongly rhythmic, with touches of waltz in no. 5 and Hungarian colouring in nos. 6 and 8; the penultimate variation, no. 9, brings this rhythmic aspect to a head in brusque, even choleric fashion. The work thereafter subsides into a *molto moderato* funeral march. But not a gloomy one: the music expands in a warm, noble E flat, Schumann's original theme returning with great delicacy in the second half to close the proceedings in a mood of profound, meditative calm. There is a strong sense here that Brahms has finally attained his own balance, and thus is able to let his friend's best qualities speak for themselves.

These duet variations had been closely preceded by a remarkable set for solo piano. Apart from various bouts of work on the Hungarian Dances, difficult to date, Brahms wrote nothing for two hands between the Variations on an Original Theme and the Variations and Fugue on a Theme of Handel, op. 24 – a gap of five years. The latter composition, completed in September 1861, was published with no dedication, but it was a birthday gift for Clara Schumann, and the manuscript is headed 'Variations for a beloved friend'. The major fruit of his first summer in Hamm, in its massive scale and exhaustive command of piano technique the work dwarfs all his previous variation sets. It is surely no coincidence that this was the first major compositional statement to appear after the débâcle of the 1860 'Manifesto'. Brahms had learned the wisdom of proclaiming his principles in music alone. This work, too, is a manifesto, consonant 'with the inner spirit of music', and infinitely more effective than any journalistic polemic. It even impressed Wagner: and his famous

---

[5] Brahms eventually published the theme itself in 1893, in the fourteenth (Supplementary) Volume of the Complete Edition of Schumann's works – but not the five variations on it Schumann had managed to complete in February 1854.

comment on the piece shows he clearly understood it as a *demonstration* of principle. It is a systematic summation of the mastery Brahms had gained through his intensive studies of the past few years: the choice of a Baroque theme, the strictness of the variations, the richness and scope of the piano technique, and the lavish display of contrapuntal learning in the final Fugue, all combine to present Brahms in the role of preserver and continuator of what Schoenberg would have called 'properly understood good old tradition'.

Some of Brahms's models in this monumental work are easy enough to identify. In the scale and ambitions of his conception both Bach's 'Goldberg' and Beethoven's 'Diabelli' Variations must have exercised a powerful if generalized influence; in specific features of form Beethoven's 'Eroica' Variations is a closer parallel. But the overall structure is original to Brahms. It has been said, rightly, that the choice of a Handel theme reflects the intensity of his identification with the past; yet there was a very contemporary model close to hand that may have sent him in that direction – the Variations on a Theme of Handel, op. 26, by Robert Volkmann. Brahms might well have known that large and often admirable work, published as recently as 1856, which Volkmann based on the so-called 'Harmonious Blacksmith' theme from the Air with Variations in Handel's E major Harpsichord Suite. There are interesting similarities between Brahms's and Volkmann's sets, such as the inclusion in each of a 'musical-box' variation harking back to harpsichord style (Volkmann's var. 8 and Brahms's var. 22); and Brahms chose his theme from a very similar source: the Air with Variations from Handel's first B flat Suite, of which he owned a 1733 First Edition.

This dapper little tune, in two four-bar periods, both repeated, has the balanced phraseology, the structural and harmonic simplicity, of an ideal variation subject. Brahms's twenty-five variations adhere rigorously to the formal basis set up by the theme (generally including the exact repetition of both halves), and confine themselves to Handel's key of B flat, with occasional excursions into the tonic minor. But this apparent constraint – which imposes a powerful structural unity – provides Brahms with a framework on which to establish and explore a widely contrasted range of moods and characters. At the same time there is a subtle but irresistible organic development of motifs, derived from the theme and steadily metamorphosed through the Variations, which often transforms Handel's harmonic background even as it counterbalances any tendency to diffuseness in the variety of the individual sections.

These are indeed almost kaleidoscopic in their approach, ranging from the 'contemporary' chromatics of nos. 2 and 9, and the organ-loft progressions of no. 20, through the free canon in octaves of no. 6, the closer and wittier canon of no. 16, to the siciliana of no. 19, the aforementioned 'musical-box' of no. 22 (apparently a homage to the French *clavecinists*), and the wonderfully ambiguous no. 13, which can be interpreted as a companion-piece to the 1855 neo-Baroque slow dances, or as a Hungarian fantasia that turns the anacruses of Handel's theme into a 'gypsy' freedom of ornamentation. Brahms is also careful to place almost centrally within his scheme, and where the floridity of no. 13 has made it most necessary, the forthright *sciolto* variation 14 which clearly re-imprints the contours of the theme on the listener's memory. Several of the variations form pairs, of which the second intensifies and develops the characteristics of the first, and the excited build-up of the last three[6] creates a thoroughly climactic introduction to the separate, concluding Fugue.

The Fugue – whose continuation of the variation process in an altogether more 'open' form makes a direct appeal to Beethoven's 'Hammerklavier' Sonata by way of the 'Diabelli' Variations – is astonishingly free in its conception (and in this wholly unlike Brahms's organ fugues of the late 1850s). Although it insists obsessively, in its great contrapuntal intricacy, upon the repetitions of the head-motif of its subject (derived from Handel's theme), Brahms's primary objective seems to have been to reconcile the *linear* demands of fugal form with the harmonic capabilities of the contemporary piano. Accordingly his hard-acquired polyphonic skills, manifest in innumerable subtleties of inversion, augmentation, and stretto, perfectly accommodate themselves to an overwhelmingly pianistic texture: the fugal voices tend nonchalantly to proliferate or dissipate into chordal inner parts, doublings in thirds and sixths and octaves, broken chords, and arpeggiated figuration. The grand sweep of the structure, however, is never lost sight of: the immense cumulative power of this Fugue, gathered up in a chiming, pealing dominant pedal, issues in a coda of granitic splendour, the vertical and horizontal demands of theme and harmony equally fulfilled in a majestic convergence of descending chords and ascending fugue-motif (Ex. 29).

To turn from this mighty work to Brahms's next (and, as it happens, last) group of piano variations – which he first performed in 1865 but wrote in 1862–3, soon after meeting its dedicatee, Carl Tausig – is to experience a salutary reminder not to pigeon-hole or circumscribe Brahms's creative outlook. If the 'Handel' set was a manifesto for the

---

[6] Compare variation 24's bravura ornamentation of variation 23 with variations 21 and 22 of Alkan's *Le Festin d'Esope* (published 1857), which this passage curiously recalls.

Ex. 29

mindful development of tradition, this op. 35 group, on the most famous of all themes by Paganini, is a bravura display of pyrotechnical virtuosity as practised by the keyboard lions of the 'New German' school; Liszt above all. Yet it would be a questionable set of criteria that immediately ranked op. 35 lower than op. 24 on account of its surface brilliance. It is equally impressive as a sheer feat of composition, and as a bold challenge to the Weimar school on their own ground.

We know the work as Variations on a Theme of Paganini, but that is only its subtitle; Brahms called it *Studien* (Studies), to emphasize its exploration of the technical aspects of keyboard virtuosity, and published it in a format appropriate for private study in two complementary Books, each containing the theme, fourteen variations, and a coda.[7]

---

[7] Indeed, a slightly different form of Book 2, variation 11, turns up as the twenty-ninth exercise in the 51 *Übungen* – studies in technical problems, collected over a long period purely for study and practice – Brahms published in 1893.

Either book is performable as an entity, or both in succession; during the later nineteenth and early twentieth centuries it was common for performers to make a selection from both books and shuffle them to their personal taste – a procedure initiated by Clara Schumann but unthinkable with any of Brahms's other variation works (and highly inappropriate for Book II at least). To Brahms's friends, however, it was the '*Hexenvariationen*' (Witchcraft Variations), an appropriately Romantic nickname for its astonishing feats of prestidigitation. It was again Clara who thus christened the work (in a letter to Brahms of October 1863, acknowledging receipt of it in manuscript): appropriately, for she herself had long ago (1834) included a *Hexentanz* among her own op. 5 – a youthful set of *Pièces caractéristiques* in the modern Romantic style that she later so despised, but which had deeply impressed Chopin.

Brahms's bold attempt to out-Weimar the Weimarites probably arose in the first instance as a gesture of friendship to Tausig: pupil and ardent supporter of Liszt, composer of a set of *Tägliche Studien* that address some of the same challenges of virtuoso technique, and a performer whose playing was an object of Brahms's freely admitted fascination. The choice of theme (from Paganini's twenty-fourth Caprice in A minor for unaccompanied violin) is likewise a gesture – Paganini, the prototypical Romantic virtuoso, and his daring Caprices, were the common imaginative property of the contending parties of musical Romanticism. Liszt several times reworked various of these pieces in forms which are themselves historic documents in the development of the literature of the piano: the *Etudes d'exécution transcendante d'après Paganini* (1834, published 1837), reissued in 1851 as *Bravour-Studien nach Paganini* – and dedicated to Clara Schuman. But even before Liszt, Robert Schumann had produce twelve Studies after the Paganini Caprices in 1832–3 (which Clara Wieck, as she then was, had first performed at her father's home). Both composers had dealt with Caprice no. 24 – so Brahms's theme, and even his use of the title *Studien*, already had a satisfyingly close connection with Clara and a long and resonant history behind it.

In yet later hands, notably those of Rakhmaninov, Lutoslawski and Blacher, the theme has since proved itself an ever-renewable source of inspiration. The very simplicity and clarity of its harmonic skeleton gives each new composer almost unlimited scope for the imposition of his own personality. Brahms's Variations open up a whole world of interpretative challenges. They include studies in double sixths (Book I, nos. 1 and 2, the second apparently a homage to Schumann's C major Toccata), double thirds (Book II, no. 1), wide leaps between hands (I/3) or with one hand (I/12), trills at the top of wide-spread chords (I/4), polyrhythm between the hands (I/5, 12; II/2, 7), octave studies (I/6–8; II/9, 11) and octave tremolos (I/9), staccato against legato phrasing (I/10), glissandi (I/13), rapid contrary motion (II/8, 11), swooping arpeggios against held notes (II/10). In many of the variations the figuration is systematically transferred from right hand to left, and vice versa. It will be noted that some of those listed above (not an exhaustive summary) combine more than one technical difficulty, and the final variations in each book, each welded to an extended tripartite coda, combine an even larger number of features, bringing both books to an end in scintillating style. Generally speaking, in Book I the technical demands occupy the foreground of the music, leaving little room for Brahms's habitual melodic developments (though the delicate arabesques of the major-key variation 12, and the Hungarian accents of no. 13, with its 'gypsy' glissandi, are delightful inventions). Book II is gentler, with compositional virtues more predominant: the dreamy waltz of variation 4, the skittish arpeggios of no. 6 with its 'diabolic' crushed-semitone acciaccaturas, the 'violinistic' no. 8 with its pizzicato effects, the cool nocturnal song of no. 12 (the only variation in either book to stray beyond A minor/major, into F) and the gently cascading thirds of its successor no. 13, all combine to make this book the more satisfying from a purely musical standpoint. But taken as a whole the two books are a stunning demonstration of compositional skill.

The 'Handel' and 'Paganini' Variations, therefore, are astonishingly contrasted approaches to contemporary piano style, looking Janus-like in opposite directions. But like Janus's faces they are aspects of a single intelligence, symbols of a gateway, of ends and beginnings. Together, these Variations constitute a double manifesto, 'ancient and modern', in which Brahms announces himself as a major new master of piano composition. His ambition and self-belief should not be underestimated: here he takes on the musical world of his time on the ground where he felt strongest – his own instrument, and the variation form which he handled better than any living composer. But characteristically, having made his point, he had no interest in labouring it. He continued to pursue the intricacies of variation form in other media, but he never again wrote a large-scale work for solo piano, preferring instead to enrich its repertoire with occasional groups of short pieces whose difficulties and profundities are not the kind to draw easy applause.

Male choruses, song cycles, and *Rinaldo*

Brahms's last pre-Viennese choral compositions are found in his op. 41, a collection of five partsongs for male voices: his only contributions to a then-popular genre in which Schubert and Mendelssohn had achieved some fine things but whose repertoire was over-supplied with low-quality music to texts of mindless jollity or militarism. Brahms's set begins with the beautiful *Ich schwing mein Horn ins Jammerthal*, a serene *a cappella* version of his song *Ich schell' mein Horn*, discussed on p. 110 (apart from the one-word difference in the first lines, the text is identical). This dates from 1860, but there follow four choruses of the soldier's life to poems by Carl Lemcke, composed in 1862. Probably no other pieces by Brahms have worn so ill. They are of course superbly composed (though the casual listener might be hard-put to guess by whom), full of rhythmic interest and vigorous declamation, and probably very enjoyable to sing. But this is the collector of tin soldiers as composer. These rhetorical apostrophes of the flag, death-or-glory, barrack life and so on belong to a Romanticized view of soldiering that perished long ago, even among soldiers. Musically we are now more familiar with the bitterly macabre survey of this territory in Mahler's settings from *Des Knaben Wunderhorn*: and the genre received its *coup de grâce* from Schoenberg, in his own op. 35 male-voice partsongs, with the frenzied drummings and pipings of *Landsknechte* ('Mercenaries'). Still, Brahms was hardly in a position to exercise our historical hindsight; though we can be grateful for his restraint in never returning to the genre. For this was a medium through which his patriotism (that identification with the nation, the 'Volk' which was a definite strand in Romanticism) could find fervent expression – an expression in which neither he nor his contemporary audience would have seen anything amiss. The true significance of op. 41, however, probably lies elsewhere: this set of choruses provided valuable experience in handling male-voice textures that bore fruit in the cantata *Rinaldo*, op 50.

Brahms's difficulties and irresolution about future courses – in music as much as in life – are presented with exceptional clarity in three much more important vocal works of this period: the aforementioned *Rinaldo* and two song collections, opp. 32 and 33. As often, the opus numbering is misleading, and conveys only the order of publication (in the case of op. 33, merely of its first half). In fact all three works were conceived within a short space of time in the early 1860s, probably in the order in which I shall discuss them (33, 50, 32), and proceeded more or less in tandem. It is symptomatic of the problems he was attempting to work out that twentieth-century critics have never been entirely happy with opp. 33 and 50, sensing at least an incongruence of musical form to Brahms's chosen texts.

The op. 33 collection, the *Romanzen aus L. Tiecks 'Magelone'*, is Brahms's biggest group of Lieder by far – there are fifteen songs,[8] most of them unusually large-scale: the first seven appeared in 1865, the remainder were still being polished until 1869. It is also a full-blown song cycle (his only overt one) in all but name, enacting a story with the final song closing the circle by quoting from the first. The dramatist and novelist Ludwig Tieck (1773–1853) had been a leading figure among the literary Romantics; his tragedy *Genoveva* had formed the basis for Schumann's only opera. He is especially notable for his adaptations of medieval Romance, and his 1812 *Wundersame Liebesgeschichte der schönen Magelone und des Grafen Peter aus der Provence* ('The Wondrous Love-story of the Beautiful Magelone and Count Peter of Provence'), a short novel whose chapters are interspersed with poems commenting on the action, drew upon a twelfth-century Provençal tale which has undergone many subsequent transformations in European literature. Brahms knew the story well: he had read another version with his childhood friend Lieschen Giesemann on his holidays in Winsen, and he probably first came across Tieck's treatment of it in Schumann's library.

The story concerns the young, fair-haired knight Peter who ventures forth from his parents' home full of youthful ardour but inexperienced in love and the ways of the world. He vanquishes all rivals at the tournaments of the King of Naples and wins the heart of the King's beautiful, virtuous daughter, Magelone. The lovers elope together, but by mischance they are separated in the forest while Magelone lies sleeping and Peter is cast adrift in the sea, only to be picked up by Moors and sold into the service of the Sultan. After two years the Sultan's daughter, Sulima, is filled with desire for him and enables Peter to escape with her by boat; but he manages to leave her behind and sets out alone, eventually returning to the forest and the shepherd's hut where Magelone has taken refuge and faithfully awaited him. They marry and live happily ever after.

Tieck's seventeen poems (Brahms omitted two) are the only completely original contribution in his treatment of the story. Although they are usually given some flimsy narrative justification (and the first, sung by a wandering minstrel, has a dramatic function in arousing Peter's desire to travel and seek adventures), they are really lyric interludes that

---

[8] They are usually all sung by a baritone if performed as a cycle; occasionally a contralto will perform nos. 11 and 13, which are ascribed to female characters.

provide, at best, emotional correlatives to the events around them. They remain separate, however; but in setting them Brahms clearly had the prose narrative continually in mind, and seems to have expected his listeners to be familiar with it too. With these *Magelone* Romances he was entering again an imaginative world of Romantic chivalry that had deeply attracted him since his youth, and to which he had already given expression in the first piano Ballade, the early Lieder about the Bonnie Earl of Moray and the Lord of Falkenstein (both are evoked in the two opening songs of the cycle, the expansive, heroic *Keinen hat es noch gereut* and the vaunting, defiant *Traun! Bogen und Pfeil*). Even more relevant is the 1858 song *Ein Sonett*, whose text derives from an actual medieval Count of Provence, and whose delicate evocation of lute-song manners foreshadows many later passages in op. 33 where Peter's lute is referred to.

It is only too easy to see that in this choice of subject he was saying something about his own life. The parallels with the fair-haired youth who had sallied forth from Hamburg, won the plaudits of the musical world, loved and parted from Clara Schumann, loved and abandoned Agathe von Siebold and returned home[9] (though not with Clara) have until their ends an over-obvious symmetry. This may not have been so clear to Brahms at the time (or perhaps he still hoped the symmetry would complete itself), but we can hardly doubt that his own life-experience drew him consciously or unconsciously to this favourite tale of his adolescence. It is more difficult to account for his musical response. Op. 33 is an ungainly work, very long as a whole and comprising mostly lengthy songs, many of them blatantly episodic, with frequent sudden changes of rhythm and material, and ambitious piano parts featuring extended prologues, interludes, and postludes. Brahms unusually avoids strophic forms or folksong elements, even when the poems suggest them. Instead he imposes cumulatively dramatic successions of melodic shapes and contrasts; there is a declamatory, even quasi-operatic element to the presentation, more appropriate to the clotted prose of Tieck's novel (the sub-text in Brahms's mind) than to his lyric verse interludes. A mass of fascinating detail is in search of an overall musical rationale. Peter's *Verzweiflung* ('Despair' – Brahms's own title for song no. 10) seems like a virtuosic Schumann *Fantasiestück* aspiring to the condition of a revenge aria; no. 13, Sulima's sole song, is set apart in character from the others by its 'exotic' modal flavouring. But by the same token this *Magelone* cycle is a very hard work not to like, prodigally filled with

[9] The penultimate song, in which Peter steers for his homeland, is said by Kalbeck to quote a popular Hamburg march which Brahms's father often played.

characteristically rich melodic lines, galloping rhythms, lute effects, and melting lullabies (*Liebe kam aus fernen Länden* and *Ruhe, Süssliebchen*, for instance), composed with an unfailing youthful exuberance and generosity of invention. All this could reasonably be defended as Brahms's characterization of Count Peter's chivalric ingenuousness, but it seems a loose and extravagant way of putting together a major song cycle. The music, though it cost Brahms considerable pains, gives the impression of craving our indulgence while its composer thoroughly enjoys himself: indeed perhaps the work, to a greater extent than most composers' products, was a *self*-indulgence in aspects of Romanticism he badly needed to get out of his system.

Less indulgent but similarly problematical is the cantata *Rinaldo*. This has long suffered in critical appraisals of Brahms's choral music from misapprehensions of its nature and place in his output, imposed by the mere appearances of chronology. First performed in 1869, it inevitably seemed far less grand, and uneasily 'operatic', in comparison with *Ein deutsches Requiem*, unveiled to the world a year before; and it signally lacks the concision and tragic force of the two short choral/orchestral scores Brahms produced a year later, the Alto Rhapsody and the *Schicksalslied*. But it has no real business in this company: apart from the final chorus, it already existed in some form in 1863 (he wrote it that summer as an entry for a competition organized by the Aachen Liedertafel), making it a far earlier (and less mature) creation than is usually acknowledged – a contemporary and kindred creation to the *Magelone* Romances.

To view *Rinaldo* in relation to Brahms's song cycle immediately clarifies some of its more experimental and incongruous features. The seemingly episodic (though in fact skilfully articulated and tonally patterned) form, the predominance of the tenor soloist in large set-pieces over the subordinate (but well integrated) male chorus, do indeed lend this 'cantata' the character of an extended series of songs, the form balanced at either end by the orchestral prelude with choir and the complex and vigorous concluding chorus. *Rinaldo* therefore is no cantata on the model of J. S. Bach (or even Schumann's *Das Paradies und die Peri*). This generally underrated and certainly under-performed work is a unique Brahmsian creation, a lyrico-dramatic effusion on a theme very close to his heart – the pull between love and duty, including the duty to use one's gifts to the full.

Once again the imagery to which he turned was that of Romanticized medieval chivalry, but this time in a darker and more concise poem by Goethe (unlike the songs and partsongs, all Brahms's choral works with orchestra are composed to texts of high poetic excellence).

The poet had, indeed, written his 'ballad' – actually a dramatic *scena*, which develops an episode from Tasso's magico-fantastical epic of the Crusades, *Gerusalemme liberata* (1581) – expressly for musical setting, and the episode itself was one that had inspired operas by Lully, Handel, Gluck, Haydn, Salieri and Rossini as well as lesser composers.

In Goethe as in Tasso the valiant knight Rinaldo (a solo tenor) has been glamoured by the enchantress Armida, and has abandoned the siege of Jerusalem to join her on her island retreat. A party of his fellow-knights (the male chorus) have journeyed there to persuade him to rouse himself and return to the war. The sole 'action' of the poem is their gradual winning of his acquiescence, breaking down his dream of love and indolence on the enchanted isle. The decisive moment comes when they show him, in a magical diamond shield, the reflected image of his moral degeneration. The unspeaking Armida appears, but her illusionary beauty withers along with that of the landscape as her magic fails. Shaken, Rinaldo joins his friends and, in the final chorus, they set sail across the dolphin-skimmed sea to renew the struggle for the Holy Land.

The autobiographical parallels in the dramatic situation are as evident here as in the *Magelone-Lieder*. Once again a knightly protagonist must free himself from an ensnaring love and find his route to freedom. This time, however, it leads not to a purer, more admirable sweetheart but to the path of duty, the exercise of his manly skills. Clearly no crude equation is possible between the figure of Armida and Agathe; but the enchantress may be standing as a symbol of women (as objects of veneration and lifelong devotion) in general – of Clara Schumann too.

But there is more to this absorbing and deeply felt composition than that. Certain moments – for example Rinaldo's first impassioned recitative – give the best existing evidence of what a Brahmsian opera might have sounded like; and despite the authentic Brahmsian accent throughout there are occasional, and appropriate, echoes of *Fidelio* and even of *Der fliegende Holländer*, the Wagner opera he most admired.[10] Though there are few overt pictorial touches (even the mysterious effects when Rinaldo sees himself reflected in the magic shield are quite subdued, more a matter of remote tonality than colour), there are psychological ones of a more subtle kind. Once Rinaldo's enchanted state has been firmly established in a lengthy aria ('Stelle her der gold'nen

---

[10] Michael Musgrave (op. cit., pp. 77–8) has also pointed out the debt to such little-known Schubert as the cantata *Lazarus*, which Brahms read in manuscript the year he composed most of *Rinaldo*.

Tage') of great beauty and impeccable ternary design, the chorus breaks in cajolingly with its insistence on immediate flight; Rinaldo interrupts them with a varied repetition of his aria's last two lines, and then moves back to its main theme as if to begin again, but is unable to hold to the melody and breaks instead into a new, more despairing strain. By such means Brahms dovetails the various sections to produce a reasonably through-composed form; that is, until the final chorus, which necessarily restores the E flat tonality in which *Rinaldo* began but is otherwise a separate, self-contained structure, dating from 1868. That it took him so long to supply the work with its required decisive culmination says much for his continuing lack of confidence about his direction in the intervening years, but the chorus itself is a magnificent structure that looks forward to the neo-Handelian glories of the *Triumphlied* while still finding room for Rinaldo's personal, less full-hearted acceptance of events. The music that greets the appearance of the dolphins is one of the least-known intoxicating moments in Brahms.

Ever since, the work has stubbornly resisted convenient pro-gramming – yet above all it is a real *tour de force* for male voices (Brahms began it as an entry for a male-chorus competition); and the critics who have longed for a female soloist to impersonate Armida gravely miss the point. Ultimately *Rinaldo* is a work *about* masculinity, about the arousal of the will and the bittersweet triumph of mastering one's destiny; it strives to give archetypal expression to concepts of male comradeship, of virility first nullified by female enchantment and later – through the decisive energy of the choral finale – given its full (but never fully happy) scope and freedom. These are unfashionable ideas, today more than ever; but they were commonplaces of Goethe's and Brahms's day, and poet and composer had no difficulty in identifying with them. They would have been less aware than us of self-Romanticizing, self-justificatory overtones. The self-pity they might have acknowledged, but would have considered it part of their manly condition.

A kind of appendix to these two works (for, though it was com-pleted and published earlier than either, it was conceived slightly later) is to be found in the 1864 set of nine *Lieder und Gesänge*, op. 32, to poems by Platen and Daumer. In no overt sense is this collection a song cycle; yet a powerful artistic unity is implied and achieved by its homogeneity of mood, and by the ordering of the chosen lyrics to suggest a progressive emotional separation from a loved one, the accompanying depressions, frustration, and sense of life wasted, and the love that endures nevertheless, undimmed. Kalbeck referred to the work, with some insight, as 'Rinaldo caught again in the old toils'; yet its differences from the Cantata and the *Magelone-Lieder* are even more striking than the resemblances, and more significant for the further development of Brahms's song style.

Aside from certain hints of recitative in some of the voice parts, all trace of 'operatic'style has disappeared: emotion is interiorized, and the piano accompaniments no longer serve a dramatic, pictorial function but a correlative one, sensitively reflecting and resonating with the singer's unquiet monologue. In place of *Magelone*'s loose, expansive form the songs are concise, sparely drawn, brooding, with a patent gain in intensity. Rhetoric has yielded to subtle rhythmic variation, harmonic shading, tonal ambiguity. Partly, of course, the choice of poetry prompts the style. These are Brahms's first settings of G. F. Daumer, a fashionable and very minor poet of whose work he became curiously fond; Daumer's verses, and the much superior ones by August Platen, both imitate the lyric compression, the point and finish of Oriental poets such as Hafiz, enjoining a similar tautness on the music. But the inequality of his poets' gifts seems to have troubled Brahms little. The tense, dark opening song to a Platen text, *Wie rafft ich mich auf in der Nacht*, conveys the sense of rootless, despairing night-wandering with an expressive restraint, an eloquent economy of gesture and rhythm, that place it among the most powerful songs Brahms ever wrote. But op. 32's concluding protestation of continuing love, to Daumer's *Wie bist du, meine Königin*, is almost equally inspired in its poised interweaving of expressive melody and the wide-ranging harmony of its central section – and has remained the more famous song.

Vocal and instrumental dances

Not only the opp. 32–3 songs, but also Brahms's earlier sets of vocal duets, are far surpassed for sheer beauty of sound and sensuous texture and harmony by his first group of vocal quartets, the three of op. 31. The latter two of these were written in 1863 as companions for the first, the wonderful *Wechsellied zum Tanze*, which dates back to 1859. To take them in reverse order (and increasing level of interest), no. 3, *Der Gang zum Liebchen*, sets a Bohemian folk poem in a choric style, the voices moving in serene hymn-like homophony to music that is an expansion (in E flat rather than E major) of the fifth of the op. 39 Waltzes on which Brahms was working at the time. *Neckereien*, a Moravian song of lovers engaged in mutual teasing, divides the voices into pairs, soprano and alto against tenor and bass, and pits them against each other in contrasted melodic statements and combatively intertwined counterpoint, all over a droll ground bass.

The jewel of the set is however *Wechsellied zum Tanze* (literally

'Alternating Song at the Dance'), to a poem by Goethe, where the voices split into two male/female duets. The text contrasts two pairs of dancers, circling around one another: 'the indifferents', intent only upon the dance, and 'the tender ones', intent only on each other. Brahms presents the former pair in the minor key, leading and following in stiff, clipped formal canon; the latter in the major, their tune contrastingly smooth and sweet in ravishing close harmony and rapt suspensions. The duets alternate to create the large-scale design; meanwhile the piano provides a beautifully ambiguous minuet accompaniment. The final section, where the two different musics intertwine and finally merge, the harmony sideslipping from major to minor and back, bar by bar, is one of the most delightful things in Brahms.

This marvellous dance-song makes a useful point of departure for consideration of the three large groups of dances, instrumental and vocal, which Brahms published during the 1860s: the aforementioned sixteen Waltzes and the first ten Hungarian Dances, both for piano duet, and the eighteen *Liebeslieder-Walzer* op. 52 for piano duet with vocal quartet.[11] These works, in deliberately 'popular' style, were overwhelmingly responsible for spreading his reputation to the general music-buying public, and became the chief source of his personal wealth. Their chronology is slightly obscure: the Waltzes appeared in 1865 but were certainly begun some years earlier (see op. 31 no. 3), while the *Liebeslieder*, published in 1869, presumably belong to the latter half of the decade. But the Hungarian Dances, which also came out in that year, have roots going back well into the 1850s.

Brahms dedicated the Waltzes to Eduard Hanslick: some writers have speculated that he thought it best not to try the famous critic's brain with anything more complicated. 'I hardly know how it was,' Brahms wrote to him. 'I was thinking of Vienna, of the pretty girls with whom you play duets, of you yourself, who like such things, and what not.' Hanslick responded handsomely in a famous review of the pieces:

> The earnest, taciturn Brahms, the true disciple of Schumann, as North German, as Protestant and as unworldly as Schumann, composing waltzes? The solution to the riddle is given in one word: Vienna.

We can accept Hanslick's 'Vienna', if we re-spell it 'Schubert', for Brahms's op. 39 is very much in the tradition of the older composer's four-handed Ländler and waltzes, though there are hints of Schumann's

---

[11] A fourth group may have been envisaged; a Clara Schumann letter of the early 1860s asks how he is progressing with a projected set of '*Deutsche Tänze*'. (She may rather have been referring to Brahms's work on a collection of 20 Schubert *Ländler*, drawn from various manuscript sources, which he eventually published in 1869.)

Carnaval in nos. 1 and 9. These are not large episodic waltzes in the Straussian sense but a sequence of miniatures relying on little more than their melodic charm. Brahms nevertheless thought well enough of them to publish two later recensions for piano solo, the second one specially simplified for pianists of moderate ability, which increased the music's widespread distribution. In its wholly unpretentious way op. 39 is an impressive demonstration of his fertile melodic invention, and his ability to compensate for an unchanging rhythmic background, with only discreet harmonic movement or contrapuntal elaboration. All sixteen waltzes are in a simple binary form with both halves repeated except for the famous no. 15 (which adds a tiny coda) and no. 16 (whose first-half 'repeat' transfers the melody to the left hand as Brahms secretly indulges in a bit of double counterpoint). Yet by the same token none is long enough to outstay its welcome, and all are subtly characterized in some way: most obviously nos. 4 and 14, which are in Hungarian vein; no. 14 even imposing a fiery *csárdás*-rhythm over the waltz metre.

This vein is of course much more comprehensively explored in the Hungarian Dances. These go back a long way, to his early enchantment with the gypsy melodies he heard from Reményi. The attraction exerted by these exotic tunes, with their supposedly direct connection to a living folk tradition, was increased by the friendship with Joachim – himself a Hungarian, and composer of at least one highly ambitious work 'in the Hungarian manner'. Brahms's sending of Hungarian tunes to Joachim has been noted on p. 80; and among his many manuscript transcriptions of folksongs, accumulated over decades, is a very early sheet dated 'Ddf. April 54' (published here, I believe for the first time, on p. 382) containing gypsy song and dance tunes which apparently interested Brahms by their irregular rhythms. As mentioned on p. 51, he played some of the Hungarian Dances as solo piano pieces to his friends in the summer of 1858, and Clara performed several in recitals during the next decade. Early in 1867 Brahms offered six dances to the Budapest publisher Dunkl, only to have them turned down; the first collection, of ten dances,[12] did not appear in print until 1869, from Simrock, and then for the fuller-textured medium of piano duet – though Brahms also issued a solo piano version in 1872 and subsequently transcribed three for orchestra. (Standard orchestrations of the rest, by other hands, soon followed, as Simrock comprehensively exploited their immense popularity).

---

[12] There were undoubtedly others. Eugenie Schumann records that at Baden he played the Schumann children 'wonderful, melancholy Hungarian melodies for which I have looked in vain among his published works; perhaps he never wrote them down.'

Brahms considered the Dances as arrangements, and though a few of the melodies may in fact be original, the bulk derive from popular gypsy tunes of the *csárdás* type, many of which could be found in Hungarian editions. No. 1, for instance, is founded on 'Isteni Csárdás', a melody attributed to Ferenc Sárkozi. Brahms was indeed accused of a measure of plagiarism from these sources, though it is likely he noted down most of the tunes by ear from Reményi's repertoire (predictably, Reményi complained of plagiarism from *him*) and later from café entertainers. Modern writers are quick to draw a somewhat puritan distinction between Brahms's taste for a 'Hungarian' music promulgated by the itinerant gypsy population for cosmopolitan consumption, and the *authentic* Hungarian folk music, as scientifically identified and collected in the field by Bartók and Kodály in the early twentieth century. It seems clear he was unaware that the tunes were not the genuine songs of the Hungarian peasantry (no more aware, that is, than Liszt in his Hungarian Rhapsodies): but that Romantic misapprehension doubtless increased his respect for them, and inspired him in his arrangements. Brahms's Hungarian Dances are not somehow inferior music because they rest upon gypsy sources. The long-running ethnomusicological resentment against gypsy music is historical (because it long diverted attention from the true folk music of which it was a distorted reflection), not aesthetic (since it ignores the extent to which gypsy music was an independently evolved idiom with an artistic worth of its own).

All this to one side, the forms and intensifications which Brahms has imposed on his favoured material are unquestionably his; the Dances are real compositions, even if he did not compose their basic material. Unlike the Waltzes, they are generally quite large-scale, multi-sectional forms, whose capricious and often fiery alternations of material, mood, and tempo re-create the traditionally passionate performance style of gypsy violinists. Brahms takes full advantage of the rhythmic freedom, the opportunities for cross-rhythm and rubato, the popular melodic style and exotically inflected cadences, that the idiom offered. It is hard to imagine anything less like the manners of a well-behaved sonata movement, but it is abundantly clear he enjoyed writing *against* his own habits of logical and conscientious development. Although all of them are worthy of mention, perhaps ultimately the most memorable dances are no. 4 in F sharp minor, with its cimbalom imitations and improvisatory feeling, and no. 9 in E minor, whose modality creates a dark harmonic colouring. Eleven further dances, a rather more personal achievement, would come some years later (see p. 267), but it is this first set which remains by far the better known.

The *Liesbeslieder-Walzer* (Love-song Waltzes) hark back to the instrumental Waltzes of op. 39 in dimensions and style. In fact, with their more elaborate piano-duet writing, they *are* primarily instrumental, but although Brahms issued a version without voices it is much less effective. Here again he presents a sequence of tiny movements, ringing resourceful changes on a single limited dance-step. But by adding a vocal quartet to the four hands at the keyboard he doubles his textural resources, and with them the opportunities for contrapuntal detail. None of the individual numbers approaches the complexity of *Wechsellied zum Tanze*; and Daumer's candyfloss verses (coy truisms and apothegms about love, translated from Russian, Polish, and Hungarian dance-songs, taken by Brahms from Daumer's 'world literature' volume *Polydora*, which also furnished him with graver texts for his op. 57 songs) are a conveniently weightless burden for the music to carry. But Brahms has some long-range structural ideas in mind, reflected not only in his rejection of some pieces that were later reworked into the *Neue Liebeslieder*, but in the careful deployment of voices – sometimes as alternating male/female duets, sometimes a chorus with tenor lead. In one (no. 9, *Am Donaustrande*, whose repeated-note idea pays covert homage to Johann Strauss's then-new *An der schönen blauen Donau*, the waltz Brahms publicly regretted not having composed), we have a low-voice trio, the soprano only joining for a few climactic bars; no. 7 is a solo alto song, no. 17 is for tenor. However, the voices are always used lyrically, never in dramatic dialogue. The forms generally echo the binary simplicities of op. 39, occasionally with varied coda; but after the unexpectedly large ternary form of no. 6 (*Ein kleiner hübscher Vogel*, perhaps the only number to have achieved something of an independent existence), the later numbers have slightly more variety. As a whole, op. 52 seems primarily intended for the enjoyment of its performers; for mere listeners it is eminently pleasant, assured, and just slightly oversweet to listen to. Brahms would not make the same mistake when he came to write its companion, op. 65 (see p. 220).

Finally we should mention one of Brahms's slightest works, the *Kleine Hochzeitskantate*, a little minuet for four-part chorus (or vocal quartet) and piano on a text by Gottfried Keller which he wrote in 1874 for the wedding of one of the poet's friends. Keller's text is a parody of the final chorus of Goethe's *Rinaldo*, but Brahms's charming treatment makes no direct allusion to his own setting of that chorus, save perhaps in the concluding rhetorical apostrophe of the wedding couple, 'Siegmund und Emilia' in the rhythm he had previously used for 'Godofred und Solyma'.

Ein deutsches Requiem

The composition of these dances surrounded a score that stands quite at the other end of the scale of importance – *Ein deutsches Requiem* op. 45 for mixed chorus and orchestra with soprano and baritone soloists: Brahms's largest single work, and the one which finally brought him widespread international recognition, not just from connoisseurs but from the great mass of concert-goers. The chronology of this supremely important creation has been a matter of intense debate. The available evidence strongly suggests the *Requiem* was effectively composed in 1865–6, following swiftly on the death of Brahms's mother; except for the present fifth movement, added only after the Bremen première in 1868. But it remains possible that Brahms had been planning a large work of memorial character for some years, had already assembled the texts for it, and that certain sections had been drafted previously. The second movement, the Funeral March 'Denn alles Fleisch es ist wie Gras', certainly has roots a decade old: according to Albert Dietrich, it incorporates material from the 'slow scherzo' of Brahms's unfinished Symphony of 1854–5 – the symphony whose first movement was written under the shadow of Schumann's tragic derangement, and eventually reworked into the D minor Piano Concerto. It is, indeed, in the Piano Concerto's slow movement that the lofty yet intimate spiritual quietus so comprehensively expressed by the *Requiem* first makes its appearance in Brahms's style. The Concerto has sometimes been considered an 'instrumental Requiem' for Schumann; the reappearance of Symphony material in the *Deutsches Requiem* suggests that Schumann is commemorated here too.[13] Nevertheless, if any single soul's passing is being mourned, Christiane Brahms remains the most likely candidate. ('We all think he wrote it in her memory, though he has never expressly said so,' Clara Schumann once told Florence May), and the added fifth movement makes the association practically explicit.

As the title *Deutsches Requiem* implies, the work has no relation to the Roman liturgy. It is 'German' in no nationalistic sense but because it is rooted in the language of the Lutheran Bible; and it is unique among requiems in that it is not an enacted prayer for the dead. The text, which Brahms himself assembled with great skill out of diverse passages from the Old and New Testaments and the Apocrypha, essentially addresses

---

[13] Brahms was certainly quite hurt when it was decided not to perform the *Requiem* in a commemorative Schumann Festival in Bonn in 1873, and he complained to Joachim, whose decision it was, that 'if you had considered the matter quite *simply* you would have known how completely and inevitably such a work as the Requiem belonged to Schumann...' (*Letters from and to Joseph Joachim*, p. 403).

the feelings of the bereaved, in a consolatory meditation on the common destiny of the dead and the living. The poignant contrast, so central to Brahms's thought in almost all his choral works, between those already in a state of grace and those barred from it and afflicted with the sense of mortality, is fully explored. Patience is exhorted in movements 2 and 3; movement 4 evokes the bliss of those now dwelling 'in the House of the Lord'; movement 5 promises comfort and future joy will replace present sorrow; movement 6 foretells the resurrection of the dead, placed within its cosmic context. Finally the living and the dead are united in the grand, circular progression of the work's thought, which began in F major in movement 1 with 'Blessed are they that mourn: for they shall be comforted' and now concludes in the seventh and last (which works its way round to a specific recall of the same music), with 'Blessed are the dead which die in the Lord from henceforth'.

The language is theistic, but at no point – as Reinthaler saw – is it explicitly Christian (any more than are Brahms's other vocal works to biblical compilation-texts). It was not the first requiem in German; precedents existed as far back as Schütz. But it was the first in which a composer had selected and shaped his text, for essentially personal resonances, to speak to a contemporary audience in a shared tongue, transcending the constraints of ritual: a prophetic sermon from individual experience, with universal application. Patience brings dignity and perspective to the mysteries of life and death, and instils a conviction of the immortality of the spirit; if there is a God, this is how He has made things, for reasons we cannot require from Him but in whose fitness we must repose some trust. It is the message Brahms was to deliver again in yet starker, more disturbing form in the motet *Warum ist das Licht gegeben?*, op. 74 no. 1.

The Lutheran Bible remained the epicentre not just of religion but of culture in Protestant-dominated nineteenth-century Germany, as it had in the seventeenth and eighteenth centuries for Schütz and Bach. In the *Deutsches Requiem* Brahms was almost inevitably mindful of their example, turned to some of the words they set and emulated some of their compositional responses. We may be sure that the texts were enhanced for him by the sense of partaking with these past masters in a shared tradition of sacred choral writing. Virginia Hancock has plausibly suggested that the fourth movement, 'Wie lieblich sind deine Wohnungen' was partly inspired by a setting of the same text in Schütz's *Symphoniae Sacrae* III no. 4, a piece illustrated and discussed at length in Brahms's much-thumbed volumes of Winterfeld's *Gabrieli*. Schütz also set portions of the texts used in the *Requiem*'s first and last movements, in works Brahms could well (though not certainly) have known: especially significant is the treatment of Brahms's 'core' text, 'Selig sind die Toten', in Schütz's 1636 *Musikalische Exequien*, where it is set in combination with a German paraphrase of the Nunc dimittis. Moreover Siegfried Ochs relates Brahms told him

> that the whole work was, essentially, founded on the chorale 'Wer nur den lieben Gott lässt walten'. Although this never comes into the foreground of the score, nevertheless several themes of the work proceed from it ...

Ochs[14] points to the work's opening (Ex. 30b) and to the second-move- ment march – which thus emerges as the seed of the entire *Requiem*, for its main theme (Ex. 30c) must have been an integral part of the early symphony's scherzo. In this use of a Lutheran chorale (Ex. 30a) Brahms seems to emulate Bach's practice in his cantatas; and Michael Musgrave has noted a significant correlation between Brahms's march theme and the first chorus of Bach's Cantata no. 27, *Wer weiss wie nähe mit mein Ende*, which uses the same chorale tune in the same 3/4 metre, with a text nearly identical to one we find in Brahms's third[15] movement. The chorale is difficult to trace in the *Requiem*'s other movements, but very many of its themes share a rising/falling arch-shape behind which the physiognomy of Ex. 30a can perhaps be descried. But it would certainly be a mistake to look for a single model for Brahms's fundamentally originally conception. It is an inspired synthesis of archaic and modern, one of the most seamless, the most infused with personal emotion, he ever achieved. His deployment of fugue (there are three altogether) to sum up movements with climatic effect, is more in the tradition of Handel and Beethoven; the masses of Haydn and Cherubini and the religious works of Mendelssohn and Schumann seem to have played their part too in orienting Brahms's idiom and structure. But there is no precedent for its overall character, which was defined in 1938 by the Marxist-mystic philosopher Ernst Bloch in *Das Prinzip Hoffnung* (The Principle of Hope) with an insight that remains resistant to paraphrase. The music of the *Requiem*, he says,

> is not lacking in restraint and in what amounts to the same thing with Brahms: a precious depth that avoids apotheoses ... Brahms's treatment of joy is even more complex than Kant's treatment of pathos (for the same un-Catholic reasons), and because his heaven has a piquancy which

[14] In his autobiography *Geschehenes, Gesehenes* (Leipzig, 1922), p. 302. The words of the chorale ('Who all his will to God resigneth') are probably not without significance to the overall spirit of Brahms's *Requiem*.

[15] Musgrave (op. cit., p. 84) says 'sixth', an example of the frequent minor slips and misprints which mar his indispensable study.

Brahms

Ex. 30

(a)

Wer   nur   den   lie - ben   Gott   lässt   Wal - ten

(b)

Ziemlich langsam und mit Ausdruck

p legato

Celli div. a 3   *p*

p

(+Basses & ad lib. organ pedal)

p legato

p legato

p legato

etc.

(c)

Langsam, marschmässig

A, T. (doubled 8ve below)

p

Denn   al - les   Fleisch   es   ist   wie   Gras   und   al - le

Herr - lich - keit   des   Men - schen   wie   des   Gra - ses   Blu - men.

prevents it from being conventional and simple-minded. These are by no means the wan joys that Nietzsche mistakenly perceived in Brahms. Nor are they a 'late autumnal light above all joys', since they display far too much ardour amid the uncertain darkness. To be sure, the happiness that turns into a mystery is manifestly enveloped in dissonance, and inherently, dissonance may in fact be a stronger expression of the mysterious than a

198

familiar triadic harmony. This music is telling us that there is a shoot – no more but no less – which could blossom into joy everlasting and will survive the darkness, which it actually constrains within itself... Within this music's darkness are glinting those treasures which are safe from rust and moths. We mean the lasting treasures in which the will and the goal, hope and its content, virtue and happiness could be united, in a world without disappointment and in the supreme good: – *the requiem encircles the secret province of the supreme good.*[16]

Less poetically expressed, this 'encircling' is due in part to the fact that though the intellectual argument of the texts develops, it is also circular, returning to its opening as it were on a higher level; and the music, while ascending up a rising chain of tonalities from movement to movement, is really symmetrically ordered. Around the central lyric vision of the blissful courts of the Lord ('Wie lieblich', no. 4 – a transfiguration of Brahms's song style into something that almost resembles a celestial *Liebeslieder* waltz) pivot two movements of teaching, built on the pattern of a soloist's exposition (baritone in no. 3, soprano in no. 5) and a choral response. While no. 3 evolves freely and culminates in a remarkable fugal invention over a continuous tonic pedal, enfolding the ecstatic variety of the polyphony (just as, in the text, the souls of the righteous remain within the hand of God), no. 5 is ternary but no less effective in its handling of its words: the thought of comfort 'like that of a mother' becomes intertwined with the repeated phrase 'I shall see you again...' in the *Requiem*'s supreme gesture of intimate tenderness. These movements are themselves encircled by the 'cosmic' perspectives of nos. 2 and 6 (universal mortality; the mystery of the Resurrection) with their unexpectedly developing forms and very different fugal climaxes. The whole grand design is introduced and rounded off by the two meditative, ternary-form choruses which propose the constant theme (no. 1, 'Blessed are they that mourn') and point the final consolatory parallel (no. 7, 'Blessed are they that die in the Lord').

The *Deutsches Requiem* therefore describes a vast, self-reflecting arch shape: almost a projection onto the largest macrocosmic level of the rising/falling contour of so many of its principal melodic ideas. However, the tonal shifts from movement to movement are always *upwards*, and the key-schemes of the individual movements are either symmetrical (in the ternary ones) or, in nos. 2, 3 and 6, brightening from a minor key to its tonic major. The trend is always towards increased radiance within a securely balanced design. When, at the end of movement 7, the music of movement 1 is reintroduced, it is at first in E flat –

---

[16] Quoted from the extract in Bloch, op. cit., pp. 240–1.

an inspired stroke which allows Brahms to delay the convergence of the material with its original F major until the very closing bars. The attainment of that key thus becomes the final upward tonal shift in a long, aspiring chain. In its very modulatory scheme, therefore, the *Requiem* enacts its spiritual message, raising itself towards the light of consolation, and closing a circle of benediction. 'Selig' ('Blessed') is the last word we hear, as it was the first.

Lieder and choral works

The first performance of the *Requiem* was followed by a summer devoted to vocal composition. Partly this was to complete unfinished business: the final *Magelone* Romances and the last chorus of *Rinaldo*. However, no less than five sets of songs, op. 43 and opp. 46–9, a total of twenty-five *Lieder* or *Gesänge*, were now put together. A few of them had been composed much earlier, and have already been mentioned; but the bulk seems to have been written in June–July 1868. Mainly setting minor poetry by Daumer and Hölty, with a leavening of folk texts from various sources, on the whole they exhibit a trend away from the dramatic tendencies of opp. 32 and 33 towards solitary meditations on love (usually star-crossed) and life (that condition famously terminable only by death). Nevertheless they present these in a highly resourceful variety of forms and with a consistent feeling for beauty that softens, or vindicates, the prevailing melancholy.

Strophic forms remain common, as in the little *Wiegenlied* (op. 49 no. 4) for Bertha Faber, celebrating the birth of her son: celebrated the world over as 'Brahms's Lullaby', it tenderly transforms a Viennese dialect love-song the mother had sung for the composer when she was Bertha Porubsky of the Hamburger Frauenchor. This exquisite miniature is in stark contrast to the austere fatalism of *Vergangen ist mir Glück und Heil* (op. 48 no. 6), one of his consciously archaic settings of an Old German text in chorale style, like the earlier *Ich schell mein Horn* (itself only published now, among op. 43). Alongside these, Brahms modifies and enlarges his strophic approach in ternary songs whose central section provides contrast by varying and developing the opening strophe, which is then recalled more exactly to round off the form: the setting of Hölty's *Die Mainacht* (op. 43 no. 2), one of whose four stanzas Brahms omitted precisely to create this desired form, is an exemplary specimen. Here the recapitulatory third part is only slightly varied; but in another Hölty song, *An ein Veilchen* (op. 49 no. 2), the suave melody and lightly dripping accompaniment of the first part are progressively transformed in the second, whose declamatory climax over throbbing chords demands an altogether darker reprise, the accompanimental pattern thickening and descending as the melody flows on into a shadowed coda. What at the beginning seemed possibly sentimental tears are revealed as symptoms of one genuinely dying for love.

This kind of varied strophic form is used on a much larger scale in the closing songs of the opp. 48 and 49 sets: two impressive nature-meditations, both to poems by Adolf von Schack and full of the sense of evanescence suggested by autumn and by evening respectively – *Herbstgefühl* (op. 48 no. 7), and *Abenddämmerung* (op. 49 no. 5). The bare textures of the former, with its plangent minor and major thirds, create a powerful sense of desolation. The misty, glimmering semiquaver figures of the latter – also dominated by thirds and pitched low in the piano's register, with a hollow, ceaselessly tolling pedal beneath – are an equally sensitive keyboard metaphor for a poem which suggests that at evening it is possible to feel closer in spirit to friends and kindred who have died. Clara was worried that Brahms, at his age, should be devoting himself to such evocations of the evening of life, but it was an expressive stance that came naturally to him after composing the *Deutsches Requiem*.

In few of these songs is there more than a perfunctory attempt at word-painting or onomatopoeic imagery; even in Hölty's *An die Nachtigall* (op. 46 no. 4) we hear not the bird's song but the poet's longing that it awakens, not the beating of its wings but his wish that it would fly away. Brahms's aim is always to render and intensify the overall mood of a poem through purely musical correlatives of line, harmony and accompanimental pattern. The ternary reprise in these modified strophic forms is thus not merely structurally cohesive but expressive, a poetically enhancing device, confirming the validity of the initial emotional response. A notable exception – because it is through-composed, and comparatively dramatic in its presentation of the argument between a village boy and his sweetheart – is the well-known *Von ewiger Liebe*, placed as the first of op. 43 but dating from 1864. Here, in what is apparently a translation from Wendish folk poetry, the girl's defiant certainty that their love must be everlasting, stronger than iron and steel, comes as a new element, a broad confident melody providing a B major resolution of the opening pages' B minor unease. The tune, poignantly enough, was taken from the choral *Brautgesang* Brahms had written for Agathe von Siebold, and then suppressed.

It was within a few weeks of the *Requiem*'s première that Brahms conceived his next choral work with orchestra, the *Schicksalslied* ('Song of Destiny'), op. 54. But though in physical dimensions this is a much smaller composition it took him three years to evolve it to his satisfaction, and it was not performed until after the completed *Rinaldo* and the later choral works opp. 53 and 55.

The *Schicksalslied* makes a significant pendant to the *Deutsches Requiem*. Brahms's short choral/orchestral works (this one, the Alto Rhapsody, *Nänie*, the *Gesang der Parzen*, and to a lesser extent the early *Begräbnisgesang* and the larger *Rinaldo*) form an almost unique and highly personal genre of their own. Awkward to programme (because of their brevity, and in some cases their vocal or instrumental requirements), they are all responses to texts of intense poetic resonance – Goethe, Hölderlin, Schiller (and the *Begräbnisgesang*'s Old German chorale) – with music of extreme evocativeness and (*Rinaldo* apart) expressive purity. In Brahms's output they occupy something of the place that religious cantatas might in another composer's; and their emotional, lyrical, and indeed spiritual intensity bespeaks the powerful significance the texts held for him. Their outlook (like that of the *Requiem* itself) is broadly non-Christian, but meditative, stoical. In their fashion, and more clearly than the *Requiem*, these works have the character of professions of metaphysical belief.

Moreover their texts all explore, from differing angles, the common theme of separation from happiness: of men (or an individual man) barred from a state of bliss (usually the preserve of God or 'the gods'). As suggested above, this idea underlies the poignancy of the *Requiem*, but it is there implied that patience may bring about a lifting of the bar. In the *Schicksalslied* and its later, even darker sister, the *Gesang der Parzen*, we find the basic quasi-philosophical statements that the Divine/human divide is in fact uncrossable. The Alto Rhapsody's human protagonist is alienated even further from his fellow men, and the work develops as an appeal (not, perhaps, very hopeful) for Divine succour. In the eponymous cantata, Rinaldo also wanders a wasteland, led astray from his comrades by the illusion of a union with a female (non-human) enchantress. In the two funeral pieces, Protestant (*Begräbnisgesang*) and Pagan (*Nänie*), individual souls have found Divine felicity – in death; and as in the *Requiem* they leave the living sorrowing for their absence.

Had Brahms not described the Alto Rhapsody as '*his* bridal-song', we might still have guessed these works to be metaphors for his own sharp awareness of absence from felicity. In *Rinaldo* and the Rhapsody we can perhaps relate the music to his separation from Agathe and from Julie Schumann; it may even be significant that the *Schicksalslied* evolved during a bitter period of disagreement with Clara; but they all surely embody a broader sense of himself as in some way fated, a man apart, able (or forced) to view his merely human aspirations dispassionately, aware of an eternal gap between them and any kind of perfection. To an extent, therefore, these are all melancholic works (in the sense of a Düreresque 'Melencolia'); but they magnificently transcend melancholy through the power of art, transmuting the emotion into a sombre joy and stoic fortitude that are among Brahms's most inspiring characteristics.

Friedrich Hölderlin's poem 'Hyperions Schicksalslied', one of his classic statements of Man's sense of alienation within the cosmos, falls into two unequal parts: an evocation of the life of the blessed spirits on high in their Elysium, followed by a bleak description of humanity below, wracked by confusion and despair. When Brahms came to compose his setting he vividly characterized these contrasted states, but the two-part structure challenged his formal sense. Musical balance and convention disposed him in favour of a ternary form, involving a repetition of the achingly beautiful opening music, and of its words; the work was, in fact, drafted in this form. But he seems ultimately to have felt that a full reinstatement of the first choral portion would nullify the effect of the grim second section and create a false sense of comfort. The solution was eventually suggested by Hermann Levi (who gave the first performance at Karlsruhe in October 1871): to reintroduce only the materials of the initial orchestral prelude, with no further contribution from the voices. This strategy confirmed the dominant role which the orchestra had in any case been assuming throughout the work.

The *Schicksalslied*, therefore, has a tragic inevitability as lucid as the 'ewiger Klarheit' ('eternal clarity') that surrounds the divine spirits. A rapt, idyllic orchestral prologue in E flat major evokes the atmosphere of everlasting peace and beauty in which the celestial gods exist – although a quiet, fateful drum-rhythm suggests a distant echo from lower, unhappier planes of being. The first principal choral section then expands serene and hymn-like in the same key, stable in rhythm and tonality. The return of the drum-rhythm signals a sudden wild plunge (closely resembling the ferocious introduction of the Last Trumpet in the *Requiem*'s sixth movement) into a harried C minor triple-time Allegro for the utterly contrasted, jagged music of blind and dwindling Mankind, whose confusion and restlessness are depicted in powerfully agitated syncopations and cross-rhythms that fall with sledgehammer blows. Brahms sets this last stanza of Hölderlin twice, the second time screwing the tonality up by a tone to D minor to intensify the hectic, driven effect.

The timpani maintain a motoric tattoo that fades eventually to a muttering rumble; at which point the radiant music of the prelude returns, reworked in richer-textured scoring and transfigured into a veiled, ethereal C major, bringing the work to a close in piercing aerial tranquillity. Many critics, from Brahms's own time onward, have rejected the premises of Hölderlin's vision and attempted to see in this coda a gesture of consolation from a more 'Christian' composer, less pessimistic than his poet. Tovey, with greater insight, wrote of its 'ruthless beauty': it seems likely that Brahms intended his conclusion, so unaffected by the minor-key anguish that preceded it, to reinforce the sense of an utter divorce between the human and the Divine. In the aftermath of that anguish it arouses a sense of hopeless longing, while the fateful drum-rhythm remains quietly persistent, even in the closing bars.

The theme of alienation is further and differently explored in the major vocal work of 1869, begun a year later but finished two years before the *Schicksalslied* in a single, intense creative effort – the Rhapsody for alto, male chorus, and orchestra. It was typical of Brahms's self-defensive humour that he spoke of this dark and deeply emotional piece as an appendix to the cosy and carefree *Liebeslieder* Waltzes; in fact it is a deeply personal lament for his isolation, and an exhortation against the dangers of misanthropy to which he must have felt himself prone: his solitary 'bridal song', occasioned by the engagement of Julie Schumann.

In choosing as his text three stanzas from Goethe's ode 'Harzreise im Winter' (actually written in 1777 on a winter journey in the Harz Mountains), Brahms seems to have been remembering a setting (also called *Rhapsodie*) of the whole poem he had seen the previous year, made in Goethe's lifetime by J. F. Reichardt. The poem is a meditation on the different kinds of life God ordains for different temperaments; the central stanzas, set by Brahms, concentrate on the fate of the man weighed down by fruitless struggles against the iron bonds of misery. A young man, turned misanthropic by sorrow, seeks solitude in the wilderness. A depiction of the desolate winter landscape into which this figure has strayed is followed by an analysis of his mental anguish and a prayer for a melody that can 'restore his heart' and bring comfort to the thirsting soul.

Brahms complemented this three-part poetic structure with a tripartite musical one which essentially reproduces (though in very 'contemporary' style) a Baroque-cantata pattern of introductory recitative, aria, and final chorus. Once he had worked out his feelings in this way he was rightly proud of the Rhapsody's compactness of expression, sombre beauty, and discreetly apposite textual illustration. The opening recitative, dark-hued in its scoring and graphic in its sense of emotional oppression, derives much of its effect from the rootless wandering around the basic C minor tonality which so aptly depicts the misanthrope's losing his way in the trackless wilderness. The sense of internal drama is further projected in the following aria, whose sinuous cross-rhythms of 6/4 and 3/2 evoke mental confusion (one of the actual melodic ideas left its mark some years later on the first movement of the Second Symphony), and whose impassioned rhetorical stress on the word *Menschenhass* (hatred of men) is one of the most 'operatic' moments in all Brahms (Ex. 31). This agonized passage returns, as he brings back the first four lines of the stanza in an intensified setting to provide the aria with a satisfactory ternary form. The modifications eventually allow a turn to the dominant major, which enables the broad, chorale-like melody of the final section to appear in a warm C major. Shared between soloist and the male chorus, this heart-easing music brings, if not fulfilment, an emotional stability that the work has sought since its outset. Religious form and gesture here limn the outlines of an inner struggle; and the supplication to 'restore his heart' is three times fervently repeated, in the manner of an Amen.

Ex.31

Brahms

([Can one] drink hatred of mankind from the fullness of love?)

The third and most extended choral work composed in the wake of the *Requiem* is utterly different from the Rhapsody and *Schicksalslied*. Whereas they are personal, even anguished, it is public, and grandiloquent. Yet the *Triumphlied*, op. 55, for double chorus, baritone solo and orchestra, is quite as important as they; that it should long have been the least-known of Brahms's major scores is an illuminating example of the irrational vagaries of taste. During Brahms's lifetime the work was widely performed and axiomatically considered a characteristic masterpiece. Fuller-Maitland thought it 'glorious', Tovey 'wonderful'; for Florence May it had

> a power, a vividness, a picturesque strength, that are not transcended, even if they are equalled, by anything ever composed in the domain of choral music for the church or the concert-room.

But around the 1914–18 War the *Triumphlied* fell clean out of the repertoire; performances in this country are prodigiously rare, and not much more common in Germany.

To excuse this phenomenon it is sometimes alleged that the work is a 'pastiche', or unpleasantly bombastic (no good performance gives this impression),[17] or that the first movement's use of the melody of 'God Save the King' (borrowed for the Prussian national anthem in 1790) somehow makes it unlistenable – though in Brahms's version the tune is hardly apparent. No valid *musical* reasons exist: the work's neglect seems to be a historical accident. As related on p. 141, Brahms – to whom the sentiment of patriotism was not unknown – composed it in 1870–1 in celebration of the victories in the Franco-Prussian War and the achievement of a German Empire, and 'respectfully' dedicated it 'Seiner Majestät dem Deutschen Kaiser Wilhelm'. Forty years later, when a considerable campaign was mounted against German music by equally patriotic British audiences and programmers during the Great War, these associations naturally rendered the *Triumphlied* utterly unacceptable. Since World War II, its 'nationalistic' overtones seem to have rendered it an embarrassment in Germany too. Yet the music magnificently transcends them, and apart from the fact that it is the hardest of all Brahms's choral works for the singers it has legitimate claims on the repertoire. The *Triumphlied* is now grossly undervalued, because grossly under-performed. To their loss, audiences remain ignorant of a work which carries to extremes certain aspects of the composer's genius, and is yet unlike anything else in his *oeuvre*.

In any case it is not as if we had to consider some tub-thumping setting of chauvinist verse (in the vein, perhaps, of the op. 41 *Männerchöre*). What Tovey called its 'hint of earthly warfare' remains only a hint: there is no endorsement of Prussian militarism. As its title implies, the work is a festal song of deliverance and victory, couched in the severe biblical terms which we find perfectly acceptable in works such

[17] The only commercial recording known to me (DG, conducted by Sinopoli) is unfortunately a travesty.

as Handel's *Israel in Egypt*. The text consists of multitudinous Hallelujahs and famous sentences from the nineteenth Chapter of the Apocalypse of St John, the vision of Divine justice visited on the nations of the Earth, which locate the *Triumphlied* upon territory adjoining Vaughan Williams's *Sancta Civitas* and Franz Schmidt's *Das Buch mit sieben Siegeln* ('The Book with Seven Seals'). Brahms deliberately omitted the passages that glorify in the destruction of God's enemies. His clear purpose was to make a contribution to a specific genre – the festive Te Deum for a great public occasion – and enlarge it with an element of apocalyptic vision and a particularly thoroughgoing creative transformation of the musical past. The result is Brahms's frankest evocation of Baroque manners. Indeed, he took Handel's Dettingen Te Deum (celebrating a different victory over the French) as a specific model, and quasi-Handelian dotted rhythms, extended sequences, melodic contours and trumpet fanfares are pervasively reproduced throughout the *Triumphlied* (which shares Handel's key of D major). But the result is manifestly no pastiche: this three-movement thanksgiving cantata gains depth and focus by exploiting pre-Classical forms with an authority and understanding none of Brahms's contemporaries could match. If there are bars which sound like Handel, every sentence or period is vintage Brahms. The harmony, the contrapuntal intricacy, the essence and overall sweep of the ideas, and the grandly through-composed structures, all bear his unmistakable stamp.

There are three closely-interrelated movements, the first virtually an enormous 'Hallelujah Chorus' (though it also sets parts of Revelations Ch. 19, vv. 1–2) in a symphonically expanded ternary form, whose prodigal invention and sheer splendour of sound put it among Brahms's most virtuosic demonstrations of his compositional skill. The spirit of the 'Handel' Variations, glorying in 'mastery of the old forms', is here writ on a vaster scale, in massive unison writing, elaborately decorated polyphony, and close antiphony and echo-effects between the choirs. The second movement has three sections (the text extracted from vv. 5–7 of Revelations 19): a calmer, meditative passage in G major, more Bachian than Handelian in effect, is followed by a return to D as fanfares and Hallelujahs herald the stirring proclamation (in a multiple imitation which mimics 'the voice of a great multitude') that the Lord God omnipotent reigneth: Luther's Bible renders 'reigneth' as 'entered into his Kingdom' (*Reich*), so a homage to the new German Empire can doubtless be detected here by critics so inclined. The movement ends in G with a chorus of gentler jubilation where expressive triplet writing in strings and chorus is counterpointed against the Lutheran chorale *Nun danket Alle Gott* in the wind instruments.

The Finale, which has some resemblances to the sixth movement of the *Deutsches Requiem*, introduces a baritone soloist to expound St John's vision of the rider on the white horse who treads the wine-press of the fierceness and wrath of Almighty God. The name written on his vesture – 'King of Kings and Lord of Lords' – becomes the text of the concluding chorus, perhaps the grandest and most contrapuntally virtuosic of them all: 'Ein König aller Könige'. Possibly while he penned it Brahms gave fleeting thought to Kaiser Wilhelm I; but Wilhelm has long been dust, while Brahms's music lives on as the most resplendent display of 'modern composition in the Handelian manner' since Beethoven's *Die Wiehe des Hauses* Overture. The *Triumphlied* speaks of no temporal Germany, but a rejoicing that (like the *Requiem*'s mourning) takes place in the universe of metaphysical realities. It has no real successors in Brahms's output, though its antiphonal effects were to be recalled much later in the *Fest- und Gedenksprüche* motets for double choir, and its Handelian energy in the Finale of the Second Symphony.

Quartets and variations

If the *Triumphlied* represents an end-point for Brahms's 'archaizing' tendencies, the two string quartets he unveiled in 1873 as his op. 51 illustrate a different kind of extremism. The remorseless logic of their construction, the derivation of so much from basic motifs, the drive to encompass his most 'advanced' and personal harmonic and contrapuntal vocabulary, admit few compromises with the chosen medium and strain it almost to breaking point. As to the medium itself, the challenge of contributing to a repertoire largely created by Haydn, Mozart, Beethoven and Schubert aroused Brahms to an even keener sense of historic responsibility than usual. Perhaps that is why the works (no. 1 especially) can seem so unrelievedly serious and hard-driven, so afflicted by the instability of the minor mode. The result has frequently been castigated as execrable quartet-writing, and Brahms's quartets have certainly never seized the unassailable prominence in the quartet repertoire that his symphonies attained in the orchestral literature. Yet they are important works by any standard, 'full of passionate intensity' and a somewhat pressurized eloquence, rich (practically clotted) with musical substance and compositional subtlety; their close-knit forms, myriad levels of contrast, malleable phrasing and tonal fluidity have exerted their fascination on generations of musical analysts.

Brahms had waited until he was forty to give a string quartet to the world. He claimed to have destroyed twenty others in the meantime – perhaps poetic exaggeration, but we know he wrote quartets in the very early 1850s and he must have continued to wrestle with the form almost constantly: it represented a challenge a composer of his ambitions simply could not decline. The op. 51 Quartets themselves likely represent several years' work and polishing: no. 1, in C minor, perhaps goes back to a quartet in that key discussed with Joachim in 1865–6, which by 1867 had at least one companion. In mid-1869 Brahms wrote to Simrock about rehearsing some string quartets to help him 'make one or the other passable' for publication. These may well have been interim versions of op. 51: when Brahms completed the two quartets that we know, in the summer of 1873, he noted it was 'for the second time'. They were further revised after private performances before he allowed them to be published, with a dedication to Billroth, his quartet-playing friend.

The layout and dimensions of their four-movement form suggests Brahms's primary model was Beethoven: the op. 18 and 'Rasumovsky' Quartets most of all, but viewed through an awareness of the last Beethoven quartets (perhaps especially opp. 130 and 132) and with a different sense of sonority, to which Schumann's quartets probably contributed. The fevered rhetoric and strenuous energy of op. 51 no. 1 has often provoked the epithet 'Beethovenian', as does the use of the older composer's 'fate' key of C minor. But in creating this genuinely (indeed, determinedly) tragic work Brahms could equally have had in mind the vigorous pathos of Mozart's G minor Symphony, and the 'orchestral' tremolando that accompanies the first movement's ardent opening theme (Ex. 32a) may stem from that source as directly as from, say, Schubert's quartet-style in such works as *Der Tod und das Mädchen*.

This movement is remarkable for its wide-ranging treatment of tonality – the immediate move by the first subject's second part (Ex. 32b) to the foreign region of F, and then to the equally exotic dominant of B minor, excited the admiration of Schoenberg, who compared the harmonic richness here to Wagner's *Tristan*. Even more remarkable is the 'motivic saturation': the theme of Ex. 32a (whose shape and rhythm already interpenetrate Ex. 32b), and the other motifs produced by first and second subjects, are ceaselessly worked over, exchanging contours and rhythms in a dazzling process of combination and transformation that produces a multiplicity of meaningful resemblances and masterly ambiguity, more susceptible to graphic analysis than verbal description. In essence Brahms has already arrived where Schoenberg was to follow forty years later in *his* official First Quartet – at a 'totally thematic' organization of his material down to the smallest motivic details.

Ex. 32

(a)

(b)

This process informs the whole Quartet: it is possible to trace further metamorphoses of Ex. 32a through the two middle movements (Ex. 32c and d) to the Finale, where it is specifically re-invoked (Ex. 32e) and, in slightly modified guise, undergoes a further bout of development. The middle movements are however overtly simpler and stabler, if hardly carefree. The oddly titled 'Romanze' has a song-like character, touched with perhaps nocturnal melancholy; but though its overall form is a straightforward A–B–A–B (in which the second A is much varied, the second B less so), the tunes are hesitant, the rhythm elusive, even prosodic, and the harmonizations almost chokingly close: as in so much of this Quartet, the scarcity of rests to aerate the texture powerfully strengthens its disturbing sense of emotional constriction. The twilit

211

world of the intermezzo-like third movement, with its pair of wan little themes (see Ex. 32d), bobbing gait and tonal vagrancy, brings no relief, despite the ghostly charm of the F major middle section. It is as if the relatively lusty dance movements of the earlier chamber works have returned in spiritualized, asceticized garb, the better to fit in with the prevailing fatalistic mood.

Ex. 32

The Finale is as strenuous as the first movement, and resumes its intensive developmental activities. A compacted sonata design with Ex. 32e as its first theme and a second subject that draws the basic motif into its axis by a different route, the movement conflates the functions of development and recapitulation so that the return of the tonic C minor (never very firmly established in the exposition in any case) is postponed dramatically, and in sonata terms almost infinitely – until well into the coda. Frustrated anticipation, teased by hints of *major* tonalities, gains at length the cruelly ironic reward of a massive tonic pedal, a firm C *minor* tonality, and a last, terse cadence (Ex. 32f) that is essentially a long-delayed resolution of the work's very first gesture: a remarkable 'closing of the circle' whose grim logic suggests the tragedy is an endless treadmill, ready to turn again.

Ex. 32
(f)

The Second Quartet, in A minor, has perhaps more points of contact with Brahms's later chamber scores. Basically more relaxed, it displays many contrasts with op. 51 no. 1 but is equally close-woven in texture and resourceful in its motivic developments; and again there is a case for regarding the themes of its four movements as varied expressions of a single motif (the links are set out in Ex. 33a–d). The work begins, however, with a 'motto-theme' seen in Ex. 33a: a form of

Brahms

Joachim's 'F-A-E' figure which is used throughout the first movement, later appearing in amicable conjunction with Brahms's personal variant 'F-A-F'. Unlike the analogous movement of the C minor Quartet, this one has quite a short development section *per se*, but a correspondingly broader exposition and recapitulation, containing some development within themselves, whose wealth of ideas suggests the example of Schubert rather than Beethoven. They include a suavely Viennese *grazioso* second subject with a *lusingando* (alluring) violin counterpoint, which shows how much greater a scope this work offers for sheer lyricism. But the sense of serious purpose, though less oppressive than in the C minor, is never absent, and exemplified by the fact that all four movements remain rooted to the basic A tonality.

Ex. 33

214

The Andante moderato, in A major, opens with a darkly pensive violin theme that greatly impressed Schoenberg by its intricate and sophisticated motivic organization, whereby the smallest phrases mirror and dovetail into each other. The subsidiary material moves into the relative minor for a brief, passionate 'Hungarian' duet for violin and cello in canon, set against smoky tremolandi; the main theme eventually returns in the 'wrong' key, F major, and is eased back to A by the intervention of the cello, closing in a spirit of uneasy calm. The third movement is marked *Quasi Minuetto*: here again one has the impression of a sad, spiritualized dance music, virtually removed from physical associations despite the cello's earthy open fifths. The Minuet alternates with a distant, contrapuntal variation of itself, a scurrying, gossamer Allegretto in 2/4 – intercalated in its turn with a brief but more recognizable variation in the original *Tempo di Minuetto*.

The Finale retains the 3/4 of the minuet and reshapes its theme into a pugnacious Hungarian dance, doubtless as a compliment to Joachim. Another sonata form, but with elements of sonata-rondo, it is remarkable for its virtuoso array of cross-rhythms and the number of transformations wrought upon Ex. 33d. These culminate in a warm major-key duet version for first violin and cello and a slow variation in *pp* block chords that leads back to the vivacious, but severe, A minor conclusion. Neither of the op. 51 Quartets is easy to love; but there is much to cherish in both, and they repay many hearings.

Apart from completing the quartets, Brahms's major compositional effort in 1873 was his Variations on a Theme of Haydn, which present-day commentators tend to call Variations on the 'St Antoni' Chorale, since Haydn almost certainly had nothing to do with the melody in question. Pedantry apart, the redesignation serves little purpose. That Brahms chose a theme (Ex. 34a) so deeply obscure (and made it one of the best-known tunes in the orchestral repertoire) reflects his own scholarly interests: it forms the second movement of a *Feld-Partita* for eight wind instruments, one of six discovered by Pohl, who showed the manuscript to Brahms in 1870 (the piece was not published until 1932: Brahms made his own copy of the movement). Though assigned the number II/46 in Hoboken's catalogue of Haydn's works, the piece is most likely by Haydn's star pupil Ignaz Pleyel – who probably took the theme, headed 'Corale St. Antonii', from some older, unidentified source. But Pohl and Brahms both presumed it to be by Haydn, whose name added lustre to it and helped to orient Brahms's conception. All his principal variation sets pay some degree of tribute to their themes' composers: the two 'Schumann' sets to his friend and benefactor and to the genre of 'fantasy-variation' he cultivated; the 'Handel' set to a master of Baroque stylization; the 'Paganini' to the early-Romantic cult of diabolic virtuosity. The 'Haydn' set is his most sustained homage to the inspiration still to be derived from Viennese Classical traditions, with Haydn as tutelary deity.

There are two versions: for orchestra (op. 56a) and for two pianos (op. 56b, despite the fact it was written earlier), identical in substance yet of greatly dissimilar importance for his *oeuvre* as a whole. Viewed simply as a two-piano work, op. 56b is a useful addition to the repertoire but hardly stretches the medium to the same heroic extent as the F minor Sonata op. 34a; more complex and searching than the piano-duet variations op. 23, it makes none of the ground-breaking demands of the 'Handel' and 'Paganini' sets, though Brahms comprehensively exploits the medium to attain full scope for contrapuntal development. But as Brahms's first transference of his beloved variation techniques to the full orchestra, op. 56a assumes greater significance. The little *Liebeslieder* Suite apart, he had written nothing for orchestra alone for fourteen years since the Serenades; but much orchestral music with chorus, refining a rich and flexible colouristic sense which is finally exploited for its own sake in op. 56a. The orchestra provides an entire layer of textural subtlety unavailable on pianos alone; although there are only eight variations and a finale, the incisive use of colour allied to a now instinctive mastery of thematic transformation sharply characterizes each, and it is in this form that the work has become one of Brahms's best-loved creations.

Ex. 34

(a)

In his initial presentation of the tune he mimics 'Haydn's' wind-instrument scoring, and the wind are prominent and sensitively used throughout. The theme's unusual phrase-structure (of $5+5+4 +4+4+4+3$ bars, the third group of 4 repeating bars 1–4 of the first 5) was clearly a prime attraction, for most of the variations

216

preserve these proportions, and stick even closer to the original key (B flat, with a few excursions into the minor) than the 'Handel' set (also in B flat). But within each variation there are subtle modifications of the original harmony and freely evolving melodic developments that derive new shapes only distantly related to the theme. Variation 1, which immediately takes up the theme's final repeated B flats and subsumes them into a quietly tolling background for quite independent string figuration (in contrary motion and rhythm), makes the tendency clear. Among many features we should note the suave leading theme (Ex. 34b) of variation 4 (whose texture shows that the supposedly academic device of strict triple counterpoint can yield the sheerest lyric poetry); the excited scherzo-like character of variation 5; the 'hunting' variation 6 with its galloping rhythms and ebullient horns (Ex. 34c); the exquisite siciliana melody of variation 7 (Ex. 34d); and the crepuscular half-lights of variation 8, whose soft, rapidly snaking melodic lines and scoring for *pp* wind and muted strings make it a ghostly invention indeed.

Ex. 34

The Finale, true to Brahms's general practice, reaches beyond the proportional confines set up by the theme to produce a through-composed design containing several further variations of a different kind. The means by which he does this, however, is new for him, and significant for his later development as a symphonist. From the 'Haydn' theme he fashions a five-bar ground bass (Ex. 34e) which is repeated, unchanging, in the manner of a Baroque chaconne or passacaglia. No less than seventeen of these five-bar variations process in an increasingly magnificent parade of seamless invention around this thematic core, climaxing in a grand clinching statement of the tune from which Brahms has derived so much inspiration.

Ex. 34

(e)

Songs, vocal quartets, duets and partsongs

Between 1871 and 1874 Brahms completed a large amount of vocal music, including no less than thirty-three songs issued in four groups, opp. 57–9 and op. 63, as well as the five *Ophelia-Lieder*, which he did not publish.[18] In general the published song sets continue and extend the range of moods explored in the Lieder of the later 1860s, with ever greater richness of technique; there is hardly one that does not deserve and reward close study of the way Brahms makes music out of poetry – often great music out of indifferent poetry. Though none of the sets are true cycles (even to the extent op. 32 was), the order of songs within each is carefully structured to secure large-scale contrasts and make expressive points within the group as a whole. The eight songs of op. 57 are the only group setting a single poet (Daumer, and Daumer's translations from Persian, Spanish and Indian sources), and the only ones to establish a discreet thematic interrelation through the use of a vocal leitmotif (which Eric Sams has plausibly suggested is another form of Schumann's 'Clara-motif'). The group extends, often tellingly, the

---

[18] Brahms wrote these at the request of the actress Olga Precheisen, for a performance of *Hamlet* in Prague in 1873. They are drastically short and simple, but not sketchy as sometimes alleged. Brahms deliberately and aptly employs his folksong-setting manners at their most laconic, securing the underlying sense of mental disturbance by irregular barring (no. 1) and unsettlingly abrupt endings (no. 4).

shadowed moods and manners of the 1868 songs, essentially exploring a single situation: that of the lover who must contain his sexual yearning with a patience that may never be rewarded.

Op. 58 starts, by contrast, with a group of lively, extrovert songs: *Blinde Kuh* (no. 1) turns to account the questing fingers in a game of blindman's-buff by giving them a neo-Baroque keyboard toccata to play around the voice-part. *Während des Regens* (no. 2) illustrates a notable exception to Brahms's general disinclination for word-painting: raindrops (as we shall see in op. 59) perennially evoked onomatopoeic effects from him, and here they patter cheerily in a shower heavy enough to keep a girl from leaving her lover's house. *O komme, holde Sommernacht* (no. 4) is a radiant anticipation of a night of love bedecked with horn-call harmonies in a glowing F sharp major. It is a crushing example of Brahms's irony that it should be followed at once by the depressive E flat minor of *Schwermut* (no. 5), which turns a feeble verse by Karl Candidus into a dour but deeply moving confession of mortal weariness. The bare, simple texture gives it something of the nobility of the 'Altdeutsch' chorale songs like op. 48 no. 6, softened by some discreet arpeggiation; and it makes explicable the succeeding bitterness of *In der Gasse* (no. 6), to a poem by Friedrich Hebbel – an expression of the futility of keeping alive mere ancient memories of love. Only with Schack's *Serenade* (no. 8) is there a kind of resolution, lightly uniting the extremes of mood in an elaborate guitar-style song whose narrator's nimble-fingered strumming recalls the keyboard bravura of *Blinde Kuh*.

The op. 59 group opens with a spacious, almost serene setting of Goethe's *Dämmerung senkte sich von oben*, a rapt evocation of evening twilight and coolness which, with the next few atmospheric songs, bespeaks the solace offered by contemplation of nature. Thus nos. 3 and 4 of this set, *Regenlied* and *Nachklang*, are rain-songs (Brahms's first settings of his friend and fellow-provincial, the poet Klaus Groth, whose nostalgic verse evoked in him an especially keen response),[19] where the raindrops first arouse piercing childhood memories and then the tears they so resemble. The two songs form a diptych, *Nachklang* literally an 'echo' of the bittersweet main part of *Regenlied*,[20] reproducing its ceaseless runnels of quaver figuration and the monotonous reiteration of the individual drops (shown in Ex. 48b on p. 280) without its more

---

[19] Groth was most celebrated for his North-German dialect poetry, but Brahms declined to set any of that because, he said, he found it 'all too personal' for music. The dialect was, of course, his own; his father spoke it all his life.

[20] This setting of *Nachklang* replaces an earlier one made separately about 1866 (when it was called *Regenlied*). Published after Brahms's death, this original version has almost no points of contact with the one in op. 59.

rhetorical later sections, which hark back almost to the style of the *Magelone* songs. The extreme thematic economy (everything in *Nach-klang*, and much in *Regenlied*, springs from the first three bars) is characteristic of a developing trend throughout the Lieder of this period. The remainder of op. 59 turns away from nature: the transition is effected in no. 5, *Agnes*, a Mörike setting that cunningly creates a 'folk' style through melodic shape and irregularly changing time-signature, its jilted heroine oblivious of her countryside surroundings. The group ends with more grieving Groth; in no. 8, *Dein blaues Auge*, a long-rejected lover looks into the eyes of the woman he has loved and finds them 'as cool as a lake' – perhaps the lake that reflected the harmony of nature in the opening Goethe setting.

Op. 63, the longest of all these song sets, alternates songs of youth and love with songs of age (with its memories of these things). Though most of them are songs of ambitious scope Brahms keeps a light touch, especially through the opening group of settings of Max von Schen-kendorf, which end with the almost Schubertian *An den Tauben* (no. 4). Then come two songs Brahms subtitles '*Junge Lieder*' to con-ventional yet stammeringly gifted love-poems by the nineteen-year-old Felix Schumann, already afflicted by the tuberculosis that was soon to kill him: Brahms's settings compensate elaborately and generously for the immaturity of the verse. Finally a triptych of Groth settings, which Brahms entitles *Heimweh* ('Nostalgia'). In other hands these rather too facile laments for lost childhood could easily have degenerated into sentimentality; Brahms rather ennobles them, and in the deeply impress-ive *O wüsst ich doch den Weg zurück* (op. 63 no. 8), a very slow monologue with uneasily murmuring figuration and a fateful, chaconne-like bass, he raises the poet's isolation upon the last empty beach of life, his backward path lost, to the level of a metaphysical statement. The final song, *Ich sah als Knabe*, then dissolves the portentous mood into lyric pathos; again a single image – this time of a wreath – refers us back to the opening song, the buoyant Schenkendorf *Frühlingstrost*.

In the winter of 1869–70, at the request of his friend the conductor Ernst Rudorff, Brahms produced a nine-movement *Liebeslieder* Suite for performance with an accompaniment of small orchestra. Eight of the movements were straight orchestrations of various numbers from the *Liebeslieder* Waltzes, but the ninth (which may of course have been sketched for it) did not in fact appear in op. 52. Instead, it resurfaced in 1874 as no. 9 of a new set for voices and piano duet, the *Neue Liebes-lieder*, op. 65. Musically, op. 65 (which contains fifteen numbers in all) is slightly superior to op. 52, although Brahms's use of the solo quartet is rather less resourceful: no less than seven numbers are solo waltz-songs, four for soprano and one each for the other voices; no. 13 is a female-voice duet, and so is no. 14 for its first half. But the actual quality of musical thought is richer, the waltz idioms ever more subordinated to individual expression.

The texts, with one signal exception, are again from Daumer's *Polydora*, but Brahms seems to wring a greater depth of emotion from some of them, such as the haunting G minor no. 12, *Schwarzer Wald, dein Schatten ist so düster!* ('Sombre wood, how cheerless is thy shadow'). The actual forms remain as circumscribed as op. 52 until no. 14, which is freely and buoyantly through-composed and prepares for the modest sensation of the epilogue, *Zum Schluss*. As if finally breaking free of his self-imposed popular-music conventions and commenting upon the realities that escape Daumer's conventionally idealized lovers, this last number sets a poet of altogether different mettle: Goethe. The final lines of his *Alexis und Dora*, beginning 'Now enough, ye Muses!' constitute a prayer for the healing of the heart wounded by love; emphasizing rather than concealing a poignant association of ideas, Brahms broadens the time to 9/4 and writes a chaconne on a familiar ground bass – the theme of the prayer (also by Goethe) for heart-healing that concluded the Alto Rhapsody. He had called that work an 'epilogue' to the *Liebeslieder*: now he enacts the jest (if such it was), and the result is a spellbinding change in the music's specific gravity, with a central canon where the pianists finally fall silent to let the singers' lingering cadence speak for itself (Ex. 35).

Shortly before the appearance of these *Neue Liebeslieder*, Brahms had published three vocal quartets with piano, op. 64, more in the tradition of the op. 31 set. Indeed the first, *An die Heimat*, probably dates from the same period. Perhaps less immediately memorable than any of that earlier group, it is nevertheless very elaborately laid out – Brahms draws a remarkable, motet-like range of colour from the four voices in harmony, treating them like a tiny chorus with canonic imitations, occasional solos and little *a cappella* passages; while to Sternau's text, a conventional praise of the poet's (unspecified) homeland, he brings a depth of feeling understandable if, as seems likely, the piece was composed during his first winter in Vienna, away from Hamburg.

There follows a setting of Schiller's *Der Abend*, a late poem full of Classical metaphor which Brahms ingeniously touches into life with male/female dialogue for Apollo and Thetis and a haunting piano accompaniment mimicking the step of the sun god's horses; there is a moment of pure magic as the horses stop (the piano falls silent) and drink cooling draughts from the sea in long female-voice phrases. Op. 64

Ex. 35

([You cannot heal the wounds] inflicted by Love...)

concludes with one of Daumer's translations from the Turkish, *Fragen*,
a set of questions put to a lover (the tenor) by the other three singers,
massed as a vocal trio. It develops into a tightly dovetailed dialogue,
carried out with a sensitive mingling of humour and pathos. Fuller-

Maitland's comment[21] that 'where a quartet-party has a first-rate tenor it is always effective' indicates what we miss in an age for which quartet-parties are a phenomenon of ancient history.

Also from this period date eight duets for soprano and contralto with piano, three published along with the much earlier *Klosterfräulein* as op. 61 in 1874, and the remainder the following year as op. 66. In these female-voice duets Brahms tends to avoid the dialogue form he had employed so successfully in the op. 28 male/female sets. The exception is *Jägerlied*, op. 66 no. 4, where the soprano's major-key questions are answered by the contralto, taking the role of the lovelorn hunter, with uniform minor-key despair. Elsewhere the texts do not generally suggest more than one voice, and Brahms merely uses two to secure effects of harmonic richness or for occasional contrapuntal intensification (most obviously by fluent canon in the central sections of Goethe's *Phänomen*, op. 61 no. 3, and Hölty's *Am Strande*, op. 66 no. 3, probably the finest songs in their respective groupings).

The piano parts are discreet but apposite to each conception, ranging in op. 61 from the droll little parlour refrain of no. 1, *Die Schwestern*, through the multicoloured arpeggios of *Phänomen* – evoking Goethe's images of rainbow, mist and rain – to the delightfully bubbling scherzo style of no. 4, *Boten der Liebe*. The second duet of op. 66 is based on a theme that clearly recalls the Minnelied, *Mir ist Leide*, as used in the slow movement of Brahms's F sharp minor Piano Sonata op. 2: the piano suggests it, then the voices take it up while the piano accompanies them in sad, 'harped' chords. As the text is full of images of burial and graves (nos. 1 and 2, both entitled *Klänge*, are to elegantly dejected poems of love and death by Klaus Groth), the music may enshrine some personal remembrance of the Schumann household more than twenty years before. Or perhaps not so long ago: Julie Schumann had died in Italy as recently as 1872. The sombre tone persists through the remainder of the set, to be partially alleviated in no. 5, *Hüt du dich!* This concluding setting from *Des Knaben Wunderhorn* is a perfect marriage of Brahms's strophic folksong style with subtle, 'art song' phrasing and a rhythmically intricate piano-part: a series of verbal variations on the old saw that Love makes a fool of the lover is melodiously set to music just too full of life to take the warning seriously enough.

During this period Brahms published only one opus for unaccompanied chorus, the seven Lieder, op. 62: a rather heterogeneous collection of secular partsongs in four to six voices, some certainly

---

[21] J. A. Fuller-Maitland, *Brahms* (London, 1911), p. 193.

composed around 1873–4 while others seem to go back to Hamburg and Detmold days. Nos. 1 and 2, the strophic *Rosmarin* and *Von alten Liebesliedern* (both on words from *Des Knaben Wunderhorn*), re-create Brahms's folksong-setting manner in rather more sophisticated idioms, while no. 7, on the Old German folk text *Vergangen ist mir Glück und Heil*, is a choral arrangement of the archaic, Dorian-mode song of the same title, op. 48 no. 6 (or more likely the song is the arrangement: the situation precisely parallels *Ich schwing' mein Horn*, which exists as both a solo song and a male chorus). No. 6, *Es geht ein Wehen in der Wald*, survives in an almost identical version from around 1860 – its curious spacing, with the basses sepulchrally reiterating a tonally ambiguous figure very low in their register, is clearly characteristic of Brahms's early approximations of Renaissance technique.

Most of the other numbers make varied use of the canonic methods Brahms had perfected in his earlier choral pieces, but these are now much more smoothly and unobtrusively assimilated into the flow of the music, most of all in the madrigal-like no. 5, *All meine Herzgedanken*, where multiple imitation is used gradually to build up the texture to a full six parts, antiphonally divided between men's and women's voices, and is then effectively disguised as natural chromatic progression. The crown of the set is undoubtedly no. 3, *Waldesnacht*, one of the most gorgeously evocative examples of the Romantic choral Lied – where the canonic writing, resulting in some plangent dissonance, is felt merely as part of an atmospheric interplay of light and shade, intensifying a mood of regretful reflection and identification with nature that is never allowed to become over-indulgent.

Apart from op. 62 we should note a single chorus which was not published in Brahms's lifetime. The dating of *Dem dunkeln Schoss der heil'gen Erde*, a short partsong for mixed voices on words from Schiller's *Lied von der Glocke*, is uncertain, but it was in existence by February 1880, and is probably a good deal earlier, from the late 1860s or early '70s. The verses are funereal, apt for a burial service, and Brahms's treatment is appropriately austere, but we do not know whether the piece was occasioned by the death of any particular friend. Writing to Wasielewski, who had requested music for the unveiling of the Schumann monument in Bonn in 1880, Brahms mentioned this chorus only to dismiss it as unfit for the occasion. Its chorale-like main tune and smooth, imitative polyphony lend it the character of a brief motet rather than a *Chorlied*.

The last piano quartet

If the op. 51 String Quartets occupied Brahms over a period of several years, the Piano Quartet in C minor, which appeared in 1875 as op. 60, emerged from a very much longer gestation. Indeed, it is a completely recomposed version of the C sharp minor Quartet he had been struggling with in 1855–6, alongside that other stillborn *magnum opus* of his youth, the D minor Symphony. Unlike the Symphony, the Quartet had been completed in at least one interim version: Brahms and Joachim tried it over in Hanover in April 1856, when it seems to have been in three movements, with a central Andante and a 'passionate' Finale. In October, Clara Schumann saw a 'wonderful' Adagio in E major, perhaps written to replace the Andante. The Quartet was again given a run-through with Joachim in November 1856; then no more was heard of it until 1868, when Brahms showed the first movement to Hermann Dieters with the words: 'Now, imagine a man who is just going to shoot himself, for there is nothing else to do' – an image he consistently developed in later remarks.

In 1873–4 he took up the Quartet afresh and fundamentally rethought it, lowering the principal key by a semitone, radically revising two of the original movements and composing two new ones. The result, he told Billroth, was 'a curiosity – perhaps an illustration for the last chapter about the man in the blue coat and the yellow waistcoat'. The man who dressed thus is the archetypal Romantic protagonist of German literature: in the last chapter of Goethe's eponymous novel, Werther shoots himself because of his anguished love for a married woman whose husband he admires. Brahms further developed the *Werther* symbolism half-jocularly in an 'instruction' to his publisher, Simrock:

> On the cover you must have a picture, namely a head with a pistol to it. Now you can form some conception of the music! I'll send you my photograph for the purpose. You can use blue coat, yellow breeches and top-boots, since you seem to like colour-printing.

These comments suggest that many of the tensions of the Düsseldorf years are still alive in op. 60, the memories made more poignant by working with it anew. Yet according to Brahms himself only the first movement and Scherzo were retained from 1856: as the contemporary correspondence makes no mention of a scherzo, what we know as the Scherzo may in fact have been the original Finale – a drastically curtailed but certainly 'passionate' one (a plausible thesis, since op. 60's Scherzo, most unusually, has no formal Trio). Michael Musgrave suggests that the 'new' Andante and Finale, begun by long solos for cello and violin respectively, may draw upon partly sketched sonatas for those instru-

ments.[22] Unsurprisingly, therefore, the C minor Piano Quartet displays
little of the close-worked motivic unity of the String Quartet in the
same key, though there are some interesting correspondences between
movements 1 and 2, and between 3 and 4. Each movement is strongly
characterized and compact in structure: if some of the material betrays
its early date, the techniques are nevertheless those of Brahms's full
maturity.

The opening, which has some of the introductory flavour of the
beginning of the Piano Quintet, immediately pitches us into a whirlpool
of Romantic tribulation (Ex. 36). The strings gasp out a two-note phrase
that seems to catch the intonations of speech. One has the distinct
impression that the violin's E flat–D semitone speaks the name 'Clara' –
an idea rendered less fanciful by the immediate unwinding of a transposed version of Schumann's 'Clara-motif'. The passage is repeated on
B flat minor, opening the tonal vista startlingly wide, before the music

Ex. 36

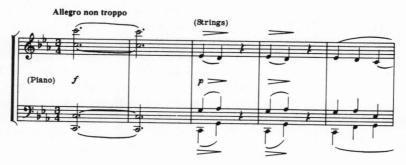

[22] Musgrave, op. cit., p. 117. Some writers still assume that the slow movement, an E
major Andante, belonged to the old C sharp minor work, but this contradicts the
testimony of Brahms's own work-list. The prominence it gives to the cello is characteristic of his chamber music at all periods, not just his early years.

226

plunges into a stormy transition that finds temporary respite in E flat major with a lyric, Schubertian second subject whose self-contained melody immediately gives rise to a little group of four variations. The development begins in E flat minor and is wrathfully strenuous. This works through to a much-altered form of Ex. 36, which therefore requires no literal recapitulation – its tonal consequences are redirected so as to lead to a more regular return of the second subject: but in the irregular key of G major, where its original variations are further developed and project the music into a bitter, strife-torn coda, finally subsiding as if in exhaustion.

Also in C minor, the Scherzo is a splendid movement in Brahms's early vein of rhythmic dynamism, with a sense of volcanic emotion barely kept under control. The tense, muttering rhythm of the opening gives prominence to a rising second as if to counterbalance the first movement's Ex. 36, and makes a similarly precipitate side-slip to B flat minor. There is a plaintive, chant-like second theme, whose pathos is the only element to interrupt the powerful rhythmic drive. The movement is through-composed: a sinuous third theme brings a brief turn to the major, but the surging scherzo character and tempo are not to be diverted from their grim purposes. The coda is defiant, vehemently embellished with trills, but brutally abrupt: if the C sharp minor Quartet ended like this, the overriding impression was surely one of angry despair.

But op. 60 has a different path to follow. The song-like cello theme that begins the Andante, the length of the melody itself (Ex. 37a is merely the opening of it), and its continuation in a rapt duet for violin and cello – all bring emotional assuagement and calm. Here is the still centre of the work, encompassed in a broad sonata form with a *dolce* second subject in B major. The start of the recapitulation, with the cello melody now in octaves on the piano accompanied by guitar-like pizzicati in cello and viola, makes wonderfully evocative use of a texture dimly and ineffectively foreshadowed in the slow movement of the B major Piano Trio.

The thesis that the opening subject of the *Allegro comodo* Finale,

Ex. 37

(a)

a long violin solo against a relentless *moto perpetuo* quaver accompaniment in the piano, may first have been intended for a violin sonata, prompts us to note that it anticipates the Finale of Brahms's then-unwritten G major Violin Sonata almost exactly in texture, rhythm, and phrase-structure. That Sonata theme was to be modelled on the song *Regenlied*, which Brahms must have written about the time he was occupied with op. 60. (All three ideas may be found in Ex. 48 on p. 280.) Whether or not the Piano Quartet Finale has a more distant, less conscious relationship to *Regenlied*, its mood of anxiety and regret matches that of the song, and steadily returns us to the restless passions of the first movement. The ceaseless quavers are augmented to create an irascible transition theme, and the second subject turns out to be an odd, quasi-religious chorale for the strings, to which the piano makes almost flippant responses. The mysterious start of the development takes the initial descending third of the first theme and turns it into a chain of them (which was the distinguishing feature of the Andante's cello theme) – a ghostly passage (Ex. 37b) that foreshadows the use of

Ex. 37

(b)

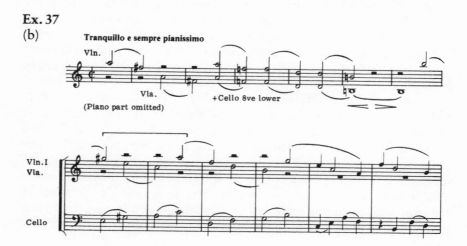

this interval in the Fourth Symphony. Development of the chorale (in a passage which we know from the manuscript was an afterthought) brings about an intensified recapitulation, the piano eventually hammering out the chorale tune in a massive, choleric C major. The major key is indeed the ultimate goal; but the Finale gradually liquidates itself with a sense of exhaustion like that which overcame the first movement; the curt final cadence (Werther pulls the trigger?) indicates that the mood of unsatisfied fatalism has triumphed.

8

'Frei aber froh'

It always seems to me rather melancholy when you write of the feeling of being lonely. I have a thorough understanding of that and hope that you are going to be careful. For I am that, too. For a long time, or for all time, I have been a somewhat lonely individual and still am!

Brahms to Billroth, 22 July 1886

Brahms had not long returned from Hamburg before he was offered the post, in succession to Anton Rubinstein, of artistic adviser and conductor to the Gesellschaft der Musikfreunde, with the promise of a large salary and a completely free hand in programming. After his customary period of hesitation he accepted, taking up the duties in the autumn of 1872. It was the last, and most prestigious, of the few official positions he held during his career. He now had access to the finest choir in Vienna, 300 strong, and a full symphony orchestra of a higher professional standard than had been available to the Singakademie. Although the administrative duties were irksome, Brahms discharged them very conscientiously, and the flourishing Society accorded him extensive decision-making powers under which he instituted a severe regime, doubling the number of choral rehearsals, insisting on sectional rehearsals for the orchestra, weeding out inadequate players and replacing them with the best musicians from the Court Opera and the Vienna Philharmonic Society, with Josef Hellmesberger as leader.

Between 1872 and 1875 Brahms conducted six concerts each season, with substantial programmes of his own devising. He presented all his own major choral works, but also a judicious selection of the contemporaries he most admired and – since his tastes were little changed since the Singakademie days – a high proportion of comparatively unfamiliarly early music. The programmes were, in short, highly demanding both for performers and audiences; but the resources were such that he could put on larger works, meticulously prepared, and as a sustained effort to improve the musical awareness of the Vienna public his concerts were of lasting significance. Whatever Brahms's gifts as a conductor – and he was admired by some of the leading conductors of his time – his understanding of his chosen repertoire was unrivalled.

His three seasons are among the most celebrated in the Society's long history, and striking evidence of his wide sympathies and concern for high musical standards. In the category of 'early music', Brahms performed such pieces as Handel's Dettingen Te Deum (as the opening item in his first concert, November 1872), *Alexander's Feast* (in 1873) and *Solomon* (1874); four of Bach's cantatas (1873, 1875) and his *St Matthew Passion* (1875); Mozart's then-unpublished Offertorium, K260 (1872) and oratorio *Davidde Penitente* (1874); as well as smaller choruses by Ahle, Eccard, Gallus and Isaac, and folksong settings. There were also Haydn symphonies, works by Gluck, Beethoven (notably the *Missa Solemnis*, and the 'Emperor' Concerto with Brahms as soloist), Schubert (including movements from the then-unpublished Mass in B flat, and the 'Grand Duo' in C, orchestrated by Joachim as a Symphony), and Cherubini's C minor Requiem. Among the more contemporary items he programmed were Berlioz's *Harold in Italy* (1874), Max Bruch's *Odysseus* (1875), Dietrich's brand new Violin Concerto (1874), Joachim's 'Hungarian' Concerto (1875), Mendelssohn's *Die erste Walpurgisnacht* (1873), Volkmann's *Concertstück* for piano and orchestra (1873) and Cello Concerto (1874), Schumann's Ballad *Des Sängers Fluch* (1873), *Manfred* music (1874) and Violin Fantasia (1875), in addition to pieces by Goldmark, Rietz, Rheinberger, Rubinstein and Hiller.

Though many of these works, even the oldest, were new to Vienna, Brahms gave very few premières as such: he placed little store on novelty for its own sake. His programmes did not immediately draw a large public (the first season had a rather Singakademie-like austerity), but the standard of performance, both vocal and orchestral, was much admired and the Gesellschaft concerts soon generated considerable interest, doing much to raise Brahms himself to a new level of popularity with Viennese audiences. His last season was enthusiastically supported, and the concert on 28 February 1875, when he conducted *Ein deutsches Requiem*, was a veritable triumph, which finally confirmed him in the eyes of musical Vienna as the foremost composer of the age.

Brahms found his position rewarding, but time-consuming; during his three years with the Musikfreunde he wrote fewer large-scale works of his own, and apart from the Variations on a Theme of Haydn the major ones that appeared – String Quartets nos. 1 and 2 and Piano Quartet no. 3 – had all been begun at an earlier date. Eventually Brahms found the duties too onerous; or at least that they interfered too much with his creative work. The Symphony in C minor which he had been drafting spasmodically since the early 1860s was finally approaching completion and he probably already had plans for its successor, and for a third string quartet. Accordingly – since Herbeck, who had been conducting the Court Opera, was agitating to resume the Gesellschaft conductorship – he resigned his post at the close of the 1874–5 season, and was rewarded with an honorary membership of the Gesellschaft der Musikfreunde.

At the beginning of 1875 he also agreed to serve, with Herbeck and Hanslick, on the Austrian Commission for the State Music Prize, a government body that bestowed grants to young, poor, and talented musicians within the Austro-Bohemian half of the Habsburg Empire. One of the first scores submitted to the Commission was a Symphony in E flat by a thirty-three-year-old from Prague called Antonin Dvořák. Brahms was much impressed with the piece, and induced his co-panel-lists to make a substantial award to the young composer – an award that was renewed each year as he sent in fresh batches of scores. Even more important, he befriended Dvořák and persuaded his own publisher, Simrock, to start publishing his music – a tremendous boost for the almost unknown Czech, who was always intensely grateful to Brahms.

Once he had resigned from the Gesellschaft Brahms took no further professional position, though he was offered Schumann's old post, that of municipal director of music in Düsseldorf, and even one that had been Bach's – Kantor at the Thomasschule in Leipzig. In the event, he felt far too contented with life in Vienna to uproot himself again. As he confided in a letter to Billroth in October 1876, at the time of the Düsseldorf offer:

> I don't want to leave Vienna, and Düsseldorf especially is a place I have taken against. My principal objections are also childish, and so cannot be revealed: the good taverns in Vienna, for instance, and the bad, coarse Rhineland tone (particularly in Düsseldorf). And – in Vienna one is free to remain a bachelor without provoking comment; in a small town an old bachelor is a standing joke. I no longer wish to marry, and yet – I've reason to fear the fair sex.

The fact that Viennese society had tolerated the bachelorhood of Beethoven and Schubert, and was even then tolerating that of Bruckner, may well have strengthened his resolve to remain there.

Of course, he continued to accept concert engagements throughout Germany, Austro-Hungary, Switzerland and Holland whenever the fancy took him, both as a conductor and – less frequently now – as a pianist: he had long ceased to practise regularly and his playing had inevitably deteriorated, although he had few problems in interpreting his own works, however difficult. Georg Henschel tells an endearing story of discovering Brahms in Koblenz in 1876, furiously practising Schumann's Concerto and the piano part of Beethoven's Choral Fantasia for a concert he was to give that night. Red in the face, he was having immense trouble playing simple diatonic runs, and kept muttering to himself 'But, Johannes, pull yourself together. Do play decently!' By the early 1880s his technique seems to have slipped even more: Clara Schumann confided to her diary in 1882 that 'Brahms plays more and more abominably. It is now nothing but thump, bang and scrabble.' It may well be that the piano pieces he wrote at the end of his life consciously address the problem of his own technical failings: though in no sense easy to play, they firmly imply an intimately expressive style of piano playing in which 'thump, bang and scrabble' have no place.

In the 1860s he had described himself as living an 'amphibian life, half virtuoso, half composer', with the virtuoso winning the greater praise. By 1875 the position was reversed. He no longer needed to give concert tours as a primary source of income, and could pick and choose among invitations from all over Europe; meanwhile his reputation as a composer was riding ever higher. In 1876 – twenty-three years after Schumann had prophesied for him a great future as a symphonist – he produced his tense and complex Symphony no. 1 in C minor, to great expectations and concentrated scrutiny from the musical world. When Hans von Bülow dubbed it 'The Tenth Symphony' – meaning that the world had finally been given a worthy successor to the nine symphonies of Beethoven, and that with this work Brahms had in effect assumed Beethoven's mantle – he was only voicing a widespread (though by no means universal) opinion. Adherents of the New Music, partisans of Wagner and of Bruckner, and intemperate critics such as Hugo Wolf, remained unconvinced by such claims, but nothing could now seriously challenge Brahms's pre-eminence in critical opinion as a composer of music in the 'abstract' forms.

After this long delay Brahms surprised the musical establishment by producing another symphony within the year: more immediately assimilable, it was a greater popular success and in a short time was being very widely performed. Brahms himself conducted an especially memorable performance in his home town in 1878, in connection with the celebration of the fiftieth anniversary of the Hamburg Philharmonic Society. Avé-Lallement and Grädener were among those who invited him; Clara was in the audience, as were members of his family, Marxsen, Gade, Grimm, Groth, Hanslick, Henschel, Kirchner, Reinthaler, and many former members of the Frauenchor. Several of Brahms's friends came to take their places in the ranks of the orchestra, among them Bargheer and Boie; Joachim was the leader; the composer received a laurel wreath to the accompaniment of a fanfare as he mounted the podium; and to his intense embarrassment was showered with roses at the end of the performance, in the course of the biggest ovation Hamburg had ever given him. The Second Symphony's natural successor was a Violin Concerto for Joachim, also on a scale seldom seen since Beethoven's. This was premièred in Leipzig on New Year's Day 1879, and the great violinist proceeded to perform it all over Europe, further spreading Brahms's fame.

Honours of all kinds began to accumulate. As early as 1874 Wagner's patron King Ludwig II of Bavaria awarded Brahms the Order of Maximilian – much to the disgust of Wagner, who nearly returned his. Britain – where both Clara and Joachim were frequent and popular visiting artists, and where Brahms's music had steadily been gathering ground – was in the forefront of the countries that sought to honour the composer. In January 1877, at the prompting of Charles Villiers Stanford, Cambridge University attempted to bestow on him an honorary Doctorate in Music. Stanford suggested that he come to conduct his new C minor Symphony; Brahms was unwilling to face the sea-crossing, but he might have gone if he could have confined himself to Cambridge and visited London quietly (he told John Farmer that what he really wanted to do there was to explore the East End and the docks, presumably because he envisaged the area as being like Hamburg). Unfortunately, as Stanford relates,[1] as soon as they got wind of the possibility of a visit the Crystal Palace authorities publicly announced that they hoped to arrange a London concert in which Brahms would conduct his works. Dreading the inevitable lionization by London society, especially as he could not speak English (though he understood and read it to a certain extent), he now declined to come to Britain at all, pleading ill-health. As the degree could not be conferred *in absentia*, Cambridge was forced to withdraw it: but instead Joachim, who received a similar degree on the day appointed, conducted the University Musical Society in the British première of Brahms's Symphony no. 1, still in manuscript (and somewhat different from its form as eventually published), as well as his own Elegiac Overture in memory of Kleist, while Stanford conducted the *Schicksalslied*. The following year the Royal Philharmonic Society of London awarded Brahms its gold medal, without requiring him to receive it in person. It was left to a German University – Breslau, in 1879 – to give him a Doctorate, not of Music but Philosophy: a degree which Brahms received in person, with a certificate referring to him as *vir illustrissimus … artis musicae severioris in Germania nunc princeps*. In thanks for which he composed his Academic Festival Overture, a work that deliberately eschews the 'severe' side of his musical nature.

---

[1] *Pages from an Unwritten Diary* (London, 1914), p. 173.

Such honours apart, the externals of Brahms's life after 1875 were uneventful, and need not be chronicled in detail – while the rich pattern of his inner life is chronicled in his music. To outward appearances he had evolved a way of life that suited him well enough. In the words of his F-A-F musical motto, which plays such a commanding role in his Third Symphony, he was 'Frei aber froh' – free but happy, with a wealth of emotional ambiguity covered by the major/minor third of 'aber'. Surely there is no antithesis between freedom and happiness – unless certain kinds of servitude accord better with one's emotional needs? Brahms was free of domestic entanglements or family ties: clearly he sometimes felt their absence as a lack of surrounding affection, through which his 'happiness' was somewhat defiantly maintained.

At all events his bachelor routine varied little from year to year. It certainly allowed him to devote the bulk of his time to his creative task. He tended to reserve the first three months of each year for fulfilling concert engagements, and to take a holiday in late spring or early autumn. His main period for original composition was the summer, which he generally spent away from Vienna at a country retreat, in Austria or elsewhere. Returning to Vienna in the autumn, he would complete the works he had already sketched and attend to their publication. Throughout the year he maintained contact with his large circle of friends, one or two of whom would usually accompany him on holiday.

His appearance was changing; though he retained a robustly healthy physique, the once slim and delicate-featured youth had an increasing tendency to stoutness that he eventually ceased to combat, and in 1878, when he was forty-five, he surprised his friends by growing the bushy and patriarchal beard that completely transformed his looks – accentuating his dignity but also his appearance of age, the more so as it rapidly went grey.

He was accumulating a considerable fortune, but used his money only for holidays, to buy books and music, and in innumerable acts of charity to friends and strangers alike. He continued to live in a very frugal manner. 'All I need is a washstand and a bed', he told his friend Maria Fellinger when she tried to help him furnish his apartment. To his small sitting-room and bedroom on the third floor of Karlgasse 4 he eventually added a third room to house his library; and when Ludovika Vogl, the last member of the family from whom he had rented them, died in 1886 he bought the Vogls' apartment as well and allowed Frau Fellinger to install a housekeeper, the widowed Celestine Truxa, in it. He became great friends with Frau Truxa's two young boys, and she looked after him faithfully and inconspicuously for the rest of his life.

Whether in Vienna or elsewhere, it was Brahms's habit to rise around 5 a.m., make himself some of his villainously strong black coffee; take an early morning walk; devote the rest of the morning to work, sometimes prolonged into the afternoon or varied with more walking; and relax with friends in the evening. He dressed simply and with little thought to appearances, remaining faithful to old clothes in which he felt comfortable after many patchings and darnings. He took his meals at humble cafés and eating-houses: his favourite haunt in Vienna being the restaurant *Zum roten Igel*, the Red Hedgehog, where he preferred to dine in a small, shabby side-room with chosen friends rather than attracting attention.

Gradually, he assumed a character of crusty self-sufficiency: a well-known public figure, approachable enough but always at the approacher's own risk. The young Italian composer–pianist Ferruccio Busoni met Brahms several times in the 1880s, and (intimidatingly acute at the age of nineteen) sketched some vivid and perceptive impressions of this mature *persona*:

> I spoke more with Brahms. He looks like a sturdy German professor. Wears a full, grey beard, rather long hair, spectacles, moves gravely and leisurely – a habit assumed with the increase of years and circumference – and walks with his hands behind his back. Even if cold and brusque in temperament, he knows how to be kind (in his own way) and takes his place merrily at a well-victualled table. Under an apparent modesty, which his temperament doesn't allow to be ruffled, he hides a good conceit of himself (mainly justified). This mask of modesty materializes in constantly repelling each word received in his praise – by a shaking of the head, or by mumbling an unfinished word, or by suddenly changing the subject. Not because he believes himself unworthy of such praise but because he often has to rebuff tributes from incompetent quarters. Also he is reluctant to give indications about performance of his works, even if asked; not because of lack of belief in his own compositions but because he evidently regards such comments as a waste of time. Such, at least, are the impressions I've received. From time to time an ill-restrained irony peeps through: thus, for example, he deals with an insincere compliment.[2]

As a bachelor with distant and diminishing family ties, Brahms had greater need than most to forge and maintain friendships which, though their immediate basis might be musical, provided him with real com-

[2] Ferruccio Busoni, 'Chiacchierata d'un musicista', article published in the Trieste newspaper *L'Indipendente*, 25 October 1885; reprinted in the Busoni number (Supplemento bimestrale, Anno IV n. 23, December 1966) of the Rome University periodical *Musica Università*, p. 7. I am grateful to Ronald Stevenson for drawing this article to my attention, and providing the translation of Busoni's Italian.

panionship and affection. He could be a difficult, moody, testy companion, but he inspired great personal loyalty in the friends he made; and the varying course of old and new friendships was one of the most important themes of his later years – the area where inner and outer life drew closest together.

In January 1874 the Leipzig Gewandhaus (scene of early disasters such as the ill-starred performance of the D minor Piano Concerto) made handsome amends by staging a 'Brahms week' in the composer's honour, in which he agreed to take part as pianist and conductor. A moving spirit in this enterprise was the president of the recently founded Leipzig Bach-Verein, Heinrich von Herzogenberg. Brahms now met Herzogenberg for the first time, and re-encountered his wife Elisabet – who a decade before, as Elisabet von Stockhausen, had so nearly turned his head that he had been forced to abandon the course of piano lessons Julius Epstein had engaged him to give her. Now she was married he could enjoy her company in safety, and there forthwith sprang up a remarkable three-cornered friendship that lasted nearly twenty years. From 1876 on, Brahms frequently stayed at the Herzogenbergs' home at Leipzig, and the three of them maintained a lively and warmly affectionate correspondence on matters musical, personal and whimsical. Heinrich and Elisabet were among the first to receive his new works in manuscript or hear them privately played by their composer, and Brahms greatly valued their comments and criticisms.

Herzogenberg was, like Brahms, a very learned musician with a passion for counterpoint, and himself a prolific and quite gifted composer of chamber, orchestral and choral music. (In 1876 he did for Brahms as Brahms had done for others, by writing a pleasant set of Variations on a Theme of Brahms for piano duet, based on the older composer's song *Die Traurernde*, op. 7 no. 5, of 1852.) But Brahms, though he liked the man, was very hard put to simulate even the slightest enthusiasm for his works, no matter how hard Elisabet pleaded and cajoled. Her husband, as Harold Truscott has remarked, had two distinct idioms – a very Brahmsian one, and another entirely his own: and it is hard to see which style bored Brahms the more. However, he confided to Clara that he could not discuss composers' work properly in letters, and an adoring wife made it impracticable to do so face to face:

> ... even in favourable circumstances, one finds it impossible to discuss an artist's work with him, and perhaps to criticize it, if his wife is listening, not to mention arguing, with one. Alone with the men, I could come to some conclusion, and then how happy I should be to enjoy the company of the ladies afterwards!

All the same, one can hardly escape the thought that Brahms was niggardly in praising the hero-worshipping Heinrich partly because he had wed such a treasure, the woman of whom (after Clara) Brahms was undoubtedly fondest.

Indeed, anyone would value the friendship of someone so warm-hearted, strong-minded, intelligent, good-looking ('not really beautiful but better than beautiful, dazzling and bewitching', thought her close friend and protégé, the young English composer Ethel Smyth) – someone so charming, humorous, enthusiastic, supportive and socially adept, who was also an excellent pianist and singer, and a divine cook. Elisabet's letters are the ones that really animate the correspondence and give it its delightfully spontaneous tone; and her voluminous discussions of Brahms's works – often from memory, after she had been forced to return the latest manuscript or pass it on to other friends – are usually amazingly perceptive, displaying a canny eye for detail and close sympathy and understanding.

Clara Schumann, who knew and liked the Herzogenbergs, felt an occasional pang of jealousy over this 'beautiful blonde aristocrat' whose domestic harmony and absence of family enabled her to steep herself in music all day long. But Brahms basked in Elisabet's approbation. A considerable musical circle gathered around 'Lisl' in Leipzig: among them Ethel Smyth, who often met Brahms at the Herzogenbergs', and left her own shrewd, unawed impressions of him in her memoirs. As she saw it, Elisabet brought out the best in him:

> His attitude was perfect...reverential, admiring and affectionate, without a tinge of amorousness. It especially melted him that she was such a splendid *Hausfrau*, and during his visits she was never happier than concocting some exquisite dish to set before the king; like a glorified Frau Röntgen[3] she would come in, flushed with stooping over the range, her golden hair wavier than ever from the heat, and cry 'Begin that movement again; that much you owe me!' and Brahms's worship would flame up in unison with the blaze in the kitchen. In short he was adorable with Lisl.[4]

Later in 1874 Brahms first made the acquaintance of the young baritone singer and composer Georg Henschel, just beginning the extraordinary career that would make him in turn the first Hans Sachs in *Meistersinger*, first conductor of the Boston Symphony Orchestra, and (as Sir George

---

[3] Julius Röntgen, the Germano-Dutch composer, was a member of the Leipzig circle and a great friend of both Brahms and Grieg; his mother was another musical lady famed for her culinary skills.

[4] Ethel Smyth, *Impressions that Remained*, Vol. I (London, 1919), pp. 263–4.

Henschel) an English knight and a Scottish Laird. They performed together on several occasions, and Brahms, greatly warming to him, suggested they spend a holiday together on the Baltic island of Rügen in the summer of 1876. The diary that Henschel then kept forms the core of his later published recollections of Brahms, especially valuable for recording the free flow of the composer's conversation on matters musical and aesthetic. Owing to a singing engagement Henschel had to leave Rügen some days before Brahms at 5 a.m. on a cold, rain-soaked morning; Brahms typically accompanied him several miles in the carriage and then set out to walk back to his lodgings:

> For a long time I looked after him out of the carriage window, in spite of the wind and the still pouring rain. It was a picture never to be forgotten. As far as the eye could reach, nothing but moor and clouds and – Brahms.

Holidaying in Switzerland two years before, Brahms had renewed his acquaintance with the poet and theologian Joseph Viktor Widmann, and this now developed into one of his closer friendships. Widmann accompanied him on several holidays, and in the late 1870s they seriously discussed collaborating in an opera. Brahms seemed especially interested in getting Widmann to make libretti for him from the magical farces of Gozzi, such as *Il re cervo* (a subject successfully treated as an opera in the mid-twentieth century, in Hans Werner Henze's *König Hirsch*); it would appear that by concentrating on light treatments of serious subjects Brahms hoped to avoid the idea that he was setting out to challenge Wagner, and the result, Widmann thought, might well have been 'a sort of second *Zauberflöte*'. However, he had great difficulty in constructing libretti from the plays Brahms suggested,[5] and the project came to nothing, without Brahms displaying any obvious signs of disappointment. Widmann, like Henschel, later published his memories of Brahms, whom he found a delightful but exhausting companion on account of his tireless physical and mental energy:

> His weekend visits were high festivals and times of rejoicing for me and mine; days of rest they certainly were not ... I have never seen anyone who took such fresh, genuine and lasting interest in the surroundings of life as Brahms, whether in objects of nature, art, or even industry. The smallest invention, the improvement of some article for household use, every trace, in short, of practical ingenuity gave him real pleasure. And

[5] Other subjects that Brahms considered for operatic treatment at different times were *Die laute Geheimnis* (a libretto which his friend Allgeyer derived from a comedy by Calderón) and Schiller's *Demetrius*, on which Joachim eventually composed a dramatic *scena*; he also discussed possible libretti with the poet Paul Heyse.

nothing escaped his observation . . . He hated bicycles . . . He was, however, glad to live in the age of great inventions and could not sufficiently admire the electric light, Edison's phonographs, etc. He was equally interested in the animal world . . .[6]

Other, younger friends included the composer–pianist Ignaz Brüll, the composer–conductor Ludwig Rottenberg and the operetta composer Richard Heuberger, another important memoirist who first got to know Brahms when he took him his compositions for comment and criticism. (Many young composers, including some future famous names – Busoni and Mahler, for example – trod the stairs to the Karlgasse apartment for this purpose, and few received outright commendation: Hugo Wolf was so wounded by Brahms's dry humour that, as critic of the Vienna *Salonblatt*, he became his most implacable enemy in print.)[7] There was the critic, poet, and translator Max Kalbeck, whom Brahms first met in Breslau in 1874 and who settled in Vienna in 1880, taking upon himself the role of Boswell to Brahms's Johnson. Kalbeck was eventually to write the biography that even today remains the standard life of the composer. There was the musicologist Eusebius Mandyczewski, a protégé of Nottebohm's, who became archivist of the Gesellschaft der Musikfreunde in succession to Pohl and was eventually to edit Brahms's own works. But by no means all his acquaintances were professional musicians. He was particularly friendly with three middle-class Viennese families whose appreciation of art and music was ardent but amateur – the Fabers (Bertha Faber was of course an ex-member of the Frauenchor), the Fellingers (Richard Fellinger was a director of the engineering firm Siemens und Haske; the world is indebted to his wife Maria, a keen photographer, for many informal pictures of Brahms in his later years),

---

[6] Florence May's translation from pp. 58–9 of Widmann's *Johannes Brahms in Erinnerungen*.

[7] Brahms had only one formal pupil: Gustav Jenner, a North German from Kiel who was passed on to him by Brahms's old teacher, Marxsen. In the case of Wolf, it may be argued in Brahms's defence that the young composer approached him with the kind of exaggerated deference that Brahms detested. An even more grievous sufferer from Brahmsian scepticism was Mahler's friend and classmate Hans Rott, who in September 1880 attempted to enlist Brahms's support by playing him his recently completed Symphony in E major – only to experience a typical rebuff. The incident obviously weighed heavily on the young man, for when Rott went insane the following month during a train journey, he claimed that 'Brahms had filled the train with with dynamite'. He spent the last four years of his life in a mental asylum, dying of tuberculosis at the age of 26. His Symphony lay unplayed until 1989, when performance proved it to be an uneven but unmistakable work of genius with amazing prefigurations of Mahler's mature symphonic style. Whether or not Brahms was aware of Rott's fate, he does seem to have treated young suppliants rather less dismissively after 1880.

and the family of Viktor von Miller zu Aicholz, another prominent industrialist. Brahms was a frequent guest at their houses, where he was able to relax in an atmosphere of sheer domestic comfort, and he usually spent Christmas with one or the other.

Almost the last female acquaintance to attract him seriously was the contralto Hermine Spies, a pupil of Stockhausen. The fifty-year-old composer first met her in Krefeld in 1883 when she took part in a performance of his new *Gesang der Parzen*. An outstanding Lieder singer with a gift for repartee to match his own, her personality entranced him and they spent much time in each other's company at Wiesbaden that summer. Her singing (and not her singing alone) undoubtedly inspired many of his finest songs of the 1880s, and Hermine in turn felt drawn to the composer, admitting to a 'Johannes-Passion'. Billroth, for one, suspected they were in love; Elise Brahms far away in Hamburg picked up rumours of an impending engagement – but in fact the relationship never seems to have progressed beyond a particularly warm and mutually stimulating friendship. One amusing element in it was that Hermine was just as ardently admired by the poet Klaus Groth, fourteen years Brahms's senior, and the two ageing romantics engaged in friendly rivalry to win her attention and company.

In the mid-1870s Brahms gained an important new champion in Hans von Bülow, whom he had already known slightly for about twenty years. In the 1850s Bülow had been a passionate adherent of Liszt and Wagner, and sceptical of Brahms, but his attitudes had gradually been changing (perhaps not unconnected with the way he had been shamelessly taken advantage of by Wagner); and the appearance of Brahms's First Symphony, which he soon conducted in Hanover and Glasgow, was the event that finally effected his conversion. He began to champion Brahms with the same wholehearted commitment he had previously accorded the 'New Germans'. Though Bülow's advocacy was hardly crucial by this stage of Brahms's career, it was certainly welcome; and when in 1880 Bülow became director of music at the ducal court of Saxe Meiningen, which boasted a fine orchestra, he put at Brahms's disposal something he had long desired – the means to try out his orchestral works semi-privately before releasing them to the wider world. The first work to be so rehearsed was the Second Piano Concerto in 1881, followed by *Nänie* and the Third and Fourth Symphonies; and the fact that the orchestra also regularly went on tour meant Brahms could count on a series of thoroughly prepared performances in major German cities, under his own or Bülow's baton. Duke George II of Saxe Meiningen himself became something of a Brahms partisan, inviting the composer to many musical events at his castle (where Brahms was particularly pleased by the absence of the usual court etiquette) and offering holidays at his country estate of Altenstein – visits which continued even after Bülow no longer conducted the Duke's orchestra.

This satisfactory state of affairs lasted until 1885, when the Meiningen Orchestra embarked on a tour of Germany and Holland with Bülow, featuring Brahms's latest Symphony (the Fourth). Brahms came along as 'supernumerary conductor', but thoughtlessly, during a short absence from the tour, allowed himself to be persuaded to conduct the new Symphony in Frankfurt, with the local orchestra. This effectively upstaged the performance Bülow had been scheduled to give there a few days later. The thin-skinned, mercurial Bülow resigned the Meiningen conductorship forthwith, cut to the quick that Brahms apparently held his own devoted efforts and those of his orchestra so lightly. Brahms seems simply not to have considered Bülow's *amour propre* in the matter (he declared that he was unable to think of concerts as 'serious affairs'), and for about a year they ceased to communicate, but their friendship was eventually fully revived.

A more serious, indeed permanent, rift arose between Brahms and his other great conductor–friend Hermann Levi. Levi's sympathies had travelled in the opposite direction to Bülow's: he had been a staunch advocate of Brahms against the Wagnerites, but had long felt his talents lay principally in the field of conducting opera. When Levi was appointed conductor of the Munich court opera in 1872 he fell directly under Wagner's spell, while his energies were perforce largely devoted to the production of Wagnerian music drama, climaxing in the first complete performance of the *Ring* cycle in 1876. Brahms himself admired Wagner, but must have been acutely conscious of Wagner's hostility towards him (though the older composer's public attack on him, in the essay 'Über das Dichten und Komponieren' was not published until 1879). The sheer comprehensiveness and passion of Levi's conversion seemed to him to denote lack of principle, rather than pure enthusiasm. In this he was mistaken, but they quarrelled violently in 1875, and though Brahms conducted the First Symphony in Munich at Levi's invitation the following year, they saw less and less of each other.

Friendship with Brahms was seldom uncomplicated. In some situations (for instance, when he wished to give financial assistance to friends normally too proud to accept it) he could show exquisite tact; but he hated dissimulation or circumlocution, and when he felt strongly about something he never bothered in private conversation or letters to temper a blunt, direct manner of expression that others could find woundingly tactless. On the other hand he was often awkward in public; his habitual self-defensiveness, and his horror of being idly praised, gave rise respectively to a crusty reserve and a withering sarcasm which repulsed many simple well-wishers and sometimes hurt even his closest friends. Serious disagreements arose even with such trusted companions as Billroth and Widmann, sometimes on matters of moral principle far more arcane than the break with Levi.[8]

Even with his nearest and dearest there were painful disruptions, though in these cases Brahms was only partly to blame. In 1879 it might have been thought his relations with Joachim had reached a new height with their collaboration on Brahms's Violin Concerto, which Joachim performed all over Europe; yet the next year their friendship was almost irreparably severed. The course of Joachim's marriage had not run smoothly, for he was a more than usually jealous husband and his continual suspicions of infidelity made life very difficult for Amalie. In 1880, alleging adultery (with Simrock!), he initiated divorce proceedings against her. Brahms, who was very fond of Amalie and well knew Joachim's capacity for getting things out of proportion, felt duty-bound to let her know where he stood and wrote her a long, chivalrously supportive letter, declaring he was certain the whole thing was a figment of his old friend's imagination.

> . . . despite a thirty year friendship, despite all my love and admiration for Joachim, despite all our artistic interests which should have bound me to him, I am very careful in my association with him, quite seldom involved in extended and confidential relations with him, and would never think of wishing to live in the same city joined with him in collaborative activity . . . I became aware of the unfortunate character-trait with which Joachim tortures himself and others so inexcusably earlier than you did. Friendship and love I will breathe simply and freely – as I will the air. I beg to be excused when fine feeling strikes me as complicated and over-refined, when it is maintained and increased by morbidly painful excitement . . . only his passionate imagination is playing a sinful, inexcusable game with the best and most holy thing that fate has granted him.[9]

He gave Amalie his consent to use the letter in any way she saw fit; but had not anticipated that she would produce it in court as a prime document in the defence of her character. Joachim's divorce suit foundered on this testimony, coming from his oldest and most famous friend, but it did nothing to save the marriage: Joseph and Amalie

---

[8] By contrast, when Simrock (to whom he had entrusted the investment of most of his wealth) confessed in fear and trembling that he had lost a large part of it in speculation on the stock-exchange, Brahms was utterly unperturbed and refused to consider Simrock's refunding the loss. He never mistook money for morality.

[9] Holde, op. cit., pp. 319–20.

1 Brahms's birthplace, no. 60 Speckstrasse, Hamburg, photographed in 1891. The Brahms family's dwelling was behind the two double windows at the left-hand end of the first floor.

2 The young Brahms, photographed in late 1853 during his first visit to Leipzig.

3 Clara Schumann, as painted by Franz von Lembach in Munich in 1878; she was then 58.

4 Joseph Joachim and Clara
Schumann performing in Berlin,
20 December 1854, painted by
Adolph von Menzel, whom
Brahms befriended 40 years later.

5 *Left:* Brahms in 1857. (*Mary
Evans Picture Library*)

6 Brahms in the 1880s, from a photograph by Hafenstängl of Frankfurt.

7 *Above:* Brahms with Hans von Bülow, photographed in Berlin, 1889.

8 *Left:* Elisabet von Herzogenberg, from a photograph by A. Meyer.

9 *Right:* The old bachelor: with Viktor
von Miller zu Aichholz's wife, Olga,
and their daughter at Gmunden in the
1890s.

10 *Below:* Squiring Alice Barbi in the
Ringstrasse, Vienna, 1892.

11 *Left:* Easter Monday: a photograph taken on 26 March 1894 by Maria Fellinger.

12 *Below:* A page from Brahms's manuscript of String Quintet no. 2, op. 111: the slow movement, showing major revision leading to the return of the main theme.

remained husband and wife in name but agreed to a separation, and Joachim, furious at Brahms's 'perfidy', broke off relations with him completely (though he continued to perform his music). After three years Brahms (aided by the Herzogenbergs, who had moved to Berlin and saw a great deal of Joachim) made moves to patch up the quarrel, and some of the old feeling gradually returned. Matters were more or less resolved when Brahms wrote his Double Concerto for Joachim and Robert Hausmann, the cellist of the Joachim Quartet; but the warmth of their original friendship never quite returned.

Tensions were built into Brahms's friendship with Clara Schumann from its beginnings, sometimes further from, sometimes nearer to the surface, occasionally breaking out into some bitter dispute. As Clara grew ever older, ill-health affected both her hands and her hearing, restricting her music-making; while misfortune continued to decimate her family (Julie died in 1872 after three years of marriage; Ludwig remained incarcerated in Colditz; Felix succumbed to tuberculosis in 1879; Ferdinand spent his last years as a morphine addict, unable to support his wife and children – who became Clara's responsibility – and died in 1891). The strains on her relationship with Brahms grew more palpable as she threw herself into preparing the Collected Edition of Schumann's works for Breitkopf & Härtel (issued between 1887and 1893), a massive task for which she needed all his friendly expertise and sympathy. It was over Schumann that they had their most bitter dispute of all.

Brahms had long admired and wished to perform the original, unpublished version of Schumann's D minor Symphony (it was not to appear in the Collected Edition; Clara had given him the manuscript as a gift), preferring its clean, uncluttered scoring to the later version which Schumann had re-scored with the weaknesses of his Düsseldorf orchestra in mind. Around 1890 he went to considerable expense to have score and parts copied and arranged for another of his principal champions, the Cologne conductor Franz Wüllner, to produce a handsome edition showing both versions laid out in parallel, page by page. Although Clara had given some kind of informal assent to the scheme at an early stage she was outraged when the edition actually appeared in 1891: she disliked Wüllner and felt that he and Brahms were making profits out of dishonouring her husband's memory, by releasing a work that Schumann had (over-modestly) described as a mere sketch. No sooner was this matter half-resolved than Brahms himself, in a depression following the death of his sister Elise, raked up and complained of Clara's intention to omit several Schumann works from the Complete Edition which he himself had edited and published in previous years.

These bitter wrangles had roots deeper than mere musicology: symbolically they touched closely upon Clara's and Brahms's relationship to the dead Schumann, and to each other – her wish to keep her husband's memory to herself, Brahms's feelings of exclusion from a position of trust and intimacy he might be felt to have earned. 'Alas,' he wrote to Clara in 1892, on her seventy-third birthday, after what must have been a particularly recriminatory meeting:

> to you more than to any other I am a pariah; this has, for a long time, been my painful conviction, but I never expected it to be so harshly expressed. You know very well that I cannot accept the ostensible cause, the printing of the Symphony, as the real cause. Years ago I had a profound feeling that this was so, though I said nothing about it at the time when the Schumann pianoforte pieces...were not included in the Complete Edition. All I could think of on both occasions was that you did not like to see my name associated with them...
>
> In my dealings with my friends I am aware of only one fault – my lack of tact. For years now you have been kind enough to treat this leniently. If only you could have done so for a few years more!
>
> After forty years of faithful service (or whatever you care to call my relationship with you) it is very hard to be merely 'another unhappy experience'. But after all, this can be borne. I am accustomed to loneliness and will need to be with the prospect of this great blank before me. But let me repeat to you today that you and your husband constitute the most beautiful experience of my life, and represent all that is richest and most noble in it.

A reconciliation was however effected, both personal – Clara saw she had gone too far – and musical: the series of piano pieces which Brahms wrote throughout 1892–4 and showed to her one after the other was a form of communication more intimate and unforced than any words. She delighted in playing them as long as she was able to use a piano, and the last years of the relationship were marked by an increased tenderness on both sides.

9

The music of the middle years, 1876–82

I want to publish my songs and should be so very much obliged if you could play them through beforehand and give me a word of advice about them. . . . write and tell me which of them pleases you and whether you dislike any of them. Particularly in regard to the last I might accept your criticism and thank you! . . . If possible write me a short comment on each. You need only give the opus or the number; for instance, Op. X, 5, bad; 6, outrageous; 7, ridiculous, and so on.

Brahms to Clara, 24 April 1877, apropos his Lieder, opp. 69 to 72.

Brahms had waited a long time to fulfil Schumann's prophecy that he would become the age's leading symphonist. With the D minor Piano Concerto, growing out of his earliest symphonic attempt, and even more with the *Requiem*, he might have been considered to have established his credentials as a master of major orchestral and choral forms. Yet the Symphony itself had long seemed beyond his reach. He well knew that anything he produced would immediately be judged by the highest standards, and found wanting on the slightest excuse. This was, after all, the Classical form *par excellence*, invested with proud tradition and enormous authority by Haydn, Mozart, Schubert, Schumann himself and, above all, Beethoven. Brahms could not avoid the feeling that here more than anywhere he was forced to challenge Beethoven on his own ground. 'You don't know what it is like', he wrote to Hermann Levi, 'always to hear that giant marching along behind me.' Yet as soon as he had finally delivered himself of his First Symphony in 1876, the next few years saw him at the summit of his creativity, producing a series of large-scale masterpieces with fluency and ease.

Two symphonies, one quartet, one motet

Brahms's Symphony no. 1 in C minor, op. 68, finally released to widespread interest and acclaim in 1876, had experienced a parturition almost as lengthy as that of Piano Quartet no. 3, and perhaps even more difficult. Kalbeck's assertion that it was conceived about the same time, in 1855–6, remains unsupported; but Brahms had certainly drafted the first movement in 1862, when he showed it to Dietrich and Clara Schumann. From then on it was an open secret he was working on a symphony – but was plainly in no hurry to finish. The primary problem confronting him seems to have mirrored his experience with the abortive D minor Symphony: the exceptionally powerful and tension-ridden first movement (shorter and more scherzo-like, but even more concentrated than that of the D minor) raised expectations that no merely orthodox symphonic structure could satisfy. The required outcome, in which the orientation of the Finale would be all-important, occupied years of thought.

It was probably in 1868 that he first saw it whole: on 12 September of that year, amidst one of his most painful periods of disagreement with Clara, he sent her a card to mark her wedding-anniversary and birthday, inscribed with the message: 'Thus blew the shepherd's horn today' and the notation of an Alphorn tune, to which Brahms added the verse 'High on the mountain, deep in the valley, I send you a thousand greetings'. It is a form of the ringing horn theme that would emerge in the Symphony's Finale (Ex. 38). Nevertheless it took him till 1876 to complete the work; and even in 1877, after performances at Karlsruhe, Munich and Cambridge, Brahms made substantial revisions – especially to the slow movement, which we know had a significantly different shape to the version eventually published. Perhaps no other work was achieved so painfully, and with so oppressive a sense of responsibility to the history of its genre: but it was labour supremely well spent.

Ex. 38

It is worth observing the First Symphony's originality in a matter we tend to take for granted: its form. In broad terms, of course, it reproduces the pattern, well-established by Brahms's day, of a sonata work that begins in minor-key striving, only to win through to a triumphant major-key finale. It manifests important affinities with the original archetype of that genre, Beethoven's Fifth Symphony (also in C minor); and with a distinguished successor, Schumann's Fourth in D minor. But the actual shape which Brahms found for his Symphony had, as far as I know, no close parallel. He rarely provided any movement with a formal introduction: this Symphony has two, for its first movement and Finale. Schumann does likewise; but the Finales of Beethoven's Fifth and Schumann's Fourth both have *transitional* introductions starting from the region of an orthodox scherzo, and neither is as elaborate as Brahms's. His begins afresh, like a fantastic intensification of the finale-introduction of his Piano Quintet, while adumbrating nearly all the important themes of the ensuing music in what Tovey called a 'magnificent cloudy procession'. The first-movement introduction, much more concise, serves a similar function, though we know it was added after the movement had been composed. Tonally stabler than its counterpart in the Finale, it performs another function too: its simple tonic–dominant–tonic progression, underlined by a throbbing timpani pulse-beat, creates the overpowering sense of tragedy, of being pinned to a fatal C minor, which the ensuing Allegro might fail to maintain on its own.

For that grim, savagely energetic first movement, despite its impressive size and sonata shape, has a pronounced scherzo-character, and indeed has more than its 6/8 metre in common with the scherzo of – again – the Piano Quintet, which dates from the period of the Symphony's earliest conception. It also has points of contact with that of the C minor Piano Quartet, given final shape while Brahms was still struggling to bring the Symphony to completion. The first movement's typical scherzo-like rhythms – with which Brahms makes great play, up to the convulsive rhythmic fusillade in the coda – deny it a certain measure of conventional first-movement gravity, although its expression is weightier than dozens of more pretentious examples. He follows it with a profound but essentially lyrical E major Andante sostenuto, whose prominent violin solo in its closing stages may have been suggested by the Romanze of Schumann's Fourth but, if so, far transcends the model; and then ensues the first of the tranquil, intermezzo-like alternatives to a scherzo for which his symphonies were to become famous, and with which he had already experimented in some chamber works.

The effect of all this is to throw the weight of expectation, and therefore of the structure, onto the Finale, which by its vast scope and vigour successfully resolves all the tensions the first movement had raised but was (magnificently) unable to dissipate. Those tensions are recalled with redoubled force in the Finale's C minor introduction: and they find their release at the moment where (after the Alpine grandeur of the shepherd's horn-call, Ex. 38, and the solemn brass chorale that follows it), C major is finally attained and the Finale proper begins with its famous, grandly striding tune (Ex. 39).

Brahms had no patience with the 'asses' who likened this to the 'Freude' theme from Beethoven's Ninth Symphony, and indeed the tune

Brahms

Ex. 39

itself is a type he had made his own since his earliest works (compare Ex. 7a, at the start of the B major Piano Trio). But its placement here invests it with a significance and sense of arrival it could never possess at the outset of a movement. The asses were not wholly wrong. Not since Beethoven's Ninth had a Symphony been so comprehensively a preparation for its Finale; and Beethoven's Finale too has an elaborate introduction (admittedly of a 'retrospective' nature not imitated by Brahms) which issues at length in a great heart-easing tune. But the uses to which Brahms puts Ex. 39 in his Finale – a movement which demonstrates the utmost fertility of his imagination – are entirely different from Beethoven. It initiates a sonata exposition, rich in substance, eventfulness and rhythmic drive, then returns (again in C major), seemingly to start the process all over again. What emerges is a counter-exposition of even greater force and invention, which merges the functions of recapitulation and development (and draws the introduction's themes back into the evolving argument with masterly contrapuntal skill). But Ex. 39's final appearance, in the coda, on saurian trombone, basses, and double bassoon, reverts to the minor-key distortions of the movement's introduction, producing one last black cloud that the music must pierce to earn its triumph; and it is the brass chorale that sets the final seal of patriarchal authority on the eventual C major victory.

The high degree of thematic integration in the First Symphony, both within and across its movements, should by now come as little surprise. The extent of that integration remains a matter of dispute, for Brahms does not conduct it in terms of surface transformation of themes such as we find in Beethoven's Fifth or Schumann's Fourth. An enormous amount proceeds from the motivic complex announced in the opening bars (Ex. 40a) – itself extrapolated retrospectively from the themes of the first movement: a fanwise chromatic progression simultaneously descending in violas, horns and woodwind and rising in violins and cellos, the latter with a rhythmic figure, (x). The double nature of the idea is itself unprecedented. As soon as the Allegro gets under way, rhythm (x) appears in counterpoint with the movement's official first

248

subject, attached to a descending turn (Ex. 40b). Brahms invests this figure with great importance, basing upon it the climax of the development and lead-back to the recapitulation, always the most dramatic juncture in a sonata design. Michael Musgrave has suggested[1] that the figure – undeniably a version of Schumann's 'Clara-motif' – underlies the whole Symphony and can be traced in many of its different themes, implying that to some extent op. 68 is Brahms's 'Clara Symphony'. Both conclusions seem acceptable, if treated with proper caution: Brahms's direct address of the horn-call Ex. 38 to Clara is supporting evidence, and he would surely never have handled 'her' motif unawares. But it seems too reductionist to attribute the totality of a work so thematically rich to a single controlling idea. Clara herself, hearing the first movement on the piano in 1862, commented how 'the interweaving of material is most interesting; the music flows on and the listener is unconscious of the workmanship'.

Ex. 40

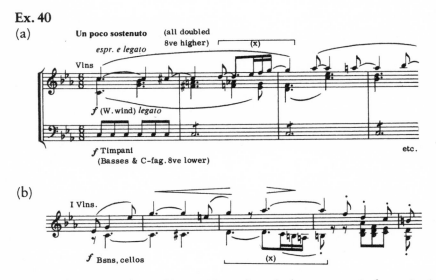

In fact a number of basic ideas, largely but not entirely springing from Ex. 40a and b, are interwoven and combined with astonishing resource, mutually reflective and mutually transforming in a manner akin to (but on a much more epic scale than) the workings of the First String Quartet. Their effect is not confined to any one movement; the

[1] 'Brahms's First Symphony: Thematic Coherence and Its Secret Origin', *Music Analysis* 2: 2, p. 117ff.

slow movement's opening theme contains within itself a reminder of the chromatic motivic complex Ex. 40a, and its central section foreshadows the characteristic melodic outlines of the following Intermezzo. A soaring theme that emerges in the course of the first-movement development, which Kalbeck likened to a chorale, is assigned by Musgrave to the 'Clara' complex but demonstrably also grows out of a staccato three-note figure in the exposition; it has been seen (by Bernard Jacobson) as the generator of much detail in the Finale, up to and including the climactic brass chorale theme. Wherever any individual thematic connection may ramify, the Symphony assuredly reflects Brahms's powers of motivic development in their highest form. Through its long maturation in his consciousness, it had emerged as the genuinely 'organic' design that every true symphonist hopes to achieve.

Finally, there is a new splendour and character in the attitude to orchestral sound. Despite all the striking and effective scoring in the early orchestral pieces and the choral works of the later 1860s, it is in this Symphony that Brahms proclaims himself a master of that greatest of instruments, the symphony orchestra. From first to last the work is conceived in authentically orchestral terms, not simply for added colour but for maximum expressive (and structural) effect. Even apparent 'miscalculations' – such as the high, isolated first-violin tessitura of the first movement – are an expression of the symphony's tensions carried into the sphere of timbre. And such famous strokes as the radiant emergence of the horn theme Ex. 38, atop a shimmering cloudscape of string tremolandi, rank among the classic orchestral moments of the nineteenth century.

Brahms celebrated the end of his toil on the Symphony by completing his Third (and last) String Quartet, in B flat, op. 67 – a work as carefree and capriciously inventive as the op. 51 Quartets had been severely logical and serious-minded. Its design is in fact a kind of comic parody of the Symphony's, beginning with a movement of even more overt scherzo-character and thereby throwing the structural weight onto the finale with hilarious consequences. Haydn and Mozart, rather than Beethoven and Schubert, seem to stand godfathers to the music now, and the work is so full of cheerful unorthodoxies that it is plain Brahms was enjoying himself throughout – to the marked benefit of his quartet style.

He opens with an exuberant 'hunting-horn' theme in 6/8: the example of Mozart's 'Hunt' Quartet has often been cited, but the music also remembers the Scherzo of Brahms's own B flat Sextet. 3/4 rhythms are immediately played off against the 6/8 pulse, and a transitional idea with florid first-violin roulades and mysterious contrary motion leads to a second dance, a prim little polka in 2/4. Soon the 6/8 rhythm is being combined with that too: in this Quartet, variants of Brahms's beloved three-against-two cross-rhythms are almost omnipresent, their long-range structural consequences only to be revealed in the final bars. Scherzo-feeling or no, these two dances are actually the principal subjects of a sonata-design: a rather odd one, whose development shuffles and interleaves them, punctuating its arguments and key-changes with rests and abrupt pauses.

The F major Andante begins like a conventionally lyrical ternary-form in 4/4, but evolves a middle section in which neo-Baroque recitative and 'Hungarian' rhythmic freedom are magically blended, briefly distorting the metre into 5/4; and the return of the opening theme is preceded by an elaborate variation of itself, widely different in texture and tonality. There is no scherzo (that was the first movement), but a strange D minor Agitato, dominated throughout by the viola, which is the only instrument allowed to remain unmuted.[2] This substantial yet shadowy piece is full of textural surprises – not least its Trio (so labelled), which begins on a real trio of two violins and cello, whose apparently self-sufficient music is revealed as a mere background pattern as soon as the viola re-enters. Schoenberg surely had this movement in mind when he wrote the viola-dominated Intermezzo for his D major Quartet of 1897.

For the first time in an output already rich in variation movements, Brahms uses a theme-and-variations form as a Finale: and his theme, in B flat and a moderate 2/4, is an ambling, *gemütlich* piece of mock-folkery. Its pawky humour conceals an intricate motivic construction, enhanced by harmonic vagrancy (towards D) and 'primitive' disproportion of phrasing. Should the viola's staccato accompanying triplets remind us of the opening movement's 6/8? We shall see. Six variations (the viola dominates the first two, as in the previous movement) retain the theme's tempo and phrase-structure, while exploiting three-against-two rhythms in different ways and roving further in tonality than Brahms usually allows himself in variations, through B flat minor and D flat to G flat. Variation 7 then reinstates B flat major – and, *doppio movimento*, the opening subject of the first movement! With his overwhelming instinct for structural unity always tempered by dislike of the musically unmotivated thematic reminiscences in Lisztian 'cyclic form', Brahms must have been delighted at bringing off this

---

[2] Brahms commented to Henschel that 'he considered [this movement] the most amorous, affectionate thing he had written'.

bravura compositional feat, whereby his Finale re-acquires first-movement material in response to the demand for variation. Nor does the
process end there – for variation 8 likewise re-acquires the first
movement's contrary-motion transition theme; and in a forgivably self-
satisfied coda Brahms presents the work's opening subject and the
finale theme in equable contrapuntal combination (Ex. 41): the Q.E.D.
towards which all the three-against-two business had been tending. It
is curious that, having written such a felicitous work, Brahms forthwith
abandoned the genre of the string quartet; but it seems he truly preferred
chamber music with piano, or at least with more than four string
instruments, where less constraint was placed upon his harmonic invention. Perhaps, too, his friendship with Dvořák, that spontaneous and
prolific quartet composer, allowed him to feel this was one genre whose
future was safe in other hands than his.

Ex. 41

The 'relaxed' nature of the Third String Quartet is more often
attributed to Brahms's next major work, his Second Symphony (in D
major, op. 73), written mainly in the summer of 1877 and thus following
his First at a distance of less than a year. That seems to suggest a
remarkably painless delivery after the complicated birth of its predecessor. (It is probable, of course, that he had been sketching its ideas
over a longer period; and just as the First has a kinship to the Piano
Quintet and other chamber music of the early 1860s, so the Second
seems not unrelated to the choral works written at the end of that
decade.)
  Conventionally it is considered Brahms's sunniest and most genial
symphony, an aspect thrown into even sharper relief when contrasted
with the C minor strenuousness of the First: it has occasionally been
dubbed his 'Pastoral'. Certainly all four movements are in the major
mode, and their material and expression is of a predominantly lyrical
nature; there are occasional echoes of the early D major Serenade. Yet

252

even that much simpler work was not all bucolic contentment; and op. 73, at any rate in its first two movements, has always seemed to me one of the darkest of major-key symphonies. True, it is a rich, introspective darkness (partly produced by the richness of the harmony, suffused with Romantic nature-symbolism), but its gravity is no less for that. The Symphony's very broad designs, yet intricately forking paths of development, allow a constant play of light and shade; and we glimpse the light as if from the heart of a forest, where we must perforce stray through some very tenebrous regions. Brahms's characterization of the work to Elisabet von Herzogenberg before she had set eyes on it –

> You have only to sit at the piano, put your small feet on the two pedals in turn, and strike the chord of F minor several times in succession, first in the treble, then in the bass (*ff* and *pp*), and you will gradually gain a vivid impression of my 'latest'.[3]

– is not much more than teasing (though minor tonalities interpenetrate and enrich its major-key orientation to a remarkable degree). But even critics wedded to the 'sunny' interpretation recognize the sombre mood of elegy in the slow movement, and Brahms told Clara that the first movement, too, was 'quite elegiac in character'. After the first performance, responding by letter to an (unidentified) friend who objected to what seemed to him the gloom and harsh dissonance of the canon for trombones in the development of this movement, Brahms pled to be excused on the grounds that the passage reflected his habitual melancholy.[4]

The melodic idioms of this Symphony are markedly different from those of the First. The first movement's leisurely unwinding of long, graceful, and even waltz-like themes is plainly influenced by Schubert rather than Beethoven. Yet Brahms's motivic thinking is no less fertile than in the previous symphony; if anything, it reaches even deeper and wider. Behind an astonishing proportion of all four movements' thematic working lies development of the three-note figure – a slow, semitonal oscillation, (x) in Ex. 42 – which the cellos announce in the Symphony's first bar, plus its inversion (y) and its four-note extension (z). Ex. 42 shows a mere handful of these derivations – a few shoots from a highly intricate motivic growth that is even more of a self-consistent organism than in Symphony no. 1.

---

[3] *Johannes Brahms: the Herzogenberg Correspondence*, ed. Max Kalbeck, trans. Hannah Bryant (London, 1909) pp. 27–8.

[4] I am indebted to Reinhold Brinkmann for bringing this still-unpublished letter to my attention.

Ex. 42

Symphony No. 2 : opening

Cellos & Basses

First movement derivations :

Second movement :

Third movement :

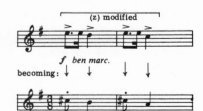

254

Figure (x)'s salient semitone, which not only shapes so many themes but is treated by Brahms as a motif in its own right, can easily be made to sound sinister. It shuts out the sunlight from the first movement's development, where the underlying elegiac quality is made manifest in agitated contrapuntal exploration of apparently innocent materials. There is a steady increase in agitation until the appearance of (x) in the stark and solemn trombone canon referred to above, introducing a troubled version of first-subject elements in alternation with a plaintive version of (x) that, to my ears at least, recalls the 'Ach, was heilet die Schmerzen' section of the Alto Rhapsody. The movement's witty scherzando-style coda, with (x) in *tranquillo* diminution on woodwind, does temporarily lighten the mood – and the preceding horn solo, used gently to 'liquidate' one of the main themes, shows how far Brahms had travelled since he first used that instrument for simple melodic statement in the D major Serenade.

Large though the movement is, its 3/4 dance-metre and introductory feeling throw the Symphony's centre of gravity forward: initially onto the Adagio non troppo, which penetrates the deepest part of the forest, if not the Wolf's Glen itself. Its eloquent and impassioned cello theme, in a very dark-hued B major with melancholic bassoon counterpoint, gives way to increasingly gnarled and knotted fugato developments of neo-Baroque polyphonic involution. Motif (x) returns as a mournful howl on bassoon, trombone, tuba and basses against shivering tremolando strings; eventually the brass launch the movement's strenuous, B minorish climax with fiercely funereal solemnity.

255

The second half of the Symphony, with its lightening of heart and glad release of energy, must be seen as a counterweight to two such troubled movements. The Allegretto grazioso is another intermezzo, the finest example of them all, lightly scored and deftly tuneful, with outbursts of high-spirited *Presto* good humour that produce capricious variants of its chief idea. Yet as this serenade-like inspiration draws to a close, the music is shadowed by major–minor cross-currents, sub-terranean echoes of figure (x) and a sighing *molto dolce* theme; and the Finale begins in *sotto voce* twilight, with grey, misty motion that could bring forth anything. What it eventually reveals is the blazing sunrise of the most athletic and ebulliently festive movement Brahms ever wrote, a virtuoso celebration of sheer orchestral power without parallel in his output: it surpasses even the *Triumphlied*, whose D major tonality it shares, whose neo-Handelian figuration it echoes at many points, and whose contrapuntal bravura it effortlessly surpasses. Even here, at the end of the development, shadow and chill invade the music; but it is swept away by the recapitulation and the resplendent, full-hearted coda, a display of power more Jupiterian than jovial.

If the Second Symphony is really as sunny as many commentators suppose, it is strange that in tandem with it, on the same holiday in Pörtschach, Brahms composed one of the grandest but darkest of his *a cappella* choral works, the motet *Warum ist das Licht gegeben?*, pub-lished in 1878 as the first of two Motets, op. 74 (the other is the much earlier *O Heiland, reiss die Himmel auf*, discussed on p. 121). Brahms was particularly proud of this potent and concentrated work; and proud too of its text, which he compiled from biblical sources – like that of the *Deutsches Requiem*, though on a much smaller scale. ('Maybe it preaches better than my [own] words', he wrote to the conductor Otto Dessoff.) Its opening passage, from the Book of Job, paints a vivid picture of human despair: 'Wherefore is life given to him that is in misery, and life unto the bitter in soul... Why is light given to a man whose way is hid, and whom God hath hedged in?' This is stilled by a verse from the Lamentations of Jeremiah: we must turn hands and hearts wholly to God. Job's patience in suffering is recalled in a quotation from the Epistle of James, with an assurance that God's purposes are merciful. Last of all come the words of the Nunc dimittis, in Luther's metrical translation, promising peace and joy; 'Death for me is turned to sleep'. As in the *Requiem*, the theme is the necessity for patience and acceptance of things are they are – something Brahms clearly found hard, to judge by the way he returned to it.

Like the earlier motets (with which it shares many features of technique, though now in intensified form), this work falls into several movements, here corresponding to the divisions of the text. The first and longest, one of the most gripping inspirations in Brahms's entire choral output, opens with the fierce major–minor chordal question 'Why? Why?' and proceeds to subject Job's agonized curse to intense canonic scrutiny, the eloquently 'speaking' line developing in magnificently expressive chromatic polyphony (Ex. 43a). The defiantly interrogative 'Warum?' chords function as a ritornello, dramatically reappearing at structural divisions in the tripartite movement, whose

Ex. 43

(a)

(Wherefore is light given to him that is in misery, and life unto the bitter in soul?)

257

central section has contrasting material with less thoroughgoing canonic features. The final section returns to the music of Ex. 43a, but in a much simplified (and non-canonic) form, in 3/4 – even so, Job's question is the last, unsatisfied word.

D minor has been the tonal focus; now, in the relative major, the second movement reveals itself as a serenely diatonic canon, its subject ascending smoothly heavenward first in four voices, and then gloriously expanding to six. The peaceful mood is maintained – with rather more internal motion – in the third movement setting the quotation from James. The texture here is in six real parts, imparting lush harmony to a texture that, despite points of imitation, is certainly not canonic; beginning in C, it moves to F, and the final line ('the Lord is very pitiful, and of tender mercy') brings a return, almost verbatim, of the glowing six-part canonic close of the previous movement. The Motet then concludes with a four-voice setting, in a Dorian D major, of the Nunc dimittis, to the chorale tune that Luther himself composed for it, *Mit Fried und Freud ich fahr dahin*. The setting itself has a Bachian feeling, and the whole idea of ending the Motet with a chorale – towards which, as it were, the composition moves and which sums up and resolves its disparate movements – resembles Bach's practice in his cantatas and some motets.[5] The origins of this superb work of Brahms's maturity, however, cast a fascinating sidelight on the operations of his creative instinct.

When in 1956 the Benedictus of his early *Missa Canonica* was published, a hundred years after its composition, it was realized that Brahms had used it as the basis for the second movement of *Warum ist das Licht gegeben?* But in 1983 the publication of the remaining Mass movements revealed his transformation of pre-existing material as much more extensive than previously suspected. Briefly stated, the opening canon in the first movement is a far-reaching recomposition of the Mass's Agnus Dei (but the 'Warum?' ritornello is new, as is the overall form of the movement); movement 2 is closely based on the material of the Benedictus, which is then superbly rethought for the concluding six-voice expansion that also appears as the ending of the third movement; the first portion of movement 3 transforms the Mass's 'Dona nobis pacem' – not quite as radically as the Agnus was transformed, but in myriad details that dispose of its original starkly canonic

---

[5] Brahms dedicated the work to Bach's biographer Spitta, but refused to be drawn on whether it was intended as a homage to Bach; indeed, he nearly withdrew the dedication, apparently because of disagreements with Spitta over the functions and content of church music.

form, and with much increased rhythmic movement of the parts. The final chorale, of course, has no original in the Mass; but it is especially remarkable that Luther's tune (Ex. 43b) nevertheless resolves the tensions of the preceding movements, and is offered as a simplification and clarification of Ex. 43a's canonic theme. Brahms must therefore have had the chorale tune in mind as the Motet's ultimate goal as he reshaped his original Agnus Dei melody (Ex. 43c), as a means of securing large-scale musical unity from what were once entirely separate ideas. It is also interesting that the expressive functions of the Motet's various movements correspond closely to the liturgical ones of their respective Mass movements: the careworn movement 1 with the imploring prayer of an Agnus Dei, the radiant calm of no. 2 with a Benedictus, and no. 3, counselling patience, with a 'Dona nobis'. We might say that *Warum ist das Licht gegeben?* represents the final, satisfactory fulfilment of Brahms's twenty-year-old desire to compose a Mass: satisfactory because eventually conceived in his own, entirely personal terms.

Ex. 43
(b)

Mit   Fried' und Freud' ich   fahr' da - hin,

(In peace and joy I pass away)

(c)

Adagio
Soprano I
p molto espress

A - - gnus De - i,   qui tol - lis pec -

- ca - ta mun - di   mi - se - re - re no - bis

Lieder and duets

Brahms's opus numbers seem to indicate that during the period covered by this chapter he wrote two widely separated groups of songs: twenty-three of them published in four sets as opp. 69–72, and a further seventeen issued in three sets as opp. 84–6. In fact, though the entire first group was indeed composed in 1875–7, there was no perceptible break in his song-writing, and Lieder eventually printed in op. 86 were being heard in manuscript by his friends as early as 1878, the year in which he produced his last true set of duets, the four *Balladen und Romanzen* op. 75. (Last 'true' set because the op. 84 songs, put together by 1881, are duets *manqués*, and can theoretically be taken by two voices.)

It is therefore convenient to deal with this large body of forty-four songs as a unit. As Brahms becomes ever more prolific in this field he affords us less and less space for detailed comment – though every song deserves it. We are dealing in almost every case with a perfection of form and verbal response that can only properly be demonstrated in a lengthy essay, and which testifies how seriously he took his own advice to Georg Henschel, when he looked over the young singer–composer's songs at Sassnitz in 1876:

> In some of [these] you seem to me too easily satisfied. One ought never to forget that by perfecting *one* piece more is gained and learned than by beginning or half-finishing a dozen. Let it rest... and keep going back to it and working at it, over and over again, until it is a complete, finished work of art, until there is not a note too much or too little, not a bar you could improve on. Whether it is beautiful also, is an entirely different matter, but perfect it *must* be. You see, I am rather lazy, but once begun I never cool down over a work until it is perfected, unassailable.

By now the texture of Brahms's song-writing style is so assured and close woven that every song is a treasury of discreet compositional subtleties. If anything, the voice parts are yet more integrated into the musical texture, developing leading motifs on a basis of equality with the piano, as in the very different settings of Goethe's amiable *Serenade* (op. 70 no. 3) and Felix Schumann's youthfully morbid *Versunken* (op. 86 no. 5), where the accompaniments derive their characteristic patterns by treating the contours of the voice part in diminution. Such refinements are to be found everywhere, even if the models for many of the songs appear to remain the strophic folksong or the artless serenade, or the very occasional 'genre' song like Candidus's *Tambourliedchen* (op. 69 no. 5) where Brahms indulges in rattling drum-roll piano effects with unexpected relish.

The numbers owing most to folksong come in op. 84, a set of dialogue songs (as, for instance, between mother and daughter or lover and sweetheart) in which the music of the strophe is modified according to the speaker. Apart from an optional second part at the end of the lilting *Spannung* (op. 84 no. 5) there is only a single vocal line, and a single singer may impersonate both characters, though Brahms's indication 'for one or two voices' allows the possibility of the songs' being performed as duets. Their ostensible simplicity belies a subtle sophistication of treatment. No. 3 of this group, *In den Beeren*, is in one of Brahms's favourite 'Hungarian' rhythms; a more 'authentic' approach is seen in the *Mädchenlied*, op. 85 no. 3, which is cast throughout in 5/4 time, and which he is known to have intended as a close imitation of the characteristics of Serbian folksong. A different kind of reference to a 'popular' style is *Minnelied*, op. 71 no. 5, in which Brahms quotes a waltz by Gungl.

Most of the songs of this period are modest in dimension and concise in their thought; the majority of the exceptions occur in the op. 69 set, which is largely devoted to folk-like poems that are given dramatic treatment – indeed, a couple of the songs here recall the sectional, descriptive writing of the *Magelone* Romances. But the technique is now much firmer: the situation depicted in no. 6, *Vom Strande* (a Spanish text translated by Eichendorff), with the poet on the shore gazing after his departing love, could easily have been found in the op. 33 cycle, but now the varied expressions of despair and passion are welded together, held within a single mood, by the continuous purling triplet semiquavers of the tide that flows so sinuously through Brahms's accompaniment. He treats the call from the shore that begins each verse of the poem as a ritornello for voice and piano, further unifying the design. The following song, *Über die See*, to a text by Karl Lemcke, is placed as if to be heard as a sequel: the lover is now alone on the deserted shore, and the many agitated notes of *Vom Strande* are replaced by a much barer, colder texture and gentler, muttering water movement as the sense of desolation grows. Brahms had a seemingly inexhaustible store of musical metaphors for the sound of moving waters; in a later Lemcke song, *Verzagen* (op. 72 no. 4), yet another abandoned lover watches waves softly foam and draw back in complex arpeggios and murmuring gruppetti, turning the accompaniment into a kind of intricate two-hand keyboard study.

As in the example of nos. 6 and 7 of op. 69, songs are often placed together to maintain a mood by parallels in their poems. Elsewhere, the connection is reinforced by overtly musical means: 'Mondescheine' ('moonlight'), the last word of the richly lyrical Heine setting *Sommerabend* (op. 85 no. 1), seems to suggest a second Heine poem, *Mondenschein* (op. 85 no. 2) in which, after an evocation of night and weariness in hollow octaves descending by a typically unquiet chain of thirds, the music of the previous song returns and is developed to a new text, apostrophizing the healing beauty of the moon's rays. This tranced nature-mood, of which Brahms was perhaps the supreme master, is

261

explored through several songs – notably in another moonlit scene, the haunting *An den Mond* (op. 71 no. 2); in the deep, elegiac lyricism of Brentano's *O kühler Wald*, with its overlapping triadic harmonies like an interlacing canopy of many wind-stirred boughs; in the exquisite *Lerchengesang* (op. 70 no. 2) with its almost Debussian colouristic textures and still, bare alternations of piano and unaccompanied voice, the piano's right hand forced into wider and wider stretches by the rise of the carolling lark (Ex. 44); and in *Feldeinsamkeit* ('Alone in the Fields', op. 86 no. 2), where the clouds pass over the sky-gazing observer in a calm, wide arch of melody, while he lies literally earthbound to a softly-pulsing octave pedal F. Perhaps the most powerful expression of this mystical affinity with nature is *Waldeseinsamkeit* (op. 85 no. 6), where in a spirit of rapt, surrendering ecstasy the poet lays his head on his lover's lap 'in the solitude of the forest', while daylight fades and a distant nightingale is heard. This last, utterly Romantic image is treated with a passionate delicacy of feeling, and that conventional bird has never been evoked with a more mystical intensity.

Ex. 44

(Ethereal, distant voices...)

It hardly matters that many of the texts are shallow, insubstantial poetastery; Brahms's settings invest them with the weight of emotion they cannot themselves reach, or bring to bear a true emotion to fill the hollow made by the poet's feigned one. More: there is a tenderness born of maturity, a wise sympathy for – as well as an instinctive identification with – the situations of young love and the piercing effect of memory. Thus Karl Candidus's automatic images of lost love in *Alte Liebe* (op. 72 no. 1) are touched into life by a spine-chilling key-change as an unseen hand seems to tap the lover on the shoulder, and the sensitivity of the keyboard writing matches the ambient, mysteriously sourceless fragrance of jasmine. In the same poet's *Sommerfäden* (op. 72 no. 2), dreams of love thread like gossamer among the trees; rather than add to the already precarious insubstantiality of the image, Brahms gives it form in the fine-spun counterpoint of the piano part, which together with the vocal line creates an almost Bachian three-part invention. Not Bach's semblance but Domenico Scarlatti's self is invoked in an earthy, diverting setting of Goethe, *Unüberwindliche* (op. 72 no. 5), which compares the irresistibility of women and wine, and the poet's inability to renounce either. Brahms bases the song on a dry, mordant little tune from Scarlatti's D major Harpsichord Sonata, L. 214, which he transposes to A and varies in an astonishing range of styles and onomatopoeic effects, the poet's grandiose renewed vow, never to succumb to either temptation again, hilariously undercut by hiccuping bass octaves.

That is perhaps the most individual of the several humorous songs which lighten the mood of these Lieder groups: but a deeper spirit is pervasive, and in a few songs gives rise to an especially personal fusion of music to poetic impulse. Chief among these are perhaps *Geheimnis* (op. 71 no. 3) – yet another Candidus setting, where the 'secret' of the title, an undeclared love, seems to have struck an especially deep chord in Brahms, who names the secret in yearning chromatic movement over a heartbeat-like bass pedal – and no less than four of the op. 86 group. In no. 1, Gottfried Keller's *Therese*, a similar pulsation turns into the distant booming of the sea, muffled by the soft pedal as the young boy puts a shell to his ear to hear what it has to say about the girl he adores. No. 3, *Nachtwandler*, to a poem by the young Max Kalbeck, has a curious bittersweet lilting piano refrain, almost Mahlerian in its major–minor harmonic sideslips. It evokes the dreamer who, unharmed, walks across the silent precipices of the unconscious, and the voice overlaps the refrain in the third verse as dream and reality become inextricably confused. Another troubled wanderer, this time immersed in memory, roves over the heath in no. 4, Theodor Storm's *Über die Heide*, with its clipped, depressive pacing rhythm, mourning the fact that life and love have flown him by. Finally no. 6, Max von Schenkendorf's *Todessehnen* ('Death-wish'), is perhaps the most explicit of all these songs about the 'secret, heavy burden' weighing down composer as well as poet. It is a very beautiful song, slow and long-breathed, whose opening four-note phrase is surely intended to evoke the chant for the dead, the 'Dies irae'; when the poem says that only in death can the poet's soul be wedded to that of 'the sisterly being', the voice intones a transposed form of the 'Clara-motif'; and the second half of the song flowers into a serenely floating metaphor of the longed-for Nirvana, 'where the language of spirits calls life by the name of love'.

While engaged upon Symphony no. 2 and the Violin Concerto, in 1877–8, Brahms wrote the four vocal duets which he published as op. 75 – his final and most important contributions to this now-neglected genre. Whereas all the previous duet groupings had been for a single pair of voices throughout (soprano and contralto in opp. 20, 61 and 62, contralto and baritone in op. 28), each number in op. 75 calls for a different combination dictated by the dramatic requirements of the texts. Thus no. 1, the ballad *Edward*, is a mother/son dialogue for contralto and tenor; no. 3, a lovers' conversation, is for tenor and soprano; the other two are mother/daughter exchanges, with the daughter naturally a soprano in each case – but while in no. 2 the mother is the expected contralto, in no. 4 she is a second, more dramatic soprano as befits her wild, eldritch nature. In musical character, too, the four pieces are all strongly contrasted.

The chosen texts are from folk sources or in folk style, and Brahms's settings superficially adopt the strophic approach that he favoured towards folk texts; but that is all. In fact the individual verses are so dramatically varied in the voice parts or piano accompaniment (in nos. 1, 2 and 3), or the whole conception is so essentially through-composed despite notional division into verse sections (in no. 4, and in no. 1), that Brahms far transcends the folksong archetype. *Edward* is a vocal realization of that same Scots Border ballad from Herder's *Stimmen der Völker* that had inspired the first of the op. 10 piano Ballades over twenty years before:[6] there is no direct quotation of the grim, measured D minor Ballade in this much more agitated F minor duet, and yet the contours of the Ballade's themes seem to hover behind its fateful progressions and speech intonations. Brahms provides a thrumming *moto perpetuo* accompaniment, restlessly twisting into new shapes and punctuated by stark chordal exclamations (where memories of the Ballade come nearest the music's surface). The first of these, the son's

---

[6] Brahms was clearly familiar with the remarkable setting of the same text published in 1824 as Carl Loewe's op. 1 no. 1, and like Loewe he makes the agonized exclamations of 'O' which end each verse into a prominent feature of his song.

admission that he has slain his father, is electrifying in its effect, but Brahms continues to build up the tension, and the song's true climax comes when he finally curses his mother in an intensified form of the same passage.

After this no. 2, *Gute Rat*, comes as light-hearted relaxation in a simpler style, though Brahms's powers of variation ring witty changes on the 'good advice' the mother gives her daughter, who finally runs after her cavalier in a delicious waltz-tempo coda. No. 3, *So lass uns wandern!*, is a tender colloquy of faithful woodland lovers in Brahms's mellowest melodic vein, the dialogue eventually giving way to contented choric agreement. Finally the hectic, broomstick-riding *Walpurgisnacht* is a miniature *tour de force* of flesh-creeping fantasy, the daughter fearfully asking her mother about the doings of the witches on the mountain, and the replies gradually revealing that the mother is a witch herself. The chromatic style of this duet strongly contrasts with the others, but is entirely appropriate, the tonality mounting inexorably, semitone by semitone, as the daughter's horrified questions lead her nearer and nearer the truth.

Piano pieces

The two collections of piano pieces Brahms published in 1879–80 – his first solo piano works since the 'Paganini' Variations fifteen years before – marked an important change of direction in this field. No more large sets of variations, still less multi-movement sonatas, would appear from his pen. The eight *Klavierstücke*, op. 76, comprising four Capriccios and four Intermezzi, and the two Rhapsodies, op. 79, inaugurate the philosophical miniatures which were to be the characteristic piano music of his last years: pieces whose comparatively small dimensions are far outweighed by the density and personal quality of their expression, the 'heroic' bravura of the earlier works now abandoned for a dedicated exploration of keyboard textures and subtleties of mood. They are, in fact, the first harbingers of Brahms's later manner, in which fewer and fewer notes came progressively to stand for richer and richer substance.

The titles of the various pieces seem not to indicate formal distinctions (Elisabet von Herzogenberg habitually referred to the A minor Intermezzo as a *Romanze* in her correspondence; the manuscript of the B minor Rhapsody calls it a Capriccio). As published, however, the Capriccii tend to be in faster tempo and more extrovert than the Intermezzi, whose character is intimate, indeed introspective, suggesting a pause for thought; the Rhapsodies are on a larger scale than either, with more exhaustive development of material. But there is nothing improvisatory or arbitrary in the structural make-up of any of them: they all relate clearly to ternary or sonata designs.

We should nevertheless remember that for Brahms form was never a matter of abstract patterning, but the palpable articulation of the ebb and flow of feeling. These pieces' relation to familiar archetypes is always individual: each appears to create its form as a natural consequence of its material – varying its ideas ever more subtly through fine gradations of harmony and rhythm. Brahm's characteristic love of cross-rhythm, 3/4 alternating with 6/8 and duplets playing against triplets, is on especially lavish display in the op. 76 pieces, nowhere more so than the powerful no. 5, a Capriccio in C sharp minor in an extended ternary form (with far-reaching variation of the basic material) which derives its dark passion from the motive energy such rhythmic ambiguities can supply. The first piece, a Capriccio in F sharp minor, is similarly turbulent and atmospheric, wrung from an obsessive, *agitato* four-note motif that Brahms wreathes in ever-changing windswept figuration.

In contrast to such sombrely Romantic outbursts, the skittish B minor Capriccio (no. 2) is much more Classical in its effect, its pattering quavers almost evoking a harpsichord piece, while the B flat Intermezzo (no. 4), though probably arising from a personal fusion of Schumann's and Couperin's keyboard styles, suggests the tranquillity and tonal ambiguity of a late Fauré nocturne. Most of the Intermezzi demand a keen sensitivity to tone-colour: in particular no. 3 in A flat, with its deliberately weak, high chords against a harp-like staccato accompaniment, and no. 6 in A major, whose central trio in F sharp minor closely anticipates the corresponding section (in the same key) of the very late Intermezzo, op. 118 no. 2. The A minor Intermezzo, no. 7, is mostly taken up with a Chopinesque central melody, but the solemn phrase that opens and closes the piece brings a far-away breath of the epic atmosphere of the op. 10 Ballades. The final Capriccio, no. 8 in C major, is perhaps the most complex piece in mood: its flowing *poco vivace* stream of quaver figuration and tolling, chordal second idea give rise to fleeting bursts of near-exultation, but the music always reins itself in and simmers down to a restrained, rather deadpan, *Adagio* coda. There are only hints here of the controlled passion that seethes throughout the Rhapsodies.

As already remarked, these are somewhat more extended than any of the op. 76 pieces, and encompass a wider range of mood. They might almost be considered extremely concise one-movement sonatas, although only no. 2 (in G minor) is actually cast in sonata form. No. 1 in B minor, the longer of the two, is a curious mixture of sonata background and ternary foreground, its fiery outer sections having two distinct subjects while the highly contrasted middle section, in B major, is based on a gentle, berceuse-like *espressivo* melody that nevertheless derives from the second of these. The G minor work is tauter in structure but more exploratory in harmony, the passionate first subject (which displays some kinship with op. 76's C sharp minor Capriccio) continuously roving with little inclination to establish the primacy of G. Although the development section begins similarly freely, Brahms creates the necessary sense of return by constructing a hypnotic, fatefully muttering internal pedal on the dominant (from a triplet figure in the funeral-march-like second subject) which builds up unremittingly from *ppp sotto voce* beginnings, and by its very persistence demands that the resolution be in G. The same figure is the focus for the coda, in which the second-subject ideas undergo a gradual, shadowed liquidation, full of mysterious tragedy.

The only other keyboard composition of this period was the second group of Hungarian Dances for piano duet, nos. 11–21. Simrock had persuaded Brahms to capitalize on the immense success of the first group by writing a follow-up, and they were issued in 1880, simultaneously with the op. 79 Rhapsodies, as Books 3 and 4. Unlike the earlier ones, these later Dances appear to be largely original compositions 'in Hungarian style', employing some of the characteristic dance styles (but no longer the previously ubiquitous csárdás), the cadential turns and sectional forms of the previous free arrangements of authentic material. Brahms himself felt these later dances showed a greater mastery of the duet medium, and indeed they allow a virtual equality between the players, made necessary by their increased contrapuntal interest. They are also harmonically and texturally richer, and perhaps more varied and subtle in character. Above all Brahms has created melodies that paradoxically seem to possess an even greater degree of 'gypsy' improvisatory freedom than in the first set. One or two numbers apart – the soulful D minor no. 14, or the skittishly prancing no. 19 in G sharp minor – they have never been as popular as the first two Books; but Elisabet von Herzogenberg, writing to Brahms on 23 July 1880 fresh from a first play-through, saw clearly enough their increased level of achievement:

Delicious as the earlier ones were, I hardly think you hit off the indescribable and unique character of a Hungarian band so miraculously then as now. This medley of twirls and grace-notes, this jingling, whistling, gurgling clatter, is all reproduced in such a way that the piano ceases to be a piano, and one is carried right into the midst of the fiddlers ... What impresses me most of all in your performance, though, is that you are

267

able out of these more or less hidden elements of beauty to make an artistic whole, and raise it to the highest level, without diminishing its primitive wildness and vigour. What was originally just noise is refined into a beautiful *fortissimo*, without ever degenerating into a civilized *fortissimo* either.[7]

Dvořák was so fond of these later dances that he orchestrated the whole of Book 4, giving them in the process a rather Slavonic tang that seems to reveal a stylistic similarity between Czech and gypsy music.

Concertos and overtures

Josef Hellmesberger's celebrated declaration that Brahms's Violin Concerto, op. 77, was concerto 'not for, but *against* the violin'[8] (and Bronislaw Hubermann's rejoinder that it is 'for violin *against* orchestra – and the violin wins!') should probably be seen as responses to the work's decidedly 'symphonic' features. It would have appeared even more so had Brahms kept to his original intention: a four-movement structure, whose sketched slow movement and scherzo (more of them later) were replaced quite late in the day by the Adagio we know. In fact the Concerto is in many ways the natural successor to Symphony no. 2 – in the same key, D major – and the similarities are especially strong in the first movement, whose resemblance to that of the Symphony Clara Schumann commented upon the first time Joachim and Brahms played it over to her. Here again is a spacious design in an apparently leisurely 3/4, warmly Romantic in its instrumental colouring, its themes built upon a triadic foundation and, though not especially extended in themselves, seamlessly evolving one from another into huge paragraphs, and seldom far removed from the character of a calm yet passionate waltz. The one true waltz theme Brahms reserves as a surprise for the very end of the exposition, as an apotheosis of the movement's majestic lyricism (Ex. 45). The development is 'symphonic' in its very exhaustiveness and strong contrapuntal interest.

Ex. 45

compare Ex. 44

---

[7] *Johannes Brahms: the Herzogenberg Correspondence*, p. 108.
[8] He had just conducted the Vienna première of the work, on 14 January 1879.

The vital difference from the Symphony, of course, is that the argument is led by and concentrated in the role of the solo violin; and Brahms never had any intention of diminishing its opportunities for brilliant display and caressing figuration. The solo part is as voluble, as rhapsodic and mercurial in mood as any 'mere' virtuoso-composer's; the effect of spontaneous improvisation is masterfully sustained, and is vocal, 'speaking' to an extent that not a single phrase is empty display. Brahms accommodates the part within – or rather, makes it the point of – his symphonic structure by the extraordinarily plastic nature of the movement's material, which allows almost imperceptible broadenings and relaxations of the momentum so that the argument may proceed by the development of ideas embodied in the soloist's musings and fioriture.

The virtuoso treatment of the violin is unprecedented in Brahms, and cunningly blent of many elements. Among these are his studies of great Classical concerti, most obviously the Beethoven but also those of a minor master, Viotti, whose Concerto no. 22 was a favourite with Joachim and Brahms. It also invokes the violin-writing of Bach, whose D minor Chaconne he had transcribed for piano the previous year; and is further influenced by his observations, over many years, of the fiery playing and upright musical character of Joachim, the soloist for whom the concerto was intended from the beginning. As is well documented, Joachim was indeed, at Brahms's urgent entreaty, intimately involved in the work's gestation. From August 1878 up to the première in Leipzig on New Year's Day 1879 they continually discussed it through meetings and correspondence as Brahms composed, and afterwards continued to refine the conception in the light of Joachim's performances until it was published the following October.[9]

Joachim was the ideal collaborator: not only a great violinist but himself a gifted composer of concertos, with Brahms's own cast of mind when it came to the integrity of musical substance. Principally Brahms involved him in the evolution of the solo part, and Joachim provided alternatives and variants to Brahms's original conception wherever he deemed a passage unwarrantably lacking in 'violinistic' qualities, or requiring enhancement in terms of the instrument's capabilities to bring out its musical essence in the most effective way. He also suggested adjustments in the orchestral textures – usually thinning them out to

[9] The process may be examined in detail in the Brahms–Joachim correspondence and in the handsome facsimile of Brahms's manuscript full score, with its multicoloured layers of progressive emendation, published by the Library of Congress, Washington DC, to mark the work's centenary in 1979.

provide a better balance so the violinist would not have to 'force' his tone in order to be heard. Nevertheless, though Brahms repeatedly sought ideas from Joachim, he did not regard him as the final arbiter, even in matters of violin technique. Often he seems simply to have wanted alternatives to choose from. Sometimes he adopted Joachim's suggestions, sometimes he retained his originals – and quite often Joachim's readings suggested a third solution, incorporating some form of his friend's ideas but raising them to a new level of compositional significance. In a gesture of homage to the Classical concerto tradition, he declined to compose a cadenza for the first movement; Joachim supplied a magnificent one, which remains the most often played, but Busoni, Tovey and others have also risen to the challenge over the years.

What it amused Brahms to call the 'feeble Adagio' in F major, substituted for the two sketched inner movements of the Concerto, has become one of his best-loved inspirations. Its opening, on wind instruments alone in rich harmony, with the main theme, full of pathos, on solo oboe, recalls the sensitive and resourceful wind scoring of the A major Serenade (but grows out of the extensive use of the wind chorus to colour the first movement). The feeling is Classical, and the movement never really descends from the lofty, almost Mozartian inner calm of these initial bars, though the tune is utterly Brahmsian in its hints of folksong and lullaby. The violin never has the main theme in its basic form apart from the first few notes, but in similarly tranced mood the soloist's virtually continuous and elaborate outpourings develop, ornament and vary the apparently artless main theme. Even when, in the movement's one brief dramatic climax, Brahms appears to propound a new theme in F sharp minor, this is but a particularly passionate melodic expansion of it. The serene coda finds the violin still rhapsodizing above a gentle string accompaniment of arpeggiated pizzicato triplets that will shortly be transformed into the first rhythmic background in the Finale.

Brahms had second and third thoughts about the tempo of the last movement: he marked it *Allegro giocoso* with the qualifying phrase *ma non troppo vivace*, which he then deleted, and later reinstated – fortunately, as too quick a tempo robs the principal theme of its characteristic mixture of fiery rhythmic excitement with a curious earthy stateliness, as of a joyous yet heavy-footed peasant dance. This Finale, in a concerto conceived for and dedicated to Joachim, is inevitably a rondo of 'gypsy' bravura, paying homage to Joachim's own Concerto in the Hungarian Manner (dedicated to Brahms).[10] It is however a taut

[10] Michael Musgrave (*The Music of Brahms*, pp. 210–11) has suggested a parallel connection to the 'alla polacca' Finale of Schumann's Violin Concerto; but since both

and complex design, owing little to the *perpetuum mobile* manner of the Finale of Joachim's Concerto, even less to the 'Rondo alla Zingarese' from Brahms's G minor Piano Quartet, but a fair amount to the last movement of that other Joachim-inspired work, the A minor String Quartet, op. 51 no. 2 – especially in its virtuosic displays of rhythmic variation and syncopation. Subsidiary ideas include a magnificently choleric dotted-rhythm figure in staccato octaves, and a suave *dolce* tune that is usually described as an entirely new element but is in fact a fairly clear variation of the rondo subject (at least, that is how I have always heard it). After an intoxicating development of the rondo theme proper that elevates the peasant dance into regions of metaphysical hilarity, a brief accompanied cadenza leads to the large and eventful coda, where the tempo finally changes to *Poco più presto* and the rondo material is wittily transformed into a rollicking bucolic march in 6/8, with the violin elatedly conjuring a stream of fresh variations above it. Eventually the energy dissipates and the violin descends contentedly to earth before the orchestra's last affirmative chords.

The Academic Festival Overture was composed in the summer of 1880 in thanks for the honorary Doctorate of Philosophy conferred upon Brahms the previous year by Breslau University, and he first performed it there at an all-Brahms concert at the beginning of 1881. 'A potpourri of student songs *à la* Suppé', he called it, presumably a reference to the overture of Suppé's operetta *Flotte Bursch* (1863), a simple medley that includes the tune of *Gaudeamus igitur*. But Brahms's overture is vastly more artful, and more humorous: a fully-worked out but unusually 'unacademic' sonata structure masquerading as a free fantasia or quodlibet.

Brahms was never formally the student of any university; but he had participated in student life at Göttingen in that wonderful spring and summer of 1853, and clearly retained great affection for it. Moreover student songs were venerable and popular enough to be counted a species of folk music, and treated with similar fondness. The overture is accordingly a student's-eye view of the nobility of learning. Imbued with an irrepressible sense of fun, it deploys immense native skill in the cause of mischief and mystification (the work's long introduction in C minor, whose stealthy initial theme is reshaped to become the first subject – the elements of the introduction themselves transformed into

Joachim and Brahms regarded that work (unjustly, I believe) as an unworthy specimen of their beloved benefactor's last period, and in consequence allowed it to remain unpublished and unperformed, I think this an unlikely influence.

271

the development and the build-up to the recapitulation). It pays lip-service to civic solemnity (presenting *Wir hatten gebauet ein stättliche Haus* as a radiant Lutheran chorale on shining trumpets); sings the praise of beauty (turning *Hört ich sing* into a gorgeous, utterly Brahmsian E major second subject); and indulges a penchant for practical jokery – the freshman's ragging song, *Was kommt dort in der Höh* first sardonically chuckling on bassoons, then bursting out uproariously on full orchestra. For parody also: does the treatment of *Was kommt dort* not recall the Apprentices' theme from *Die Meistersinger*, and is the whole work not a kind of Brahmsian rejoinder to Wagner's *Meistersinger* Overture (also in C major) – a personal tribute to the values of counterpoint and 'holy German art', seen entirely from the Apprentices' point of view? Certainly the final glorification of *Gaudeamus igitur* is achieved in a most un-Brahmsian (but typically Wagnerian) texture, the tune grand and chorale-like on full wind chorus, festooned with rushing demi-semiquaver string scales, as Brahms makes a merry noise with the largest orchestra he was ever to employ, complete with cymbals, triangle and bass drum.

The companion work he completed in the same summer of 1880, the Tragic Overture, is of very different mettle. Brahms's carefully generalized title gives no hostages to the musico-literary ideals of the 'New German' school and avoids parallels with Joachim's various overtures (which he admired) inspired by specific tragic dramas. Kalbeck associates the work with the plans of the Viennese *Dramaturg* Franz von Dingelstedt to stage both parts of Goethe's *Faust*, with incidental music by Brahms, at the Burgtheater: a project for which Brahms felt considerable enthusiasm even though it fell through. However, the overture's substantial second-subject group is reworked from a sketch clearly dating from the late 1860s: found, indeed, on the back of sketches for that other Goethean conception, the Alto Rhapsody. Whatever its origins, the Tragic Overture seems curiously to divide opinion among Brahms's commentators: even such a sympathetic writer as Karl Geiringer found it 'colourless', and Latham was inattentive enough to think it 'conventional in cut'. Musgrave, with seeming inconsistency, declares its 'formal logic and balance' to be 'unassailable', yet finds the nature of the form 'incongruous', reflecting an 'uneasy relationship' between programmatic ideas and their 'sonata context'.[11]

To Tovey and others – the present writer included – Brahms here creates a compelling musical image of human defiance against dark destiny that can be appreciated entirely on its own terms without reference to any literary archetype. The adaptation of sonata form is

[11] Ibid., pp. 218–19.

quite as unorthodox as in the Academic Festival Overture, but along
entirely different lines – and so musically self-sufficient that some critics
(notably Harold Truscott) have gone so far as to see it as, in essence, a
highly concise one-movement Symphony. In fact, the sketch-material
which became the second subject has affinities of mood with the First
Symphony, and the sketch itself (which indicates an exposition repeat)
may well have been intended for a symphony rather than an overture.

Ex. 46

The work starts (Ex. 46a) with a veritable hammer-blow of fate,
(figure (x)) from which a wiry, tensile theme arises, swiftly growing with
great energy and determination into a first subject-group packed with
forcefully dramatic motivic ideas. This is linked to the second group
(which opens with a warmly Romantic melody (Ex. 46b) but soon
produces a further series of terse and stormy figures, among them figure
(z ii) from the first group) by an exceptionally broad transition. This
slowly modulates upon a wintry carpet of string sonority while strange
cries sound upon solo woodwind and horns: perhaps the only passage
in Brahms that foreshadows the mature symphonic style of Sibelius.

When we arrive at the development, marked clearly enough by expansions of the hammer-blow (x) and a return of the hollow unison theme (y) in the tonic, D minor, the restless activity evaporates and the tempo is halved: the development is conducted in slow motion, becoming indeed a kind of 'slow movement', a creeping invention on figures (z i) and (z ii), groping forward in crepuscular instrumental half-lights. The sense of pathos and lost direction is overwhelming, almost Beethovenian (see Ex. 46c). When the original *Allegro* tempo is restored the activity becomes even more minimal, disguising the fact in a grey, dawn-like stillness: Brahms here anticipates Sibelius's characteristic mastery of imperceptible changes in symphonic motion, and this very passage is a skeletal version of the exposition's 'Sibelian' transition. Only when the Romantic tune Ex. 46b reappears in the tonic major do we realize a foreshortened recapitulation is under way. The bulk of the first subject is held back until the coda, where (z ii) turns into an angry cadence-figure, bringing the tragedy to a grimly punctual end.

Ex. 46

(c)

At Pressbaum near Vienna, on 7 July 1881, Brahms put the finishing touches to something he had been working on at intervals over the past four years, and which he described to Elisabet von Herzogenberg that same day as 'a tiny, tiny piano concerto with a tiny, tiny wisp of a scherzo'. He posted the score to Billroth with the laconic message 'I am sending you a few small piano pieces', and later declared he had needed to introduce a scherzo (based on the one originally sketched for the Violin Concerto) because the first movement was 'too harmless' (*simpel*). A more accurate gauge of the importance he attached to the piece is the fact that he dedicated it 'to his beloved friend and teacher Eduard Marxsen' – as if he had finally produced something worthy of presentation to his old master. In fact Brahms had written one of the most imposing of all his works, the Piano Concerto no. 2 in B flat major, op. 83: even longer in duration than the huge D minor Concerto, op. 15, even more 'symphonic' with its design enlarged to four movements by the hardly 'tiny' scherzo, and even more demanding in the strenuousness and bravura of its piano writing. Its 'harmlessness' is the innocence of the lion, an intermittently lazy and gentle creature. Spiritually, too, op. 83 is hardly the smaller work: if the D minor Concerto brings to mind a Faust or Manfred raging against implacable fate, the B flat inhabits a level of Olympian majesty and largeness of mind no less impressive and far more mature.

It is, nevertheless, a paradoxical score. Precisely because of its sustained serenity, its apotheosis of the genial B flat major that had served so well in the op. 18 Sextet and the op. 67 Quartet ('this udder', as Brahms called the key, 'which has always yielded good milk before'), the Concerto's moods appear relatively uncomplicated, with little inherent drama except in the Scherzo – the only movement not in B flat. Yet it poses any soloist enormous challenges. In a sense it takes on directly from the melding of symphonic and concerto principles we observed in the Violin Concerto, creating a very broad architecture to accommodate seemingly rhapsodic solo writing of immense technical accomplishment. Here Brahms was dealing with his own instrument, and needed no one to advise him: in its massive chording, wide stretches, vigour, richness and textural variety the piano writing is the most elaborate result of his lifelong fascination with virtuoso technique – the logical next step along the path signposted by the 'Handel' and 'Paganini' Variations, whose array of bristling difficulties it elaborates upon and refines.

On the other hand the work's character is almost as much a kind of '*Überkammermusik*', a chamber-musical intimacy of discourse writ large into the orchestral medium. The Concerto seems partly to extend the line of Brahms's works for strings and piano, especially the Piano Quartets: there are clear parallels between the slow movement and that of op. 60, and arguable ones between the Scherzo and Finale and those of op. 26. Above all, the role of the soloist is fluid, not fixed in a single rhetorical posture; he or she must indeed dominate with the utmost

Brahms

power at certain junctures, but other moments call for extreme delicacy and limpidity of touch, the reticence and self-effacement of the ideal accompanist. The Finale demands a raffish yet never unstylish sense of fun; and the very start of the work requires the ability to be a precisely equal partner in creating the most Romantic of all concerto openings, where the stillness of mountain and forest resound to the notes of Oberon's horn (Ex. 47).

Ex. 47

WEBER: *Oberon* Overture

That preliminary airing of the first theme arouses a fiery piano cadenza in Brahms's most muscular and sinewy vein, itself merely preparation for a fervent and full-hearted orchestral tutti. The strategy is reminiscent of (and probably inspired by) Beethoven's in his E flat

276

Concerto, which is indeed the progenitor of Brahms's work; but here the expressive effect is entirely different. Brahms's exceptionally spacious movement is certainly a sonata design, but its prodigious amount of thematic material, much of it of striking beauty, appears to grow organically, root and branch, ramifying into a vast tonal network of interconnected ideas. The piano does not merely repeat or comment upon the themes of the tutti but engages in a wide-ranging dialogue by continual variation of them. As in the similarly 'relaxed' Second Symphony, darkness and passion have their place, the former represented by sudden glimpses of far-off tonal areas (such as B minor, at the start of the development), and the latter by the more choleric and forceful of the piano's eloquent monologues.

The ensuing D minor Scherzo is the nearest the Concerto approaches tragic expression, and is an extremely concise sonata form, in contrast to the opening movement's expansive one. Its first subject (mainly on piano and low strings) is nervous and hard-driven, closely related to the ghostly Scherzo in the early D major Serenade but imbued now with impetuous zeal; the second (high strings, piano following) a haunting little tune full of submissive pathos. These contrasts are fixed more firmly by a *da capo* repeat of the exposition, and then dissolved in an angry development. This rises to a new pitch of tension, with the second subject's 'little tune' proving as full of fighting spirit as the first. Rescue is at hand in the shape of a pealing, Handelian D major theme that bursts in at the height of the storm and transforms the mood to one of robust and vigorous hilarity, expanding to create a very unorthodox central Trio for the movement. Sonata logic demands, however, that the driven scherzo music should return: it does so in a recapitulation that essentially continues the processes of development, much of the piano's original contribution being assigned to the orchestra while the soloist reinforces the texture with resonant octaves. Urgent and volatile to the last, but just enabled by the Trio to avoid real tragedy, the movement storms to an ending of breathtaking concision.

Brahms never wrote a cello concerto, although he twice said that another composer's example (first Volkmann's, then Dvořák's) had showed him how it might be done. Op. 83's Andante begins with an easeful, singing cello solo that shows he had no need of instruction, and makes us regret he did not make the attempt. (Was he perhaps thinking of the prominence given to the cello in the central Romanze of Clara Schumann's own Piano Concerto of 1833–5?) The piano never has this tune; instead it wreathes it, and muses upon its harmonic background, in filigree passage-work and decoration of the utmost plasticity, carefully contrived to give the impression of self-communing extemporization while in fact carrying motivic development to the point of deliquescence. Piano and orchestra engage in a more agitated dialogue, showing that the tensions of the Scherzo have not entirely evaporated; then the piano has an F sharp major episode of the utmost tenderness, and the solo cello returns with its theme in that key before gently descending to the tonic B flat to usher in the reprise of the ternary form, rounding off the movement in the same mood of analeptic calm with which it began.

The *Allegretto grazioso* Finale is a complex mixture of rondo and sonata that wears its complexity with playful insouciance. Brahms never wrote a movement that was more of an unalloyed entertainment, nor more feline in its humour; the proportions remain kingly, but the lion now moves with a kitten's lightness and a cat's precise, unconscious grace. The piano strews lilting, instantly memorable themes before our ears in seemingly innocent profusion: but great art is everywhere, in the extraordinary number of subtle rhythmic contrasts, in the 'gypsy' languor of the main first-episode (or second-subject) tune, which echoes the metre and key (A minor) of the eighth Hungarian Dance, in the positively Mozartian wit and point of the epigrams bandied between piano and favoured orchestral soloists, in the relaxed mastery of the orchestra that allows Brahms to write grand, full-hearted tuttis without once requiring trumpets or drums. The *Poco più presto* coda is an improbable and wholly convincing blend of skittishness and grandeur, setting the final seal on the achievement of a concerto unique in design, spirit, and sensibility. 'Civilization' can be an ambivalent concept. In its best sense it denotes something like Brahms's B flat Piano Concerto.

Three chamber works

Between 1879 and 1882 Brahms wrote three important chamber works whose confident artistry reflects the optimistic mood of the post-First Symphony period in contrasting but clearly related ways. The lyricism of the G major Violin Sonata combines with a strong constructivist impulse in the F major String Quintet, which takes a mature look at the perennially fascinating problems of formal dances and fugue; while in the C major Piano Trio the lyrical approach gives rise to a powerful and concentrated four-movement form which nevertheless flows with magnificent spontaneity.

The G major Sonata for violin and piano, op. 78,[12] was composed

---

[12] Generally called 'Violin Sonata no. 1', though it is thought three or four others were drafted and suppressed in the years separating it from the early (and likewise discarded) A minor Sonata of 1853.

at Pörtschach in the summer of 1879 and presented to Joachim even as
he was still helping Brahms to refine the details of the Violin Concerto.
Comparatively modest in its violinistic demands, and unaffectedly lyrical
though not entirely untroubled in mood, it has often been seen as a
gentler appendix to that work. Their connection may be more intimate
than is generally supposed: I have certainly occasionally wondered
whether the weightiest portion of the Sonata, its central Adagio in E
flat, makes use of materials from the Concerto's original, supplanted
slow movement (as we know Brahms used the rejected Scherzo for the
B flat Piano Concerto). E flat would be an unlikely key in the context
of op. 77, but B flat would have been possible – as would, unmodified,
the B minor of the movement's most 'symphonic' element, a funeral-
march-like Andante whose grim dotted rhythms could plausibly be
related to ideas in both the Concerto's outer movements. There is no
shred of external evidence to support the hypothesis, but the textures
of this Adagio often convey an 'orchestral' effect wholly unlike the pure
chamber music of the two movements with which Brahms has framed
it.

Ex. 48

(a)

Perhaps it was the dotted rhythms of the funeral-march passage
(say in a figure such as Ex. 48a) which put him in mind of the plangent
head-motif of his two op. 59 songs to Klaus Groth's 'rain' poems,
Regenlied and *Nachklang*. Whether or not this provided the spur, the
Sonata's Finale begins as a recasting of these songs' shared principal
idea into purely instrumental terms. Ex. 48 shows (b) the opening of
Nachklang (the corresponding music in *Regenlied* is identical); and (c)
the start of the Sonata's Finale – identical again save for change of key,
re-notation into smaller note-values, and details of phrasing. Compare
these with Ex. 48d, the first subject from the finale of the C minor Piano
Quartet, op. 60: also allotted to violin and piano, and a strikingly similar
conception save that it lacks the dotted rhythm – I strongly suspect
Brahms had this passage at the back of his mind when he decided to

279

develop Ex. 48b into a violin-sonata movement. But it is precisely the dotted-rhythm figure, bracketed as (x) in Ex. 48b and c, that provides a unifying motif for the whole of op. 78. Not only is it prominent in the Adagio, but the first movement seems to flower spontaneously from the initial lyric utterance of Ex. 48e, a 'little phrase' whose artlessness is of the kind that conceals art. The very simplicity of the piano part throughout the first-movement exposition, largely eschewing contrapuntal working for quiet chords and arpeggiated accompaniment, allows the violin to articulate the form as if engaged in a rhapsodic flow of melody, when in fact the contours of a sonata design are meticulously drawn, and the ardent second-subject tune (Ex. 48f) also embodies figure (x), merely filling in its rests.

Despite the serene tunefulness of its opening paragraph, the Sonata is not quite as limpid and sunny as its reputation suggests. The development soon quits the major key and grows impassioned; the shadowed

Ex. 48

(b)

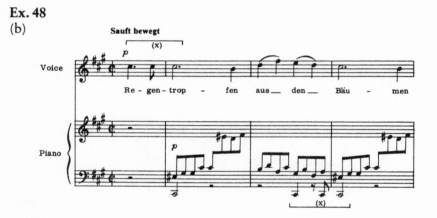

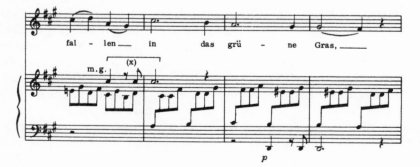

(c)

Allegro molto moderato

p dolce

p dolce

m.g.

(d)

Allegro comodo

Vln.

p

p leggiero

281

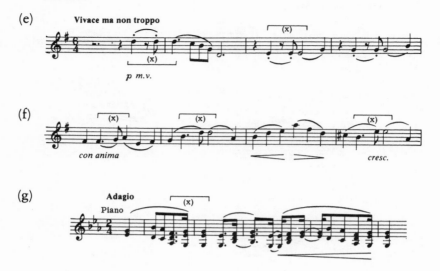

rhetoric of the slow movement's B minor funeral march has already been mentioned, and its E flat main theme (Ex. 48g) is nothing if not pensive. And of course the op. 59 'rain' songs are themselves hardly carefree: they evoke a yearning nostalgia for childhood innocence across a years-wide gulf of experience. That yearning the Finale intensifies, adopting the songs' unsatisfied minor-key restlessness and divorcing figure (x)'s raindrop symbol from its verbal context while finding enlarged use for its plangent tolling. The movement evolves as a rondo, but with surprising structural consequences: its principal episode takes up the *Adagio* theme, Ex. 48g, and develops it within the context of the rondo's obsessive, wandering figuration – an unprecedented formal move. The coda of the whole work is an even richer synthesis of ideas, scraps of themes from the Finale and slow movement interwoven as the harmony melts back into the long-abandoned G major and the piano textures thin out, repetitions of figure (x) recalling, with no necessity for explicit statement, the leisurely Ex. 48e with which the entire composition began. The circle closes on a finally tranquil major-key diminuendo.

Around the time that he was completing his two overtures, in June 1880, Brahms was also sketching two piano trios, one in E flat and the other in C major. Though he showed the first movements of both to Billroth, the E flat work was eventually abandoned; but in the spring of 1882, at Ischl, Brahms returned to the C major, finishing it that July. 'You have not so far had such a beautiful trio from me and very probably have not published one to match it in the last ten years', he wrote to

Simrock with uncommon satisfaction at the way the piece (eventually published as op. 87) had turned out.

He had come a long way since the B major Trio of 1854. The C major is no less opulent – probably even more so – in its profusion of material, but the working-out is masterly in its economy, so that the entire work is of moderate compass, with scarcely a wasted note. Although there are few dark moods Brahms finds no superficial brightness in C major: the key brings forth from him virile, good-humoured music with a strong sense of purpose. The sense of sonority is different, more purely functional, than in op. 8. The violin and cello are generally treated as a single unit, doubling each other in octaves or thirds, in order effectively to counterbalance the piano. Indeed they begin the work alone, propounding an opening theme of almost Handelian robustness against a piano accompaniment that only gradually assumes shape and body. When we reach the second group the piano gets the largest share of it: but both groups are so full of constituent ideas, swiftly following one another in contrasts of rhythm, texture and outline and so cunningly phrased as to elide seamlessly into one another, that all players are kept fully occupied and the music has a majestic, inevitable sweep.

With such a large number of themes affording promising material for development, it is perhaps a surprise to find that in the development itself Brahms broadens and simplifies the pace of his thought. He devotes fully half the space to a lyrical *espressivo* transformation of the opening theme in large rhythmic augmentation (marked *animato* to avoid any loss of momentum), as a serene, waltz-like dialogue in D flat for cello and violin over a flowing triplet accompaniment in the piano. But his sure architectural sense (so different from the comparable movement of op. 8) had taught him the necessity of relaxation, even at a point where textbooks presuppose the greatest activity; in fact he evidently decided that the proper place for dealing with the movement's many ideas in sequence was during the recapitulation, which performs its function of return while 'developing' all of them by a greater or lesser degree of variation. Brahms then finds a further use for the waltz-like variant of the opening theme, to introduce the coda.

The slow movement, in A minor, is a set of five variations, composed with all Brahms's perennial mastery of that genre, on a plaintive theme of distinct folk-like character and strong rhythmic profile, whose prominent 'Scotch snaps' are probably intended to suggest Hungarian 'gypsy' music. The piano accompaniment, syncopated on the weak beats, constitutes a counter-theme that is itself to be extensively varied; and this idea of two parallel but separate thematic entities is explored in different ways throughout the movement, notably in variation 3 where the two strings and piano are pitted against each other in short, pugnacious chordal phrases, and the major-key fourth variation, whose *dolce* version of the main tune presages the Trio of the ensuing Scherzo. The variations are wide-ranging in character, but until the last all adhere to the dimensions of the theme and to its unusual seven-bar cadence figure, a conflation of two four-bar phrases, one the inversion of the other. Brahms extends the final variation to provide a languid coda in which the cadential bars, and the idea of lines in inversion, are deliciously developed.

The *Presto* Scherzo, in C minor, is one of his briefest, and centres on a shivering *pianissimo* repeated-semiquaver figure in the strings which the piano turns into nervous arpeggios and hollow octave tremolandi, like a keen wind stirring the reeds on a lake in winter. Out of these cold surroundings soars the Trio, a radiant arch of melody in the warmest possible C major – an intoxicating tune even for Brahms, among his most full-hearted love-music; and he utterly refuses to linger over it, bringing back the silvery chill of the Scherzo without delay.

The Finale creates several parallels with the first movement. It is cast in sonata form, with an unusually large number of themes, but an altogether more relaxed, rondo-like tone, the piano's tramping quavers (actually a theme in their own right) imparting a genial downrightness of utterance from the start. The codetta of the exposition features some very delicate piano writing in rapid contrary motion, the hands leaping an extra octave to opposite ends of the keyboard at the climactic point of each phrase. The coda is a large one, occupying almost a quarter of the movement; a very tender penultimate passage echoes the first movement by treating the main theme in luxurious augmentation, before a development of the wide-spanning keyboard textures whips up an ending, in glad and vigorous C major, of almost symphonic sweep and finality. At the very end Brahms welds the first subject – whose opening phrase has throughout been treated almost interchangeably with its inversion and whose intervallic configuration has proved very malleable – into a triumphantly plunging stepladder of thirds (which I quote on a later page as Ex. 51c) as the work's final thematic statement.

Brahms had delayed finishing the C major Trio in order to compose, during that same spring of 1882 at Ischl, a String Quintet in F major, his op. 88. Unlike the F minor String Quintet drafted twenty years before and variously reworked into the Sonata for two pianos and the Piano Quintet, the F major is for the Mozartian rather than Schubertian quintet ensemble, adding not a second cello but a second viola to the standard string quartet and freeing viola I for plentiful solo writing. He was even more pleased with this piece than with the Piano Trio. 'You

have never before had such a beautiful work from me', Brahms told
Simrock; and in a letter to Clara of 1890 he called it 'one of my finest
works'. Such expressions of pride, very different from his habitual ironic
deprecation of his music, indicate that op. 88 stood unusually high in
his affections. Yet it is nowadays perhaps the least familiar of his major
chamber works, and most critics seem to regard it with cold admiration
rather than love. Since the Quintet has always been a favourite of mine
I find this difficult to understand, especially as it unites features of some
of the best-loved earlier chamber scores, such as the op. 36 Sextet and
op. 38 Cello Sonata, with presages of the autumnal warmth of the works
Brahms was to produce a decade later. Certainly it begins with as
gorgeous a tune as he ever wrote (Ex. 49), instinct with the burgeoning
of Spring.

Ex. 49

The real contrast to this melody is provided by an energetic dotted-
rhythm transition theme – which may remind some listeners of the
Tragic Overture, recalled elsewhere also (cf. figure (z ii) in Ex. 46,
p. 273) – before the lyrical second subject proper makes its appearance
in A major, the first of many relationships between tonal areas a third
apart that Brahms exploits with impeccable logic in this score. The
second subject's triplets introduce rhythmic complications that are
exhaustively explored in the development, which also begins in A but
is driven towards its climax, over a vast pedal-point on C, by the
dotted-rhythm figure, which becomes more aggressive at this juncture.

Throughout this movement Brahms obtains a wonderfully full sonority from his five instruments, with none of the sense of strain that sometimes oppresses the String Quartets, and this is nowhere more apparent than at the moment of recapitulation. Ex. 49 originally appeared over a harmonization in viola II and cello that was essentially a drone-fifth pedal on F and C; the tune is recapitulated in sixths on both violins, with viola II and cello now doubling the drone, the F and C duplicated an octave higher but rhythmically differentiated, while viola I provides a double-stopped inner harmony in pulsating triplets.

In the G major Sextet Brahms had derived the initial idea of his third movement from one of his very early neo-Baroque keyboard dances, the A minor Gavotte. The F major Quintet only has three movements, but the second, a complex fusion of slow movement and scherzo, is a similar but far more extraordinary feat of transformation, founded on two more of those keyboard dances, the A major Sarabande and the Gavotte in the same key. Whereas in thè Sextet Brahms merely used one theme as a starting-point for an entirely new movement, in the Quintet he makes use of most of the material in the original dances – but he re-fashions, expands, develops and strengthens it, and continually puts it in fresh tonal perspectives. The result is one of his most refined creations, and one now wholly conceived in terms of strings. The movement falls into five clearly-defined sections, creating an A–B–A–C–A form, more correctly understood as A_1–B_1–A_1–B_2–A_2. The first section, marked *Grave ed appassionato*, is evolved from the first half of the Sarabande, transposed into a wistful equivocation between C sharp major and minor, with a new continuation developing the theme's triplet figure, and a haunting chromatic pendant heard in canon between cello and violin II. This is interrupted by the second section, a delicate, pastoral, gigue-like Allegretto vivace in A major. The *Grave* resumes and is developed once again in C sharp major/minor; then the key switches back to A, for a Presto in 4/4 which we recognize as a variation of the previous Allegretto vivace. Except this Presto is, in fact, a newly developed form of Brahms's early A major Gavotte! So the Allegretto vivace must have been composed as a variation on it rather than the other way around – not that such considerations should interfere with our experiencing the movement, from moment to moment, as a slow movement with two fast and intimately-related trios. In the last section, the *Grave* appears for the third time, beginning now in A major; but as it moves onto C sharp it finally departs from the first half of the Sarabande and instead develops its *second* half – the floridly-decorated portion that I have quoted on p. 89 as Ex. 12. This figuration suddenly seems always to have been intended for strings, and provides the movement with an exquisite dying fall that carries it back to a soft ending, not in C sharp but in A major.

The *Allegro energico* Finale is an example of a structure with which Brahms had first experimented in the E minor Cello Sonata: a union of fugue and sonata form. The model here is almost certainly the Finale of Beethoven's third 'Rasumovsky' Quartet (of which Brahms had made a now-lost piano transcription), although Heinrich von Herzogenberg believed it might have been his own String Trio in F which he had sent to Brahms shortly before. Yet the head-motif of Brahms's fugue subject – two explosive opening chords, spanning a falling fourth – are also, remarkably enough, a transposed form of the initial motif of the Tragic Overture (cf. Ex. 46, figure (x)). After a vivacious fugal exposition in F the first violin propounds a sweet and rhythmically supple variation of the fugue theme in A which does duty as a second subject and leads to a development in D minor. Here, both subjects are combined, with a vigorous stretto eventually bringing a recapitulation in which fugal style is increasingly cast aside in favour of more massively homophonic treatment of the opening theme. The coda tightens the tempo to a skittish *Presto* in 6/8, involving rhythmic variation of the main subject and bringing the movement, a nonchalant display of easy mastery, to a genial and brilliant end.

Two 'Classical' choral works

At the beginning of the 1880s Brahms wrote what proved to be his last compositions for chorus and orchestra, *Nänie* (1880–81) and the *Gesang der Parzen* (1882) – two of his profoundest short works, both intensely elegiac in tone; the former certainly, and the latter probably, composed in a spirit of mourning. Astonishingly seldom performed, they are his final statements on the theme of human/Divine separation he had been exploring through the choral/orchestral medium since the early *Begräbnisgesang*. 'I am quite willing to write motets', he wrote to Elisabet von Herzogenberg in July 1880,

> or anything else for chorus (I am heartily sick of everything else!); but won't you try and find me some words? One can't have them made to order unless one begins before good reading has spoilt one. They are not heathenish enough for me in the Bible. I have bought the Koran but can find nothing there either.[13]

Probably he was already contemplating a musical memorial to the painter Anselm Feuerbach, who had died the previous January. Elisabet

---

[13] *Johannes Brahms: the Herzogenberg Correspondence*, p. 106

advised him to look once more in the Psalms, but instead Brahms's choice soon went in the 'heathen' directions he desired, and fell upon a great German re-creation of the pagan Classical spirit, Schiller's *Nänie* ('Threnody'). Almost certainly his attention had first been drawn to this by a setting by Hermann Goetz, performed at the Musikfreunde in early 1880: and indeed Goetz, whom Brahms had known and liked, had himself died young a few years before.[14] The poem's fine-spun network of mythical allusion made it an apt choice in view of Feuerbach's own statuesque Classicism of style and subject – Brahms had particularly admired the painter's huge 'Battle of the Amazons', which had been savaged by the art critics when exhibited in Vienna, and he had sat to Feuerbach for a portrait which the artist did not live to complete. He composed his setting in Ischl and Pressbaum, for SATB chorus and an orchestra that includes the bardic timbre of a harp but omits the brighter one of trumpets, and dedicated it to Feuerbach's stepmother Henriette.

Nänie is a profound but reposeful lamentation that seldom strays from the major key – indeed Brahms seems to take his cue from Schiller's penultimate line: 'Even a dirge, on the lips of a loved one, is glorious'. He never found a more tender melody than the D major oboe line that opens the work, immediately developed in graceful and flexible canon by the chorus to the words 'Even the Beautiful must die...'. For sheer heart-breaking beauty of sound and line, *Nänie* is possibly the most radiant thing he ever wrote. He found Schiller's hexameters difficult, but they inspired from him the poised, long-breathed 6/4 motion he handled so well, and a large, unhurried ternary form whose reprise is compressed to admit further motivic and textural developments. The poem's range of reference – the separation through death of Orpheus and Eurydice, of Venus and the wounded Adonis (in lines that immediately recall the folk text Brahms had set long ago in his song *Vom verwundeten Knaben*), of Thetis and the dead Achilles – strikes repeatedly to the heart of Brahms's perennial theme of Mankind's separation from bliss. Yet here, for once, the roles are reversed, and Heaven is not uncaring: Thetis and the sea-goddesses rise from the triplet-patterned waves in a lambent, majestically mourning F sharp major whose broad and lyrical theme is soon set to the astonished observation: 'Lo, they are weeping, the gods... for the Beautiful fades, for perfection must die'. The intense awareness of the transience of beauty, sometimes conventionally attributed particularly to British composers of the early

---

[14] Both Geiringer and Musgrave find actual musical resemblances between Goetz's and Brahms's settings, which raises the possibility that Brahms may have intended a double memorial.

twentieth century, is here given archetypal expression by the composer who of all composers was perhaps best equipped to feel it. His example was not in vain. The mature choral styles of Parry and Elgar, to look no further, are full of echoes of this gravely luminous work.

The *Gesang der Parzen* ('Song of the Fates'), whose D minor evocation of Classical mythology parallels and clearly develops the impulse behind the D major *Nänie*, paints an altogether darker picture of human destiny. A setting of the blank-verse monologue of the Priestess from Goethe's drama *Iphigenie* (another great example of the German Pre-Romantics' obsession with Greek Classical drama and poetry), Brahms composed it for six-part chorus and orchestra at Ischl in 1882. He had recently seen the play produced at the Vienna Burgtheater with the great actress Charlotte Wolter in the title role. A remarkable feature of the sombre text of the Priestess's monologue is the closeness with which its imagery echoes that of the Hölderlin poem Brahms had set in the *Schicksalslied*, especially through its depiction of the blessed life of the immortals on high. In *Gesang der Parzen*, however, the essential separation of human and divine is made the more bitter by limited contact between the two planes of existence: and by the essentially arbitrary nature of the gods' judgements, even towards 'him whom they raise up'. Brahms may have been thinking of himself as an example, or still of Feuerbach (whose brooding 'Iphigenia' is one of his most famous paintings); but it is equally possible that he had Schumann in mind. The lines later in Goethe's text, where the gods deny favour to an entire later generation, would then be all too apt. By now the two Schumann children to whom Brahms had felt closest – Julie, and his godson Felix – were dead, Ludwig was incarcerated in a mental asylum, Ferdinand a broken man. The final stanza refers to 'an outcast, an old man', who 'listens in caverns of darkness' to the Fates' song, 'thinks of children and those to come, and shakes his head'.

Whatever personal associations lie behind his choice of words, Brahms was moved to produce one of his most powerful, monumental and concentrated expressions of tragic grandeur. The brief, granitic orchestral introduction (Ex. 50a) sets the tone with a neo-Baroque rigour and stern inevitability of pace; and the prominent three-note figure (x) is rhythmically varied throughout the work with astonishing resourcefulness. After the contrapuntal idiom of most of the earlier choral works, the choral writing in *Gesang der Parzen* is homophonic to a surprising degree, but exceedingly rich in texture, consistently darkened by the division of contraltos and basses, and the addition to the orchestra of contrabassoon and bass tuba, whose characteristic timbres open black abysses beneath the music's striding gait. Formally the work is a rondo, with two major-key episodes that serve to accentuate the unremitting gravity of the main sections. The coda (Ex. 50b) is notable not only for its spine-chilling scoring (piccolo and muted strings suggesting bleak alpine immensities of distance), but the extraordinary harmonic circularity by which it finally attains its hollow, tenebrous conclusion on an archaic-sounding bare fifth on D.[15] In the prophetic darkness of this magnificent work, whose mood strikingly anticipates the Fourth Symphony, Brahms's gift for symphonic elegy receives its finest expression.

Ex. 50
(a)

[15] This passage, whose tonal movement describes an arc of major thirds connected by augmented sixths, excited the admiration of Anton Webern, who used it in his 1933 Lectures, 'The Path to the New Music', as prime evidence that Brahms had anticipated the developments of the Second Viennese School: 'the cadences found here are astonishing', Webern declared, 'and so is the way its really remarkable harmonies already take it far away from tonality!... The chromatic path has begun' – the path, he meant, of Schoenberg, Berg and Webern.

Ex. 50

(b)

10

The final phase

That you continue to study my beloved [Volkslieder] is a great joy to me...
Has it ever occurred to you that the last of the songs comes in my Opus 1...?
It really ought to mean something. It ought to represent the snake which bites
its own tail, that is to say, to express symbolically that the tale is told, the
circle closed. But I know what good resolutions are, and I only think of them
and don't say them aloud to myself. At present, now that my sixtieth year has
passed, I should like to be as sensible as I was at twenty...

Brahms to Clara Schumann, August 1894

During the most creative stage of his compositional process – the actual
sketching or drafting of works rather than their revision or fair-copying –
Brahms liked to be in rural, not urban surroundings, preferably of
considerable natural beauty. Thus he spent his summers at various small
resorts or hideaways, working out his music in his head during his
habitual early morning walks. After the 1876 summer in Rügen, with
its beechwoods and desolate moorlands and frogs croaking in their
'yearning, mournful C flat' (as Brahms described it to Henschel), he
preferred lakeland or mountain scenery. From 1877 to 1879 he summered
at Pörtschach, on the Wörthersee, where Symphony no. 2, the Violin
Concerto, and the G major Violin Sonata were all brought to birth. In
1880 and 1882 he based himself in the Upper Austrian resort of Ischl in
the Salzkammergut, at that time very fashionable as it was patronized
by Emperor Franz Josef, and there wrote his two overtures, the C major
Piano Trio, F major String Quintet and *Gesang der Parzen*.

The summers of 1881 and 1883 were spent respectively in
Pressbaum, a suburb of Vienna, and the spa town of Wiesbaden, where
he completed his Third Symphony; and those of 1884 and 1885 at the
picturesque village of Mürzzuschlag in the Styrian Alps, where he wrote
his Fourth. There followed three consecutive summers in Switzerland,
at Hofstetten near Thun in the canton of Berne. Here he rented a villa
with a view over the lake, and was near enough to Widmann to visit
him regularly, while Klaus Groth and Hermine Spies were among his
own guests. Here, too, he produced the C minor Piano Trio, F major
Cello Sonata, A major Violin Sonata, the Double Concerto for violin
and cello, the *Zigeunerlieder* and many songs. After 1889 he no longer

ventured so far afield, but almost invariably spent the summer months at Ischl, where his last dozen or so major works were composed.

For all his much-declared fondness for Vienna Brahms never seemed sorry to be away from it, either on these long, productive summer retreats or on the yearly holidays which he pursued with such vigour and interest. In April 1878 he made his first visit to Italy in the company of Billroth and their composer-friend Karl Goldmark. Brahms discovered that he adored the country, the climate, the Italian temperament, and the innumerable examples of medieval and Renaissance art; and during the next fifteen years he took no less than nine holidays throughout the peninsula and in Sicily, doing a great deal of walking and cultural sightseeing, and usually staying at modest inns rather than hotels patronized by tourists. 'One travels through the whole of Italy as though it were a most beautiful garden', he once wrote to Clara, 'and to my mind it often rises to the heights of a paradise'

His companions on these trips included, at different times, Billroth, Widmann, Ignaz Brüll, Kirchner, Nottebohm and Simrock, and with them he ranged far and wide. Thus, for example, in 1881 with Billroth and Nottebohm he visited Rome, Naples, Messina, Palermo, Siena, Florence and Pisa. 'We are a peculiar three-leafed clover; on the streets we are seldom together', Billroth reported to his wife:

> Brahms, as the youngest, always ahead, always jolly, looking into all the stores, and amused about everything; ten or fifteen paces after him come I, somewhat more slowly; then thirty or fifty paces back is Nottebohm, very slowly! We meet on corners and discuss the map of the city. Brahms bubbles with desire to speak Italian, has studied the grammar for months and learned all the irregular verbs; however, he seldom finds just what he needs for the moment and looks at me with astonishment when I toss all varieties of words about me.

Usually a careless and taciturn correspondent, Brahms waxed lyrical in his reports to Clara. 'If you stood', he wrote from Rome,

> for only one hour in front of the facade of the cathedral at Siena you would be beside yourself with joy and agree that this alone made the journey worth while. And, on entering, you would find at your feet and throughout the church no single corner than did not give you the same joy. On the following day in Orvieto you would be forced to acknowledge that the cathedral was even more beautiful, and after all this to plunge into Rome is an indescribable joy!... Every little detail rewards one for the journey, and the more slowly and the more comfortably it is taken, the more enjoyable it is ... At night on the steamer returning from Sicily Billroth helped a little stranger into the world! It made him forget his seasickness and everything, but he was successful although the operation is

not his speciality . . . next time I shall not allow anybody, not even myself, to mention going home.

In 1884 he stayed at the beautiful Villa Carlotta on the shores of Lake Como with Rudolf von der Leyen, an amateur musician whose friendship he had made some years before in Krefeld, as guests of the Duke of Meiningen. In 1888 Widmann and Brahms explored Verona, Bologna, San Marino, Rimini, Ancona, Loretto and Turin; and in 1890 they visited Parma, Cremona, Brescia and Vicenza.

Brahms's last Italian journey was undertaken in 1893. Wishing himself as far as possible from Vienna on his sixtieth birthday, to avoid the inevitable fuss and celebrations, he set off in April with Widmann and two mutual friends from Zurich, the violinist and conductor Friedrich Hegar and the pianist Robert Freund. They travelled from Milan to Genoa, where they were to have taken a steamer to Sicily, but as Brahms did not like the idea of a long sea-journey (and perhaps also because he had contrived to lose all his money) they made a leisurely way down the peninsula by train instead, stopping at Naples and Sorrento before getting the ferry to Palermo. In Sicily they visited Catania, Syracuse, Taormina and Messina; on the return journey by ferry to Naples Widmann was caught by a heavy loading chain and broke his foot, so Brahms spent the day of his sixtieth birthday looking after his friend in a Naples hotel room, while Freund and Hegar went off to see Pompeii.

'The doctor's performances', Widman later recalled,

> which gave me little pain, excited him fearfully, though he tried to conceal this by making jesting remarks, as when he muttered between his teeth: 'If it should come to cutting, I am the right man; I was always Billroth's assistant in such cases'. When we were alone he provided for my comforts like a deaconess . . .

Brahms returned to Vienna via Venice, which he visited with Robert Freund. This was his last foray beyond the confines of the Austro-German Empire.

Since Wagner's death in 1883 Brahms had been generally recognized as the leading German composer, and as yet the younger generation posed no challenge to his pre-eminence.[1] Honours continued to be

[1] He met the young Richard Strauss, whom Bülow had appointed his deputy, at Meiningen in 1885, at a performance of Strauss's youthful Symphony in F minor. 'Very pretty (*ganz hübsch*), young man', observed Brahms, 'but too full of thematic irrelevancies. There is no point in piling up themes which are only contrasted rhythmically on a single triad.' (Strauss never really took the advice, but learned over the years to turn this weakness to advantage.)

showered on him. He was elected honorary president of the Vienna society of musicians, the Tonkünstlerverein, while Eusebius Mandyczewski took over most of the routine tasks associated with the post. He was elected an honorary member of the French Academy of Arts, and received the Prussian order 'Pour le Mérite'; Cambridge once again attempted to give him a Doctorate, with no better success than in 1877; on his return from Italy in 1893 he found that his friend Viktor Miller zu Aichholz had induced the Gesellschaft der Musikfreunde to strike a gold medal in honour of Brahms's sixtieth birthday. In 1889 Franz Josef awarded him one of the principal decorations of the Austrian Empire, the Order of Leopold; and in the same year he received a tribute much closer to his heart, the honorary freedom of the city of Hamburg. As a mark of gratitude Brahms composed the three motets *Fest- und Gedenksprüche*, which he dedicated to the Burgomaster who had made the award, and these were performed at the Industrial and Commercial Exhibition held in the city in September 1889. By now Hamburg had certainly made restitution to her leading musical son; but in 1894 the post that Brahms had once so eagerly hoped for, and twice been disappointed in, was finally put within his grasp – the Hamburg Philharmonic Society asked him to become its conductor.

By now, however, it was much too late to tempt him. Brahms was over sixty, settled in his ways, and had no intention of leaving Vienna. His letter of refusal was one of regret, with a touch of even-yet unhealed pride at the irony of the situation:

> ... Had things gone according to my wish, I might today be celebrating my jubilee with you, while you would be, as you are today, looking for a capable younger man. May you find him soon, and may he work in your interests with the same good will, the same modest degree of ability, and the same wholehearted zeal, as would have done yours very sincerely,
>
> J. Brahms

The sombre tone of this letter was probably partly caused by thoughts of mortality. For a gregarious man with such a need of friendship, Brahms's latter years were cruelly shadowed by the accumulation of losses within his circle. Tausig and Feuerbach were among the first of his friends to die, in 1877 and 1880 respectively. Brahms was at Gustav Nottebohm's bedside when his old friend expired at Graz in 1882, paid for his funeral and delivered the funeral oration for the lonely scholar–composer. Grädener followed in 1883. His old teacher Marxsen, and Pohl, one of his kindest and most considerate friends, both died in 1887; in the same year Billroth contracted pneumonia that nearly killed him, and was never his old self afterwards. To Brahms's deep grief, Lisl von Herzogenberg succumbed to a heart complaint at the age of forty-four in January 1892; later that year he lost his own sister Elise – Brahms had now outlived all his blood relations, as his brother Fritz had died as early as 1886. Then in 1893 death carried off the merry and invigorating Hermine Spies, who had married only the year before, at the age of thirty-six. In 1894, shortly before Brahms received the Hamburg offer, these blows seemed to rise to a climax: within the space of a few weeks Billroth, Spitta and the faithful Bülow were all taken from him.

In such circumstances it is hardly surprising if his thoughts began to be oppressed with a sense of his own mortality; and indeed for the past few years he had been talking of giving up composing entirely. When he completed the G major String Quintet, op. 111, in 1890, he declared it would be his last work – though he was only fifty-seven – and in 1891 he drew up a will, in the form of a letter to Simrock (the so-called 'Ischl testament') which left most of his money to two charitable associations for needy musicians in Hamburg and Vienna, as well as a number of bequests to individuals and the bulk of his library and musical effects to the Gesellschaft der Musikfreunde.[2] He began to go through his unpublished manuscripts, destroying everything he considered unworthy of publication. Much of what he did publish in the next few years had the character of 'legacies' accumulated over the years: the thirteen choral canons (including the Rückert setting discussed in the Prologue to this book), the fifty-one piano exercises, and the monumental collection of forty-nine *Deutsche Volkslieder* discussed on pp. 152–6. These he sent first in manuscript to Clara for criticism, commenting, in what seems an allusion to their own relationship:

> I think you will find them quite easy... I don't suppose the texts will always please you. But you will certainly be interested by one or two; for instance by *Schwesterlein*, if you picture yourself in the position of the jealous girl. As for Gunhilde and the story on page 6, think of [Schumann's *Paradise and the*] *Peri* and the meaning of the tears of repentance. The man and the woman lead perilous lives, but as they repent and do penance,

[2] In 1896 Brahms revised this testament, leaving everything to the Gesellschaft, which was also to administer a bequest for his stepbrother Fritz Schnack; but as he made the revisions on the manuscript of his original letter, and neglected to sign the legal document drawn up for him on this basis by Richard Fellinger, it was claimed that Brahms died intestate and the will was disputed by no less than twenty-two distant relatives, some of them in the USA and most of whom had never had any contact with him. Litigation dragged on until 1915: in the end Brahms's fortune was indeed divided between the relatives, but his library, and the bulk of his musical effects and correspondence, were acquired by the Gesellschaft, where they are still preserved.

the lilies bow their heads and an angel prays for the sinner. Well – so it
goes.

I am very anxious you should not take the stories too seriously.
Besides they are often incomplete...

Fortunately, however, he had no sooner decided to lay down his
composing pen than he received a fresh stimulus to take it up again.
Visiting Meiningen with Widmann in March 1891 to hear the orchestra
under its new conductor Fritz Steinbach, Brahms was impressed by the
beauty of the playing of the clarinettist Richard Mühlfeld, with whom
he now struck up a friendship and discussed the technique of the
instrument with a keen interest. It is to Mühlfeld's refined and aristocratic playing, therefore, that the world owes Brahms's last four chamber
compositions – the Clarinet Quintet and the Trio for clarinet, cello and
piano, both written at Ischl in the summer of 1891, and the two Clarinet
Sonatas, op. 120, composed in 1894. The Trio and Quartet were both
premièred in Berlin in December 1891 at one of Joachim's Quartet
concerts, and the Quintet especially was hailed as perhaps the finest
work for the clarinet since Mozart's. In the audience on this occasion
was the German engraver and painter Adolph von Menzel, a spry and
vigorous seventy-six-year-old whom Brahms had met the previous year,
and who now became one of the composer's closest friends.

There was one further flutter of the heart, typically over a young
singer. Alice Barbi fitted the time-honoured pattern in being pretty,
intelligent, of a cheerful disposition, and a fine contralto, and she had
the added advantage of being Italian. Brahms first met her in 1890;
when, in April 1892, she included some of his songs in a recital, he
declared: 'I had no notion of how beautiful my songs are. If I were
young, I would now write love songs.' There is no suggestion that their
relationship was anything other than one of his typically deep, musically
based friendships, but they were often seen together in the next few years;
Brahms acted as Alice's accompanist on several occasions, including her
farewell concert in Vienna's Bösendorfer Saal shortly before her marriage to an Austrian nobleman at the end of 1894.

The composition of his clarinet sonatas seemed to invigorate
Brahms, for in 1895 he undertook a concert tour with Mühlfeld, performing them in several German cities, and professionally this was
perhaps the most eventful of his latter years. The Emperor awarded him
the Medal for Art and Science. In January he conducted both his piano
concertos in a single concert at a 'Brahms week' held in Leipzig, with
the young Scottish-born virtuoso Eugen d'Albert as soloist. In
September, Fritz Steinbach and the Meiningen orchestra mounted a

297

festival of the music of the 'Three Great Bs' – Bach, Beethoven and Brahms; and the following month Brahms conducted his *Triumphlied* in Zürich, at a concert inaugurating the city's new concert hall – whose painted ceiling carried his portrait, side by side with those of Beethoven and Mozart.

In January 1896 he again conducted his piano concertos with d'Albert, this time in Berlin – the last occasion on which he appeared before the public as a conductor. Joachim gave a dinner in his honour, and proposed a toast to 'the greatest composer'; before he could finish, Brahms called out 'Quite right, here's to Mozart's health!' and insisted on walking round clinking glasses with the entire party. Shortly afterwards, in Leipzig, he spent some merry evenings with Henschel, the conductor Artur Nikisch, and the Norwegian composer Edvard Grieg, whom he had first met some years before (in the company of Tchaikovsky) but who now became a good friend.

The previous autumn, returning from Meiningen to Vienna, he had paid a brief visit to Clara at Frankfurt, staying only twenty-four hours. On the morning of his departure, Clara played for him, including the E flat minor Intermezzo from the group of piano pieces he had composed for her in the past few years; when she had finished her daughter Eugenie found them sitting together, obviously overcome by deep emotion. Brahms never saw Clara again. In March 1896 she suffered a stroke. Brahms gave up a projected Italian holiday and stayed near Vienna to await news of her recovery. Probably he suspected there would be none: during the next two months he composed the *Vier ernste Gesänge*, the most profound of all his meditations on death and 'last things'. 'I have often thought Frau Schumann might survive all her children, and me –', he wrote to Joachim:

> but I have never wished that she might do so. The thought of losing her cannot frighten us any more, not even me who am so lonely and to whom so little is left in the world.
>
> And when she has left us, will not our faces light up with joy at the thought of the splendid woman whom it has been our privilege and delight to love and admire throughout her long life?
>
> Only thus let us grieve for her.[3]

Clara failed to rally; she managed to pencil a couple of lines in greeting on his sixty-third birthday, but less than a fortnight later, on 20 May, she died at the age of seventy-seven. Brahms had gone to Ischl; a telegram found him there and he left immediately by train for Frankfurt to attend the funeral service. In his agitation he took the wrong con-

[3] *Letters from and to Joseph Joachim*, p. 453.

nection and so had to retrace part of the journey; as a result he got to Frankfurt too late for the service, and immediately dashed on to Bonn where the burial was to take place. He arrived only just in time to pay his last respects, unkempt and utterly exhausted after travelling continuously for forty hours. The physical and emotional strain left its mark, and Brahms, who had rarely ever been ill, suffered a severe chill. Upon his recovery he made his way back to Ischl, where during the summer he composed his last music, the eleven Chorale Preludes for organ – further meditations on endings and eternal verities, couched in almost the most archaic, and yet most personal, of his re-creations of strict Baroque manner.

During that summer his appearance underwent a marked change. The stout, sturdily built composer began to lose weight, and his skin colour became distinctly sallow. Several friends noticed it, and Richard Heuberger urged him to consult a doctor. Brahms at length agreed, as long he was not told anything 'unpleasant'. The doctor at Ischl diagnosed a mild attack of jaundice but called in a Viennese specialist. Both of them recommended that Brahms should go to the spa of Karlsbad to take the waters for a cure; to Heuberger, however, they confided that there was only small hope of recovery – the composer had a very grave disorder of the liver.

Brahms therefore went to Karlsbad in the early autumn in the company of Richard Fellinger, and enjoyed himself in congenial company and surroundings, although the spa water made no perceptible difference to his complaint. He returned to Vienna in October, but was clearly going into a decline. The Karlsbad doctor had kept his diagnosis from Brahms, yet it is difficult to believe that he was unaware of what was happening to him: he was dying of cancer of the liver, just like his father. But in answer to all enquiries after his health he continued to speak of his 'jaundice', and even explained his thinning figure as a deliberate attempt to slim. Thus he contrived to set at least some people's fears at rest. Joachim, having heard rumours that he was seriously ill, wrote to Hanslick and received a reassuring report, which he then passed on to Stanford:

> Brahms . . . has not yet recovered from his attack of jaundice. But as he feels no pain whatever, has an excellent appetite, frequents the 'Rother Igel' every afternoon and evening as usual, and goes about a good deal, we hope he will soon be quite well again.

Doubtless that was what Brahms wished people to think. But his vigour was much diminished: he could no longer walk everywhere as he used to, and was grateful to be taken for carriage rides by friends. Nevertheless he bore himself with as much dignity and habitual good cheer as he could muster. Grieg spent much time with him this autumn, and urged him to come to Norway for his health, where he was sure the mountains would inspire a Fifth Symphony.

Probably the last photograph of Brahms was taken on 11 December at a party at the home of the von Miller zu Aichholz family, and shows him in the centre of a gathering of old friends, among them Hanslick, Julius Epstein, Mandyczewski, and all four members of the Joachim Quartet. Brahms sits at ease in the centre, cigar in hand; but the face is drawn, the skin unnaturally darkened (it was now not so much yellow as brown). He passed Christmas in Vienna with the Fellingers; and in January 1897 went on stage to acknowledge the applause after the Joachim Quartet gave a performance of the G major String Quintet. Joachim noted the 'unusual gratitude and warmth' with which he expressed his appreciation: 'it was almost as if he was satisfied with his work'.

On 7 March he sat in the directors' box at the Gesellschaft der Musikfreunde to hear a concert conducted by Hans Richter, including Dvořák's Cello Concerto and his own Fourth Symphony. The Fourth had always been judged too severe for Viennese tastes before, but on this occasion there was applause after every movement, and at the conclusion of the performance Brahms, standing in the box with tears running down his cheeks, received a tremendous ovation from the entire audience: there was a palpable sense of farewell. He appeared in public only once more, to attend the première of his friend Johann Strauss's operetta *Die Göttin der Vernunft*, but felt so unwell he could not stay to the end. He last left Karlgasse on 25 March, when he lunched with Mandyczewski and Mühlfeld at the Millers; the next day he was too weak to rise from his bed, though he wrote to his stepmother that he was merely 'trying a spell lying down' to see how his jaundice would respond to that.

Frau Truxa, usually with the assistance of some of Brahms's friends, looked after him during the last days of the illness. He sank slowly and apparently without much pain, or much consciousness of what was going on around him. In the early morning of 3 April Arthur Faber called, to find Brahms barely conscious but asking for wine. He gave him a little to drink, and Brahms said: 'That was good. You are a kind man' – his last words. About two hours later, having struggled, with Frau Truxa's help, to prop himself up in bed, he died without being able to speak again.

'Poor Brahms! No: lucky Brahms!' wrote Grieg later that day to their mutual friend Julius Röntgen:

He didn't suffer much, and – he didn't outlive himself. How different the person we call Brahms now suddenly appears to us – more flexible, as it were, than before his death! Now for the first time I see and feel how *whole* he was both as an artist and as a human being as far as I knew him. How glad I am to have been so fortunate as to have known him!

With his simple tastes and Protestant upbringing, Brahms would probably have ridiculed the events of the next few days, when he could no longer protest against the spirit of lionization he had so long striven to keep at bay. Henschel, who arrived in Vienna only later on the 3rd, found the death-chamber transformed into a Catholic chapel of rest, with silver crosses and candelabra, the room filled with flowers. The funeral, which took place on 6 April, was one of the most elaborate Vienna had ever seen; the crowds thronged the streets to follow the immense cortège, and musical representatives came from all over Germany to pay their last respects as well as from London, Cambridge, Paris, Amsterdam, and other cities which felt they had a stake in Brahms's fame. No close relations remained alive to attend the exequies; Joachim was in England, and Stockhausen too ill to come to Vienna. Brahms would have been glad, however, to know that Alice Barbi was among his mourners, and that a group of twelve friends – among them Brüll, Dvořák, Faber, Fellinger, Henschel, Heuberger, Mandyczewski, Miller and Simrock – bore torches behind his coffin, which, after a eulogy by another torch-bearer, the conductor Richard von Perger, was laid to rest in the Zentralfriedhof, near to the graves of Beethoven and Schubert. Far off in Hamburg, at the hour of the funeral, every ship of every nation in the harbour lowered its ensign to half-mast, in a last tribute to the former child of the Gängeviertel.

11

The later music, 1883–96

I should choose this movement for my companion through life and in death.
Elisabet von Herzogenberg, on the Andante of Symphony no. 4

Last orchestral works

The last dozen years or so of Brahms's creative life brought no startling
change of style – but his tendency, from at least the mid-1860s onward,
always to create an organic unity, with every greater motivic economy
and tonal fluidity yet increasing potency of ideas, had solidified by now
into a 'late manner' which combined a masterly concision of structure
with remarkable freedom and richness of thought. A striking illustration
is the Third Symphony, in F major, op. 90, completed at Wiesbaden in
1883. The work scored an immediate public success – for a short
time, to Brahms's irritation, it threatened to overshadow his other
compositions in critical esteem. Of all his orchestral compositions, it is
the one in which instrumental colour is most often enjoyed for its own
sake as well as for structural point; and the manuscript shows how
sensitively Brahms – presumably in his rehearsals with the Meiningen
Orchestra – adjusted even the smallest details of scoring and tonal weight
to achieve the particularly golden glow that suffuses the orchestration.

The Third is the shortest of the symphonies, and the development
sections in its sonata-form movements (there are three) are notably
brief. By contrast the expositions and recapitulations, especially of first
movement and Finale, are expansive and generously supplied with
memorable ideas; while internal and cross-movement unity is secured
both by the use of a 'motto' figure and its associated theme, and
by significant development in the Finale of elements from the slow
movement. As in the other symphonies, though less overtly because of
the powerful first movement, the Finale is the culmination of the whole
argument. The work's subtly interlocking structure flows with such an
untrammelled spontaneity and passion that Hans Richter was moved
to dub it 'Brahms's *Eroica*'. The spiritual parallels to Beethoven's Third
are about as elusive as the structural ones; yet Brahms's work does
suggest a man taking stock (he was now fifty), and confronting his

destiny, whatever it might be, with magnificent intellectual resources but an unquiet heart.

Though any interpretation of no. 3 as a symphonic self-portrait requires to be treated with due Brahmsian scepticism, it does make extensive and significant use of a version of the musical cypher F-A-F, which Kalbeck claimed was the composer's personal motto: *Frei aber froh*, 'Free but happy'. Michael Musgrave has questioned whether Brahms ever meant the figure to be thus understood (and observes that its initial presentation, in Ex. 51a, parallels the opening modulation of Schubert's C major String Quintet). But the motif clearly existed, early in Brahms's career, as a rejoinder to Joachim's F-A-E, *Frei aber einsam* (the two motifs are combined, with obvious symbolic significance, in the first movement of the A minor String Quartet), and the melodic shape, whatever its transpositions, resounds across Brahms's entire *oeuvre*: an *echt*-Brahmsian idea, if not a cypher for 'Brahms himself'. In this Symphony it receives special prominence from the very first bars (Ex. 51a), where the bold statement of the 'motto', surging upwards in brass and woodwind, unleashes a *passionato* descending theme in the strings with which the motto figure remains intertwined.

There is further symbolism here: as many listeners must have noticed for themselves, the *passionato* theme echoes the opening tune of Schumann's Third Symphony, the 'Rhenish'. (More precisely, the reference seems to be to a variant that Schumann presents during his recapitulation: Ex. 51b. J. Barrie Jones has pointed out[1] that the falling-thirds gesture with which Brahms concludes the C major Piano Trio – given here for comparison as Ex. 51c – may also be an aggrandized

Ex. 51

(a)

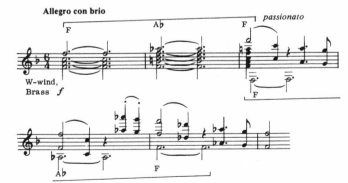

[1] J. Barrie Jones, 'Beethoven and Schumann: some literary and musical allusions', *Music Review*, Vol. 49 no. 2 (May 1989), p. 119.

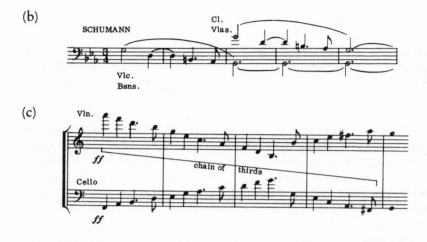

quotation of Schumann's theme, and the three ideas display close kinship when set side by side.) Brahms of all people would hardly be unaware of the resemblance, so in all likelihood this proud-hearted opening carries us back to the Rhineland town of Düsseldorf in 1853, where Schumann and the young Brahms had played with musical cyphers for Joachim's amusement. But Brahms now uses the minor-key version of his cypher, with its A generally flattened, undermining the official major mode to express the more complicated feelings of a mature personality.

It is this persistent minor-key inflection which gives the music such capacity for tonal mobility; so, too, does the sinister tritone, B natural, that appears in the harmony as early as the second bar; and indeed the 'motto' almost immediately develops a 4-note variant, F–A flat–F–B (*Frei ABer FroH*?) which is employed almost as extensively. Ex. 51a inaugurates a stormy exposition, whose one island of calm is a delicate, dance-like second subject in A, largely assigned to solo woodwind over drone fifths in violas and cellos; its relatively carefree character does not last, however, and the music has been swept up into a towering passion long before the end of the exposition.[2]

The mood of turbulent, irascible exhilaration carries through into the development, where violas, cellos and bassoons suddenly transform

---

[2]Brahms directs that the exposition (like those of Symphonies nos. 1 and 2) should be repeated, though until comparatively recent years the repeats of all three symphonies were usually omitted in performance and recording. Their reappearance nowadays seems more because of a prevailing move towards 'completeness' in performance rather than any strong belief in the necessity of the repeats themselves. Yet Brahms's repeats

the dance-like second subject into a swirling, tragic waltz in C sharp minor, calmed by a solo horn bringing back an *expressivo* version of the 'motto' in E flat. The colouring is darkened by a contrabassoon; then in slightly slower tempo a gaunt, mysterious statement of the descending theme from Ex. 51a, in bare octaves, intensifies into a (fortuitous?) reminiscence of a phrase from the climax of the early *Begräbnisgesang* (see Ex. 20 on p. 114) – a work which I have already opined may have connections with Schumann – and therefrom to a blazing brass restatement of the 'motto' and a full-scale recapitulation, in which all the previous material returns with many significant changes of tonal disposition. The coda is principally based on Ex. 51a and its immediate consequences, the 'motto' contrapuntally combining with most elements in a massive demonstration of polyphonic vigour. However, after a fervent climax the movement closes quietly (they all do in this symphony – even the Finale, an effect its first audiences must have found much more startling than we do) with Ex. 51a transfigured in wide, seerene chord-spacings.

There is no real slow movement, rather two of lyrical, intermezzo-like character and moderate pace: the first of them, a C major Andante, is slightly the slower and structurally the larger, as it enacts a full sonata design. Its opening subject, for woodwind and horns with only brief phrases of assent for the strings, has a delicacy of wind-scoring worthy of the A major Serenade, and is one of Brahms's most inspired sublimations of foksong style. Its simple gravity and hymn-like seriousness create a highly refined Brahmsian equivalent of the kind of 'village band' episodes sometimes found in Dvořák's symphonies (for example, in the slow movement of his Eighth). The 'pastoral' quality which early commentators discovered here is certainly present, and so is an indefinable sense of inner landscape, partly inhabited but including areas of brooding, solitary space. After the strings have joined in for a gorgeously decorated version of the opening theme (the decoration principally a simple, rocking semiquaver figure), we arrive at one of these: a melancholy chant-like theme on clarinet and bassoon, with a very gentle pattern of repeated chords under it in the strings (Ex. 52a).

A slightly different form of this theme will arise in the Finale, where it has an important role: Tovey ascribes this not-especially obscure

are by no means unthinking imitations of Classical convention, any more than is the celebrated first-movement repeat of Mahler's Symphony no. 6; and there is ample evidence – see for instance the Tragic Overture and the C minor Piano Trio – that he always carefully pondered the need for a repeat, weighing up the nature of each movement as a whole.

observation to Edward Elgar, a passionate admirer of the Third Symphony. Yet Neville Cardus, in a frequently reprinted record sleeve-note, dismissed this as a 'fanciful connection' or at best a cross-reference 'subconsciously come by; we do injustice to creative imagination to think of it as having need for logical deliberation'. We do it equal injustice in withholding recognition of its conscious constructive power: there is nothing 'fanciful' about the connection, for it is not simply the woodwind theme in Ex. 52a, but its accompanying repeated-chord idea, in the rhythm I have marked (x), which has far-reaching consequences later.

Ex. 52

(a)

(b)

Before long, indeed, Brahms takes that idea on its own and creates from it a wonderfully bare, evocative texture, with the (x) rhythm echoing by isolated two-chord groups in widely spaced registers, now high, now low, like some plaintive natural cry, heard through a kaleidoscopic spectrum of harmonies: Ex. 52b. This proves to be a transition into the development, which mainly concerns the decorated version of the opening theme, and during which the rocking semiquaver figure becomes a motif in its own right and accumulates an intensity of passion that the movement's opening would never have suggested. After this the recapitulation of the first theme proceeds sedately on wind instruments, with the semiquaver figure on the strings, omnipresent but reduced to a continual woodland rustling. The chant-like theme of Ex. 52a does not return, but Ex. 52b does, its plaintive harmonies transposed now to the tonic and its evocative effect magnified by still wider spacing. It arouses that feeling of stillness and utter solitude in a vast place which both enhances sensory awareness and admits a tremor of fear.

The ensuing Poco Allegretto, a simple ternary form, is the most intimate of all Brahms's symphonic intermezzi: it could almost be titled 'Romanze'. Its yearning, exquisitely shaped cello theme with its florid gypsy-style cadential turn, the discreet wind chording, the strings' *leggiero* triplet-semiquaver patterns that turn the previous movement's rustling accompaniments into a soft background murmur, all combine in one of his most memorably twilit elegies. The central section brings another sublimated echo of peasant wind-music; the bass is taken by bassoons and cellos – the latter syncopated, so they are a persistent semiquaver behind the wind. But if Brahms thus intended some gentle humour, the shadows return with the opening motif of the main theme sounding out as a desolate woodwind call. The reprise is led by solo horn in a deepening atmosphere of nocturnal mystery; the rising/falling melodic curve of the ending is like an expansive orchestral sigh.

The start of the Finale recalls that of Symphony no. 2: a *sotto voce* theme in bare octaves with a ghostly, dactylic running motion. Across its shadowed path falls a solemn patriarchal chant (Ex. 52c) very definitely related to Ex. 52a and b. The repeated-note summons of (x) in the trombones provokes an angry *fortissimo* response from full orchestra, compounded from the opening theme and an abrupt, angular, skeletal version of it. This main part of the exposition proceeds with that choleric vigour which makes Brahms such an exhilarating composer even in his grimmest moods; and a valorous, singing C major tune in striding triplet-rhythm on cellos and horn (quoted in Ex. 67 on p. 406) does duty as second-subject contrast. But the second group consists of much more than this, becoming ever more hectic and impassioned in its rhythmic drive and tensile polyphonic energy.

Ex. 52

(c)

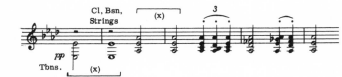

(d)

The ghostly running theme returns, and the mood grows ever more mysterious, straying into a haunted A flat minor. Then suddenly the main development bursts out with Ex. 52d, an awesome new version of the chant-like idea from the slow movement, its vehement, pounding reiterations of figure (x) in brass and woodwind surrounded by seething triplet figuration in the strings. As the rhythms tighten and overlap in a magnificent stretto, the tonality shifts from E to a climactic and overwhelming cadential F, major turning to minor as fatefully as in any Mahler symphony, and precipates us into the recapitulation – which is regular, but intensified in both tonality and sonority, and starts immediately with the angular version of the opening theme. When its fury has subsided, a husky, wavering triplet version of the initial theme creeps in on muted violas from distant B minor, initiating a coda of unexpectedly mellow beauty that turns finally to F major, its tenderness of expression still disturbed by the occasional minor-key chill in the harmony. For the 'motto' returns (in its four-note form); so does the Finale's initial theme in lyrical augmentation, and a quiet and now almost benedictory version of Ex. 52c; the last word is the descending, 'Rhenish' idea from Ex. 51a, reduced to a tranquil, fluttering string tremolo – gently describing, so it seems, the fall of autumn leaves.

Brahms's last Symphony, the Fourth, in E minor, op. 98, followed swiftly – it was composed at Mürzzuschlag in the summers of 1884 and 1885. Yet the work – or at least its Finale – had clearly been contemplated for some years before that. The conductor Siegfried Ochs records a conversation at his Berlin home, about 1880, where Brahms demonstrated to a sceptical Hans von Bülow the latter's ignorance of the vast majority of J. S. Bach's church cantatas (the great conductor had declared complacently that he knew 'seven or eight of them very well'). One of Brahms's prime illustrations was the final chorus of Cantata no. 150, *Nach Dir, Herr, verlanget mich*: a work that had never yet been published, but which he possessed in a fine copyist's manuscript – a gift from Spitta, who had interested him in its striking application of Chaconne form to choral music.

> ...in order to demonstrate what a work of art the piece was, [Brahms] went to the piano and played part of...the Chaconne, which forms the climax and conclusion of the 150th Cantata. Brahms first played the bass, upon which the whole piece is built... Then he proceeded to the Chaconne itself. Bülow listened to all this with only cold admiration, and made the objection that the great climax, which was clearly Bach's intellectual conception of it, could hardly be brought out with the desired force by singing voices. 'That has occurred to me, too,' said Brahms. 'What would you think of a symphonic movement written on this theme some day? But it is too heavy [*klotzig*], too straightforward [*geradeaus*]. It would have to be chromatically altered in some way.'
>
> I immediately wrote down this conversation: and now one may compared the Finale of Brahms's E minor Symphony with that of the aforementioned Cantata...[3]

One may indeed: see Ex. 53a and b. (Ochs, in an omitted portion of the above quotation, actually misquotes the Bach subject.) Brahms adapted Bach's theme, transforming it into an eight-bar phrase and providing a chromatic degree which functions as a sensationally emphasized leading-note to the dominant, and used it as the basis of a passacaglia[4] – boldly reviving a strict Baroque polyphonic form in the context of late-

[3] Ochs, op. cit. pp. 299–300. The story is usually credited to Richard Specht's Brahms biography (1928, English translation 1930), but Ochs's autobiography (1922) is the first-hand source. The manuscript full score of Bach's Cantata 150 which Brahms owned survives, now incomplete and mutilated, in the collection of the Vienna Stadt- und Landesbibliothek. In her description of this copy Virginia Hancock (op. cit., pp. 68–9) erroneously states Brahms made no annotations in the Chaconne. Its surviving pages are in fact as closely annotated and corrected as the rest of the score, which bears witness throughout to close study.

[4] Passacaglia and chaconne are closely related forms, both involving a continuous stream of variations upon a strictly repeated 'ground'; the generally accepted distinction being that in a chaconne the ground is always confined to the bass, whereas in a passacaglia it may appear in other parts of the texture.

Ex. 53

(a)   BACH

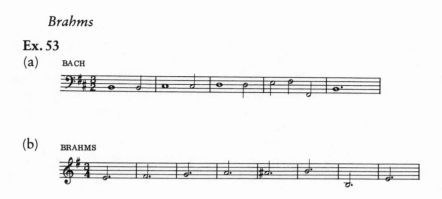

(b)   BRAHMS

nineteenth-century symphonism. However, the important point is that he was contemplating this revival some years before he found its proper context – the symphonic design to which such a movement would be the structurally essential conclusion. In all Brahms's symphonies the Finales assume enhanced importance as areas where the musical arguments are finally resolved, their logic and impetus most graphically demonstrated. This is especially true of the Fourth, which – in the Classical grandeur of its proportions and expression, the richness and intricacy of its internal working, and its passionately elegiac argument, wrought from what might appear the most abstract of musical premises – must be adjudged Brahms's supreme achievement in instrumental music, and one of the supreme creative acts of the Romantic era, in which reverence for old forms gives birth to a new symphonic language.

Brahms was afraid the work would appear too stern to the general public. 'It tastes of the climate hereabouts', he wrote to Bülow from Mürz, 'the cherries are hardly sweet here, you wouldn't eat them!' But he was dismayed that even his friends received the symphony with initial incomprehension. When he and Ignaz Brüll played through the first movement for Hanslick on two pianos the critic complained, 'All through I felt I was being thrashed by two terribly clever men.' Kalbeck, amazingly, urged Brahms to throw the Scherzo in the wastepaper basket, publish the passacaglia as a separate work, and write the second half of the symphony afresh! Even Clara Schumann and Elisabet von Herzogenberg were puzzled by it at first, but the letters in which the latter came to terms with the symphony's greatness are among the treasures of the Brahms–Herzogenberg correspondence. Brahms stuck to his convictions ('the piece does not altogether displease me', he told Clara), and the series of performances soon enthusiastically inaugurated by Bülow and Joachim rapidly established the work as, if one of his austerer creations, also one of his very greatest.

The 'archaic' nature of the passaglia-finale was clearly a major critical stumbling-block. The last of the Variations on a theme of Haydn had been a kind of chaconne; Brahms's admiration for Bach's D minor violin Chaconne is well attested (see p. 150); and in 1883 he was studying an organ passacaglia by Georg Muffat. There were also some important post-Baroque works employing the principle of variations on a ground: notably Beethoven's 32 Variations in C minor and Mendelssohn's *Variations sérieuses*. Yet with one recent exception,[5] there was no precedent for using a passaglia as the Finale for a four-movement sonata structure. However, we should probably consider Brahms's Symphony no. 4 in a wider perspective, of symphonies that employ sets of variations to round off their emotional and intellectual argument: the classic examples were Beethoven's 'Eroica' and Ninth Symphonies. Those variation-finales are much freer (immensely so in the Ninth) than the strict form which Brahms adopted. But both the Beethoven movements include as part of the variation process a form which is both polyphonically strict and of Baroque origin: fugue. And the fugal symphonic finale was itself a long-established tradition, for example in Mozart's 'Jupiter' Symphony; a magisterial instance, adjacent in time to Brahm's Fourth (though not yet published or played) was Bruckner's Fifth, whose Finale combines a fugue and chorale, and an homage to the Finale of Beethoven's Ninth.

The reasons for composing fugal finales are probably as diverse as their composers; but the effect of the tradition that accumulated through such individual contributions was a general acceptance that works with movements in sonata form (a structure characteristic of the Classical era and after, whose essential nature is harmonic, in the sense that it operates through large-scale tonal contrast) could effectively conclude with a fugue (a form characteristic of an earlier period, where tonal contrast is subordinate to contrapuntal activity). Brahms had already blended fugal and sonata types in the Finales of the First Cello Sonata and First String Quintet. In Symphony no. 4, whose first three movements are all fundamentally sonata designs, his creation of a variation-finale in a contrapuntal form comparable in strictness and archaic authority to a fugue, effected a fusion of the two traditions in a manner comparable to Beethoven's fusion of fugue and variations in the Finale

---

[5] Josef Rheinberger's Organ Sonata no. 8 (in the same key as Brahms's symphony) was published in 1882 and has for finale a passacaglia on an original theme. Brahms was well acquainted with Rheinberger, and probably studied the work. It is just conceivable that, whereas in 1880 he had talked only of 'a symphonic movement' [*Sinfoniesatz*], Rheinberger's example helped him to decide the movement's position in a symphonic scheme.

of the 'Hammerklavier' Sonata – a work with several striking points of contact to Brahms's Symphony,[6] not least the way much of its material derives from a chain of descending thirds.[7] That last element, however, was already an authentic Brahmsian fingerprint, and it can be found employed for poetic effect in closely contemporary Lieder: for example *Mit vierzig Jahren*, op. 94 no. 1 (1884), where it clearly symbolizes the ineluctable decline into old age. No text helps us assign meaning to the opening of Symphony no. 4, but the falling thirds of the first theme we hear (Ex. 53c: although inversion disguises some as rising sixths, the accompaniment confirms the downward trend) have an inscrutable poise that is soon revealed as elegy of the noblest kind.

No study shorter than book length may even begin to demonstrate the extraordinary subcutaneous motivic connections of this Symphony, whose thematic integration far exceeds the other three. Here I only hint at a few of them. The first four notes of Ex. 53c already adumbrate the curiously sombre added-sixth harmony that colours much of the work. Within this movement the salient pitch (C in the example) is often treated as an augmented dominant, and is thus an aspect of the tension between augmented and diminished intervals built into the yearning phrases of the theme's continuation (Ex. 53d) and exploited throughout with enormously expressive dissonant effect. But C's Neapolitan relationship to the actual dominant, B, hints at the two Neapolitan inflections of the Phrygian mode, whose flattened second is used at the start of the slow movement deceptively to suggest the key of C major – which in its turn prepares for the true C major of the Scherzo. Meanwhile the prominent augmented fourths in this opening thematic complex foreshadow the vital tritone, A sharp, of which Brahms makes such a point in the theme of the final passacaglia (Ex. 53b) – indeed, the cadential bars of Ex. 53d precisely outline the second half of that theme, long before we actually encounter it. One of the symphony's mysteries is how the falling-third motion of Ex. 53c is gradually transformed into

[6]Brahms owned Beethoven's sketches for the 'Hammerklavier'. I have explored the relations between the two works in more detail in a lecture delivered at the Open University in Cardiff in 1986, whose substance will form part of a projected monograph on this Symphony. I have also suggested the possibility that as the first major work Brahms conceived after the death in late 1882 of his friend Gustav Nottebohm, no. 4 may on one of its many levels of meaning be a symbolic memorial to the great musicologist: investigator of Beethoven's sketchbooks, connoisseur of early music, and composer of a set of variations on a Theme by Bach.

[7]It may not be without significance that the first movement of Bach's Cantata 150 also yields a notable chain of descending thirds, at the words 'Lass mich nicht zu Schanden werden' ('Let me never be confounded').

the ascending conjunct motion of the passacaglia theme; and the process, which involves myriad equivocations between adjacent pitches, and the 'filling-in' of third intervals to provide scalic fragments that move up or down, begins already in the opening bars.

Ex. 53

So does preparation for the very form of that most unusual Finale. As soon as Ex. 53d has been heard Brahms, instead of moving towards a second subject, restates Ex. 53c in a varied guise, a framework for ornamental woodwind counterpoints. This was a passage whose purpose frankly baffled such savants of musical structure as Joachim and Clara Schumann. In fact it admits, at the very outset of an ostensibly sonata form movement, the role of variation – variation of strict proportions, where the principal theme recedes into the background of new contrapuntal developments (and therefore behaves like the ground of a passacaglia). Similar events occur at many junctures in this movement, which is deeply interpenetrated by the variation principle in a way that anticipates the processes of the Finale and immensely broadens the music's expressive scope.

For, dry as these features may appear in cold print, this is at once the most powerful and the most poetic of Brahms's symphonic first movements, afire with a sense of heroic inevitability and an irrepressible lyric impulse that wells up in even its darkest and most combative music. The variation process continually reveals the material in strange new lights, unattainable by any orthodox sonata behaviour. The initial phrase of Ex. 53c is reshaped to give rise to the urgent, thrusting fanfare-figures which are one of the principal elements of the second subject; the glorious, impassioned cello theme which is the more directly melodic element is accompanied (in abrupt, choppy rhythms deriving from the fanfare-idea) by further sequences of descending thirds.

Alone among Brahms's symphonic first movements, that of no. 4 has no repeat of the exposition. The music is so powerfully organic and continuously unfolding that he probably felt one would have disastrously retarded the progress of his argument; but after concluding the exposition he does restate Ex. 53c in its original key, thus alluding (with the characteristic structural ambiguity of his later work) to the possibility of an exposition repeat, even while making it the starting-point for an unusually wide-ranging development section. Chains of thirds can be found almost everywhere, in subordinate voices if not in the thematic foreground, sometimes disguising their identity by the 'filling-in' of an intermediate second which often functions as an appoggiatura. Sometimes, as in Ex. 53e (a passage long ago foreshadowed in the B major Piano Trio, and quoted in my description of it as Ex. 7c), this appoggiatura is inflated to draw such attention to itself that the basic span of a third is all the clearer.

Ex. 53
(e)

In his early sonata first movements (for instance, that of the First Piano Concerto), Brahms had reinforced tradition by making the moment of recapitulation the point of greatest drama. Now it is the point of greatest mystery: Ex. 53c sounds out in solemn, crepuscular augmentation in hollow, reedy octaves and soft, luminous wind chords enshrouded by nebulously swirling string figuration – a thematic transformation so radical and atmospheric we are simply unaware the recapitulation has begun. From this mystical withdrawal the music gathers force and splendour all the way through to the passionate aspiration and tragic vehemence of the coda, the most dramatically 'developmental' of all Brahms's endings in its dynamically evolving variation of Ex. 53c and d.

The bardic unison horn-call that opens the Andante with overtones of epic mystery seems to suggest C major, but when the theme it presages enters smooth and meditative in E major, in luminous thirds on clarinets and pizzicato strings, the opening is revealed (even if we do not know the name for the effect) as in the Phrygian mode, on the symphony's keynote of E. The movement is a straightforward though compressed sonata design (with only brief development, and no formal recapitulation of the first theme, which is already restated within the 'exposition' section); but its continual play with the austere colouring of the old church mode, as against the Romantic warmth of a fully developed E major, gives the harmony a deep-hued patina and a uniquely threnodic atmosphere. The Phrygian is the only Gregorian mode to include a semitone interval above both tonic and dominant pitches: both features have been anticipated in the first movement, especially through the use of an augmented dominant. Brahms frequently made use of modal elements, whether those inherent in folk sources or in pre-Classical music: here he boldly promotes such archaism to the forefront of a highly developed symphonic argument to secure a particular tonal mobility and expressive character.

His conception of the Phrygian mode may well have arisen early: in his copy of Winterfeld's *Gabrieli* he had marked a long (and highly Romantic) paragraph expatiating on the nature of the individual church modes. According to Winterfeld the Phrygian is the darkest of them all, expressing profound need and remorse – but the deeper man's sin, the more fervently he feels the heavenly comfort (*himmlischer Trost*) of redemption, and thus the Phrygian has traditionally been used both for penitential psalms but also for songs of praise. Something of Winterfeld's characterization may linger in Brahms's movement, which from its austere beginning eventually derives (by variation: that principle operates here as in the first movement) its heart-easing second subject in B major, one of his most glorious tunes. (The process is shown in Ex. 53f, g, h, and the tune itself may well have a Bachian origin.)[8] After a sternly striving and muscularly contrapuntal development of Ex. 53f and g, the recapitulation of Ex. 53h, in assuaging glory in the tonic, and in a sumptuous eight-part string texture, is the most gorgeous assertion of the '*himmlischer Trost*' of E major in Brahms's output. The shadows fall again in the coda, where the fusion of diatonic tonality and modal austerity is at its most intense and sombrely glowing.

[8] In his commentary to the Schott–Goldmann edition of the Symphony (Mainz, 1980), p. 237, Christian Martin Schmidt plausibly sees Ex. 53g as derived from the aria *Gottes Engel weichen nie* ('God's angels waver never, they compass me about'), from Bach's Cantata no. 149 – finally published by the Bach–Gesellschaft, along with no. 150, in 1884, and immediately acquired by Brahms (who then discarded his MS copy of the latter).

Ex. 53

(f)

(g)

(h)

In Winterfeld's disquisition on the modes, cited above, stands the following remarkable sentence: *Mit dem hellen, heiteren Ionischen darf das trübe Phrygische unmittelbar verschmelzen* – 'In the face of the bright, cheerful Ionian the gloomy Phrygian must utterly melt away'.[9] The Ionian mode corresponds precisely to the diatonic C major scale: and in C major the Allegro giocoso, Brahms's only symphonic scherzo, proceeds to disperse the magnificent miasma of the slow movement. Bright and cheerful it certainly is, but also amazingly concentrated, and possessed of an intoxicating physical energy and rhythmic urge that Tovey justly characterized as 'tiger-like'. In his judgement, this is 'perhaps the greatest scherzo since Beethoven'; the qualification is surely redundant.

Brahms was of course a master of the scherzo as a musical type, but this – the only occasion on which he admitted one to a symphonic scheme – is structurally the most original of all, a terse sonata form with no hint of trio save a brief, mysterious pre-recapitulation reverie where hitherto distinct themes deliquesce (by variation) into one another. We know that the movement was the last to be written, and Brahms

---

[9] Winterfeld, *Johannes Gabrieli und sein Zeitalter*, pp. 87–8. Virginia Hancock (op. cit., p. 97) has drawn attention to the surrounding passage (but not to this sentence) in the context of Brahms's general partiality for the Phrygian mode, without direct reference to the Fourth Symphony.

calculated its effects to a nicety. Even that 'frivolous' instrument, the triangle, makes its sole appearance in his symphonic *oeuvre* to intensify the steely brightness of mood, not to lighten or cheapen its impact. While powerful enough not to be dwarfed by the grandeur of its surroundings (as a mere intermezzo would have been), the Scherzo in a sense accomplishes the dynamic, sonata development of the symphony's ideas that might have been demanded of a finale, thus leaving the real Finale free for a different level of development entirely. Sly anticipations of the Finale are nevertheless infiltrated throughout it. The pouncing main theme (Ex. 53i) takes its place as a stage in the evolution of themes with emphatic scalic motion; it is often heard in near-exact inversions, one of which (Ex. 53j) supplies the first half of the Finale theme Ex. 53b; a further development (Ex. 53k) gives us that theme's distinguishing chromatic segment – with a reference right back to the symphony's opening chain of thirds; and finally, in a choleric passage of massive, slamming chords, wrathfully spanning the heights and depths (Ex. 53l), the passacaglia theme is climactically presaged (and simultaneously concealed by octave displacement) up to its all-important augmented fourth. This is the penultimate event in a thrilling coda which has built an enormous sense of impetus over a long, pulsating dominant pedal; and whose closing bars are as exultant as anything Brahms ever wrote.

Ex. 53

(i)

(j)

(k)

Brahms

(l)

ff sempre

Exultation, of a grimmer kind, colours much of the passacaglia Finale, his supreme display of mastery in variation technique. Trombones are heard for the first time in the Symphony, with the stark, severe wind chords that proclaim the passacaglia theme Ex. 53b, its E/A sharp tritone dramatically emphasized by timpani at bar 5. True to the nature of the form, and the Symphony's motivic saturation, the theme is not first presented in the bass, but harmonized over an independent bass-line with prominent descending thirds[10] which is itself to be developed later. However, Ex. 53b remains the principal focus of development throughout the ensuing thirty variations and coda.

Variation as such now becomes the predominant and self-evident structural principle. Unlike most of Brahms's other variation works, however, the Finale is built not from a series of deliberately contrasted character-variations but from a tightly interwoven sequence of eight-bar units, each of which contributes to the discourse a subordinate clause rather than a complete sentence; and from these Brahms is able to fashion large paragraphs which suggest a semblance of sonata shape. Clearly this has to be done without reference to the customary tonal contrasts and hierarchies of sonata style, since, with only occasional remission, the passaglia theme pins the music immovably to the tonic. However, variations 1–9 have a pronounced 'expository' character, with even a sweeping, impassioned tune of 'second-subject' type (Ex. 53m) emerging in variation 4 (as the passacaglia theme recedes to the bass) to keep the idea of the descending thirds firmly if covertly in the mainstream of the argument. Variations 10 and 11 function as a calming and modulating transition, leading to variations 12–15. In 3/2 time, at half the speed of the rest of the movement, and all but the first in E major, these four appear more as 'central episode' than 'development', though we may remember the slow development section of the Tragic Overture.

[10] Musgrave (op. cit., pp. 226) sees this as related to Bach's D minor violin Chaconne. It should be noted that the penultimate chord of the harmonization features a 'Phrygian' F natural in the bass-line, creating a Neapolitan cadence onto the final E.

318

Ex. 53

(m)

They are also perhaps the heart of the entire Symphony, its lapidary core, their major-key contrast as poignant a choice for lament as the main tonality in *Nänie*. Variation 12 transforms the mood to the pathos of Greek tragedy with one of the most poignantly expressive flute solos ever written, and in nos. 14 and 15 the trombones return for the first time since the beginning of the movement, with unmistakably funereal import, their soft, solemn chords seeming to bear a catafalque to the rhythm of a stately sarabande. After this, variation 16's fierce E minor restatement of Ex. 53b, intensified by fervent string counterpoint, clearly signals a kind of 'recapitulation' that occupies the succeeding variations up to 30 – but a recapitulation that heightens the process of continuous development, transforming earlier events even as it refers to them, as variations 19 and 20 do to nos. 8 and 9, or nos. 24–6 to nos. 1–3.

As Brahms applies ever-increasing pressure to his theme to disclose its infinite latent possibilities he creates the symphony's most gripping music, with variations 24–5 as a dramatic climax of stark, granitic force. The music then relaxes momentarily towards C major, taking on a lyrical, waltz-character. However, in variation 29 a soft chain of pizzicato descending thirds, at the very pitch of the symphony's opening, prompts the astonishing logical demonstration of variation 30, where a plunging canon on this third-chain at one beat's distance (Ex. 53n) transforms Ex. 53c into a variation on Ex. 53b – a feat of unification that far surpasses earlier examples, such as the assimilation of first-movement material within the Finale of the Third String Quartet.

The listener may remain quite unaware of what the music is doing, save for its sudden access of decision; but anyone can hear the grandiose ritardando which this last variation provokes, heralding a change of

Ex. 53
(n)

direction, and the sudden *Più Allegro* eruption of Brahm's greatest coda.
An ardent tutti blazons forth the passacaglia theme up to its fifth bar
(the one with the tritone); the bar is repeated; and suddenly the second
half of the theme, treated in gaunt and magnificent canon against a
blizzard of string figuration, breaks into a thrilling series of modulations,
as if finally releasing energy pent up by the hitherto monolithic insistence
on E. Now vigorously varying Ex. 53b in outline and proportion, the
coda drives to its end in grim splendour, the theme still defiantly growing
and reshaping itself even as it is terminated by the iron punctuality of
the final cadence.

Brahms's output is generously supplied with masterpieces, yet there
can be little question that Symphony no. 4 is his greatest instrumental
work; and so comprehensively does it succeed in terms of purely musical
and architectonic drama that we need hardly feel surprised he completed
no further symphonies – though he made sketches for possibly two
more, whose material ended up in later chamber and piano works.
Indeed, he produced only one further orchestral composition, but one
that has a special place in his output, and in its warmth and fantasy may
be considered Symphony no. 4's antithesis, or rather, its complement: the
Double Concerto for violin, cello and orchestra in A minor, op. 102,
written in 1887 at Lake Thun. He announced it to Clara in August as
an 'amusing idea':

> If it is at all successful it might give us some fun. You can well imagine
> the sort of pranks one can play in such a case. But do not imagine too
> much! I ought to have handed on the idea to someone who knows the
> violin better than I do (Joachim has unfortunately given up composing).[11]
> It is a very different matter writing for instruments whose nature and
> sound one only has a chance acquaintance with, or only hears in one's
> mind, from writing for an instrument that one knows as thoroughly as I

[11] Not quite true: he was writing his Third Violin Concerto, using a theme by Bettina
von Arnim and dedicated to the memory of her daughter Gisela, his great friend of
the 1850s.

know the piano. For in the latter case I know exactly what I write and why I write it as I do. But we will wait and see. Joachim and Hausmann want to try it...

Clara delightedly dismissed the 'chance acquaintance':

> Surely this wonderful combination has never been tried before? I discussed it a good deal with Joachim who paid me a visit the other day, and we are tremendously pleased about the work. My idea is that one who has written such Symphonies, such Sonatas for violins and violoncellos must know these instruments to their inmost core, and must be able to conjure unsuspected harmonies from them.

She was privileged to hear the Concerto first rehearsed, in Baden-Baden, by Joachim and Robert Hausmann (the great cellist of the Joachim Quartet), accompanied by Brahms at the piano.

Brahms had in fact conceived the work from the first with Joachim and Hausmann in mind; and it proved to be his means of ultimate reconciliation with Joachim since their quarrel seven years before. The first movement makes his intention plain in symbolic terms, for the heartfelt second subject (anticipated in the violin's very first entry) is shaped so as to suggest to Joachim a theme from an obscure work they both relished, Viotti's Violin Concerto no. 22. Flattered that Brahms should once again compose a work specifically for him, and drawn unresistingly into consultation about the solo parts just as with the Violin Concerto, Joachim abandoned his correct but distant manner of recent years and threw himself into the task of promoting the new piece, which he and Hausmann performed under Brahms's direction in many German cities within the first year of its existence.

Not that it had an altogether easy reception: the novelty of the medium, and the fact that Brahms treated it both with an astonishing fantasy of instrumental invention, and in his most concentrated symphonic style, struck contemporary audiences and critics as reckless obscurity. Even so sympathetic a friend as Billroth made the astonishing confession to Hanslick that he found the Concerto

> tedious and wearisome, a really senile production. If the *Zigeunerlieder* had not been composed later, one might almost believe it was all up with our Johannes! I do not know of a less important work of our good friend, and yet just this particular one is dear to his heart.... I would rather not go to the concert at all...

Significantly shorter than Brahms's other concertos, it took many years to be accepted as their equal, and it is still the least frequently heard, largely owing to the economic and logistic barriers against engaging two mutually compatible soloists for the same concert. No precise precedent existed for a violin/cello concerto. Concertante works involving the latter instrument were still rare,[12] but Brahms's fondness for it made it rather more than an equal partner in the Double Concerto, where the cellist propounds the majority of the themes. His models probably included Bach's Double Violin Concerto, Mozart's Sinfonia Concertante for violin and viola, and pre-eminently the Triple Concerto of Beethoven. Yet it also builds upon a firm tradition of passionate sonata discourse by violin, cello and accompaniment which Brahms had already built up in his Piano Trios: in some respects the Concerto is a natural successor to the C minor Trio, op. 101, though the scope of its argument and the high-profile virtuosity demanded of the strings surpasses anything in the chamber works. In op. 102 he asserts his individuality in the most sovereign terms, combining an especially warm and passionate Romanticism with gypsy elements; and the bravura of the solo parts, brilliant though these are, is outstripped by the sheer *compositional* virtuosity of the conception.

Far from being the least, the Double Concerto is without question the most Romantic of all his concertos, perhaps of all his orchestral works, and in a way that springs from the nature of the instruments themselves. Treated as co-equal soloists the two string instruments, so alike in construction and so different in character, inevitably suggest dialogue – and male/female dialogue at that. The violin is a sometimes assertive female and the cello a sometimes pliant and dreamy male, but the fundamental polarities are built into their sonority. And what, in the Romantic universe, do male and female talk about? Tautly symphonic and incredibly rich in construction though it is, it is hardly fanciful to characterize the Double Concerto as virtually continuous love music. Brahms had spent a lifetime writing love-songs, but some of his most intimate and deeply felt had always been without words: perhaps the first of these was the violin/cello reworking of Beethoven and Schumann in the 1854 Piano Trio (see Ex. 8), and thirty-three years later he now took up the idea of wordless string dialogue on an incomparably grander scale. On previous pages I have suggested that *Rinaldo* and the Alto Rhapsody variously provide hints of what a Brahms opera might have sounded like; but in one sense we get a far better idea if we view the Double Concerto as an opera without words, and with only two protagonists.[13]

[12] Schumann's Concerto of 1850 lay unplayed; those of Volkmann and C. A. F. Eckert (1820–79) had had only modest success, though Brahms admired the former and Clara had praised the latter to him.

[13] Curiously, the prevailing rumour in 1887 was that Brahms was writing an opera – and when the Landgrave of Hesse asked Brahms if this were true, he replied 'I am

The first movement is possibly Brahms's most perfect fusion of symphonic dynamism and lyrical ardour, achieved in a design that combines rhapsodic freedom of utterance (involving not one but two introductory cadenzas, cello and violin anticipating first and second subjects respectively) with a taut and very powerful sonata form rich in highly characterful and subtly interrelated themes, and a tonal fluidity that further develops the modal tendencies inherent in Symphony no. 4. Among its most memorable ideas is a forcefully rhythmic theme (Ex. 54a) that is a notable example of Brahms's love both of syncopation and strong dissonance. But even more striking as an instance of his powers of thematic development is the way he utterly transforms it, just before the recapitulation, into a passage of infinite and mysterious tenderness

Ex. 54

(a)

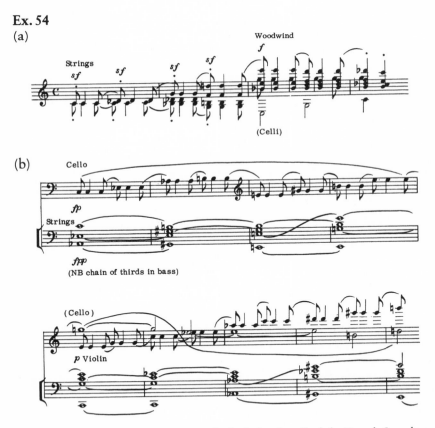

(b)

composing the entr'actes'. However, he had also described the Fourth Symphony to Bülow as 'a few entr'actes'.

(c)

Violin

f (Cello 8ve lower)

(Ex. 54b); and a third version of the theme, fervent and sonorous, touches off the dramatic coda (Ex. 54c).

Beginning with two introductory bars whose rising-fourth call outlines the first notes of the main theme, the serene central Andante in D major is comparatively simple in construction, a ternary form whose gorgeous, song-like principal tune is given out by the soloists in octave unison, and whose second strain proves to be its own (inexact) inversion. The middle section is built on a grave and glowing chorale-type theme in F for woodwind, which the soloists decorate in their most blissfully conversational vein. Here the impression of a love-duet is especially difficult to dispel, and Verdi himself could hardly have built a more soaringly vocal culmination than Brahms, intensifying the effect by violin octaves, creates for his soloists out of the reappearance of the rising-fourth figure. The lyrical main theme returns, expanded, and the second section is recalled in a radiant coda, soaring fourths and all.

The Finale is a Hungarian rondo with sonata elements, on a droll yet graceful subject which Brahms treats with humour, fiery rhetoric, occasional ceremoniousness, and a measured but irresistible rhythmic impetus. It is first announced by the cello, which also propounds the majestically ascending second subject in sonorous double-stopping. The rondo return wittily peters out into fragments, and an impassioned, D minorish theme, contrasting abrupt dotted rhythms and triplets, strides across the course of the music. This is the first part of an extended episode, itself ternary in form. At its centre is a calmer theme in F with a noticeably syncopated rhythm; when the soloists take it up more forcefully, as Ex. 54d, it appears to me a clear reference back to the syncopated theme of the first movement, as developed in Ex. 54a–c, thus emphasizing the organic unity of the work as a whole. Admittedly this is primarily achieved by means of rhythmic similarity, but Brahms presumably felt rhythm to be no less important a source of thematic definition than interval-cells. The dotted-rhythm theme returns, leading back to the rondo tune and the second subject, which now appears in the tonic major – and in A major the music remains throughout the coda. This begins with a slower form of the rondo subject, decorated by the soloists in a dialogue of paradisiac roulades, before a triumphant return to *Tempo primo* for the final bars.

Ex. 54
(d)

Last works for chorus

Apart from the *Tafellied*, op. 93b, for six-part choir and piano (discussed for convenience on p. 355 in connection with its close cousins the vocal quartets), all Brahms's late choral pieces are unaccompanied, and fall conveniently into two groups, secular and sacred. Two sets of partsongs, opp. 93a and 104, are followed by two triptychs of motets, opp. 109 and 110; they represent Brahms's most spare and concentrated contributions respectively to the line of the romantic *Chorlied* and to that of the neo-Renaissance polyphonic techniques he had been exploring since the 1850s.

The six *Lieder und Romanzen*, op. 93a, written in 1883–4, are for four-part SATB choir and concern themselves with a variety of Romantic texts, similar to those of op. 62, but now with a profoundly economical and formally concentrated musical idiom. There are three 'folk' poems, and three by major writers of the Romantic movement. The set begins with *Der bucklichte Fiedler* – a robust setting of words from a Lower-Rhenish folksong whose tune Brahms had arranged before and was to arrange again (see p. 153); but here he provides a tune of his own, in similar rhythm, and a triple-time development of it, for the central witches, dance, whose Lydian mode and stark bare fifths give the piece an unexpectedly twentieth-century air. No. 2, *Das Mädchen*, to a Serbian poem translated by Siegfried Kapper, is possibly the jewel of the entire set. Alternating 3/4 and 4/4 to suggest the seven-beat metres of Serbian folksong, and ravishingly contrasting a solo soprano against a background of mixed-voice harmony, this song represents the antithesis of Brahms's usual strophic approach, evolving seamlessly by continuous development of a single gentle motif announced at the outset and brightening from an initial B minor to a glowing B major climax. The treatments of another Serbian poem, *Der Falke*, and of *O süsser Mai* and *Fahr wohl* (short lyrics by Achim von Arnim and Rückert respectively) are perhaps more conventional – but the unfailing beauty and close integration of melody and harmony avoid any sense of routine: the music is clearly deeply felt, even when its sentiments (notably in *Fahr wohl*, which was to be sung during Brahms's funeral procession) are unremarkable; and the fluid cross-rhythms, major/minor equivocations and long-drawn-out final cadence of *O süsser Mai* have a melting beauty remarkable even for Brahms. After such sweetness the supple and strenuous polyphony of the final setting, a superb canonic treatment of Goethe's aphorism *Beherzigung* ('Encouragement'), is all the more striking.

A few years later the mood is already different. In the five *Gesänge* of op. 104, all but one composed in 1888, beauty of sound and relaxed mastery of medium combine with texts of almost uniformly nostalgic import to produce one of Brahms's most exquisitely despondent works. Op. 104 indulges a mood of melancholy which he must often have experienced after he turned fifty (and had anticipated many times before then), and here communicates with palpable intensity of feeling. The poems tell us that no loving heart opens to the poet's heartfelt whispers; that spring turns to autumn; that youth is fled; that hopes remain unfulfilled; they also link night, and surrender to sleep, with the acceptance of death. At once resigned and ravishing, Brahms's partsongs raise these regrets to the status of high art. The first three of them are cast for six-part choir, SAATBB, which Brahms deploys in the kind of male/female polyphonic exchanges he usually reserved for his sacred choruses; in this sense the op. 104 set, with its fluid and tightly woven antiphony, forms a bridge to the techniques of his last motets, and like them reconciles such archaic devices with the full force of Romantic harmony in a highly effective way. There is little direct word-painting – an exception is the horn and echo imitations in the second of the two Rückert settings called *Nachtwache* that open the set – but a very close correlation of mood with musical movement, and a wonderful richness of vocal colour, especially in these glowing nocturnes (the first of which features some discreet yet plangent dissonance) and in the highly concentrated *Letztes Glück*, an autumnal-twilight evocation which greatly intensifies the effect of Max Kalbeck's poem. Contrast to the generally slow pace is found in the fourth partsong, *Verlorene Jugend* ('Lost Youth', a Bohemian poem, set for SATBB), which alternates two tempi, one vigorous and canonic for the heedless days of youth, the other slower and more Romantically homophonic for the piercing sense of their loss.

The culmination of this group (and indeed of Brahms's secular choral writing)[14] is an SATB chorus written two years before the others, a powerfully depressive setting of Klaus Groth's *Im Herbst* ('In autumn'), itself a *tour de force* of gloom-shrouded nostalgia. Autumn and evening symbolize the end of life; the man watching the sunset foresees his death; but the tears that fill his eyes are blessed: 'the heart's most sacred effusion'. Brahms sets it strophically, in C minor, with great chromatic intensification of the harmony (Ex. 55). The second verse duplicates the music of the first, but the third transfigures it into an equally chromatic C major, recasting the harmony to match the miasmal exaltation of Groth's last lines. (In fact the piece was originally composed a third lower, in A, with an even darker effect.) Various shades of regret remain to be explored in Brahms's late music: but in this undeniably impressive opus he shows himself eloquently unreconciled to the fact of growing old.

Ex. 55

(Autumn is grave, and when the leaves fall the heart sinks too...)

[14] The six-part canon for female voices *Einförmig ist der Liebe Gram*, discussed at the beginning of this book and among the canons published as op. 113, may date from a year or so later.

For the festival concerts that opened the Hamburg Industrial Exhibition of 1889 and in acknowledgement of the award of the freedom of his native city, Brahms composed a group of three motets for double choir which he entitled *Fest- und Gedenksprüche* (Festal and Commemorative Sentences), op. 109, and dedicated to the Mayor of Hamburg. The texts are another of his deft compilations of Bible verses, suggesting in broad terms that house, nation, and people are ultimately sustained by mindfulness of God; and the music, as befits the words and the occasion, is forthright, public and sonorously collective in its utterance. Nevertheless the work has its share of paradox, deploying diatonic formulae of the utmost apparent plainness in three ternary designs (imposed upon the texts for purely architectural considerations) of masterly concision, the vocal textures luxuriantly rich and yet without a wasted note.

In their very varied explorations of antiphonal exchanges these motets return to Brahms's interest in Renaissance music, perhaps enhanced by a renewed study of Schütz (whose Gesamtausgabe had begun to appear under Spitta's editorship); yet the result is a vastly experienced fusion of personal sensibility with ancient techniques. All three movements make extensive use of imitation, especially canon and echo effects, usually in close and complex stretto; and Brahms moves effortlessly between ceremonial decorum and graphic Romantic word-painting. The latter is especially striking in the central section of the second motet, *Wenn ein starker Gewappneter*, where the desolation of the Kingdom divided against itself is evoked by sudden diminished-seventh harmony, and the fall of the House divided is accomplished in a hectic multiple stretto bringing deliberate rhythmic confusion in its train (Ex. 56).

While the mood was on him, Brahms went on to compose three further motets, op. 110, probably the last choral music he ever wrote. To judge by his correspondence he held a higher opinion of these than of op. 109. Their texts are no longer applicable to collective experience but are far more personal, returning once again to the theme of human fallibility and the need for trust in God already eloquently explored in op. 74 no. 1; their forms are more concise and economical than any of his previous motets, and they display his part-writing and responsiveness to the sense of his texts at a peak of flexibility and richness.

The first and third motets of op. 110 are for eight-part double chorus, as in op. 109; but the second – *Ach, arme Welt* ('Ah, base world, you deceive me', by an unknown poet) is only for four-part chorus, largely homophonic in texture, with a suggestion of Dorian modality; it treats the poem strophically, creating a solid, 'hymn-like' central panel

Ex. 56

(... falls upon another)

for the triptych. From this point of view it has most in common with Brahms's early choral works. Nevertheless the individual parts move with great fluidity, the tune itself featuring a segment of whole-tone scale, and the third strophe is varied and brightened in texture. Also its suave 6/4 metre echoes – of all things – the *Liebeslieder* Waltzes. The flanking choruses are by contrast through-composed and use a highly sophisticated polyphonic style that is leavened in subtle ways with chant-like or homophonic passages in Renaissance manner. The smooth transitions between these textures, or their dovetailing by antiphonal effects, as well as the ease with which Brahms deploys a remarkable range of canonic and imitative devices, point even more clearly than op. 109 to his study of Schütz. Indeed at the end of no. 1, possibly the most beautiful of Brahms's motets, *Ich aber bin elend* ('But I am poor', on verses from Psalm 69 and the Book of Exodus) his setting of the final line 'deine Hulfe schütze mich' ('Let thine aid protect me') so stresses the verb 'schütze' that one is tempted to wonder if he is not paying a punning homage to the old master.

The final motet of op. 110, *Wenn wir in höchsten Nöten sein* ('When

329

we are in direst need') sets a sixteenth-century text (by Paul Eber), well known in Bach's famous setting; but Brahms ignores Bach's major-key chorale tune and constructs instead a dark, chromatically inflected C minor canonic texture, based on a more angular chorale-like phrase, which he contrasts with broad block chords in rhythmically lively major-key homophony: the separation of these idioms to characterize alternate verses of the poem (though the two treatments are closely related motivically) recalls the way the earlier motets divided into separate movements, but here produces an A–B–A–B structure with a 'coda' combining elements of A and B. In that section Brahms introduces a chant-like treatment of the line 'and be obedient to thy Word' which he reiterates until it quite counterbalances the expressions of praise in the rest of the final verse, creating the uneasy feeling that the praise is enforced rather than freely given.

Brahms's progress from his first sacred choral works of the 1850s to these glorious and sophisticated motets of more than thirty years later provides a remarkable study in the ever more sensitive and meaningful adaptation of Renaissance choral techniques to the expression of a latter-day and utterly different religious sense. Only one other nineteenth-century master achieved a similarly personal synthesis in this field, and that was Anton Bruckner. But as a Catholic church musician Bruckner was already to some extent born within an unbroken Renaissance tradition, whereas Brahms was forced to approach it from the outside. And whereas Bruckner's Latin motets are among the most wholly integrated expressions of mystical belief since the Renaissance itself, Brahms's German ones – though clearly alluding to the forms, idioms, and thought of the Lutheran sacred-music tradition – are instinct with a detached agnosticism even while fervently expressing the emotional need for submission and consolation. They are not so much personal acts of faith as moving symbols of his admiration for the musical spirituality of Bach and Schütz, to which his heart went out even as his intellect refused to accept it.

Chamber music

Brahms's first summer at the Swiss resort of Hofstetten near Thun, in 1886, was remarkably productive, for in rapid succession he wrote three of his most important chamber works, the Second Cello Sonata, op. 99, Second Violin Sonata, op. 100, and Piano Trio in C minor, op. 101. While the latter two scores both display an increasing desire for compression and essentialization of argument the F major Cello Sonata, though partly sharing these features, is relatively expansive in form and extroverted in character. With its highly dramatic four-movement design and much more adventurous approach to the cello, increasingly reliant on high registers and use of pizzicato and tremolando to produce an eloquently 'speaking' effect, it stands in graphic contrast to the E minor Sonata of over twenty years earlier.

The opening of the Allegro vivace has an almost symphonic sweep, with the cello proposing a leaping, passionate theme (Ex. 57a) over a thunderous tremolando in the piano. Many contemporary listeners found the theme's voluble asymmetry and syncopation, its abrupt, crowing phrases, perversely difficult to understand. As for the tremolando, so often thought 'poor style' in piano writing except as an approximate transcription of orchestral textures, Brahms makes it the binding agent that holds the theme together, and its thrumming, vibrant sonority is fundamental to the excited, emotional nature of the movement. The cello takes up the tremolando imperiously at the end of the exposition (which is repeated); and the whole of the mysterious development section, which shifts the tonal focus unexpectedly to what looks like the mediant major but is treated as a subdued F sharp minor, is built on it – the piano first providing a background to a more reflective version of the first subject, then changing to a more 'pianistic' texture that essentially develops the harmony of the tremolando in more rhythmically defined form. As the recapitulation approaches, the tremolando transfers to the cello, while the piano takes up Ex. 57a in soft chordal augmentation, creating a sense of suspended time and rhythm that looks forward thirty years to the opening of Debussy's Violin Sonata. Tremolandi in both instruments are naturally a prominent feature of the movement's coda.

Ex. 57

(a)

The following Adagio affetuoso goes further along the path of Neapolitan relationships indicated by the first movement's development, for it opens in the far-off key of F sharp major, and with a double theme: a kind of grave procession in the piano, shadowed by padding pizzicato semiquavers in the cello. A warmly lulling *dolce* pendant flowers in the cello as the piano echoes the pizzicato idea in detached chords. For a more conventionally lyrical subsidiary theme, Brahms makes yet a further drastic tonal shift, to F minor; and at the return of the double theme the cello's pizzicati are plangently developed, sounding out in high and low registers, before the cello has the piano's tune for the only time in the movement. Its tense pizzicato patterns stalk yet more depressively in the coda.

The Scherzo, a fiery Allegro appassionato in C minor, is in Brahms's most turbulent and rhythmically hard-driven vein and demands a virtuoso pianist. It is a direct descendant of the C minor Scherzo he had written long ago for the 'F-A-E' Sonata, but now with an incomparably greater mastery of pounding 6/8 metre, bracing cross-rhythm, and a continuous cross-fire of motivic interplay and development between the two players. The main subject is cousin to that of the Finale of the Third Symphony, though Michael Musgrave seems to me over bold in suggesting that they are the same idea. The sweetly singing, smoothly flexible tune of the F major Trio is a radiant contrast; and, as in previous movements, carries the tonality as far as F sharp.

The three movements so far have all been ambitious in scale and serious in utterance; the Finale – marked *Allegro molto*, though its cheerful main tune has too much downright rhythmic and harmonic aplomb to sound really fast – offers a relaxed and melodious rondo that has struck some listeners as too lightweight. The structural parallel here is with the B flat Piano Concerto; once again the final words of wisdom are all the better for being expressed with wit and grace. The equable mood is disturbed only once, by a gustily sighing subsidiary theme in B flat minor (Ex. 57b). Many commentators compare this tune with one of the most celebrated arias from Leoncavallo's *I Pagliacci*: fruitlessly so, as that work was not yet written. Rhythmically and motivically, however, it offers interesting points of contact with Brahms's opening theme Ex. 57a. The ensuing rondo return puts its own gloss on the Sonata's F/F sharp tonal polarity by occurring in G flat major; in this case the tune is on the piano with a pizzicato cello counterpoint; and in the delightful coda the cello takes it over again, but in a tongue-in-cheek pizzicato variant complete with cheeky Scotch snaps.

Unassuming throughout in its utterance, the Violin Sonata no. 2 in A major resembles its G major forebear in no structural particular yet parallels its almost wholly lyrical character, and likewise derives some of its material from contemporary Lieder. Brahms himself acknowledged that the first movement's second subject was developed from a motif of the Klaus Groth song *Wie Melodien zieht es mir*, later published as

Ex. 57

(b)

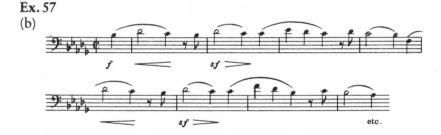

op. 105 no. 1, but even that is rhythmically varied and gives rise to quite different melodic consequences. With less certainty, other writers have seen quotations from *Komm bald* of the op. 97 group in the same movement, and from two other op. 105 songs, *Immer leiser wird mein Schlummer* and *Auf dem Kirchhofe*, in the Finale.

If we could be sure of all these identifications (and they are not inherently impossible) we might see this Sonata as something of an improvisation on pre-existent themes – as near to a spontaneous, unstructured reverie as Brahms's music ever comes. But we cannot. It is however surely true that, to a greater extent than his other chamber music, the textures of Brahms's violin sonatas are predominantly song-like, in both melody and accompaniment. This situates them very near to his song-writing impulse, and ideas and phrases similar and occasionally identical to those of near-contemporary songs are almost bound to occur in the sonatas' very different structural contexts. Probably it is permissible to relate the music to the text – and perhaps even more the sub-text – of those songs. In *Wie Melodien* the poet speaks of melodies growing like flowers within his imagination and wafting away like scent: an apt image for the delicate play of themes in this sonata, and one that also conjures up the flowering garden of the villa in Thun, where Brahms awaited the visits of Hermine Spies, meanwhile composing *Wie Melodien* and the other op. 105 songs for her to sing. Not for nothing did he give the first movement the unusual tempo-marking *Allegro amabile*.

All the same, he integrated such possibly autobiographical elements into a lyrical sonata structure by reserving his song quotation for the second group, writing instead a broad and flowing first subject melody initially given out by the piano in four-bar phrases, the violin adding a fifth-bar pendant that banishes any hint of squareness. The *Wie Melodien* tune occurs in the orthodox dominant but is by no means the only element in the second subject, which also includes an ardently aspiring figure in dotted rhythm and an important motif of two repeated notes

333

and three triplet quavers. This motif features prominently in the development, where its repeated-note rhythm does much to pace the music's progress; while the dotted-rhythm figure initiates an expansively Romantic coda, whose last word is the *Wie Melodien* tune in the violin's highest register.

The second movement, in F, combines the characteristics of slow movement and scherzo in alternating sections, as in the central movement of the F major String Quintet. The opening *Andante tranquillo* portion is a cool, poised melodic complex with an almost Baroque formality, in whose simultaneous unwinding violin and piano have an equal share. This is discreetly developed on each of its appearances, which are interspersed with a delicate D minor *Vivace* element in the style of a lively yet slightly melancholy Slavonic dance.[15] The second time it occurs the *Vivace* is a skeletal variation of itself, its tune 'deconstructed' into isolated pizzicati whose confident deployment echoes the use of pizzicato cello in op. 99. Though the *Andante* music then returns for a third time, the merest wisp of the *Vivace* is used to round the movement off.

Brahms qualified the *Allegretto grazioso* tempo-indication of the Finale with a parenthetical (*quasi Andante*) to ensure its momentum should be sufficiently easy and relaxed. This is an unusually gentle and improvisatory-sounding Rondo, its gracious singing melody (whose germinal figure resembles, but hardly decisively, a climactic phrase in *Immer leiser wird mein Schlummer*) freely varied at each appearance. The first episode also sounds curiously extemporized and colouristic for Brahms, the violin's theme very low-lying and enwrapped in a piano texture dominated by dark, mysteriously rippling arpeggios in diminished-seventh harmony. The piano subsequently takes up the violin's theme here in high, bare octaves; a later melody is more conventionally impulsive and eloquent, while the movement eventually concludes in a peaceful coda, resonant with warm, ecstatic double-stopping from the violin, and in a rhythm that recalls the dotted-note figure from the first movement, achieving a feeling of unity and integration as effective and as understated as at the end of the previous Violin Sonata.

With the modest dimensions of the Second Violin Sonata allied to an emotional turbulence at least as high-powered as that of the Second Cello Sonata, and a structural concision greater than either, the C minor Piano Trio, op. 101, is probably the crowning panel of this 1886 triptych of chamber works. Formally and technically superb, it shows Brahms

[15] Herzogenberg found it 'Norwegian', and implied Brahms might have taken a leaf out of Grieg's op. 8 Violin Sonata.

utterly the master of his medium. Yet there is evidence here of a struggle, perhaps to master himself. Though full of beautiful ideas, the Trio's dominant moods are of defiance, unease and that caustic humour which could catch even his closest friends on the raw.

The opening of the first movement has an explosive wrath that had hardly been heard in Brahms's chamber music since the Piano Quintet, and it inaugurates a structure all the more impressive for its terseness in handling ideas of elemental impetus. 'Smaller men', commented Herzogenberg, 'will hardly trust themselves to proceed so laconically without forfeiting some of what they want to say.' ('Laconic' indeed, Brahms even cancelled a proposed repeat of the exposition.) A transition theme features the obsessive staccato dotted-rhythms that characterized much of the Tragic Overture, and the second subject proper, though technically in 'lyrical' contrast (since it is a sweeping and instantly memorable *cantando* tune), in no way relaxes the high-pressured fervour of the argument. The development (whose latter part takes place in the distant key of C sharp minor) is brief, and unusually concentrated because the two main subjects are developed simultaneously, the first on the piano, the second in the strings; while the recapitulation is foreshortened, beginning with the dotted-rhythm theme. It is this theme, too, which Brahms makes the basis of his coda, after an expansive C major apotheosis of the second subject, ending the movement in the minor, in a mood of grim, tragic determination.

Also in C minor, the *Presto non assai* Scherzo is one of the most delicate Brahms ever wrote, and yet a profoundly uneasy movement of grey half-lights, rapid stealthy motion, and suppressed sadness. The first section is concerned with a sinuously unwinding theme, mainly in bare octaves on the piano, counterpointed against broken phrases in the strings. The central section (it is hardly a trio) goes into F minor, with plangent pizzicato arpeggios against *agitato* syncopated chords sustained in the piano. The reprise of the opening section transfers most of the piano's material to the strings, in canon, against rippling piano figuration, and the coda allows a brief lyrical flowering, in sighing 'gypsy' thirds.

The extremely concise slow movement, a serene C major Andante grazioso, is remarkable for its irregular rhythm, freely fluctuating between bars of 3/4 and 2/4 (the commonest pattern is $3 + 2 + 2$, creating a kind of 7/4; it was originally sketched as such), and for its antiphonal treatment of strings and piano. In the op. 87 Trio Brahms had experimented a little with using violin and cello unaccompanied, but now strings and piano alternate in much bolder fashion, first six bars of each, then fifteen: and from this point arise the characteristic solo string textures of the Double Concerto, to be composed the next year. A *quasi animato* central section supervenes, developing the opening idea in compound time, the metrical irregularities changing to 9/8 and 6/8 (generally one bar of each, 9+6, suggesting a 15/8 rhythm). When the first section is recapitulated the strings and piano remain separate but are intercut every few bars; and a tiny coda then recalls the *poco agitato* music.

The *Allegro molto* Finale is actually a superb example of Brahms's 6/8 'scherzo' vein (which he could apply to other kinds of movements, like the first movement of the First Symphony, also in C minor) at its most serious. With a display of wiry energy that every now and then bubbles up into something like anger, it manifests a kinship with the third movement of the F major Cello Sonata, though its form is more that of an extremely flexible sonata design with no very definite second subject group. Towards the end the tonality brightens to C major and the movement's main theme appears in a sonorous *espressivo* transfiguration, but there is no hint of any easy apotheosis: it is more like a glimpse of the warm heart and noble nature lurking beneath an outwardly depressive and argumentative personality, and it is concealed again in the vigorous and saturnine coda. Perhaps this is what Elisabet von Herzogenberg meant when she commented that the Trio was 'better than any photograph, for it shows your *real* self'.

In that same summer of 1886 Brahms sketched yet one more chamber work, a Violin Sonata in D minor, but did not complete it until 1888, when it was published as op. 108. It may well have been conceived as a contrasting companion to the A major Sonata, for it is entirely different from that work (and, indeed, the G major) in character and structure. The design now encompasses four movements, though their forms are so taut and economical that the Sonata is no longer than its fellows. It is, on the other hand, closely related to the C minor Trio, whose inner movements are equally exiguous, and whose Finale likewise exploits a scherzo character. Lyrical utterance is subordinated, at least in the outer movements, to an argument of considerable tension and drama; and the Finale so effectively re-creates – for almost the last time – the *Sturm und Drang* atmosphere of the instrumental works of Brahms's Romantic youth, that it is sometimes suspected to have been salvaged from some much earlier composition. Yet it shares with the other movements the concise structure, with elements of elision, that distinguish Brahms's latest manner.

The opening Allegro starts *sotto voce*, the violin's high singing line unfolding above an uneasy, syncopated piano part – full of a suppressed passion and anxiety that soon breaks out into eloquent rhetoric. The swiftly flowing exposition makes do with two themes, linked by a short transition motif that turns up again in the second subject and is then used to provide a codetta. But this economy makes possible a great expansion elsewhere. Without pause the music passes into the extraordinary development, which may be interpreted as a single immense cadence: this entire portion of the movement, concerned only with elaborating the first subject tune, takes place over a quiet, insistently tolling dominant pedal in the piano's bass, imitated by the violin through a plangent repeated A in quavers across two strings, an apparently colouristic effect that soon reveals itself as a highly decorated form of the first subject. Precisely because of the severe limitations Brahms sets upon this development, the recapitulation is much more expansive than the exposition, typically permitting some real development of elements not previously so treated; and a reminiscence of the development section, with the tolling pedal and the violin's rocking figure now on the tonic D, becomes the basis for the coda.

The D major Adagio is formally Brahms's simplest slow movement, not even a ternary design but a long accompanied melody followed by its decorated and tonally adjusted restatement. The tune is, however, of such cool intricacy and aristocratic refinement, and its reworking so resourceful, that few listeners will feel any lack of artistry. The violin's sighing thirds towards the end of the first statement recur with a wild, gypsy intensity during the second, providing the movement with a highly effective climax. There follows a curious little intermezzo-cum-scherzo in F sharp minor, which Brahms marks *Un poco presto e con sentimento* to make sure we do not take it too seriously. Certainly its charming opening, with playful, stammering figures of two repeated quavers, promises nothing weighty. However, before long it gives rise to a choleric and dramatic passage in D minor – not a formal trio, as it continues the development of the movement's opening portion – that eventually requires dissolution in a lengthy calming passage back to the initial mood and key, with the violin now delicately pizzicato. The way the movement evaporates in the tiny coda, like a spiral of smoke, is one of Brahms's wittiest conclusions.

The *Presto agitato* Finale is one of the darker manifestations of his galloping 6/8 scherzo style. It is also the most extroverted movement in any of the Brahms violin sonatas, and texturally the weightiest, featuring heavy chordal piano writing and a broad chorale-like second theme (introduced at first on the piano alone), which so closely recalls the big tune in the Finale of the early F minor Piano Sonata that one suspects a deliberate reference. The exposition closes with the first subject in the dominant but rapidly switching back to the tonic; however Brahms almost immediately drops this restatement in favour of a mysteriously subdued development full of obsessive syncopations. This eventually rises to a climax, whereupon the restatement of the opening material resumes at precisely the point where it was previously abandoned, and now functions as an abbreviated recapitulation that leads to a full-blooded, grimly passionate coda.

In the spring of 1888, a few months before Brahms completed this Sonata, Simrock had acquired the rights to his early works published by Breitkopf & Härtel, who had long ago allowed them to go out of print. Brahms was more amused than gratified. 'You expect me to congratulate you?' he wrote on 1 April, wishing the whole thing was 'an April Fool joke':

> ...but I think it exceedingly unwise of you to buy Härtel's things at goodness knows what high prices, music that cost them approximately a hundred Louis d'or, and which in the near future won't be worth powder and shot... But to prove my sympathy with you or rather my commiseration for your great sympathy, I suggest and propose, truly and seriously, that henceforth I receive no honorarium but that you place a certain sum to my credit, which I can claim in case of need, but which is simply cancelled by my decease. You...are aware that I can live very well without receiving any further fees... After my death, however, I should really leave everything to you, so that you would get a trifle out of the deal with Härtel.[16]

Simrock offered Brahms the opportunity to revise any of the early pieces that now displeased him, and the composer averred that he would, 'and to such an extent that you will be justified in announcing the fact on the title page'. He toyed with the idea of rewriting the F minor Piano Sonata, but in the event left all the works as they were, except for the B major Piano Trio (described in Chapter 4), on which he imposed a revision so comprehensive that it amounted to a recomposition. 'You would never guess what childish amusement I have used to while away the gorgeous summer days,' he wrote to Clara from Ischl on 3 September 1889: 'I have rewritten my B major Trio and can now call it Opus 108 instead of Opus 8.[17] It will not be as wild as it was, but whether or not it will be better –?'

[16] Quoted from Karl Geiringer, *Brahms: his Life and Work* (2nd ed., London, 1948), pp. 364–5.
[17] It might have been a good thing if he had, but the new version shares the old opus number, and Violin Sonata no. 3 became op. 108.

338

Far from 'childish amusement', the idea of recasting this loosely structured yet intensely personal youthful outburst to achieve late-Brahmsian organic coherence was a compositional problem of the first order, and just the kind of creative and craftsmanly challenge he relished. Three weeks later he played the result to Clara, who confided to her diary that 'the Trio seems to be much improved.' Yet when she heard a concert performance in Baden a few months later, she confessed: 'The entire Trio strikes me as being much better proportioned, but I don't like all of it...the second theme of the last movement seems to me to be quite ghastly.' Elisabet von Herzogenberg, too, felt at first that 'you had no right to impress your masterly touch on this lovable, if sometimes vague, product of your youth...because no one is the same after all that time...' She was soon reconciled to the new version, however; while her husband retained some doubts, writing to Brahms on 28 February 1891 that 'In the 1st [movement] I cannot get rid of the impression of its being a collaboration between two masters who are no longer quite on a level. It is probably my own fault, for I still shed a tear each time for the dear departed E major subject.'

It was not until later that year that Simrock was able to publish the new version of the Trio, for Brahms held on to the manuscript until he had given a large number of performances and assessed audience reaction. 'With respect to the modernized Trio,' he warned his publisher, 'I must categorically state that the old one is bad, but I do not maintain that the new one is good.' His revision had been so thorough that Simrock had the expense of making an entirely new set of plates, as for a brand-new work. Nor did Brahms even now disown the original version:

What about the old edition? There is no point in discussing it, but all I would say is: if it is requested, send it, and if you find it necessary and advisable to reprint it one day, then do so.

He even suggested that the two versions should be advertised together. All this indicates he recognized that the 1854 Trio remained valid, even if it now dissatisfied him, and that he considered the 1889 one was (as it is) an essentially independent work using some of the same material. While he obviously felt the later version better represented him to the public, he equally clearly did not anticipate the present-day situation in which his original version has retreated into musicological obscurity, while the 1889 recomposition is a staple of the repertoire, usually presented and received as the lightly adjusted work of a twenty-one-year-old.

In fact the only portion of the early Trio which could be transferred to the new work relatively intact was the Scherzo. Its one blemish – the curiously ineffective slow ending with pizzicato figures – was removed, and a new coda substituted, growing naturally and fluidly out of the piano's characteristic falling-arpeggio figure. Otherwise in 1854 this had been an impressive specimen of Brahms's early mastery of the form, and it had least to benefit from major surgery, though many subtle details of phrasing and register were overhauled. It was also concise enough not to warrant shortening, whereas the other three movements are considerably compressed: at the same time their range of tonal reference is enlarged by the use of a broader spectrum of keys. All three begin very nearly as they did in 1854, but soon diverge widely from their original incarnations.

The episodic form of the 1854 Adagio is abandoned for a simple ternary design, nearly sixty bars shorter. The opening chorale-like theme now leads not to the subdominant major but to G sharp minor, where a new and eloquent cello tune completely replaces the music that had resembled Schubert's *Am Meer*. The elaborated return of the first theme, which previously occurred as a central developmental passage, is retained almost exactly but now functions as a decorated reprise of the opening, linking directly to the coda: the intrusive Schumannesque *Allegro* music has disappeared.

Changes to the first and last movements were even more drastic, since these remain sonata designs but acquire completely new second subject groups; the logic of this necessitates wholesale recomposition as soon as the opening portion of the exposition has been left behind. The first movement therefore begins with the grand opening tune Ex. 7a (but now marked *Allegro con brio* rather than *con moto*) and continues with the first sixty-two bars of the 1854 Trio, pruning only a few contrapuntal irrelevances. It was far too good an idea to waste. The same could not be said of its sequel, the jerky transition to relative minor and the flaccid second subject group – unison piano theme, chromatic invention, and concluding country dance. In 1889 Brahms ditched them all, and nothing thereafter resembles what he had written thirty-five years before. Just as the first subject draws to a close the piano makes covert allusion to the original transition figure; but immediately a fresh, swift-moving transition boils up and sweeps the music along on an irrepressible triplet rhythm that carries us into the new second subject. Though this has two halves (and begins on the piano in octave unison), it is in no sense a series of heterogeneous inspirations but a broadly conceived paragraph of vintage Brahmsian lyricism that grows in resolution and direction as it proceeds, rather than dissipating its energies. With the breadth of the first subject as a 'given', Brahms could hardly aim for the terseness of his recent C minor Trio, yet this movement is still 200 bars shorter than the 1854 one, and the new second group, half the length of its predecessor, contrives to balance Ex. 7a much more effectively. The triplet-rhythm idea returns in a short codetta and carries straight over into the beginning of the development, which is dramatic and impassioned (and wholly different from that of 1854). The opening of the recapitulation is effectively masked, Ex. 7a and the triplet idea appearing inextricably entwined with one another in G sharp minor (the key in which the second subject appeared), and only gradually assuming the solidity of the tonic B major. There are no post-recapitulation fugal experiments; instead the coda transforms Ex. 7a into a gorgeous *tranquillo* reverie from which it is only roused in the very last bars.

The Finale is re-designated plain Allegro, shedding its *molto agitato*, and the galloping dotted rhythms of the opening theme begin to sound driving rather than driven. A new and much briefer transition leads to the D major second subject that Clara found 'quite ghastly' (Ex. 58). A terse idea in octaves, underpinned by a hammered pedal D that hardly counts as Brahms's most imaginative left-hand piano part, it is nonetheless characteristically muscular and well integrated into the movement's overall dynamism. It is only when we remember what it replaces – the lyrical F sharp major ardour of Ex. 8c, the tune developed from Beethoven via Schumann, addressed to (and certainly recognized by) Clara – that her negative reaction to its replacement becomes fully explicable. But to the mature Brahms Ex. 8c must have seemed insufficiently motivated and embarrassingly confessional, and perhaps this is why Ex. 58 seems to want almost literally to stamp out all memory of it. With such a second subject, the Finale falls into a much more

Ex. 58

concise and regular sonata shape, nearly 200 bars shorter than its obsessive 1854 counterpart, with no formal recapitulation of the first subject but a restatement of Ex. 58 in the tonic B major. The coda nevertheless remains faithful to the overall thrust of the 1854 Trio, and ends as before in the minor – not so histrionically, it is true, but with a hard-bitten resolve.

The result is, of course, a masterpiece; and if we had to choose only one version of Brahms's op. 8 few would regret with Herzogenberg the 1854 first movement, or the Adagio, though sensitive souls might allowably shed a tear for the F sharp major subject in the 1854 Finale. But why ought we to choose? The 1854 Trio is fascinating music in its own right, and deserves a permanent place in the repertoire, even if we locate it distinctly behind its later counterpart.

Though Brahms's G major String Quintet arose out of a request by Joachim for a companion to op. 88, it was premièred by the Rosé Quartet (who were destined to introduce Schoenberg's Sextet *Verklärte Nacht* and first two mature String Quartets to the Viennese public). When he wrote it at Ischl in summer 1890, Brahms was seriously contemplating retirement from creative work, and conceived the Quintet, which bears the same opus number as Beethoven's last Piano Sonata, as a kind of farewell. We must be grateful that he reversed his decision, but it would have been a fittingly magisterial piece with which to sign off, showing him at the very height of his inventive powers and crammed with matter to give future composers food for thought. Above all, there is a plasticity of ideas and a quality of bold, abandoned virtuosity in the handling of the ensemble that seem to develop from the solo writing of the Double Concerto and to surpass all the other chamber music for strings alone. The first movement presents an especially kaleidoscopic range of texture and sonority in which all five instruments have an equal share of the argument: very different though the structural approach and musical character may be, the sheer textural bravura already anticipates that of *Verklärte Nacht*.

The magnificent opening (Ex. 59) requires a first-rate cellist to project the vaunting, steadily evolving and tonally vagrant first subject tune against the exciting tremolo background on the other four strings. (At Joachim's urging, Brahms sketched a less massive alternative, but eventually allowed his first thoughts to stand, an eternal challenge to performers' confidence.) The effect was criticized as 'orchestral' (cellists must yearn for a few supporting horns), and Kalbeck believed it had originally been sketched for a Fifth Symphony. Yet whatever its origins, Brahms makes it the starting point for a movement of extraordinary textural invention, where the tremolo attains a structural and even thematic significance of its own. The second subject is an utter contrast achieved with a masterly minimum of transition, and contains a suave and delicate waltz on the two violas and a rhythmically fluid *dolce* idea beginning with a rising third. In both these subjects, and elsewhere in the Quintet, there is more than an occasional echo of Dvořák, whose chamber music Brahms studied closely and whose spontaneity of invention perhaps encouraged his own here.

Ex. 59

Tremolandi begin to invade the end of the exposition, which should certainly be repeated (as Brahms directs) to give full effect to the extraordinary opening of the development. An unexpected modulation to F brings a withdrawal from the extrovert music heard so far into an uncanny passage of *pianissimo* rustlings (developed from the opening tremolo) and mystic, abstracted wisps of melody echoing the second subject's rising third. (Elgar clearly remembered it at salient points in his *Introduction and Allegro* for strings and Violin Concerto.) The rest of the concise yet highly eventful development returns to the heroic, full-

343

blooded, full-textured character of the opening, with much ingenious variation of the multi-voiced tremolo as a builder of climaxes; but there are also quiet episodes which recall that magical, inward moment in spirit if not in technique. The recapitulation is reached in a mood of high excitement; the coda features another pensive, withdrawn passage, dominated this time not by tremolandi but by *dolce* versions of the cello theme's first phrase, before further development of Ex. 59 is brought to a scintillating conclusion.

In contrast to this elaborate and ebullient movement, the D minor Adagio is short but suffused with intense melancholy, as is immediately apparent from the husky viola theme in gypsy manner, with its sighing cadential turn, presented over a richly ambiguous harmonic background. This and a short pendant in the violins are almost the only material, but they are developed with great emotional and textural resourcefulness. Towards the middle of the movement comes a slow, mysteriously beautiful chordal sequence, fanning out in contrary motion and dying away almost to the borders of silence as it suggests myriad tonalities in a few bars' space. Ending on G minor, it unleashes a passionate developmental climax (in which 'orchestral' tremolandi again play an important role) ending in a voluble quasi-cadenza for viola I that anticipates the idiom of the Clarinet Quintet, before the original theme returns on violin I, its depression unhealed but eased enough to allow the movement to conclude in D major.

The tense yet exquisite Un poco Allegretto, in G minor, is a more expansive cousin to some of Brahms's symphonic intermezzi (that of the Third Symphony comes especially to mind). As Elisabet von Herzogenberg observed, 'It relieves the strain without displaying – as do so many Allegrettos – more sprightliness than is musically justifiable'. Its main portion has something of the character of a plaintive waltz, violin I taking the lead throughout most of it. Duets of violas and violins then dovetail in a graceful G major dance whose faint Slavonic tang may make us think of the middle movement of the A major Violin Sonata; a bare reminder of the dance serves as coda.

The inner movements' discontent is banished in the concluding Vivace ma non troppo presto – the last of Brahms's 'gypsy' finales, and one of the finest, a concise and spirited fusion of rondo and sonata. Elisabet von Herzogenberg opined that 'the person who invented it all must have felt very light-hearted'.[18] The first subject contrasts a scurrying semiquaver idea (which provides much of the movement's dashing

---

[18] 'Brahms in the Prater?', Kalbeck suggested at a rehearsal: humouring him, the composer said 'You've hit it! And all the pretty girls there, eh?'

momentum), opening in the relative minor, with a rollicking, foot-stamping dance in G; the second features a more indulgent violin solo in sinuous triplets against an accompaniment with off-beat emphases. The development, nimbly threading its way between major and minor, mainly concerns the first-subject group. Spirits rise even higher as the contrapuntal working becomes more intense and brilliant; after an enriched recapitulation the first subject seems about to come round again but the music dissolves into a *pianissimo* haze, from which suddenly erupts a stream of unison semiquavers, an interrupted cadence, and a hectic gypsy dance for coda, the first violin (Brahms clearly pictured Joachim in headscarf and gold earrings) dominating proceedings with true *Zigeuner* élan.

Late Lieder and vocal quartets

As in the 1870s, the opus numbers of the songs from the following decade suggest two separate bouts of activity which were in fact by no means so distinct: the group opp. 94–7 derives essentially from the period 1884–5, and opp. 105–8 from 1886–8, with an overlap in op. 106 which includes two songs of 1885, written before some of op. 97. Prior to all these stands a work unique in Brahms's output, the two *Gesänge*, op. 91 for alto voice, viola and piano: his only example of 'vocal chamber music'. The first song dates from 1884, but the second is much earlier in its origins – it is the *Geistliches Wiegenlied* (Sacred Lullaby), to a German translation of a Spanish text, which Brahms had first produced in 1864 to celebrate the birth of Joachim's first child. It had remained unpublished, though apparently quite well known among his circle. Twenty years later, in the wake of Joachim's divorce proceedings against Amalie, Brahms revised it, composed a companion piece to a poem by Rückert, *Gestillte Sehnsucht* ('Longing Assuaged'), and issued the two songs partly as a peace-offering to the embittered Joachim and partly as a means of reuniting him with his estranged wife, at least on the concert stage; but though Amalie did sing these *Gesänge*, it was never with Joachim as violist.

To some extent op. 91 is a highly refined essay in colour, the viola's timbre being exploited for its likeness to that of the alto voice, and its part assuming a prominence equal to that of the vocal line. Compositional subtlety and love of fine-shaded sonority blend with the enhancement of poetic meaning to produce two of Brahms's greatest songs – both of them unusually extended, quite comparable in scale to slow movements in a sonata. In the *Geistliches Wiegenlied*, its peaceful berceuse-rhythm not unshadowed by hints of future suffering for the child Jesus, the viola provides a cantus firmus and free counterpoint based on the fourteenth-century German carol *Joseph, lieber Joseph mein*, from which Brahms derives many of the music's motifs and a rondo theme capable of expressive variation. In *Gestillte Sehnsucht*, one of Brahms's most impressive nature-meditations, the viola's role is even more elaborate: in a long instrumental prelude it introduces the principal theme, answered and later adopted by the voice – then vies with the singer in searching counterpoint and yearning arpeggios, dominating in interludes and the closing bars. Rückert's is among the finest of many poems that Brahms set which combine the imagery of sunset, evening birdsong, and the onset of sleep, all presaging a drift towards death. The plangently spiritual tones of the viola, and the polyphonic possibilities it opens up within the music, makes of this setting an archetypal exposition of Romantic metaphysics, untouched (as some of his other songs are not) by any hint of sentimentality.

Rückert also stands, with symbolic force, at the beginning of the late Lieder with piano: op. 94 no. 1 is an impressive B minor setting of his poem *Mit vierzig Jahren* ('At Forty'). Brahms had passed fifty when he wrote it, but that was the point: at forty, says the text, one has climbed the mountain, finally turned one's back on childhood and youth, but there is a further ridge to climb and much ground to cross before one finds the way leading downward, easily, almost imperceptibly. Brahms had reached a stage where he could perceive that declivity, and illustrates it in the piano part with another shadowy chain of descending thirds. A shorter chain of four steps then becomes an important bass figure in the next song, Friedrich Halm's *Steig auf, geliebter Schatten*, evoking restless memories of a dead (or at least long-departed) beloved.

In these Lieder of the 1880s the predominant moods are often of regret and imperfect resignation to fate, of piercing awareness of the fleeting moment and the lost opportunity. Doubtless they helped to fuel Nietzsche's jibe[19] that Brahms's inspiration was 'the melancholy of

---

[19] In *Der Fall Wagner* (1888). Nietzsche had tried, without success, to interest Brahms in his own compositions, and after Brahms refused the dedication of Nietzsche's cantata *Hymnus an das Leben* he abandoned the idea that Brahms might be a suitable antidote to his youthful love of Wagner. He took instead to crying up the 'neo-Mozartian' music of his friend and editor Heinrich Köselitz, who composed under the name of Peter Gast. (On the basis of his few published works, the best one can say of Köselitz is that he was not entirely talentless.) Brahms retained a wary respect for the philosopher's writings – perhaps because of the enthusiasm of his friend J. V. Widmann – while careful always to maintain, with a phrase of the youthful Beethoven, 'Perhaps the reverse may be true'. See D. Thatcher, 'Nietzsche and Brahms: a Forgotten Relationship', in *Music & Letters*, Vol. 54 (1973), pp. 261–80.

impotence', but he egregiously mistook their significance. The music is highly potent but irresolute, its strength subsumed into the greater potency of the natural world as it strives to give precise, memorable expression to the ambiguous and dissatisfied moods so central to the composer's experience of life. As a couplet has it from the text of op. 95 no. 6, his friend Paul Heyse's *Mädchenlied*: *O Herzeleid, du Ewigkeit! Selbander nur ist Seligkeit!* ('O heartache, you Eternity! Only the after-life is like you!').

Briefly to characterize opp. 94–7, the even-numbered groups contain the grimmer and more ambitious songs, in Brahms's most developed idiom, while the odd-numbered are lighter and more diverse, with several examples of his *volkstümlich* manner. Op. 94 therefore continues with *Mein Herz ist schwer* ('My heart is heavy'), to verses by Emanuel Geibel – whose image of the insomniac poet kept sleepless by the sighing wind and memories of lost youth is evoked on the keyboard by the restless roving of the hands in contrary motion, and hollow, repeated chords. There follows one of Brahms's most admired songs, the *Sapphische Ode*, a warmly mellifluous D major setting of a very slight poem by Hans Schmidt (sometime tutor to Joachim's children) whose only literary interest lies in its imitation of the Classical Greek 'Sapphic' metre (11 + 11 + 16 syllables). Brahms effortlessly accommodates this within the subtle flexibility of his song's accentual structure. The op. 94 group ends with Halm's *Kein Haus, kein Heimat* ('No house, no home-land') – a bitter song whose theme of spiritual exile is treated with clipped, epigrammatic brevity.

Halm is the author of three of the poems among the seven Lieder, op. 95, but they are less anguished and more folk-like, yielding in *Beim Abschied* (no. 3) an experiment in uneasy rhythmic disjunction (the voice in 3/8 against a 2/4 accompaniment),[20] and in no. 4, *Der Jäger*, a strophic setting in Brahms's cheerfullest folk idiom. The other texts actually stem from various folk-sources, mediated through translation; and no. 1, *Das Mädchen*, is in fact an arrangement of the partsong of that title in the op. 93a *Chorlieder*. The 'heartache' of Heyse's *Mädchenlied* mentioned above (translated from a Spanish original), is rendered in a sensuously graceful setting in F major; but a darker note is sounded again by no. 7, in F minor – *Schön war, das ich dir weihte* ('It was beautiful, my gift to you'), one of Daumer's translations from the Turkish. The final thought that the lover who brings such a gift deserves a better reward than he has in fact received gives rise to a concentrated and powerfully discontented song.

[20] Not as originally published; Brahms's revision to the present form was not printed until 1926.

The six Lieder of op. 97 are on balance even lighter, containing as they do a warm and delicate nocturne (no. 1, *Nachtigall*) with hints of onomatopoeic birdsong; the glowing lyricism of no. 5, Klaus Groth's *Komm bald* ('Come soon'), a song of delighted anticipation that may have lent an idea to the A major Violin Sonata;[21] the frankly merry no. 2, *Auf dem Schiff*, one of the few songs to imply a glad release from care; and the lusty medievalism of the ballad-like no. 3, *Entführung* ('Elopement'), whose armoured knight having lain awake six nights in the marshes because of his Lady Judith, carries her off to the sound of galloping hooves and trumpet-calls. If there is any regret here – for not having done what the song so wittily and enthusiastically celebrates – the composer keeps it to himself. There are also two genuine folk texts, both of them (no. 4, *Dort in den Weiden*; no. 6, *Trennung*) from folksongs Brahms arranged more than once in his career, finally as nos. 31 and 6 respectively of the 1894 *Volkslieder*. Here (as in *Der bucklichte Fiedler* in the op. 93a partsongs) Brahms produces settings of folk character but on new tunes, with sophisticated variations of accompaniment and piano preludes which point towards his treatment of the original folk-tunes in the 1894 collection.

But it is the four Lieder, op. 96, which communicate most power-fully, and remind us that Brahms was simultaneously involved with the Fourth Symphony. Three of them are settings of the mordant and lyrical Heinrich Heine, and represent his most sustained encounter with that most astringent of the major Romantic poets. Indeed, he had planned a complete Heine group, but suppressed a fourth song which Elisabet von Herzogenberg thought of inferior quality, and substituted instead, as op. 96 no. 2, a retreat to the comfortable certainties of Daumer. Yet the music in which Brahms clothes the latter's *Wir wandelten* (a picture of two lovers walking side by side, their inmost thoughts unspoken) is of such tenderness and refinement – the accompanimental patterns appropriately in canon, right and left hands occasionally mirroring their intervals by inversion, and a delicately syncopated right-hand carillon for the bells resounding in the poet's mind – that the song implies no lowering of artistic tone. No. 3, *Es schauen die Blumen*, is an ambiguous love-song turned into a miniature Schumannesque scherzo, the continual flickering cross-rhythms of the piano part giving it the appearance of a keyboard study. It seems almost weightless, in contrast to the immense gravity of the first and last songs of the set. No. 1, *Der Tod, das ist die*

[21] Groth sent the poem as a tribute on Brahms's fifty-second birthday, posting a copy simultaneously to Hermine Spies. Brahms composed the song in a single day, and also sent it to Hermine: she received poem and setting by the same post.

kühle Nacht ('Death is the cool night' – a famous poem, already memorably set for chorus by Brahms's friend Cornelius), provides him with a particularly concise interfusion of the images of death, night, sleep, and a nightingale's love-song that invades the poet's dreams. Brahms's almost Wagnerian setting (parallels to *Tristan* are sometimes adduced) deploys hypnotically lapping rhythms in a very slow 6/8, and a richly chromatic harmony whose modulations seem to draw the singer ever deeper into shadow and slumber. Its dark intensity is, however, equalled and even surpassed by no. 4, *Meerfahrt* ('Sea voyage'), one of Brahms's greatest songs. The 6/8 time of *Der Tod, das ist die kühle Nacht* returns in a barcarolle as anguished as any that bore a lugubrious Lisztian gondola (Ex. 60). Heine's lovers venture out in their boat to the ghostly island where spirits dance in moonlit mist (and where Brahms gives them a darkly glowing waltz music); but they are carried past it, 'comfortless on the wide sea'; and despairingly the song ebbs away, with remorseless restraint, into a fateful, featureless A minor night.

Ex. 60

Brahms

Most songs in the last three sets, opp. 105–7 (of five Lieder each, mainly to minor poets), cultivate ever more closely a sense of spontaneous utterance and lyric intimacy, with ever greater simplicity of material and maturity of means. But there are striking exceptions. Op. 105 no. 5, *Verrat* ('Betrayal'), uses a ballad-style text by Carl Lemcke in which a jealous lover murders a rival on the heath; Brahms's treatment harks back to his early dramatic ballad-songs like *Das Lied vom Herrn von Falkenstein*, yet is incomparably more developed in technique. The progressive variation of the main tune verse by verse, and its intertwining with the accompaniment, are far more radical than anything he would have attempted thirty years before. *Auf dem Kirchhofe*, op. 105 no. 4, to words by Liliencron, is also dramatic, but as a Caspar Friedrich landscape may be, with nature aspiring to the condition of spiritual symbolism. The poet visits an abandoned graveyard on a stormy winter day, the wind gusting through Brahms's turbulent C minor arpeggios and the declamatory word-setting. But a turn to C major evokes the thought that under the frozen headstones the departed ('Gewesen') have in fact been healed ('Genesen') of life's troubles. The identical wordplay occurs in the text of Brahms's *Begräbnisgesang*; here a chorale melody flowers, *gravely* serene – and based on the Lutheran Passion Chorale *O Haupt voll Blut und Wunden*, so that the song begins to anticipate the spiritual atmosphere of the *Vier ernste Gesänge*. Similarly rhetorical but less successful in establishing a distinctive profile is *Ein Wanderer* (op. 106 no. 5), originally composed in 1885 as a companion-piece to *Nachtigall*, op. 97 no. 1, some of whose ideas it transforms – another stern F minor song on the theme of homelessness, real or metaphorical. But overall the emotional dissatisfaction so palpable in opp. 94–7 is much eased in opp. 105–7 – though slumber, sorrow, death and waning time are united in the other-worldly calm of *Immer leiser wird mein Schlummer* ('Ever fainter grows my slumber', op. 105 no. 2), a song about a dying girl; with infinite pathos, it recalls as if in dream the main theme of the slow movement of the B flat Piano Concerto.

But compare it with the deathly oblivion of op. 96 no. 1: in the later song, at least the speaker knows her beloved will live to kiss another after she is dead. Like many of this group, *Immer leiser* grew directly out of the ageing Brahms's romantic friendship with the young singer Hermine Spies (who did not in fact outlive him). To their affectionate camaraderie may be ascribed the greater contentment and sometimes youthful ardour of these later Lieder: he can sing once again (in *Ständchen*, op. 106 no. 1) of students serenading a fair lady, wittily rendering their affable music of 'flute and fiddle and zither' into a fledgling sonata-design of keyboard staccati and 'harped' chords, with a near-quotation

350

from the Academic Festival Overture. The urbane and sensuous melodiousness of several numbers recalls a composer with whom Brahms's name is seldom linked but with whom he had much in common in song, piano and chamber music – Gabriel Fauré. *Auf dem See* (op. 106 no. 2) is as much a barcarolle as op. 96 no. 4, but a Fauréian not a Lisztian one – elegant, lilting, quietly ecstatic, a love-song upon unruffled lake waters with an emotionally ambiguous ending. The Fauréian impression of peace and liquid grace, underscored by a strain of dark nostalgia, is equally strong in *Meine Lieder* (op. 106 no. 4), to a poem by Adolf Frey in praise of the sound of the song itself; a more characteristically Brahmsian form of it inhabits *Wie Melodien zieht es mir* ('It seems as if melodies'), op. 105 no. 1, to a poem by Klaus Groth – a song whose soaring opening tune found its way into the second subject of the A major Violin Sonata. The last of all Brahms's Groth settings, *Es hing der Reif* ('The hoar-frost hung') contrasts the imagery of summer and winter, passion and rejection, with astonishing economy of means and a bleak, haunting repetitiveness prophetic of some of Debussy's piano *Préludes*: the entire piece is essentially developed from two chords and a four-note bass arpeggio.

Even here there are folk-like settings, largely congregated in op. 107, though *Klage*, op. 105 no. 3, is as simple a strophic treatment (of a Lower Rhenish folk text) as any Brahms had written, the same music sufficing for all three verses. In op. 107 the simplicity of design is offset by the sophistication of the piano parts – illustrating, for instance, the flight of the swallow in no. 3, *Das Mädchen spricht*, a song which Elisabet von Herzogenberg found 'a pretty enough piano piece'. The last of this set, another *Mädchenlied* by Heyse, felicitously combines the folksong manner with the stylized conventions of the 'spinning-song'; it begins strophically, then freely develops in its second half, the piano throughout suggesting the motion of the girl's spinning-wheel, the harmony her loneliness, unproposed-to by any man she likes.

On this sympathetic note of tuneful pathos closes Brahms's immense contribution to the mainstream art song. (Only the 1894 *Volkslieder*, discussed on p. 152, and the *Vier ernste Gesänge*, Lieder of a radically different kind, were still to come.) As at its outset one remains impressed by his variety and inventiveness of approach to word-setting, and his ability to identify with the emotional truth behind often undistinguished poems and place them in a setting that imparts the memorable resonance lacking in the words themselves. Eric Sams's comment on the 1894 folksong setting *Verstohlen geht der Mond auf* may profitably be applied to the vast bulk of Brahms's Lieder output:

Two hearts under the moon, a sweet sentimental sampler embroidered with silver clouds and roses and forget-me-nots, depicting home and country, house and garden; this was the illustrated family reading of the whole nineteenth century. But that is the world of Brahmsian song, created from unassuaged passion and dedicated devotion. His music finds and illuminates the reality behind the sentiment. His art embraces both lovers, man and woman, in life and death. Much frustration and loneliness went into that warm knowledge, much corrective bitterness into those sweet thoughts.[22]

Brahms's vocal quartets had never been a mere appendix to his contemporary Lieder; and indeed, the 1880s undoubtedly produced his finest contributions to this now-neglected form, whether treated (as in the four Quartets, op. 92) as a multi-voice Lied – with expressive possibilities equal or even superior to the solo kind for exploring Brahms's favourite Romantic convention of nature as a correlative for human emotion – or as an exotic dance-song genre, as in the *Zigeunerlieder*, op. 103. The final group of six Quartets, op. 112, features both approaches, since its last four numbers form a kind of appendix to op. 103.

The op. 92 Quartets were all written in 1884 except for the first, *O schöne Nacht*, which dates from 1877 and opens the set in a balmy E major, celebrating Brahms's amicable passion for Elisabet von Herzogenberg with the most ravishing of all his settings of G. F. Daumer. The words amount to a tissue of Romantic commonplaces – moon, stars, dew-strewn grass, a nightingale's song, a boy on his way to his girl – but Brahms weaves from them a sumptuous nocturne,[23] spaciously constructed with vocal solos, duets, antiphonies and choral refrains, all over a delightfully varied piano part that has no qualms about painting the starlight in high syncopated octaves, or echoing the nightingale in liquid trills. Then *Spätherbst* ('Late Autumn') turns to E minor with a palpable chill and a poem whose imagery of grey mist, silence and dying greenery is practically a denial of Daumer's. Here Brahms transforms the left-hand piano figuration and triplet rhythms occasionally heard in *O schöne Nacht* into a continuous, plaintively monotonous keyboard

---

[22] Eric Sams, *Brahms Songs* (London, 1972), pp. 63–4.

[23] His original title was *Notturno*, and the piece was an offering to Elisabet von Herzogenberg, who had criticized his song *Willst du, dass ich geh?* (op. 71 no. 4) on the grounds that its text was of a kind that could only be treated 'in *Volkslied* style' (which Brahms had for once eschewed). In mild mockery, he sent her a specially copied autograph of the *Notturno* (which is manifestly no 'Volkslied' despite its pseudo-folk text – and borrows a theme of her husband's to boot), where the setting of Daumer's line about the boy and girl is followed by a blank space and the words: 'Stop, Johannes my son, what's this? These matters are only to be treated in *Volkslied* style; you have forgotten *again*...'

accompaniment, above which the voices spin a fine-woven texture that contrasts and then entwines the soprano with the other three, all four parts saturated throughout by a swirling triplet turn-figure. In *Abend-lied*, an F major invocation of the healing power of sleep, the voices develop a drooping figure over a calmly rotating chordal idea, with a hushed, mysterious, partly unaccompanied central section in longer note-values that is recalled in the quiet, evanescent close. Like the contemporary group of *Chorlieder*, op. 93a, the op. 92 Quartets end with a knottily contrapuntal setting of a Goethe aphorism. At least, *Warum?* (no relation to the great op. 74 motet) begins quite strenuously, with forceful dotted-rhythm piano interludes among the vocal pol-yphony and abrupt modulation; but its second part dissolves into a graceful 6/8 dance-song, radically varying the motivic material of the first. Why do songs soar up to heaven? asks Goethe, and replies: to draw the gods down to us. Accordingly the Quartet concludes with a melting cadence built on Brahms's favourite pattern of a potentially endless ladder of descending thirds.

The eleven *Zigeunerlieder*, op 103, composed in 1887 at the same time as the Double Concerto, are a very different proposition. No one could imagine Brahms capitulating to commercial considerations, yet these 'gypsy songs' skilfully combine the appeal of his two most popular and successfully marketed works, the Hungarian Dances and the *Liebes-lieder* Waltzes. Like the latter, though on a slightly more elaborate scale, they form a sequence of dance-songs for vocal quartet; but now in the rhythms and exotic harmonic shading of the former. In fact Brahms, who at this stage in his life had more than sufficient money for his needs, must have written them for sheer enjoyment (he described them to Elisabet von Herzogenberg as 'excessively gay'), and they are further testimony to the extraordinary fascination and fertilizing effect of gypsy music on his musical language. A Viennese friend of his, Hugo Conrat, had translated the texts of twenty-five Hungarian folksongs for an edition published in Budapest with piano accompaniments by Zóltan Nagy. Brahms only occasionally and glancingly referred to the original tunes but chose freely from Conrat's German versions of the words, producing a concentrated song sequence that rings as resourceful a set of changes on the 2/4 csárdás-rhythm as the *Liebeslieder* had upon waltz-time, and is perhaps even more resourceful in flexible contrasts of vocal texture. The 'national' idiom, though seldom obscured, is other-wise rather diffuse, and some of the songs – notably the beautiful nos. 7 and 8 – resemble strophic Lieder with Slavic colouring; indeed Brahms later published eight of the set in alternative versions as solo songs. The theme of the opening song, *He, Zigeuner!*, returns in varied form as the theme of the last, *Rote Abendwolken*; and in no. 10 the piano part produces an uncanny imitation of the cimbalom (Ex. 61) that recalls and at once surpasses a similar effect in the early Variations on a Hungarian Song: compare it with Ex. 9 on p. 81:

Ex. 61

etc.

Four years later Brahms returned to Conrat's verse translations and wrote four more *Zigeunerlieder*, which he published as nos. 3–6 of his final and oddly heterogeneous set of Vocal Quartets, op. 112. The first of them, *Himmel strahlt so helle und klar*, is formally somewhat more elaborate than the op. 103 settings, and the 'gypsy' style is further diluted; otherwise the same general remarks apply. The principal interest in op. 112 focuses instead on nos. 1 and 2, settings of short, depressive poems by Franz Kugler which Brahms had composed in 1888, about the time of his equally melancholic partsongs, op. 104. These are the darkest thoughts he ever committed to the vocal-quartet medium. *Sehnsucht*

('Yearning'), a bitter little meditation on how desire remains unsatisfied as life passes in solitude, prompts an act of intense personal identification in F minor, and considerable textural diversity in a small space, the poet's memories moving glumly in chromatic canon by inversion. The D minor *Nächtens* ('At night'), an evocation of uneasy slumber, uses the irregularities of a 5/4 metre, a depressive chant-like figure (which recurs in different forms in the op. 114 Clarinet Trio and the first of the *Vier ernste Gesänge*) and a nervously shimmering demi-semiquaver figuration in the accompaniment to achieve a similarly desolate effect, undispelled by the perfunctory arrival of a D major dawn through an appoggiatura in the very last bar.

It remains to mention a strictly occasional work, the *Tafellied* for six-part chorus (or solo voices) and piano, a glee composed in 1884 in celebration of the fiftieth anniversary of the Krefeld Singverein in January 1885, and published as op. 93b. Brahms's delightful setting of Eichendorff's poem in praise of song and wine subtitled 'Dank der Damen' ('The ladies' toast') is a more elaborate affair than his earlier occasional piece, the *Kleine Hochzeitskantate*. The text itself, a gallant dialogue, suggests the basic form of exchanges in his most blithely melodious vein between male and female vocal groups, the two sexes joining together for the jubilant toast proclaimed in the final verse.

Last piano pieces

Brahms's final compositions for his own instrument continued, after a long interval, the line of miniatures begun in the op. 10 Ballades and refined in the op. 76 Piano Pieces. Though some of them may have been drafted in the intervening years, it seems likely that the four collections of pieces he issued as opp. 116–19 were mainly compiled from a large group composed near the time of their publication in 1892–3. (We know he wrote more than the twenty that were eventually printed.) They stand at the furthest possible remove from the rhetoric of the early sonatas or the pugnacious challenge of the large-scale variation sets. Though a few of them afford brief glimpses of the old fire and energy, the predominant character is reflective, musing, deeply introspective, and at the same time unfailingly exploratory of harmonic and textural effect, of rhythmic ambiguity, of structural elision and wayward fantasy. They are among the most personal piano music ever written, in that they seem a product of the composer's self-communing, something to play to himself or at most to a few close friends (Clara Schumann was the first to see them in manuscript). This does not mean they are unsuitable for concert performance. They merely present the pianist with some of the greatest interpretative challenges in the repertoire: the goal must be to get far beyond their purely technical problems (and though they contain much of Brahms's most grateful piano writing, they are no less difficult for that) and create the necessary ambience of shared intimacy.

A slight distinction may be drawn between the seven pieces of op. 116, to which Brahms gave the overall title *Fantasien*, and the op. 117–19 groups, which he simply designated *Klavierstücke*. Not that their component movements are greatly different, but op. 116 presents a mix of vigorous 'Capriccii' and reflective 'Intermezzi' along the lines of op. 76; after that the intermezzo character becomes pre-eminent, and there are no further 'Capriccii'. Op. 117 is a triptych of three Intermezzi, but op. 118 offers variety with a 'Ballade' and a 'Romanze', and op. 119 concludes with the fine flourish of Brahms's last Rhapsody. Unlike these following groups, op. 116 seems less a compilation than a self-consistent entity, beginning and ending with passionate and volatile Capriccii in D minor that enclose four Intermezzi and another Capriccio in carefully structured mutual tonal relationships. Like the op. 10 Ballades, but in a far more allusive and tangential way, these *Fantasien* resemble a multi-movement sonata, with the G minor Capriccio (no. 3) serving as a brief but powerful scherzo and the ensuing three Intermezzi (nos. 4–6) as a 'slow movement' in E major, with a central contrast (no. 5) in E minor. Even more persuasive is the motivic unity: the material of all three Capriccii is fashioned out of chains of descending thirds, which also feature more covertly in the other movements.

Both the D minor Capriccii use the thirds-motif most inventively in the context of diminished-seventh harmony, and the first, marked *Presto energico*, is an agitated rhythmic study, with strong accents on the weakest beat of the bar. A similarly mercurial syncopation is found in no. 7, with a more melodic central section but with wide-ranging variation of the original material, in the manner of a toccata, in the reprise. The truest ternary shape emerges in the scherzo-like G minor Capriccio, where the flickering fires of Brahms's youthful Romanticism blaze up most fiercely in the impulsive outer sections, with their chromatically inflected figuration; its central portion, however, is a noble, full-hearted E flat tune in massively diatonic chordal writing and with a triumphant march-character that gains power from pervasive and trenchant triplet rhythms – his very last utterance in the grand and generous public manner.

A withdrawn and gentle pathos is more typical of the Intermezzi, and the simplest ternary form among those is found in no. 6, the second E major specimen, which resembles a plaintive minuet whose tune occurs in the inner voices of its otherwise largely chordal texture. Brahms often indulges his partiality for assigning the melody to inner parts, and sometimes half-concealing it there, and nowhere more strikingly than in the E minor Intermezzo, no. 5 – whose hesitant rhythm of two quavers, accented on the weak beat, plus quaver rest, with the left hand an almost exact mirror inversion of the right in motion and intervals, creates an impression of twentieth-century rigour.[24] Most intimate of all is the other E major Intermezzo, no. 4, which grows fantasia-like from a peaceful melody (resembling the opening of Symphony no. 4, Ex. 53c, though without the chain of thirds) over a cradling left-hand figure which calls upon the right hand to cross over and touch the deepest bass notes. Throughout the entire piece Brahms displays extreme sensitivity to niceties of keyboard colour and pedalling.

The three Intermezzi comprising op. 117 may be considered a triptych of lullabies, subdued yet infinitely tender. Here too there are links to the op. 10 Ballades, but of a different kind: no. 1 in E flat is headed by lines from an actual Scots lullaby – 'Lady Anne Bothwell's Lament' in Herder's translation from *Stimmen der Völker* – and its unforgettable tune, a middle voice gently rocked between a repeated octave span, fits the words like a glove. The central section of the piece descends into a shadowed E flat minor that increases the poignancy of the lulling reprise with its cunningly interwoven imitations. A ballad-character is also evoked by no. 3 in C sharp minor, a comparatively spacious work beginning sombrely and *sotto voce* with a quintessentially Brahmsian theme presented in severe octaves. On later appearances this too is consigned to an inner voice against a harmonic background of unusual richness, and there is a highly contrasted A major middle section whose gently syncopated figuration and octave displacements create a twilit world of almost impressionistic gleams and half-lights. At once one of the darkest and most beautiful of the late piano pieces, it seems to have had an especially personal significance for Brahms, who referred to it in an unguarded moment as 'the lullaby of all my griefs'. The intervening Intermezzo, in B flat minor, wrings music of rare and plaintive delicacy from a simple falling-arpeggio figure, melting through a range of tonalities with fluid grace: and it traces a miniature sonata design, with a more smoothly flowing second idea in D flat. Development and reprise merge into one another in the spiralling arpeggio figuration, and the coda finally imposes stability in the shape of an uneasy pedal F, over which the second idea dies away.

[24] Musgrave (op. cit., pp. 258–9) has compared it to the opening of Webern's op. 27 Piano Variations.

357

The stormy, passionate A minor movement which opens the six op. 118 *Klavierstücke* also calls itself an Intermezzo, which shows how widely Brahms defined the term – or, more likely, that strict categorization was a matter of indifference to him. Op. 118 no. 1 resembles an emotionally afflicted yet ardent concert waltz, exuberant in manner yet drastically curtailed in form: two unequal halves of tune, both repeated, over powerful left-hand arpeggios, swiftly dissolving into a fantasia-like coda where the arpeggios sweep upward and then precipitously descend. The succeeding A major Intermezzo conforms more closely to the expectations set up in the previous sets: once again it is a kind of cradle-song, wistfully yet broadly conceived, with especially fine harmonic shading, poignant use of major/minor cadences, and touches of canonic imitation. As in the late songs, one senses a parallel with Fauré: Brahms cultivates the infinite subtleties of expression available to a single miniature genre, the Intermezzo, as tenaciously as did Fauré with the Nocturne and Barcarolle. Here too, and throughout these late pieces, Brahms displays infinite resource in strategies of transition: especially, in ternary designs, the lead-back to the opening idea, which almost always returns in some imaginative and unexpected fashion, and yet with perfect ease and naturalness.

Op. 118 no. 3, in G minor, styles itself a Ballade, and provides bold contrast with its strong galloping rhythms. Yet there is something playful about its pugnacity,[25] and for its B major middle section it quietens down for a suave little csárdás. After a 'false return' of the opening, wittily abandoned when it discovers itself in the wrong key of D sharp minor, the first bars are reused differently to modulate neatly back to the dashing main section, after which the coda is a swift fade on a mere wisp of the csárdás idea. The F minor Intermezzo, no. 4, is an altogether more enigmatic piece, with a frail initial idea of obsessive triplet pulsations opening onto a wealth of delicately opalescent harmonic colouring. Even stranger is the texture of the A flat central section, largely compounded of isolated chords and single notes deep in the bass, necessitating much crossing of hands and a flawless pedal technique. Yet both ideas are disguises for the simplest of figures, a rocking octave rise and fall, around which canonic imitations cluster (canonic chordal textures in the middle section). In the coda the octave alternation peals out boldly in a texture new enough to give the impression of a fresh melodic idea, and the imitative cadential bars give rise to an almost Expressionistic sense of anguish. Throughout, the piece is a standing

[25] It is worth passing on William Murdoch's delightful description of it – in his *Brahms* (London, 1933) – as 'this battle-horse of aspiring school-girls'.

358

challenge to the sensitive exercise of rubato, not marked but surely expected by the composer, whose own use of rubato we know was lavish – in the authentic performing style of the mid-nineteenth century.

Brahms called the fifth item of op. 118 a Romanze, and of all these late pieces it is perhaps the most directly melodic in its appeal, suggesting a song without words; yet also one of the most strict in construction. The *Andante* main section (much curtailed in its reprise) has something of the character of a folksong setting, the main tune in the middle of a largely homophonic texture that conceals the casual exercise of double counterpoint. The central *Allegretto grazioso*, in D flat, is virtually a tiny chaconne, based on the idea of progressively more florid, pseudo-Bachian embellishment of a contrasting melodic idea over an ostinato bass. This decoration makes increasing use of trills, and a sudden subdued, major/minor equivocation of trills rising from the bass register provides the lead-back to the folk-like initial idea.

All the pathos in the late Intermezzi is summed up and surpassed in the last piece of op. 118, the desolately beautiful Intermezzo in E flat minor – if ever an 'Intermezzo' could convey such grim finality. This is perfect piano music, and at the same time rich in intimations of orchestral effect (Clara took it at first for a movement of a Sonata; Kalbeck believed it was originally intended for a Symphony). The very opening (Ex. 62), based on a wavering turn-figure, conjures up lonely clarinet

Ex. 62

and horn solos over harp arpeggios as profoundly plangent as those in the early *An eine Äolsharfe*. Despite this figure's similarity to the first idea of the Clarinet Quintet (cf. Ex. 63a below), its import is more bitter, and as it is many times reiterated in different registers we surely note a distinct affinity to the 'Dies irae' chant. Doubling in thirds (with the unmistakable effect of flutes) only intensifies its bittersweet eloquence. A staccato, bitingly rhythmic music begins muttering in G flat – an idea in Brahms's most irascible vein: it starts *sotto voce* and grows in decisiveness and vigour, with massive yet clipped chordal textures. But at the very moment of climax the 'Dies irae' theme is recalled, inextricably bound up with it, and this inspired work subsides into its former tragic monologue, dying out eventually in exquisite but bleak despair.

Precisely contemporary with op. 118, the four op. 119 *Klavierstücke* seamlessly continue with their predominant lyrical and colouristic concerns. Seeking to find words for the elusive hue of the B minor Intermezzo which opens the set, Clara characterized it to Brahms as 'a grey pearl. Do you know them? They look as if they were veiled, and are very precious.' This ravishing Adagio makes the frankest use in all these pieces of the chain of falling thirds variously exploited in op. 116 – its main thematic cell is a downward arpeggio of thirds whose individual notes are held into wonderfully ambiguous vertical sonority, suggesting both B minor and D major, the tonal focus of a slightly contrasting central idea. The second and third pieces, also Intermezzi, both begin with rhythmic figures involving repeated notes: but whereas in no. 2 (in E minor) it is a nervous pulse-beat in dactylic rhythm like a charming stammer, in no. 3 (C major) it is a skittish 6/8 quaver metre, with a nonchalant melody in the middle voice. No. 2 also evolves a fairly large form, transforming its main idea by successive variation into an elegant E major waltz for central section – a mere ghost of which returns to round off the coda; whereas no. 3 is shorter, with deft touches of humour, capriciously dissolving towards the end into fragile, rainbow-like arpeggios.

The solo piano output ends with a final flourish of indomitable Brahmsian spirit.[26] The Rhapsody in E flat, op. 119 no. 4, is very much in the heroic mould expected of its key, and in the virile manner of the op. 79 Rhapsodies ('rough, crude, brutal' were epithets he used to describe it to Clara). Yet, though the most extended of all the late piano pieces, it is still more compressed than the earlier Rhapsodies, and

[26] The 51 *Übungen*, or technical exercises, were published later than op. 119, but had been compiled over many years.

creates its own form with a freedom and spontaneity appropriate to its late date. As foil to the principal tune – a muscular, pounding affair in 2/4 with a 'Hungarian' five-bar rhythm – it evolves a subsidiary idea of tolling repeated crotchets with dissonant descending harmonies beneath, and a highly characteristic second theme of powerful triplets in C minor that echoes the early D minor Ballade. A deliciously contrasting *grazioso* section follows in A flat, almost a parody of salon style with its harped chords and tripping grace-notes; then the triplet theme returns, with only a hint of the main subject. So strong and forthright is the latter that Brahms is in no hurry to reinstate its original form, but instead presents wittily allusive variations of it in new guises, including a teasing *pianissimo* one in broken staccati in C major, further developed over a reverberant G pedal. The repeated-crotchet figure initiates a long lead-back to the opening, producing chordal progressions that acquire chains of falling thirds in the bass. When the first tune finally reappears climactically in its original guise and key it is only for a brief space until Brahms takes it apart again in the coda – whose closing stage provides a sprightly triplet variant before the composer dismisses his piano output with a massive chordal cadence that curtly and unexpectedly ends this otherwise ebullient work in the minor.

Four works with clarinet

Brahms's last four chamber works form an unusually self-contained group, as they all feature the clarinet – an instrument of which he was very fond, but which he had not previously used outside orchestral scores – and were inspired by the artistry of the principal clarinettist of the Meiningen orchestra, Richard Mühlfeld. Just as the world owes Mozart's Clarinet Concerto and Quintet to the virtuoso playing of Anton Stadler, it owes to Mühlfeld Brahms's Clarinet Trio in A minor, op. 114, his B minor Quintet for clarinet and string quartet, op. 115 and the two Sonatas for clarinet and piano which form his op. 120. Originally a violinist at Meiningen, Mühlfeld had taught himself the clarinet and moved to the woodwind section in 1876. Brahms especially admired the polish and feminine sensitivity of his playing (for which he nicknamed Mühlfeld 'my Primadonna'); and the works he wrote for him offer comparatively few opportunities for displays of vertiginous bravura, but continual ones for the exercise of refined musicality, intimate expression, and beautiful tone.[27]

[27] Mühlfeld's clarinets, made in boxwood by Georg Ottensteiner, are still preserved in Meiningen, and a recent article by Nicholas Shackelton and Keith Puddy ('Mühlfeld's

Brahms

This is overwhelmingly the aim of the Clarinet Quintet, which was composed simultaneously with the Trio at Ischl in the summer of 1891 and first performed publicly together with it at one of Joachim's Berlin concerts that December – both works having been thoroughly rehearsed at Meiningen the previous month. The Quintet was much the better received of the two, became a great favourite of Joachim's, and has since remained one of Brahms's most popular works in any medium, for its perfect expression of a spirit of mellow reflection, tinged with autumnal melancholy.

There is a paradoxical touch of extremism about its sweetness. No other work of Brahms is more consistently euphonious in sonority; yet the lush string writing develops directly out of the op. 111 String Quintet, and the characteristic textures of early Schoenberg are only a hand's-breadth away. It shows Brahms at the summit of his powers of organic development and motivic variation, yet nowhere else does he so res-olutely suppress strong contrasts in favour of a quiescent sensuousness of mood and colour that is almost cloying – though that impression may partly have been fostered by the performing tradition: over the years, ensembles have vied with each other to extract from the score every super-refined shade of silver-grey regret, and created in the process an air of over-indulged pathos, dangerously near to sentimentality. The Quintet's darker and more vigorous elements – in the first movement, in the fantastic gypsy-music at the heart of the Adagio, throughout the second variation in the Finale, at the very end – need to be very strongly characterized to strike an emotional balance. Even so, there is a depressive tinge to the music's bone-deep nostalgia, as if the aching beauty keeps something deeper than mere melancholy at bay.

Everywhere the tendency is towards unification – of emotion, colour, tonality, and thematic substance – while creating a sense of rhapsodic freedom and reverie. The clarinet functions less as a 'solo' instrument than as *primus inter pares* (with obvious exceptions, such as the central portion of the slow movement).[28] Three of the four movements are in the tonic B minor, in each case coloured by an ambiguous pull towards D major, apparent from the work's very first

Clarinets', *The Clarinet*, May/June 1989, pp. 33–6) comments on their very warm tone and closeness to modern concert pitch. (When Brahms first played the Sonatas with Mühlfeld for Clara Schumann, her piano had to be retuned to Mühlfeld's pitch.)
[28] We should note that Brahms sanctioned (as in the other three works discussed in this section) the replacement of the clarinet by a viola if necessary. Though very rarely followed, this substitution does less violence to the Quintet's character than might be expected, whereas in the Trio it is highly unsatisfactory; the more complex case of the Sonatas is discussed on p. 368.

bars (Ex. 63a). The exception is the Adagio, which is in the tonic rather than the relative major, reverting to B minor in its central section. The effect is both subtly coloured and monolithic. As for the motivic material, figures (x) and (y) in Ex. 63a are the initial seeds for distinct yet inter-dependent families of themes which grow root and branch throughout the entire Quintet, as Ex. 63 shows. Almost all of them (Ex. 63c is the principal exception) have a gentle, unassertive quality which maintains the prevailing sense of ripe reflectiveness, and Ex. 63a is an unusually relaxed opening for a major Brahmsian structure. Figure (y) immediately gives rise to the subsidiary theme shown in Ex. 63b (note the inspired texture, the clarinet low in its chalumeau register and the cello above the viola), whose adaptation of figure (x) is further modified into staccato quavers in the forceful transition theme Ex. 63c, and then legato for the smoothly flowing Ex. 63d, the second subject proper. The development begins with a mystical withdrawal (based on Ex. 63a) analogous to that in the first movement of the G major String Quintet; figure (x)'s semiquavers work up to a kind of climax but the music passes onto a *Quasi sostenuto* variation of Ex. 63c that removes its contrast with the other material by transforming it into a slumberous, Romantic shadow of itself. Ex. 63b is used to lead into the recapitulation, which curtails the return of Ex. 63a so that theme may attain its apotheosis in the coda, where a sudden display of passion evaporates in a depressively hushed final cadence.

Ex. 63

(a)

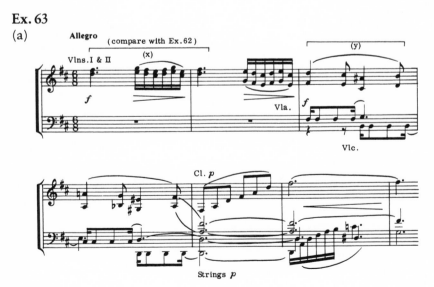

Brahms

The ternary-form Adagio, with the clarinet's sighing principal theme recumbent against a rhythmic and melodic chiaroscuro of muted strings, is the *ne plus ultra* of Brahmsian Romanticism, evoking a profound mood of nature-mysticism whose tradition in his work goes back as far as the slow movement of the First Serenade. Ravel himself could not have surpassed the impressionistic blending of tone colour here; and despite his fascination with gypsy music, he never equalled the achievement of the movement's long *Più lento* central section, Brahms's last and most extraordinary homage to the *Zigeuner* style. Prefaced by a clear reference back to the work's opening (Ex. 63e), it is a desolately beautiful series of florid clarinet arabesques that spiral and swoop over a fantastic string texture of rustling tremolandi. The effect is of wild, spontaneous improvisation and yet the structural logic is undiminished: the thematic focus of the clarinet roulades (Ex. 63f) is essentially an expansion of figure (y), and its mournful string pendant (Ex. 63g) a version of figure (x), the two elements now appearing as variants of each other through their new similarity of rhythmic profile. The nocturnal scene-painting of Schoenberg's *Verklärte Nacht* clearly derives from this plangently expressive passage, and the uneasy atmosphere of early Bartók (for example, the slow movement of his Orchestral Suite no. 2) is implicit here too.

364

Ex. 63

(e)

(f)

(g)

The brief third movement begins *Andantino*, with an ambling, lyrical theme (Ex. 63h) in B minor with the inevitable pull to D major. Before long, however, this serenade-like music cadences on D and gives way to a hurrying yet delicate *Presto non assai* (significantly qualified *ma con sentimento*, whose main theme (Ex. 63i) is a clear variant of the *Andantino*'s. Though the transformation recalls the Intermezzo of

Ex. 63

(h)

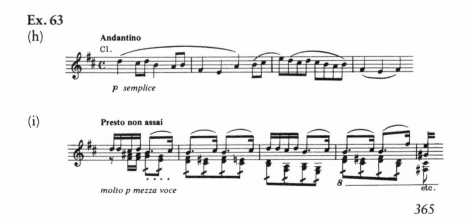

(i)

365

Symphony no. 2, here the *Presto* is no episode but the main portion of the movement – the most ethereal of all Brahms scherzos, developing its own self-contained sonata form and ending in D major with the briefest of glances back to Ex. 63h.

The *Con moto* Finale is Brahms's last-but-one set of variations. Both in terms of the Quintet and of Brahms's *oeuvre* the design is retrospective, and most closely resembles the last movement of the B flat String Quartet; but the strict form of the thirty-two-bar tune with verbatim repeat of the second sixteen bars, adhered to throughout the five variations, is handled with all the marvellous plasticity and harmonic resource of Brahms's late manner. The tune itself (which begins as Ex. 63j) reflects and sums up many of the thematic entities we have encountered in the work, and its variations seek still further to refine and underline the Quintet's predominant mood of almost hallucinatory tranquillity. The only contrast is the intense, agitated variation 2, which alludes to the gypsy character of the slow movement. No. 4, the major-key variation, turns the theme into a version of the accompanimental figure shown in Ex. 63i; variation 5 returns to the minor and becomes a nostalgically impassioned waltz in 3/8. Its six-semiquaver patterns inevitably recall the work's very opening – and, on cue, Ex. 63a reappears, mingling with fragments of the waltz in an allusive coda rendered suddenly sombre by hesitations and silences. Thus the Finale hints at all three previous movements, the first appearing last. This closing of the circle is rendered beautifully unemphatic by the nature of the themes themselves, and accords entirely with the work's deceptive spirit of rhapsody. A last echo of Ex. 63b, high on solo clarinet, leads to a closing cadence which almost exactly reproduces that of the first movement, but with a sudden *forte* stress on the penultimate B minor triad that finally reveals the winter chill in the autumnal glow.

Ex. 63

(j)

Brahms, unlike posterity, thought as highly of the Clarinet Trio as of his Quintet, but its sardonic wisdom has never attained the popularity of the latter's lambent melancholy: in many respects the logical successor to the C minor Piano Trio, the work's emotional range is much wider than the Quintet, and far less amenable to merely comfortable interpretations. Standing at the very end of his long line of concerted chamber music with piano, it exhibits all the resource and subtlety of his late style, further stimulated by the contrasting characters of the three instruments, which permit little of the Quintet's blended sonority. Here the cellist has equal importance, and in some stretches the work resembles a cello sonata with clarinet obbligato.

The cello, indeed, opens the proceedings unaccompanied, with an eloquent, high-lying melody, varied by the clarinet and balanced by a muttering triplet motif in the piano, recalling the mood of the G minor Piano Rhapsody. These ideas constitute an expository introduction, such as in the Piano Quintet, before the passionate tutti statements of the same material which form the first subject of the exposition proper. The lyrical E minor second subject, arrived at via C major, is also presented by the cello, and then heard in canon by inversion with the clarinet. The terse development evolves new thematic entities from the original material – a sombre, chorale-like phrase, and whispering *pianissimo* semiquaver scales against wide-spaced piano chords – and the recapitulation is notably flexible in its reshaping of the elements of the exposition. In the brief, uneasy coda, the 'chorale' idea suddenly emerges as a disquieting presage of the first of the *Vier ernste Gesänge*; and the music evanesces into imitation of the passionless beauty of an Aeolian harp, with the semiquaver scales in liquid contrary motion on clarinet and cello.

A more serenely philosophical mood, tinged with fantasy, prevails in the D major Adagio, a pearl even among Brahms's slow movements. An astonishing amount of matter is packed into its fifty-four bars, so that it seems relaxed and expansive despite (perhaps because of) its masterly compression. It is a kind of foreshortened ternary form, the calm opening *dolce* clarinet tune returning briefly to form a six-bar coda but varied (in augmentation, with delicious cello pizzicato figuration) within the larger central section, which has the character of a free but intense development. Brahms's intricate elaboration of the smallest motifs, his resourceful exploration of subdivisions of the beat (right down to rippling demisemiquavers), and the subtle oppositions of instrumental colour – mediated by very full yet sensitive piano writing – yield textures and thematic working of unusual richness.

The following Andantino grazioso in A major is the Brahmsian 'intermezzo' carried into realms of wry self-mockery. The artless innocence of the clarinet's opening waltz tune has brought some English commentators up short: Fuller-Maitland thought it could have been written by Balfe. He was confusing Victorian sentimentality with

367

German sentiment, and missing the knowing humour that winks roguishly from every turn and sigh of this delightful movement. Isn't it sad to be an old bachelor, and isn't it fun! Here for the last time Brahms evokes the manner of the *Liebeslieder* Waltzes, but now in a complex, organic form whose sophistication quite belies the well-wined tearfulness of the opening tune. A ternary design made fluid and elusive by variation, it traverses much tonal ground in a short space, evolves three closely related themes, and nonchalantly reduces the initial waltz theme into a schematic version of itself on the way – an object-lesson in the fruitful development of an apparently unpromising idea.

The Finale returns us to the minor and features the most strenuous music in the work, in yet another sonata form transformation of Brahms's 'driven' scherzo manner. This one gains its bracing rhythmic suppleness from the informal alternation of equal-length bars of 6/8 and 2/4, while contrasting areas of relaxation are provided by the subsidiary idea of the first subject (which recalls the opening of the Clarinet Quintet) and the main melody, in 9/8, of the second subject (presented, like that of the first movement, by the cello, and then by clarinet and cello in canon by inversion). The development is very concise, and notable for its rapid modulations, achieved by the use of two extraordinarily extended examples of Brahms's favourite chains of descending melodic thirds – one of no less than thirty steps, and the other of fifteen. This adds an air of mystery and instability even to the more cheerful passages of the movement, and any shallow optimism seems decisively banished in the choleric bravura of the coda, all three instruments joining in a curt, wintry dismissal of the idea that had recalled the Quintet.

Three years later, in 1894, Mühlfeld was the recipient of the two Sonatas for clarinet and piano, op. 120. Brahms's final chamber works, they contain his last sonata form movements, his last intermezzo, his last scherzo, and his last set of variations, and embody his compositional technique in its ultimate taut, essentialized yet marvellously flexible manner. In their way they are, like the Double Concerto, pioneering: since there were virtually no Classical models for such a combination, he was establishing a new genre with pieces which have remained cornerstones of the clarinet repertoire ever since. And not only the clarinet repertoire: with minimal alterations to the solo parts, Brahms produced alternative versions for viola and piano – creating at a stroke the first important sonatas for that instrument too[29] – and went on to adapt them for violin also (a more far-reaching recomposition which

---

[29] Joachim had written some important chamber music for viola, but no sonata.

involved some rewriting of the piano parts). These three parallel versions argue that he wanted the music to have the widest possible dissemination; yet while the Sonatas are known to virtually all clarinettists and violists, and the violin versions are not totally forgotten, the works are much less performed than the three Violin Sonatas – their only real forebears in Brahms's output, although in sheer musical substance they are probably superior. In the following pages I shall refer to them as clarinet sonatas, though my personal preference is for the versions with viola, whose darker, huskier tone seems to suit their elusive moods even better than the veiled and silken clarinet.

They make a fascinating study in contrasts. No. 1, in F minor, has something of the turbulent passion that key always evoked in Brahms and is the more orthodox in outline, a four-movement design with active outer movements and balancing relaxation in the slow movement and intermezzo. No. 2, in E flat, is a fantasia-like conception in three movements, none of them really slow: an unusually relaxed sonata form, and an equally unusual set of variations, flanking a large and unexpectedly powerful scherzo. Within these broad confines the works display a kaleidoscopic range of colour and emotion, a propensity for mercurial shifts of texture and harmony – indeed they are prime examples of that 'economy, yet richness' which Schoenberg so admired in Brahms. Even the piano writing veers between an extreme parsimony of means, the intimacy of the late piano pieces, and a new structural application of the sonorous, full-blooded bravura that had erupted again in the op. 119 Rhapsody.

The First Sonata's opening *Allegro appassionato* manages to convey an impression of gravity and tensile strength without compromising the predominantly lyrical nature of its ideas, typified by the yearning, wide-spanned clarinet melody that follows the brief piano introduction. Highly economical yet apparently expansive, with a large number of distinct themes, it carries Brahms's tendency to reduce the contrasts between different portions of a sonata form movement almost to the ultimate stage (the Second Sonata carries it further). The recapitulation section, arrived at via a 'false' return of the opening subject in F sharp minor as the climax of the development, is so varied that it can be regarded as a second-stage development, ending in spare, ominous minor-key chords from which grow an assuaging *sostenuto* coda that finally brings major-key calm.

The exquisite Andante un poco Adagio, in A flat, begins as a still, tranced nocturnal song, just touched into movement by the clarinet's melancholy, rhapsodic turning figures and the slow-motion descending arpeggios of the piano. The mood of ecstatic reverie is never broken,

369

though the movement evolves a kind of ternary form, with an equally gentle subsidiary idea closely derived from the main tune, the two combining in the moonlit quiescence of the closing bars. Likewise in A flat, there follows an intermezzo-like Allegretto grazioso, in the manner of an Austrian Ländler, which develops a certain peasant vigour in its second strain, and a delicate F minor central section exploiting the clarinet's lowest register.

No diminishing of Brahmsian energy is discernible in the *Vivace* Finale, a bracing and sometimes pawky rondo in F major with occasional flashes of the choleric strength that can enliven the composer's cheerfullest moods. Even more important than the chuckling rondo theme is the chiming figure of three repeated minims which serves the movement for opening fanfare: Brahms finds innumerable functions for this simple device, and it tolls and peals its way through the fabric of rondo theme and episodes alike. The final rondo statement is considerably varied, and the Sonata ends with the fierce and joyous *élan* of a composer still young at heart.

No such strenuousness invades the *Allegro amabile* first movement of the E flat Sonata, the most unassuming of Brahms's sonata structures and yet one of the subtlest. The apparently artless beauty of the material and its dreamy, musing, song-like character conceal considerable art: the design carries to its extreme his concern with continuous development and interrelation of themes. There are no clearly audible divisions between exposition, development and recapitulation, and the discourse accumulates delightful parentheses whose main focus seems to be the exploration of colour – whether of instrumental timbre or in shifts of harmony, such as the *frisson* of the final sideslip from E major into E flat for the *tranquillo* polyrhythmic texture of the coda.

The second movement is Brahms's last scherzo, in the same key and 3/4 time as his first, the E flat minor piano work of 1850: another example of 'the snake which bites its own tail'? The Sonata's Scherzo has something of the character of a heroic waltz: over four decades the passion remains undimmed, but burns now with a steadier, warmer flame (and equally fiery pianism). The function of the trio is assumed by a broad *sostenuto* melody – in B major, as was the second Trio of op. 4 – harmonized largely in thirds and sixths and cast with smooth asymmetry in seven-bar phrases. There is an analogy here with the big E flat tune in the G minor Piano Capriccio, op. 116 no. 3 (in identical relationship to its movement's tonic), but for all Brahms's *dolce e ben cantando* marking this later tune is darker and more subdued, the clarinet seldom rising clear of the lower-lying piano part.

The broad and glowing theme of the Finale, *Andante con moto*, has a Classical poise, solidity of rhythm, intriguing asymmetry (fourteen bars, with no repeats) and opulence of harmony that would seem to offer enormous potential for variation. In fact Brahms's last variation set seems primarily concerned to simplify rather than elaborate, paring the theme down to its smallest note-values and exploring its possibilities in modest contrapuntal textures of almost Mozartian clarity. This comparative restraint, practised in the first four variations, leads to an outburst of passionate energy in the fifth and last, a minor-key *Allegro* dominated by the piano's virile cross-rhythms; and flows directly into a *Più tranquillo* coda that returns to the major, develops the theme's cadence figure, and climaxes in a brief display of gleeful virtuosity for both instruments.

Last words

On 26 March 1896 Clara Schumann suffered the stroke from which she never recovered, though she lingered until 20 May. During her last illness, apparently prompted by the inevitability of her death, Brahms composed the *Vier ernste Gesänge*, op. 121: four 'Serious Songs' for low voice and piano, completing them on 7 May, his sixty-third and last birthday. Spacious, profoundly moving and penetrating settings of biblical words, they extend the Lied tradition to accommodate the searching ethical idealism previously explored in his sacred choral works, particularly the *Requiem* and the motets. Indeed they themselves constitute a kind of Requiem – not interceding for the dead but addressing, as in op. 45, the bereaved and the unhappy – which powerfully fuses the characters of his choral and instrumental music within an overall song-conception. But Brahms labelled the work 'Serious', not 'Sacred'. Typically, he chose texts that were essentially undogmatic – meditations on death, on the fragility of human life, on the transcendent power of love – and which easily admit agnostic interpretations. The result, he told Herzogenberg, was 'a trifle...which may cause you to attack my unchristian principles'; and he habitually called the songs 'my godless harvesters' revels'.

Though Clara's last illness was clearly the creative spur that produced this extraordinary work, it would be a mistake to define it too narrowly as a 'memorial' to her, composed before the event.[30] 'Some such words as these have long been in my mind', he wrote to Clara's daughter Marie. More likely the imminence of Clara's demise served to crystallize a long-growing mood of elegy, previously manifested in works

[30] Brahms did not dedicate it to her memory, but to the artist Max Klinger, whose 'Brahms-phantasie' etchings had given him great pleasure.

such as *Nänie* and *Gesang der Parzen* but intensified since then by the deaths of so many that were dear to him: Elisabet von Herzogenberg, Hermine Spies, Billroth, Bülow. (It is also possible that he was adapting a somewhat earlier conception – as discussed below, p. 377.) In a sense the *Gesänge* are for all of them, and for everyone: a private lamentation for the tragedy at the heart of everyday life, in whose coils we are all enmeshed.

The intimate interpenetration of verbal meaning and musical structure sets these songs apart from all Brahms's previous Lieder (parallels might be adduced with the free-ranging forms of the *Magelone* Romances, but those were mere youthful rhapsodies compared with the iron control manifested in every aspect of op. 121). Here is no generalized response to a dominant mood aroused by the personal associations of significant images, but an almost oracular use of motif and tonality to expound and indeed interpret every line. The resonant prose of Luther's Bible in any case demanded very different treatment from a closed verse-form. Gone is any hint of strophic repetition, and anything beyond a distant intimation of ternary reprise: the songs evolve organic forms of virtually symphonic scope and contrapuntal sinew, while the vocal lines attain a new freedom and flexibility of declamation that pivots between expressive arioso and nobly heightened recitative.

Brahms was initially uncertain about the order of the first two *Gesänge* (both on texts from Ecclesiastes), and the manuscript shows that what is now no. 1, *Denn es gehet dem Menschen* ('for that which befalleth the sons of men befalleth beasts'), was originally placed second. This D minor song begins with a soft, remorseless funeral-march theme (Ex. 64a) developed from an opening piano ostinato and presented in

Ex. 64

(a)

(For that which befalleth Men befalleth the beasts)

372

bare octaves against a solemnly tolling dominant pedal. This fateful idea relates clearly to the march-like second movement of *Ein deutsches Requiem* (compare Ex. 30c). Contrasted with it is a surging, angry 3/4 *Allegro* music beginning in D major with rushing triplet writing but continuing to rely on the insistently tolling crotchet rhythm in the bass for the message that all are of the dust. A stirring chordal climax is reached at the words 'Who knoweth the spirit of man that goeth upward, and the spirit of the beast that goeth downward to the earth?', in an idiom that recalls rather the *Requiem*'s sixth movement. But here there is manifestly no faith in resurrection; and Brahms deepens the sense of doubt by providing a prominent *descending* bass line at the mention of 'upward', and a *rising* one at 'downward'. The bass line at the beginning of this passage is important, too (Ex. 64b). Although it may sound here like a mere descending triad it is the first[31] intimation of another

Ex. 64
(b)

(Who knoweth the spirit of man that goeth upward?)

exploitation of the sequence of falling thirds of which extraordinarily thoroughgoing use will be made in the two succeeding songs. The slow march Ex. 64a returns, brightening very slightly towards the major with the advice that a man should rejoice in his own works. The *Allegro* music comes round again, but its triplet figuration is soon diverted and constricted into a long, slow trill that persists within the texture of a sternly mysterious coda broadening into 9/4 time over the tolling pedal-note: what comes after us, we shall not see, say the last two emphatic chords with fierce finality.

[31] Perhaps not the first: the Allegro's triplets swirl in diminished sevenths created by rapid third chains.

Ex. 64

(c)

(I turned me, and saw...)

The second song, *Ich wandte mich* ('I turned, and saw all the injustice that is done under the sun'), opens with the descending figure from Ex. 64b in both piano and voice (Ex. 64c). Of the four *Gesänge*, this is the most starkly pessimistic. No one has yet claimed Brahms as a composer of social protest: but as a sensitive man raised in poverty and slum surroundings, he had no illusions about the world's changeless injustice and endless waste of human resources. Rigorously logical in its contrapuntal structure, his setting of the words 'and behold the tears of the oppressed, who had no comforter; and might was on the side of their oppressors, but they had no comforter', with its aching melisma on *Tränen* ('tears'), attains a depth of all-encompassing pity and regret unequalled in his music. During this very passage the bass has begun to shape Ex. 64c into a chain of thirds (precisely on the recurrences of *Unrecht*, 'injustice'). Finally at 'Wherefore I praised the dead' this ever-more obsessive pattern of Brahms's later years coincides with the first of its two fated texts (Ex. 64d). It remains present in the piano part for much of the coda, which turns to G major but derives small comfort from it: more fortunate than the dead are those still to be born, who have not yet seen evil.

In E minor, the key of the Fourth Symphony, the third song, *O Tod, wie bitter bist du* (on words from Ecclesiasticus) strikes in with what could well be seen as a new version of the Symphony's opening theme – and an ultimate demonstration of the depth of meaning Brahms could extract from a simple chain of falling thirds (Ex. 64e). It is a famous passage, much analysed by Schoenberg and others. Brahms's command of strict contrapuntal working, in imitation, inversion, and

374

Ex. 64

(d)

(Wherefore I praised the dead...)

(e)

(O death, o death, how bitter art thou when a man thinks on thee...)

augmentation, allows the basic motif of the falling third to saturate the vertical and horizontal aspects of the music, its harmonic and melodic spheres. Everything may be regarded as development of that initial cell. And this occurs at – indeed makes possible – one of the most profoundly moving movements in all Brahms. Yet the shape of this song is not so much the exact palindrome that such motivic self-consistency inspired in a successor such as Webern, but rather a V-shape, of which the opening music forms the descending arm. The tonality warms to E major, and the falling thirds become calm rising sixths, though the thirds still link them together (Ex. 64f). Death may be bitter to the vigorous and prosperous man, but to the old man who foresees no better days, it is 'well enough'. The music, its motivic logic undimmed, contrives to find consolation in the thought, and give stoic assent.

Ex. 64
(f)

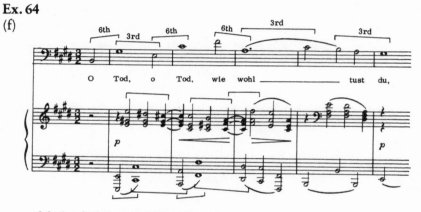

(O death, o death, how acceptable art thou...)

The final song, *Wenn ich mit Menschen und mit Engelzungen redete*, a setting of the words of St Paul in I Corinthians, Ch. 13, is radically different in character from the other three, and has sometimes been considered an unsatisfactory companion – not because it is weaker, but because it manifests no obvious motivic links with them, and its grand apostrophe of Love has been thought at variance with this grim context. Brahms has been accused of not having the courage of his own pessimistic convictions, and providing his audience with a comparatively facile consolation (though no one has accused the song itself of facility). He might well have retorted that the provision of consolation was a duty: the lack of comfort inherent in the human condition and depicted in *Ich wandte mich*, enjoined it as a moral imperative on the creative

376

artist. In any case this ardent, aspiring final song confirms the trend begun by Ex. 64f: the depressive drooping motion of the first two songs has given way to rising, positive phrases. And as for motivic correspondence, the rising sixth introduced by Ex. 64f finds two plain echoes very early in the vocal line, as a leap up to the vital words 'speak' and 'Love', and both these leaps occur in phrases which are essentially chains of descending thirds (Ex. 64g).

Ex. 64
(g)

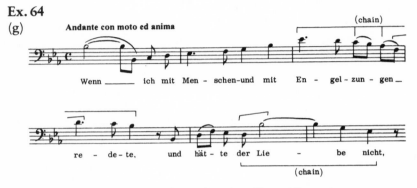

(Though I speak with the tongues of men and angels, and have not Love...)

All these points acknowledged, *Wenn ich mit Menschen* still stands somewhat apart from the first three *Gesänge*, and probably for reasons that raise the question of op. 121's creative origins. A page of sketch material, associated with Brahms's manuscript, offers confusing clues. One side carries the beginning of an orchestral movement in short score, with some indications of instrumentation, which alludes to motifs familiar from some of the songs, including a form of Ex. 64e. The other seems to carry drafts for two different portions of the fourth song, but each partly to a different text, namely a *Trauerlied* by Rückert, and a poem by Heyse called *Nixe im Grundquell* ('The sprite in the spring') whose imagery recalls the Lieder of the 1870s and 80s associated with Elisabet von Herzogenberg – such as *Sommerabend* (op. 85 no. 1), with its parallel image of a fairy bathing in a brook. Kalbeck believed Brahms may have sketched settings of these poems during the years when he felt closest to Elisabet, and that after her death in 1892 he began a 'symphonic cantata' for voice and orchestra in her memory, reworking the Rückert and Heyse settings into a single song, to biblical words, and probably now conceiving the others, hinting at them in the unfinished orchestral movement (which may have been a prelude). For some reason the work did not progress[32] until 1896, when under the pressure of Clara Schumann's illness it found its proper form as the *Vier ernste Gesänge*.[33]

However this may be, it is certainly fascinating that Brahms should have drawn upon overtly secular Lieder, love-songs even, in composing his exalted setting of I Corinthians 13. The Greek *agape*, translated in the King James Bible as 'charity' – a word which loses its force unless we are Classically-minded enough to remember the Latin *caritas* – is rendered by the Lutheran Bible as an all-encompassing 'Liebe'. The love that Brahms had hymned throughout his song output was always the earthly kind, and his Bible drew no distinction between *eros* and *agape*. So *Wenn ich mit Menschen* remains a love-song, a song to Love itself as the only thing worth having, the only thing as strong as the Death which so enshrouds the three previous *Gesänge*.

Perhaps the opening portion of the song, with its energetic, aspiring E flat music, remains a little too close to the impulsive love-song archetype. But it accumulates stature as it proceeds, attaining its full *gravitas* in the expansive and richly mysterious B major central section, with its harped arpeggios, 'for now we see through a glass darkly...' The climactic thought that 'I shall know even as I am known' brings a cadence of agonized intensity. As the E flat music resumes, much broader in tempo, the vocal line expands in a great, ecstatic curve, the last flowering, and one of the finest, of Brahms's passionate lyricism (Ex. 64h). The harp-like music returns, in E flat, leading to the serenely glowing conclusion that states love's surpassing and abiding excellence.

These astonishing songs stand alone in Brahms's output, yet sum up much of what his music represents. They have sometimes been called the swansong of the German Lied, yet they are also a new beginning, bringing to the voice-and-piano medium a formal concentration and philosophical profundity from which many twentieth-century vocal masterpieces derive their ancestry. Moreover, as the final work he published, they occupy a powerfully symbolic position as premonitions of his own death, and testaments of the faith (in humanity, if not Divinity) that survives even unbelief.

Yet there was time for one further work, of comparably symbolic sigificance. In May–June 1896, following Clara's death, Brahms turned

---

[32] Possibly because Herzogenberg commemorated his wife in his own cantata, *Totenfeier*. Perhaps it is not without significance that he published in 1895 (and sent to Brahms) a set of *Elegischer Gesänge* to words by Eichendorff.

[33] Kalbeck's argument is difficult to paraphrase (it occupies pp. 445–54 of Volume IV of his Brahms biography, including musical examples from the sketches) and perhaps over-hypothetical. But it is clear that the orchestral sketch is not simply the 'draft of an orchestration' of op. 121 to which Geiringer and other writers glancingly refer.

Ex. 64
(h)

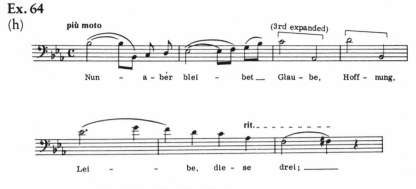

(Therefore abide Faith, Hope, Love, these three)

for the first time in nearly forty years to composition for the organ, and occupied himself at Ischl in writing a set of eleven Chorale Preludes. Though he played them privately (on the piano) to friends such as Heuberger he made no effort to have them printed,[34] and six years elapsed before they were published posthumously as op. 122. Perhaps arising – as had some of the late *Klavierstücke* – out of the love of keyboard improvisation with which he beguiled the loneliness of his final years, they are his last and most comprehensive identification with the Baroque manner, upon tunes deeply rooted in German Protestant culture which had been a lifelong part of his mental universe. Like the *Vier ernste Gesänge*, the Preludes forge links with his earlier choral music, but much more closely and specifically with the motets based on polyphonic treatment of chorale tunes. Some of them harmonize and decorate the basic melody; the others employ it as a cantus firmus, with fugal preludes and/or interludes on figures derived from the chorale. In the tradition of Schütz, Scheidt, Pachelbel, and above all J. S. Bach, Brahms puts his contrapuntal art, in its purest and most concentrated form, at the service of tunes which represented for him the timeless continuity of music itself.

But not exactly in those composers' spirit. The fusion of Baroque polyphonic discipline with Romantic harmony, so perfectly achieved, which bathes these pieces in such a steady, ambiguous glow, signals the

[34] He did commission a fair copy of the first seven, which would have been a first step to a printed edition. He alluded to the work in a letter to Herzogenberg as 'less compromising' than the *Ernste Gesänge*, 'but not for publication'. It is possible one or two may be earlier than 1896; no. 1 especially recalls the manner of the op. 27 Motets.

working of a different sensibility – indeed, a deeply sceptical one. One is reminded of the equally agnostic Busoni, who had already begun issuing his Bach transcriptions (and was to transcribe some of Brahms's Preludes to coincide with their first publication). Yet the profoundly equivocal attitude implicit in op. 122 is a consistent development of what may be sensed in Brahms's motets – and also in the *Vier ernste Gesänge*, since over half of the chorales Brahms selected treat of the prospect of death. Whereas for Bach, whose techniques (especially from the *Orgelbüchlein*) are so often recalled here, the chorale melodies would have been symbols of faith and their treatment an artistic reinforcement of Christian doctrine, Brahms seems rather to regard them as symbols of an idealized state attainable, if at all, only in the actual exercise of musical craft. In this sense, his Chorale Preludes constitute a kind of 'high art' counterpart to the 1894 collection of *Deutsche Volkslieder*.

Within the group they are in fact very varied in character and treatment, ranging from such monumental, neo-Bachian contrapuntal structures as no. 1, *Mein Jesu, der du mich*, which prefaces each line of chorale with a new fugal exposition, to tender Romantic miniatures such as the famous no. 8, *Es ist ein Ros entsprungen*, whose appeal is almost entirely harmonic, the melody interred within an inner voice. In no. 4, *Herzlich tut mich erfreuen*, whose chorale praises the 'glorious summertime' in which God shall renew the Heavens and all creation, we catch a last echo of Brahms's ardent love of nature, expressed in falling-arpeggio patterns that recall typical textures of the *Klavierstücke*. The suavely beautiful no. 5, *Schmücke dich, o liebe Seele* ('Adorn thyself, o soul') is literally adorned with added polyphonic voices which imitate the opening phrase throughout in diminution and inversion.

One of the less familiar of the series, no. 6, *O wie selig sind*, is also one of the most personal, for its chorale harks back to the *Requiem* with the message 'Blessed are the dead', and Brahms provides an unbroken stream of pastoral 12/8 in contemplation of a paradisal state that appears very nearly to be a static, featureless Nirvana. By contrast no. 7, *O Gott, du frommer Gott*, is addressed to the living (the text prays for health and a clear conscience), and is emotionally one of the most intense. Brahms creates quite a substantial and intricate form whose salient thematic motif is a sighing figure of a falling (and occasionally rising) third. This is not at first presented as a link in a chain, yet echoes of the Fourth Symphony seem to be present, as well as a faint Phrygian colouring. As the Prelude moves into its second half with impressive, trombone-like chords, a chain appears in the bass to lend the music its sense of severe mystery (Ex. 65), and is developed in various ways within the close-woven fabric of the final page.

Ex. 65

Two chorale-tunes are treated twice, in different settings. Nos. 9 and 10 work another Phrygian-mode tune, *Herzlich tut mich verlangen* ('My heart longs for a blessed end') as a clearly contrasted pair, the first grimly contrapuntal, the second a study in veiled, seraphic textures created by virtually continuous semiquaver figuration and inner pedal notes. Nos. 3 and 11 are based on *O Welt, ich muss dich lassen* ('O world, I must leave thee'), the first a spacious but gently serene polyphonic setting reminiscent of the last movement of the *Deutsches Requiem*. No. 11, though equally contrapuntal, is a heartfelt valediction that creates its effects more by harmonic means. Each phrase of the chorale begins solidly and commandingly on full organ, only to melt into a gentle cadential dying fall, always twice echoed in a way that suggests a desire to linger, a deep reluctance to move on to the end.

But it was indeed time to leave the world, and *O Welt, ich muss dich lassen* was, with moving and perhaps conscious appropriateness, the last music Brahms ever wrote. Whether or not he realized how short a span was left to him before he must personally confront the mystery of death, in the Chorale Preludes he had created – in a form so time-hallowed it was almost impersonal – a uniquely personal testament to his craft, his historical insight, and his passionate belief in the spiritual value of his art.

The rest is silence. There is no evidence that Brahms engaged in any further creative activity during the autumn and winter months that remained to him. If he had plans for new pieces, he did not mention them; if he made any sketches, he took care to destroy them. At sixty-three he was old before his time, and may consciously have thought of the Chorale Preludes as a final work. Yet had cancer not intervened he might well have lived out the Biblical span of seventy years – or even Joachim's seventy-six, which would have made him a contemporary of the first Expressionist works of Schoenberg. And if he had lived, he would surely have continued composing. Op. 122, so determinedly – even eccentrically – archaic, is no reliable guide to his future development. In all likelihood he would have continued to explore the motivic saturation and ever more concentrated, tight-knit structures we find in the last chamber works and the *Ernste Gesänge*; but his music would hardly have mutated into Reger, or Schoenberg. Even in his own time Brahms, as a composer, was an increasingly isolated figure. Doubtless he would have seemed even more so in the first years of the twentieth century, but his commitment to his compositional ideals would never have wavered.

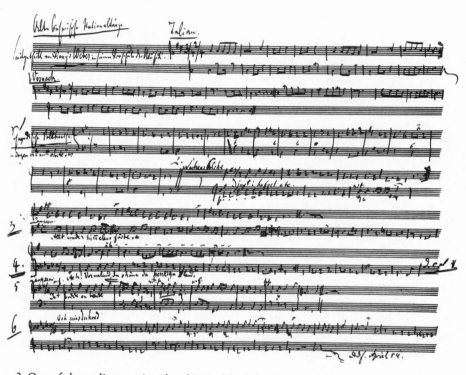

3 One of the earliest entries (dated Düsseldorf, April 1854) written out by Brahms in a manuscript collection of folksongs from many countries which he assembled over more than 20 years. Among the items on this page are several Bohemian dance-tunes, and the well-known Swedish folk-song 'Ack Varmeland, du sköna'.

12

Music and *Menschenbild*

I speak through my music. The only thing is that a poor musician like myself
would like to believe that he was better than his music.

Letter to Clara Schumann, September 1868

In his own estimation, Brahms was a self-taught composer. Despite his
prodigious natural talent, honed by Marxsen's intensive training in
certain aspects of technique,[1] the young Brahms felt painfully deprived
of a general musical culture. Many years later he commented to Richard
Heuberger that Schumann, Wagner, and he himself had all been forced
to find their own (quite separate) paths to mastery because they lacked
the kind of strict education in a living tradition that Mendelssohn, say,
had acquired from Zelter in Berlin, or his French contemporaries at
the Paris Conservatoire under the powerful aegis of Cherubini. The
voracious studies of older music and pre-Classical technique which
Brahms undertook in the 1850s, although they established the predilections of a lifetime, began as a desperate course of self-improvement.
Thus it is a fundamental error to imagine Brahms as a composer of
'conservative' instincts who wished to turn back the clock to the practice
of the past masters. His instincts were Romantic, but he needed their
knowledge in the here and now, so that he might be a better contemporary.

As a result, his music is imbued with a stronger sense of history
than that of any composer before him; indeed, with a qualitatively
different sense that was a product of his period, in which the systematic
investigation and comparison of past cultures had, for the first time,
become a significant intellectual pursuit for its own sake. Brahms continually looks to music of former times – both to actual technical
features, and with a generalized Romantic passion for the past as a

[1] The precise extent and suitability of Marxsen's training has been much debated, and
doubt on the topic was exacerbated by Brahms's destruction, after his teacher's death,
of almost the entire Brahms–Marxsen correspondence. However pedantic Marxsen
may have been, his breadth of musical culture is worth stressing, and his links with
the Vienna Schubert circle must have had significance for Brahms. It seems sensible to
take at face value the esteem implied by the dedication to Marxsen of the Piano
Concerto no. 2.

source of wisdom, of primal emotion, and of spiritual harmony.

There was an element of make-believe in this identification with the past. When he drew up the rules of the Hamburg Frauenchor in the macaronic language of an eighteenth-century theorist like Mattheson, that was an antiquarian jest. When he carefully copied and lettered the score of his *Geistliche Chöre* to resemble a seventeenth-century edition, with archaic Latin designations of the canonic devices employed therein, one can see the young musician play-acting, in Hoffmannesque fashion, at being a Renaissance composer. This element never entirely disappeared: in fact we might claim that the op. 122 Chorale Preludes are the most perfect 'impersonation' of Baroque manners he ever carried out.

Generally, though, Brahms's use of the past is 'modern' in its eclectic range and freedom of reference – whether reviving 'archaic' forms such as passacaglia or chorale prelude in new structural and expressive contexts, applying 'old' polyphonic methods to modern material, using Baroque or Classical themes as bases for variation, or obliquely recalling and emulating specific themes or formal models out of his unparalleled knowledge of the tradition from Schütz to Schumann. His famous retort – '*Das seiht jeder Esel!*' (Any ass can see that!) – when his attention was drawn to the 'resemblance' of the finale theme of his First Symphony to that of Beethoven's Ninth, was no disclaimer of the connection, but annoyance with the mentality that saw in such resemblances merely plagiarism or lack of originality; that could not see deeper, to the continuous network of allusion and divergence by which Brahms's music binds itself into the fabric of tradition, referring to and drawing upon the examples of great predecessors, and proclaiming its individuality by its different use of related vocabulary, or different solutions to related problems. In his work, much of musical history recapitulates itself – but is also transformed.

The time-honoured forms and gestures arise now from different premises, to articulate new orders of material and the concerns of a sceptical, questioning, mid-nineteenth-century sensibility. Brahms's harmony could be as chromatically complex as Wagner's, though usually arrived at from a more diatonic basis; and his treatment of tonality in large-scale forms seldom fulfils traditional expectations. In an age when the interplay of line had been subordinated to chordal progression as the chief agent of harmonic definition – and when more subtle forms of rhythmic organization had been subordinated to the regular stress of the strong beat – Brahms's study of early music led him to create an enriched polyphonic texture in which each contrapuntal voice has an increased independence and life of its own. His success in this was due to the plasticity of his melodic gift and, especially, to his subtle and all-pervasive mastery of rhythm to point up contrasts of line and shifts of pulse. Thus he was less a reborn Classicist than 'the first of the moderns', the initiator of that drive for absolute polyphonic freedom which became such a concern of Schoenberg and other twentieth-century composers. Schoenberg himself, in his essay 'Brahms the Progressive', was in no doubt that 'the progress towards an unrestricted musical language' was inaugurated by Brahms.

Brahms's individuality is perhaps most clearly felt, even on first acquaintance, in his handling of rhythm as a distinct musical area equal in importance to melody and harmony. Even his earliest published works display, especially in their fast movements, a strongly individual rhythmic profile, and predilections – notably for strongly-emphazised triplet formations and the energy derived from cross-rhythm and hemiola – which persisted throughout his entire creative evolution. Indeed the characteristic rhythmic vitality of Brahms's music surely stems from a new balance between the regular pulses of beat and bar and the musical elements that can be played off against them. As he attained creative maturity he acquired and absorbed an impressive armoury of devices (many of them discovered in pre-Baroque polyphony) for enhancing rhythmic variety and interest – ranging from small modifications of pulse to complex polyrhythmic superimpositions or multiplicities of accent designed to confuse the ear, for necessary reasons of local or structural ambiguity, as to where the beat actually falls.

These devices include, most obviously, the combination of triple rhythms with duple ones within a melodic line, or their superposition to produce polyrhythms of three-against-two or three-against-four (see Ex. 9, from the Variations on a Hungarian Song, for simple examples of both; a more sophisticated melodic use is Ex. 24, the opening of the A major Piano Quartet). There is a large variety of shifts of accent, some of which may be classified under the general heading of syncopation (displacement of the strong accent, by rests or ties or phrasing, to weak beats or off-beats of the bar: see Ex. 1b from Piano Sonata no. 1, or Ex. 1 from the Ballade, op. 10 no. 3) – and others, growing out of the triple/duple combinations, under that of hemiola (the substitution of three beats for two, for instance by the interplay of an implied 3/4 time against an official 6/8, or 3/2 against an official 6/4; or phrasing across the barline, for example three minims across two bars of 3/4; or by explicit changes of metre, e.g. from 6/8 to 2/4 as in the Piano Quintet's Scherzo, see Ex. 25j and k). Canonic writing and other forms of imitative counterpoint routinely involve ambiguity of accent when one voice shadows another at something other than a full bar's distance, as at the opening of the motet *Warum ist das Licht gegeben?*, Ex. 43a. There are expansions or contractions of pulse by means of changing time-signatures (e.g. from 6/8 to 9/8); and rhythmic dislocations, for instance the consistent anticipation of the beat (see the start of the Scherzo of the Piano Quintet, Ex. 25i, where the first violin is always a quaver ahead of the beat). One finds examples of off-beat accompanimental patterns; irregular rhythmic groupings; repetitions of phrases in changing relations to the predominant beat, where the metre can be clearly felt but the behaviour of the thematic elements pose contradictions to it (compare bars 7–8 with 9–10 of Ex. 18, the first theme of the D major Serenade, for a very simple instance). Furthermore, there are melodic phrases that are themselves irregular (say of five bars rather than the standard four, as in the chaconne-subject of the last of the Variations on a Theme of Haydn, Ex. 34e), or are irregular in relation to the chosen metre, such as a five-beat phrase in 3/4 time, or a three-beat one in 2/4; and even phrases so fashioned within the flow of the melodic line that they look simultaneously forwards and backwards, perhaps echoing or seeming to conclude a previous melodic span even as they initiate a new one (an obvious example is the theme of the slow movement of String Quartet no. 2, Ex. 33b, for which Schoenberg provided a famous analysis, illustrating its wealth of such features).

Brahms invented none of these techniques (it is remarkable how many of them Schoenberg was able to trace back to Mozart, popularly conceived as the supreme exponent of Classically-balanced phrasing). But his comprehensive deployment of them in so many compositional situations throughout the whole range of his output was unparalleled, and gave a new importance to the rhythmic dimension of music at precisely the moment when, under the impact of Wagner, the harmonic aspect was becoming all-powerful and beginning to tend towards a state of chromatic saturation. If it is possible to speak of a 'rhythmic texture' (created through stress, accent, metre, phrasing, harmonic and thematic pulse), then Brahms's is freer, more flexible, more multifaceted and pointedly ambiguous, than that of any composer before him – and probably any composer since.

His approach to harmony, and through harmony to tonality, is likewise a subtly individual blend of old and new elements. His studies of early music and folksong gave him a taste for archaic modes other than the diatonic major and minor, and these can often colour whole movements – not necessarily in their own right, but as a foil to and added means of modulation within a harmonic idiom as sophisticated as any in the latter half of the nineteenth century. The slow movement of the Fourth Symphony, with its juxtaposition of orthodox E major against the Phrygian mode on E – whose flattened supertonic, F, draws into the orbit of E the distant tonality of F major (the so-called 'Neapolitan' relationship) – is only the most celebrated instance of this tendency. It is important to note that the ambiguity of mode and key at the start of this movement (see p. 315) is not, for Brahms, a mere local harmonic sensation. It has long-range structural consequences which colour the entire movement, nowhere so intensely as in its final bars; and the appearance of this ambiguity is prepared by previous ambiguities in the preceding movement, and has consequences for the movements that follow.

For Brahms, as for all the great Classical composers, harmony and tonality impinged directly upon form, but his predilection for employing 'remote' keys and tonal areas often has effects more far-reaching than they derived from it. A fine example is the F major Cello Sonata, op. 99. As I noted on p. 331, the Adagio of this work is in F sharp major, an astonishing leap from the F major close of the first movement; but in fact that 'distant' key (spelt enharmonically as G flat in the Finale) features significantly in all four movements, and is brought into varying Neapolitan relations to the principal tonality by the use of alternating major and minor forms both of the tonic F and of the F sharp itself. No composer was more aware that in music, context is everything. Brahms was very fond of the duality or juxtaposition of major and minor modes, of Neapolitan (semitonal) connections and also relationships by thirds; and he loved to use them as agents of tonal ambiguity, where the sense of key fluctuates or is capable of more than one interpretation in relation to the passages surrounding it.[2] At the opening of the Second String Sextet, for instance, the persistent semitonal inflexions create a G minor tinge to the nominal G major tonality, and appear to establish a counterpoise with its flattened submediant, E flat. Such tonal ambiguities might be compared with Brahms's rhythmic ambiguities and both of them

---

[2] It has sometimes been claimed that the late works of Schubert were the most significant influence on these aspects of his tonal thinking – Tovey even asserted that 'the influence of Schubert is far greater than the combined influences of Bach and Beethoven' – and it is certainly the case that Brahms was the first great composer to appreciate and assimilate Schubert's significance as an inheritor and transformer of Classical tradition. Yet it is surely unwise to assign predominant importance to any single figure, when Brahms was so thoroughly steeped in them all. Most of the features cited above may be found in Beethoven, if less often concatenated together; while the ultimate inspiration for the use of a distant Neapolitan region for a sonata slow movement may well have been the resonant precedent of Haydn's great E flat Piano Sonata (Hoboken no. 52), with its E major second movement.

linked to his motivic and thematic working, where – as in the examples I have given from the First and Second Symphonies, and the Clarinet Quintet – themes of later movements are allowed to be both 'themselves' and to transform or allude to material in earlier ones. They might further be related to ambiguities of large-scale structure, such as the union of sonata and variation principles in different ways throughout Symphony no. 4. In fact at every level of Brahms's mature style one encounters a whole range of fascinating ambiguities. None of them results from imprecision in his thought: they are agents of double or sometimes triple meaning, and a prime cause of his music's incredible richness, by which his works yield new meaning, even after many years' acquaintance. And in a sense they mimic the central ambiguity of his position in history, poised between past and future. Self-evidently Brahms is a strongly 'tonal' composer, using the Classical hierarchy of tonal relationships with a force and confidence scarcely heard since Beethoven. He does not undermine the power of triadic harmony with *Tristan*-esque chromaticism; yet in modifying its function to attain multiplicity of meaning or to serve the purposes of his very wide-ranging thematic working, he suggests new principles of coherence. (In truth, it is Brahms, not Schoenberg, who should be labelled the 'conservative revolutionary'.)[3]

This is especially true when he allows a motif from the beginning of a work to have repercussions throughout its structure: all four Symphonies provide examples of this at the thematic level; the role of the D flat–C semitone, traced throughout my discussion of the Piano Quintet, affects the large-scale tonal events also; the most far-reaching exploitation of a motif in both thematic and tonal spheres is seen in the Fourth Symphony, through the role Brahms assigns to the chain of descending thirds.

A large book waits to be written on 'Brahms and the third': his fascination with this most basic element of diatonic tonality – as melodic interval, as harmony in its own right and in the building of more complex harmonies, as agent of key-relations – may be traced throughout his life's work from op. 1 to op. 122, and his treatment of it is staggering in variety and resourcefulness. Doubling a melodic line in thirds, often redoubled at a higher or lower octave, is among the most characteristic

---

[3] Willi Reich's phrase, the title of his critical biography *Schönberg oder Der konservativ Revolutionär* (Zürich, 1968), has by now passed into general currency. In my volume on Schoenberg for the 'Master Musicians' series (1976), I have suggested that it would be more accurate to see Schoenberg as a 'a revolutionary conservative'. So much for word-play.

sources of warmth in his orchestral scoring; high thirds against low fifths or octaves add a chill austerity to his keyboard textures, as in Ex. 10.

Whole movements are often related by shifts of a third: a commonplace in Classical structural thinking yet one capable of startling effect when, for instance, the relationship is by a *major* third in a *minor-key* work. The example of Beethoven's C minor Piano Concerto, with its wonderfully impressive move to E major for the slow movement, manifestly affected Brahms's thinking – indeed the relationship is mimicked by his C minor Piano Quartet, which arrives at an E major slow movement after not one but two C minor movements. Beethoven's equally daring stress upon A flat in his Finale (a major third down from C, as E was a third above) is also alluded to in Brahms's Finale by the A flat pedal that precedes the introduction of the second subject.

Yet it was the special tonal and colouristic properties of the formation to which I have often drawn attention in previous chapters – thirds arranged in a descending chain – which seems to have had special significance for Brahms. If any single work demonstrated to him the constructive power with which such material might be treated, it was probably the 'Hammerklavier' Sonata, and indeed the development section of Beethoven's slow movement throws up, as a natural consequence of its working, the opening theme of Brahms's Symphony no. 4. In Brahms's *oeuvre*, the 'chain' idea emerges very early as a theme in its own right: the opening subject of the slow movement of the F minor Piano Sonata (Ex. 4a) derives its rainbow-tinted beauty precisely from this shape.

Yet, from the first, Brahms thought of it harmonically as well as melodically – and it led him to the idea of a chain of tonalities. One of his most powerful and characteristic modulatory effects is to juxtapose a bold sequence of triads which describes a succession of major keys, each a descending third apart – usually with an element of contrary motion, the music's melodic profile aspiring upwards. Ex. 66 cites four examples, all (perhaps significantly?) from finales. That from the First Piano Sonata (Ex. 66a) demonstrates how the modulation is present even in Brahms's earliest works, and occurs in the context of development of the theme originally quoted as Ex. 1b, adding tonal breadth to its scherzo-like vigour, although limited to a chain of three keys, C–A–F. Ex. 66b, from the coda of the First Piano Concerto, is a notable use of this formula in virile triumph, the chain extended (in the rhythm of the first bar of the rondo theme Ex. 17b) to four steps, C–A–F–D, to cadence into the work's tonic key. Ex. 66c, shortly before the coda of the Violin Concerto, gains the same key by a five-step sequence, E–C–A–F–D,

389

while developing the main finale theme in a state of climactic exhilaration. Finally Ex. 66d, from the closing bars of the G major Violin
Sonata, uses the formula to gain an effect of quiet rapture, G–E–C.

What must especially have appealed to Brahms about the 'third-
chain' was that it was such a profoundly ambiguous symbol of tonal
stability. A single step of a third presents the kernel, major or minor,
of a diatonic triad; two steps span the triad to its fifth, giving the tonic–

Ex. 66

(a)

(b)

(See also Ex.54b)

dominant relationship by which a key defines itself. Yet three steps give a major or diminished seventh, agents of dissonance and tonal change, and further steps lead to ninths, elevenths, thirteenths – increasingly rarefied dissonance and increasingly tenuous sense of directed tonality. That these steps should be downward increases their ambiguity: the root of their overall harmony is not heard at the outset but constantly expected as the final tone in the descending series, and the longer the series the weaker the gravitational pull of the root. Theoretically the stepladder of thirds is endless – or rather, in musical terms, it might encompass all twelve pitches of the chromatic scale without repetition (as Liszt used one of ascending thirds in his 'Faust' Symphonie). It need not, and Brahms generally uses a milder form, where (if he gets that far) the pitches start to repeat at the eighth note after spanning two octaves. But even a four- or five-step segment of the chain is sufficient to introduce ambiguity of key, the sense of tonal perpetual motion.

The prime examples of the use of the chain of thirds to determine melody, harmony, and even long-range structure are of course in the Fourth Symphony (Ex. 53) and the *Vier ernste Gesänge* (Ex. 64): but sequences of falling thirds abound throughout Brahms's output, often linked to specific verbal images in songs and choral music. Their occurrences in the *Ernste Gesänge*, especially at Ex. 64d and e, have led several commentators, notably Peter Latham in the previous 'Master Musicians'

Brahms, to speak of a 'Death Motif', calling in support the falling thirds that occur in the song *Feldeinsamkeit*, op. 86 no. 2, where the poet compares himself to one long dead; in *Mit vierzig Jahren*, op. 94 no. 1, where he speaks of the declining years of life; and in *Nänie*, at the words 'for the beautiful fades, for the perfect must die'. The 1894 folksong setting *Es reit ein Herr und auch sein Knecht*, might be cited as a further instance: but in fact the chain of thirds seen there is comparatively disguised when the Knight's death is described – it is clearest at the beginning of the song (quoted as Ex. 22b), apparently to create a fateful atmosphere.

Indeed, if the lines by Sternau prefacing the slow movement of the F minor Piano Sonata are taken at face value, then Ex. 4a is intended only to evoke the image of moonlight. The coincidence of falling thirds and moonlight is found again, much later, in the Heine setting *Mondenschein* (op. 85 no. 2) – and though the tone of the poem is anguished, the thirds here echo a chain in the immediately foregoing Heine song, *Sommerabend*, where a beautiful elf (possibly to Brahms's imagination Elisabet von Herzogenberg) bathes in a brook, her arms and neck shimmering in lunar radiance.[4] Clearly the wordless passages cited in Ex. 66 have nothing to do with death, though they stamp themselves on the mind with almost symbolic force; and neither do the remarkable chains of 'infinite modulation' by falling thirds in the development sections of the Finales of the C minor Piano Quartet (see Ex. 37b) and the Clarinet Trio. Here, surely, Brahms employs the chain as an agent or image of destabilization, of change. Indeed, even in some of its textual assocations it may stand for change as such, transformation of spiritual state, a turn of life's wheel, rather than death in particular. The 'imperceptible downward slope' in *Mit vierzig Jahren* leads by implication towards death, but it is the slope, the change from ascent to descent, that Brahms illustrates. And the descending third as an obsessive figure in the following song of op. 94, *Steig auf, geliebter Schatten*, is ambiguous indeed: the poem addresses a ghost, who can still refresh her lover's spirits as she did when alive – and he calls on her to infuse his soul with energy, make him young again. Changes of life, altered states (with death the greatest alteration), the other-worldly, impermanence, perhaps even by paradox a symbol of Eternity, changefully unchanging – it seems that Brahms's falling thirds may have signified to him all of these.

He leaves it to us to work these things out for ourselves. In a period when poetical description of all kinds was routinely applied to music

---

[4] 'I never saw a more beautiful neck and shoulders; so marvellously white were they...': Ethel Smyth on Elisabet von Herzogenberg.

(Schumann even provided picturesque interpretations of the Preludes and Fugues of Bach's *Wohltemperierte Klavier*, as if they were Romantic genre-pieces), Brahms was almost unique in placing no reliance on extra-musical metaphor to suggest his meaning. Indeed, he sometimes remarked that music generally did not suggest any pictorial or literary images to him (though the contrary process clearly took place with the poetry that inspired his songs and choral music). Nevertheless he suffered with seeming tranquillity the metaphorical interpretations of Clara, Elisabet von Herzogenberg, Kalbeck and others; and he was much taken with the etchings his works inspired from Max Klinger, with their harps, lyres, sphinxes, nereids, dolphins, eagles, rock-strewn seashores, Greek masks, grand pianos and nude male figures.

Even where settings of poetry offer clues, Brahms's songs come nearer to instrumental music in their approach to a text than do those of any other great nineteenth-century composer. The language of the late Lieder allowed easy transference into violin sonatas, just as the early B major Trio could accommodate instrumental fashionings of Beethoven and Schubert songs. His attitude is the antithesis of Hugo Wolf's, whose songs – under the influence of Wagner – strive to underline the poem's every significant word by super-charged harmony and a vocal line that is the apotheosis of heightened recitation. Nor did Brahms attempt the miraculous synthesis of music and poetic meaning achieved by Schumann. It could be argued that his literary taste was inferior to either; but he preferred poems whose expression of a predominant emotion, whether couched in first-rate words or not, was strong enough to allow the elaboration of that emotion in music flowing freely according to its own dictates. In his attachment to strophic forms, formal rather than dramatic variety, and to lyric melody for its own sake he is the natural successor to Schubert, 'blending elevated style with popular feeling', in Eric Sams's phrase. Brahms's identification with folksong idioms gives added integrity to the 'popular' areas of his output, and as Sams points out, songs like the *Wiegenlied* for Bertha Faber became 'folksongs' in his own lifetime.[5]

The songs demonstrate that the infrequency of conscious poetic or pictorial correlatives in his music certainly does not rule out the presence and development of powerful emotion, or personal symbolism of a musical kind, such as that hinted at in my discussion of Brahms's use of falling thirds. When he told Clara 'I speak in my music', he clearly meant what he said. He also wrote to her, in 1893:

[5] Sams, op. cit., p. 6.

Of your interest in my music and sympathy with it I feel I can always rest assured. But the artist cannot and should not be separated from the man. And in me it happens that the artist is not so arrogant and sensitive as the man, and the latter has but small consolation if the work of the former is not allowed to expatiate his sins.

Nearly two decades before he had commented, in conversation with Henschel:

How few true men there are in the world! The two Schumanns, Robert and Clara, they are two true, beautiful *Menschenbilder*. Knowledge, achievement, power, position – nothing can outweigh this: to be a beautiful *Menschenbild*.

The term *Menschenbild* is a decidedly Romantic concept which Henschel translates literally as an 'image of man', but by which Brahms presumably meant an exemplar of humanity at its best. If 'nothing could outweigh' that as a goal, it follows that even being a great composer was no substitute for the moral integrity of the *Menschenbild*, and explains Brahms's comment to Clara that he wished to 'believe that he was better than his music'. This attitude was diametrically opposed to that of a composer like Wagner and of many creative artists down to the present day who, having nothing to declare but their genius, travel unencumbered through a life which is felt to owe them sympathy and livelihood on their genius's account.

'Arrogant and sensitive' Brahms may have been, but not because of his musical achievements, about which he seems to have felt little insecurity. His faults of character, if one may call them that – his occasional rudeness, taciturnity, apparent thoughtlessness and indulgence of melancholy, which could distress old friends as much as strangers – probably stem from that 'egocentricity' which Joachim diagnosed in him as early as 1854: the self-absorption and social awkwardness which caused him to draw back from full emotional commitment in a relationship, jealously guard his personal independence, and seldom reveal his deepest feelings. That he was sometimes misunderstood he seems to have accepted as the lesser of two evils: 'It is easy to attribute all sorts of motives to a man who is not keen on answering and explaining', he wrote of himself to Joachim in 1873.

Probably this reticence arose from a fear of emotional hurt. In the area of human relationships he clearly strove to be a good man, while painfully aware that he was an imperfect one. The Schumann/Joachim circle sometimes seem rather priggish in their attitudes of artistic dedication: Clara's verdict on Anton Rubinstein (whom she personally liked) was 'What he lacks above all is sacred seriousness'. Brahms apparently agreed – he preferred Rubinstein the man to Rubinstein the composer – but the phrase 'sacred seriousness' was not one that was likely to fall from his lips. He simply felt Rubinstein did not take enough trouble over his compositions.

Brahms was never a man to sit in moral judgement over other people, but the actions of his day-to-day life demonstrated a high moral idealism. He appears to have judged himself by the most stringent standards while looking leniently and with sympathy at the behaviour of others. The unassuming frugality of his life-style; his indifference to social convention or class divisions; his love of children; his unstinting generosity with money – extending even to beggars, and often anonymous when it involved his friends; even the terseness and casualness of much of his correspondence, so clearly functional and dashed down without a thought to posterity:[6] all testify to the basic simplicity and rectitude of his personal principles. It was the reflection of this attitude that so attracted him in the painter Adolph von Menzel, whom he befriended in his last years. 'What I like about him', he wrote to Clara in February 1896,

> ...is that he is the only one of our famous men who lives in the most humble bourgeois circumstances. His rooms are not half as high or as big as yours, and you have never seen a studio furnished with such supreme simplicity. The vitality and *joie de vivre* of this little octogenarian would certainly amuse you. When I am in Berlin he always comes towards midnight to my tavern or wherever else I happen to be – Joachim and others would like to do the same!

Brahms valued *joie de vivre*, cloaking even his most serious thoughts in dry wit or self-deprecating irony, and his letters have little of Clara's or Joachim's solemnity. It is moreover remarkable that in such a religiose age his ethical conduct appears to have had no specifically religious basis. His knowledge of Scripture was deep and subtle; theological topics interested him and he liked to argue them with such people as Reinthaler and Spitta; yet the Bible seems to have furnished him merely with patterns and standards of human conduct, and in his daily life there is no shadow of specifically Christian belief or even any tenuous sense of an after-life. He shared this stoic agnosticism – expressed so

---

[6] And this although he was an indefatigable and often delightful correspondent. 'I am passionately fond of reading letters from wise, good, and dear people,' he wrote to the conductor Otto Dessoff in 1878. '...I even have a secret passion for writing letters, but it is very secret indeed and completely evaporates in front of the notepaper. Never in my life have I written a letter easily or comfortably.' (Quoted from Geiringer's *Brahms: his Life and Work*, 2nd ed., (London, 1948), p. 362.)

powerfully in the *Schicksalslied* and *Gesang der Parzen* – with Clara: in their voluminous correspondence, even when she was beset with domestic tragedy, there is never a mention of religion.[7]

He was if anything rather proud of his 'heathenish' tendencies, though they made some of his orthodox friends unhappy. 'Such a great man! Such a great soul!' sorrowed Dvořák, with simple Catholic piety, 'And he believes in nothing!' That was not quite true. He believed in the best aspects of humanity – in the *Menschenbild* – and in music's power to give it transcendent and autonomous expression. The late nineteenth- and early twentieth-century commentators who attempted to discover a Christian spirit of comfort in the *Requiem* and *Schicksalslied* were thus not wholly wrong: the comfort is there, but it is human, not spiritual, designed for this world not the next. Brahms's religious sense was unmediated by Christian myth and the conventions of orthodox religion; paradoxically this increases his significance as a religious composer, for this very 'earthly' faith is often expressed most intensely in his settings of scriptural texts, which he clearly valued as a source of his national culture, and understood as metaphors for the human predicament.[8] The paramount example is the *Vier ernste Gesänge*, which proclaim with such supreme poignancy that all things are uncertain save death itself, that a man should rejoice in his works, and that the only thing worth having is love, whose source may be Divine but whose expression is human.

[7] It is this lifelong silence even in the most emotional circumstances that renders incredible the account of Brahms given by Arthur M. Abell in his curious book *Talks with Great Composers* (New York, 1955). Abell, a German–American violinist, lived in Europe from 1890 to 1918 and certainly did make Brahms's acquaintance; some writers have accepted without qualm his evidence that Brahms professed an interest in the music of negro minstrels, from the rhythmic point of view. Written over fifty years after the event (supposedly at Brahms's insistence), the bulk of his book purports to record a long conversation with Brahms and Joachim in Vienna in the autumn of 1896 about the psychic and religious sources of musical inspiration. Although Abell was doubtless sincere, and though one can imagine some of the remarks could have been made by Brahms, the general tone is so utterly and uncharacteristically fulsome, even evangelical, so conveniently supports Abell's own Spiritualist convictions, and is so closely reproduced in further 'conversations' with Puccini, Bruch, Grieg, and others, that it is difficult to accept seriously. Abell claimed that he was working from a verbatim record in German, taken by a stenographer from the American Embassy in Vienna: but I am not aware that such a document has emerged since his book appeared.

[8] See Wilhelm Furtwängler's comment jotted down in his notebooks for 1940: 'Has it ever occurred to anyone that the great "earthly" artists of the nineteenth century, that Brahms, indeed Wagner and Verdi, were the *only* ones who were able to put truly religious content into music?' (*Notebooks 1924–1954*, trans. Shaun Whiteside, London, 1989, p. 122).

Brahms's love for Clara Schumann was perhaps the central fact of his adult existence; in the nature of things hers for him, though very deep, could not be quite so central. Whether or not their early passion was ever physically consummated, whether either of them found it easy that their lives should essentially go separate ways, the tensions that clearly underlay their relationship were only an exacerbating factor for the more general unresolved tensions in Brahms's attitudes to women. The depth of his feeling for Clara might sufficiently explain his failure to marry Agathe von Siebold or any of the other women nearer his own age to whom he felt strongly attracted, but almost certainly it was not the only cause. The testimony of the singer Max Friedländer, as presented by Robert Schauffler in his somewhat sensationalized book *The Unknown Brahms*, is in essence all too believable: that Brahms in unguarded moments sometimes spoke of women in general in extravagantly misogynistic terms, under pressure of bitter childhood memories. When on one occasion Friedländer remonstrated with him for the offensiveness of his language Brahms retorted that compared to his own childhood, the singer had been 'reared in cotton-wool', and he simply could not indulge in conventional romantic homage of women after seeing the sailors in the St Pauli *Animierkneipe*, fresh off their ships after months at sea, flinging themselves on women 'like beasts of prey', and after being himself treated as a sexual plaything by 'the lowest sort of public women – the so-called "Singing Girls"'.[9]

One hardly needs a training in psychology to realize that, if Brahms's memories of these early experiences remained so painful even in his fifties, they must have driven a wedge in his mind between love and sex, from his first years of physical maturity; which could only have been widened by the strength of his passion for the loving but unattainable Clara. To use a modern term, he had suffered childhood sexual abuse, whose victims are often unable to integrate love and sexuality in their maturity. The strong bond of family affection, especially with his mother, of which he spoke so movingly to Kalbeck, probably helped to preserve his balance: but on its own it does not seem to have been

---

[9] Schauffler, *The Unknown Brahms* (New York, 1933), pp. 224–6. Friedländler is also the source of a story of peculiar pathos. Once he was dining with Brahms and some friends at a rather shabby café which was invaded by some prostitutes with their men-friends: one of the girls hailed Brahms familiarly and asked him to play them something to dance to. To his friends' surprise Brahms went to the neglected upright piano and played while the couples danced; to their puzzlement it was dance-music in an unfamiliar, quaintly old-fashioned style. Afterwards Brahms told Friedländer that it had been his nightly repertoire from the *Animierkneipe*; he had not played it for over forty years, and had wanted to see if he could still remember it.

enough, and may even – in his relations with Clara, maternal in age and fecundity – have confused matters. (Ethel Smyth, seeing them together, thought that 'to Frau Schumann he behaved as might a particularly delightful old-world son'.) As we have seen, he formed deep and tender friendships with many other talented, intelligent women; but the sensual side of his nature, so evident in the virile strength and harmonic richness of his music, seems only to have found its physical outlet in occasional encounters with prostitutes: transactions recorded in gossip but, of their nature, generally lacking firm documentation.

This double image of woman, the pure object of adoration and the sexually threatening predator, is to some extent dramatized in the *Magelone* Romances, where Peter must choose between the virtuous Magelone and the oriental sensuality of the Sultan's daughter Sulima. It is even more central to that much-misunderstood work *Rinaldo*: Goethe's text surely struck Brahms with the force of a personal myth, nowhere more strongly than in the passage where the scales fall from the hero's eyes and he sees the object of his passion, the enchantress Armida, 'utterly transformed – she looks and acts exactly as demons do', and her magical visions 'together with all love . . . scattered as dust'.

Even in normal society his attitude to women was equivocal, for while he treated Clara, Elisabet and other favoured friends with the utmost gentleness and respect, his behaviour towards less intimate acquaintances sometimes amounted to what would nowadays be considered an appalling display of male chauvinism. That pioneer feminist Ethel Smyth noted with distaste that he constantly referred to women with a 'detestable' word, *Weibsbilder* (a vulgar usage, very different indeed from *Menschenbild*!), and that

> If they did not appeal to him he was incredibly awkward and ungracious; if they were pretty he had an unpleasant way of leaning back in his chair, pouting out his lips, stroking his moustache, and staring at them as a greedy boy stares at jam tartlets. People used to think this rather delightful, specially hailing it, too, as a sign that the great man was in high good humour, but it angered me . . .[10]

If this tendency to regard women as sweetmeats (which, as Ethel Smyth notes, was common enough in the Germany of his time) may be taken as a sign of immaturity in emotional relations, we ought perhaps briefly to consider the possible physical immaturity implied by Brahms's curiously high-pitched voice. Many contemporaries noted it, and he is known to have taken voice-production lessons in his mid-

[10] Smyth, op. cit., p. 264.

twenties in an attempt to bring his speaking voice lower, apparently without success. The piping quality is obvious in the only known recording of Brahms playing (a primitive Edison cylinder made in the early 1890s, on which he announces and then plays part of the first Hungarian Dance, the latter largely inaudible except for the piano's pedal-action, but clear enough to convey his immense rubato). It has been suggested to me that this odd vocal quality might possibly be a symptom of retarded growth, perhaps of impotence, caused by a severe childhood illness such as German Measles. It must be said that what little we know of Brahms's childhood medical history provides no supporting evidence. Apart from his accident at the age of ten, when his chest was nearly crushed, and bouts of severe headache throughout his teens, he seems to have been a very healthy child – remarkably so for someone brought up in such an unhealthy area as the Gängeviertel. If indeed he was sexually inhibited – which would give ironic, if poignant, force to Nietzsche's famous jibe (p. 346) – perhaps this was a result of his experiences in the *Animierkneipe*. This is possibly already further than speculation can legitimately be taken.

It would be too facile, and based on evidence far too flimsy, to speak of emotional or psychological compensation in Brahms's music. But even in his teens he had used music and literature as a refuge from his sordid surroundings, and this must have encouraged him to think of artistic creation as a countervailing ideal state, the nearest approach to human perfection (see his advice to Henschel on composing: 'Whether it is beautiful . . . perfect it *must* be'). Does it overstate the case to say that only in his music, with its powerful will to the union of drama and lyricism, to the integration of contrasting elements across a large design, was he truly able to reconcile the conflicting strands of his personality, and to 'speak' as a wholly rounded and fulfilled human being? If the conflicts were as deep and scarring as Friedländer's evidence suggests, then the goodness and uprightness of his character was a triumph over emotional adversity, a solitary heroism; and his occasional selfishness and wounding sarcasm should be better understood as signs of a sometimes intolerable strain.

Perhaps that gives a clue to the imperishable appeal of his music. Unlike Wagner, he was no impetuous revolutionary, in art or politics: he manned no barricades. Unlike Beethoven he was no obviously heroic figure, nor a tragic one like Schumann or Hugo Wolf. Unlike Schubert or Chopin, he did not die young and Romantically from disease, or in unjust poverty, like Mozart. After the excitements of the 1850s his life was devoid of high drama, and to outward appearances he became the embodiment of solid, comfortable bourgeois conservatism, albeit endowed with musical gifts which raised it to the rank of genius. Yet behind the tranquil mask of his public and professional eminence he clearly felt much unhappiness, frustration, shyness, loneliness, self-doubt, and lack of emotional fulfilment. In his late years especially, outliving all his near family, he often regretted never having married, never having had children of his own. Yet he knew he had never felt himself able to make the necessary commitment, though in conversation with Widmann he offered a different rationalization:

> At the time when I might have married a girl, my stuff was being whistled at in the concert hall, or at best received with icy coldness. Now I could bear that perfectly well on my own, since I knew exactly how little it was worth and how the tide would eventually turn... But if in such moments I had had to go back to face a wife, to see her questioning eyes anxiously judging me, and to have to say to her 'again, nothing' – that I could not have endured.

Private, unexciting problems: but so are those of most people in any age, like the peasant lovers evoked and treated with such sympathy in his many folksong settings. None of the great composers is more human and understanding than Brahms, and none is more comforting an example of the power of creative mastery to transcend and ennoble human frailty. With Beethoven he shares the secret of projecting intimate feeling onto the largest symphonic canvas (as in the sumptuously amorous Double Concerto). Sometimes not even Beethoven seems to have quite his ability to scale his concerns down to everyday dimensions, without in any sense relaxing his artistic standards (one thinks of the *Wiegenlied*, op. 49 no. 4, or the A flat Waltz). We should remember what G. K. Chesterton said of Brahms's near-contemporary, Charles Dickens: 'Dickens did not write what the people wanted. He wanted what the people wanted'. A man of the people, Brahms knew that ordinary human beings are capable of being better than their circumstances, and ultimately his music is an assertion of that fact. This was a quality well captured by the great *Manchester Guardian* critic, Samuel Langford who, writing of a performance in the early 1920s of the B flat String Sextet, made the point (which Brahms would surely have relished) that his art itself attains something of the universality of folk music:

> How noble is the great variational ballad which forms the slow movement of this sextet! That is a folk-music the like of which is not to be found anywhere else. It has a sweep and breadth and a pride in its lowly inspiration and origin that goes as far as the best political theories to show us in what way men may be equal. And the grace of the last

movement, in which all that is gracious in the closing movements of Beethoven is brought to the service of a large romantic melody that has the heart of Schumann in its fullness – how warm and mild its tone, and yet how noble its bearing! We do well to honour such music, and to love the genius and nobility of heart which went into its making.[11]

The 'young eagle' who was 'fated to give the highest expression to the times' did so in terms which despite their immense technical skill, remain comprehensible to the widest possible audience. Aware of the tragedies, paradoxes, and imponderables of existence, Brahms wrote to provide sustenance for the here and now. His music seeks to give beauty, nobility, a sense of meaning, to the brute fact of human transience.

[11] Quoted from *Samuel Langford: Music Criticisms*, ed. Neville Cardus (Oxford, 1929), p. 120.

13

A Music of the Future

We can see from our vantage-point of 1966 that Schumann was wrong: Brahms was not to be the prophet of a new age. He is no founder of a new dynasty, not even an intermediate name in a long continuous line, but the very last of the classical Caesars... Schoenberg, who was beginning to compose in the nineties, owes in his early works much to Wagner, something perhaps to Schubert, nothing to Brahms.

Peter Latham, Brahms (rev. ed., 1966)

From *Brahms* [I learned]:

1. Many of the things that I acquired unconsciously from Mozart – especially uneven numbers of measures, extension and contraction of phrases.
2. Plasticity in moulding figures; not to be mean, not to stint myself when clarity demands more space; carrying each figure through to the end.
3. Systematic construction of movements.
4. Economy, yet richness.

Arnold Schoenberg, Zu Nationale Musik
(typescript dated 24 February 1931)

One day during the last summer of Brahms's life, he took a walk along the shore of the Traunsee near Ischl with Gustav Mahler, who was trying to enlist Brahms's support for his candidacy as conductor of the Vienna Hofoper. It is not certain how much of Mahler's music Brahms knew,[1] but he admired him as a conductor, declaring a performance of *Don Giovanni* Mahler had given in Budapest in 1890 the best he had ever heard. As they walked Brahms, who was often in poor spirits that summer, gave vent to his disenchantment with the latest musical developments, bewailing what he saw as a progressive decline that could only lead to 'the end of music'. They came to a stream running into the lake, crossed by a bridge, on which they paused:

> Suddenly Mahler siezed him by the arm and with his other hand pointed down excitedly into the water: 'But look, Herr Doktor, look!'
> 'What is it?' asked Brahms.

---

[1] He had been a member of the committee that, in 1881, had rejected Mahler's cantata *Das klagende Lied* as an entry for the Gesellschaft der Musikfreunde's Beethoven Prize. According to Kalbeck (IV, p. 454) he had been shown the 'Resurrection' Symphony (no. 2) in MS, but his opinion of it is not recorded.

'Look there – there goes the last wave!'
Whereupon Brahms retorted: 'That's all very well – but perhaps the real point is whether the wave flows into the lake, or into a bog'.[2]

The anecdote appears a typical confrontation between progressive youth and reactionary old age; according to authorial standpoint one may approve Mahler's spirit of adventure or Brahms's wise caution – or indeed both. Behind Mahler's irreverent mockery of Brahmsian fatalism lay decades of debate between the conservers of tradition, for whom Brahms seemed the natural figurehead, and the supporters of the 'Music of the Future'. Mahler may have valued Brahms's approval, but his sympathies lay with the latter party. 'I have gone through all of Brahms pretty well by now', he wrote to his wife Alma in 1904. 'All I can say of him is that he's a puny little dwarf with a rather narrow chest. Good Lord, if a breath from the lungs of *Richard Wagner* whistled about his ears he would scarcely be able to keep his feet'.

The double image of Wagner as the 'progressive' superman, breaking utterly new musical ground, and Brahms as the timid conservative clinging to tradition, was standard-issue ammunition to the champions of the 'New German' school; it had been promulgated by Wagner himself, and enthusiastically developed by Hugo Wolf in his journalism. Brahms was careful to keep out of the debate, but his adherents were equipped with inferior weapons. They maintained that Wagner and Liszt were poor composers, or hardly composers at all; and history has proved them wrong. And in fact – although the debate soon ceased to matter, as the early twentieth century yielded fresh issues that produced even more radical polarization of musical attitudes – in terms of critical orthodoxy the 'New Germans' clearly won the argument. When he made the pronouncement quoted at the head of this chapter, Peter Latham obviously felt he was stating no more than an axiomatic truth. Brahms the conservative, the Classical composer born too late, the last of his line – this was the accepted interpretation of his achievement for over fifty years after his death: accepted even by musicians who admired him profoundly.

This was no doubt because his desire to restore the form-building power of Classical music appealed to composers with much more conservative instincts than his own, and it was these who became the 'Brahmsians', whose works – though undeniably technically skilled and sincere – reproduced Brahms's manner, and the outward workings of his structures, in an essentially ossifying form. Herzogenberg at his weakest was one such. Another was Robert Fuchs, who occupied

---

[2] Richard Specht, *Johannes Brahms* (Hellerau, 1928), p. 382.

Brahms's old position at the Gesellschaft der Musikfreunde and wrote fluent, graceful, forgettable music in most of the Brahmsian forms, including the clarinet quintet and the orchestral serenade, of which he composed so many that he was nicknamed 'Serenaden-Fuchs'. Nevertheless Fuchs, a professor at the Vienna Conservatoire, was a gifted teacher, whose pupils included Mahler, Franz Schreker, and Zemlinsky. Even more thoroughly forgotten Brahmsians were such once-respected figures as the symphonists and chamber-music composers Wilhelm Berger and Ewald Straesser, and the choral composer Otto Taubman. It was perhaps inevitable that the historical sense, the formal intricacy and apparent absence of dangerous revolutionary tendencies which characterized Brahms's music made it self-recommending to composers of an academic cast of mind, and that it rapidly became the symbol of an orthodoxy, taught in conservatoires and universities, against which the rising generation instinctively reacted. Brahms was identified with their teachers.

That was certainly the pattern in Britain, where Brahms's music had been increasingly warmly accepted throughout the latter half of his life, to the extent that a vital part of that post-1880 transformation of British musical life which we call 'the British Musical Renaissance' was the re-emergence of composers able to master complex instrumental forms, who naturally found in Brahms a vital contemporary model.

It may be that Brahms himself had some inkling of this development. The Manchester-born composer John Foulds, who as a cellist in the Hallé Orchestra became a protégé of Brahms's friend and interpreter Hans Richter, and whose own early works (notably a cello sonata and cello concerto) are clearly influenced by Brahms, was told by Richter that Brahms had once declared to him and the violinist Adolf Brodsky: 'for the next great step forward in music, to England look'.[3] According to Richter, Brahms gave as one reason

> the fact that this country was in a better position than any other in Europe to survey Russian, German, French, Italian, and other characteristic music, and distil therefrom, as it were, the next forward urge in art.[4]

Though Brahms never visited England he knew a good deal about it from Joachim and Clara Schumann, who performed there almost every

---

[3] John Foulds, *Music To-day: Its Heritage from the Past, and Legacy to the Future* (London, 1934), p. 17.

[4] John Foulds, 'Does the Public like Good Music?', article in *Music Masterpieces*, ed. Percy Pitt (London, 1925), p. 67. It should be noted that in the previously cited (but later, and therefore perhaps less accurate) source, Foulds attributes these latter remarks to Brodsky rather than Brahms.

year, and he had met many British musicians: two of his favourite interpreters of his Piano Concertos were the Glasgow-born Eugen d'Albert and the young Londoner Leonard Borwick. Moreover he was acquainted with the twin figureheads of the early years of the 'Musical Renaissance', Hubert Parry and Charles Villiers Stanford.

Stanford had been instrumental in inviting him to Cambridge in 1877, and in the same year had dedicated to Brahms a collection of his settings of Irish folksongs. Parry, who had tried unsuccessfully to become Brahms's pupil, composed a powerful orchestral memorial to him, the *Elegy for Brahms*. By the early twentieth century these composers' music was already passing out of fashion, and they were long remembered as virtually identical Brahms disciples: a judgement pretty inaccurate in the case of Stanford (whose music owes much more to Mendelssohn and Schumann), and unjust in that of Parry, a sensitive and resourceful eclectic who indeed absorbed much from Brahms in the fields of chamber and choral music but who blended this with an early awareness of Liszt and Wagner that yielded a distinctive synthesis in his orchestral works, notably the *Symphonic Variations*. But as leading musical educators in Oxford, Cambridge, and at the RCM in London, they were enormously influential in setting up Brahms's music as a standard of excellence. Even more influential was Parry's pupil Donald Tovey, a gifted pianist and composer who – as a protégé of Joachim – had direct access to the Brahmsian traditions of performance and musical thought. Tovey's own compositions were entirely side-lined by the way musical language developed (though the prelude to his opera *The Bride of Dionysus* is a beautiful act of osmosis in combining Brahmsian with Wagnerian styles; the Cello Concerto, written as late as the 1930s in a largely Brahmsian vocabulary, is a kind of masterpiece; and Brahmsian structural precepts infuse his often impressive chamber works). However, through his educative writings, especially the mis-named and perennially popular *Essays in Musical Analysis*, he succeeded in conveying to a very large lay audience how the standard repertoire might be understood from a viewpoint that situated Brahms approximately at the centre of the musical universe. Here again the result was to establish the idea of Brahms's music as a noble orthodoxy, an achieved and established style; and it left talented and exploratory-minded younger composers with little alternative but to react against it.

However, admiration of Brahms was by no means confined to academic figures – as shown by the example of Elgar, a virtually self-taught composer who, apart from some lectures at Birmingham School of Music, did no teaching whatever. Elgar's primary orientation, especially in *The Dream of Gerontius* and his subsequent oratorios, was towards the methods of Wagnerian music drama, above all as exemplified in *Parsifal*; but he revered Brahms, especially the symphonies (he once said he felt 'like a pygmy' before his favourite, the Third, and he seems to have been the first person to point out the thematic cross-connection between the second and fourth movements of that work). The effect of this reverence can be felt in his own symphonic and chamber works. A striking instance is the way a famous theme from the Finale of his First Symphony is clearly modelled directly on an equally famous one in the analogous place in Brahms's Third (Ex. 67): yet the effect here is not one of imitation but of characteristically Elgarian inspiration.

Ex. 67

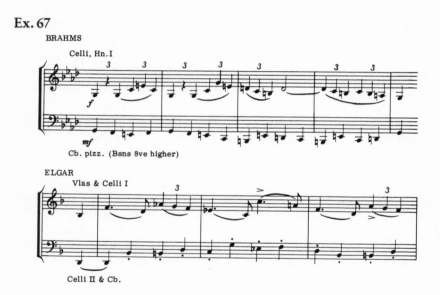

Meanwhile some of the post-Elgar generation, sustainedly exposed to Brahms's music through study with Parry or Stanford, began to assimilate it in ways that strengthened their own creative personalities. We can see this in the chamber and piano works of Stanford's pupil John Ireland; less obviously but more profoundly it is true of Vaughan Williams, who studied with both mentors. Certainly his music seldom *sounds* like Brahms; but temperamentally and intellectually they had much in common, starting with reverence for Bach, admiration for pre-Classical music and love of folksong. One particular Brahms work had demonstrably important repercussions on Vaughan Williams's output: the Fourth Symphony. Parry's own Fourth (1889), in E minor, is an almost immediate reaction to Brahms's in the same key; and his pupil's two E minor symphonies (nos. 6 and 9) variously reflect many of Brahms's structural features, while his Fifth imitates to the extent of a passacaglia finale. But Brahms's Fourth left its clearest imprint on the work which is generally (and justly) considered one of the first coherent expressions of Vaughan Williams's strong individuality – the Fantasia on a Theme of Thomas Tallis (1910). In this comprehensive exploration of the potential of the Phrygian mode within a modern harmonic framework,[5] Vaughan Williams must surely have taken the Andante of Brahms's Symphony as inspiration and partial model. The English composer's work is on an even larger scale than Brahms's movement, and yet more thoroughgoing in its use of modal alternatives to diatonic tonality. It is possibly a coincidence (since a derivation might be demonstrated from Tallis's tune), but if so a delightful one, that one of Vaughan Williams's most haunting themes is essentially Brahms's second subject, 'purified' from the major to the Phrygian mode (Ex. 68). Or is it perhaps a salute?

Ex. 68

If the case of Vaughan Williams shows how a composer could safely invoke Brahmsian models if his subject-matter and national idiom were sufficiently distinctive, that of Elgar begins to suggest how Brahms's influence could be fruitfully absorbed by the generations who finally resolved the Brahms–Wagner antithesis by daring to learn from both masters: as indeed they were virtually forced to, if their interests lay elsewhere than the field of music drama. As the nineteenth century drew to its close, the more vigorous creative personalities began to see that the primary problem facing them was how a post-Wagnerian sense of chromatic harmony might be combined with a post-Brahmsian feeling for intricate structure and polyphonic movement.

[5] On this aspect of Vaughan Williams's Fantasia, see Lionel Pike, 'Tallis – Vaughan Williams – Howells' in *Tempo*, 149 (1984), pp. 2–13.

To begin with the individual solutions were by no means even-handed. The music of Max Reger, for example, has an obvious Brahmsian orientation: he clearly followed Brahms's example in his passionate cultivation of chamber music, large-scale variation sets, and the use of strict Baroque forms, but attempted (sometimes with striking success) to graft them onto a yet more complex harmonic idiom. On the other hand Mahler, as we have seen, considered himself principally a disciple of Wagner, whose ideals he developed in symphonic form. His spacious Adagios and Ländler-type scherzi owe much to Bruckner; yet the actual polyphonic texture of his symphonic movements owes little to either of those masters, and in some instances (perhaps the most striking examples are the Finale of the Fifth Symphony and the Rondo-Burleske of the Ninth) approach an intensity and intricacy of contrapuntal working that suggest Brahms in technique, though remaining thoroughly Mahlerian in character. Nor is it difficult to find resemblances in contour in their melodic invention (Mahler always admired the beauty of Brahms's themes, even when he deplored what seemed to him the tiresome manner of their working-out). This was perhaps because their melodic sense was affected by their common interest in folksong and folk-models, which came to interfuse Mahler's 'art music' language with *volkstümlich* character just as deeply as it did Brahms's. As noted in Chapter 6, however, Mahler's response to folksong was more ironic and alienated: indeed his overt, referential use of such 'popular' elements was one of the first critical stumbling-blocks for audiences attempting to come to grips with his symphonies.

A special relation exists between Brahms's music and that of Ferruccio Busoni: because Busoni, more than any composer named so far, shared many of Brahms's musicological interests and attitudes, and was similarly agnostic, subtle-minded, and intellectually inclined. Also, unlike Elgar, Mahler, or Reger, he consciously rejected Wagner, though his music could no more remain entirely free of Wagnerian influence than any music of the late nineteenth and early twentieth centuries.

Busoni's music derives in part from a development of the later works of Liszt; but significantly he began studying Bach while still a child, and absorbed the influence of pre-Classical polyphony very early indeed. Brahms himself provided a third crucial element in his early musical evolution. Busoni was still a child-prodigy pianist–composer when he met Brahms in Vienna in the late 1880s, and the older composer is reputed to have been so impressed that he said 'I will do for Busoni what Schumann did for me', though no Brahmsian version of 'Neue Bahnen' followed. Brahms's keyboard manner is digested and partly reproduced in Busoni's impressive set of six Etudes, op. 16, written in

1883 and dedicated to Brahms. It is here that his piano technique begins to acquire the dark, heavy chording, the richly resonant use of the bass registers, that is the colouristic antithesis of what he learned from Liszt and is exploited throughout much of his mature piano music.[6] Op. 16 was swiftly followed by the even larger *Etude in Form von Variationen*, op. 17, also dedicated to Brahms, and it was as a composer of variations that Busoni began his personal development of the Brahmsian legacy, notably in his Variations and Fugue (*'in freier Form'*) on Chopin's C minor Prelude, op. 22, whose principal model would appear to be Brahms's 'Handel' Variations. Though still a derivative work, Busoni's 'Chopin' Variations stands at the beginning of the process that was to lead to his *Fantasia Contrappuntistica* of 1910 – a comprehensive polyphonic masterpiece, containing within itself a completion of the unfinished fugue from Bach's *Die Kunst der Fuge*, that would have fascinated Brahms. In Busoni's piano studies and his editions and piano transcriptions of Bach, he trod paths on which Brahms had preceded him, but Busoni went much further. He also – as the *Fantasia Contrappuntistica* illustrates – went as far as to incorporate 'transcriptions' into his 'original' works, and transferred to instrumental music the chorale techniques which Brahms had exploited more in his choral compositions.

Although in later years Busoni tended to speak rather slightingly of Brahms as a composer, and to discount his influence, Brahms's B flat Piano Concerto was clearly one of the principal progenitors of his own gigantic C major Concerto of 1903, and only the previous year he had performed a very special Brahmsian 'homage' by providing sensitive piano transcriptions of six of Brahms's op. 122 Chorale Preludes for simultaneous publication along with the organ originals. Moreover, while a Brahmsian sense of sonority in relation to structure remained a vital element of Busoni's keyboard writing, Brahms's motivic preoccupations with chains of thirds (in the Fourth Symphony, *Vier ernste Gesänge*, and elsewhere) became a Busonian preoccupation as well, ever more entwined in the musical symbolism that finally gave birth to his potent masterwork, the opera *Doktor Faust*.

In 1896, the same year that Brahms and Mahler disputed the

---

[6] Brahms's characteristic piano writing naturally exercised a continuing fascination upon succeeding generations of composer–pianists. Even a composer so seemingly distant from the Austro-German tradition as Percy Grainger acknowledged Brahms's influence, citing for instance the 1894 folksong setting *Du mein einzig Licht* as a direct model for his *Sussex Mummer's Christmas Carol*. Grainger recorded a superb performance of Brahms's F minor Piano Sonata, and towards the end of his life made 'simplified' and 'less simplified' versions of part of the 'Paganini' Variations.

significance of 'the last wave', Brahms's attention was attracted by a Trio in D minor for clarinet, cello and piano composed, in obvious but highly gifted emulation of his own Clarinet Trio, by the twenty-four-year-old Alexander von Zemlinsky, who had studied at the Gesellschaft der Musikfreunde and was now a member of the Tonkünstlerverein (of which Brahms was honorary president). Brahms not only gave Zemlinsky advice but, in one of his last acts of generosity to a young musician, induced Simrock to publish the Trio and its equally impressive successor, the First String Quartet. Until recently Zemlinsky was a practically forgotten and unknown composer, so this fact was of very little interest. But his critical stock has appreciated sharply in the last decade or so, and he must now be generally regarded as at least a minor master, and a significant linking figure between Brahms and the man whose brother-in-law and sole teacher he became: Arnold Schoenberg. Zemlinsky's Clarinet Trio is not merely derivative. Its large structures are handled with skill, it attempts (with considerable success) the kind of subtle thematic integration Brahms practised in his latest works, and it even wittily and gracefully reproduces his 'gypsy' manner in its Finale. A year later Zemlinsky completed his Second Symphony – a far lesser example of the genre than Brahms's Fourth, but perhaps the first to follow in Brahms's footsteps with a finale in passacaglia form. Six years further on he produced a far more significant piece in what had been the 'New German' form *par excellence*, the symphonic poem *Die See-jungfrau* – yet he told Schoenberg that he was composing it 'in the spirit of Brahms'. For the time, this was a paradoxical statement, and superficially the work (which is indeed symphony-sized, in three separate movements) seems to owe far more to Strauss and Mahler in its lavish and colourful orchestration. But Zemlinsky seems to have recognized that to retain a convincing musical form, even 'programmatic' works now needed to manifest the subtle and far-reaching structural unity that characterized Brahms's compositions; and he extended this principle further, into his operas, thus to some extent fulfilling Schoenberg's prophecy that Brahmsian techniques had a potentially important role to play in the development of music drama.

But it was Schoenberg himself who accomplished the most radical application of Brahmsian principles to new musical conditions. This may sound a perverse claim. Surely it was Schoenberg who, by his advance into the realm of 'atonality' in the early years of the twentieth century, and his subsequent creation of a 'method of composition with twelve notes related only to one another', made the two decisive breaks with musical language as previously understood? Compared to that, surely the 'revolution' initiated by the 'New Germans' Wagner and Liszt was a mild deviation from Classical tradition. Yet Schoenberg and his followers – the so-called 'Second Viennese School'[7] – were nothing if not traditionalists: they merely maintained that tradition could not be kept alive unless its implications were recognized, acted upon, and pursued to their logical conclusions.

Schoenberg discovered many of these implications in Brahms. His oft-repeated assertion that his development was not just the result of an irresistible creative necessity, but the logical next step in the evolving musical language, found acceptance only slowly outside his own circle. His music is still often seen as a phenomenon without a past, or only as an extreme end-point, perhaps an intellectual extrapolation, of the highly emotional late-Romanticism of Wagner, Strauss and Mahler. Although these composers did strongly influence Schoenberg, especially in such early works as the *Gurrelieder* and the symphonic poem *Pelleas und Melisande*, that does not explain how the essentially *polyphonic* language of twelve-note music could have arisen out of the essentially *harmonic* one of post-Wagnerian chromaticism: or indeed why the works mentioned already utilize many contrapuntal devices that were to become characteristic of twelve-note usage.

Schoenberg's pupil Alban Berg gave a good, if provocative answer to that question when he took the assessment of J. S. Bach in Riemann's *Musiklexicon* ('belongs with equal right to the period of polyphonic music, of the contrapuntal, imitative style that lay behind him, and to the period of harmonic music') and rewrote it to apply to Schoenberg ('belongs with equal right to the period of harmonic style that lay behind him, and of the contrapuntal, imitative style that sets in again with him'). The idea of an antithesis between harmonic and contrapuntal ways of composing is of course a drastic over-simplification, but using those terms with proper caution it becomes apparent that Berg's definition of Schoenberg's special role in musical history might equally apply directly to Brahms, who had already renewed the function of the 'contrapuntal, imitative style' even as the post-Classical 'harmonic style' (in which, for the sake of argument, we may include Wagner) was at its height (see p. 386).

Born in 1874 before Brahms had completed his First Symphony,

---

[7]The term seems only to be used in English-speaking countries. It is a moot point whether there ever was a 'First Viennese School', though the term employed in Austria and Germany, 'Wiener Schule' or 'Neue Wiener Schule', seems to have arisen by analogy with the group of very early symphonic composers who operated in Vienna in the mid-eighteenth century, such as Monn, Vanhal and Wagenseil. It has no connection to the great Classical trinity: Mozart and Beethoven were not Haydn's disciples in the sense that Berg and Webern were Schoenberg's.

Schoenberg was still a child when Wagner died; whereas, throughout his adolescence and early twenties in his native Vienna, Brahms was an ever-present public figure. It was Brahms, above all, who represented the 'new music' that was evolving in Schoenberg's immediate vicinity, as the leading practitioner of the art of subtle and long-ranging transformation of musical ideas, the technique which Schoenberg himself was later to call 'developing variation'. 'In my youth', he once wrote,

> living in the proximity of Brahms, it was customary that a musician, when he heard a composition for the first time, observed its construction, was able to follow the elaboration and derivation of its themes and its modulations, and could recognize the number of voices in canons and the presence of a theme in a variation... That is what music critics like Hanslick, Kalbeck, Heuberger... and amateurs like the renowned physician Billroth were able to do.[8]

The implication is that hearing and studying Brahms's late works, as they appeared, shaped Schoenberg's own awareness of what music should be; and indeed the features he lists are precisely those that he considered important for his own compositions.

Unlike his friend Zemlinsky, the virtually self-taught Schoenberg lacked the proper connections to meet Brahms, but he admired him intensely from afar. Only a few months after Brahms's death he scored his first public success with a String Quartet in D major (owing debts in about equal measure to Brahms and Dvořák) performed under the aegis of the Tonkünstlerverein and extravagantly praised by no less a Brahmsian than Hanslick. It is fascinating to learn that Brahms had, in fact, seen the score, possibly the last piece of new music he ever studied:

> When Zemlinsky... showed Brahms [Schoenberg's] String Quartet (in D), Brahms, who was usually uninterested in musical beginners, began to display some interest. He inquired about this Schoenberg, and when Zemlinsky informed him that since the age of 18 Schoenberg had been earning his bread by writing and copying-work, to Zemlinsky's astonishment, Brahms offered to pay the money to enable Schoenberg to attend the Vienna Conservatoire. That was the greatest honour that Schoenberg ever experienced in his life. But Schoenberg would not accept a loan.[9]

Forty years later, Schoenberg produced a superb musical homage to Brahms in his lovingly virtuosic orchestral transcription of the G minor Piano Quartet, op. 25. Ten years after that came an even more

---

[8] Arnold Schoenberg, 'New Music, Outmoded Music, Style and Idea', English-language version (1946) of a lecture given in Prague in 1933; cited here from the 2nd ed. of *Style and Idea* (London, 1975), pp. 120–21.

[9] Hanns Eisler, *Materialen zu einer Dialektik der Musik* (Leipzig, 1973), p. 206.

significant tribute: the essay to which he gave the deliberately controversial title 'Brahms the Progressive'[10] – a statement of his view of Brahms's unique importance as the creator of 'great innovations in musical language'. Though sometimes tendentiously selective in its arguments, and partly intended as a justification of the principles underlying his own musical evolution, Schoenberg's essay remains a landmark in the understanding of Brahms, and dealt a body-blow to the conventional estimation of Brahms as the conservative antipope to Wagner.

On his own admission Schoenberg was a 'Brahmsian' before he met Zemlinsky, and it was in fact Zemlinsky who opened his eyes to the virtues of the 'New Germans', whose programmatic principles and treatment of instruments were thoroughly absorbed in his first masterpiece, the string sextet *Verklärte Nacht*. But the very idea of using a chamber ensemble for a 'programmatic' composition was a new departure showing adherence to a Brahmsian medium, and Schoenberg himself long afterwards pointed to the work's use of 'Brahms's technique of developing variation . . . Also to Brahms must be ascribed the imparity of measures'[11] (phrases with an odd number of bars, including half-bars). It is difficult to escape the conclusion that Brahms was Schoenberg's first artistic father-figure (briefly to be succeeded by Mahler, after which no further father-figure was necessary).

Indeed, Brahms and Schoenberg clearly shared a common attitude of responsibility to the musical material they worked with, and a common tenor of musical thinking: and it is arguable that, by absorbing Brahms's innovations at a profounder level than any of his contemporaries, Schoenberg was enabled to transform his own musical language rather than imitate a stylistic model. What he considered he had learned from Brahms he set out in the quotation given at the head of this chapter. But (to judge from many other writings) what he most admired in Brahms were his inexhaustible variety of phrase-lengths; his immense contrapuntal and rhythmic, indeed polyrhythmic, skill; his mastery of the techniques of variation, not only in formal variation sets but in 'developing variation' of motifs as a continuous compositional texture; and the concomitant ability – well illustrated in the symphonies and string quartets – to evolve themes, periods, and structures out of the smallest motivic units, providing whole movements or even works

---

[10] It was originally written as a Brahms birth centenary lecture delivered on Frankfurt Radio in February 1933, and reformulated in English in 1947 for the fiftieth anniversary of his death. Currently it is available in the 2nd ed. of *Style and Idea* (London, 1975), pp. 398–441.

[11] 'My Evolution', article in English dated 1949; quoted from the 2nd ed. of *Style and Idea* (London, 1975), p. 80.

with what Schoenberg termed a 'subcutaneous' organic unity. None of these traits is original to Brahms – they are features that he himself found in the Classical and pre-Classical masters, rescued and refined – but his music presents them all in highly developed forms, more central to (and consciously a part of) his discourse than they had been in earlier composers. They became the life-blood of Schoenberg's music: principles that allowed it to function despite his far more dissonant harmonic language. Significantly, works such as Brahms's *Vier ernste Gesänge* provide examples of simultaneous motivic elaboration in melodic and harmonic spheres (see Ex. 64e) that can be interpreted as direct forerunners of Schoenberg's serial method, whereby all themes, motives, and harmonies in a piece spring from the permutations of a single fixed series of notes. It could be said that the ultimate source of such an attitude is the cantus firmus technique of medieval and Renaissance composers, which stand in an obvious relationship (mediated through the Bachian chaconne) to a movement such as the passacaglia of Brahms's Fourth Symphony; and which undergoes more flexible and wide-ranging transformation in Brahms's use of the descending-thirds chain to haunt so much of the symphony as a cantus firmus of a ghostlier kind, thus creating a large-scale yet allusive unity between the work's four movements. It was in such ways that Schoenberg felt Brahms had extended the versatility of musical language itself.

Some writers have complained of the 'narrowness' of Schoenberg's outlook, asserting that he takes insufficient account of the binding unity that Brahms's tonal harmony provides for his intricate motivic developments. But while it is true that in 'Brahms the Progressive' Schoenberg discussed Brahms's thematic working and melodic asymmetries in virtual isolation, he was certainly well aware of the properties of Brahmsian harmony, many passages of which are penetratingly analysed as models in his textbook *Structural Functions of Harmony* (posthumously published 1954). On the contrary, Schoenberg was fascinated by the tonal language of Brahms's music, and especially the freedom and fluidity of the harmonic relationships he could create or suggest within a relatively small compass. Far from ignoring this aspect, it is more likely that he viewed it as a further justification for the totally chromatic idiom he adopted around 1908–9 and later rationalized through the twelve-note method; for he never ceased to maintain that this was not 'atonality' but a natural further stage in the development of tonality itself, one in which the maximum number of harmonic relations were suggested in the minimum possible space.

Veneration of Brahms became an article of faith among the 'Second Viennese School', who were always acutely aware of the need to explain how their music grew naturally out of the existing Austro-German traditions. We have noted (on p. 290) Anton Webern's admiration for the *Gesang der Parzen*; in the same series of lectures he observed: 'Brahms is a much more interesting example than, for instance, Wagner. In Wagner, harmony is of the greatest importance, but Brahms is in fact richer in harmonic relationships'. Webern's own op. 1, the Passacaglia for orchestra, is clearly inspired by the Finale of Brahms's Fourth Symphony, and almost certainly it was the complex, multi-functional forms of some of Brahms's movements which prompted Webern to synthesize Classical formal principles with polyphonic structures – for instance in the first movement of his op. 21 Symphony, which is at once a ternary form and a four-voice canon, or the Finale of his op. 28 String Quartet, which is both a scherzo and a fugue.

A very different Schoenberg pupil, the committed Marxist Hanns Eisler, absorbed the precepts of his master's twelve-note method and made intermittent use of it: but for his mass choruses and political songs he needed a much more direct, diatonically simple idiom. It seems to me demonstrable that one of his chief models for this was Brahms's approach to the strophic *Volkslied*, though one must of course relate Eisler's works to the broader *volkstümlich* tradition within German music. Even Eisler's most truculent political ballads display a Brahmsian refinement and subtlety of construction, and he certainly added to the Brahmsian tradition of formal exploration in casting his 1936 Brecht cantata, *Gegen den Krieg*, as a large-scale set of theme and variations for unaccompanied chorus.

Eisler is one of those composers – Hindemith and Kurt Weill were others – whose music represented a reaction againt the more self-indulgent and overblown forms of late Romanticism. Partly of course they were affected by the 'neo-Classicism' of Stravinsky, whose slogan of 'Back to Bach!' appeared to overleap Brahms, and indeed the Classical tradition entirely; yet consciously or unconsciously their ideals and methods aligned them with the 'archaizing' aspect of Brahms's achievement. Hindemith's attempted presentation of himself as a neo-Baroque composer, producing works 'for everyday use' in all the main instrumental forms, employing a severely polyphonic language with many canons, fugues and passacaglias, and making 'much of little' through rigorous development of limited basic material, is no direct emulation of Bach, but of Bach understood through the medium and precedent of Brahms (and indeed of Reger).

Although the reputations of Weill and Eisler have been rising steadily in recent years, and that of Hindemith, once so celebrated for his 'modernism', may rise again, it was the 'post-Webernian' developments from the twelve-note method which appeared to represent the new avant-garde orthodoxy in the years after World War II. The 'total serialism' of Stockhausen and Boulez – which sought to derive not just melody and harmony, but rhythm, dynamics, structural proportions, tempi, register, and even instrumentation from the premises of a single note-row – was justified by them, and by associated theorists, as an extrapolation from Webern's musical language: one that Webern, had he lived, was unlikely to have recognized or approved, not least because of its total lack of historical perspective. Yet if we restore that perspective, admitting (as the 1950s Darmstadt avant garde seemed incapable of doing) that Webern's own music rested on a solid foundation of Austro-German tradition (was, indeed, simply the 'last wave' on Mahler's stream) – then we may see that 'total serialism' was in a curious way the pseudo-logical extreme (arrived at via Schoenberg and Webern) of Brahms's concern with structural unity, with 'pure' music that secures organic cohesion through development, by harmonic and polyphonic variation, of the smallest basic motifs. The first movement of Brahms's Second Symphony and (say) Stockhausen's *Kontrapunkte* have perhaps much more in common than meets the eye or ear.

Nevertheless the highly restrictive nature of 'total serialism' is ironic, considering that Schoenberg's view in 'Brahms the Progressive' was that Brahms had inaugurated 'a development of the musical language towards an unrestricted, though well-balanced presentation of musical ideas'. The retreat from 'total serialism', which represented a historical moment impossible to sustain, has indeed been in 'unrestricted' directions – but towards a 'post-modern' cultural pluralism to which Brahms has seemed to have little direct relevance except as symbol of nostalgia for a less confusing tonal past. Yet some of his characteristic gestures have continued to haunt composers who may at first appear to have little in common with him. The tremendous opening of the First Symphony, with its long melodic line struggling to rise against the fateful beat of the timpani, is one such powerful auditory image – surely being re-created in personal terms at the beginning of Carl Ruggles's tone-poem *Sun-Treader* (1932), and very differently at the start of Bernd Alois Zimmermann's opera *Die Soldaten* (1960).

With his highly Expressionist creative stance, uncompromising use of collage techniques and fascination with jazz, Zimmermann might seem about as far removed from Brahms as it is possible to be while still remaining within the overall Austro-German tradition; yet his last work, the deeply pessimistic Cantata *Ich wandte mich, und sahe* (1970), on the same text as the second of the *Vier ernste Gesänge*, affirms Brahmsian roots even as it agonizingly deconstructs the basis of its musical dialectic.

416

Meanwhile, in the USA, Brahmsian precept seems to stand behind not only the steely polyphony of Ruggles but the 'metrical modulation' techniques of Elliott Carter, which might be considered a systematization of the accentual and polyrhythmic complexities which flow with such naturalness in Brahms's discourse. Carter, moreover, is supremely a contextual composer, in whose music all elements are essentially defined in relation to all the others: a principle which operates in Brahms to stronger effect than any composer before him.

Even today, erstwhile members of the avant garde feel compelled to make an occasional 'Homage to Brahms', as György Ligeti has subtitled his Horn Trio. Luciano Berio has orchestrated the F minor Clarinet Sonata as a Concerto, reverently securing an astonishingly authentic Brahmsian orchestral sound except where he has unwisely added some introductory bars in what he imagines to be Brahmsian style. Even Mauricio Kagel, a master of absurdist music-theatre, has produced his own eccentric orchestral version of the 'Handel' Variations. Too much time has passed for Brahms to seem 'conservative' any more; his music continues to have relevance because of the way he faced problems that all composers with a sense of history and stylistic awareness must face. It has become inescapable, interwoven into the very fabric of musical history.

Brahms therefore is not 'the last of the Caesars'. He is something greater. He is Janus (Johannes?), the spirit of beginnings and endings, who looks both ways at once, to the past and to the future. His keenly developed historical sense made him aware of the irrecoverability of the past, yet his strong imaginative identification with aspects of earlier music conditioned his approach to creating for his own times, and made him in truth the first of the moderns. But all issues of old and new apart, Brahms ranks as the peer of Beethoven, Bach, Mozart, and Schubert because like them he shows to the highest degree what may be done with musical ideas – how they may simultaneously be developed in the manner of the highest philosophical truth, and reflect a profound humanity.

> Here they talk and talk; he is silent. There the almighty racket of oh-so progressive and fine-sounding theories. Here active silence, silent action. There chatter about the future; here action in the interest of maintaining the future. (Nothing says more for the importance of Schoenberg's mind than the fact that he found the connection from Wagner to Brahms.) Brahms knew what Goethe knew: that there can be no development without man, beyond man. As a result he became the arch-enemy of all illusions.[12]

[12] Furtwängler, op. cit., p. 212.

417

Appendix A

Calendar

Year	Age	Life	Contemporary musicians and events
1833	0	Johannes Brahms born 7 May at no. 24 Specksgang (later no. 60 Speckstrasse), in the Gängeviertel district of Hamburg, son of Johann Jakob Brahms (27), town musician, and Johanna Henrike Christiana Nissen (44), seamstress. Baptized 26 May at the Michaeliskirche.	Borodin born 12 November. Alkan aged 19, Auber 51, Balfe 25, Bellini 32, Berlioz 30, Bronsart von Schellendorf 3, Bruckner 9, Bülow 3, Burgmüller 23, Cherubini 73, Chopin 23, Chrysander 7, Cornelius 9, Czerny 42, David 23, Dietrich 3, Donizetti 36, Erkel 23, Field 51, Franck 11, Franz 18, Gade 16, Pauline Garcia (later Viardot-Garcia) 11, Glinka 30, Goldmark 3, Gounod 15, Grädener 21, Henselt 18, Hiller 22, Hummel 55, Joachim 2, Kalkbrenner 48, Kiel 12, Kirchner 10, Liszt 22, Litolff 15, Loewe 37, Lortzing 30, Macfarren 20, Marschner 38 (*Hans Heiling* prod. 24 May), Fanny Mendelssohn 27, Felix Mendelssohn 24 (writes 'Italian' Symphony), Meyerbeer 42, Moscheles 40, Nicolai 23, Nottebohm 16, Offenbach 14, Onslow 49, Paganini 42, Pierson 18, Potter 41, Raff 11, Reicha 63, Reinecke 9, Rosenhain 19, Rossini 41, Rubinstein 3, Schumann 23 (writes 2nd set of 'Paganini' Studies), Smetana 9, Spohr 49, Spontini 59, Johann Strauss (I) 29, Johann Strauss (II) 8, Thalberg 21, Verdi 20,

Brahms

Year	Age	Life	Contemporary musicians and events
			Volkmann 18, Wagner 20, Samuel Wesley 67, Clara Wieck 13, Zuccalmaglio 30. Marxsen (27) gives his first concert in Hamburg. Kaspar Hauser dies, 17 Dec.
1834	1		Ponchielli born, 31 Aug., Reubke born, 23 Mar. Berlioz (31), *Harold in Italy*; Schumann (21) founds *Neue Zeitschrift für Musik* and writes 1st version of *Etudes Symphoniques*; Winterfeld's *Gabrieli* published.
1835	2	Brother Friedrich (Fritz) born, 26 March	Bellini (34) dies, 24 Sept., Cui born 18 Jan., Draeseke born 7 Oct., Ebenezer Prout born 1 Mar., Saint-Saëns born 9 Oct. Schumann (25), *Carnaval*; Clara Wieck (15), Piano Concerto.
1836	3		Burgmüller (26) dies 7 May, Delibes born 21 Feb., Reicha (66) dies 28 May. Schumann (26), Fantasy in C and *Kreisleriana*; Clara Wieck (16) plays her *Hexentanz* to Chopin (26)
1837	4	The family moves to no. 38 Ulricusstrasse	Balakirev born 2 Jan., Field (55) dies 23 Jan., Hummel (59) dies 17 Oct., Jensen born 12 Jan., Samuel Wesley (71) dies 11 Oct. Berlioz (34), *Grande Messe des Morts*. Chopin (27) publishes op. 25 *Etudes*; Schumann (27) the *Davidsbündlertänze*.
1838	5		Bizet born 25 Oct., Bruch born 6 Jan. Alkan (24) publishes *Trois Grandes Etudes*. Vol. I of the Kretzschmer/ Zuccalmaglio *Deutsche Volkslieder* appears.
1839	6	Begins to learn music from his father. Attends the	Gernsheim born 17 July, Mussorgsky born 21 Mar.,

420

Year	Age	Life	Contemporary musicians and events
		Privatschule of Heinrich Friedrich Voss in the Dammthorwall.	Rheinberger born 17 Mar. Chopin (29) publishes the 24 Preludes.
1840	7	Continues studies with father as training for an orchestral player's career.	Goetz born 17 Dec., Paganini (58) dies 27 May, Svendsen born 3 Sept., Tchaikovsky born 7 May. Schumann (30) composes *Frauenliebe und –leben* and marries Clara Wieck (20).
1841	8	Begins piano lessons with Otto Cossel (28)	Chabrier born 18 Jan., Dvořák born 8 Sept., Pedrell born 19 Feb., Sgambati born 28 May, Spitta born 7 Dec., Tausig born 4 Nov. Gade (24), 'Ossian' Overture; Schumann (31), 'Spring' Symphony; Wagner (28), *Der fliegende Holländer*. Ludwig Feuerbach (37) publishes *Das Wesen des Christentums*.
1842	9	The family moves to no. 29 Dammthorwall, while Cossel (29) takes over the rooms in Ulricusstrasse. A great fire (8 May) destroys much of the old town.	Boito born 24 Feb., Cherubini (82) dies 15 Mar., Massenet born 12 May, Sullivan born 13 May. Mendelssohn (33), 'Scottish' Symphony.
1843	10	First appearance as pianist (at private benefit concert) leads to offer of American tour. Cossel (30) induces Eduard Marxsen (37) to intervene and take Brahms for advanced study.	Grieg born 15 June, Herzogenberg born 10 June.
1844	11	Attends secondary school. Plays (improvises?) a piano sonata of his own to Louise Japha (18)	Rimsky-Korsakov born 18 Mar. Henselt (30), Piano Concerto. Wagner (31), *Tannhäuser*. Nietzsche born 15 Oct.
1845	12	Now entirely a pupil of Marxsen (39)	Fauré born 12 May, Widor born 24 Feb. Mendelssohn (36), Violin Concerto.
1846	13	Studying theory and composition with Marxsen, earns money playing in	Brüll born, 7 Nov. Berlioz (43), *La Damnation de Faust*; Clara Schumann (26), Piano Trio;

Year	Age	Life	Contemporary musicians and events
		dockside *Animierlokale*.	Robert Schumann (36), Symphony no. 2 in C.
1847	14	His health impaired, he spends the summer at Winsen an der Lühe, where he conducts a male-voice choir. First public concert, 20 Nov.	Fuchs born 15 Feb., Augusta Holmès born 10 Dec., Mackenzie born 22 Aug., Fanny Mendelssohn (41) dies 17 May, Felix Mendelssohn (38) dies 4 Nov. Liszt (36), *Magyar Dallók*. Alkan (34) publishes *Grande Sonate* and 12 *Etudes dans les tons majeures*.
1848	15	Hears Joachim (17) play Beethoven Violin Concerto in Hamburg, 11 Mar. Spring in Winsen. First solo concert (21 Sept.) includes a Bach fugue.	Donizetti (51) dies 8 Apr., Duparc born 21 Jan., Parry born 27 Feb.
1849	16	Second solo concert includes Beethoven's 'Waldstein' Sonata and his own *Phantasie über einem beliebten Walzer* (14 Apr.). Takes some piano pupils and starts writing potpourris for Cranz as 'G. W. Marks'.	Chopin (39) dies 17 Oct., Kalkbrenner (64) dies 10 June, Nicolai (39) dies 11 May, Johann Strauss I (45) dies 25 Sept. Liszt (38), *Totentanz* (first version). Riemann born 18 July.
1850	17	*Souvenir de la Russie*(?) and song composition. Meets Eduard Reményi (20), 14 Aug.; fails to meet the Schumanns (Clara 30, Robert 40) when they visit Hamburg in Dec.	Fibich born 21 Dec., Henschel born 18 Feb., F. X. Scharwenka born 6 Jan. Liszt (39) completes the first 'symphonic poem', *Ce qu'on entend sur la montagne*; Schumann, 'Rhenish' Symphony.
1851	18	More studies and hack-work. Composes Scherzo in E flat minor, which he plays to Litolff (33); also songs and first attempts at chamber music, some played at a private concert with Gade (34) on 5 July.	d'Indy born 27 Mar., Lortzing (48) dies, 21 Jan., Spontini (77) dies 14 Jan. Verdi (38), *Rigoletto*. Liszt (40) starts issuing the Hungarian Rhapsodies.
1852	19	F sharp minor Piano Sonata (op. 2) and more songs.	Stanford born 30 Sept. First volume of the Bach-Gesellschaft edition published. Messager born 30 Dec., Onslow (69) dies 3 Oct. Liszt
1853	20	C major Piano Sonata (op. 1). Concert tour with Reményi	

Year	Age	Life	Contemporary musicians and events
		(23) in Apr.–May; performs the 'transposition feat' at Celle on 2 May. Meets Joachim (22) in Hanover and Liszt (42) at Weimar (12 June), with Cornelius (29) and Raff (31). June–Aug. with Joachim at Göttingen. Walking tour of the Rhineland in Sept., making new friends at Bonn. Visits Hiller (42) and Reinecke (29) at Cologne. 30 Sept. to Düsseldorf, where Robert (43) and Clara (33) Schumann welcome him into their circle. Collaborates with Schumann and Dietrich (24) on 'F-A-E' Sonata. Returns to Göttingen. Schumann hails Brahms in 28 Oct. issue of *Neue Zeitschrift für Musik*. To Leipzig (mid-Nov.) where he meets Moscheles (60), David (43), Grimm (26) and Berlioz (50), and has opp. 1, 3 and 6 published in Dec. Christmas in Hamburg.	(42), Piano Sonata in B minor; Clara Schumann (33), Variations on a Theme of Robert Schumann, *Romanzen* and *Jucunde Lieder*; Robert Schumann (43), Violin Concerto.
1854	21	Meets Bülow (24) in Leipzig. Opp. 2, 4 and 5 published. 27 Feb. Schumann (44) tries to drown himself and is confined to Endenich Sanatorium. Brahms returns to Düsseldorf to aid Clara (34). Composes op. 8 Trio, 'Schumann' Variations and other 'Kreisler' piano pieces, op. 10 Ballades; also works on a D minor Symphony. In Dec. visits Hamburg with Clara.	Humperdinck born 1 Sept., Janáček born 4 July, Köselitz (Peter Gast) born 10 Jan. Liszt (43), 'Faust' Symphony; Wagner (41), *Das Rheingold*. The Grimm brothers begin compiling the *Deutsches Wörtbuch*.
1855	22	Lives in Düsseldorf, but makes concert tours with Clara (35) and Joachim (24) as pianist and conductor. The op. 8 Trio is premiered in New York (27 Nov.).	Chausson born 21 Jan., Liadov born 11 May, Röntgen born 9 May.

423

Year	Age	Life	Contemporary musicians and events
1856	23	Continuing concert activity. Meets Rubinstein (26). Stays in Hamburg until Spring and starts counterpoint studies with Joachim, then moves to Bonn to be near Schumann. Works on op. 21/1 Variations, organ pieces, *Missa Canonica*, perhaps A major Trio. Meets Julius Stockhausen (30) and gives concerts with him (May). On Schumann's death returns to Düsseldorf to support Clara; in Sept. they holiday in Switzerland with some of her children and Brahms's sister Elise (25). Returns to Hamburg in Oct., then visits Detmold. Unfinished symphony resolves into a Piano Concerto. C sharp minor Piano Quartet (early form of op. 60) composed. Becomes a subscriber to the Bach-Gesellschaft Edition.	Martucci born 1 Jan., Schumann (46) dies 29 July, Sinding born 11 Jan., Taneiev born 25 Nov. Liszt (45), 'Dante' Symphony; Volkmann (41), 'Handel' Variations; Wagner (43), *Die Walküre*. Heine (59) dies 17 Feb., Freud born 6 May.
1857	24	Composition and teaching in Hamburg. Second Detmold visit (May) leads to court appointment in autumn conducting and teaching piano.	Bruneau born 1 Mar., Czerny (66) dies 15 July, Elgar born 2 June, Glinka (53) dies 15 Feb., Kienzl born 17 Jan. Alkan (43) publishes Cello Sonata and *12 Etudes dans les tons mineurs*. Wagner (44) breaks off work on *Siegfried*.
1858	25	In Hamburg, works on Piano Concerto and Nonet. Summer in Göttingen with Grimm (31), Joachim (27) and Clara (38). First Hungarian Dances, also many folksong arrangements. Becomes deeply attached to Agathe von Siebold. Second autumn in Detmold: *Ave Maria* and *Begräbnisgesang* composed; Piano Concerto rehearsed at Hanover (Mar. and Oct.). Nonet rescored as a	Leoncavallo born 8 Mar., Puccini born 22 June, Reubke (24) dies 3 June, Hans Rott born 1 Aug., Ethel Smyth born 23 Apr. Joachim, Concerto in the Hungarian Manner; Wagner (45), *Wesendonck Lieder*. Chrysander (32) founds the Handel-Gesellschaft Complete Edition (Brahms subscribes from inception.)

Year	Age	Life	Contemporary musicians and events

'symphonic serenade'.

1859	26	Secret engagement to Agathe, soon broken off (Jan.). Piano Concerto no. 1 premièred in Hanover, 22 Jan., repeated in Leipzig and Hamburg; Serenade premièred in Hamburg 28 Mar. Forms and conducts the Hamburger Frauenchor, which premières *Marienlieder* and Psalm 13 (19 Sept.). Last season at Detmold – composes Serenade no. 2 and many vocal works.	Ashton (Algernon) born 9 Dec., Foerster born 30 Dec., Spohr (75) dies 22 Oct. Berlioz (52), *Les Troyens*; Verdi (46), *Un Ballo in Maschera*. Franco-Austrian War in Italy.
1860	27	Leaves Detmold in Jan. for Hamburg; conducts Serenade in A there 10 Feb. Final version of Serenade in D premièred in Hanover, 3 Mar. Press manifesto against 'New German' school published 6 May. June–Aug. in Bonn with Joachim (29); composes Sextet no. 1; meets Fritz Simrock (23) who is to become his publisher and business adviser. Otherwise much occupied with the Frauenchor: op. 17 Partsongs and op. 27 Motets composed.	Albéniz born 29 May, Charpentier born 25 June, Mahler born 7 July, Paderewski born 6 Nov., Reznicek born 4 May, Wolf born 13 Mar.
1861	28	Living in Hamburg, composing and performing. In summer to Hamm. Works on Piano Quartets and 'Handel' Variations, performed by both Brahms and Clara (41) in Hamburg (Nov., Dec.).	Arensky born 11 Aug., Chaminade born 8 Aug., Loeffler born 30 Jan., MacDowell born 18 Dec., Marschner (66) dies 14 Dec., Thuille born 30 Oct.
1862	29	Spring in Hamburg, with concerts in Oldenburg. Works on *Magelone-Lieder*, String Quintet and beginnings of C minor Symphony in summer. In Sept. to Vienna where he gives recitals and makes his base for the winter. Meets new	Debussy born 22 Aug., Delius born 29 Jan., Emmanuel (Maurice) born 2 May, Halévy (62) dies 17 Mar. Bismarck becomes Chief Minister of Prussia.

Brahms

Year	Age	Life	Contemporary musicians and events

friends including Hanslick (37), Nottebohm (45), Pohl (43) and Tausig (21). Stockhausen (36) becomes conductor of the Hamburg Philharmonic.

1863 30 Returns to Hamburg in spring; composes most of *Rinaldo* in summer. Appointed conductor of Vienna Singakademie for one season. First concert (15 Nov.) features Bach, Schumann, Isaac and Beethoven.

Mascagni born 7 Dec., Emanuel Moór born 19 Feb., Pierné born 16 Aug.

1864 31 Piano pupils include Elisabet von Stockhausen (17). Meets Wagner (51) at Penzing, 6 Feb. through mutual friends Tausig (23) and Cornelius (40). On 20 March conducts Bach's Christmas Oratorio, Vienna. In spring resigns from Singakademie. Summer at Lichtenthal with Clara (45); meets Hermann Levi (25), Viardot-Garcia (43) and Turgenev (46). Bases himself in Vienna for winter.

d'Albert born 10 Apr., Meyerbeer (73) dies 2 May, Guy-Ropartz born 15 June, Richard Strauss born 11 June. Bruckner (40), Mass in D minor. Ludwig II crowned King of Bavaria.

1865 32 Brahms's mother dies, 2 Feb. In Vienna, works on *Ein deutsches Requiem*. Summer in Lichtenthal; composes Horn Trio and meets Feuerbach (36). Concert tours in autumn and winter; premières 'Paganini' Variations in Zürich, 25 Nov.

Dukas born 1 Oct., Glazunov born 10 Aug., Magnard born 9 June, Nielsen born 9 June, Sibelius born 8 Dec. Liszt (64), *Missa Choralis*. Première of *Tristan und Isolde* (Munich, 10 June).

1866 33 Brahms festival at Oldenburg (Jan.) with Dietrich (36); visits Switzerland with Joachim (35). Works on *Requiem* at Karlsruhe and Winterthur. Summer near Zürich, where he meets Billroth (37). Sextet no. 2 completed. Back to Vienna in autumn; Christmas at Oldenburg.

Busoni born 1 Apr., Satie born 17 Mar. Bruckner (41), Symphony no. 1 and Mass in E minor; Liszt (55), *Christus*; Smetana (41), *The Bartered Bride*. Austro-Prussian War. Rückert dies.

426

Year	Age	Life	Contemporary musicians and events
1867	34	Concert tours of Austrian provinces in spring and autumn, the latter with Joachim (36). Summer walking tour with father (61) and Gansbacher (38) in Austrian Alps. Three movements of *Requiem* performed in Vienna 1 Dec., without success.	Granados born 27 July, Koechlin born 27 Nov., Sechter (79) dies 10 Sept. Marx (49) publishes vol. I of *Das Kapital*.
1868	35	Tours in Germany and to Copenhagen with Stockhausen (42) in Feb.– Mar. 10 Apr.: *Ein deutsches Requiem* premièred in Bremen Cathedral. At Lower Rhine Festival in Cologne (May); June–July in Bonn; concerts in autumn with Clara (48) and Stockhausen. *Schicksalslied* begun.	Bantock born 7 Aug., Berwald (72) dies 3 Apr., Rossini (76) dies 13 Nov. Max von Schillings born 19 Apr. Grieg (25), Piano Concerto
1869	36	*Rinaldo* premièred in Vienna; final version of *Requiem* in Leipzig (28 Feb.). Summer in Lichtenthal; engagement of Julie Schumann (24) and composition of Alto Rhapsody. Tour to Budapest with Stockhausen. *Liebeslieder* Waltzes composed. Hungarian Dances published. Settles in Vienna, autumn.	Berlioz (66) dies 8 Mar., Dargomizhky (56) dies 17 Jan., Loewe (73) dies 20 Apr., Pfitzner born 5 May, Roussel born 5 Apr. Bruckner (44), F minor Mass; Bruch (31), Violin Concerto no. 1. *Das Rheingold* 1st perf., Munich. Joachim (38) becomes Director of the Berlin Hochschule. Vienna Hofoper opens on the Ringstrasse.
1870	37	Alto Rhapsody premièred in Jena, 3 Mar. In Munich (July) attends performances of *Das Rheingold* and *Die Walküre* (1st production).	Balfe (62) dies 20 Oct., Godowsky born 13 Feb., Lehar born 30 Apr., Mercadente (75) dies 17 Dec., Novak born 5 Dec., Schmitt born 28 Sept. Franco-Prussian War breaks out. Schliemann discovers Troy.
1871	38	First part of *Triumphlied* performed in Bremen (7 Apr.) in memory of war dead. Summer in Lichtenthal, teaching Florence May (26). The *Schicksalslied* premièred in Karlsruhe, 18 Oct. In Dec.	Auber (89) dies 12 May; Stenhammar born 7 Feb., Thalberg (59) dies 27 Apr., Tansig (29) dies 17 July. Verdi (58), *Aida*. Establishment of German Empire under Wilhelm I.

Brahms

Year	Age	Life	Contemporary musicians and events
		moves into Karlsgasse 4 in Vienna, his permanent home.	
1872	39	Brahms's father dies 11 Feb. in Hamburg. Complete *Triumphlied* in Karlsruhe, 5 June. Summer in Baden, where he meets Nietzsche (28). Becomes Director of Gesellschaft der Musikfreunde concerts, following Rubinstein (42). Six concerts per season for next three years (see text for highlights).	Hausegger born 16 Aug., Skriabin born 6 Jan., Vaughan Williams born 12 Oct., Zemlinsky born 4 Oct. Bizet (34), *L'Arlésienne*. Bruckner (48), Symphony no. 2.
1873	40	Completes String Quartets nos. 1 and 2 and Variations on a Theme of Haydn. In Aug. attends Schumann-Festival in Bonn under Joachim (42); visits Vienna World Exhibition in autumn.	Rakhmaninov born 1 Apr., Reger born 19 Mar., Séverac born 20 July. Bruckner (49), Symphony no. 3; Dvořák (32), Symphony no. 3.
1874	41	In Leipzig (Jan.), meets Herzogenberg (31) and wife (27) as well as Spitta (33). Meets Henschel (24) at Lower Rhine Festival in Cologne. Summer near Zürich where becomes friendly with Widmann (32). Completes C minor Piano Quartet, op. 60.	Cornelius (50) dies 26 Oct., Holst born 21 Sept., Ives born 20 Oct., Franz Schmidt born 22 Dec., Schoenberg born 13 Sept., Suk born 4 Jan. Bruckner (50), Symphony no. 4 (1st version); Dietrich (44), Violin Concerto; Liszt (63), *Glocken vom Strassburg*; Mussorgsky (35), *Boris Godunov*; Smetana (50), *Vltava*; Verdi (61), the Requiem.
1875	42	Last Gesellschaft concerts (resigns 18 Apr.). In summer works on Symphony no. 1 in Heidelberg and near Zürich. Becomes aware of Dvořák (34), to whom he directs government grants. Wagner (62) retrieves the MS of *Tannhäuser* from an unwilling Brahms. Estrangement from Levi (36).	Sterndale Bennett (59) dies 1 Feb., Bizet (37) dies 3 June, Coleridge-Taylor born 15 Aug., Glière born 11 Jan., Reynaldo Hahn born 19 Aug., Ravel born 7 Mar., Roger-Ducasse born 18 Apr., Tovey born 17 July. Bizet (37), *Carmen*; Goldmark (45), *Die Königin von Saba*; Tchaikovsky (35), Piano Concerto no. 1. Jung born 26 July.

Year	Age	Life	Contemporary musicians and events
1876	43	Visits Holland, Mannheim, Koblenz Jan.–Feb. Completes Symphony no. 1 in spring and String Quartet no. 3 in summer, on holiday with Henschel (26) at Sassnitz, Isle of Rügen. Symphony no. 1 premièred in Karlsruhe under Dessoff (41) on 4 Nov.; Brahms conducts it in Mannheim and Munich.	Havergal Brian born 29 Jan., Falla born 23 Nov., Goetz (36) dies 3 Dec., Wolf-Ferrari born 12 Jan., Ruggles born 11 Mar. Tchaikovsky (36), *Swan Lake*; Herzogenberg (34), Variations on a Theme of Brahms. First complete *Ring* cycle, Bayreuth, 13–17 Aug.
1877	44	Joachim (46) gives Symphony no. 1 in Cambridge (8 Mar.) after Brahms declines to receive a degree there; the work is afterwards revised. Summer in Pörtschach and Lichtenthal, composing motet *Warum ist das Licht gegeben?* and Symphony no. 2, premièred in Vienna by Hans Richter (34) on 30 Dec.	Dohnányi born 27 July. Saint-Saëns (42), *Samson et Dalila* (prod. Weimar, 2 Dec.); Bruckner (53), Symphony no. 5; Dvořák (36), Symphonic Variations. Böhme publishes his *Altdeutsches Liederbuch*
1878	45	First Italian holiday, April with Billroth (49). Offered post of Thomaskantor, Leipzig. At Pörtschach begins Violin Concerto, continued in consultation with Joachim (47); also op. 76 *Klavierstücke*. Hugo Wolf (18) seeks Brahms's advice on composition; not liking it – Brahms told him to study counterpoint with Nottebohm (61) – he becomes an implacable enemy.	Boughton born 23 Jan., Holbrooke born 6 July, Palmgren born 16 Feb., Schreker born 23 Mar. Tchaikovsky (38), Violin Concerto and Symphony no. 4; Dvořák (37), Slavonic Dances.
1879	46	Violin Concerto premièred in Leipzig, 1 Jan., repeated Vienna 14 Jan. Breslau University awards Brahms an Honorary Doctorate, Mar. Summer in Pörtschach: writes G major Violin sonata and op. 79 Rhapsodies. Tours Hungary, Transylvania and Poland with Joachim (48) in autumn. Wagner (66) attacks	Bridge born 26 Feb., Ireland born 13 Aug., Jensen (42) dies 23 Jan., Karg-Elert born 21 Nov., Respighi born 9 July, Alma Schindler (later Mahler) born 31 Aug., Cyril Scott born 27 Sept. Bruckner (55), String Quintet; Dietrich (50), *Robin Hood* (Brahms attends Frankfurt première); Franck (57), Piano Quintet;

Year	Age	Life	Contemporary musicians and events
		Brahms in 'Über das Dichten und Komponieren'.	Tchaikovsky (39), *Eugene Onegin*. Einstein born 14 Mar.
1880	47	Attends unveiling of Schumann memorial in Bonn, Feb. First summer at fashionable resort of Ischl, where he meets Brüll (34) and J. Strauss II (55) and composes the Tragic and Academic Festival Overtures. Books 3 and 4 of Hungarian Dances published. Serious rift with Joachim (49) over his suit for divorce, owing to Brahms's support for Amalie (41) in private letter of Dec.	Bloch born 24 July, Foulds born 2 Nov., Medtner born 24 Dec., Offenbach (61) dies 5 Oct., F. G. Scott born 25 Mar., Pizzetti born 20 Sept. Mahler (20), *Das klagende Lied*; Dvořák (39), Symphony no. 6; Rott (22), Symphony in E.
1881	48	Academic Festival Overture premièred at Breslau, 4 Jan. Jan. – Feb. tours Holland and Hungary, where he again meets Liszt (70) through the prompting of Bülow (51). Apr.– May, holidays in Italy and Sicily with Billroth (52) and Nottebohm (63). Summer at Pressbaum where he completes *Nänie* in memory of Feuerbach, who had died (50) 10 Jan. 1880, and Piano Concerto no. 2, which he premières in Budapest on 9 Nov. after rehearsals with Bülow's ducal orchestra in Meiningen.	Bartók born 25 Mar., Enescu born 19 Aug., Miaskovsky born 20 Apr., Mussorgsky (42) dies 28 Mar. Bruckner (57), Symphony no. 6; Fauré (36), Ballade.
1882	49	Introduces the new Piano Concerto in many German and Dutch centres on tour. Summer at Ischl; completes C major Piano Trio, F major String Quintet, and *Gesang der Parzen*. Holiday in Italy (Sept.) with Billroth (53), Brüll (36) and Simrock (45). With Nottebohm (64) when he dies in Graz on 29 Oct.	Grainger born 8 July, Kodály born 16 Dec., Malipiero born 18 March, Raff (60) dies 24 June, Stravinsky born 17 June, Szymanowski born 6 Oct. Liszt (71), *Von der Wiege bis zum Grabe*. *Parsifal* premièred at Bayreuth (25 June). Hugo Riemann (33) publishes his *Musiklexicon*.

Year	Age	Life	Contemporary musicians and events
1883	50	Summer in Wiesbaden, where he forms a close attachment to Hermine Spies (26) and completes Symphony no. 3, premièred 2 Dec. in Vienna under Richter (40).	Bax born 8 Nov., Casella born 25 July, Grädener (71) dies 10 June, Hauer born 19 Mar., Varèse born 22 Dec., Wagner (69) dies 13 Feb., Webern born 3 Dec. Bruckner (59), Symphony no. 7; Dvořák (42), *Scherzo Capriccioso*. Karl Marx (65) dies 14 Mar.
1884	51	Spring in Italy; Summer at Mürzzuschlag with Hanslick (59) where he begins Fourth Symphony. Close friendship with the Fellinger family in Vienna begins. Winter tour as pianist and accompanist for Hermine Spies (27).	Griffes born 17 Sept., Rott (25) dies 25 June, Smetana (60) dies 12 May. Bruckner (60), *Te Deum*; Debussy (22), *L'Enfant prodigue*; Mahler (25), *Lieder eines fahrenden Gesellen*. Schütz Edition begins under editorship of Spitta (43).
1885	52	Completes Symphony no. 4 at Mürzzuschlag in summer. Conducts première at Meiningen, 25 Oct., where he meets Richard Strauss (21); then goes on tour with the orchestra. Rift with Bülow (55) over performance in Frankfurt.	Berg born 7 Feb., Butterworth born 12 July, Hiller (73) dies 10 May, Kiel (64) dies 13 Sept., Riegger born 29 Apr., Wellesz born 21 Oct. Dvořák (44), Symphony no. 7; Franck (63), *Variations Symphoniques*; Liszt (73), *Bagatelle without Tonality*; Wolf (25), *Penthesilea*.
1886	53	Summer in Hofstetten near Thun, where Cello Sonata no. 2, Violin Sonata no. 2, and Piano Trio no. 3 are composed. Elected Honorary President of the Wiener Tonkünstlerverein.	Liszt (74) dies, 31 July, Ponchielli (51) dies 17 Jan., Schoeck born 1 Sept. Fauré (41), Requiem; Franck (64), Violin Sonata; Goldmark (46), *Merlin*. Ludwig II of Bavaria dies. Nietzsche (42) writes *Jenseits von Gut und Böse*.
1887	54	Spring holiday in Italy with Simrock (50) and Kirchner (64). Summer at Thun, where he composes *Zigeunerlieder* and Double Concerto, premièred by Joachim (56) and Hausmann (35) in Cologne, 18 Oct. Pohl (67) dies 28 Apr., and is succeeded by Mandyczewski (30) as archivist of the	Van Dieren born, 27 Dec., Borodin (53) dies 28 Feb., Madetoja born 17 Feb., Toch born 7 Dec., Fartein Valen born 25 Aug., Villa-Lobos born 8 Feb. Bruckner (63), Symphony no. 8; Goldmark (47), *Ländliche Hochzeit* Symphony; Verdi (74), *Otello* (prod. 5 Feb.).

431

Year	Age	Life	Contemporary musicians and events
		Gesellschaft der Musikfreunde. Celestine Truxa (??) becomes housekeeper at Karlgasse 4.	
1888	55	Meets Grieg (45) and Tchaikovsky (48), 2 Jan. Spring in Italy with Widmann (46); meets Martucci (32) in Bologna. Summer in Thun, where composes Violin Sonata no. 3.	Alkan (74) dies 29 Mar., Max Butting born 6 Oct., Marxsen (81) dies 18 Nov., Vermeulen born 8 Feb. Franck (66), Symphony in D minor; Satie (22), *Gymnopédies*; Tchaikovsky (48), Symphony no. 5. Wilhelm II becomes German Emperor.
1889	56	Awarded freedom of city of Hamburg, 23 May; composes *Fest- und Gedenksprüche* in response, also op. 110 motets. Summer at Ischl, near Goldmark (59) and J. Strauss II (64). Order of Leopold conferred by Emperor Franz Josef (59). Revises op. 8 Piano Trio.	Henselt (75) dies 10 Oct., Shaporin born 8 Nov. Dvořák (48), Symphony no. 8; Franck (67), String Quartet; Mahler (29), Symphony no. 1; Strauss (25), *Don Juan*. Adolf Hitler born 20 April.
1890	57	Spring holiday in Italy with Widmann (48). Summer at Ischl; composes String Quintet no. 2. Meets Alice Barbi (28).	Franck (67) dies 8 Nov., Gade (73) dies 21 Dec., Ibert born 15 Aug., Frank Martin born 15 Sept., Martinů born 8 Dec., Nyström born 13 Oct. Busoni (24), *Konzertstück*; Strauss (26), *Tod und Verklärung*; Wolf (30), *Spanisches Liederbuch*.
1891	58	Hears Mühlfeld (35) at Meiningen. Visits Berlin in spring. Makes will ('Ischl testament') in May. Composes Clarinet Trio and Quintet. Friendship with Adolph Menzel (76).	Bliss born 2 Aug., Delibes (55) dies 16 Jan., Prokofiev born 13 Apr. Fauré (46), *La Bonne Chanson*; Rakhmaninov (18), Piano Concerto no. 1; Wolf (31), *Italienisches Liederbuch*.
1892	59	Death of Elisabet von Herzogenberg (44), 2 Jan. Spring in Italy. Death of sister Elise (61), June. In Ischl, begins composing piano pieces of opp. 116–19.	Honegger born, 10 Mar., Howells born 17 Oct., Jarnach born 26 July, Kilpinen born 4 Feb., Lalo (69) dies 22 Apr., Milhaud born 4 Sept., Rosenberg born 6 June, Sorabji born 14 Aug. Dvořák (51), Te

Year	Age	Life	Contemporary musicians and events
			Deum; Nielsen (27), Symphony no. 1; Sibelius (27), *Kullervo* and *En Saga* (orig. version).
1893	60	Hermine Spies (36) dies. Holiday in Italy and Sicily (Apr.–May) to avoid sixtieth birthday celebrations, with Widmann (51). Summer at Ischl, working on opp. 118 and 119 *Klavierstücke*.	Erkel (83) dies 15 June, Goossens born 26 May, Gounod (75) dies 18 Oct., Hábá born 21 June, Merikanto (Aare) born 29 June, Tchaikovsky (53) dies 6 Nov. after writing Symphony no. 6. Dvořák (52), Symphony no. 9, 'From the New World'. Verdi (80), *Falstaff*, first perf. 9 Feb.
1894	61	Shaken by deaths of Billroth, Bülow and Spitta. Summer at Ischl, where composes Clarinet Sonatas nos. 1 and 2. Publishes the *Deutsche Volkslieder* in seven volumes. Offered, but refuses, conductorship of the Hamburg Philharmonic. On 21 Dec. accompanies Alice Barbi (32) in her farewell concert.	Bülow (63) dies 12 Feb., Chabrier (53) dies 13 Sept., Heseltine born 30 Oct., Moeran born 31 Dec., Pijper born 8 Sept., Piston born 20 Jan., Rosenhain (81) dies 21 Mar., Rubinstein (64) dies 20 Nov., Spitta (52) dies 13 Apr. Debussy (32), finishes *Prélude à l'après-midi d'un faune*.
1895	62	Tours German cities with Mühlfeld (39) performing the Clarinet Sonatas (Jan. – Feb.) Summer at Ischl. Meiningen Festival of the 'three B's' (Sept.); visits Clara (76) at Frankfurt; then conducts in Zürich.	Castelnuovo-Tedesco born 3 Apr., Hindemith born 16 Nov., Orff born 10 July. Dvořák (54), Cello Concerto; Mahler (35), Symphony no. 2; Puccini (37), *La Bohème*; Rakhmaninov (22), Symphony no. 1; Satie (29), *Messe des pauvres*; Sibelius (30), *Lemminkäinen Legends*; Strauss (31), *Guntram*.
1896	63	Conducts both piano concertos in Berlin (10 Jan.) with d'Albert (32) as soloist. Composes *Vier ernste Gesänge*. Forty-hour journey to Bonn to attend Clara's funeral, 24 May. Summer at Ischl, composing Chorale Preludes for organ. Alarming deterioration in health; goes to Karlsbad to take the waters.	Bruckner (72) dies 11 Oct., leaving Symphony no. 9 unfinished; Gerhard born 25 Sept., Clara Schumann (77) dies 20 May, Sessions born 28 Dec., Thomas (85) dies 12 Feb., Vogel born 29 Feb. Elgar (39), *King Olaf*; Foulds (16) uses quarter-tones in a string quartet; Mahler (36), Symphony no. 3; Nielsen (31),

Brahms

Year	Age	Life	Contemporary musicians and events

Returns to Vienna in Oct. but continues to decline. Attends funeral of Bruckner, 14 Oct.

Hymnus Amoris; Reger (22), Suite for organ, (dedicated to Brahms); Strauss (32), *Also sprach Zarathustra*; Zemlinsky (24), Clarinet Trio (Brahms recommends to Simrock).

1897   63   Revises his will. Last public appearance at a performance of Symphony no. 4 under Richter (54), 7 Mar. After this rapid physical deterioration. Dies in Vienna of cancer of the liver, 3 Apr. Public funeral on 6 Apr.

Cowell born 11 Mar., Korngold born 29 May, Saeverud born 17 Apr. Albéniz aged 37, Arensky 36, Ashton 38, Balakirev 60, Bantock 29, Bartók 16, Bax 13, Berg 12, Bliss 6, Bloch 17, Boito 54, Boughton 19, Brian 21, Bridge 18, Bronsart von Schellendorff 66, Bruch 59, Brüll 50, Busoni 31 (writes Violin Concerto); Butterworth 12, Casella 14, Coleridge-Taylor 22, Cui 62, d'Albert 33, Debussy 35, Delius 35, Dietrich 67, Dohnányi 20, Dukas 32, Duparc 49, Dvořák 56, Elgar 40, Emmanuel 35, Enescu 16, Falla 20, Fauré 52, Fibich 47, Foulds 17, Fuchs 50, Gerhard 1, Gernsheim 58, Glazunov 32, Glière 22, Godowsky 27, Goldmark 66, Grainger 15, Granados 30, Grieg 54, Griffes 13, Hahn 22, Hauer 14, Herzogenberg 54, Hindemith 2, Holbrooke 19, Holmès 50, Holst 23, Honegger 5, Humperdinck 43, d'Indy 46, Ireland 18, Ives 22, Janáček 43, Joachim 66, Karg-Elert 19, Kienzl 40, Kirchner 74, Kodály 14, Koechlin 29, Köselitz 43, Léhar 27, Leoncavallo 39, Liadov 42, Loeffler 36, Magnard 32, Mahler 37, Malipiero 15, Frank Martin 7, Martinů 6, Martucci 41, Mascagni 33, Massenet 55, Medtner 17, Merikanto 4,

Year   Age   Life

Miaskovsky 16, Milhaud 5,
Moór 34, Nielsen 32, Orff 2,
Paderewski 37, Parry 49
(writes *Elegy for Brahms*),
Pedrell 56, Pfitzner 28, Pijper 3,
Piston 3, Pizzetti 17, Prokofiev
6, Prout 62, Puccini 39,
Rackmaninov 24, Ravel 22,
Reger 24, Respighi 18,
Reznićek 37, Rheinberger 58,
Rimsky-Korsakov 53, Röntgen
42, Roussel 28, Ruggles 21,
Saint-Saëns 62, Satie 31,
Scharwenka 47, Schillings 29,
Schindler 18, Schmidt 22,
Schoenberg 23 (writes String
Quartet in D), Schreker 19,
Cyril Scott 18, F. G. Scott 17,
Séverac 24, Sgambati 54,
Sibelius 31, Skriabin 25, E.
Smyth 39, Sorabji 5, Stanford
45, Stenhammar 26, J. Strauss
II 71, R. Strauss 33, Stravinsky
15, Sullivan 55, Szymanowski
15, Thuille 36, Tovey 22, Valen
10, Varèse 11, Vaughan
Williams 25, Verdi 84,
Vermeulen 9, Villa-Lobos 10,
Webern 13, Wellesz 11, Widor
53, Wolf 37, Ysaÿe 39,
Zemlinsky 25.

Appendix B

List of works

Brahms sometimes allowed many years to elapse before committing his works to print, with an inevitably confusing effect upon their chronology. In the following list, works are generally dated by their year(s) of composition, or of publication if this is believed to have followed swiftly on completion of the music; but a separate publication date is given when that was delayed for an appreciable period. Although in Brahms's own lifetime no work reached publication which had not satisfied his own intense self-criticism, numerous items, not all of them minor, have come to light and found their way into print since his death. Several of these were already included in the standard edition of his music, sponsored by the Gesellschaft der Musikfreunde in Vienna, the twenty-six-volume *Johannes Brahms: Sämtliche Werke*, ed. Eusebius Mandyczewski and Hans Gál (Breitkopf & Härtel, 1926–8). More have been discovered since, and the process is unlikely to be at an end. The present catalogue is intended, as far as possible, to bring it up to date. In an attempt to give a fuller picture of Brahms's creativity, it also includes those now-missing works which he did not allow to survive, but of whose one-time existence there is reasonable documentary evidence. Undoubtedly there were many others of which we know nothing. The most compendious listing yet attempted of Brahms's output will be found in D. and M. McCorkle, *Brahms Thematisch-Bibliographisches Werkverzeichnis* (Munich, 1984), a catalogue which, like all others of its kind, must be used with a certain degree of caution. A new critical edition of the complete works is to be published by G. Henle Verlag, Munich under the aegis of the Johannes Brahms Gesamtausgabe e.V., founded there in 1983.

ORCHESTRAL MUSIC

1854–5		Symphony in D minor (unfinished, and lost in this form; only first movement orchestrated; material eventually worked into Piano Concerto no. 1 and *Ein deutsches Requiem*)
1856–9	op. 15	Piano concerto no. 1 in D minor (piano reduction pub. 1861; score pub. 1871)
1859–60	op. 11	Serenade no. 1 in D major (derived from Nonet of 1858; 1859 version for small orchestra lost)
1860	op. 16	Serenade no. 2 (for orchestra without violins; rev. 1875)

1873	op. 56a	Variations on a Theme of Haydn (*Chorale St Antoni*)
1873		Hungarian Dances nos. 1, 3 and 10 (arranged for orchestra)
1862–76	op. 68	Symphony no. 1 in C minor (possibly begun earlier; rev. 1877)
1877	op. 73	Symphony no. 2 in D major
1878	op. 77	Violin Concerto in D major
1879	op. 80	Academic Festival Overture
1880	op. 81	Tragic Overture (on sketches going back to late 1860s)
1880		Overture in F major (lost; probably not completed)
1881	op. 83	Piano Concerto no. 2 in B flat major
1883	op. 90	Symphony no. 3 in F major
1884–5	op. 98	Symphony no. 4 in E minor
1887	op. 102	Double Concerto in A minor for violin, cello and orchestra

CHAMBER MUSIC

	12 Trumpet Studies (late 1840s or early 1850s if genuine, but of doubtful authenticity; pub. 1928)
c1851	Duo for cello and piano (lost)
c1851	Phantasie in D minor for violin, cello and piano (lost)[1]
c1852–3	String Quartet in B flat major (lost)
c1852–3	Violin Sonata in A minor (originally op. 5; lost)
1853	Hymne, 'Zur Verherrlichung des grossen Joachim' (Trio for 2 violins and double bass or cello; pub. 1976)
1853	Scherzo in C minor for violin and piano (for the 'F-A-E' Sonata jointly composed with Schumann and Dietrich; pub. 1906)
1854 op. 8	Trio no. 1 in B major for violin, cello and piano (original version; the work was recomposed 1889, and is almost exclusively known in this later form, pub. 1891)
1855–6	Quartet in C sharp minor for piano, violin, viola and cello (possibly not completed; lost, but material reused in op. 60)
c1856?	Trio in A major for violin, cello and piano (possibly earlier; pub. 1938; authenticity disputed)

[1] This two-movement work is mentioned in correspondence with Joachim and Schumann in late 1853; Schumann suggested it should be published as Brahms's op. 1. It is possible, but by no means certain, that this was the Trio by Brahms performed in 1851 under the pseudonym of 'Karl Würth'.

1858		Nonet in D major for wind and string instruments (early version of Serenade no. 1; lost in this form; conjectural restorations by Jorge Rotter, 1987 and Alan Boustead, 1987
1859–60	op. 18	Sextet no. 1 in B flat major for 2 violins, 2 violas and 2 cellos
?1859–61	op. 25	Quartet no. 1 in G minor for piano, violin, viola and cello
1861–2	op. 26	Quartet no. 2 in A minor for piano, violin, viola and cello
1862		Quintet in F minor for 2 violins, viola and 2 cellos (lost in this form; conjectural restoration by Sebastian Brown pub. 1947)
1864	op. 34	Quintet in F minor for piano, 2 violins, viola and cello (recomposition of 1862 Quintet via Sonata for 2 pianos, op. 34b)
1864–5	op. 36	Sextet no. 2 in G major for 2 violins, 2 violas and 2 cellos
1862–5	op. 38	Cello Sonata no. 1 in E minor
c1862		Adagio for cello and piano (lost; original slow movement of op. 38; copyist's MS last seen in 1930s)
1865	op. 40	Trio in E flat major for violin, horn (or cello, or viola) and piano
c1868–73	op. 51 no. 1	String Quartet no. 1 in C minor[2]
c1868–73	op. 51 no. 2	String Quartet no. 2 in A minor
1875	op. 60	Quartet no. 3 in C minor for piano, violin, viola and cello (radically recomposed version of C sharp minor Quartet of 1855–6)
1876	op. 67	String Quartet no. 3 in B flat major
1879	op. 78	Violin Sonata no. 1 in G major[3] (an arrangement for cello and piano, pub. 1897 and sometimes mistakenly ascribed to Brahms, is the work of Paul Klengel)
1880		Trio in E flat major for piano, violin and cello (one mvt. only; lost)
1882	op. 87	Trio no. 2 in C major for piano, violin and cello
1882–3	op. 88	String Quintet no. 1 in F major for 2 violins, 2 violas and cello (incorporates material from Sarabande no. 2 and Gavotte no. 2 for piano)
1886	op. 99	Cello Sonata no. 2 in F major
1886	op. 100	Violin Sonata no. 2 in A major
1886	op. 101	Trio no. 3 in C minor for piano, violin and cello

[2]Brahms claimed to have composed and destroyed '20 string quartets' prior to the publication of this work.
[3]Brahms composed at least two other, lost sonatas for violin and piano between this work and the early A minor Sonata.

1886–8	op. 108	Violin Sonata no. 3 in D minor
1890	op. 111	String Quintet no. 2 in G major for 2 violins, 2 violas and cello
1891	op. 114	Trio in A minor for clarinet (or viola), cello and piano
1891	op. 115	Quintet in B minor for clarinet (or viola), and string quartet
1894	op. 120 no. 1	Sonata no. 1 in F minor for clarinet (or viola) and piano (also revision for violin and piano, 1895)
1894	op. 120 no. 2	Sonata no. 2 in E flat major for clarinet (or viola) and piano (also revision for violin and piano, 1895)

PIANO MUSIC

(Solo piano unless otherwise indicated; 'piano duet' signifies four hands at one piano)

1844		Piano Sonata (possibly in G minor; lost)[4]
1849		*Phantasie über eine geliebten Walzer* (lost)
c1850		*Souvenir de la Russie* (fantasy-transcriptions on Russian and Bohemian airs, for piano duet; pub. as 'op. 151' by 'G. W. Marks')
		1 *Hymne national russe de Lvoff*; 2 *Chansonette de Titoff*; 3 *Romance de Warlamoff*; 4 *'Le Rossignol' de A. Alabieff*; 5 *Chant bohémien*; 6 *'Koca' – chant bohémien*
1851	op. 4	Scherzo in E flat minor
1852	op. 2	Piano Sonata no. 2 in F sharp minor
1852–3	op. 1	Piano Sonata no. 1 in C major[5]
1853	op. 20 no. 2	Variations on a Hungarian song (pub. 1861)
c1853		*Rákóczi-Marsch* arrangement (Aug. at latest; unpub. and no longer complete)
1853	op. 5	Piano Sonata no. 3 in F minor
1854		Sonata in D minor for 2 pianos (unfinished and lost; became basis of D minor Symphony)
1854		*Blätter aus dem Tagebuch eines Musikers* (by 'Johannes Kreisler Junior', Volume I; lost)[6]
		1 *Menuett oder?* in A flat minor; 2 *Scherzino oder?* in B minor; 3 *Piece* in D minor; 4 *Andenken an M.*[endelssohn] *B.*[artholdy] in B minor
1854	op. 9	Variations on a Theme of Schumann

[4] Louise Japha claimed that such a work was played to her by Brahms at the age of eleven. He may, of course, have improvised it.

[5] At least two other sonatas preceded opp. 1 and 2; the former is designated '*Vierte Sonate*' in the MS.

[6] Volume II, also lost, is known to have included the op. 9 'Schumann' Variations and possibly Sarabande no. 1.

Brahms

1854	op. 10	4 Ballades (pub. 1856)
		1 in D minor; 2 in D major; 3 in B minor; 4 in B major
1854–5		2 Gavottes (pub. 1979)[7]
		1 in A minor; 2 in A major
1854–5		2 Sarabandes (pub. 1917)
		1 in A major; 2 in B minor
1855		2 Gigues (pub. 1927)
		1 in A minor; 2 in B minor
1855		Prelude and Aria in A minor (lost; originally combined with some of the above dance movements in a 'Suite in A minor')
c1856–7	op. 20 no. 1	Variations on an Original Theme (pub. 1861)
1859–62		Piano piece in B flat major (pub. 1979)[8]
1860		Theme and Variations in D minor (arrangement of the slow movement of String Sextet no. 1; pub. 1927)
1861	op. 24	Variations and Fugue on a Theme of Handel
1861	op. 23	Variation on a Theme of Schumann for piano duet (version for solo piano by Theodor Kirchner, 1878)
1862–3	op. 35	Studies (Variations on a Theme of Paganini; pub. 1866)
1864		Canon in F minor (pub. 1979)[9]
1863–4	op. 34b	Sonata in F minor for 2 pianos (recomposition of 1862 String Quintet; pub. 1871)
1865	op. 39	16 Waltzes for piano duet (arranged for solo piano 1867; simplified arrangement with nos. 13–16 in new keys, also 1867; four numbers also arranged for 2 pianos)
1868		Variation on a Theme of Schumann (*Albumblatt* for Marie Wieck; same theme as op. 9; pub. 1902)
1858–68		Hungarian Dances, Sets 1 and 2, for piano duet (also version for solo piano, probably partly earlier than duet form, pub. 1871)
		Set 1:
		1 in G minor; 2 in D minor; 3 in F major; 4 in F sharp minor; 5 in G minor
		Set 2:
		6 in D major; 7 in A major; 8 in A minor; 9 in F major; 10 in F major
	op. 52a	*Liebeslieder* Waltzes for piano duet (see VOCAL DUETS AND QUARTETS)

[7] Gavotte no. 2 is now incomplete; the edition includes a completion by Robert Pascall, by analogy with the String Quintet, op. 88.

[8] Possibly a musical joke.

[9] No instrumentation is specified for this canon; the edition (by Robert Pascall) offers a possible realization as a piano piece.

1873	op. 56b	Variations on a Theme of Haydn for 2 pianos
	op. 65a	*Neue Liebeslieder* for piano duet (*see* VOCAL DUETS AND QUARTETS)
1871–8	op. 76	8 Pieces

Set 1:
1 Capriccio in F sharp minor; 2 Capriccio in B minor; 3 Intermezzo in A flat major; 4 Intermezzo in B flat major

Set 2:
5 Capriccio in C sharp minor; 6 Intermezzo in A major; 7 Intermezzo in A minor; 8 Capriccio in C major

| 1879 | op. 79 | 2 Rhapsodies |

1 in B minor; 2 in G minor

Hungarian Dances, Sets 3 and 4, for piano duet (pub. 1880)

Set 3:
11 in D minor; 12 in D minor; 13 in D major; 14 in D minor; 15 in A flat major

Set 4:
16 in F major; 17 in F sharp minor; 18 in D major; 19 in A flat minor; 20 in E minor; 21 in E minor

| 1891–2 | op. 116 | 7 Fantasias (possibly earlier) |

Set 1:
1 Capriccio in D minor; 2 Intermezzo in A minor; 3 Capriccio in G minor

Set 2:
4 Intermezzo in E major; 5 Intermezzo in E minor; 6 Intermezzo in E major; 7 Capriccio in D minor

| c1892 | op. 117 | 3 Intermezzi (possibly earlier) |

1 in E flat major; 2 in B flat minor; 3 in C sharp minor

| 1892–3 | op. 118 | 6 Pieces (possibly earlier) |

1 Intermezzo in A minor; 2 Intermezzo in A major; 3 Ballade in G minor; 4 Intermezzo in F minor; 5 Romanze in F major; 6 Intermezzo in E flat minor

| 1892 | | Piano Piece in C minor (lost)[10] |
| c1893 | op. 119 | 4 Pieces (possibly earlier) |

1 Intermezzo in B minor; 2 Intermezzo in E minor; 3 Intermezzo in C major; 4 Rhapsody in E flat major

51 *Übungen* (Exercises; pub. 1893; probably accumulated over many years)[11]

[10] Shown to Clara Schumann, October 1892; presumably intended for opp. 118–19.
[11] There were many more, some of which may still survive in private hands.

Brahms

Cadenzas

Bach: Keyboard Concerto in D minor (pub. 1927)
Beethoven: Piano Concerto in G major (2 cadenzas, pub. 1907)[12]
Mozart: Piano Concerto in G major, K453 (pub. 1927)
Mozart: Piano Concerto in D minor, K466 (pub. 1927; this is founded on a cadenza for the same work by Clara Schumann)[13]
Mozart: Piano Concerto in C minor, K491 (pub. 1927)

Keyboard arrangements and reworkings of pieces by other composers[14]

1852	2 Studies (pub. 1869)
	1 Etude after Chopin's F minor Etude, op. 25; 2 Rondo after Weber (Finale of Sonata in C, op. 24)
	Litolff: Overture to *Maximilien Robespierre*, op. 55, arranged for piano and harmonium (?early; fragment only)
1854	Schumann: Piano Quintet, op. 44, arranged for piano duet (pub. 1887)
1854	Scherzo from Schumann's Piano Quintet arranged for piano solo (pub. 1983)
1854	Joachim: Overture to Shakespeare's *Henry IV*, op. 7, arranged for 2 pianos (pub. 1902)
?1854–5	Joachim: Overture to Grimm's *Demetrius* arranged for 2 pianos (unpub.)
	Study after Schubert (Impromptu in E flat; early, pub. 1927; authenticity doubtful)
	Beethoven: Finale of Third 'Rasumovsky' Quartet, op. 59 no. 3, arranged for solo piano (performed 1867; lost)
1871	Gavotte in A major (from Gluck's *Iphigenie en Aulide*, originally intended for *Paride ed Elena*)
1877	3 Studies (pub. 1879 as nos. 3–5 of 5 Studies, with reprint of Studies 1 and 2 above)
	3 Presto after Bach (Violin Sonata in G); 4 Presto after Bach (second version); 5 Chaconne for the left hand alone (after Bach, D minor Violin Partita)

[12] A cadenza for Beethoven's C minor Piano Concerto, published in 1927 in the Brahms *Sämtliche Werke* is in fact by Moscheles.

[13] The authenticity of another cadenza for this Concerto (pub. 1980; ed. Paul Badura-Skoda) is extremely doubtful.

[14] Brahms routinely made 2-piano, piano duet or solo piano arrangements of his orchestral and larger chamber works; these are not listed here.

442

ORGAN MUSIC

1856		2 Preludes and Fugues (pub. 1927)
		1 in A minor; 2 in G minor
1856		Fugue in A flat minor (pub. 1864)
1856		Chorale Prelude and Fugue on O *Traurigkeit, o Herzeleid* (pub. 1882)
1896 and earlier	op. 122	11 Chorale Preludes (pub. 1902; NB solo piano versions of nos. 4, 5, 8, 9, 10 and 11 by Ferruccio Busoni also pub. 1902)

1 *Mein Jesu, der du mich*; 2 *Herzliebster Jesu*; 3 *O Welt, ich muss dich lassen* (I); 4 *Herzlich tut mich erfreuen*: 5 *Schmücke dich, o liebe Seele*; 6 *O wie selig seid ihr doch*; 7 *O Gott, du frommer Gott*; 8 *Es is ein Ros' entsprungen*; 9 *Herzlich tut mich verlangen* (I); 10 *Herzlich tut mich verlangen* (II); 11 *O Welt, ich muss dich lassen* (II)

CHORAL MUSIC

With orchestral or instrumental ensemble accompaniment

1858	op. 12	Ave Maria (version for SSAA female chorus and orchestra; pub. 1861)
1858		*Brautgesang* (Uhland) for soprano solo, female chorus and orchestra (only fragment extant; orchestral portion lost)
1859	op. 13	*Begräbnisgesang* (Michael Weisse) for mixed chorus, wind and timpani
1859	op. 27	Psalm 13 (version for SSA female chorus and organ or piano with string orchestra *ad libitum*, 1863)
1860	op. 17	4 *Gesänge* for SSAA female chorus, 2 horns and harp

1 *Es tönt ein voller Harfenklang* (Ruperti); 2 *Lied von Shakespeare* (from *Twelfth Night*, trans. A.W. von Schlegel); 3 *Der Gärtner* (Eichendorff); 4 *Gesäng aus 'Fingal'* (Ossian/Macpherson, trans. anon.)

1863	op. 50	*Rinaldo* (Goethe), cantata for tenor solo, TTBB chorus and orchestra (final chorus 1868)
1863–7	op. 45	*Ein deutsches Requiem* (Lutheran scripture) for soprano and baritone soli, SATB chorus and orchestra (possibly begun earlier; mvt 5 added 1869; mvt 2 incorporates material from D minor Symphony of 1854–5)
1869	op. 53	*Rhapsodie* (Goethe) for contralto solo, TTBB chorus and orchestra

Brahms

1869–70		*Liebeslieder* Suite from op. 52 (nos. 1, 2, 4–6, 8, 9, 11) with one new number (later op. 62 no. 9) arranged for 4 solo voices (or SATB chorus) and small orchestra (also performable without voices; pub. 1938)
1868–71	op. 54	*Schicksalslied* (Hölderlin) for SATB chorus and orchestra
1870–71	op. 55	*Triumphlied* (Book of Revelations) for baritone solo, double SATB chorus, and orchestra[15]
1880–81	op. 82	*Nänie* (Schiller) for SATB chorus and orchestra
1882	op. 89	*Gesang der Parzen* (Goethe) for SAATBB chorus and orchestra
	op. 121	*Vier ernste Gesänge* (*see* SOLO SONGS; Brahms is known to have begun sketching an orchestral version; complete orchestrations have been published by, among others, Sir Malcolm Sargent and Erich Leinsdorf)

Vocal/orchestral arrangements of other composers

1862	Schubert: *An Schwager Kronos*, D369 (Goethe); *Geheimes*, D719 (Goethe); *Memmon*, D541 (Mayrhofer); arranged for voice and orchestra (pub. 1933)
1862	Schubert: *Nachtstück*, D672 (Mayrhofer), arranged for voice, piano or harp, and small orchestra (only fragment extant)
1873	Schubert: *Ellens zweiter Gesang*, D838 (Storck, after Sir Walter Scott) arranged for solo soprano, female chorus, 4 horns and 2 bassoons (pub. 1906)
	Schubert: *Gruppe aus dem Tartarus*, D583 (Schiller), arranged for voice (or unison chorus) and orchestra (pub. 1937)
	Schubert: *Greisengesang*, D778 (Rückert), arranged for voice and orchestra (unpub.)

Chorus and keyboard accompaniment (piano or organ)

1856		Kyrie in G minor for SATB chorus and continuo (pub. 1984)
1856	op. 30	*Geistliches Lied* (Paul Flemming) for SATB chorus and organ (or piano duet; pub. 1864)
1858	op. 12	Ave Maria for SSAA female chorus and organ
1859	op. 27	Psalm 13 for SSA female chorus and organ (or piano)
1859–60	op. 44	12 *Lieder und Romanzen* for SSAA female voices with piano *ad libitum* (pub. 1866; *see also* Unaccompanied chorus)

[15] Brahms is known to have sketched a setting of Psalm 22 for baritone, chorus and orchestra in 1870, presumably intended as a further movement of the *Triumphlied*.

Part I:
1 *Minnelied* (Voss); 2 *Der Bräutigam* (Eichendorff); 3 *Barcarole* (trad. Italian); 4 *Fragen* (trad. Slav); 5 *Die Müllerin* (Chamisso); 6 *Die Nonne* (Uhland)

Part II:
1 *Nun stehn die Rosen*; 2 *Die Berge sind spitz*; 3 *Am Wildbach die Weiden*; 4 *Und gehst du über den Kirchhof* (all from Heyse's *Jungbrunnen*); 5 *Die Braut* (Müller); 6 *Märznacht* (Uhland)

op. 52	*Liebeslieder* Waltzes (*see* VOCAL DUETS AND QUARTETS)
op. 65	*Neue Liebeslieder* (*see* VOCAL DUETS AND QUARTETS)
1874	*Kleine Hochzeitskantate* (Keller) for SATB chorus and piano (pub. 1927)
1884 op. 93b	*Tafellied* ('Dank der Damen', Eichendorff), drinking glee for SAATBB chorus and piano

Arrangements of other composers for chorus and keyboard

Schubert: Mass in E flat for chorus and orchestra, reduction for chorus and piano (pub. 1865)
Mozart: *Offertorium de venerabili sacramento*, K260 (now K248a), for double chorus and organ, realization of organ accompaniment (pub. 1873)

Folksong arrangements for chorus and piano

c1859–60	*In stiller Nacht*, arranged for SSAA chorus and piano (pub. 1938)
1894	*Deutsche Volkslieder* Book VII (nos. 43–9) for voice and piano with SATB chorus *ad libitum* (for Books I–VI *see* **Folksong arrangements for voice and piano**)

43 *Es stunden drei Rosen*; 44 *Dem Himmel will ich klagen*; 45 *Es sass ein schneeweiss Vögelein*; 46 *Es war einmal ein Zimmergesell*; 47 *Es ging sich unsre Fraue*; 48 *Nachtigall, sag*; 49 *Verstohlen geht der Mond auf*

Unaccompanied chorus

1847	A, B, C, partsong for SATB chorus (lost)
1847	*Postillions Morgenlied* (anon.), partsong for SATB chorus (lost)
1856–61	Mass in C major for SSATB chorus ('*Missa canonica*', probably not completed; Credo lost; Benedictus pub. 1956; Sanctus, 'Hosanna', Agnus Dei and 'Dona nobis pacem' pub. 1984, with

rearrangement of the Sanctus for SSATBB by Julius Otto Grimm, 1857)

1859	op. 22	*Marienlieder* (trad. German) for SATB chorus (no. 3 ?1860; pub. 1862; the songs were originally for female chorus and this version of no. 2 still survives)

    1 *Der Englische Gruss*; 2 *Marias Kirchgang*; 3 *Marias Wallfahrt*; 4 *Der Jäger*; 5 *Ruf zur Maria*; 6 *Magdalena*; 7 *Marias Lob*

op. 37   3 *Geistliche Chöre* for SSAA female chorus (nos. 1–2 1859 or earlier, no. 3 by 1863; pub. 1865)

    1 O bone Jesu; 2 Adoramus te; 3 Regina coeli
2 Canons for mixed voices (no. 1 1859, no. 2 probably later; pub. 1927; no. 1 previously pub. in facsimile)

    1 *Töne, linderner Klang* (anon.); 2 *Zu Rauch* (Rückert)

c1859–60   *Wenn ich ein Vöglein wär'* (folksong text), part-song for SSA female voices (pub. 1968)

op. 29   2 Motets for mixed chorus (no. 1 1860, SATB; no. 2 1857–60, SAATBB; both pub. 1864)

    1 *Es ist das Heil* (Paul Speratus); 2 *Schaffe in mir, Gott* (Psalm 51)

1859–60 op. 42   3 Partsongs for 6-part mixed chorus

    1 *Abendständchen* (Brentano); 2 *Vineta* (Müller); 3 *Darthulas Grabgesang* (Ossian/Macpherson, trans. Herder)

c1860   *Dar geit en Bek* (Plattdeutsch text by Klaus Groth), partsong for female voices (version of op. 44 no. 9 with different text; pub. 1952)

1860   *Dein Herzlein mild* (Heyse), partsong for female voices (pub. 1938; no relation to op. 62 no. 4, which has the same text)

1860–62 op. 41   5 Partsongs for male voices (pub. 1867)

    1 *Ich schwing' mein Horn ins Jammerthal* (Old German); 2 *Freiwillige her!*; 3 *Geleit*; 4 *Marschieren*: 5 *Gebt Acht!* (all by Lemcke)

op. 62   7 Partsongs for SAATBB chorus (nos. 4–6 c1860; 1–3, 7 from period 1860–3; pub. 1874)

    1 *Rosmarin*; 2 *Von alten Liebesliedern* (both from *Des Knaben Wunderhorn*); 3 *Waldesnacht*; 4 *dein Herzlein mild*; 5 *All meine Herzgedanken*; 6 *Es gehet ein Wehen* (all from Heyse's *Jungbrunnen*); 7 *Vergangen ist mir Glück und Heil* (Old German)

op. 74   2 Motets for mixed chorus (no. 1 1877 or earlier, SSATBB; no. 2 from period 1863–70, SATB; both pub. 1878)

1 *Warum ist das Licht gegeben?* (Lutheran scripture); 2 *O Heiland, reiss die Himmel auf* (anon.)

Dem dunkeln Schoss der heil'gen Erde (Schiller), partsong for SATB chorus (1880 at latest, probably much earlier; pub. 1927)

3 Canons for female voices (1881 or earlier)
 1 *Mir lächelt kein Frühling* (anon., puzzle-canon, pub. 1881); 2 *Grausam erweiset sich Amor* (Goethe, pub. 1927; for 3-voice version, *see* op. 113); 3 *O wie sanft* (Russo-Polish song, trans. Daumer, pub. 1908)

c1883	op. 93a	6 *Lieder und Romanzen* for mixed chorus 1 *Der bucklichte Fiedler* (Rhenish folksong); 2 *Das Mädchen* (Kapper); 3 *O Süsser Mai* (Arnim); 4 *Fahr wohl!* (Rückert); 5 *Der Falke* (Kapper); 6 *Beherzigung* (Goethe; Brahms's title)

Wann? Wann? (Uhland), canon for SA female voices (pub. 1885)

1886–8	op. 104	5 Partsongs for SAATBB chorus 1 *Nachtwache* (I); 2 *Nachtwache* (II) (both by Rückert); 3 *Letztes Glück* (Kalbeck); 4 *Verlorene Jugend* (Wenzig, from the Czech); 5 *Im Herbst* (Groth)
1888–9	op. 109	*Fest- und Gedenksprüche*, 3 motets on biblical sentences for double SATB chorus 1 *Unsere Väter hofften auf dich*; 2 *Wenn ein starker Gewappneter*; 3 *Wo ist ein so herrlich Volk*
1889	op.110	3 Motets for SATB and SSAATTBB chorus 1 *Ich aber bin elend* (Luther); 2 *Ach, arme Welt* (anon.); 3 *Wenn wir in höchsten Nöten sein* (Paul Eber)
	op.113	13 Canons for female voices (nos. 3–5 1858; nos. 1, 2, 8, 10–12 1860–63; no. 9 c1868; pub. 1894; all for SSAA except nos. 2, 4, 12 (SSA) and 13 (SSSSAA)) 1 *Göttlicher Morpheus*; 2 *Grausam erweiset sich Amor* (both Goethe); 3 *Sitz a schöns Vögerl*; 4 *Schlaf, Kindlein, schlaf*; 5 *Wille, wille, will* (all folksong texts corresponding to nos. 2, 11 and 5 of *Deutsche Volks-Kinderlieder* respectively); 6 *Solange Schöneit* (Greek, trans. Fallersleben); 7 *Wenn die Klänge nahn*; 8 *Ein Gems auf dem Stein* (both Eichendorff); 9 *Ans Auge* (Arabic, trans. Rückert); 10 *Leise Töne der Brust*; 11 *Ich weiss nicht* (both Rückert);

12 *Wenn Kummer hätte* (Arabic, trans. Rückert); 13 *Einförmig ist der Liebe Gram* (Rückert)

Arrangements of other composers for unaccompanied chorus

Johann Rudolf Ahle: Chorale *Es ist genug* (from Cantata of same title) arranged for 6-part chorus (pub. 1933)

J. S. Bach: Chorale *Ach Gott, wie manches Herzeleid* from Cantata no. 44 (pub. 1877)

J. S. Bach: Chorale *Es ist genug* from Cantata no. 60 (pub. 1933)

c1859–60   Johann Eccard: *Marienlied* arranged for SSAA female chorus (pub. 1943)

Folksong arrangements for chorus

c1859–60   10 *Volkslieder* for 3- and 4-part female chorus (pub. 1938–40, ed. Drinker)[16]

Altes Lied (Minnelied); Der todte Gast; Ich hab' die Nacht geträumet; Altes Liebeslied; Es waren zwei Königskinder; Spannung; Mit Lust tät ich ausreiten; Guten Abend; So will ich frisch und fröhlich sein; Der tote Knabe

c1859–60   20 *Volkslieder* for 3- and 4-part female chorus (pub. 1964, ed. Kross; some nos. duplicate the 1940 group; only the unduplicated ones are listed below)

3 *Schwesterlein*; 4 *Ich hörte ein Sichlein rauschen*; 5 *Es stunden drei Rosen*; 6 *Ich stand auf hohem Berge*; 7 *Gunhilde*; 8 *Der buckligte Fiedler*; 9 *Die Versuchung*; 11 *Altes Minnelied*; 12 *Die Wollust in den Maien*; 13 *Da unten im Tale*; 14 *Der Jäger*; 15 *Scheiden*; 16 *Zu Strassburg auf der Schanz*; 18 *Wach auf, mein Hort*; 19 *Es ritt ein Ritter*; 20 *Ständchen*

c1859–60   26 *Volkslieder* for female voices (pub. 1968, ed. Gotwals and Keppler)[17]

1 *Die Entführung*; 2 *Minnelied*; 3 *Gang zur Liebsten*; 4 *Schifferlied*; 5 *Erlaub mir, feins Mädchen*; 6 *Der Gang zum Liebchen*; 7 *Schnitter Tod*; 8 *Die Bernauerin*; 9 *Das Lied vom*

---

[16] These came out in several numbers of the 'University of Pennsylvania Choral Series'; and like all the subsequent female-voice groups, here listed in order of publication, they derive from the surviving part-books of the Hamburger Frauenchor.

[17] No. 26 in this group is *Wenn ich ein Vöglein wär*, listed in this catalogue as an original composition. It also appears as no. 27 in 27 *Volksliedbearbeitungen* for female chorus (pub. 1970, ed. Helms), which contains no arrangements not already represented in the previously published collections, though titles sometimes differ.

eifersüchtigen Knaben; 10 *Der Baum in Oden-wald*; 11 *Des Markgrafen Töchterlein*; 12 *Die stolze Jüdin*; 13 *Der Zimmergesell*; 14 *Gar lieblich hat sich gesellet*; 15 *Ich schwing' mein Horn*; 16 *Heimliche Liebe* (2 versions); 17 *Mein Herzlein thut mir gar zu weh!*; 18 *Dauernde Liebe*; 19 *Während der Tren-nung*; 20 *Sehnsucht*; 21 *Morgen muss ich fort vom hier*; 22 *Scheiden*; 23 *Sonntag*; 24 *Vor dem Fenster*; 25 *Verstohlen geht der Mond auf*

c1859–60   Additional arrangements for female chorus (partly missing or lost; tunes pub. 1968)

Ade von hinnen; *Mein feins Lieb*; *Die wun-dergefündene Tochter*; *Gottesgericht*; *Liebes-klage*; *Pfaffenschlich*

Deutsche Volkslieder nos. 1–14 for SATB chorus (nos. 2, 3, 8–11 and 13 1857, remainder 1863–4 or earlier; pub. 1864)

1 *Von edler Art*; 2 *Mit Lust tät ich ausreiten*; 3 *Bei nächtlicher Weil*; 4 *Von heiligen Mär-tyrer Emmerano*; 5 *Täublein weiss*; 6 *Ach lieber Herre Jesu Christ*; 7 *Sankt Raphael*; 8 *In stiller Nacht*; 9 *Abschiedslied*; 10 *Der tote Knabe*; 11 *Die Wollust in den Maien*; 12 *Mor-gengesang*; 13 *Schnitter Tod*; 14 *Der eng-lischer Jäger*

Deutsche Volkslieder nos. 15–26 for SATB chorus (nos. 15–20 1857, 21–2 c1873, remainder 1863–4 or earlier; nos. 23–6 pub. 1926 along with 28 arrangements for voice and piano, q.v. below, as nos. 1, 2, 5 and 28 of 32 *Neue Volkslieder*, ed. Friedländer; repub. with nos. 15–22 in *Sämtliche Werke*, 1927)

15 *Scheiden*; 16 *Wach auf!*; 17 *Erlaube mir*; 18 *Der Fiedler*; 19 *Da unten im Tale*; 20 *Des Abends*; 21 *Wach auf!* (2nd version); 22 *Dort in der Weiden*; 23 *Altes Volkslied* ('Verstohlen geht der Mond auf'); 24 *Der Ritter und die Feine*; 25 *Der Zimmergesell*; 26 *Altdeutsches Kampflied*

VOCAL DUETS AND QUARTETS WITH PIANO

1858–60   op. 20   3 Duets for soprano and alto (pub. 1862)

1 *Weg der Liebe* (I); 2 *Weg der Liebe* (II) (Herder, from *Stimmen der Völker*); 3 *Die Meere* (trad. Italian)

1860–62	op. 28	4 Duets for alto and baritone (pub. 1864)

        1 *Die Nonne und der Ritter* (Eichendorff); 2 *Vor der Tür* (Old German); 3 *Es rauschet das Wasser* (Goethe); 4 *Der Jäger und sein Liebchen* (Hoffmann von Fallersleben)

op. 31   3 Quartets for SATB soli (no. 1 1859, others 1863)

        1 *Wechsellied zum Tanze* (Goethe); 2 *Neckerein* (trad. Moravian); 3 *Der Gang zum Liebchen* (trad. Czech)

1868–9   op. 52   *Liebeslieder* Waltzes (Daumer, from *Polydora*) for SATB (*ad libitum*) and piano duet (also pub. 1875 as Waltzes for piano duet without voices, op. 52a)

        1 *Rede, Mädchen, allzu liebes*; 2 *Am Gesteine rauscht die Flut*; 3 *O die Frauen*; 4 *Wie des Abends*; 5 *Die grüne Hopfenranke*; 6 *Ein kleiner, hübscher Vogel*; 7 *Wohl schön bewandt*; 8 *Wenn so lind dein Auge mir*; 9 *Am Donaustrande*; 10 *O wie sanft die Quelle sich*; 11 *Nein, es ist nicht auszukommen*; 12 *Schlosser auf*; 13 *Vöglein durchrauscht die Luft*; 14 *Sie, wie ist die Welle klar*; 15 *Nachtigall, sie singt so schön*; 16 *Ein dunkeler Schacht ist Liebe*; 17 *Nicht wandle, mein Licht*; 18 *Es bebet das Gesträuche*

op. 61   4 Duets for soprano and alto (no. 2 1852, rest 1873–4)

        1 *Die Schwestern* (Mörike); 2 *Klosterfräulein* (Kerner); 3 *Phänomen* (Goethe); 4 *Die Boten der Liebe* (Wenzig, from the Czech)

op. 64   3 Quartets for SATB soli (no. 1 1862, others 1874)

        1 *An die Heimat* (Sternau); 2 *Der Abend* (Schiller); 3 *Fragen* (Daumer)

1874   op. 65   *Neue Liebeslieder* Waltzes for SATB soli and piano duet (also pub. 1875 as Waltzes for piano duet without voices op. 65a)

        1 *Verzicht, o Herr, auf Rettung*; 2 *Finstre Schatten der Nacht*; 3 *An jeder Hand die Finger*; 4 *Ihr schwarzen Augen*; 5 *Wahre, wahre deinen Sohn*; 6 *Rosen steckt mir an die Mutter*; 7 *Vom Gebirge Well auf Well*; 8 *Weiche Gräser im Revier*; 9 *Nagen am Herzen*; 10 *Ich kose süss*; 11 *Alles, alles in den Wind*; 12 *Schwarzer Wald, dein Schatten*; 13 *Nein, Geliebter, setze dich*; 14 *Flammenauge, dunkles Haar* (all Daumer); 15 *Zum Schluss* (Goethe)

1873–5   op. 66   5 Duets for soprano and alto

        1 *Klänge* (I); 2 *Klänge* (II) (both Groth); 3 *Am*

Strande (Hölty); 4 *Jägerlied* (Candidus); 5 *Hüt du dich!* (*Des Knaben Wunderhorn*)

| 1877–8 | op. 75 | 4 *Balladen und Romanzen* for 2 voices |

1 *Edward* (Herder, *Stimmen der Völker*; AT); 2 *Guter Rat* (*Des Knaben Wunderhorn*; SA); 3 *So lass uns wandern!* (Wenzig, from the Czech; ST); 4 *Walpurgisnacht* (Alexis; SS)

| | op. 84 | 5 *Romanzen und Lieder* (*see* SOLO SONGS) |
| | op. 92 | 4 Quartets for SATB soli (no. 1 1877, rest 1884) |

1 *O schöne Nacht* (Daumer, from the Hungarian); 2 *Spätherbst* (Allmers); 3 *Abendlied* (Hebbel); 4 *Warum?* (Goethe)

| 1887 | op. 103 | *Zigeunerlieder* (Conrat, after Hungarian originals) for SATB soli (nos. 1–7 and 11 also pub. 1889 in version as solo songs) |

1 *He, Zigeuner, greife in die Saiten ein*; 2 *Hochgetürmte Rimaflut*; 3 *Wisst ihr, wann mein Kindchen*; 4 *Lieber Gott, du weisst*; 5 *Brauner Bursche führt zum Tanze*; 6 *Röslein dreie in der Reihe*; 7 *Kommt dir manchmal in den Sinn*; 8 *Horch, der Wind klagt*; 9 *Weit und breit schaut niemand mich an*; 10 *Mond verhüllt sein Angesicht*; 11 *Rote Abendwolken ziehn am Firmament*

| | op. 112 | 6 Quartets for SATB soli (nos. 1–2 1888, rest 1891) |

1 *Sehnsucht*; 2 *Nächtens* (both Kugler); 4 *Zigeunerlieder*: 3 *Himmel strahlt so helle und klar*; 4 *Rote Rosenknospen*; 5 *Brennessel steht an Weges Rand*; 6 *Liebe Schwalbe, kliene Schwalbe* (all Conrat, after Hungarian originals)

SOLO SONGS

• (With piano unless otherwise stated)

(Many early songs, including Eichendorff settings, from late 1840s onwards, lost)

| 1852–3 | op. 3 | 6 *Gesänge* for tenor or soprano |

1 *Liebestreu* (Reinick); 2 *Liebe und Frühling* (I); 3 *Liebe und Frühling* (II) (both Hoffmann von Fallersleben); 4 *Lied aus 'Ivan'* (Bodenstedt); 5 *In der Fremde*; 6 *Lied* (both Eichendorff)

| 1852–3 | op. 6 | 6 *Gesänge* for soprano or tenor |

1 *Spanisches Lied* (Heyse); 2 *Der Frühling* (Rousseau); 3 *Nachwirkung* (Meissner); 4 *Juchhe* (Reinick); 5 *Wie die Wolke nach der Sonne*; 6 *Nachtigallen schwingen* (both Hoffman von Fallersleben)

| 1853 | | *Die Müllerin* for soprano (Chamisso; no longer |

		complete; pub. 1983, completed Draheim)
	op. 7	6 *Gesänge* (no. 6 1851, rest 1852–3)
		1 *Treue Liebe* (Ferrand); 2 *Parole*; 3 *Anklänge* (both Eichendorff); 4 *Volkslied*; 5 *Die Trauernde* (folksong); 6 *Heimkehr* (Uhland)
		Mondnacht (Eichendorff, pub. 1854)
1858	op. 14	8 *Lieder und Romanzen* (pub. 1861)
		1 *Vor dem Fenster* (Volkslied); 2 *Vom verwundeten Knaben*; 3 *Murrays Ermordung*; 4 *Ein Sonett* (all from Herder, *Stimmen der Völker*); 5 *Trennung*; 6 *Gang zur Liebsten*; 7 *Staïdchen*; 8 *Sehnsucht*(all folksong texts)
1858–9	op. 19	5 *Gedichte* (pub. 1862)
		1 *Der Kuss* (Hölty); 2 *Scheiden und Meiden*; 3 *In der Ferne*; 4 *Der Schmeid* (all Uhland); 5 *An eine Äolsharfe* (Mörike)
c1857–9		*Spruch* (Hoffmann von Fallersleben), canon for voice and viola
1864	op. 32	9 *Lieder und Gesänge von Aug. v. Platen und G. F. Daumer*
		1 *Wie rafft ich mich* (Platen); 2 *Nicht mehr zu dir* (Daumer); 3 *Ich schleich umher betrübt und stumm*; 4 *Der Strom, der neben mir verrauschte*; 5 *Wehe, so willst du mich wieder*; 6 *Du sprichst, dass ich mich täuschte* (all Platen); 7 *Bitteres zu sagen*; 8 *So stehn wir*; 9 *Wie bist du, meine Königin* (all Daumer)
1861–9	op. 33	15 *Romanzen aus L. Tiecks 'Magelone'* (nos. 1–6 pub. 1865, nos. 8–15 pub. 1869)
		1 *Keinen hat es noch gereut*; 2 *Traun! Bogen und Pfeil*; 3 *Sind es Schmerzen, sind es Freuden*; 4 *Liebe kam aus fernen Landen*; 5 *So willst du des Armen*; 6 *Sie soll ich die Freude*; 7 *War es dir, dem diese Lippen bebten*; 8 *Wir müssen uns trennen*; 9 *Ruhe, Süssliebchen*; 10 *Verzweiflung*; 11 *Wie schnell verschwindet so Licht als Glanz*; 12 *Muss es eine Trennung geben*; 13 *(Sulima) Geliebter, wo zaudert dein irrender Fuss*; 14 *Wie froh und frisch*; 15 *Treue Liebe dauert lange*
	op. 43	4 *Gesänge* (1864, 1866, 1859, 1857 respectively; pub. 1868)
		1 *Von ewiger Liebe* (Hoffmann von Fallersleben);[18] 2 *Die Mainacht* (Hölty); 3 *Ich schell mein Horn ins Jammerthal* (Old German); 4 *Das Lied vom Herrn von Falkenstein* (Uhland)

[18] In all editions the poem is misattributed to Joseph Wenzig.

1866	*Regenlied* (Groth; pub. 1908; earlier setting of the text of *Nachklang*, op. 59 no. 4)
op. 46	4 *Lieder und Gesänge* (no. 1 1864, rest 1868)
	1 *Die Kränze*; 2 *Magyarisch* (both Daumer); 3 *Die Schale der Vergessenheit*; 4 *An die Nachtigall* (both Hölty)
op. 47	5 *Lieder und Gesänge* (no. 5 1858, no. 3 1860, rest *c*1868)
	1 *Botschaft*; 2 *Liebesglut* (both Daumer, after Hafiz); 3 *Sonntag* (Uhland); 4 *O liebliche Wangen* (Flemming); 5 *Die Liebende schreibt* (Goethe)
op. 48	7 *Lieder und Gesänge* (no. 2 1855, no. 5 1858, rest 1867–8)
	1 *Der Gang zum Liebchen* (Wenzig, from the Czech); 2 *Der Überläufer*; 3 *Liebesklage des Mädchens* (both from *Des Knaben Wunderhorn*); 4 *Gold überwiegt die Liebe* (Wenzig, from the Czech); 5 *Trost in Tränen* (Goethe); 6 *Vergangen ist mir Glück und Heil* (Altdeutsch); 7 *Herbstgefühl* (Schack)
op. 49	5 *Lieder und Gesänge* (pub. 1868)
	1 *Am Sonntag Morgen* (Heyse); 2 *An ein Veilchen* (Hölty); 3 *Sehnsucht* (Wenzig, from the Czech); 4 *Wiegenlied* (v. 1 *Des Knaben Wunderhorn*, v. 2 Scherer); 5 *Abenddämmerung* (Schack)
op. 57	8 *Lieder und Gesänge von G. F. Daumer* (pub. 1871)
	1 *Von waldbekränzter Höhe*; 2 *Wenn du nur zuweilen lächelst* (after Hafiz); 3 *Es träumte mir* (from the Spanish); 4 *Ach, wene diesen Blick*; 5 *In meiner Nächte Sehnen*; 6 *Strahlt zuweilen auch ein mildes Licht*; 7 *Die Schnur, die Perl an Perle* (from the Sanskrit); 8 *Unbewegte laue Luft*
op. 58	8 *Lieder und Gesänge* (pub. 1871)
	1 *Blinde Kuh* (Kopisch, from the Italian); 2 *Während des Regens* (Kopisch); 3 *Die Spröde* (Kopisch, from the Calabrian); 4 *O komme, holde Sommernacht* (Grohe); 5 *Schwermut* (Candidus); 6 *In der Gasse*; 7 *Vorüber* (both Hebbel); 8 *Serenade* (Schack)
op. 59	8 *Lieder und Gesänge* (no. 1 1871, rest 1873)
	1 *Dämmerung senkte sich von oben* (Goethe); 2 *Auf dem See* (Simrock); 3 *Regenlied*; 4 *Nachklang* (both Groth); 5 *Agnes* (Mörike); 6 *Eine gute, gute Nacht* (Daumer, from the

1873		Russian); 7 *Mein wundes Herz*; 8 *Dein blaues Auge* (both Groth)
		5 *Ophelia-Lieder* (Shakespeare, *Hamlet*, trans. A. W. Schlegel) for contralto (pub. 1935)
		1 *Wie erkenn ich dein Treulieb*; 2 *Sein Lechenhemd, weiss wie Schnee*; 3 *Auf morgen ist Sankt Valentins Tag*; 4 *Sie trugen ihn auf der Bahre bloss*; 5 *Und kommt er nicht mehr zurück?*
1873–4	op. 63	9 *Lieder und Gesänge*
		1 *Frühlingstrost*; 2 *Erinnerung*; 3 *An ein Bild*; 4 *An die Tauben* (all Schenkendorf); *Junge Lieder* (I, II) (F. Schumann): 5 *Meine Liebe ist grün*; 6 *Wenn um den Holunder*; *Heimweh* (I–III) (Groth): 7 *Wie traulich war*; 8 *O wüsst ich doch den Weg zurück*; 9 *Ich sah als Knabe*
	op. 69	9 *Lieder und Gesänge* (pub. 1877)
		1 *Klage* (I); 2 *Klage* (II); 3 *Abscheid*; 4 *Des Liebsten Schwur* (all Wenzig, from the Czech); 5 *Tambourliedchen* (Candidus); 6 *Vom Strande* (Eichendorff, from the Spanish); 7 *Über die See* (Lemcke); 8 *Salome* (Keller); 9 *Mädchenfluch* (Kapper, from the Serbian)
	op. 70	4 *Lieder und Gesänge* (no. 4 pub. 1875, rest 1877)
		1 *Im Garten am Seegestade* (Lemcke); 2 *Lerchengesang* (Candidus); 3 *Serenade* (Goethe); 4 *Abendregen* (Keller)
	op. 77	5 *Lieder und Gesänge* (pub. 1877)
		1 *Es liebt sich so lieblich* (Heine); 2 *An den Mond* (Simrock); 3 *Geheimnis* (Candidus); 4 *Wilst du dass ich geh?* (Lemcke); 5 *Minnelied* (Hölty)
	op. 72	5 *Lieder und Gesänge* (nos. 1, 2 and 5 1875; pub. 1877)
		1 *Alte liebe*; 2 *Sommerfäden* (both Candidus); 3 *O kühler Wald* (Brentano); 4 *Verzagen* (Lemcke); 5 *Unüberwindlich* (Goethe)
	op. 84	5 *Romanzen und Lieder* for 1 or 2 voices[19] (pub. 1882)
		1 *Sommerabend*; 2 *Der Kranz*; 3 *In den Beeren* (all Schmidt); 4 *Vergebliches Ständchen*; 5 *Spannung* (both Lower Rhenish folk texts)
	op. 85	6 *Lieder* (nos. 3 and 6 1878, nos. 1 and 2 1879; pub. 1882)
		1 *Sommerabend*; 2 *Mondenschein* (both

[19] These are all dialogue-songs, and no. 5 includes an optional passage that may be sung in duet.

Heine); 3 *Mädchenlied* (Kapper, from the Serbian); 4 *Ade* (Kapper, from the Czech); 5 *Frühlingslied* (Geibel); 6 *In Waldeseinsamkeit* (Lemcke)

op. 86   6 *Lieder* for low voice (no. 5 1873, no. 3 1877, no. 2 1879; pub. 1882)

1 *Therese* (Keller); 2 *Feldeinsamkeit* (Allmers); 3 *Nachtwandler* (Kalbeck); 4 *Über die Heide* (Storm); 5 *Versunken* (F. Schumann); 6 *Todessehen* (Schenkendorf)

op. 91   2 *Gesänge* for alto, viola and piano (no. 1 1884, no. 2 1864, rev. 1882)

1 *Gestillte Sehnsucht* (Rückert); 2 *Geistliches Wiegenlied* (Geibel, after Lope de Vega)

op. 94   5 *Lieder* for low voice (no. 3 1879, rest 1884)

1 *Mit vierzig Jahren* (Rückert); 2 *Steig auf, geliebter Schatten* (Halm); 3 *Mein Herz ist schwer* (Geibel); 4 *Sapphische Ode* (Schmidt); 5 *Kein Haus, kein' Heimat* (Halm)

1884   op. 95   7 *Lieder*

1 *Das Mädchen* (Kapper, from the Serbian); 2 *Bei dir sind meine Gedanken*; 3 *Beim Abschied* (2 alternative versions); 4 *Der Jäger* (all Halm); 5 *Vorschneller Schwur* (Kapper, from the Serbian); 6 *Mädchenlied* (Heyse, from the Italian); 7 *Schön war, das ich dir weihte* (Daumer, from the Turkish)

1884–5   op. 96   4 *Lieder*

1 *Der Tod, das ist die kühle Nacht* (Heine); 2 *Wir wandelten* (Daumer, from the Hungarian); 3 *Es schauen die Blumen*; 4 *Meerfahrt* (both Heine)

1885   op. 97   6 *Lieder*

1 *Nachtigall*; 2 *Auf dem Schiffe* (both Reinhold); 3 *Entführung* (Alexis); 4 *Dort in den Weiden* (Lower Rhenish folk text); 5 *Komm bald* (Groth); 6 *Trennung* (Swabian folksong)

1885   *Wie der Mond* (Heine); *Winternacht* (Halm); *Brautlied* (Heyse) (intended for opp. 96–7; lost)

op. 103   *Zigeunerlieder*, version for solo voice and piano (*see* VOCAL DUETS AND QUARTETS)

1886–8   op. 105   5 *Lieder* for low voice

1 *Wie melodien zieht es mir* (Groth); 2 *Immer leiser wird mein Schlummer* (Lingg); 3 *Klage* (Lower Rhenish folksong); 4 *Auf dem Kirchhofe* (Liliencron); 5 *Verrat* (Lemcke)

op. 106   5 *Lieder* (nos. 2 and 5 1885, rest 1888)

1 *Ständchen* (Kugler); 2 *Auf dem See* (Rein-

		hold); 3 *Es hing der Reif* (Groth); 4 *Meine Lieder* (Frey); 5 *Ein Wanderer* (Reinhold)
1886–9	op 107	*5 Lieder*

1 *An die Stolze* (Flemming); 2 *Salamander* (Lemcke); 3 *Das Mädchen spricht* (Gruppe); 4 *Maienkätzchen* (Liliencron); 5 *Mädchenlied* (Heyse)

| 1896 | op. 121 | *Vier ernste Gesänge* for bass voice |

1 *Denn es gehet dem Menschen* (Ecclesiastes 3); 2 *Ich wandte mich, und sahe* (Ecclesiastes 4); 3 *O Tod, wie bitter bist du* (Ecclesiasticus 41); 4 *Wenn ich mit Menschen- und mit Engelzungen redete* (I Corinthians 13)

Folksong arrangements for voice and piano

1858   28 *Deutsche Volkslieder* (pub. 1926 with 4 choral arrangements – q.v. under **Folksong arrangements for unaccompanied chorus** – as 32 *Neue Volkslieder*; the numbering below follows the 1928 *Sämtliche Werke*, Vol. XXI)

1 *Die Schnürbrust*; 2 *Der Jäger*; 3 *Drei Vögelein*; 4 *Auf, gebet uns das Pfingstei*; 5 *Des Markgrafen Töchterlein*; 6 *Der Reiter*; 7 *Die heilige Elisabeth*; 8 *Der Englische Gruss*; 9 *Ich stund an einem Morgen*; 10 *Gunhilde*; 11 *Der tote Gast*; 12 *Tageweis von einer schönen Frauen*; 13 *Schifferlied*; 14 *Nachtgesang*; 15 *Die beiden Königskinder*; 16 *Scheiden*; 17 *Altes Minnelied*; 18 *Der getreue Eckart* (2 versions); 19 *Die Versuchung*; 20 *Der Tochter Wunsch*; 21 *Schnitter Tod*; 22 *Marias Wallfahrt*; 23 *Das Mädchen und der Tod*; 24 *Es ritt ein Ritter wohl durch das Ried*; 25 *Liebeslied*; 26 *Guten Abend, mein tausiger Schatz*; 27 *Die Wollust in den Maien*; 28 *Es reit' ein Herr und auch sein Knecht*

1858   14 *Volks-Kinderlieder*

1 *Dornröschen*; 2 *Die Nachtigall*; 3 *Die Henne*; 4 *Sandmännchen*; 5 *Der Mann*; 6 *Heidenröslein*; 7 *Das Schlaraffenland*; 8 *Beim Ritt auf dem Knie* (with alternative Plattdeutsch text); 9 *Der Jäger im Walde*; 10 *Das Mädchen und die Hasel*; 11 *Wiegenlied*; 12 *Weinachten*; 13 *Marienwürmchen*; 14 *Dem Schutzengel*

1882   *Neapolitanische Canzonetta* (trad. Italian; unpub.)

1894   49 *Deutsche Volkslieder* in 7 books (for nos. 43–9 (Book 7) *see* **Folksong arrangements for chorus and piano**)

Book 1:
  1 *Sagt mir, o schönste Schäf'rin mein*;
  2 *Erlaube mir, feins Mädchen*; 3 *Gar lieblich
  hat sich gesellet*; 4 *Guten Abend*; 5 *Die Sonne
  scheint nicht mehr*; 6 *Da unten im Tale*;
  7 *Gunhilde*

Book 2:
  8 *Ach, englische Schäferin*; 9 *Es war eine
  schöne Jüdin*; 10 *Es ritt ein Ritter*; 11 *Jung-
  fräulein, soll ich mit euch gehn*; 12 *Feins-
  liebchen, du sollst*; 13 *Wach auf, mein Hort*;
  14 *Maria ging aus wandern*

Book 3:
  15 *Schwesterlein*; 16 *Wache auf mein Her-
  zensschöne*; 17 *Ach Gott, wie weh tut Scheiden*;
  18 *So wünsch ich ihr ein gute Nacht*; 19 *Nur
  ein Gesicht auf Erden lebt*; 20 *Schönster Schatz,
  mein Engel*; 21 *Es ging ein Maidlein zarte*

Book 4:
  22 *Wo gehst du hin, du Stolze?*; 23 *Der Reiter*;
  24 *Mir ist ein schön's braun's Maidelein*;
  25 *Mein Mädel hat ein Rosenmund*; 26 *Ach
  könnt ich diesen Abend*; 27 *Ich stand auf
  hohem Berge*; 28 *Es reit ein Herr und auch sein
  Knecht*

Book 5:
  29 *Es war ein Markgraf überm Rhein*; 30 *All
  mein Gedanken*; 31 *Dort in der Weiden*; 32 *So
  will ich frisch und fröhlich sein*; 33 *Och Moder,
  ich will en Ding han*; 34 *Wie komm ich denn
  zur Tür herein?* (with alternative Plattdeutsch
  text); 35 *Soll sich der Mond nicht heller
  scheinen*

Book 6:
  36 *Es wohnet ein Fiedler*; 37 *Du mein einzig
  Licht*; 38 *Des Abends kann ich nicht schlafen
  gehn*; 39 *Schöner Augen schöne Strahlen*;
  40 *Ich weiss mir'n Maidlein hübsch und fein*;
  41 *Es steht ein Lind*; 42 *Verstohlen geht der
  Mond auf*

MISCELLANEOUS EDITIONS OF OTHER COMPOSERS' WORKS

Schumann: Cantata, *Vom Pagen und der Königs-
tochter*, op. 140 (pub. 1857)
C. P. E. Bach: 5 Concerti for clavier and strings
(pub. 1862)
J. S. Bach: Cantana no. 21, with organ continuo
by Brahms (performed 1863; lost)

C. P. E. Bach: Sonatas in B minor and C minor for violin or oboe (with continuo realizations; pub. 1864)

W. F. Bach: Sonata in F for 2 claviers (pub. 1864)

Schubert: 12 Ländler, op. 171 (pub. 1864)

Handel: 7 Duets and 2 Trios (with continuo realizations), for Handel-Gesamtausgabe Vol. XXXII

Schumann: Scherzo and Presto Passionato, op. posth. (pub. 1866)

Schubert: Impromptus in E flat minor, E flat major and C major (pub. 1868–9)

Schubert: 20 Ländler, for piano solo and for piano duet (anthology collated 1865–9; pub. 1869)

Schubert: *Quartettsätz* in C minor (pub. 1870)

Couperin: *Pièces de clavecin*, Vol. IV of Chrysander's *Denkmäler der Tonkunst* (pub. 1871)

Schumann: *Etudes symphoniques*, 3rd ed., with first publication of 5 discarded variations (pub. 1873)

Mozart: Requiem, K626, as Supplement to the Complete Edition (pub. 1877)

Schubert: *Der Strom* (Lied, D565; pub. 1877)

Chopin: Piano Sonatas 1–3, Mazurkas, Fantasia in F minor, Barcarolle, for Vols. III, VIII, X and XIII of Complete Works (pub. 1878–80)

Handel: 6 Trios (with continuo realizations), for Handel-Gesamtausgabe Vol. XXXII (2nd ed., pub. 1880)

Schubert: Symphonies 1–8, for Schubert-Gesamtausgabe Vols. I and II (pub. 1884–5)

Schumann: Symphony no. 4 (original version), as an 'Anhang' to the Collected Edition, in collaboration with Franz Wüllner (pub. 1891).

Schumann: Vol. XIV of the Complete Works under the editorship of Clara Schumann (includes the Andante and Variations for 2 pianos, 2 cellos and horn, the suppressed *Etudes symphoniques*, the Scherzo and Presto Passionato, and the 'Theme in E flat' on which Brahms based his op. 23; pub. 1893)

LITERARY AND MUSICAL ANTHOLOGIES

?1850–54

Des jüngen Kreislers Schatzkästlein, anthology of quotations (pub. 1919, ed. Krebs)

Oktaven u. Quinten u. A., anthology of contrapuntal examples (pub. 1933, ed. Schenker)

Appendix C
Personalia

Allgeyer, Julius (1829–1900) was an engraver and photographer whom Brahms first met in Düsseldorf in 1853 and who remained one of his closest friends. He was a passionate enthusiast both for Brahms's music and for the painting of their mutual friend Feuerbach, and his most notable work was a critical biography of the artist. Eugenie Schumann describes him as 'painfully slow in speech and movements'.

Arnim, Bettina von (1785–1859) was the sister of one leading Romantic poet, Clemens Brentano, and the widow of another, Ludwig Achim von Arnim (d. 1831); as a child she corresponded with Goethe. In her own right she was a noted memoirist and an essayist on social questions. Brahms met her in 1853. Her daughter Gisela (1827–89), a close friend of Joachim's in the 1850s, married another of their friends, the playwright and essayist Hermann Grimm (1828–1901), son of the folklorist Wilhelm Grimm.

Avé-Lallemant, Theodor (?–1890) was a Hamburg music-teacher, pianist and conductor who befriended Brahms in the 1850s and was an important source from whom he acquired editions of old music. He was closely associated with the Hamburg Philharmonic Society, and a supporter of Brahms's unsuccessful campaign to be appointed conductor of the orchestra.

Barbi, Alice (1862–1948) was an Italian mezzo-soprano who first made a reputation in her native country, where she was admired (and written for) by the composers Martucci and Sgambati. She toured widely and from 1892 became a friend and favourite interpreter of Brahms, who often accompanied her in recitals. She married an Austrian nobleman.

Bargiel, Woldemar (1828–97) was Clara Schumann's half-brother and a composer respected by Brahms; he studied in Leipzig and later taught in Berlin, Cologne and Amsterdam. He wrote much chamber music and several large choral works.

Billroth, Theodor (1829–94) was a leading surgeon whom Brahms first met in Switzerland in the early 1860s and who in 1867 became Professor and Director of Operations at Vienna University. A well-known public figure and amateur musician of very wide general culture, he became one of Brahms's closest friends and was the dedicatee of the op. 51 String Quartets.

Brüll, Ignaz (1846–1907) was a Viennese composer and pianist, born in Moravia – his works included ten operas, of which *Das goldene Kreuz* (1875) had some contemporary success. A remarkable sight-reader, he often partnered Brahms in preliminary play-throughs of his works to their circle of friends.

Bülow, Hans Guido von (1830–94) was a composer, pianist and conductor who achieved significant results in all three fields. A piano pupil of Clara

Schumann's father Friedrich Wieck, he became a protégé of Liszt, whose daughter Cosima he married. He was an outstanding champion of Wagner, who nevertheless relieved him of Cosima and shamelessly plundered Bülow's symphonic poem *Nirwana* in the composition of *Tristan und Isolde*. After his divorce in 1869 Bülow became an equally enthusiastic advocate of Brahms. As a conductor, especially with the small but highly disciplined Meiningen orchestra, he pioneered a new standard of faithfulness to the score, and his tours with the orchestra were instrumental in making Brahms's orchestral works known across Germany.

Chrysander, Karl Franz Friedrich (1826–1901) was one of the outstanding musicologists of his age. He lived for some years in England researching his partly published but never completed biography of Handel, and practically single-handed edited what remains today the only 'complete' edition of Handel's music. He also edited other series of early music editions and various musical journals.

Cossel, Otto Friedrich Willibald (1813–?) was a Hamburg pianist and pupil of Marxsen. A conscientious and idealistic pedagogue, he was Brahms's first teacher (1841–5) and induced Marxsen to take over his tuition to avoid him being exploited as a *Wunderkind*.

Daumer, Georg Friedrich (1800–75), by profession a teacher and homeopathic doctor, is generally considered a mediocre poet who would have been entirely forgotten had not Brahms set so many of his verses in the *Liebeslieder* Waltzes and elsewhere. Yet Daumer was an interesting figure whose early theological studies led him to publish an attack on orthodox Christianity, *Religion des Lebens*. After flirting with Mohammedanism he became a Rosicrucian. He was the first mentor and educator of the 'wild boy', Kaspar Hauser, who appeared in his native Nuremberg in 1828. A gifted translator, he was stimulated by the ideals of Herder and Goethe, and in his collection *Polydora* he drew together poems of Classical Greece and Rome, China, Madagascar, India, Malaya, Persia, Turkey, Serbia, Russia, Hungary and many other countries in an idealistic attempt to envision a future 'world literature'. Brahms met him only once, in 1872, and discovered that the aged poet had never heard of the composer who had made him famous throughout Europe.

Dietrich, Albert Hermann (1829–1908) was a German composer and conductor, a pupil of Schumann; Brahms first met and became firm friends with him in Düsseldorf in 1853. He collaborated with Schumann and Brahms in the composition of the 'F-A-E' Sonata for Joachim. From 1861 he was musical director at the court of Oldenburg, where he introduced many of Brahms's works. His own music includes a Symphony, an opera *Robin Hood*, a violin concerto, horn concerti, and chamber works; he published some important recollections of Brahms.

Door, Anton (1831–1919) was an Austrian pianist who studied with Czerny and Sechter. After teaching in Moscow he became a professor of piano at the Vienna Conservatoire, and frequently performed Brahms's piano works.

Dustmann, Marie Luise (1831–99), née Meyer, was a German soprano singer, attached to the Vienna Hofoper; Brahms greatly admired her, and she was

one of those who persuaded him to come to Vienna. She also taught singing
at the Conservatoire.

Epstein, Julius (1832–1918) was an Austrian pianist from Croatia and one of
Brahms's earliest acquaintances and supporters during his first visits to
Vienna. Epstein was professor of piano at the Conservatoire there from 1867
to 1901.

Faber, Bertha (?–?), née Porubsky, was a Viennese singer who became a founding
member of Brahms's women's choir in Hamburg while on an extended stay
in that city. She was the first person to interest him in visiting Vienna, and
she and her husband, the industrialist Arthur Faber, were among his closest
friends after he settled there. Brahms dedicated the *Wiegenlied*, op. 49 no. 4,
to her on the birth of her second son.

Farmer, John (1836–1901) was a Nottingham-born composer and music teacher
who studied at Leipzig and taught in Zürich and subsequently at Harrow
School and Oxford. One of Brahms's earliest British champions, he composed
chamber works, a Requiem for dead Harrovians and a fairy-tale opera
Cinderella, and edited several educational music anthologies.

Fellinger, Richard (1848–1903) was a Viennese industrialist, director of an
engineering firm. He and his wife **Maria** (1849–1925) were among Brahms's
closest friends in Vienna, and towards the end of his life he often spent
Christmas with their family. Maria Fellinger was an enthusiastic photographer, to whom we owe many delightful informal snapshots of Brahms in his
later years.

Feuerbach, Anselm (1829–80), one of the leading German painters of the so-
called 'Roman' group, was the eponymous grandson of the great Bavarian
jurist (who, like Daumer, had been a protector of Kaspar Hauser), and a
nephew of the religious philosopher Ludwig Feuerbach. A late developer,
and evidently a vain and difficult man, he spent much of his career in Italy,
but was a Professor at the Vienna Academy of Art during 1873–6, where his
paintings aroused critical hostility. Brahms first got to know him in the early
1860s when they were introduced by their mutual friend Allgeyer; and after
Feuerbach's death in Venice he composed *Nänie* in his memory. Few modern
commentators have accepted Feuerbach's estimation of himself as a misunderstood genius, but his best paintings, mainly of Classical subjects, in a
monumental style that nevertheless suggests intense personal emotion and is
suffused by a warm, dark palette of colour, shed an interesting light on the
qualities Brahms admired in art.

Friedländer, Max (1852–1934) was a German baritone singer, a pupil of Stockhausen, who later taught singing in Berlin and Harvard. He knew Brahms
in his latter years in Vienna, and in 1922 published an important study of
Brahms's entire song-output.

Gade, Niels Vilhelm (1817–90) was a prolific Danish composer and violinist
who succeeded Mendelssohn as conductor of the Gewandhaus concerts in
Leipzig and was later Director of the Copenhagen Conservatoire. His works
include eight symphonies and various pieces, including a well-known
overture, after James Macpherson's *Ossian*; he was a pioneer in introducing
national colour and folksong into his music. He participated in one of

Brahms's earliest concerts in Hamburg, and they remained on good terms for the next forty years.

Gansbacher, Josef (1829–1911) was an Austrian cellist and teacher of singing who became a professor at the Vienna Conservatoire. He was instrumental in securing Brahms's appointment as conductor of the Singakademie, and was the dedicatee of his First Cello Sonata.

Goldmark, Karl (1830–1915) was a prolific composer of Jewish extraction, born in Hungary, who taught in Vienna from 1850 onwards. He is best remembered for his *Ländliche Hochzeit* Symphony, though in his own day his operas such as *Die Königin von Saba* and *Merlin* had some success. Brahms and he were good friends, and he accompanied the former on some of his Italian travels.

Grädener, Karl Georg Peter (1812–83) was a German cellist, conductor, and composer whom Brahms got to know well in Hamburg in the 1850s. He was a professor at the Vienna Conservatoire in 1862–5, and later returned to Hamburg.

Grimm, Julius Otto (1827–1903), whom Brahms first befriended at Göttingen in 1853, was a pianist, choral conductor, and composer. He and his wife **Philippine** (d. 1895) were close friends of Agathe von Siebold. In 1860 he was one of the signatories of the 'Manifesto' against the New German School.

Groth, Klaus (1819–99) was a poet from Heide, where Brahms's father was born; much of his work is in Low German (*Plattdeutsch*) dialect. He taught literature at Kiel University. Brahms and he were good friends, and some of the composer's finest songs are to his texts.

Hanslick, Eduard (1825–1904) made himself the most influential Austrian music-critic of his generation through his articles in the *Neue freie Presse*, and lectured on musical history at Vienna University. He is notorious for his hostility to Wagner (who satirized him as Beckmesser in *Die Meistersinger*) and Bruckner; after initial reservations he became a strong partisan for Brahms.

Hellmesberger, Joseph (1828–93) was an Austrian conductor, teacher, and violinist, leader of his own string quartet. An infant prodigy, he became Director of the Vienna Conservatoire at twenty-three and remained there until his death, conducting the Gesellschaft concerts until 1859, after which he was leader of the orchestra of the Hofoper. From 1877 he was chief Kapellmeister to Kaiser Franz Josef.

Henschel, Georg, later Sir George (1850–1934), was a German baritone singer, composer and conductor. In a long and eventful career he created the role of Hans Sachs in the first (concert) performance of *Die Meistersinger* in Leipzig and was much in demand in both the oratorio and recital repertoire. In 1881 he became the first conductor of the Boston Symphony Orchestra, settled in London in 1884, conducted the Scottish Orchestra 1893–5, was knighted in 1914, and ended his days as Laird of Alltnacriche in Inverness. He became friendly with Brahms at the Lower Rhine Festival of 1874, and in 1876 they spent a holiday together at Rügen; Henschel's diary of it forms the core of his important reminiscences of Brahms. As a composer his principal works included many songs and a Requiem in memory of his first wife.

Herbeck, Johann (1831–77) was an Austrian conductor and composer who succeeded Hellmesberger as conductor of the Vienna Gesellschaft der Musikfreunde in 1859. He became associated with the Hofoper in 1863 and its Director in 1870, but resigned in 1875 and took over the Gesellschaft concerts again in succession to Brahms. He discovered the original score of Schubert's 'Unfinished' Symphony, which he premièred in Vienna in 1865.

Herzogenberg, Heinrich Picot de Peccaduc, Freiherr von (1843–1900) was a Vienna-born composer and conductor descended from a French aristocratic family. He was conductor of the Leipzig Bach-Verein, 1872–85, and then taught composition at the Berlin Hochschule. A connoisseur of Baroque music and an ardent admirer of Brahms, he wrote much choral, orchestral, instrumental and chamber music; towards the end of his life he concentrated on providing music for the Evangelical church, suitable for communal worship. His wife **Elisabet** (1847–92), née Stockhausen, was the daughter of a Bavarian diplomat who had studied with Chopin; she herself was a fine amateur pianist and singer, and studied briefly with Brahms in Vienna before her marriage. After some years' break she and her husband resumed Brahms's acquaintance in Leipzig, and she became one of his closest and most trusted friends, whose rare insight into his music is demonstrated in their voluminous correspondence.

Heuberger, Richard (1850–1914) was a Viennese critic and composer, mainly of operettas, among which *Der Opernball* remains famous. He had some informal composition lessons with Brahms and thereafter became a good friend. His important recollections of conversations with Brahms were only published in the early 1970s.

Heyse, Paul (1830–1914) was a once-fashionable German poet, dramatist, essayist and novelist; he won the Nobel Prize for Literature in 1910. Brahms found him a highly attractive personality, and set several of his poems as songs.

Hoffmann, Ernst Theodor Amadeus (1776–1822) was a German novelist, composer, opera director and music-critic, one of the pivotal figures of the German Romantic movement. His music includes the influential 'magic opera' *Undine*, and his grotesque novellas present the Romantic view of music in especially powerful form. He was the teenage Brahms's favourite author.

Japha, Louise (1826–1910) was a pianist who befriended Brahms when he was still a child and started to interest him in Schumann. She was a pupil of both Robert and Clara Schumann in Düsseldorf, where her sister Minna was studying painting, and where Brahms renewed their acquaintance in 1853. She was later active in Paris, where she gave the French première of Brahms's Piano Quintet in 1868.

Jenner, Gustav Uwe (1865–1920), born on the island of Sylt, studied briefly in Hamburg with Marxsen, who passed him on to Brahms in Vienna. He was Brahms's only formal pupil, and also studied with Mandyczewski. From 1895 Jenner was Musical Director and conductor at Marburg; as a composer he seems to have confined himself to chamber music and small-scale choral and vocal pieces. He published two volumes of Brahms recollections in 1902–3.

Joachim, Joseph (1831–1907) was a Hungarian violinist, composer and conductor, internationally famous from his teens, who lived successively at Leipzig, Weimar, Hanover and Berlin. At first an adherent of the 'New German' school and a protégé of Liszt, he later renounced these early tendencies, partly as a result of his discovery in 1853 of Brahms, whose close friend and leading champion he became. He was a frequent visitor to Great Britain, and was instrumental in spreading Brahms's fame there. In 1869 he founded the Joachim Quartet and became head of the Music Department at the Berlin Academy of Arts. His own works include several dramatic overtures and three violin concertos. His wife **Amalie** (1839–98), née Schneeweis, who used the professional name Weiss before her marriage, was an alto singer who first made her name in opera, but as Amalie Joachim confined her activities to the concert stage. She became a notable interpreter of Brahms's Alto Rhapsody, and he also wrote the op. 91 songs with viola for her. She separated from her husband in 1884 after his attempt to divorce her failed, chiefly because Brahms offered Amalie support which she made public. His friendship with Joachim revived after a few years, but never with their old closeness.

Kalbeck, Max (1850–1921) was an Austrian music-critic and writer and translator of opera libretti. He first met Brahms in Breslau in 1874, and after settling in Vienna in 1880 became one of the composer's most frequent companions. Brahms set two of his early poems; his chief achievement was the monumental standard biography of Brahms, published 1904–11, and he edited several volumes of Brahms's correspondence.

Keller, Gottfried (1819–90) was a Swiss poet, novelist, and short-story writer of remarkable stylistic range, whose autobiographical novel *Der grüne Heinrich* is the last notable example of the Goethean *Bildungsroman*. Brahms, who first met him in Switzerland in the 1860s, set some of his poetry, and Keller was among the writers with whom he tentatively discussed collaboration on an opera.

Kirchner, Fürchtegott Theodor (1823–1903) was a German organist, pianist and composer, principally of piano pieces, active in Switzerland 1843–73 and later in Leipzig, Dresden and Hamburg. A pupil of Schumann, he first met Brahms in 1856 and became a lifelong friend and an enthusiastic advocate; he was an early performer of the D minor Piano Concerto.

Klinger, Max (1857–1920) was a painter, etcher and sculptor whose work seems partly influenced by the French Symbolist school. In 1880 he dedicated to Brahms a cycle of etchings entitled *Amor and Psyche*, and in 1894, as a belated sixtieth birthday tribute, followed this up with his *Brahmsphantasie* cycle of forty-one etchings inspired by Brahms's works. Brahms responded with the dediction of the *Vier ernste Gesänge*. From 1905 to 1909 Klinger sculpted the large Brahms monument which stands in the Hamburg Musikhalle.

Levi, Hermann (1839–1900) was a German conductor and a strong advocate of Brahms, whom he befriended when Music Director in Karlsruhe. Later, as conductor of the Court Theatre in Munich (1872–96), he became more closely associated with Wagner – with a concomitant cooling of his relations with Brahms – and conducted the première of *Parsifal* in 1882. He was a pioneer in the revival of Mozart's operas.

Mandyczewski, Eusebius (1857–1929) was an Austrian musicologist who succeeded Pohl as keeper of the Archives of the Vienna Gesellschaft der Musikfreunde in 1887, and was later a professor at the Conservatoire, where he himself had studied under Nottebohm and Fuchs. He was one of Brahms's most favoured friends among the circle of younger Viennese musicians in whom he took an interest, and acted as his assistant in various capacities. He was in charge of the Complete Edition of Schubert's works, began the (never finished) Complete Edition of Haydn, and co-edited Brahms's complete works with Hans Gál in 1926–28.

Marxsen, Eduard (1806–87) was a German pianist and composer, born near Hamburg, who studied in Vienna from 1830 with Seyfried and Bocklet. He returned to Hamburg in 1834 and devoted himself mainly to teaching; Brahms was his most famous pupil – he studied with Marxsen 1845–52, and dedicated his Second Piano Concerto to him.

May, Florence (1845–1915) was an English pianist, daughter of the organist and singing-teacher Edward Collett May. In 1871, as a pupil of Clara Schumann, she underwent a course of study with Brahms to improve her keyboard technique, and this laid the foundations of a friendship which eventually resulted in her two-volume biography of the composer, first published in 1905.

Menzel, Adolph von (1815–1905) was a distinguished historical painter who, like Brahms, was a holder of the Prussian order 'Pour le Mérite'. Their friendship – as two peppery old bachelors – began in 1891 when Menzel made a sketch of Mühlfeld at the premières of Brahms's Clarinet Quintet and Trio.

Miller zu Aichholz, Viktor von (18?–19?) was a Viennese industrialist and friend of Brahms who originated the idea of the gold medal struck in honour of the composer's sixtieth birthday. After Brahms's death he devoted much of his energy to perpetuating his memory: he was first president of the Vienna Brahms-Gesellschaft, and opened a Brahms Museum at his villa in Gmunden, where Brahms had often been a guest.

Mühlfeld, Richard (1856–1907) studied as a violinist, but was from 1873 the principal clarinettist in the grand-ducal orchestra at Meiningen, and from 1884 to 1896 was also principal clarinet at Bayreuth. Brahms wrote the Clarinet Quintet, Trio, and the two Sonatas for him.

Nottebohm, Gustav (1817–82) was a German musicologist and composer who knew Mendelssohn and Schumann in Leipzig and settled in Vienna in 1846, where Brahms first met him in 1862 and became a close friend. He compiled thematic catalogues of the works of Beethoven and Schubert, and published a pioneering book on Beethoven's sketches; he was also an avid and scholarly collector of early music, much of which Brahms inherited. His works include some fine chamber compositions and sets of variations for piano, such as the Variations on a Theme of Bach for piano duet.

Ochs, Siegfried (1858–1929) was a celebrated German choral conductor, who founded the Berlin Philharmonic Choir. His memoirs include some important observations of Brahms, whom he knew.

Pohl, Carl Ferdinand (1818–87) was a German organist, bibliographer and musicologist, who studied with Sechter in Vienna and in 1866 became librarian to the Vienna Philharmonic Society. He wrote much on Mozart and Haydn, notably the standard biography of the latter (which he did not live to finish).

Reinthaler, Karl Martin (1822–96) was a German conductor and composer who came to music via the study of theology; from 1858 he was in charge of the music at Bremen Cathedral, where he was responsible for mounting the première of Brahms's *Ein deutsches Requiem*.

Reményi, Eduard (1830–98), originally called Hoffmann, was a Hungarian violinist who studied in Vienna as a classmate of Joachim and took part in the 1848 revolution. He met Brahms in Hamburg in 1850, and his playing of Hungarian gypsy music made a deep impression on him. They formed a violin–piano duo in 1853, and their tour of Germany brought them to Weimar, where Reményi fell under the spell of Liszt and their ways parted. For the rest of his career Reményi toured widely in Europe and the USA: he died in San Francisco.

Richter, Hans (1843–1916) was a Hungarian-born conductor who became a noted Wagnerian and conducted the first *Ring* cycle in 1876. He was also an important exponent of Brahms and Bruckner. He was conductor of the Vienna Hofoper from 1880 to 1898, and became well known in England, conducting the Hallé Orchestra 1899–1911, and the Birmingham Triennial Festivals from 1885.

Rietz, Julius (1812–77) was a German conductor and composer, a pupil of Zelter and Bernhard Romberg. He succeeded Mendelssohn as conductor of opera in Düsseldorf, and during the period 1847–60 conducted the Gewandhaus concerts in Leipzig (including the disastrous early performance of Brahms's Piano Concerto no. 1). His works included two symphonies and four operas.

Rosenhain, Jacob (1813–94) was a German pianist and composer, a protégé of Schumann, who spent much of his career in Paris; he wrote three symphonies, three operas, a piano concerto and much chamber music. He and his wife were good friends of the Schumann family, and Brahms got to know them well during the summers of the 1860s at Lichtenthal.

Rubinstein, Anton (1829–94) was a prolific Russian composer–pianist of German and Polish descent. A pupil of Liszt, he was active in many musical centres, including Vienna, where he conducted the concerts of the Gesellschaft der Musikfreunde immediately before Brahms assumed that position, but from 1858 was most concerned with music in St Petersburg, whose Conservatoire he founded in 1862. His works include many operas and stage oratorios, six symphonies, five piano concertos, ten string quartets and many other works. Brahms liked him as a man but was unimpressed by his compositions.

Scholz, Bernhard (1835–1916) was a German conductor and composer, conductor of the court theatre in Hanover, where he became a friend of Joachim. Along with Brahms, Joachim, and Grimm he was the only other signatory of the ill-fated 'Manifesto' of 1860. He later worked in Berlin and Breslau, eventually becoming Director of the Frankfurt Conservatoire.

Schumann, Clara (1819–96), née Wieck, was the leading woman pianist of the nineteenth century and a composer in her own right. Trained as a child prodigy in Leipzig by her tyrannical father Friedrich Wieck, she gave her first public concert at the age of nine and later toured widely. Despite Wieck's strong opposition, she married Robert Schumann in 1840, becoming his artistic assistant and ideal interpreter as well as mother of their large family. Following Schumann's suicide attempt in 1854 she was strongly drawn to the young Brahms, but opted for a resumption of her professional career although he remained the most important man in her life after Schumann's death. Many of Brahms's piano and chamber works were written with her in mind. Brahms helped look after her seven surviving children during the 1850s, and later advised her on their welfare; he was especially fond of **Julie** (1845–72), to whom he dedicated the op. 23 'Schumann' Variations for piano duet, and **Felix** (1854–79), three of whose poems he set as Lieder.

Siebold, Agathe von (1835–1909), was the daughter of a Göttingen professor and a friend of Brahms's friends Julius and Philippine Grimm. Brahms was greatly attracted to her in the summer of 1858, but was unable to commit himself to marriage, and they never saw one another again after a painful parting in January 1859. In old age she wrote a novelization of the episode, under the title *Erinnerungen*.

Simrock, Fritz August (1837–1901) was junior partner in the Bonn music-publishing firm of N. Simrock when he first met Brahms in 1860 and began to acquire his works for publication. In 1870 he became head of the firm and engineered its relocation in Berlin, becoming Brahms's principal publisher. He was also a good friend and became his principal financial adviser, taking charge of the investment of his capital (not always with success).

Spies, Hermine (1857–93) was a German contralto singer who specialized in Lieder, a pupil of Stockhausen. Her first professional appearance was at Wiesbaden in 1882, when she greatly attracted Brahms, many of whose late songs were written with her in mind.

Spitta, Julius August Philipp (1841–94) was a German musicologist who studied in Göttingen, became professor of music history at Berlin University in 1875, and in 1882 Director of the Hochschule für Musik. He corresponded a great deal with Brahms on the subject of early music, especially Bach – on whom he wrote a classic two-volume critico-biographical study – and Schütz, whose complete works he edited. He also edited those of Buxtehude, and was co-editor with Adler and Chrysander of the quarterly *Vierteljahrsschrift für Musikwissenschaft*.

Stockhausen, Julius (1826–1906) was a German baritone singer, born in Paris, who divided his activities between French opera and German song. He met Brahms in the 1850s and became the first and one of the most important exponents of his Lieder, such as the *Magelone* Romances. From 1862 to 1869 he was conductor of the Hamburg Philharmonic concerts (a post Brahms had coveted), and later taught in Stuttgart, Berlin and Frankfurt.

Tausig, Karl (1841–71) was a Polish pianist–composer of Bohemian origin, a protégé of Liszt in Weimar. He based himself in Vienna in 1862, where he and Brahms struck up a warm friendship despite Tausig's leanings towards the 'New German' school. Together they gave the première of Brahms's Sonata for two pianos and Brahms wrote the Variations on a Theme of

Paganini with Tausig in mind. In 1865 he settled in Berlin, where he opened a school of advanced piano playing.

Volkmann, Friedrich Robert (1815–83) was a German composer from Saxony who studied in Leipzig and was active in Prague and Budapest before settling in Vienna in 1854; in 1878 he returned to Budapest as professor of composition at the National Music Academy there. A gifted composer of chamber, piano, and orchestral music, some of it in a 'Hungarian' style, he was admired by Brahms, who performed some of his works.

Wasielewski, Joseph Wilhelm von (1822–96) was a violinist, conductor, and critic of combined German–Polish extraction. He studied with Mendelssohn and welcomed Brahms to Bonn in 1853, convincing him that he should make the acquaintance of Schumann. His books include the first biography of Schumann (disliked by both Clara and Brahms) and various studies of instruments and instrumental music.

Widmann, Joseph Victor (1842–1911) was a Swiss poet, playwright and critic of German descent who lived in Berne. Brahms and he met in Zürich in 1874 and soon became firm friends. Widmann, whose memoirs contain many recollections of the composer, was among the writers with whom he discussed possible opera collaborations, and was one of Brahms's most frequent companions on his Italian holidays in the latter part of his life.

Appendix D

Select bibliography

The literature on Brahms is inevitably very large, and still expanding. This Bibliography confines itself to necessary standard works in addition to items which have been of assistance in writing this book. It has been compiled with English-speaking readers in mind, but of course English is only the second language of Brahms studies: the first is German, and the selection to some degree reflects this fact.

THEMATIC CATALOGUES AND BIBLIOGRAPHIES

Braunstein, Joseph (ed.), *Thematic catalog of the collected works of Brahms* (New York, 1956). An expanded edition and translation of the 5th (1910) edition of the Simrock catalogue of Brahms's works, first published in 1887 and progressively enlarged.

Hofmann, Kurt, *Die Bibliothek von Johannes Brahms, Bücher- und Musikalienverzeichnis* (Hamburg, 1974).

Kross, Siegfried, *Brahms-Bibliographie* (Tutzing, 1983).

McCorkle, Donald and Margit L., *Brahms Thematisch-Bibliographisches Werkverzeichnis* (Munich, 1984).

Quigley, Thomas, *Johannes Brahms: an annotated bibliography of the literature through 1982* (Metuchen, N.J., 1990)

CORRESPONDENCE

Sixteen Volumes of Brahms's letters to and from various correspondents were published under the editorship of the Deutsches Brahms-Gesellschaft in the series *Johannes Brahms Briefwechsel* (Berlin, 1906–22), as follows:

Vols I and II with Heinrich and Elisabet von Herzogenberg (ed. Max Kalbeck); English version *Johannes Brahms: The Herzogenberg Correspondence*, (London, 1909);

Vol. III with Reinthaler, Dietrich, Bruch, Reinecke, Bernhard Scholz, and others (ed. Wilhelm Altmann);

Vol. IV with J. O. Grimm (ed. Richard Barth);

Vols V and VI with Joachim (ed. Andreas Moser);

Vol. VII with Levi, Gernsheim, and the Hecht and Fellinger families (ed. Leopold Schmidt);

Vol. VIII to Widmann, Schübring and others (ed. Max Kalbeck);

Vols IX–XII to Simrock (ed. Max Kalbeck);

Vol. XIII with Engelmann (ed. Julius Röntgen);

Vol. XIV with publishers other than Simrock (ed. Wilhelm Altmann);

Vol. XV with Wüllner (ed. Ernst Wolff);

Vol. XVI with Spitta and Dessoff (ed. Carl Krebs).

Further principal collections of correspondence are as follows:

Billroth und Brahms im Briefwechsel, ed. Otto Gottlieb-Billroth (Berlin, 1935); English version *Johannes Brahms and Theodor Billroth: letters from a musical friendship*, trans. and ed. Hans Barkan (Norman, Oklahoma, 1957).

Briefe der Freundschaft Johannes Brahms Klaus Groth, ed. Volquart Pauls (Heide, 1956).

Clara Schumann Johannes Brahms Briefe aus den Jahren 1853–1896, ed. Berthold Litzmann (Leipzig, 1927); shortened English version *Letters of Clara Schumann and Johannes Brahms 1853–1896* (2 vols., London, 1927).

Johannes Brahms an Julius Spengel. Unveröffentliche Briefe aus den Jahren 1882–97, ed. Annemarie Spengel (Hamburg, 1959).

Johannes Brahms in seiner Familie. Der Briefwechsel, ed. Kurt Stephenson (Hamburg, 1973).

Johannes Brahms und Fritz Simrock. Weg einer Freundschaft. Briefe des Verlegers an den Komponisten, ed. Kurt Stephenson (Hamburg, 1961).

Johannes Brahms und Julius Allgeyer. Eine Künstlerfreundschaft in Briefen, ed. Alfred Orel (Tutzing, 1964).

Johannes Brahms und Mathilde Wesendonck. Ein Briefwechsel, ed. Erich H. Müller von Asow (Vienna, 1943).

Johannes Brahms an Max Klinger (Leipzig, 1924).

Letters from and to Joseph Joachim, selected and trans. Nora Bickley (London, 1914).

A Working Relationship: The Correspondence between Johannes Brahms and Robert Keller, ed. and trans. George S. Bozarth and Wiltrud Martin (Washington, forthcoming)

In addition, the following articles contain material supplements to the correspondence:

Einstein, Albert, 'Briefe von Brahms an Ernest Frank' (*Zeitschrift für Musikwissenschaft*, IV, 1921–2).

Geiringer, Karl, 'Johannes Brahms im Briefwechsel mit Eusebius Mandyczewski' (*Zeitschrift für Musikwissenschaft*, XV, 1932–3).

——'Brahms and Wagner. With unpublished Letters' (*Musical Quarterly*, XXII, 1936).

Holde, Artur, 'Suppressed Passages in the Brahms–Joachim Correspondence Published for the First Time' (*Musical Quarterly*, XLV, 1959).

Further biographical and correspondence material has been appearing since 1975 in a series of volumes issued by the Hamburg Brahms-Gesellschaft under the title *Brahms-Studien*

GENERAL STUDIES

Bozarth, George S. (ed.), *Brahms Studies: Analytical and Historical Perspectives* (Oxford, 1990)

Bruyr, José, *Brahms* (Paris, 1965).

Culshaw, John, *Brahms: an outline of his life and music* (London, 1948).

Dale, Kathleen, *Brahms: a concertgoer's companion* (London, 1970).

Frisch, Walter (ed.), *Brahms and His World* (Princeton N.J., 1990)

Fuller-Maitland, J.A., *Brahms* (London, 1911).

Gál, Hans, *Johannes Brahms, his work and personality* (London, 1963).

Geiringer, Karl, *Brahms: His Life and Work* (original version, Vienna, 1934–5; 2nd English ed., London, 1948).

Grasberegr, Franz, *Das kleine Brahms-Buch* (Salzburg, 1973).

Keys, Ivor, *Brahms* (London, 1989)

Musgrave, Michael (ed.), *Brahms 2: biographical, documentary and analytical studies* (Cambridge, 1987).

Neunzig, Hans A., *Johannes Brahms. Der Komponist des deutschen Bürgertums* (Vienna/Munich, 1976).

—— *Johannes Brahms, mit Selbstzeugnissen und Bilddokumenten* (Reinbek, 1973).

Pascall, Robert (ed.), *Brahms: documentary and analytical studies* (Cambridge, 1983).

Rostand, Claude, *Brahms* (Paris, 1954–5, 2nd ed., 1978).

Schmidt, Christian Martin, *Johannes Brahms und seine Zeit* (Regensburg, 1983).

BIOGRAPHY AND REMINISCENCES

Dietrich, Albert, *Erinnerungen an Johannes Brahms* (Leipzig, 1898); English ed., *Recollections of Johannes Brahms* (London, 1899).

Drinker, Sophie, *Brahms and his Women's Choruses* (Merion, Pa., 1952).

Erb, Lawrence, *Brahms* (London, 1905, rev. ed. 1934).

Henschel, George, *Personal Recollections of Johannes Brahms* (Boston, 1907; several subsequent eds).

Heuberger, Richard, *Erinnerungen an Johannes Brahms. Tagebuchnotizen aus den Jahren 1875 bis 1897*, ed. Kurt Hofmann (Tutzing, 1976).

Hofmann, R. and K., *Johannes Brahms: Zeittafel zu Leben und Werk* (Tutzing, 1983).

Jenner, Gustav, *Johannes Brahms als Mensch, Lehrer und Künstler* (Marburg, 1905).

Kalbeck, Max, *Johannes Brahms* (Berlin, 4 vols., 1904–14).

May, Florence, *The Life of Johannes Brahms* (London, 1905; 2nd ed., 1948).

Michelmann, Emil, *Agathe von Siebold. Johannes Brahms' Jugendliebe* (Göttingen, 1930).

Pulver, Jeffrey, *Brahms* (London, 1926).

Reich, Nancy B., *Clara Schumann: The Artist and the Woman* (London, 1985).

Schauffler, Robert H., *The Unknown Brahms, his Life, Character and Works* (New York, 1933).

Schumann, Eugenie, *Erinnerungen* (Stuttgart, 1925); English ed., *Memoirs of Eugenie Schumann* (London, 1927).

Smyth, Ethel, *Impressions that Remained* (2 vols., London, 1919).

Brahms

Specht, Richard, *Johannes Brahms. Leben und Werk eines deutschen Meisters* (Hellerau, 1928); English trans. as *Johannes Brahms* (London, 1930).
Stanford, Sir Charles V., *Brahms* (New York, 1912; English ed., London, 1927).
Widmann, J. V., *Erinnerungen an Johannes Brahms* (new ed., Zürich, 1980).

THE MUSIC

Drinker, Henry S., *The chamber music of Johannes Brahms* (Philadelphia, 1932).
Dalhaus, Carl, *Between Romanticism and Modernism: Four Studies in the Music of the Later Nineteenth Century*, trans. Mary Whittall (Berkeley/London, 1980).
Dunsby, Jonathan, *Structural Ambiguity in Brahms: Analytical Approaches to Four Works* (Ann Arbor, 1981).
Evans, Edwin, *Historical, Descriptive and Analytical Account of the Entire Works of Johannes Brahms* (4 vols., London, 1912–35).
Floros, Constantin, *Brahms und Bruckner: Studien zur musikalischen Exegetik* (Wiesbaden, 1980).
Friedländler, Max, *Brahms' Lieder. Einführung in seine Gesänge für eine und zwei Stimmen* (Berlin/Leipzig, 1922; English trans. Oxford, 1928).
Fritsch, Walter M., *Brahms and the principle of developing variation* (Berkeley, Calif., 1984).
Hancock, Virginia, *Brahms's Choral Compositions and His Library of Early Music* (Ann Arbor, 1983).
Harrison, Julius, *Brahms and his four symphonies* (London, 1939).
Horton, John, *Brahms Orchestral Music* (London, 1968).
Jacobson, Bernard, *The Music of Johannes Brahms* (London, 1977).
Keys, Ivor, *Brahms Chamber Music* (London, 1974).
Kraus, Detlef, *Johannes Brahms – composer for the piano* (Wilhelmshaven, 1988).
Kross, Siegfried, *Die Chorwerke von Johannes Brahms* (Berlin-Halensee 1958; 2nd ed., Tutzing, 1963).
Krümmacher, Friedhelm and Steinbeck, Wolfram, (eds), *Brahms-Analysen* (Kassel, 1984).
Mason, Daniel Gregory, *The chamber music of Brahms* (New York, 1933; 2nd ed., Ann Arbor, 1950).
Matthews, Denis, *Brahms Piano Music* (London, 1978)
Morik, Werner, *Johannes Brahms und sein Verhältnis zum deutschen Volkslied* (Tutzing, 1965).
Murdoch, William, *Brahms: with an analytical study of the complete pianoforte works* (London, 1933).
Musgrave, Michael, *The Music of Brahms* (London, 1985).
Sams, Eric, *Brahms Songs* (London, 1972).
Tovey, Donald F., *Essays in Musical Analysis* (6 vols., London, 1933–9)
——'Brahms's Chamber Music', in *Essays and Lectures on Music* (Oxford, 1949).
Zaunschirm, Franz, *Der frühe und der später Brahms* (Hamburg, 1988).

472

ARTICLES

Adler, Guido, 'Johannes Brahms: His achievement, his personality and his position' (*Musical Quarterly*, XIX, 1933).

Behrmann, Martin, 'Die A-cappella Kompositionen von Johannes Brahms und das Problem des Romantischen' (*Musica*, 43, 1989).

Boyd, Malcolm, 'Brahms and the *Four Serious Songs*' (*Musical Times*, July 1967).

Boyer, Thomas, 'Brahms as Count Peter of Provence: A Psychosexual Interpretation of the *Magelone* Poetry' (*Musical Quarterly*, LXVI, 1980).

Bozarth, George S., 'Brahms's duets for soprano and alto, op. 61: A study in chronology and compositional process' (*Studia musicologica*, Vol. 25, 1983).

——'Brahms's Lieder Inventory of 1959–60 and Other Documents of his Life and Work' (*Fontis Artis Musicae*, Vol. 30, 1983).

——'A New Collected Edition for Johannes Brahms' (*The American Brahms Society Newsletter* 6/1, 1988).

Brown, Peter, 'Brahms's Third Symphony and the New German School' (*Journal of Musicology* 2, 1983).

Clapham, John, 'Dvořák's Relations with Brahms and Hanslick' (*Musical Quarterly*, LVII, 1971),

Deutsch, Otto Erich, 'The first editions of Brahms' (2 parts, *Music Review*, May and August 1940).

Fiske, Roger, 'Brahms and Scotland' (*Musical Times*, December 1968).

Forte, Allen, 'Motivic Design and Structural Levels in the First Movement of Brahms's String Quartet in C minor' (*Musical Quarterly*, LXIX, 1983).

——'Motive and Rhythmic Contour in Brahms's Alto Rhapsody' (*Journal of Music Theory*, Vol. 22, 1983).

Frisch, Walter, 'Brahms, developing variation, and the Schoenberg critical tradition' (*19th Century Music*, V, 1981–2).

Garlington, Aubrey S., '*Harzreise als Herzreise*: Brahms's Alto Rhapsody' (*Musical Quarterly*, LXIX, 1983).

Geiringer, Karl, 'Brahms as Reader and Collector' (*Musical Quarterly*, XIX, 1933).

——'Brahms as a Musicologist' (*Musical Quarterly*, LXIX, 1983).

Hancock, Virginia, 'Brahms's Performances of Early Choral Music' (*19th Century Music*, VIII, 1984).

Helms, Siegmund, 'Johannes Brahms und Johann Sebastian Bach' (*Bach-Jahrbuch*, 57, 1971).

Hiebert, Elfrieda, 'The Janus figure of Brahms: A future built upon the past' (*Journal of the American Liszt Society*, No. 16, 1984).

Hill, William G., 'Brahms' Opus 51: A diptych' (*Music Review*, Vol. 13, 1952).

Hollander, Hans, 'Die Terzformel also musikalisches Bauelement bei Brahms' (*Neue Zeitschrift für Musik*, Vol. 133, 1972).

Klenz, William, 'Brahms, Op. 38: Piracy, pillage, plagiarism or parody? (*Music Review*, Vol. 34, 1973).

Kross, Siegfried, 'Johannes Kreisler's Certificate of Apprenticeship' (*19th Century Music*, IV, 1982).

——'The choral music of Johannes Brahms' (*American Choral Review*, Vol. 25, 1983).

Brahms

Küchler, Stephan, 'Das Klaviertrio in H-Dur, op. 8 von Johannes Brahms. Ein Vergleich der beiden Fassungen': in *Professor Rudolf Stephan zum 3. April 1985 von seinen Schülern* (Berlin, 1985).

Lesznai, Lajos, 'Auf den Spuren einer ungarischen Intonation in den Werken von Johannes Brahms' (*Musik und Gesellschaft*, Vol. 21, 1971).

Mason, Colin, 'Brahms's piano sonatas' (*Music Review*, Vol. 5, 1944).

Musgrave, Michael, 'Historical Influences in the Growth of Brahms's Requiem' (*Music & Letters*, Vol. 53, January 1972).

——'Frei aber Froh: A reconsideration' (*19th Century Music*, IV, 1980).

——'Brahms's First Symphony: Thematic coherence and its secret origin' (*Music Analysis*, 2, 1983).

Neighbour, Oliver, 'Brahms and Schumann: Two Opus Nines and Beyond' (*19th Century Music*, VII, 1984).

Newman, Sidney, 'The Slow Movement of Brahms's First Symphony' (*Music Review*, Vol. 29, 1948).

Pascall, Robert, 'Some special uses of sonata form by Brahms' (*Soundings*, Vol. 4, 1974).

——'Ruminations on Brahms's chamber music' (*Musical Times*, August 1975).

——'Brahms's First Symphony Slow Movement: The Initial Performing Version' (*Musical Times*, October 1981).

——'Brahms and Schubert' (*Musical Times*, 1983).

Pisk, Paul A., 'Dreams of death and life: A study of two songs by Johannes Brahms': in *Festival Essays for Pauline Alderman: a musicological tribute* (Provo, Utah, 1976).

Redlich, Hans, 'Bruckner and Brahms Quintets in F' (*Music & Letters*, Vol. 36, 1955).

Reynolds, Christopher, 'A Choral Symphony by Brahms?' (*19th Century Music*, IX, 1985–6).

Rosen, Charles, 'Influence: Plagiarism and inspiration' (*19th Century Music*, IV, 1981).

Sams, Eric, 'Brahms and his Clara themes' (*Musical Times*, May 1971).

Schachter, Carl, 'The first movement of Brahms's Second Syymphony: The first theme and its consequences' (*Music Analysis*, 2, 1983).

Schoenberg, Arnold, 'Brahms the Progressive': in *Style and Idea* (New York, 1950, 2nd ed. London, 1975).

Schwarz, Boris, 'Joseph Joachim and the genesis of Brahms's Violin Concerto' (*Musical Quarterly*, LXIX, 1983).

Sisman, Elaine, 'Brahms and the Variation Canon' (*19th Century Music*, XIV, 1990).

Truscott, Harold, 'Brahms and sonata style' (*Music Review*, Vol. 25, 1964).

Walker, Alan, 'Brahms and Serialism' (*Musical Opinion*, Vol. 81, 1958).

Webster, James, 'Schubert's sonata form and Brahms's first maturity' (*19th Century Music*, II, 1978–9, and III, 1979–80).

——'The C sharp Minor Version of Brahms's Op. 60' (*Musical Times*, February 1980).

474

Appendix E

Who wrote the A major Trio?

In 1924 Ernst Bücken, Professor of Music at Cologne University, received a collection of manuscripts from the estate of a Dr Erich Preiger of Bonn. Among these was the score of a Piano Trio in A major, whose title-page was missing, and which carried no composer's signature or other ascription. It was not in Brahms's hand; but, arguing from stylistic grounds alone that this was a copyist's manuscript of an early composition of Brahms, Bücken arranged for the work to be performed at the 1925 Rhenish Chamber Music Festival and later collaborated with Karl Hasse on an edition of it, published by Breitkopf & Härtel in 1938. (A reprint was issued in 1982.) Since Bücken's own death the autograph has not been located. According to Hasse's editorial report, at the end of the first-movement coda another hand had sketched a revision of one bar into two: this hand was not Brahms's, but neither is the revision in any way an improvement of the musical sense.

The Trio has since become the Cinderella of Brahms scholarship. Though Bücken's arguments were cautiously accepted by continental scholars, and the ascription to Brahms has brought the work a couple of commercial recordings over the years, it has been treated with scant interest by most commentators – who feel safe in dismissing it as 'inferior' Brahms since Brahms clearly had no interest in publishing it. English-speaking writers have been more sceptical: Ivor Keys in *Brahms Chamber Music* (London, 1974) dismisses it in a footnote as a work that 'can safely be regarded as spurious'; Musgrave does not discuss it, except to assign it among 'Dubious Works' in his work-list, but the epithet '(Spurious)' stands against it in his Index. Bozarth (op. cit., p. 76) cautiously, and justly, opines that 'a full-length analytical study' of the piece 'in relationship to the stylistic characteristics of Brahms's music through the early 1860s' is needed properly to assess its authenticity.

Though I have not undertaken such a study, and though I have no theories as to why the work should have been silently abandoned by its composer, I am prepared to accept that the A major Trio is by Brahms. Lacking all but internal evidence, Bücken was surely right to trust his ears. It is very well composed, and certainly sounds like Brahms – albeit with those echoes of Beethoven, Schubert, Mendelssohn and Schumann which in differing balances and to different degrees can be found in almost all his early works. The inner movements are the most obviously characteristic, especially the Scherzo and Trio, a fine example of a form in which he had established an individual manner from the first; the slow movement compares favourably with that of the op. 8 Trio in its 1854 version, and has a similarly Schubertian flavour. The outer movements impress by their fluent structure, confident use of contrapuntal device including canon and augmentation (the latter to striking thematic effect in the Finale), rich piano chordal writing reminiscent of the early keyboard works, fondness for two-against-three cross-rhythms and other typical features. The first movement's opening theme (to my ears at least) presages in different ways those of the Piano Quintet and the F major String Quintet; for musical cryptographers, the second limb of the Finale's opening theme yields a version of the 'Clara motif' (particularly clear in the violin, bars 9–10); and the Finale also contains a tune in overtly 'Hungarian' style.

Most writers who have accepted the Trio's authenticity have argued for a very early date, either the Hamburg period pre–1853, or (as Bücken thought) from Brahms's sojourn in Bonn and Mehlem shortly before his first meeting with Schumann. Brahms returned to Bonn several times in the 1850s; equally, the fact that the manuscript emanated from Bonn does not inevitably mean it was written there. The actual copying appears to have taken place in the 1860s. In the main text of this book I have tentatively placed the work two or three years later than 1853. Compared to op. 8, composed in early 1854, the A major Trio is much tauter in form, and could plausibly be regarded as an early reaction to op. 8's wilder structural and emotional excesses. Like op. 8 it manifests a 'Bachian' chromatically contrapuntal element, but this is worked out in the Finale (on the theme I have quoted as Ex. 15) rather than interrupting the first movement which is here a concise and, if anything, understated sonata form. Moreover the Schumannesque touches, seldom found in Brahms's works before late 1853, are considerably more assimilated than in op. 8.

The question of dating, like that of authenticity, has to remain open, of course, in the absence of any scrap of documentary evidence. As to the quality of the music, it certainly lacks some of the sumptuous tunefulness and high Romanticism of op. 8, but the work is clearly and perhaps consciously of different orientation: we might compare the pairing a few years later of the fiery G minor Piano Quartet with its more poised, Apollonian A major companion. Certainly on long acquaintance I have found the A major Trio a score of many subtleties, which repays study and repeated hearings.

The fact remains that, whoever wrote it, the quality of the music is consistently high. Though not in the first rank of nineteenth-century trios, it has a fair claim to be numbered in the second; and if we dismiss the ascription to Brahms we are forced to argue the existence of an otherwise entirely unknown minor master of chamber music who wrote in a manner closely resembling his. Which is easier to believe? I may mention in conclusion that, as an incorrigible player of that parlour-game which involves forcing one's musical friends to 'guess the composer', I have many times tried out a recording of the A major Trio, and have yet to find anyone who has not, within thirty seconds and as first choice, confidently identified the piece as by Brahms.

Index

Aachen Liedertafel, 187
Abegg, Meta, 34
Abell, Arthur M., 396
Adler, Guido, 148, 467
Ahle, Johann Georg, 148, 230
Alabiev, Alexander, 61
d'Albert, Eugen, 297–8, 405
Albrechtsberger, Johann Georg, 7
Alkan, Charles-Valentin, 23, 62, 69
    Douze Etudes dans les tons mineurs,
      100, 180
    Grande Sonate, 67
    Trois Grandes Etudes, 62
Allgemeine Musikalische Zeitung, 136
Allgeyer, Julius, 40, 131, 133, 238, 459, 461
Altenstein, 241
Altona, 7, 9, 46
Amsterdam, 301
Ancona, 294
Arbeau, Thionot, 147
d'Arien, 11
Arminius, 50
Arnim, Bettina von, 17, 36, 320, 459
Arnim, Gisela von, 20, 36, 40, 320, 459
Arnim, Ludwig Achim von, 23, 25, 151,
    326, 459
Arnold, Friedrich Wilhelm, 151
Asch, 34
Austro-Prussian War, 141
Avé-Lallemant, Theodor, 48, 126, 232, 459

Bach, Carl Philipp Emmanuel, 147
Bach, Johann Sebastian, 10, 28–9, 33, 55,
    76, 88, 92–3, 113, 120, 132, 143–4,
    148, 174–5, 187, 196–7, 230–1, 258,
    263, 269, 298, 309, 330, 379–80, 387,
    406, 409, 415, 417, 467
    Cantata no. 4, 114, 148
    Cantata no. 21, 129, 148
    Cantata no. 27, 197
    Cantata no. 149, 315

    Cantata no. 150, 146, 309–10, 312
    Chaconne in D minor, 158, 311, 318
    Christmas Oratorio, 129
    Chromatic Fantasia and Fugue, 92
    Double Violin Concerto, 322
    English Suites, 88
    'Goldberg' Variations, 179
    Die Kunst der Fuge, 33, 76, 93, 174, 409,
      411
    Musikalisches Opfer, 175
    Orgelbüchlein, 380
    St Matthew Passion, 101, 230
    Sonatas for bass viol, 174
    Das wohltemperierte Klavier, 393
Bach, Wilhelm Friedemann, 147
Bach-Gesellschaft, 143, 145–6, 174
Baden-Baden, 129, 131–2, 175, 192, 321
Balfe, Michael, 367
Banchieri, Adriano, 147
Barbi, Alice, 297, 301, 459
Bargheer, Karl Louis, 50–1, 232
Bargiel, Woldemar, 18, 37, 49, 51, 59,
    459
Bartók, Béla, 23, 193, 364
Beethoven, Ludwig van, 19, 23, 25, 31–3,
    35, 48, 53, 57, 62–5, 125, 127, 129,
    136, 147, 161, 197, 209–10, 214, 231,
    233, 245, 248, 250, 253, 298, 301, 312,
    341–2, 387, 393, 399–401, 411, 417,
    465, 475
    An die ferne Geliebte, 79
    Cello Sonatas op. 102, 174
    Choral Fantasia, 231
    'Diabelli' Variations, 179–80
    'Eroica' Variations, 179
    Fidelio, 188
    Missa Solemnis, 230
    Piano Concerto no. 3, 389
    Piano Concerto no. 4, 46, 49
    Piano Concerto no. 5, 'Emperor', 22, 46,
      99, 230, 277

Piano Sonata op. 106, 'Hammerklavier', 65, 144, 180, 312, 389
Piano Trio op. 97, 'Archduke', 75
Quintet op. 16, 7
'Rasumovsky' Quartets, 210, 287
Septet, 105
Symphony no. 2, 107
Symphony no. 3, 'Eroica', 302, 311
Symphony no. 5, 32, 168, 246, 248
Symphony no. 6, 'Pastoral', 106
Symphony no. 7, 119
Symphony no. 9, 99, 247–8, 311, 384
Triple Concerto, 322
Variations in C minor, 311
Violin Concerto, 10, 233
Violin Sonatas, 7, 12
Die Wiehe des Hauses, 209
Berg, Alban, 290, 411
Berger, Wilhelm, 404
Berio, Luciano, 417
Berlin, 41, 45, 49, 59, 135, 139, 297, 309, 383
Berlioz, Hector, 20, 23, 27, 58, 61, 70
Harold in Italy, 230
'Rákóczy' March, 61
Symphonie Fantastique, 27
Bernsdorf, Edward, 53
Billroth, Theodor, 133–4, 210, 225, 231, 240, 242, 274, 293–6, 321, 372, 412, 459
Bismark, Otto von, 141
Bizet, Georges, 149
Carmen, 149
Blacher, Boris, 182
Bloch, Ernst, 3, 197
Blom, Eric, vii, ix
Blume, 10
Bocklet, Carl Maria von, 7, 465
Böhme, Franz, 152
Böhme, Jakob, 26
Boie, John, 232
Bologna, 294
Bonn, 14, 47, 123, 137, 224, 299
Bononcini, Giovanni, 147
Borwick, Leonard, 405
Boulez, Pierre, 416
Bozarth, George, 20, 475
Brahms, Caroline (Schnack), 133–4, 142
Brahms, Christiane (née Nissen), 5–7, 128, 131–2, 175, 195

Brahms, Elise, 5, 47, 128, 142, 240, 243, 296
Brahms, Fritz, 6, 19, 128, 131–2, 142, 296
Brahms, Johann, 4–5
Brahms, Johann Jakob, 4–9, 21, 128, 131–6, 142, 186
Brahms, Johannes

WORKS

Chamber music
Cello Sonata no. 1, 172–5, 285, 287, 311, 462
Cello Sonata no. 2, 292, 330–3, 334, 336, 387
Clarinet Quintet, 297, 344, 360–8, 388, 465
Clarinet Sonata no. 1, 297, 361, 368–70, 417
Clarinet Sonata no. 2, 297, 361, 368–71
Clarinet Trio, 297, 355, 361–2, 366–8, 392, 465
Duo for cello and piano, 73
Hymne zur Verherrlichung des grossen Joachim, 14, 73–4
Horn Trio, 119, 133, 175–7
Nonet, 51, 105
Phantasie Trio, 73
Piano Quartet no. 1, 50, 124, 160–4, 271, 412, 476
Piano Quartet no. 2, 96, 124, 162–4, 275, 385, 476
Piano Quartet no. 3, 160, 225–8, 230, 245, 247, 275, 279, 281, 389, 392,
Piano Quartet in C sharp minor, 45, 90, 160, 225, 227
Piano Quintet, 132, 164–71, 226, 247, 252, 335, 367, 385–6, 388, 463, 476
Piano Trio no. 1 21, 46, 74–80, 90, 93, 95–6, 100, 102, 113, 161, 227, 248, 283, 314, 322, 393, 475–6
(revised version, 1889), 338–42
Piano Trio no. 2, 278, 282–4, 292, 303, 335
Piano Trio no. 3, 292, 322, 330, 334–6, 341, 366
Piano Trio in A major, 75, 95–8, 108, 475–6
Piano Trio in E flat, 282
Scherzo for 'F-A-E' Sonata, 17, 74, 303, 332

String Quartet no. 1, op. 51/1, 139, 209–13, 230, 248

String Quartet no. 2, op. 51/2, 139, 209–10, 213–15, 230, 271, 303, 386

String Quartet no. 3, op. 67, 250–2, 275, 319, 366

String Quartet in B flat, 19, 73

String Quintet no. 1, 88, 278, 284–7, 292, 311, 334, 476

String Quintet no. 2, 296, 300, 342–5, 362

String Quintet in F minor, 125, 129, 164–6, 284

String Sextet no. 1, 50, 52, 123–4, 158–60, 170, 172–3, 250, 275, 400–1

String Sextet no. 2, 88, 132, 170–3, 285–6, 387

Violin Sonata no. 1, 228, 278–82, 292, 336, 390

Violin Sonata no. 2, 292, 330, 332–4, 336, 344, 348, 350

Violin Sonata no. 3, 336–8

Violin Sonata in A minor, 19–20, 73

Choral works

Alto Rhapsody, 140, 187, 202, 204–6, 221, 253, 272, 322, 464

Ave Maria, 55, 113, 129

Begräbnisgesang, 56, 113–15, 202, 287, 305

Canons op. 113, 1–2, 51, 56, 91, 113–15, 202, 296, 327

Dem dunkeln Schoss der heil'gen Erde, 224

Ein deutsches Requiem, 26, 99, 114, 132–8, 141, 157, 187, 195–203, 209, 230, 245, 256, 371, 373, 396, 466

Fest- und Gedenksprüche, 209, 295, 325, 328–9

Geistliche Chöre, 56, 91, 384

Geistliches Lied, 90–1

Gesang der Parzen, 119, 202, 240, 287, 289–92, 372, 396, 415

4 Gesänge, op. 17, 56, 118–19, 123, 176

Kleine Hochzeitskantate, 194, 355

Kyrie in G minor, 91–2

Liebeslieder Suite, 216, 220

6 Lieder und Romanzen, op. 93a, 153, 325–6, 348, 353

12 Lieder und Romanzen, op. 44, 117

5 Männerchöre, op. 41, 184, 207

Marienlieder, 56, 116, 129

Mass (*Missa Canonica*), 91–2, 102, 258–9

2 Motets op. 29, 56, 119–21, 129, 379

2 Motets op. 74, 91, 119–22, 196, 256–9, 328, 353, 386

3 Motets op. 110, 325, 328–30

Nänie, 202, 240, 287–9, 319, 372, 392, 461

3 Partsongs op. 42, 56, 117–18

7 Partsongs op. 62, 223–4, 325

5 Partsongs op. 104, 325–7, 354

Psalm 13, 56, 115–16

Rinaldo, 52, 128, 137, 139, 184–5, 187–9, 200, 322, 398

Schicksalslied, 137, 187, 201–4, 233, 289, 396

Tafellied, 325, 355

Triumphlied, 141, 189, 206–9, 256, 298

Organ music

Chorale Prelude and Fugue on O *Traurigkeit*, 92–3, 120

11 Chorale Preludes op. 122, 92, 143, 299, 378–81, 384, 409

Fugue in A flat minor, 92–3

2 Preludes and Fugues, 92

Orchestral works

Academic Festival Overture, 233, 271–3, 350

Double Concerto, 243, 292, 320–5, 336, 342, 368, 400

Piano Concerto no. 1, 50, 53–4, 57–8, 71, 90, 99–104, 107–8, 114, 123–4, 133, 164, 195, 245, 275, 389, 464, 466

Piano Concerto no. 2, 106, 163, 240, 274–9, 314, 332, 350, 383, 409, 465

Serenade no. 1, 50–1, 54–5, 104–9, 252, 255, 277, 364, 386

Serenade no. 2, 50, 56–7, 96, 105, 107–9, 123–4, 126, 270, 305

Symphony no. 1, 63, 125, 169, 230, 232–3, 240–1, 245–50, 252–3, 278, 304, 336, 384, 388, 411

Symphony no. 2, 205, 209, 233, 252–6, 264, 268–9, 277, 292, 304, 306, 365, 388, 416

Symphony no. 3, 35, 234, 240, 292, 302–8, 332, 344, 406

Index

Orchestral works – *contd*

Symphony no. 4, 76, 104, 146, 153, 228, 240–1, 292, 300, 308–20, 323, 348, 374, 380, 387–9, 391, 406–7, 409–10, 414–15

Symphony in D minor, 45, 50, 71, 90, 99, 114, 195, 225, 246

Tragic Overture, 272–4, 285, 287, 305, 318, 335

Variations on a Theme of Haydn, 215–18, 230, 311, 386

Violin Concerto, 233, 242, 264, 268–71, 275, 278, 389

Piano music

Ballades, op. 10, 40, 84–8, 90, 110, 186, 264, 355–7, 385

Blätter aus dem Tagebuch eines Musikers, 83–4

7 Fantasien, op. 116, 355–7, 370

2 Gavottes, 46, 88, 172, 286

2 Gigues, 88

Hungarian Dances, 51, 138, 162, 177–8, 191–3, 267, 278, 353

8 Klavierstücke, op. 76, 265–7, 355–6

3 Klavierstücke, op. 117, 355–7

6 Klavierstücke, op. 118, 355–6, 358–60

4 Klavierstücke, op. 119, 355–6, 360–1, 369

Phantasie über eine geliebten Walzer, 10, 60

Prelude and Aria, 88

2 Rhapsodies, op. 78, 265–7, 360, 367

2 Sarabandes, 46, 88–9, 286

Scherzo, op. 4, 11, 13, 19–20, 60, 62–3, 370

Sonata no. 1, op. 1, 13, 15, 19–20, 63–6, 385, 389

Sonata no. 2, 19–20, 62–4, 66, 223

Sonata no. 3, op. 5, 14, 19, 45, 66–71, 75, 79, 337–8, 389, 392, 409

Sonata for 2 pianos in D minor, 71, 99

Sonata for 2 pianos in F minor, op. 34b, 129, 147, 164–5, 216, 467

Souvenir de la Russie, 61, 177

51 Übungen, 181, 296, 360

Variations and Fugue on a Theme of Handel, 124, 126, 130, 159, 178–81, 183, 208, 215, 275, 409, 417

Variations on a Hungarian Song, 80, 82, 94, 354, 385

Variations on a Theme of Paganini, 181–3, 216, 265, 275, 409, 467

Variations on a Theme of Schumann, op. 9, 30, 35, 40, 74, 80–4, 90, 94, 177, 215

Variations on a Theme of Schumann, op. 23, 124, 177–8, 215–16, 467

Variations on an Original Theme, 80, 90, 93–5

16 Waltzes, 190–3, 400

Songs

Deutsche Volks-Kinderlieder, 51, 109, 152

28 Deutsche Volkslieder (1858), 109, 153

49 Deutsche Volkslieder (1894), 152–6, 292, 296, 348, 351, 380, 392, 409

4 ernste Gesänge, op. 121, 153, 298, 350–1, 355, 367, 371–9, 382, 391, 396, 409, 414, 416, 464

6 Gesänge, op. 3, 12, 19, 71–3

6 Gesänge, op. 6, 71–3

6 Gesänge, op. 7, 71–3, 236

8 Lieder und Romanzen, op. 14, 51, 109–11, 152, 186, 288

5 Gedichte, op. 19, 51, 109–11, 360

9 Lieder und Gesänge, op. 32, 184, 189–90

Magelone Romances, op. 33, 3, 52, 112, 124–5, 184–90, 200, 220, 261, 372, 398, 467

4 Gesänge, op. 43, 110, 186, 200–1

4 Lieder und Gesänge, op. 46, 200–1

5 Lieder und Gesänge, op. 47, 111, 200

7 Lieder und Gesänge, op. 48, 200–1, 219, 224

5 Lieder und Gesänge, op. 49, 200–1, 393, 400, 461

8 Lieder und Gesänge, op. 57, 218–19

8 Lieder und Gesänge, op. 58, 218–19

8 Lieder und Gesänge, op. 59, 218–20, 279–80

9 Lieder und Gesänge, op. 63, 218, 220

9 Lieder und Gesänge, op. 69, 259–61

4 Lieder und Gesänge, op. 70; 259–62

5 Lieder und Gesänge, op. 71, 259–63, 352

5 Lieder und Gesänge, op. 72, 259–63

5 Romanzen und Lieder, op. 84, 259–60
6 Lieder, op. 85, 259, 261, 392
6 Lieder, op. 86, 259–60, 262, 392
2 Gesänge (with viola), op. 91, 132, 345–6, 464
5 Lieder, op. 94, 312, 345–7, 392
7 Lieder, op. 95, 345–9
4 Lieder, op. 96, 345–51
6 Lieder, op. 97, 333, 345, 347–8, 350
5 Lieder, op. 105, 332–4, 345, 350–1
5 Lieder, op. 106, 345, 350–1
5 Lieder, op. 107, 345, 350–1
5 Ophelia-Lieder, 218
Regenlied, 219, 228

Transcriptions
Bach: Chaconne in D minor, 150, 269
Bach: Presto in G major, 150
Beethoven: 'Rasumovsky' no. 3 finale, 287
Chopin: Etude, 60
'Rákóczy' March, 61
Weber: Rondo, 60

Vocal duets and quartets
4 Balladen und Romanzen, op. 75, 264–265
3 Duets, op. 20, 51, 112, 264
4 Duets, op. 28, 112–13, 223, 264
4 Duets, op. 61, 112, 223, 264
4 Duets, op. 66, 223, 264
Liebeslieder Waltzes, 112, 139–40, 191, 193–4, 199, 204, 220–1, 329, 353, 368, 460
Neue Liebeslieder, 194, 220–2
3 Quartets, op. 31, 129, 190–1, 194
3 Quartets, op. 64, 221–3
4 Quartets, op. 92, 352–3
6 Quartets, op. 112, 352, 354–5
Zigeunerlieder, 112, 292, 321, 352–4

Writings
Des jungen Kreislers Schatzkästlein, 24, 33
Oktaven und Quinten, 148–9

Brahms, Peter, 4
Brahms, Peter Hinrich, 4
Breitkopf & Härtel, 17, 19, 62, 73, 81, 123, 146, 148, 243, 338, 475

Bremen, 46, 134–5, 141
Brendel, Franz, 20, 58
Brentano, Clemens, 23, 25, 151, 262, 459
    Des Knaben Wunderhorn, 151, 223–4
Brescia, 294
Breslau, 233, 239, 271
Brinkmann, Otto, 14, 73
Brinkmann, Reinhold, 253
Brodsky, Adolf, 404
Bronsart von Schellendorff, Hans, 35
Bruch, Max, 59, 136–7, 396
    Odysseus, 230
    Symphony no. 1, 137
Bruckner, Anton, 23, 120, 231–2, 330, 408, 466
    Symphony no. 5, 311
Brüll, Ignaz, 293, 301, 310, 459
Brunsbüttel, 4
Bücken, Ernest, 475
Budapest, 41, 139, 192, 402
Bülow, Hans von, 21, 57–8, 146, 232, 240–1, 294, 296, 309–10, 323, 372, 459–60
Burgmüller, Norbert, 38
    Rhapsody, 38
    Symphonies, 38
Busoni, Ferruccio, 150, 235, 239, 270, 380, 408–9
    Doktor Faust, 409
    Etudes, 408–9
    Fantasia Contrappuntistica, 409
    Piano Concerto, 409
    Variations and Fugue on Chopin's C minor Prelude, 409
Buxtehude, Diderik, 146–7
Byrd, William, 55, 147

Caldara, Antonio, 55, 147, 149
Callot, Jacques, 40
Cambridge, 233, 246, 295, 301, 405
Campra, André, 147
Candidus, Karl, 219, 260, 263
Cardus, Neville, 306, 401
Carissimi, Giacomo, 146–7
Carter, Elliott, 417
Catania, 294
Cavalli, Francesco, 147
Celle, 12
Cesti, Antonio, 147
Cherubini, Luigi, vii, 149, 197, 383
    Requiem in C minor, 230

Index

Chesterton, G. K., 400
Chopin, Frédéric, 23, 28–9, 62, 66, 84, 148, 182, 399, 463
 Ballades, 84
Chrysander, Friedrich, 145–8, 460, 467
Clemens non Papa, Jacobus, 149
Clementi, Muzio, 7, 29, 124
Colditz, 141, 243
Cologne, 15, 47, 136, 139, 243
Conrat, Hugo, 353–4
Copenhagen, 135
Corelli, Arcangelo, 146–7
Cornelius, Peter, 13, 130, 349
Cossel, Otto, 6–8, 460
Couperin, Louis, 146–7, 266
Cramer, Johann Baptist, 7
Cranz, August, 10, 60
Cuthullin, 119
Czerny, Carl, 7, 460

Dandrieu, Jean François, 147
Dante Aligheri, 27
Danzig, 46
Daumer, Georg, 139, 189–90, 194, 200, 218, 221, 347–8, 352, 460–1
 Polydora, 194, 221–2, 460
David, Ferdinand, 19–20
Debussy, Achille-Claude, 331
Deichmann, 14–15
Denkmäler der Tonkunst, 146
Denkmäler deutscher Tonkunst, 146
Dessoff, Otto, 256, 395
Detmering, 5
Detmold, 48–51, 55–6, 113, 120, 144, 151, 158, 161, 224
Dickens, Charles, 400
Dieters, Hermann, 136, 150, 225
Dietrich, Albert, 17–20, 36, 39, 59, 123–5, 133–7, 177, 195, 245, 460
 Symphony, 36
 Violin Concerto, 36, 230
Dingelstedt, Franz von, 272
Dittmarschen, 4, 46
Dohler, Theodor, 10
Door, Anton, 46, 460
Dowland, John, 147
Dresden, 36, 135
Dunkl, 192
Dürer, Albrecht, 203
Düsseldorf, 15–19, 21–2, 39–41, 43–7, 49–

50, 73, 123, 125, 131, 151, 231, 243, 304
Dustmann, Luise, 125, 460–1
Dvořák, Antonin, 172, 231, 252, 268, 277, 301, 305, 396, 412
 Cello Concerto, 300
 Symphony no. 3, 231
 Symphony no. 8, 305

Eber, Paul, 330
Eccard, Johann, 55, 129, 148, 230
Echo, 59
Eckert, Carl Florian, 322
Eichendorff, Joseph von, 1, 71, 73, 112, 118–19, 261, 378
Eisler, Hanns, 415
 Gegen den Krieg, 415
Elgar, Edward, 108, 289, 306, 343, 405–8
 The Dream of Gerontius, 405
 Introduction and Allegro, 343
 Symphony no. 1, 406
 Violin Concerto, 343
Endenich, 22, 39, 44, 47
Epstein, Julius, 125, 236, 300, 461
Erb, Laurence, vii, ix
Erbach, Dionigi, 147
Erk, Ludwig, 152

Faber, Arthur, 300–1, 461
Faber, Bertha, 45, 55, 125, 133, 200, 239, 393, 461
Farmer, John, 136, 233, 461
Fauré, Gabriel, 66, 266, 351, 358
Fellinger, Maria, 234, 239, 461
Fellinger, Richard, 239, 296, 299, 300–1, 461
Feuerbach, Anselm, 131, 287–9, 295, 459, 461
Feuerbach, Henriette, 288
Flemming, Paul, 90
Florence, 293
Förster, Georg, 147
Foulds, John, 404
Franco-Prussian War, 141, 207
Frankfurt, 45, 153, 241, 298–9, 413
Franz, Robert, 18, 24
Franz Josef I, Emperor of Austria, 292, 295, 462
Frederike, Princess of Lippe-Detmold, 49
Frescobaldi, Girolamo, 147

Freund, Robert, 294
Friedländer, Max, 397, 399, 461
Friedrich, Caspar David, 26, 350
Frey, Adolf, 351
Froberger, Johann Jacob, 147
Fuchs, Robert, 403–4, 465
Fuller-Maitland, J. A., 207, 222–3, 367
Furtwängler, Wilhelm, 396, 417

Gabrieli, Giovanni, 55, 114, 117, 129, 145, 149
Gade, Niels, 11, 18, 24, 59, 135, 232, 461–2
Gál, Hans, 465
Gallus, Jacobus (Handl), 55, 230
Gansbacher, Josef, 132, 173, 462
Garbe, Laura, 56
Geffcken, Johannes, 6
Geibel, Emanuel, 37, 347
Geiringer, Karl, 272, 288, 338, 378, 395
George, King of Hanover, 12
George II, Duke of Saxe Meiningen, 240–1, 294
Gernsheim, Friedrich, 37, 136
Gersau, 47
Gesellschaft der Musikfreunde, 62, 126, 129, 134, 139–40, 142, 144, 229–31, 239, 295–6, 300, 402, 410, 463, 465–6
Giebichstein, 27
Giesemann, Adolf, 9–10
Giesemann, Lieschen, 9–10, 185
Glasgow, 240
Gleich, Ferdinand, 53
Gluck, Christoph Willibald, 31, 149, 188, 230
Goethe, Johann Wolfgang von, 25–8, 33, 91, 111–13, 187–91, 202, 204, 219–21, 223, 225, 260, 263, 326, 353, 398, 417, 459
   Alexis und Dora, 221
   Faust, 27, 272
   Harzreise im Winter, 140, 204
   Iphigenie, 289
   Rinaldo, 187–9, 194, 398
   Werther, 225, 228
Goetz, Hermann, 288
Goldmark, Karl, 230, 293, 462
Goldschmidt, Otto, 11
Göttingen, 12, 14, 50–1, 112–13, 271
Gould, Glenn, 102
Gozzi, Carlo, 238

Grädener, Karl, 37, 48, 55, 59, 125, 151, 295, 462
Grainger, Percy, 409
Graz, 295
Grieg, Edvard, 237, 298, 300–1, 396
   Violin Sonata no. 1, 334
Grimm brothers (Jakob Ludwig and Wilhelm Karl), 25, 459
Grimm, Hermann, 36, 459
Grimm, Julius Otto, 19–20, 29, 39, 46, 51, 59, 91, 99, 105, 135, 232, 462, 466–7
Grimm, Philippine, 51, 135, 462, 467
Groth, Klaus, 4, 9, 46, 219–20, 223, 232, 240, 279, 292, 327, 332, 348, 351, 462
Grund, Wilhelm, 56
Gungl, Joseph, 261

Hafiz, Shams al-Din Muhammud, 190
Hallé Orchestra, 404
Halm, Friedrich, 346–7
Hamburg, 4, 9–13, 17–18, 21, 37, 43, 45–51, 54–6, 60, 91–2, 112–13, 123–8, 132, 134–5, 137, 139, 142, 161, 186, 221, 224, 229, 232–3, 295–6, 301, 328
Hamburger Frauenchor, 55–6, 91, 116, 118, 123, 128, 136, 151, 153, 200, 232, 384
Hamburger Nachrichten, 54
Hamm, 55, 178
Hammerschmidt, Andreas, 120
Hancock, Virginia, ix, 119–20, 196, 309, 316
Handel, Georg Frideric, 143, 146–7, 149, 179–80, 188, 197, 208–9, 277, 283, 460
   Acis and Galatea, 129
   Alexander's Feast, 229
   Dettingen Te Deum, 208, 230
   Duets and Trios, 146
   Harpsichord Suites, 179
   Israel in Egypt, 208
   Messiah, 136, 143, 146
   Solomon, 230
Hanover, 3, 12, 18, 20–1, 39, 46, 50, 53, 56–7, 59, 128, 240
Hanseatic League, 4
Hanslick, Eduard, 125, 127, 129, 134, 191, 231–2, 299, 300, 321, 412, 462
Harold, Edmund von, 118
Härtel, Raimund, 19–20, 338
Hasse, Johann Adolf, 147

Hasse, Karl, 475
Hassler, Hans Leo, 55, 149
Hauer, Ottilie, 130
Hauser, Kaspar, 460–1
Hausmann, Robert, 243, 321
Haydn, Franz Josef, 7, 23, 32, 105, 125,
  129, 144, 146, 149, 188, 197, 209, 215–
  16, 230, 245, 251, 411, 465–6
  Piano Sonata no. 52, 387
Hebbel, Friedrich, 219
Hegar, Friedrich, 133, 294
Heide, 4
Heidelberg, 34
Heine, Heinrich, 27, 78, 261, 348–9, 392
Heller, Stephen, 18
Hellmesberger, Josef, 126, 229, 268, 462
Henschel, Georg, 231–2, 237–8, 251, 260,
  292, 298, 301, 394, 399, 462
Henze, Hans Werner, 238
Herbeck, Johann von, 126, 129, 134, 139–
  40, 230–1, 463
Herder, Johann Gottfried, 25, 33, 37, 39,
  84, 110, 118, 357
  Briefwechsel über Ossian, 25
  Stimmen der Völker, 25, 37, 40, 112,
    151, 264, 357
Herz, Henri, 7, 10
Herzogenberg, Elisabet von, 45, 62, 130,
  236–7, 243, 253, 265, 267, 274, 287,
  296, 310, 336, 339, 344, 348, 351–3,
  372, 377–8, 392–3, 398, 463
Herzogenberg, Heinrich von, 130, 236,
  243, 287, 334–5, 339, 341, 352, 371,
  378–9, 403, 463
  Elegischer Gesänge, 378
  String Trio, 287
  Totenfeier, 378
  Variations on a Theme of Brahms, 236
Hesse, Alexander Friedrich, Landgrave of,
  322
Hesse, Anna, Landgräfin of, 131
Heuberger, Richard, 239, 299, 301, 383,
  412, 463
Heyse, Paul, 37, 238, 347, 351, 377, 463
Hildesheim, 12
Hiller, Ferdinand, 15, 28, 59, 137, 139, 149,
  230
Hindemith, Paul, 415
Hoboken, 215
Hoffmann, Ernest Theodor Amadeus, 9,
  14, 23–4, 28–33, 40, 62, 83, 144, 384,
  463
  Kater Mürr, 9
  Kreisleriana, 30, 40
  Mass, 31
  Miserere, 31
  Piano Sonatas, 31
  Symphony, 31
  Undine, 31, 463
Hoffmann, J. F., 6
Hoffmann von Fallersleben, August Hein-
  rich, 73, 112
Hofmann, Kurt, 44
Hofstetten, 292, 330
Hohenthal, Countess Ida von, 19
Hölderlin, Friedrich, 26, 137, 202–3, 289
Holstein, 4
Hölty, Ludwig, 200–1, 223
Hubermann, Bronislaw, 268
'Hungarian' style, 12, 162, 164, 180, 215,
  251, 261, 267, 283, 324, 344–5, 361,
  364, 468, 476

Ireland, John, 406
Isaac, Heinrich, 55, 129, 143, 230
Ischl, 282, 284, 292–3, 296, 298–9, 342, 402

Jacobson, Bernard, 250
Jahn, Otto, 145
Japha, Louise, 11, 17, 463
Japha, Minna, 463
Jena, 140
Jenner, Gustav, 239, 463
Jensen, Adolf, 37
Joachim, Amalie, 112, 128, 136, 140, 242,
  344
Joachim, Johannes, 132, 344
Joachim, Joseph, 10–14, 17–18, 20–2, 29–
  30, 36–7, 39–42, 45–51, 53–4, 57–9,
  71, 73–4, 80, 83, 99–100, 104–5, 123,
  127–8, 132, 134–5, 139, 144, 146, 150,
  158, 161–2, 178, 192, 195, 210, 214–
  15, 225, 230, 232–3, 242–3, 268–71,
  279, 297–301, 303–4, 310, 313, 321,
  342, 344, 347, 362, 368, 381, 394–6,
  404–5, 459–60, 463–4, 466
  Concerto in the Hungarian Manner, 37,
    123, 230, 270–1
  dramatic overtures, 36–7, 58, 272

Elegiac Overture in memory of Kleist, 37, 233
Violin Concerto no. 3, 320
Joachim Quartet, 243, 300, 321, 464
Johnson, Robert, 147
Jones, J. Barrie, 303

Kagel, Mauricio, 417
Kalbeck, Max, viii, 8, 186, 189, 239, 245, 272, 303, 310, 326, 342, 344, 359, 377–8, 393, 397, 402, 412, 464
Kant, Immanuel, 197
Kapper, Siegfried, 325
Karlsbad, 299
Karlskirche, 142
Karlsruhe, 131, 133, 140, 203, 246
Keiser, Reinhard, 147
Keller, Gottfried, 133, 194, 263, 464
Kerll, Johann Casper, 147
Kerner, Justinus, 112
Keys, Ivor, 475
Kiel, 46, 135
Kiel, Friedrich, 37
Kirchner, Theodor, 18, 36, 44, 59, 124, 133, 138, 233, 293, 464
Klindworth, Karl, 13
Klinger, Max, 371, 393, 464
Koblenz, 231
Kodály, Zoltán, 193
Köselitz, Heinrich, 346
Krefeld, 240, 294, 355
Kretschmer, August, 151
Kreuznach, 125
Kugler, Franz, 354

Langford, Samuel, 400
Lassus (Orlando di Lasso), 145, 149
Latham, Peter, vii–ix, 272, 391, 402–3
Laurens, J.-B., 17
Leipzig, 17, 19–21, 45–6, 53–4, 80, 123, 136, 236–7, 269, 297–8
Leipzig Bach-Verein, 236
Lemcke, Carl, 184, 261, 350
Leoncavallo, Ruggiero, 332
I Pagliacci, 332
Leopold II, Prince of Lippe-Detmold, 48, 50
Lessing, Gotthold Ephraim, 33
Levi, Hermann, 131, 133, 139–40, 203, 241, 245, 464

Leyen, Rudolf von der, 294
Lichtenthal, 129, 131, 133, 138–41
Ligeti, György, 177, 417
Liliencron, Detlef von, 350
Liszt, Franz, 12–15, 20–1, 23, 27–9, 35–7, 42, 46, 53, 57–9, 62–3, 125, 131, 133, 150, 162, 181–2, 193, 240, 349, 351, 391, 403, 405, 408–9, 461, 464, 466–7
Bravour-Studien nach Paganini, 182
Etudes d'exécution transcendante d'après Paganini, 182
'Faust' Symphony, 391
Hungarian Rhapsodies, 80, 193
Piano Sonata, 13, 67
Litolff, Henri, 11
Loewe, Carl, 264
London, 88, 136, 232, 301, 405
Loretto, 294
Lotti, Lorenzo, 55
Lowenherz, Aaron, 10
Ludwig II, King of Bavaria, 233
Lully, Jean Baptiste, 147, 188
Lüneburg, 12
Luther, Martin, 256, 258–9, 372
Lutheran chorales, 6, 197, 258–9

Macpherson, James, 25, 118
Fingal, 118
Ossian, 25, 118, 461
Magdeburg, 45
Mahler, Alma, 403
Mahler, Gustav, 23, 156, 174, 239, 263, 308, 402–4, 408–11, 413
Das klagende Lied, 402
Des Knaben Wunderhorn, 156, 184
Symphony no. 2, 402
Symphony no. 5, 408
Symphony no. 6, 305
Symphony no. 9, 408
Manchester Guardian, 400
Mandyczewski, Eusebius, 146, 239, 295, 300–1, 463–5
Mannheim, 133
Marchand, Louis, 147
Marenzio, Luca, 145, 149
'Marks, G. W.', 60
Marmorito, Count Victor Radicati di, 139–40
Marschner, Heinrich, 23, 28, 62
Hans Heiling, 62

485

Index

Martucci, Giuseppe, 259
Marxsen, Eduard, 7–8, 10, 13, 60, 136, 232, 239, 275, 295, 383, 460, 463, 465
Mason, William, 12, 46
Mattheson, Johann, 384
May, Florence, 5–6, 141–2, 158, 195, 207, 465
Mayntzisch Gesangbuch, 93
Mehlem, 14, 33
Méhul, Etienne Nicolas, 107, 149
Uthal, 107
Meiningen Orchestra, 240–1, 297–8, 302, 361–2, 465
Mendelssohn, Dorothea, 28
Mendelssohn, Felix, 14, 19, 22–3, 27–9, 53, 65, 73, 111–12, 116–19, 143, 147, 177, 197, 383, 405, 461, 465, 468, 475
Die erste Walpurgisnacht, 230
A Midsummer Night's Dream, 77
Variations sérieuses, 311
Menzel, Adolph von, 297, 395, 465
Messina, 294
Meyerbeer, Giacomo, 23
Meysenbug, Carl von, 143
Meysenbug, Laura von, 48
Michaeliskirche, 6, 55
Milan, 294
Miller zu Aichholz, Viktor von, 240, 295, 300–1, 465
Minnesingers, 151
Monn, Georg Matthias, 411
Monteverdi, Claudio, 145
Mörike, Eduard, 111, 118
Moscheles, Ignaz, 19
Mozart, Wolfgang Amadeus, 7, 23, 28, 31–2, 46, 57, 125, 143, 145, 147–9, 209, 245, 250, 278, 284, 297–8, 386, 399, 411, 417, 464–5
Clarinet Concerto, 361
Clarinet Quintet, 361
Davidde Penitente, 230
Divertimenti, 105
Don Giovanni, 32, 73, 131, 402
'Hunt' Quartet, 250
Le Nozze di Figaro, 10
Offertorium, K260, 230
Piano Concerto in D minor, K466, 46
Requiem, 147
Sinfonia Concertante, K364, 322

Symphony no. 40 in G minor, 131, 144, 210
Symphony no. 41, 'Jupiter', 311
Die Zauberflöte, 238
Muffat, Georg, 311
Mühlfeld, Richard, 297, 300, 361–2, 368, 465
Müller, Wilhelm, 117
Munich, 241, 246
Munster-am-Stein, 125
Murdoch, William, 358
Mürzzuschlag, 292, 308, 310
Musgrave, Michael, ix, 118, 171, 176, 188, 197, 225–6, 249–50, 270, 272, 288, 303, 318, 332, 357, 475

Nagy, Zoltán, 353
Naples, 294
Neapolitan relationships, 92, 165–6, 169, 312, 330, 387
Neighbour, Oliver, 82
Neue Zeitschrift für Musik, 18, 20, 57–9, 125
'New German' School, 13, 21, 53, 57–8, 136, 181, 240, 272, 403, 410, 413, 464, 467
Nietzsche, Friedrich, 198, 346, 399
Der Fall Wagner, 346
Hymnus an das Leben, 346
Nikisch, Artur, 298
Nottebohm, Gustav, 35, 125, 146–7, 239, 293, 295, 312, 465
Variations on a Theme of Bach, 35, 312
Novalis (Friedrich von Hardenberg), 23, 26, 30, 33

Ochs, Siegfried, 197, 309, 465
Oldenburg, 124, 133, 137
Orvieto, 293
Ostwald, Peter, 16
Ottensteiner, Georg, 361
Oxford, 405

Pachelbel, Johann, 147, 379
Paganini, Niccoló, 23, 27, 181–2
24 Caprices, 182
Palermo, 293–4
Palestrina, Giovanni Pierluigi da, 31, 55, 91, 121, 143, 146, 149
Missa Papae Marcelli, 91

Paris, 12, 20, 123, 301, 383
Parma, 294
Parry, Sir Charles Hubert Hastings, 289, 405–6
  Elegy for Brahms, 405
  Symphonic Variations, 405
  Symphony no. 4, 406
Pasquini, Bernardo, 147
Perger, Richard von, 301
Pike, Lionel, 171
Pisa, 293
Platen, August, 189–90
Playford, John, 147
Pleyel, Ignaz, 215
Pohl, Carl Ferdinand, 146, 215, 239, 295, 465–6
Pompeii, 294
Pope, Alexander, 33
Pörtschach, 256, 279, 292
Porubsky, Bertha, see Faber, Bertha
Porubsky, Emil, 55
Potter, Cipriani, 136
Praetorius, Michael, 149
Prague, 41, 218
Precheisen, Olga, 218
Preiger, Erich, 475
Pressbaum, 274, 288, 292
Puccini, Giacomo, 396

Quagliati, Paolo, 147

Rakhmaninov, Sergey, 182
Raff, Joachim, 13, 57
Rameau, Jean Philippe, 147
Ravel, Maurice, 364
'Reading Rota', 1
Reger, Max, 408, 415
Reich, Willi, 388
Reichardt, Johann Friedrich, 27, 204
Reinecke, Carl, 15, 136
Reinick, Robert, 73
Reinthaler, Karl Martin, 134–7, 196, 233, 395, 466
Reissiger, Karl Gottlieb, 36
Reményi, Eduard, 11–13, 20, 80, 162, 192–3, 466
Reuter, Marie, 56
Rheinberger, Joseph, 230, 311
  Organ Sonata no. 8, 311
Rhine Music Festival, 123, 125, 136

Richter, Hans, 300, 302, 404, 466
Richter, Jean-Paul, 33
Riemann, Hugo, 411
Rieter-Biedermann, 123, 136
Rietz, Julius, 53, 59, 230, 466
Rimini, 294
Rochlitz, Friedrich, 145
Romberg, Bernhard, 174, 466
Rome, 293
Röntgen, Julius, 237, 300
Röntgen, Frau, 237
Rosé Quartet, 342
Rosen, Charles, 28–9, 105
Rosenhain, Jacob, 10, 37, 131, 466
Rosing, 124
Rossini, Gioacchino, 29, 188
Rott, Hans, 239
Rottenberg, Ludwig, 239
Rotterdam, 45
Rousseau, Jean-Jacques, 24
Rovetta, Giovanni, 129
Royal Philharmonic Society, 233
Rubinstein, Anton, 46, 131, 140, 229–30, 394–5, 466
Rückert, Friedrich, 1–2, 91, 296, 326, 344–5, 377
Rudorff, Ernst, 220
Rügen, 238, 292
Ruggles, Carl, 416–17
Ruperti, 118

Sahr, Heinrich von, 19
St Paul, 376
St Pauli, 8, 397
St Petersburg, 136, 142
Salieri, Antonio, 188
Salonblatt, 239
Sams, Eric, 34, 76, 218, 351–2, 393
Samson, Jim, 84
San Marino, 294
Sárkozi, Ferenc, 193
Sassnitz, 260
Sayn-Wittgenstein, Princess Carolyne von, 13
Scarlatti, Domenico, 29, 263
Schack, Adolf von, 201
Schauffler, Robert, 397
Scheidt, Samuel, 146, 379
Schelling, Friedrich von, 23
Schenkendorf, Max von, 220, 263

Index

Schenker, Heinrich, 148
Schiller, Friedrich, 20, 24–5, 27, 33, 202, 221, 224, 238, 288
Schlegel, August Wilhelm, 23
Schlegel, Friedrich, 23, 26, 28
Schleswig, 3
Schmidt, Christian Martin, 315
Schmidt, Franz, 208
  Das Buch mit sieben Siegeln, 208
Schmidt, Hans, 347
Schnack, Fritz, 134, 142, 296
Schoenberg, Arnold, vii–viii, 23, 162, 179, 184, 210, 215, 251, 290, 362, 374, 381–2, 385–6, 388, 402, 410–17
  Gurrelieder, 411
  Pelléas und Mélisande, 411
  String Quartet no. 1, 210, 342
  String Quartet in D, 251, 412
  Verklärte Nacht, 342, 364, 413
  'Brahms the Progressive', viii, 385, 413
  Structural Functions of Harmony, 414
Scholz, Bernhard, 59, 466
Schreker, Franz, 404
Schubert, Franz, 1–2, 7, 22–3, 25, 38, 63, 71, 73, 75, 111, 118, 125, 127–8, 144, 146–8, 150, 156, 158–9, 167, 177, 191, 209–10, 231, 245, 253, 284, 301, 383, 387, 393, 399, 417, 465, 475–6
  Am Meer, 78, 340
  Grand Duo in C, 230
  Lazarus, 128, 188
  Mass in B flat, 230
  Octet, 105
  Ossian settings, 25, 118
  Piano Quintet ('The Trout'), 49
  String Quintet, 161, 164, 171, 303
  Symphony no. 8 ('Unfinished'), 463
  Der Tod und das Mädchen, 210
  'Wanderer' Fantasy, 65
  Die Winterreise, 1–2
Schübring, Adolf, 127
Schumann, Clara, ix, 11, 15–17, 19–22, 34, 37–52, 55–7, 76, 79–83, 88, 90, 92, 102, 120, 123–4, 126, 129, 131, 133, 137–41, 144, 148, 150, 158, 161–2, 164, 170, 172, 177–8, 186, 188, 191–2, 195, 201–2, 226, 233, 236–7, 243–6, 249, 253, 268, 285, 293, 296, 298, 310, 313, 320, 339, 341, 355, 359–60, 362, 371, 378, 393–8, 404, 459–60,

463, 465, 466–8
  Lieder aus Jucunde, 37
  Piano Concerto, 277
  Piano Trio, 37
  Pièces caractéristiques, 182
  Preludes and Fugues, 37, 92
  Romanzen, 37
  Variations on a Theme of Robert Schumann, 37, 81, 83
Schumann, Eugenie, 141, 192, 298, 459
Schumann, Felix, 41, 138, 220, 243, 260, 289, 467
Schumann, Ferdinand, 141, 243, 289
Schumann, Julie, 48, 138–40, 177, 202, 204, 223, 243, 289, 467
Schumann, Ludwig, 138, 141, 243, 289
Schumann, Marie, 15, 371
Schumann, Robert, 11, 14–24, 28–9, 33–51, 53, 57, 63, 66, 70, 73–5, 79–83, 86–8, 90, 93, 99–100, 102, 111, 115, 118, 130, 136, 143–5, 150–1, 177–8, 182, 185–6, 191, 195, 197, 210, 218, 224, 226, 231, 243–5, 249, 289, 303–5, 322, 341, 383–4, 393–4, 399, 401, 405, 408, 463, 465, 466, 468, 475–6
  'Abegg' Variations, 34
  Bunte Blätter, 81–3
  Carnaval, 34, 83, 191
  Cello Concerto, 322
  Concertstück, op. 92, 118
  Davidsbündlertänze, 82, 144
  Des Sängers Fluch, 230
  Etudes symphoniques, 35, 148
  Fantasia for violin, 22, 230
  Fantasiestücke, 33, 40
  Fantasy in C, 34–5, 79
  Genoveva, 76, 185
  Impromptus on a Theme of Clara Wieck, 35, 83
  Introduction and Allegro, 17, 118
  Kreisleriana, 14, 29, 33
  Das Paradies und die Peri, 21, 187, 296
  Piano Concerto, 34, 231
  Requiem für Mignon, 129
  Studies after Paganini, 182
  Symphony no. 3, 'Rhenish', 34–5, 303, 308
  Symphony no. 4, 22, 144, 148, 243–4, 246–8
  Toccata, 183

Violin Concerto, 178, 271
Zigeunerleben, 144
'Neue Bahnen', 18, 73
Schütz, Heinrich, 55, 129, 144–6, 149, 196–7, 328–30, 379, 384, 467
Scottish ballads, 84, 109–10, 264
Sechter, Simon, 460, 465
Second Viennese School, 411, 414
Senff, 19
Senfl, Ludwig, 147
Seyfried, Ignaz, 7, 465
Sgambati, Giovanni, 259
Shakespeare, William, 25, 27–8, 118–19
  Hamlet, 218
  Twelfth Night, 118
Sibelius, Jan, 274
Siebold, Agathe von, 45, 51–3, 56, 170, 186, 188, 201–2, 397, 462
Siena, 293
Signale, 53
Simrock, Fritz, 107, 116, 123, 192, 210, 225, 231, 242, 267, 283, 285, 293, 296, 301, 338–9, 410
Sinopoli, Giuseppe, 207
Smyth, Ethel, 237, 392, 398
Sorrento, 294
Specht, Richard, 309, 403
Speratus, Paul, 120
Spies, Hermine, 45, 240, 292, 296, 333, 348, 350, 372
Spina, Carl Anton, 127–8
Spitta, Philipp, 146, 148, 258, 296, 309, 328, 395
Spohr, Ludwig, 28–9
Stadler, Anton, 361
Stanford, Charles Villiers, 233, 299, 405–6
Stegmayer, Ferdinand, 128
Steinbach, Fritz, 297
Sternau, 68, 221, 392
Stevenson, Ronald, 235
Stockhausen, Bodo Albrecht von, 62
Stockhausen, Elisabet, see Herzogenberg, Elisabet von
Stockhausen, Julius, 46–7, 54, 123, 126, 128, 135–6, 139, 240, 301
Stockhausen, Karlheinz, 416, 461, 467
Storm, Theodor, 263
Straesser, Ewald, 404
Strauss, Johann (II), 131, 192, 194, 300
  Die Göttin der Vernunft, 300

Strauss, Richard, 294, 410–11
Stravinsky, Igor, 23, 28, 415
Suppé, Franz von, 271
  Flotte Bursch, 271
Süssmayr, Franz Xaver, 148
Syracuse, 294

Tasso, Torquato, 188
Taormina, 294
Taubmann, Otto, 404
Tausch, Julius, 17
Tausig, Carl, 125, 127, 129–30, 164, 181–2, 295
  Tägliche Studien, 182
Tchaikovsky, Peter, 298
  Overture '1812', 61
Teutoberger Forest, 50
Thalberg, Sigismond, 42
Thibault IV, Count of Provence, 109
Thun, Lake, 320, 330, 333
Tieck, Ludwig, 3, 23, 26, 185–6
  Genoveva, 185
  Wundersame Liebesgeschichte der schönen Magelone und des Grafen Peter aus der Provence, 185
Titelouze, Jean, 147
Titov, Nikolai, 61
Toggenburg, Kraft von, 63
Tovey, Donald Francis, 101, 204, 207, 247, 270, 272, 305, 387, 405
  The Bride of Dionysus, 405
  Cello Concerto, 405
  Essays in Musical Analysis, 405
Traunsee, 402
Truscott, Harold, 36, 236, 273
Truxa, Celestine, 234, 300
Turgenev, Ivan, 131–2
Turin, 294

Uhland, Ludwig, 25, 45, 71, 111, 117
Utrecht, 136

Vanhal, Johann Baptist, 411
Varlamov, Alexander, 61
Varus, Publius Quinctilius, 50
Vaughan Williams, Ralph, 208, 406–7
  Fantasia on a Theme of Thomas Tallis, 407
  Sancta Civitas, 208
  Symphonies, 407

Index

Venice, 294
Verdi, Giuseppe, 23, 324, 396
Viardot-Garcia, Pauline, 131, 140
Vicenza, 294
Vienna, 8, 11, 41, 55, 125–9, 132, 134–6,
    139–42, 191, 229–31, 234–5, 274, 288,
    292, 294–301, 309, 383
Vienna Burgtheater, 272, 289
Vienna Conservatoire, 125–6, 465
Vienna Hofoper, 229, 402, 460, 463, 466
Vienna Singakademie, 128–30, 148, 151,
    153, 229–30, 462
Vienna Tonkünstlerverein, 295, 412
Vierteljahrsschrift für Musikwissenschaft,
    148
Vieuxtemps, Henri, 12
Viotti, Giovanni Battista, 269
    Violin Concerto no. 22, 269, 321
Vivaldi, Antonio, 147
Vogl, Ludovika, 142, 234
Vogt, Hans, 38
Völckers, Betty, 56, 124
Völckers, Marie, 56, 124, 136
Volkmann, Robert, 36, 59, 179
    Cello Concerto, 230, 277, 322
    Concertstück, 230
    Piano Trios, 36
    Symphony No. 1, 36
    Variations on a Theme of Handel, 36,
    179

Wagenseil, Georg Christoph, 411
Wagner, Friedchen, 55
Wagner, Richard, 23, 27–8, 31, 33, 36, 58,
    71, 127, 130, 133, 144, 178, 188, 232–
    3, 238, 240–1, 272, 294, 346, 349, 383–
    4, 386, 393, 396, 398, 403, 405–8, 410–
    12, 415, 417, 460, 462, 464
    Der fliegende Holländer, 28, 188
    Lohengrin, 28
    Die Meistersinger von Nurnberg, 28,
    127, 237, 272, 462
    Parisfal, 406, 464
    Der Ring des Nibelungen, 28, 241, 466
    Symphony, 36
    Tännhauser, 144
    Tristan und Isolde, 28, 127, 132, 210,
    349, 388, 460
Walther, Johann, 147

Wasielewski, J. W. von, 14, 20, 61, 224
Weber, Arnold, 14, 73
Weber, Carl Maria von, 23, 31, 276
Webern, Anton, 290, 357, 411, 415–16
    Passacaglia, 415
    Piano Variations, 357
    String Quartet, 415
    Symphony, 415
Weill, Kurt, 415
Weimar, 12–13, 20, 53, 57, 62, 182
Wesendonck, Mathilde, 133
Wesselbüren, 4
Widmann, Joseph Viktor, 133, 238, 242,
    292–4, 297, 346, 400
Wiesbaden, 292, 302
Wilhelm I, Emperor of Germany, 207, 209
Wilhelmshaven, 137
Willaert, Adrian, 147
Wieck, Friedrich, 16, 19, 460, 466
Wieck, Marie, 19, 49, 81
Winsen an der Lühe, 9–10, 12, 61, 185
Winterfeld, Carl von, 145, 315–16
    Johannes Gabrieli und sein Zeitalter,
    145, 196, 315–16
Winterthur, 124
Wolf, Hugo, 232, 239, 393, 398, 403
Wolter, Charlotte, 289
Wüllner, Franz, 243

Young, Edward 33

Zarlino, Gioseffe, 147
Zelter, Carl Friedrich, 28, 383, 466
Zemlinsky, Alexander von, 116, 404, 410–
    413
    Clarinet Trio, 410
    Die Seejungfrau, 410
    String Quartet no. 1, 410
    Symphony in B flat, 410
Zigeuner, see 'Hungarian' style
Zimmermann, Bernd Alois, 416
Zirler, 147
Zuccalmaglio, Anton Wilhelm von, 65,
    151, 156
    Deutsche Volkslieder mit ihrem
    Original-Weisen, 151–3
Zum roten Igel, 235
Zürich, 298